CURRENT COMPETITION LAW

Volume IV

Edited by

PHILIP MARSDEN
and
MICHAEL HUTCHINGS

THE BRITISH INSTITUTE OF INTERNATIONAL AND COMPARATIVE LAW

Published and Distributed by
The British Institute of International and Comparative Law
Charles Clore House, 17 Russell Square, London WC1B 5JP

© *The British Institute of International and Comparative Law 2005*

British Library Cataloguing in Publication Data
A Catalogue record of this book is available from the British Library

ISBN 1–905221–00–2

Typeset by Cambrian Typesetters
Frimley, Surrey
Printed in Great Britain by Biddles Ltd
King's Lynn

CURRENT COMPETITION LAW

VOLUME IV

PREFACE

With this fourth volume of *Current Competition Law* we have almost caught up with events. The competition law programme at the British Institute is a busy one, and over the past months we have accelerated the publication of this volume, so that the fascinating discussions that we have here are available for deeper consideration and comment by a broader audience in a timelier manner. This issue brings together for the first time, papers and speeches from all three of our annual competition law conferences held in the 2004/2005 academic year.

We begin with the proceedings and papers presented at our Competition Litigation conference held on 15 October, 2004. This involved a very interesting discussion amongst European, Canadian and American experts of pressing issues, including private enforcement, class actions, injunctive relief, parallel proceedings, discovery/evidentiary issues and remedies. There was also an interesting discussion of extraterritoriality and other jurisdictional issues, as well as a roundtable discussion on agency perspectives on private enforcement.

Our next section comes from our 3rd annual Merger Conference, held on 6 December 2004. At this conference, competition officials and experts from the private sector engaged in a frank discussion about case referrals within the European Competition Network; the use of Devil's Advocate panels; Remedies; Vertical and Conglomerate Mergers; and the use and abuse of economic evidence. We were also very fortunate to learn the views of Judge Bo Vesterdorf, President of the Court of First Instance, with respect to the standard of proof to be applied in merger cases.

Our final section is comprised of the content of our 5th annual Trans-Atlantic Antitrust Dialogue, held on 9–10 May, 2005. Here, as has been the case for the last three years, we benefited from the key insights into the development of US antitrust law offered to us by Assistant Attorney General for Antitrust, R Hewitt Pate. Director General Philip Lowe of the European Commission gave us a look into the operations of DG-Comp in the Kroes regime, and Judge Diane Wood of the US Court of Appeals (7th Circuit) presented an enjoyable keynote speech of a welcome comparative nature. Panel topics including Competition Policy and Intellectual Property; Rights of complainants and third parties; Economics in Court—with a panel of leading judges; Monopolization/Abuse—towards effects based tests; and Unilateral effects analysis, and we closed with ever-lively round-table discussion amongst the heads of various agencies. I hope you find this fourth volume to be a helpful research resource, and I thank all of our contributors for their time and effort. Extremely capable research assistance was provided by our Junior Fellows in Competition Law, Ms Hedvig Schmidt and Mr Peter Whelan. I look forward to seeing you at our competition workshops, meetings, and conferences and welcome suggestions as we develop our programme further.

Dr Philip Marsden
Director Competition Law Forum
and Senior Research Fellow, British Institute

CONTENTS

PART ONE

Litigation Conference
15 October 2004

Developments in Competition Litigation: A Comparative Perspective

Philip Marsden

Welcome to the British Institute and to our international visitors, welcome to London. I direct the competition law programme at the Institute. It gives me great pleasure to welcome you to this session. For the last two or three years we had a Current Developments in Competition Litigation workshop in the evenings and it was very successful, but we thought that we could do more. In those workshops we would focus on a couple of specific issues relevant to UK and EU law in an 'update' fashion. But of course, in keeping with the focus of the Institute on international and comparative law itself, we thought that the important developments in the law this year, in particular, in a range of jurisdictions, meant that we should expand the programme. And that's what we've donetoday. The great number of attendees we have is testament to the fact that obviously this is an area of increasing interest.

I am grateful to Sir Christopher Bellamy and the panellists for participating today, in particular thanks to Surbata Bhattacharjee, from Canada, who has very much collaborated with me in putting on the programme.

Finally, it gives me great pleasure to invite Sir Christopher Bellamy, the President of the Competition Appeal Tribunal, a very great supporter of our Institute and our Chairman today to begin our discussions. Thank you all for coming.

SIR CHRISTOPHER BELLAMY

The points I would like to make very briefly concern the damages aspect of private enforcement. Private enforcement, of course, has got both the aspect of injunctive relief and the aspect of damages. We shall come on to injunctive relief, but I would like to start with damages.

Damages, of course, is something that is being thought about a great deal at the moment across Europe and the first point I would like to make is that one needs to try to think of this problem in terms of an EU perspective, rather than a national perspective. The Commission is proposing to publish a green paper next year on the conditions necessary for a more effective regime of private enforcement across the EU. As a first step in that direction, they have recently completed and now put on the website a study on the conditions of claims for damages in case of infringement of EC competition rules, which you are probably all familiar with.[1] It is prepared on their behalf by Ashursts, and is in my view a very comprehensive and detailed account of where we are at the moment, in all the 25 member states, based on national reports and a great deal of analysis. The overall picture, I think, is very like the map of Africa in the 19th century as seen through European eyes. That is to say, there are one or two out-posts on the coasts that have been identified but there is a great deal of terra incognita. Although there are one or two rivers leading to the dark interior, they are pretty much inhabited by crocodiles and other wild animals and we don't quite know how far we can get up the river without being snaffled by a crocodile or two.

I would also draw your attention if I may to the Seventh Amendment to the German Law on Competition, which will come into force in a few weeks time, which in the German context is intended to strengthen private rights of enforcement. In Germany, those are fairly well known already—certainly on the injunctive side—but Germany has thought pretty hard as to what sort of structure you need, and although there is probably not time to go into detail today, that is certainly a background point that one would need to think about in terms of principles.

The Commission's approach, of course, will also to some extent at least, involve tackling that most intractable of subjects, which is the difference between the various Member States in terms of procedure. All European experience, I think to date, is that it is not in the end so difficult to harmonize the substantive law, but procedure, generally speaking, absolutely defies harmonization and that is going to be one of the particular challenges for the future.

Skipping over the various reasons for the moment, as to why we don't have much private enforcement in the EEC as compared with the United States and without looking at this stage in detail into the pros and cons of a better system of private enforcement in Europe, I for my part, would just like to make some very short comments about the sorts of questions that we might in principle be asking ourselves.

First of all, what is the balance, the right balance between public enforcement and private enforcement? And is there any way in which one can hit the balance? As you know a small step was taken in the Enterprise Act 2002, which gave the Competition Appeal Tribunal jurisdiction to deal

---

[1] Denis Waelbroeck, Donald Slater and Gil Even-Shoshan 'Study on the Conditions on Claims for Damages in Cases of Infringement of EC Competition Rules, Comparative Report' Ashurst, 31 August 2004 <http://www.europa.cu.int/comm/competiton/antitrust/others/private_enforcement/comparative_repott_clean_enpdf>.

with so-called follow-on actions for damages where liability has already been established by an action of the public authorities. I am given to understand that a fairly high proportion of litigation in the United States is a follow-on from some kind of public enforcement action although no doubt we will hear a bit more about it.

Follow-on actions, of course depend on having something to follow on from and that, of course, pre-supposes a certain degree of activity on the part of the public enforcement agencies. If one is going to go beyond follow-on actions, one perhaps needs to think at least briefly, about some aspects of the laws of unintended consequences. It could be said in some respects that over-deterrence in this field has, or might have, a certain cost. One can think of respects in which fear of damages actions might, in some circumstances, inhibit innovation, might inhibit forming a joint venture, might inhibit certain kinds of pricing policies, might even in certain circumstances inhibit competition itself if one is on the border-line in between a proper competition response and some allegation of predatory pricing.

One would not, I think, want to finish up with a situation in which loss has been suffered, essentially as a result of a bad or misguided management decision, which is then converted into a cause of action in damages. That is one general idea to think about.

The second area to think about is the whole question of actions for damages in circumstances where the law is uncertain, or not yet fully developed. You may say that the law in what we now called 'hard core cartels' is fairly developed and there would be no particular policy or other reason to limit actions for damages in some way or other against companies who have been participating in hard core cartels. But once we move outside that particular area, we get into issues such as dominance and abuse. Is the position so clear? It is perhaps not without interest the cases that the OFT at least has so far taken to the Competition Appeal Tribunal have been cases of very high market shares. If one is talking about a wide degree of dominance, of which probably the best example so far is *Virgin*,[2] were British Airways in that case over the course of the proceedings went down from 42 per cent of the market to 37 per cent of the market. If you are going to bring actions for damages in borderline cases of dominance, one might have to ask one's self whether that might turn out to be a counter-productive move.

If one is going to develop such actions in relation to abuse, at the moment at least, the exact parameters of abusive dominance are somewhat under-developed in European jurisprudence, despite more than 40 years of case law. Indeed, having, I think, sorted out Article 81 and having sorted out its

---

[2] T-219/99 *British Airways v Commission*, judgment of 17 Dec 2003.

approach to mergers, the next think that the Commission has got on the stocks, is to sort out or produce new guidelines on abuse under Article 82.

What I think those reflections might lead up to, is whether you need some kind of a differentiated approach, in which it is fairly clear that damages actions are available for certain kinds of activity, but for three kinds of activity, one leaves it to the regulatory authorities, at least until the law is clear.

One should perhaps also bear in mind that there are gradations or degrees of different situations, in which one might want to have, as it were, a flexible armoury of remedies available. To give one example, it may be in certain circumstances, that what you really what to achieve is simply to stop a certain activity. You don't necessarily want to penalize it, and you don't necessarily want to give rise to claims for damage. You just want it to stop, because that is where the public interest lies.

If you just want it to stop, it may not be appropriate for example, to be applying the same standard of proof that you may wish to apply if you are going to impose penalties. You may want to develop the law in a particular area for example.

So one may need to have different degrees and coax a bit in a slightly more sophisticated way than one might otherwise do. One might want to differentiate a little between different situations.

That I think just takes me on to my last point from, as it were, a judicial point of view, although I am thinking for the moment, from the point of view of the civil judge. If we were to find ourselves in a situation where cases were being brought, where the courts felt uncomfortable about the underlying basis for the case, what you are going to find, I think, if the introduction of damages actions has an effect on the substance, because what the courts can do if they don't want to allow a particular case to succeed in damages, is to modify or restrict the substance. You might find yourself finishing up with rather restrictive rulings, on what is abuse or what is dominance in particular cases, because the judges in that particular case, didn't want that particular claim to succeed.

It is, therefore, in my view, important that this whole subject starts off on the basis of a substantive law that is soundly based and is well based. If you have to a substantive law that is well based, you can perhaps arguably and justifiably, add on to that substantive law a right of action for damages, for reasons of equity, for reasons of deterrence, for reasons of completing the system . . . for all kinds of reasons.

If, however, your substantive law is doubtful or questionable before you start, then adding on an action for damages, simply compounds the errors and makes everything worse and causes the transfers of resources in direction that you wouldn't really wish to see. You have really reinforced the law of unintended consequences, which is where I started these rather preliminary remarks. So in my humble view, a number of those things need to be thought about.

Now today, we have the great advantage of hearing from various speakers who have practical experience of other systems that are up and running and indeed, experience of our own systems, who have no doubt thought about some of these things and have actually seen in action a number of the issues that we are going to discuss.

Panel 1—Private Enforcement of Competition Laws: Comparative Overview

Kevin Grady

It is a pleasure to be here this morning. There is one thing that I want to set everybody straight on: The issue of antitrust damages is not a major issue in the presidential campaign in the US. For some reason that has not captured the attention of the public.

I realize I am the token 'Yank' on this panel on damages. I thought Sir Christopher's questions were very good questions. For an American antitrust attorney to be speaking to a group of English members of the bar about antitrust damages reminds me of the comment that I think Senator John Kerry made the other night in a debate with President Bush. Being an American talking to you about damages is like Tony Soprano talking about Law and Order. I am not sure that we are in the best position to talk to you about exactly the most appropriate legal structure for remedies.

Commissioner Mario Monti gave a recent speech about the need to consider more private rights of action to enforce the EU competition laws. I also want to clarify that Philip Marsden did not pay him to say that in order to increase the attendance at this conference. I know that this programme has attracted a lot of people because of Commissioner Monti's views. When he and I were together recently, he said to me 'Kevin, I did say that I wanted more private causes of action, but I didn't say like in the US.' I want to make sure you understand that.

You can not discuss the damage system in the US without understanding the interrelatedness between both the civil and the criminal side. The treble damage civil provisions are innately linked to the criminal sanctions as Sir Christopher mentioned. There are a lot of follow-on civil class actions in the US. If there are grand jury indictments, or even if there are rumours of grand jury investigations, you will often see immediately antitrust class actions filed. We also have overlapping jurisdiction in the US, which again is a real factor in terms of our whole damage system. Not only do we have the Federal causes of action, we also have more than 50 states and territories that also have their own antitrust laws.

One of the big criticisms of the US antitrust civil damages system is the requirement of awarding treble damages to a prevailing plaintiff. Let me again set the record straight: We didn't invent this concept all on our own. The English Statute of Monopolies in 1623, which may have been a dark day here in England, basically started the idea of treble damages. Our problem may be that we have emulated the English for so long in so many things that we just don't know when to stop!

In any event, right now it has been estimated that over 90 per cent of the antitrust actions in the US involve civil actions seeking treble damages. A vast majority of those actions are filed after Government enforcement actions, but not all of them follow that pattern. The philosophy behind the treble damage actions in the US is that they are incentives for private Attorneys General to enforce the antitrust laws. The idea is that consumers themselves are more knowledgeable about when they have been harmed than State or Federal enforcers, and so, therefore the possibility of recovering treble damages is a great incentive to enforce the antitrust laws.

In the US currently we are having a big debate among members of the antitrust bar over whether our system is fatally flawed, or whether it can be corrected. I have just finished serving this year as Chair of the ABA Section of Antitrust Law. One of the things that we did this year was to put together a Task Force on remedies. We also had a set of hearings on remedies at our Spring Meeting in 2003. I don't know whether many of you have been to our Spring Meeting. It is a small, little gathering of 1,750 antitrust attorneys, and there are no egos in that room, I can tell you! They are very humble, mild-mannered, obsequious individuals.

If you go to the Section's website,[1] you can see transcripts of the set of hearings we had at the 2003 Spring Meeting, where people gave their views about the pluses and minuses of our current system of remedies. They discussed exactly the issues that Sir Christopher was raising in his question about striking the right balance.

Also this past year, as I mention in my paper, I appointed a Task Force on Remedies to develop a legislative proposal indicating how we might address the issue constructively. We have talked about the issue of antitrust remedies for so many years that it's almost gotten to be like a perpetual topic for a debating society.

Well, I put together a Task Force of people from our Section, both from the plaintiff's side and the defendant's side. They came up with a potential bill that they thought might be able to serve as a compromise. This is not anything the Section has endorsed. We make it very clear that we are not proposing this as legislation. Again, it should be on our website. If you go to it, you can read it.

---

[1] <http://www.abanet.org/antitrust/home.html>.

One of the things we did was look at the issue of providing incentives to remove cases from a state court to federal court much easier than can be done now, to eliminate the perfect diversity that you need to have to be in federal court on non-federal claims, to allow the Court that has a case transferred to it, for discovery purposes, to be able to retain the case for trial. Right now, as established under a Supreme Court decision called 'Lexecon',[2] if cases are filed all over the country, they can get transferred to one court to handle the pre-trial proceedings, including discovery. That court, which has become the most familiar with all of the issues, however, then has to send all the cases back to the original jurisdictions to be tried. It doesn't make a whole lot of sense from a management standpoint. The draft legislation suggested by the Task Force would change that wasteful result.

The legislative draft proposed various other things. One of the incentives to the plaintiff's side was to grant pre-judgment interest from the time of filing the complaint, which is something that is not available now. Indeed, pre-judgment interest is only from the time the complaint is actually filed in the US. Even then, it is awarded very rarely.

What our Section was trying to do is strike a balance, or give some creative thought to what people might be able to do with respect to remedies and damages in the US, if they put their minds to it. It is not a perfect proposal. It reflects compromises from both the plaintiffs' and the defendants' bar, but it is a start. We gave up on the idea of trying to say there can be no state antitrust causes of action. That is not workable in the US system. Why? Because under our Constitution and concepts of federalism, it is very difficult to convince a state attorney general that you are not trenching on a state's right in terms of being able to establish their own causes of action. The Supreme Court has made that very clear as well, acknowledging the fact that states can go beyond what the federal antitrust laws cover.[3]

I just want to make you aware that there is a move afoot in the US to try to re-examine the issue of antitrust remedies. Recently, Congress passed legislation forming a politically bi-partisan Antitrust Modernization Commission. It is supposed to file a report in three years on various aspects of the antitrust laws, including whether they should be modernized or not. Again, the Antitrust Section prepared a paper on 1 October, (again it is on the Section's website) in which we laid out several issues that the Commission may want to consider. One of these was the issue of remedies and damages. Whether the Commission ever accomplishes anything or not

---

[2] *Lexecon, Inc v Milberg Weiss Bershad Hynes & Lerach*, 523 US 26 (1998).

[3] *Exxon Corp v Governor of Maryland*, 437 US 117 (1978); *New Motor Vehicle Bd v Orrin W Fox Co*, 439 US 96 (1978); *California v ARC America Corp*, 490 US 93 (1989).

I think is still up in the air, and it of course depends on whether Congress ever implements the Commission's final recommendations, if any. There are a lot of Commissions that make reports and nothing happens. This could well be one of them. I am not trying to predict that help is on the way. I am not sure it necessarily is.

I also want to follow up on the very good point Sir Christopher made about the judiciary taking steps to reign in abusive uses of the antitrust laws. In the US, we have developed concepts about 'antitrust injury' and 'antitrust standing.' A lot of people have referred to the whole concept of antitrust injury as a basic 'morass' in terms of trying to figure out exactly what is the difference between the two concepts, and when can a plaintiff bring an antitrust case. Is your injury the type of injury that the antitrust laws were meant to prevent? This discussion all stems from a Supreme Court decision—*Brunswick*[4]—back in the late seventies. Many of the decisions that the US Supreme Court has made in the antitrust area have narrowed the ability of plaintiffs to prevail. In proving an antitrust agreement illegal, the court has heightened the standards of evidence that a plaintiff needs. Similarly, the court has increased the standards for plaintiffs to survive a summary judgment motion in the US.[5] These are standards, I think, that the Supreme Court has developed primarily as a way to dispose of a lot of private antitrust actions. The whole issue of 'antitrust standing' is another concept that the courts have used for the very reason that you said, Sir Christopher. I think they are concerned about opening the Courthouse doors too much.[6] You will find this whole substantive area that, if you hit the antitrust laws cold, it is like reading a different language when you get into the issues of standing, injury, and evidentiary standards necessary to establish an 'agreement.'

Another puzzling aspect of the antitrust laws to many people is the concept of proving damages and antitrust injury. In the US it is done primarily by duelling expert economists with their attendant costs. What I love to tell our clients is that 'If you don't like my hourly rates, wait until you see our economic experts' rates!' They make us look modest in terms of what we charge. Obviously, there are very good economists, and if any economist is reading this transcript, please take no offence!!

Non-US attorneys often are puzzled by this battle of duelling experts. As part of the exercise of being able to show either damages or antitrust injury, the courts will often entertain what is known as a 'Daubert motion'.

[4] *Brunswick v Pueblo Bowl-O-Mat, Inc* 429 US 477 (1977).
[5] *Monsanto Co v Spray-Rite Service Corp*, 465 US 752 (1984); *Celotex Corp v Catrett*, 477 US 317 (1986); *Matsushita Elec Indus Co v Zenith Radio Corp*, 475 US 574 (1986).
[6] *Cargill, Inc v Monfort of Colorado, Inc*, 479 US 104 (1986).

Daubert[7] is the Supreme Court decision in the early 1990s that established how you can basically flesh out expert testimony and determine when expert testimony should or should not be allowed into evidence.

Daubert challenges are now almost a cottage industry in private civil litigation under the antitrust laws. 'Daubert motions' basically determine whether economists' testimony is going ultimately to be heard by a jury. Expert economic opinions are extremely important in antitrust cases in the US. One of the things you are going to face if you develop a private cause of action to recover antitrust damages in the EU is exactly how you go about proving a claim, and what standards will apply to permit the recovery of damages. As much as those in the private bar may be salivating over private causes of action coming to the EU en masse, I would think all of the economic consulting firms would be even more eager because they know that they have a minefield here . . . a gold minefield!

There are a few other things I wanted to mention to you briefly in my limited time here. In terms of changes in the US law, right now there have been two major significant developments.

One is a move away from treble damages towards single damages in certain situations. There are two examples that I set out in the paper. One was a bill that was passed in the House of Representatives this past fall, dealing with standard setting organisations. It was titled 'Standards Development Organization Advancement Act of 2004' which amended the National Cooperative Research and Production Act.[8] In the US, trade associations often try to develop certain industry standards, and there has been concern over potential antitrust liability for such actions from those who believe they are competitively disadvantaged by the adoption of such industry standards. There was a very limited Congressional hearing to provide the factual rationale for this statute. Two or three people testified that they were mortified about the fact that they could be sued for antitrust treble damages because they were a standard-setting organization, and it really impinged on their ability to help their industry move forward. Based on that anecdotal evidence, the House of Representatives passed this bill. Under the bill, If a standard setting organization gives notice to the agencies in advance of its standard setting, and it later is sued, it can only be liable for single damages, not treble damages. This limitation only applies to the standard setting organization. It doesn't apply to the parties who participated in the standard setting organization. Consequently, you have to ask yourself how much relief it really is going to give to people. In any event, this legislation is an

---

[7] *Daubert v Merell Dow Pharmceuticals, Inc* 509 US 579 (1993).
[8] 15 USC § 4301.

example of trying to cut back, if you will, on treble damages in certain situations. There are a couple of other statutes like that in the US.

Once the bill went from the House to the Senate, a pending Senate bill[9] to increase the criminal penalties for antitrust violations was added as an amendment to the House bill. The amendment was accepted in the Conference Committee, in which there was a substantial increase in criminal fines in the US: a corporation's liability went from $10m to $100m, prison time went from three years to ten years for an individual, and private liability went from $1m to $10m.[10] There were no hearings. There was no attempt to ask the bar what they thought, and no discussion whether such a drastic increase might result in over-deterrence, as you pointed out, Sir Christopher. One interesting aspect of the amendment was that if a party participated in the government's amnesty or leniency programme, ie if you were given leniency by the US Government for being the first to report a possible criminal violation of the antitrust laws, and if you were later sued in a follow-on treble damage civil action, you would only be liable for single damages, not treble damages, and your liability would not be joint and several with all the other defendants, so long as you co-operated with the Plaintiffs' Counsel.

The standards for cooperation are not set forth in the Act. It is a piece of legislation that, I think, is flawed at best. We don't know the impact of it, but again, it's another example of what is going on in the US with respect to attempts to whittle down if you will, the treble damage aspect of antitrust causes of action, at least in certain areas.

In closing I would remind you, as I say in the paper, as far as one US antitrust practitioner is concerned, I do not think I would recommend this model to the EU. I don't know of many people who would recommend our model, but we are stuck with it. I don't foresee any major changes in the near future, unless the Antitrust Modernisation Commission somehow galvanises public sentiment and all of a sudden in the last 17 days of the presidential race, both Senator Kerry and President Bush decide this is the cutting edge issue that is going to bring all these undecided voters off the fence. I don't hold a great deal of hope that we are going to change any time soon. I have been wrong in the past, however, and I hope I'm wrong about this in the future.

---

[9] Antitrust Criminal Penalty Enhancement and Reform Act of 2003 Pub L No 108–237, 118 Stat 661.
[10] 15 USC §§ 1,2, 4301–5.

SIR CHRISTOPHER BELLAMY

To tell us how we are to avoid the mistake we apparently made in 1623, when we started all this, Subrata Bhattacharjee will now come in and tell us a little bit about the perhaps less exuberant, but on the other hand, more measured approach in Canada.

SUBRATA BHATTACHARJEE

I should first of all preface by saying when we appear before an audience outside of North America, the first question I can predict most of you asking is, why do I care about what is happening in Canada? The answer in this particular context , and following from what Kevin has just said, is that when we decided to look at whether or not we would have the right of private actions for damages under our Competition Act,[11] we had the benefit of the extents of US experience in that regard. The choice that Parliament took in the mid-1970s, which is when a limited right of private action was added to our act, was actually to leave the balance of enforcement of the Canadian competition laws largely in the hands of public enforcement with a very circumscribed right of enforcement for private parties. This is not to say we have no rights of private action, but the cornerstone of our act in Section 36 confers a very limited right of private action. Now, in comparison to the features of the US regime, what we have in Canada, is a section that can be asserted by private plaintiffs, only when there has been a breach of the criminal provisions of the Act. So for example, in Canada, conspiracy, predatory pricing, price maintenance for example, conduct that would contravene those sections would be potentially subject to a private action, or as I put it, more contemporary concerns of competition law, abuse or dominance, certain distribution practices would not be subject to private actions. So we first of all took the decision to limit the types of matters for which you could see damages.

We then took the additional step of saying, well we are not actually going to allow for treble damages, we are only going to allow for single damages, and we will restrict the damages to the measure required to compensate the injured parties.

We also have costs and costs sanctioned in place, and in addition to that, we allow successful plaintiffs to recover the costs of investigation. So we took a slightly more restrictive view on how to approach the issue.

There are no punitive damages under our Section 36 and we do however, have pre-judgement interest that is available and is customarily awarded in

---

[11] RSC 1985, c C-34 as amended.

Canadian courts to successful plaintiffs. I think this is a significant difference for the US, because I think Kevin has suggested that in the few cases where you get pre-judgment interest, it extends from the time the complaint has been filed; in Canada we get pre-judgment interest from the commencement of the conduct in question.

The bottom line on damages for us is that we have tried to avoid what we perceive to be a potential windfall effect that has characterized the private enforcement system in the US. We have tried to do that by limiting the types of conduct for which you can get damages for and the varying level of damages that you can receive.

Sir Christopher Bellamy

Thank you very much indeed Subrata. Just while we are on that point before we lose it, I just want to put one question, if I may to Kevin. I was at a meeting yesterday in Paris discussing these issues in an OECD context, when it was being asserted that the treble damage suit in the US has to be seen in the light of the fact that pre-judgment interest is not normally available in US civil litigation. Of course, it is available certainly in English litigation, in most common law countries outside the US and pre-judgment interest can in practice very often lead, depending on how long it takes to get to trial of course is enormously long, to sort of double damages, if not treble damages. No, it won't lead to treble damages normally, but it will substantially increase the amount of damages and that is perhaps a relevant thought to feed into when trying to compare the two systems.

Kevin Grady

The question was, am I right generally speaking that there is very little pre-judgment interest available?

There is no doubt about that. I mentioned this point in the paper as well. You are exactly right. The key difference though, the real incentive for US antitrust actions, is the treble damages, as I pointed out in the paper. There is a real debate in the US about whether private parties really do recover treble damages or not. In Robert Lande's article that I cited in the paper,[12] based on his calculations the actual damages plaintiffs ultimately recovered are somewhere between 0.75 per cent of actual damages and 100.4 per cent of the damages. You can debate that.

---

[12] Robert H Lande *Are Antitrust 'Treble' Damages Really Single Damages?*(1993) 54 Ohio St LJ 115.

I believe Sir Christopher that the bigger difference between the US and other jurisdictions, is that in the US, the loser does not pay. If you were to have a private right of action and still maintain that the loser pays, I think you would have a huge weeding out of non-meritorious cases, a process that we don't have in the US right now. So, if you are thinking about building in some disincentives to prevent non-meritorious law suits from taking up a lot of time and legal expenses for defendant businesses, that is what I would focus on.

SIR CHRISTOPHER BELLAMY

The normal costs rule in this country and in Canada too, I am sure, is that the loser pays.

Right, we now move over to the home-team as it were, Aidan Robertson from Brick Court Chambers will now give us some short views from that respect.

AIDAN ROBERTSON

Thank you very much Sir Christopher. I should say, as a dual UK/Canada citizen I am perhaps not such a member of the home-team as it might appear. I thought what I would do is just sketch out a little bit about what we know about damages actions in the EU, but particularly from a UK perspective because that is what I certainly have most experience of.

As Sir Christopher said, there is a very detailed research paper published on the European Commission website, research carried out by Ashurst, for the European Commission,[13] which goes in to far greater detail than I can possibly do from a pan EU perspective.

I think the starting point is damages are available as a remedy in the UK and indeed elsewhere in the EU, that is whether by way of claim, or by way of counter-claim. As a counter-claim, it doesn't necessarily defeat whatever claim it is that you are facing. The competition damages don't necessarily entitle you to set them off against whatever the claimant is claiming against you. I saw a recent case called '*Three-con Europe*'. I should say that I don't have a handout, but there is an article that is shortly to be published in the *Competition Law Journal*, published by Jordans, edited by Dan Beard and Ben Rayment from Monckton Chambers in which I cover a lot of cases that I will be mentioning.

---

[13] Denis Waelbroeck, Donald Slater, and Gil Even-Shoshan 'Study of the Conditions on Claims for Damages in Case of Infringement of EC Competition Rules, Comparative Report' Ashurst, 31 August 2004 <http://www.europa.eu.int/comm/competition/antitrust/others/private_enforcement/comparative_report_clean_en.pdf>.

So damages are available as a remedy. The purpose of damages is compensatory, so it is the ordinary tort approach. The door is ajar for claims for exemplary or punitive damages. There is a House of Lords decision three years ago called '*Cuddes and the Chief Constable of Leicestershire*', which is obviously in an entirely different context, but there are different expressions of judicial opinion from their Lordships as to the desirability of expanding the currently very restricted scope for exemplary damages in English law.

In principle, competition damages claims are perceived by way of normal commercial litigation. That is to say essentially three elements: You have got to establish a breach of a statutory duty owed by the defendant to the claimant; secondly, you have got to show causation of loss rising from the breach, and the third element is assessing the quantum of the loss.

Now looking at those three stages. The first, establishing a breach is in principle, problematic, because, unlike ordinary commercial litigation, the breach may depend on factors going beyond the knowledge of the claimant. That is to say you may have to carry out an assessment of market power and that is when you do get into the realms of instructing expert economists, the duelling economists that Kevin Grady referred to.

The *Arkin* case[14] is a good example of some of the difficulties that arise. Their claim for damages was dismissed in High Court because the claimant was unable to establish abuse. These are difficult questions. What it essentially comes down to is what is normal competition? What is anti-competitive? Those are economic judgments, much more than legal judgments. This is applied industrial economics. So it is a difficult task for a court to carry out.

However, again unlike normal commercial litigation, the court may save the problem of deciding those questions, because a public agency will have already carried out a task for it. The claimant may be suing on the back of a decision of a competition authority, the follow-on action that we have already discussed. That can be relied upon, certainly in the UK, by a claimant as being definitive if that is a decision of the European Commission or of the Office of Fair Trading: the principle first set out of the *Iberian* case[15] by Mr Justice Laddie, now enshrined in Section 47A of the Competition Act 1998.

Which brings us to a particular element, a particular feature of competition litigation in the UK, which differentiates it from I think pretty much anywhere else in Europe and that is that we now have the specialist court,

---

[14] *Arkin v Borchard Lines & Ors* [2003] EWHC 687 (Comm), 14 July 2004.
[15] *Iberian UK Ltd v BPB Industries Plc* [1996] 2 CMLR 601 [1996] ECC 467 [1997] Eu LR 1 [1997] ICR 164 Times, 15 May 1996, 1996 WL 1093340.

the Competition Appeal Tribunal, invested with particular jurisdiction to hear damages claims in follow-on actions. The first two of those claims are currently before the Tribunal in claims brought by vitamins purchasers, against members of the Vitamins Cartel. Those cases are on the Appeal Tribunal's website, the *BCL* case that was formerly *Buxton Chicken* and the *Deans Food* case.[16]

On causation, this is also problematic because unlike the US, at least Federal US law, the European Union law permits the possibility of the passing on defence. That is to say, someone who has been the victim of anti-competitive practices, as a result has had to pay higher prices, if they passed on those higher prices to consumers and themselves suffered no loss, then they can't claim damages.

For a domestic jurisdiction within the European Union to legislate to remove that principle, it is arguable, it is enshrined in EU law under the San Georgio Pinciple.

Finally, on quantum. This, following on from causation is also problematic. It is not a unique problem, trying to work out what would have happened had the anti-competitive action not taken place. Typically that is what one has to do in tort or contract actions—work out what would have happened, had it not been for the particular breach in question, but the passing on issue does particularly complicate this issue in competition law.

I think, for a good illustration of the differences of problems that can arise in relation to quantum, just look at the *Crehan* litigation.[17] Mr Crehan lost in the High Court, but the Judge there calculated the damages that he would have won had he succeeded in the High Court to be a figure some ten times higher than was actually awarded by the Court of Appeal, where of course, Mr Crehan did succeed in proving his claim.

So I think the above is a sketch map of where we currently are in the UK, at least, as I say, within this jurisdiction, within the European Union. I will now hand over to Elizabeth.

CHRISTOPHER BELLAMY

Elizabeth Morony from Clifford Chance gives us the litigator's point of view.

---

[16] *Deans Food Ltd v Roche Products Ltd, Hoffman-La-Roche and Aventis SA* Competition Appeals Tribunal, Case No. 1029/5/7/04.
[17] *Crehan v Inntrepreneur Pub Company (CPC)* [2004] EWCA Civ 637, judgment on 21 May 2004.

ELIZABETH MORONY

I think it is very important to actually put the status of antitrust litigation and the state of it's growth in this jurisdiction into context when we have these debates, because sometimes it seems as if we are talking about something which is a sort of foetal stage of development, and sometimes when we listen to the US lawyers, I sort of have images of some withered old woman, smoking a fag, with a heroin addiction!

KEVIN GRADY

I've been called a lot of things, but that is a first!

ELIZABETH MORONY

I am hoping Kevin isn't a defamation lawyer as well!

I think we are somewhere in the middle. I see that the state in growth of antitrust litigation in Europe, in England in particular, because it is my phobia and has been for many years that we are years ahead of the other Member States. We are at sort of 21 on my analogy. Antitrust litigation has been in existence in this country really since the decision of the House of Lords in the *Garden Cottage* cases[18] and I think although it is currently, and has suddenly become, hugely fashionable, it has been out there, it has been going on since the early 1990s and I think in particular since the Beer Litigation.

Crehan is a good example of the fact that you can't take a view as to the volume of litigation simply by looking at the number of judgments that there have been. Most of the cases out there are settled. If you are a cartelist and you have got a decision against you that has been concluded by the European Commission or now by the OFT, and in circumstances where in the old days by means of argument in the very sensible decision of Mr Justice Laddie in Iberian, these days actually by statute, that decision will be binding in a court against you, why on earth would you end up in trial? You will have two years in litigation, you will have an incredibly expensive disclosure process, witness statements, expert reports, it would cost you more than £1m and two years later, you will almost certainly go down.

---

[18] *Garden Cottage Foods Ltd v Milk Marketing Board* [1984] AC 130 [1983] 3 WLR 143 [1983] 2 All ER 770[1983] Com LR 198 [1983] 3 CMLR 43 [1984] FSR 23 (1983) 127 SJ 460 1983 WL 215814 and *Garden Cottage Foods Ltd v Milk Marketing Board* [1982] QB 1114 [1982] 3 WLR 514 [1982] 3 All ER 292 [1982] 2 CMLR 542 (1982) 126 SJ 446 1982 WL 222182.

So these cases are settled and they have been settled for many years and I think it is very important to bear that in mind. You simply cannot consider the state of antitrust litigation and its growth and where it is going without bearing that in mind. I think at the same time, we need to look at this. I certainly look at this from the commercial perspective. I often hear discussions of antitrust litigation, really focusing on the public policy issues of an enforcement of competition law, should we enforce competition law via the OFT and the other regulators; should it be done by private parties; and again, more nightmarish tales of grasping lawyers and huge costs and treble damages and all the rest of it.

I think obviously there are public policy concerns from the perspective of the regulators. Lawyers such as myself shouldn't be getting in the way of the effective enforcement of competition law. Personally, I don't think I do. I think I add to it. But it is not in my view, an either or situation. Indeed I think the perfect situation which often does actually happen is that the private litigation adds to what is going on in the public enforcement side. It is an add-on to regulatory enforcement and therefore, very much in the public interest. So if you go back to the most obvious example of antitrust litigation, a follow-on claim against a cartel, that in my view is the right situation. The cartel is defined by the regulators, but if there is no way of recovering the losses that the cartelists have actually imposed on others, that is not a very satisfactory solution. Those who have suffered from increased prices imposed by cartels ought to be able to recover those losses as a matter of public policy.

Another point there is that it is not just about what we want, what the regulators want, what Government wants. My clients are commercial entities who if they feel they have suffered harm from a cartelist from extreme abuse, they want to recover that loss and they come to me to ask how they do that. Quite frankly, we can talk about the pros and cons of antitrust litigation and treble damages and how we avoid becoming like the Americans, but at the end of the day, commercial entities are going to want to recover those losses. And they can do it in other ways. At the moment, these claims, I would say are usually pleaded in the alternative as conspiracy claims. I think if somehow we choose to do away with antitrust litigation for fear that we will end up like the States, I suspect that lawyers such as myself and others will find an alternative way of pleading. They can be pleaded as conspiracy to defraud and that is not going to stop.

Obviously US antitrust litigation is inspiring for us, not least commercial litigation lawyers because for obvious reasons—it is a very appealing area of law in all sorts of ways, not least the fees, but again, I think it is terribly important not to be terrified by the US procedure. Antitrust litigation in this country is not based on the US model, any more than our commercial litigation generally is based on the US model. There are some extreme and terribly important differences that I should think we should highlight. We don't have jury trials. The damages awards are decided by a judge. We don't have treble damages. I agree with Aidan there is a possibility for claiming exemplary damages. There is no authority for that in the context of arbitration, advantage for us, but I will come to arbitration in a second, but one can imagine that if there were actually to be evidence of a calculation by a cartelist for example, that the additional profit would not be recovered in subsequent litigation.

I can see in those circumstances an argument for exemplary damages, but that I think is going to be extremely rare indeed. We don't have a plaintiff's bar. I advise plaintiffs; I advise defendants. We don't have 'no win, no fee'. Our contingency fee arrangements are deeply unattractive to me as a lawyer and I would think it extremely hard to think of any situation in which I would be willing to take on a large claim on a contingency fee basis.

We don't really have class actions. We have got the introduction of representative claims in the amended Competition Act, but they are aimed at consumers. I am not convinced that anybody is going to be terribly interested in representative claims other than consumer associations.

Probably most importantly of all, as was mentioned earlier, the loser pays. Why on earth would you want to bring a hopeless claim against a defendant when it is going to cost you—your own costs will be probably at least £0.5m in a major claim, which is going to go to trial, possibly £2m. If you face the risk of actually paying the opponent's fees on top of that, I simply don't understand why we spend too much time worrying about what is essentially seen as being vexatious litigation. In a sense, there is going to be a self-defining market in antitrust litigation. So I don't worry about that too much.

I do think that the move towards having specialist judges and a specialist court currently CAT, but I agree with a view of many people, including Aidan, I think what we ought to do is end up with a specialist division of the High Court to decide these cases. I think that would be an excellent development.

One talks about a 30 per cent litigation risk. However good your claim, you are only ever likely to have a 70 per cent chance of winning, just because you get the judge on a bad day. I think in antitrust litigation, you have probably got a 40–50 per cent litigation risk, which isn't very appealing, because you might find yourself in front of a judge who hasn't got a clue. I remember in 1993 in the Manchester District Registry, trying to persuade a judge in one of the beer cases that yes, you really did have to apply EU law in his Court. It was quite surreal.

Just quickly, on the forum shopping issues, others will talk about *Empagran*[19] today, but obviously that is hugely important and the decision of the Supreme Court recently was a very pleasing one, because, for obvious reasons. I don't think it is to our advantage, or to the advantage of the US courts or consumers to have the US as the world-wide antitrust court, so I hope that the last remaining tag in that case is decided the right way.

Disclosure—we only have it to any degree comparable within the US to this jurisdiction within Europe. There is no such thing as disclosure in the continent. Even if you have a decision by the European Commission or the OFT, the ability to get the opponent's documents in order to prove your position on causation, prove your position on quantum, is absolutely essential. This is why in my view, we are far ahead of other continental jurisdictions.

When the European Commission talks about somehow trying to equate litigation procedure across the continent, well all I can say is dream on. I don't think any litigators in this country are going to support that.

The last thing I would mention is arbitration. Often forgotten, but I think we have now gone beyond the thrilling debate about the arbitrability of competition law. I think we all know it is arbitrable. What is slightly disappointing, is that the arbitration community has got terribly excited about it's ability to apply competition law and has sort of gone too far the other way now and rather like Mr Justice Park, in Crehan, is not entirely open to the fact that they should find themselves bound by decisions of national competition authorities, which I think is a very important move that we need to see in the arbitration community as well.

KEVIN GRADY

If I could, Sir Christopher, I would just like to make a couple of comments.

One point on private actions: Elizabeth made the point that most cases in England are settled. Most cases in the US are also settled. There are very few trials, particularly trials of antitrust cases, in the courts. Probably less than 1 per cent I would think. Cases are rarely tried to a jury. What happens though is that the make or break point in antitrust cases usually occurs in the US on summary judgment motions. What you have in the US is the development of antitrust law through private causes of action. Summary judgment opinions written by trial court judges may often get appealed, and

---

[19] *Hoffmann-La Roche Ltd et al, Pertioners v Empagran SA et al*, 542 US—(2004), case no 03-724, decided 14 June 2004.

then you have circuit court opinions. Those opinions can then get appealed to the Supreme Court, but we have had very few Supreme Court opinions recently in the antitrust area. This previous Supreme Court term we had three pure antitrust cases, and then we had *Intel*,[20] which was antitrust-related. Four cases. You would have thought Christmas had come for the antitrust bar in the US! The Supreme Court took four antitrust cases.

The point however, is that the law in the US is able to evolve because you do have District Court opinions coming down, primarily in the summary judgement area. If defendants lose on summary judgment, then the case gets settled very quickly after that. Same is true on class actions, in particular. If the class is certified, that is the big battle usually that leads to settlements.

One of the recent cases, for example, that is not in my paper, is a very good opinion that I would commend to you by the Third Circuit in the *Flat Glass* Litigation[21] that just came down little over a week ago, in which the court discusses the issue of how to prove a conspiracy, at least in the Third Circuit. It discusses what evidence is necessary to show 'conscious parallelism–plus' in an oligopolistic industry. It is a very worthwhile opinion to review. Again, it is an example of how private causes of action provide the opportunity to develop the law, as opposed to relying on your government enforcement authorities, who may be a little bit like the Wizard of Oz, standing behind the curtains and then making the decision. They may come down with some pronouncements or some settlements, and you have basically to divine what a violation is, or what it should be, from the perspective of a government enforcement agency.

One of the real values to having private litigation, and I think this is the point that Mario Monti was talking about, is that it does allow the law to develop more freely and quickly. I am not saying you have to adopt our system, but I do think there is something fundamentally vibrant about having private causes of action to allow courts to be making decisions and developing the law, as opposed to government bureaucrats telling you what the law is from their perspective.

Sir Christopher Bellamy

Thank you very much Kevin. What I suggest is that we go round the panel now and we move off across to injunctive relief and that any comments on what has been said about damages are sort of wrapped up in that. I am just going to make one comment that has nothing to do with the topic today, which is that it was interesting that we were reminded by Elizabeth of the

---

[20] *Intel Corporation v Advanced Micro Devices, Inc* 124 S Ct 2466 (2004), No 02-572.
[21] *In re Flat Glass Antitrust Litigation,* 385 F3d 350 (3d Cir 2004).

possibility that a cartel is also pleadable as a conspiracy to defraud., It reminds me of the school of thought that although we have recently made cartel activity a criminal offence, there is a perfectly respectable body of opinion that it always has been a criminal offence, and certainly under Restrictive Practices Acts, a conspiracy to commit an unlawful act always was criminal and I certainly recall seeing an opinion from Treasury Counsel at the Old Bailey about 30 years ago. It may not be quite so revolutionary as we imagine.

However, that is a side issue, which has nothing to do with what we are talking about today. Kevin, do you want to do injunctions first?

KEVIN GRADY

With respect to injunctive relief in the US, it is available; private parties have the right to seek injunctions, not just the governmental entities. There is a lower threshold of proof for injunctions. A plaintiff seeking an injunction only needs to show threatened loss, not actual loss, and even if the plaintiff is unable to show monetary damages, the plaintiff is still able to obtain injunctive relief in the right circumstances.

You still have to show the causal connection between harm to the plaintiff and the alleged anti-competitive conduct. The issue of injunctive relief is very important. I will give you one example. There was a major law suit that was filed against most of the major US medical schools and teaching hospitals in the US.[22] It challenged the 'matching programme' in which medical school graduates are selected to go on to graduate residency training in the US. The claim for damages would have just been astronomical. Congress came in and attached an amendment to legislation dealing with pensions (again, without any hearings) basically that exempted the medical schools and teaching hospitals participating in the residency match programme from antitrust liability. The case then was dismissed. One of the key issues in the case, however, was not necessarily over the damages. Damages were potentially huge, but most observers felt 'Well, they're not going to bankrupt every medical college in the US.' Instead, the defendants' real concern was, if the court granted injunctive relief to prevent the match programme from working, determining how medical residents would be selected in the future. The lawsuit challenged the very foundation on which medical education is conducted in the US. Therefore, the injunctive aspect of this particular case was a very real concern of the defendants. This concern motivated the legislative effort to create a special immunity.

---

[22] *Jung v Association of American Medical College*, 2004 WL 1803198 (DDC, 12 Aug 2004).

Courts can issue preliminary injunctions in the US. Under the federal antitrust laws, Section 16 of the Clayton Act, specifically provides for the possibility of injunctive relief.[23] Under Rule 65 of the Federal Rules of Civil Procedure, there are four basic factors that a party needs to show to obtain preliminary injunctive relief: (1) a likelihood of success on the merits, (2) a threat of irreparable harm for which there is no adequate remedy at law, (3) the injury to the plaintiff outweighs the harm the injunction may impose on the defendant, and (4) the preliminary injunction is in the public interest. Those are the four basic criteria for preliminary injunction that the federal courts apply.

The Seventh Circuit Court of Appeals, as I pointed out in the paper, through the judicial creativity of Judge Richard Posner, has developed a sliding scale, if you will. Where irreparable harm is established and the balance of hardships favours the plaintiff, then the burden of showing the likelihood of success on the merits is somewhat lessened. The plaintiff can show either a probable success on the merits or a serious question of law going to the merits. This is similar to a standard the Federal Trade Commission (FTC) has, when the FTC goes into court to seek injunctive relief. The FTC has an administrative right of action called Part III Adjudication, where the FTC staff can bring their own cause of action before their own administrative judges. If they are going to a federal court, however, in order to seek an injunction so they can get the matter put in Part III Adjudication, all the FTC staff has to really show is a serious question going to the merits of the matter.

The FTC, thus has a lower burden of proof for injunction cases in federal courts. Indeed, that is one of the things that distinguishes the FTC from the Department of Justice, which has a higher burden to obtain a preliminary injunction than the FTC. Most judges, I think, in practice basically apply the same standard, although technically the FTC has a lighter burden for a preliminary injunction.

Permanent injunctions are also available, obviously after judgment in a case. Oftentimes, when a suit may be brought for an alleged boycott or illegal standard setting activities, the defendants may say, 'OK, we'll stop setting standards, or we'll stop the boycott. Let us just go home. Leave us alone.'

Well, the Court could take them at their word, but usually the Court has to be convinced that the cessation of activity is effective, that it is going to be permanent and that the parties are basically sincere in saying that. Most courts I think are dubious. So if you're hit with an antitrust suit for alleged

---

[23] 15 US C § 26 (2004).

conspiratorial conduct and you say 'We promise, we won't do that again,' the chances are you are still going to remain before a court, particularly if the Federal Government comes after you with respect to a Department of Justice investigation or FTC investigation. The agencies will hardly ever abandon an investigation without seeking some type of consent order in which parties commit that they are not going to continue the conduct being challenged.

The last and most drastic of the equitable remedies in the US is divestiture. Such relief is available under Section 16 of the Clayton Act. There is a Supreme Court decision, *California v American stores*,[24] in which the Supreme Court talks about the necessity of divestiture as part of the whole remedial scheme in the US. It was used by the Government more often in merger challenges prior to the Hart-Scott Rodino Act[25] (HSR) coming into effect in 1976. Prior to that time the Government would have to go after mergers that had already occurred. Whereas under the current HSR regime the agencies go in preliminarily to stop a merger if they have some concerns about it.

There are two other examples I want to bring to your attention—you may or may not be aware of them. Currently the FTC has a challenge to a hospital merger, the *Evanston Northwest Healthcare* court case[26] in the Chicago area for a hospital merger that occurred several years ago in which they claim that as a result of the merger having gone through, prices have been raised and consumers had been harmed, so it is a retrospective challenge to a merger that has already occurred.

Similarly, the Department of Justice challenged an acquisition in the *Dairy Farmers* case[27] where the party had acquired ownership a couple of years before. The DOJ for some reason found out about it late and it wasn't reportable under Hart Scott and so they went into court. The Eastern District of Kentucky in a decision at the end of last month, I believe, rejected the Government's challenge.[28] We will see if they appeal or not.

Those are examples of the Government still being able to come in for injunctive actions after mergers have already occurred.

SUBRATA BHATTACHARJEE

In Canada, the availability of injunctive relief under Section 36 is unclear.

---

[24] *California v American Stores Co* 495 US 271 (1990).
[25] Hard–Scott–Rodino Antitrust Improvements Act, 15 USC § 18(a).
[26] *In re Evanston Northwestern Healthcare Corp*, No. 9315 (FTC, filed 10 Feb 2004).
[27] *United States v Dairy Farmers of Am, Inc*, No 6:03-206 (ED Ky Filed 24 Apr 2003).
[28] *United States v Dairy Farmers of Am, Inc* No CIV. A. 03-206KSF 2004 WL 2186215 (ED Ky 31 Aug 2004).

If you take a look at the paper that is in the materials, it explains a little bit about some of the cases that have gone on, but I'm not going to go into those here for obvious reasons.

You should know, however, that private parties have a limited right of access to our Competition Tribunal. I have not spoken about the Tribunal because the Tribunal does not have the power to order damages and the right of private applicants to go to the Tribunal to get a remedial order including perhaps injunctive relief, is restricted to cases of tied selling, exclusive dealing, market restriction and refusal to deal and that's it. So there is a potential route for complainants who are worried about that type of conduct to seek relief from the Tribunal.

If you go back to Section 36, which is a civil damages provision that I spoke about in my first round of comments, that section does not contain any clear reference to injunctive relief. Courts have wrestled with that issue in Canada in a number of cases. There are indications that a limited form of injunctive relief is possible. The substantive test in Canada, by the way, is very similar to that used in the UK. There are no significant departures from that.

It appears that at least one court in Canada has taken the view—although our Section 36 is silent about injunctive relief that provincial superior courts do have the power as part of their inherent jurisdiction as Superior Courts to grant interim relief for anti-competitive conduct and so there is some authority at least to suggest that interim relief is available under Section 36 action. It appears that at the moment we have no authority to suggest that any other form of injunction is available, although I suspect that it is possible that a court could try to rely on its inherent jurisdiction to achieve that result.

One related point and this actually follows up from something Elizabeth mentioned, and I thought it was a very good point. Obviously allegations of anti-competitive conduct are not something that you plead solely under competition laws, and in Canada it is very common to see these cases, as Elizabeth pointed out, where you have a pleading in conspiracy, you have got a pleading for unlawful interference in economic relations, and then you have got a throw-in about a Section 36 action.

The common sense way is that you throw everything at the wall and see what sticks. However, the reality in Canada is that the scope of some of these parts is not entirely clear and so you don't necessarily get out of the forest simply by saying 'well I completed some common law causes of action', because even those actions may not get you where you want to go including injunctive relief.

AIDAN ROBERTSON

From an EU perspective in this jurisdiction, I think the basic starting point is that injunctive relief is available, as it would be in any other type of commercial litigation that stems from the basic principle of the effectiveness of Community law. That means you can get injunctive relief, both at the interim stage and at final trial. Typically, most competition cases involving injunctive relief have been applications for interim relief. Normally, a claim for an interim relief is going to be brought before the Chancery Division of the High Court.

Now interim relief is in principle available from the Office of Fair Trading, but has yet to be granted. They came close to it in the *Genzyme* case,[29] Ofcom has declared it's intention to seek interim relief in certain cases, but never has. You can also when you have got appeal proceedings in front of the tribunal obtain interim relief and there are a couple of incidences of that at least, the *Albion Water* case[30] being the most recent one. Also *Genzyme*.

There are obstacles to getting interim relief, both in cases under Article 81/ Chapter 1 Prohibition, Article 82/Chapter 2 prohibitions. In Article 81 /Chapter 1 cases, one of the biggest obstacles is that very often what is being challenged isn't an agreement, it is the termination of an agreement. Courts in this jurisdiction are going down the approach that the decision to terminate an agreement is essentially unilateral and therefore, doesn't fall within the scope of the Chapter 1 prohibition. See the case *Clover Leaf Cars v BMW (GB) Ltd* [1997] EuLR 535, more recently *Frazer v Nissan*[31] and see I think, very importantly, although it is not a termination of agreement case, the *Unipart v O2* decision[32] of the Court of Appeal applying Bayer, handed down on 30 July this year.

In relation to Article 82/Chapter 2 cases—abuse of dominance cases, the biggest problem there has been for claimants of injunctive relief to demonstrate to the court's satisfaction at the interim stage, dominance. You have got cases like *Norbain v Dedicated Micros*,[33] the Landrover case in which in both of those cases, the judge indicated he had a lot of sympathy with the abuse element of the claim, but in both those cases they were decided

---

[29] *Genzyme Ltd*, Decision of Director General of Fair Trading, No CA98/3/03, 27 Mar 2003.

[30] *Albion Water Ltd v Director General of Water Services* 1031/2/4/04, judgment 29/04/2004.

[31] *Frazer (Willow-Lane) Ltd v Nissan Motors (GB) Ltd* [2003] EWHC 3157 [2004] Eu LR 445 2003 WL 23192244.

[32] *Unipart Group Ltd v O2 (UK) Ltd (formerly BT Cellnet Ltd)* [2004] EWCA Civ 1034, 2004 WL 1640358.

[33] *Norbain SD Ltd v Dedicated Micros Ltd* [1998] ECC 379 [1998] Eu LR 266, 1997 WL 1103820.

against the claim of injunctive relief because they weren't able to establish dominance to the requisite degree of proof at the interim stage.

ELIZABETH MORONY

Yes, I would certain support that. It is perfectly clear that you can obtain an injunction to prevent an abuse generally, it would tend to be. I suppose it would apply to an illegal agreement as well, either on a final basis or on an interim basis and indeed for many years this was actually the most common form of antitrust litigation and a classic example of cases, which will usually settle, rather than go to court.

I think probably the most important point, I would make about interim injunction interim relief applications is the critical importance of considering the facts. Lawyers love law obviously, but I think the facts are rather more important on an injunction interim application in circumstances where you have to show that damages are an inadequate remedy. My rough and ready rule of thumb on that is basically, if your client wants to get an injunction, and is not prepared to tell you that if they fail to get an injunction it is either going to kill them off or have such an appalling effect on their reputation that they are never going to cover it again, then they are very unlikely to manage to get an injunction.

Many years ago when British Airways set up its low cost airline 'Go!', 'Easyjet' started off some rather inventive litigation, alleging that British Airways was abusing it's allegedly dominant position by cross-subsidizing 'Go!' which was a subsidiary of British Airways. They amended their original claim for a final injunction and sought an interim injunction. We all took off to court for a full day's hearing the day before 'Go!' was due to launch, and we had a very interesting debate about whether cross-subsidization was an abuse, whether British Airways was dominant and whether we could split these two things, but the slight problem that Easyjet had, was that when it came to actually looking at whether damages were an adequate remedy for Easyjet or not, the route that Go! had announced the previous day were not the same as Easyjet. They weren't actually flying to any of the same destinations whatsoever, and despite the fact we tried to persuade Easyjet of this in correspondence, they chose to ignore it. I think, it was actually some good, and relatively cheap publicity for them. So they carried on with that, but it was a somewhat hopeless case.

Also beware tactically of how you use a remedy such as an injunction. I once was instructed on a Friday afternoon by a client whose major supplier had written to my client saying that they were going to terminate the supply agreement. The effect of this was basically that my client would have been put out of business by Tuesday morning and somewhat to my amusement, I saw a letter written on another law firm's headed paper, I won't tell you which firm, and it said 'Our client has a dominant position in the supply of "X", and we have entered into an exclusive supply agreement for ten years with your client and therefore, this agreement is void and supply will be terminated tomorrow.'

So we did spend the weekend drafting our injunction application, but I had much more fun writing a letter saying 'Are you seriously going to turn up to court on Monday morning and argue this?' and surprise, surprise by Monday morning we had a letter saying that our agreement was going to carry on.

So it can be quite fun the tactical issues that can come up.

SIR CHRISTOPHER BELLAMY

Thank you very much. We have a lot of things to cover during the morning, so what I am going to do now if I may, is just ask each of our panellists to have perhaps five minutes each just to draw to our attention the particular points, they would like to underline, either on the topics we have already covered or on the topics we haven't got time to cover in the depth that we would like.

KEVIN GRADY

Thank you very much. The big fear, at least that I sense, from people in the EU about private litigation, is the discovery costs. They believe that this is going to be absolutely the rack and ruin of the EU. In the US we have the full panoply of discovery weapons: Depositions, interrogatories, document requests, requests for admission, third party subpoenas and depositions of third parties. It comes as a shock to a lot of people that you can bring third parties in and go through their documents. In many cases there are fights about protective orders, in order to make sure the proprietary information does not fall into the public domain.

In the US current antitrust litigation on the private side is heavily focused on summary judgment motions. The key battle is to have enough facts, if you are plaintiff, that will allow you to survive defendants' motion for summary judgment, thus convincing a trial court that you should be able to take your case to trial. That's the key, and that's really where the battles come down on the civil side.

The Supreme Court itself has changed the burdens of surviving summary judgment motions for plaintiffs. If you go back and look at the *Poller* case,[34] which is in the materials, the Supreme Court said that it didn't want to shut the door to trying antitrust cases because the evidence of conspiracies is usually in the hands of the conspirators. Therefore, the Court was not going to weed out these cases early. The Court basically discouraged summary judgments in antitrust cases and encouraged trial courts to give antitrust plaintiffs a chance to convince a jury of the merits of their claims.

Then you have a series of decisions in 1986 by the Supreme Court: the Matsushita[35] Anderson[36] and Celotex[37] cases. These cases reflect a major change in attitude. The Court made it much easier for defendants to prevail on summary judgment motions. It shifted the burden with respect to summary judgment motions.

Yes, we have discovery in the US. The big battle, however, is on summary judgement, not so much on trials. If you can find experienced antitrust attorneys who have tried over ten antitrust cases in their careers, you could put them all in this room and still have room to invite all their extended families. Antitrust trials simply don't happen that often.

I wanted to follow up on a point that Elizabeth alluded to about the issue of prima facie evidence if there is an adverse government decision. We have the same position in the US, and that is why the Government resolves many cases by way of consent decrees. In such settlements, there is no admission of liability by the defendants. Therefore, the adverse judgment or consent decree can not be admitted against the defendants in later actions. For example, when the Government ultimately prevailed in the *Microsoft* case, that adverse decision was used by other private parties against Microsoft as prima facie evidence of Microsoft's liability. I have set forth in the materials the Microsoft follow-on cases and the Fourth Circuit's decision in which the court basically allowed offensive collateral estoppel.[38] The court, however, limited it to the earlier case's factual findings that were necessary—meaning critical and essential—in the earlier case. Only those findings were preclusive in the subsequent case.

Therefore, in the US you have both prima facie evidence from Government actions, as well as collateral estoppel from civil actions. The issue here is based on the primary principle of collateral estoppel, emphasizing judicial efficiency and economy, thus not having to prove the same facts again if a party has already been found liable. This aspect of collateral estoppel is an evidentiary issue in the US that perhaps you don't have in the EU.

---

[34] *Poller v Columbia Broadcasting System, Inc* 368 US 464 (1962).
[35] *Matsushita Electric Industrial Co v Zenith Radio Corp* 475 US 574 (1986).
[36] *Anderson v Liberty Lobby, Inc*, 477 US 242 (1986).
[37] *Celotex Corp v Catrett* 477 US 317 (1986).
[38] 355 F3d 322 (4th Cir 2004).

Parallel proceedings are a big issue, as reflected in the *Intel* case,[39] I know that Jim Lowe and Don Baker are going to be talking about this subject later. There was this absolutely incredible fear, I think, that the *Intel* case was going to allow all cases in jurisdictions outside the US to come into the US judicial system for discovery purposes. Many people feared the US courts were going to thumb their noses at comity, and trial court judges would open the door for discovery. I doubt seriously that these fears will be realized. In fact, in the *Intel* case, when it was remanded to the trial court,[40] the trial court followed the four factors that Justice Ginsburg set forth in the *Intel* opinion and concluded: 'No, we're not going to let you have the documents.' This was a pure and simple reaffirmation of the fact that the US courts will not simply be a back door vehicle for discovery in EU judicial or administrative actions.

So to the extent that there has been a lot of discussion about the impact of Intel, I would tell you to rest easy at night. The US courts are not going to be going out of their way to require extensive discovery if a foreign jurisdiction or tribunal comes in and says it doesn't want the court's help. I believe this will be the key factor.

The other case that I would touch on before I close is the *Empagran* case. Elizabeth talked about the view that this is a great decision and, several other speakers on our program have said it was a great decision. In my view, I think the jury is still out on *Empagran* because, particularly when you are dealing with international cartels, I think Justice Breyer gave a road map in terms of how a plaintiff can satisfy the allegations in terms of talking about the inter-connectedness and inter-dependency of the conspiracies in the US and outside the US. There is a recent decision by a District Court in Connecticut, just about two or three weeks ago, in which it dealt with a resale price maintenance claim against Du Pont in Bhopal, India.[41] It was filed in the District Court of Connecticut by the former Du Pont distributor against Du Pont, and it used the magic words of interconnectedness. Following the language in the Empagran decision, the District Court concluded that a resale price maintenance claim in India had satisfied the *Empagran* requirement, at least for pleading purposes, to remain in federal court.

In conclusion, I believe that the *Empagran* case has not closed the door on access to US courts for all kinds of conspiracy claims. Therefore, I would encourage you to keep your eyes and ears open for such cases.

---

[39] *Intel Corporation v Advanced Micro Devices, Inc* 124 S Ct 2466 (2004).
[40] *Advanced Micro Devices, Inc v Intel Corp*, No C 01-7033, 2004 WL 2282320 (ND Cal 4 Oct 2004).
[41] *MM Global Servs, Inc v Dow Chem Co*, 329 F Supp 2d 337 (D Conn 2004).

SUBRATA BHATTACHARJEE

I would like to spend my five minutes briefly talking about the evidentiary issues I think that are critical under our private actions. The key words in Canada are 'follow-on actions' and that is because the majority of private actions that we have seen have been follow-ons. That is because the structure of Section 36 means that it is very difficult for plaintiffs to prove in the absence of a conviction, or a guilty plea in many cases, to meet the standard of proof required under the relevant substantive sections of the Competition Act. For example, our conspiracy provisions are, for a lack of a better term, a modified rule of reason provision. In other words, you have got to show in addition to the conduct in question that the conduct complained of results in, or is likely to result in an undue lessening of prevention of competition.

So in order for a plaintiff to succeed in a Section 36 case in Canada, you have got to prove all the elements of the criminal offence, which underlies the cause of action in order to establish liability. Now obviously we have resorted to the same sorts of pre-trial discovery procedures that are available in the US—not quite as extensive, but we obviously have discoveries or examinations for discovery, and we have an extensive documentary production process in most provinces rules.

Nonetheless, it is extremely difficult as a practical matter for a plaintiff to secure the proof they need in the absence of a conviction. The Act makes it easy for plaintiffs to bring their cases once there has been a conviction and that is because there is a deeming provision that says if there has been a conviction or a contempt order, then that is taken to be proof of loss of damages for the purposes of the Section 36 action.

On top of that, the record of those proceedings is admissible in court as evidence. So if you have got a conviction, or you have got an agreed statement of facts, you can rely upon those to bring your case as a private plaintiff. It is important to note, however, that depending how carefully the parties to a guilty plea draft the statement of facts that may, of course, not assist a plaintiff, depending on how good they are.

So this is the reason why in Canada we have not seen a lot of cases that have been brought independently of Governmental action.

AIDAN ROBERTSON

I think if we just stand back and look at it from the perspective of this jurisdiction, I have been in the practice of the bar for eight years now, and the position has changed out of all recognition to that applied in the 1990s.

Then competition law was seen as being as a little bit cherchez operating under somewhat antiquated statutes. If you tended to rely upon the Treaty of Rome you were told that is from the continent and we are an island so forget about EU law. Most cases were lost on lack of effect on interstate trade. Competition law is now taken very seriously indeed by the English courts and by policy makers generally. Witness, for example, the establishment of the tribunal and its various jurisdictions.

Cases now, if they are genuine competition cases, are likely to survive some prejudgment summary dismissal procedures in the English courts. The Court of Appeals decision in the *Intel* case[42] is particularly important in this respect. Competition law raises difficult questions of mixed fact and law, which generally speaking will go to final trial. That means that evidential issues are important, disclosure is particularly important in cases where you're not relying on a follow-on action, and you haven't got an underlying decision. I think a case that is well worth looking at for some remarks about the importance to be attached to competition law cases is the *Bim Kemi v Blackburn Chemicals* case[43] a judgment by Mr Justice Cooke, in which he said this was a very important policy that the courts must take very seriously indeed.

There is, I think, sometimes a misconception that one can avoid evidential issues by relying upon expert economic evidence. Expert economic evidence is very important, but it is not a substitute for facts and if you want to want to see a good illustration of that, look at the *Leeds City Council v Watkins* case,[44] in which Mr Justice Peter Smith had some particularly devastating things to say about the claimant's witness evidence from an alleged expert in that particular case.

ELIZABETH MORONY

I would just add very briefly to that in the context of the discussion about disclosure that email disclosure is increasingly critical in any commercial litigation case, but I think it is going to be particularly important and common in antitrust litigation in circumstances where, certainly in a cartel case, you are effectively looking at a conspiracy, which is very likely to be

---

[42] *Intel Corp v VIA Technologies Inc* [2002] EWCA Civ 1905 [2003] UKCLR 106 [2003] ECC 16 [2003] Eu LR 85 [2003] info TLR 136 [2003] FSR 33 (2003) 26(2) IPD 26007, 2002 WL 31784489.

[43] *Bim Kemi AB v Blackburn Chemicals Ltd* (Application to strike out) [2004] EWHC 166 [2004] UKCLR 364 [2004] Eu LR 575, 2004 WL 62167.

[44] *Leeds City Council v Watkins* [2003] EWHC 598 [2003] UKCLR 467 [2003] Eu LR 490 [2003] 14 EGCS 122 [2003] NPC 42 Times, 9 Apr 2003, 2003 WL 1202660.

evidenced in emails. None of us use emails as we ought to, and certainly too many of my clients don't. This is another way in which it is going to put up the cost, and therefore in a way actually discourage the vexatious claims, so we can watch that space as well.

Private Enforcement of Canadian Competition Laws

Subrata Bhattacharjee* and Gregory Sullivan**

I. INTRODUCTION

Private enforcement of competition laws in Canada has been markedly restrained in comparison to such enforcement in the United States, despite the fact that both countries have had competition laws for roughly the same period of time. Unlike the US, where the ability of private parties to seek damages for antitrust violations has been a cornerstone of antitrust policy for many decades, the right of private parties to enforce provisions (indeed, only certain provisions) of the Canadian *Competition Act*[1] has only existed since 1976, and even since that time, that right has been sparsely exercised. Prior to the widespread availability of class actions in the various provinces, private actions for damages under the Act were extremely rare. Few private actions proceeded to trial. As a result, Canadian courts have had a limited role in the development of Canadian competition law, at least with respect to cases other than those directly involving the criminal provisions of the Act. This task has, by and large, been left to the Commissioner of Competition[2] (and the Competition Bureau,[3] of which she is head) and, to a lesser degree, the Competition Tribunal,[4] a specialized administrative tribunal composed of judges and lay persons. Nonetheless, the Canadian approach to private enforcement represents a deliberate policy choice on the part of Parliament with respect to the enforcement of the Act. In a comparative context, the Canadian choice and, more saliently, for the purposes of this discussion, the practical features of that choice, may be informative.

There are many factors which explain why the Canadian experience has been different from that of the US. A comprehensive review of these factors is beyond the scope of this brief survey paper. Rather, this paper provides

---

* Co-Chair of Heenan Blaikie LLP's National Trade & Competition Group and a Partner in the Litigation Department in the firm's Toronto Office. This paper has been revised following presentation on 15 Oct 2004, and is current to 1 Dec 2004.

** Associate, Heenan Blaikie LLP (Toronto).

[1] RSC 1985, c C-34, as amended [hereinafter the *Act*].

[2] Hereinafter the *Commissioner*. Ms Sheridan Scott currently holds this position.

[3] Hereinafter the *Bureau*.

[4] Hereinafter the *Tribunal*.

an overview of private actions for damages under the Act.[5] In particular, this paper considers class proceedings, discovery/evidentiary obstacles facing potential litigants, and the availability of injunctive relief under the Canadian regime. In our view, the structure of the Canadian legislation, the existence of obstacles which impede class proceedings, the difficulty of proving claims, and limitations (and in some cases, sheer uncertainty) with respect to the availability of remedies, are instructive in explaining the comparatively limited nature of private enforcement in Canada.

II. THE LIMITED RIGHT OF PRIVATE ACTION

A. Overview

The Act is federal legislation that applies across all industries, with certain limited exceptions. The Act establishes the Commissioner as the independent authority responsible for the administration and enforcement of the legislation. The Commissioner is the head of the Bureau, which carries out investigations of contraventions of the Act.

The Act contains both criminal provisions and those subject to review by the Tribunal. The criminal provisions are contained in Part VI of the Act, and include conspiracy, bid-rigging, price maintenance, price discrimination, predatory pricing, misleading advertising, and deceptive telemarketing.[6] Reviewable provisions include more 'contemporary' preoccupations

---

[5] While claims for damages under the Act are limited to breaches of the criminal provisions of the legislation, individuals who suffer loss or damage as a result of conduct which infringes one of the civil reviewable provisions are granted a *limited* right to bring a claim to the Tribunal. Such claims are restricted to alleged violations of the section dealing with refusals to deal and that dealing with exclusive dealing, tied selling, and market restriction. It is important to note that in order to commence a claim, a potential plaintiff must first obtain leave from the Tribunal. The Tribunal, in *National Capital News Canada v Canada (Speaker, House of Commons)* [2002] CCTD No 38, established the following test for when leave should be granted:

> In order to exercise its discretion to grant leave, the Tribunal must therefore be satisfied that it has reason to believe that: (1) the applicant is directly and substantially affected in the applicant's business by any practice referred to in section 75 or 77 or the Act; and (2) the alleged practice could be subject to an order under that section.

This test has subsequently been applied by the Tribunal in *Robinson Motorcycle Limited v Fred Deeley Imports Ltd*, 2004 Comp Trib 13 and *Quinlan's of Huntsville Inc v Fred Deeley Imports Ltd*, 2004 Comp Trib 15.

The Tribunal is *not* empowered to award damages. The only remedy available to a successful claimant is a remedial order.

[6] Bill C-19, *An Act to amend the Competition Act and to make consequential amendments to other Acts*, was given first reading in the Canadian House of Commons on 2 Nov 2004. The Bill proposes to decriminalize most pricing practices, including price discrimination, geographic price discrimination, predatory pricing, and promotional allowances. Conduct that would presently be examined under these provisions would likely be examined under the civil

of competition law, such as abuse of dominance, tied selling, exclusive dealing, market restriction, and refusals to deal. In addition, mergers which result, or are likely to result, in a substantial lessening or prevention of competition are potentially reviewable, as are deceptive marketing practices (including ordinary price representations and other similar conduct). Leaving aside the civil damages remedy which will be discussed in the body of this paper, conduct that violates the criminal provisions is punishable by fine and/or imprisonment, while conduct that falls within the scope of the reviewable practices provisions is *not* illegal unless performed in the face of an order from the Tribunal or an existing court order.

The dichotomy between the criminal and civil provisions has been characterized as 'the genius' of the Act.[7] Specifically, it has been suggested that by restricting enforcement of the civil provisions (which relate largely to vertical distribution arrangements) to the Commissioner and, in those limited circumstances discussed above,[8] to those who have obtained leave from the Tribunal, strategic litigation on the part of competitors is deterred. The structure of the Canadian legislation seeks to minimize such conduct on the part of competitors and, in turn, foster business activity which has positive effects on the economy. Fear of strategic litigation has been the most cited reason for opposing further expansion of private rights of action in Canada.

Section 36 of the Act contains a limited right of action for private litigants. The provision has restricted the development of private enforcement of the Act, and stands in sharp contrast to the American antitrust regime, which permits private parties to litigate and, if successful, receive (in theory, at least) treble damages for antitrust injury.[9] Section 36 provides that any person who has suffered loss or damages as a result of (a) conduct contrary to the criminal provisions of the Act or (b) the failure of any person to comply with an order of the Tribunal or another court under the Act, may sue for and receive 'an amount equal to the loss or damage proved to have been suffered by him, together with any additional amount that the court may allow', provided this amount does not exceed the full cost to that

---

abuse of dominance provisions, provided that the other requisite elements of the abuse of dominance provisions are met. Should the Bill be enacted into law, the result will be that conduct previously subject to the affected pricing provisions but pursued under the abuse of dominance provisions will generally attract enforcement only from the Commissioner, as individuals are not permitted to bring claims to the Tribunal for alleged violations of the abuse of dominance provisions of the *Competition Act*.

[7] JB Musgrove, 'Private Antitrust Actions in Canada: A Brief Overview' (paper presented to the Canadian Bar Association Annual Fall Conference on Competition Law, Sept 1998) at 186.   [8] *Supra* note 5.

[9] Section 4, *Clayton Act* (15 USCA s 15(a)). For a lucid overview of the private enforcement regime in the US, see Sullivan and Grimes, *The Law of Antitrust: An Integrated Handbook* (West Group St Paul 2000) at ch XVII.

person of an investigation in connection with the matter and proceedings under the section.

Actions under section 36 may be brought in either the Federal Court of Canada or a provincial superior court.[10] However, such actions cannot be brought:

(a) in the case of an action based on conduct contrary to the criminal provisions of the Act, after two years from a day in which the conduct was engaged in or the day on which any criminal proceedings relating thereto were finally disposed of, whichever is the later;[11] or

(b) in the case of an action based on the failure of a person to comply with an order of the Tribunal or another court, after two years from a day on which the order of the Tribunal or court was violated, or the day on which any criminal proceedings relating thereto was finally disposed of, whichever is the later.[12]

The section 36 right of action is limited in the following ways. First, the section is limited to claims arising out of breaches of the criminal provisions of the Act, or violations of orders made pursuant to the Act. Section 36 does not contemplate a private right of action for injury suffered as a result of a reviewable practice, although other provisions in the Act permit private parties to seek leave to bring an application to the Tribunal for a remedial order as a result of an alleged breach of the reviewable refusal to deal or exclusive dealing/tied selling/market restriction provisions.[13] The significance of this limitation varies, given the nature of the conduct in question— it is entirely possible that certain types of conduct which could be characterized as reviewable conduct could also be characterized as conduct under Part VI of the Act (subject, of course, to the differing substantive elements that must be proven). Concerted conduct may, for example, be subject to the abuse of dominance provisions if an allegation of joint dominance could be made out.[14] However, that same conduct may also raise concerns under the conspiracy provisions of the Act, thereby providing the basis for a section 36 action.[15]

---

[10] Act, above n 1 at s 36(3).

[11] See *Bérubé v Makita Power Tools Canada Ltd* (1991), 40 CPR (3d) 108 (FC TD).

[12] Above n 1 at s 36(4).   [13] Above n 5.

[14] There have only been two cases involving the concept of joint dominance under the Act: *Canada (Director of Investigation and Research) v Bank of Montreal* (1996), 68 CPR (3d) 257 (Comp Trib) and *Canada (Director of Investigation and Research) v AGT Director Ltd et al.* [1994] CCTD No 24. The *Enforcement Guidelines on the Abuse of Dominance Provisions* note that the wording of the Act 'clearly contemplates cases where a group of unaffiliated firms may possess market power even if no single member of the group is dominant by itself'.

[15] For further discussion on this point, see DB Houston et al, 'Private Remedies for Anticompetitive Conduct' (paper presented to the Canadian Bar Association Annual Fall Conference on Competition Law, Sept 1998) at 203–5.

Secondly, section 36 actions are difficult to prove. The section essentially requires that a plaintiff prove all of the elements of the relevant Part VI offence, albeit on a civil standard of proof.[16] Furthermore, section 36 also makes it difficult for plaintiffs to prove damages suffered as a result of the impugned conduct. This is particularly evident when considering examples such as price fixing, where an injured party would presumably have to prove not only the prices paid during the period of a conspiracy, but also what those prices would have been in the absence of the conspiracy.[17]

III. FEATURES OF SECTION 36 ACTIONS

A. *Damages*

The wording of subsection 36(1) limits the remedies available to potential litigants by providing that an individual who has suffered loss or damage may 'sue for and recover . . . an amount equal to the loss or damages proved to have been suffered by him'.[18] It is generally accepted that this subsection limits a successful plaintiff to an award of compensatory damages. Claims for punitive damages under subsection 36(1) have been expressly rejected by Canadian courts.[19] Note, however, that such damages are available if a litigant combines a claim under section 36 with a claim in tort, such as conspiracy or unlawful interference with economic interests.[20]

In addition to compensatory damages, the Act provides that successful plaintiffs can recover the costs of investigating the matter in question and of the proceedings under section 36. Given that in a typical civil action, cost awards cover only a small fraction of the costs actually incurred by the successful party, the prospect of recovering the full expense of an investigation of a section 36 claim provides an important incentive for individuals to pursue private enforcement.[21] There is little, if any, case law that clarifies the scope of a section 36 plaintiff's right to costs.

It is important to note, however, that there are two features of the Canadian legal system which mitigate the restrictive nature of section 36, at least with

---

[16] But see JB Musgrove 'Civil Actions and the Competition Act' (1994) 16 Adv Q 94 at 105, in which the author suggests that as a practical matter, a plaintiff will likely be required to meet an 'intermediate' burden of proof, between 'balance of probabilities' and 'beyond a reasonable doubt'.

[17] See generally, DB Houston et al, above n 15.

[18] Above n 1.

[19] See, eg, *Westfair Foods Ltd.* v *Lippens Inc* (1987), 44 DLR (4th) 145 (Man QB), aff'd (1989) 30 CPR (3d) 209 (Man CA) and *Wong v Sony of Canada Ltd*, [2001] OJ No 1707 (Sup Ct J).

[20] Above n 15 at 208.

[21] C M Flavell and CJ Kent, *The Canadian Competition Law Handbook* (Carswell Scarborough 1997) at 187.

respect to remedies. First, and as is the case in England, Canadian courts apply a 'loser pays' costs rule. Though in practice, a successful litigant in a civil action usually recovers a portion of out of pocket costs (even on the highest scale of awardable costs), a successful section 36 plaintiff could supplement an entitlement to costs with reimbursement of the investigating costs. Secondly, Canadian courts routinely award prejudgment interest to successful litigants at a commercial rate from the commencement of the conduct complained of.[22]

It is worth noting that the requirement of antitrust injury, which, in our understanding, is required under US law for a plaintiff to sustain a damages claim, is not a prerequisite to a section 36 action. As discussed below, however, Canadian courts have considered and rejected the US *Illinois Brick* doctrine, which limits recovery to plaintiffs who have direct dealings with the defendants.

B. *Injunctive Relief*

The availability of injunctive relief to address anti-competitive conduct under section 36 is unclear.[23] While subsection 36(1) provides expressly for awards of compensatory damages, no such provision is made with respect to injunctive relief. The practical result is that a plaintiff with a strong prima facie case may be left in the unpleasant situation of having to wait for trial to obtain relief from conduct injuring, and perhaps even destroying, its business.[24]

The Federal Court (Trial Division) has made conflicting rulings with respect to the availability of interlocutory injunctions for conduct actionable under section 36 of the Act. In *ACA Joe International v 147255 Canada Inc et al*,[25] for example, the Court held that such relief was not available under section 36. However, in *Industrial Milk Producers Assn v British Columbia (Milk Board)*,[26] Justice Reed declined to strike out a claim for injunctive relief under the Act, stating that the availability of the remedy was 'a debatable legal issue',[27] though this was in *obiter*.

---

[22] See, eg, *Ontario Courts of Justice Act*, RSO 1990, ch C-43, s 128.

[23] See, eg, N Finkelstein and R Kwinter, 'Section 36 and Claims to Injunctive Relief' (1990), 69 Cdn Bar Rev 298.

[24] Note, however, that interim relief is available from the Tribunal. However, as discussed above, access to the Tribunal is limited to claims involving refusals to deal and exclusive dealing, tied selling, and market restrictions and is subject to a leave requirement.

[25] (1986), 10 CPR (3d) 301 [hereinafter *ACA Joe International*].

[26] (1988), 47 DLR (4th) 710.

[27] ibid at 728.

Rulings of provincial superior courts have been similarly inconsistent. In *947101 Ontario Ltd v Barrhaven Town Centre Inc*,[28] for example, the Ontario Court held that interlocutory relief was not available under section 36. The plaintiff in that case sought an interim injunction to prohibit the defendant from establishing a pharmacy in the same shopping complex as that in which the plaintiff carried on business. Among its various claims, the plaintiff alleged that the defendant would, upon opening its pharmacy, be in breach of the predatory pricing provisions of the Act as a result of its planned pricing policy. In refusing to grant the injunction, the Court stated:

> The Act does not provide for any other relief, such as injunctive relief, for a person who has suffered damage as a result of predatory pricing and it does not provide for any relief for a person who has not yet suffered any damage as a result of such conduct, but may reasonably expect to do so in future.[29]

The decision in *947101 Ontario Ltd* has subsequently been followed.[30] A more recent decision, however, suggests that interim relief may be available to address anti-competitive conduct. In *Mead Johnson Canada v Ross Pediatrics*,[31] the plaintiff and defendant were competitors in the infant formula market. In marketing its new brand of infant formula, the defendant's promotional materials included representations that the formula was superior to other formulas, that it was similar to breast milk, and that it was clinically proven to strengthen a baby's immune system. The plaintiff alleged that these representations were false and misleading, contrary to section 52 of the Act (the criminal misleading advertising provisions), and, consequently, sought an interlocutory injunction restraining the defendant from promoting the sale of its new formula. In its analysis of the issue, the Court referred explicitly to the decision in *947101 Ontario Ltd* and concurred with the judge's view in that case that the Act did not confer jurisdiction to grant injunctive relief. Nonetheless, the Court in *Mead Johnson* held that it was empowered to grant interlocutory injunctions to restrain breaches of the Act by virtue of a provincial superior court's inherent jurisdiction to do justice between the parties.

It should be noted that the cases discussed speak only to interlocutory and not permanent injunctive relief. As with interlocutory injunctions, it is unclear whether permanent injunctions are available under section 36. There is at least one case where a court struck out a claim for a mandatory

---

[28] [1995] OJ No 15 (Gen Div) [hereinafter *947101 Ontario Ltd*].
[29] ibid at para 40.
[30] See eg *UL Canada Inc v Procter & Gamble Inc* (1996), 65 CPR (3d) 534 (Ont Gen Div).
[31] (1996), 70 CPR (3d) 189 (Ont Gen Div) [hereinafter *Mead Johnson*].

injunction on the basis that section 36 was restricted to claims for damages.[32] It is also noteworthy that the Court in *ACA Joe International* suggested (in *obiter*) that permanent injunctions were not available under section 36.

As with claims for punitive damages, a potential plaintiff can avoid the uncertainty surrounding the right to injunctive relief under section 36 by combining his or her claim with a claim in tort, such as conspiracy or unlawful interference with economic interests. This avenue has received the approval of at least one Canadian Court:

> no injunction can be obtained by a party . . . against a breach of [the Act] . . . unless, in the circumstances of the case, the person seeking the injunction can establish that the conduct complained of would give rise to a cause of action in favour of the plaintiff independently of any rights the plaintiff might have to damages under s. 36 of the Competition Act.[33]

C. Discovery/Evidentiary Issues

The bulk of recent section 36 cases have followed convictions secured by the Attorney General. This raises two issues: the burden of proof required under section 36 and the availability of evidence gathered by the Bureau to assist in a private action.

Actions under section 36 of the Act can be difficult to prove. The conspiracy provisions of the Act, for example, include a requirement that the unlawful restraint of trade will or will be likely to result in an unlawful prevention or lessening of competition. This test has been interpreted to require proof of market power.[34] The predatory pricing provisions contain a broadly similar requirement.[35] Private actions seeking damages for breach of these provisions of the Act therefore face the hurdle of demonstrating that competition in the relevant market has been prevented or lessened.

In all actions under section 36, the plaintiff must prove all of the elements of the criminal offence which underlie the cause of action in order to establish liability. While the Crown in a criminal proceeding must prove its case beyond a reasonable doubt, the burden imposed on a claimant under section 36 is the lower standard of proof on a balance of probabilities.[36]

---

[32] *Price v Panasonic Canada Inc* [2000] OJ No 3123.
[33] *947101 Ontario Ltd*, above n 28 at para 42.
[34] *R v Nova Scotia Pharmaceutical Society* (1993), 49 CPR (3d) 289 (NS SC).
[35] See above n 6.
[36] *Continental Insurance v Dalton Cartage Co* [1982] 1 SCR 164.

Despite the alleviated burden, such claimants face the daunting task of presenting economic evidence to define the relevant market, must establish that he or she has suffered actual loss as a result of the defendant's conduct, and, in certain situations, demonstrate that competition in the relevant market has been negatively affected.

The Act does provide plaintiffs with some assistance in proving claims for damages. In the first place, subsection 36(2) deems proceedings in any court in which a person was convicted of an offence under Part VI of the Act, or convicted of or punished for failure to comply with an order of the Tribunal or another court under the Act as *proof* of loss or damage for the purpose of a section 36 action. The same provision also states that evidence given in such proceedings (ie proceedings resulting in a conviction or, arguably, contempt sanctions), is admissible as evidence of such loss or damage. As one commentator has noted:

> the record of proceedings in such a case could constitute the plaintiff's entire case in a damages action. While the record of proceedings does not constitute irrefutable evidence of the conduct, once it is introduced the burden shifts to the defendant. Particularly in the case of a criminal conviction, absent new evidence, the evidence of a conviction will be difficult to rebut.[37]

The assistance provided by subsection 36(2) can be limited in cases involving prior guilty pleas. In *R v Canada Pipe Co*,[38] for example, the agreed statement of facts filed in the criminal proceedings included a provision stating that there was no evidence that the conspiracy in question had been implemented. As a result, the proceedings in that case were of little use to consumers who might have wished to pursue a claim under section 36.[39]

In addition to cases involving prior criminal convictions, potential plaintiffs may benefit where the Commissioner has conducted an inquiry into the impugned conduct. The information collected by the Commissioner during such an inquiry may be a 'gold mine' for a plaintiff contemplating an action under section 36.[40] While there is little doubt that such information would be useful to a claimant, several obstacles inhibit access to the Commissioner's files. The most notable of these are the requirement in

[37] JB Musgrove, above n 16 at 106.
[38] (1995), 64 CPR (3d) 182 (FCTD).
[39] Note should also be taken of the potential applicability of s 69 of the Act, which contains provisions that permit a plaintiff to prove that agents of a defendant were acting on authority of the defendant, without calling any evidence; that a defendant had deemed knowledge of the contents of any record on its premises; or that anything recorded as done, said or agreed on by the defendant was so done, said or agreed.
[40] DB Houston et al, above n 15 at 206.

subsection 10(3) of the Act that requires that inquiries be conducted in private and the confidentiality provisions contained in subsection 29(1).

In particular, subsection 29(1) of the Act provides that:

> No person who performs or has performed duties or functions in the administration or enforcement of this Act shall communicate or allow to be communicated to any other person except to a Canadian law enforcement agency or for the purposes of the administration or enforcement of this Act
> (a) the identity of any person from whom information was obtained pursuant to this Act,
> (b) any information obtained pursuant to section 11, 15, 16, or 114;[41]
> (c) whether notice has been given or information supplied in respect of a particular proposed transaction under section 114;
> (d) any information obtained from a person requesting a certificate under section 102; or
> (e) any information provided voluntarily pursuant to this Act.[42]

The protection afforded by subsection 29(1) to information collected by the Commissioner during inquiries has been the subject of extensive debate. That debate focuses largely on the exception contained in that subsection which provides that the protection may be overridden where the disclosure of the confidential information is 'for the purposes of the administration or enforcement of this Act'.

There have been differing judicial responses to the issue of the disclosure of information ostensibly protected under subsection 29(1). In *Forest Protection Ltd v Bayer AG*,[43] for example, the Bureau did not oppose the plaintiff's motion and the Court ordered the disclosure of the documents in question. The Court took the position that a private action is initiated 'for the purposes of the administration or enforcement of [the] Act' and, consequently, held that the exception contained in subsection 29(1) was applicable. In *British Columbia's Children Hospital et al v Air Products Canada Ltd et al*,[44] the Bureau opposed the plaintiff's motion for the disclosure of confidential documents. The Court dismissed the plaintiff's application, concluding that it was premature to seek disclosure from the Bureau since discoveries had not yet taken place and distinguishing the decision in *Bayer*

---

[41] The sections listed contemplate information obtained by the Commissioner through the exercise of her extensive investigatory powers, including the power to obtain written and oral discovery from an individual and the power to obtain a search warrant.

[42] Above n 1.

[43] (1996), 68 CPR (3d) 59 (NB QB) [hereinafter *Bayer*].

[44] [1997] BCJ No 494 (BC SC).

on the ground that the Bureau in the present case opposed the application. However, the Court indicated that a further motion could be brought by the plaintiff after the completion of the discoveries.

In previous policy statements,[45] the Bureau took the position that it would assist private litigants by providing confidential information in cases where its investigation is no longer on-going. Subsequently, however, the Bureau has stated that it will provide confidential documents to private parties only in response to a court order.[46] Ultimately, while confidential information could theoretically be disclosed pursuant to the exception enumerated under subsection 29(1), it would appear that it cannot be assumed that private plaintiffs will have a right to such information in the absence of a court order.

D. Class Proceedings

The Canadian experience with respect to class actions in the competition law context has been limited. Class proceedings in general are a relatively recent phenomenon in Canada. It was only in 1993, for example, that the Ontario *Class Proceedings Act*[47] came into force. Similar statutes have been enacted in other Canadian provinces. A small but growing number of class proceedings have been commenced in various Canadian provinces.

Under the Ontario legislation, for example, a court must certify a class if the following criteria are met:

(i)   The pleadings disclose a cause of action;
(ii)   An identifiable class of two or more persons exists;
(iii) The claims or defences of the class members raise common issues;
(iv)   A class proceeding is the preferable procedure for the resolution of the common issues; and
(v)   There is a representative plaintiff or defendant who, *inter alia*, would fairly and adequately represent the interests of the class.[48]

These requirements are broadly similar to class proceedings legislation in other Canadian provinces. Indeed, the general Canadian framework for class proceedings is similar in many respects to that under the US Federal Rules of Procedure with one significant exception—it is not the case (in the Province of Ontario anyway) that the court must find that the questions of

---

[45] Industry Canada 'Communication of Confidential Information Under the Competition Act' (May 1995).
[46] Industry Canada 'Bulletin—Immunity Program Under the Competition Act' (Sept 2001).
[47] RSO 1992, c 6.
[48] ibid at s 5(1).

law and fact common to the members of the class predominate over questions affecting individual members.[49] This may generally imply that all other factors being equal, certification in Canadian courts may be easier to obtain than under the US Federal Rules of Procedure.

One of the most significant issues with respect to class proceedings is whether a group of indirect purchasers can be certified as a class in a claim under subsection 36(1) of the Act. This issue was considered by the Ontario Court of Appeal in *Chadha v Bayer Inc*[50] In that case, the plaintiffs were recent purchasers of homes containing coloured bricks and paving stones. The defendants were the major manufacturers and suppliers to the Canadian market of the iron oxide pigments used to colour concrete brick and paving stones. It was alleged by the plaintiffs that the defendants had engaged in a price-fixing scheme, thereby illegally increasing the price of bricks and paving stones. While the plaintiffs were not the direct purchasers of iron oxide from the defendants, they alleged that as a result of the price-fixing activities on the part of the defendants, they overpaid for their homes.

In holding that the class should not be certified, the Court of Appeal noted that an element of liability under subsection 36(1) was that the plaintiff suffered loss or damage as a result of the impugned conduct. Certification was, in the opinion of the Court, contingent on whether liability could be proven as a common issue. The plaintiffs in *Chadha* presented no economic evidence as to how loss could be proven on a class-wide basis and instead assumed that the overcharge caused by the price-fixing scheme had been passed on to the ultimate purchasers of the homes. The Court took issue with the plaintiff's assumption and held that liability could not be proven as a common issue. Similarly, the Court reasoned that a class proceeding was not the preferable procedure to deal with the dispute, as it would require individual trials to establish whether each class member had suffered any actual harm or loss. A class action in such circumstances (given that the number of potential plaintiffs was estimated to be 1.1 million persons) would have been 'unmanageable'.[51]

While the decision in *Chadha* presents a serious obstacle to class proceedings involving indirect purchasers, such individuals are not completely disenfranchised. The Canadian courts have chosen not to follow the example set by the United States Supreme Court in *Illinois Brick Company v Illinois*.[52] It would appear that a class of indirect purchasers could be certi-

---

[49] US Fed R Civ 23(b)(3).

[50] (2003), 63 OR (3d) 22, application for leave to appeal to the Supreme Court of Canada dismissed [hereinafter *Chadha*].

[51] ibid at para 56.

[52] 431 US 720 (1977).

fied so long as an economic methodology for establishing loss on a class-wide basis is offered. Another method for circumventing the result in *Chadha* is to define the proposed class so as to include *all* purchasers (both direct and indirect). Such an approach would eliminate the requirement of presenting an economic methodology for establishing that the over-charge in question had been passed on to the indirect purchasers. This approach has been endorsed by the Canadian courts.[53]

IV. CONCLUSION

In Canada, private enforcement of competition laws remains a comparably minor feature of the overall enforcement of the competition regime, at least in comparison to the robust state of private enforcement in the US This was clearly the intention of Parliament, given the relatively late stage at which actions for damages were made available (and notwithstanding the recent half-hearted attempt to explore expanding private access to the Tribunal). The limited nature of the section 36 right with respect to remedies, limitation periods and standards of proof only underlines the desire of Parliament to keep enforcement of the Act in public hands. Notwithstanding this, however, the availability of class proceedings has breathed life into a previously moribund section of the Act, and class plaintiffs have shown a willingness to be creative and squeeze the maximum benefit from the existing provisions of the Act. Only the passing of time will reveal the extent to which this may change the existing balance between public and private enforcement of Canadian competition laws.

---

[53] See, eg, *Vitapharm Canada Ltd v F Hoffman-La Roche Ltd*, [2000] OJ No 4594 (Sup Ct J) and *Mura v Archer Daniels Midland Co* [2003] BCJ No 1086 (SC).

Panel 2—Jurisdictional Issues: Reflections on Extra-territoriality

SIR CHRISTOPHER BELLAMY

We are now moving to jurisdictional issues, and this next panel is going to be essentially directed to extra-territoriality, particularly after the *Empagran* decision[1] and in view of the *Provimi* case.[2] What I thought we might do now, since we have now got two panels in succession before lunch, is hear from our four distinguished speakers on this panel, who will take 12–14 minutes each to cover their various topics. Then I think we may have a period of questions from the floor, because I am sure some of you are dying to ask at least some questions—both on this panel and the panel that we have just finished, and then we will proceed to the last panel. But we might, as it were, cut into the last panel a bit in order to allow time for questions on the first two panels that we have had.

So let us press on with this panel, and I will ask first, if I may, James Lowe, Wilmer Cutler Pickering Hale and Dorr from the Washington office of that very distinguished firm to give us his views.

JAMES F LOWE

Good morning, and it is an honour and pleasure to be here. I am here to deliver some good news and bad news from the States of which Kevin Grady gave us a preview. I am here to talk about *Empagran* and to a lesser extent, *Intel*, an issue that is under control, whereas *Empagran* is an issue that, unfortunately, I must report is not yet under control.

Let me start briefly with *Intel*. As many of you know *Intel* is a case that involves the question of how US courts can be used to obtain discovery in non-US actions, be it court actions or actions of an administrative nature. The Ninth Circuit Court of Appeals in a somewhat oddly worded opinion ruled that AMD, a competitor of Intel, might seek discovery from Intel for a complaint that AMD had brought in the European Commission.

That decision went to the Supreme Court and the Supreme Court, in a decision that was not surprising to those of my colleagues who are expert in

---

[1] *Hoffmann-La Roche Ltd. et al, Pertioners v Empagran SA et al*, 542 US—(2004), case no 03-724, decided 14 June 2004.

[2] *Provimi Ltd v Aventis Animal Nutrition SA* [2003] EWHC 961, [2003] 2 All ER (Comm) 683 [2003] UK CLR 493 [2003] ECC 29 [2003] Eu LR 517 2003 WL 21236491.

comity and act of state and international law, ruled that the Ninth Circuit had, in fact, perhaps for some of the wrong reasons, gotten the statute correct, namely there is the ability for District Courts in their discretion under certain conditions to order the discovery of the sort that AMD was seeking. But the Court made it clear that there were four factors that had to be applied by the District Court in determining whether that discovery was appropriate in any particular case. Those four factors were quite clearly derived from the statute and its amendments.

Ten days ago now, the District Court which had originally denied discovery to AMD—issued its decision on remand and applied the four factors laid out by the Supreme Court. It found that three of those four factors urged against allowing AMD discovery of Intel and therefore, decided that no discovery would be ordered in this case.

I think that the District Court opinion will be used as an example by other District Courts, or at least I certainly hope it will be, as the way to apply the statute, 28 USC 1782. Therefore, I suspect this is an issue, which I know drew a lot of attention on this side of the Atlantic that will fade largely into the background over time.

Empagran is a more complex issue; indeed it was a more complex issue to begin with and remains so in my view. Elisabeth expressed in the last panel the hope that the Supreme Court's decision would resolve some of the apparent efforts of US plaintiff's lawyers to create a world antitrust court in the US. As Kevin said, and I agree with him, the jury is still very much out on this question.

A little background here for those who may not have been aware of the history here. For more than 50 years, US courts have asserted that the US antitrust laws have extra territorial jurisdiction when the effect of the conduct at issue intentionally affects US markets and that comes principally from a case in 1945, *US v Alcoa*.[3] That position was developed over time in a variety of cases leading up to 1982.

In 1982, the Congress for reasons that are somewhat mysterious, at least to me, decided that it needed to clarify the scope of extra territorial jurisdiction of the US antitrust laws and also simultaneously, somewhat ironically, legalize US export cartels.

Accordingly, they passed the misnamed Foreign Trade Antitrust Improvements Act,[4] a statute which is a modicum and example of poor congressional drafting. It is a statute that one can read, as I have done

---

[3] *US v Aluminum Co of America*, 148 F2d 416 (2d Cir 1945).
[4] Foreign Trade Antitrust Improvements Act of 1982, 15 USC 6(a).

unfortunately, repeated times without fully understanding what Congress intended, meant, or could possibly have been thinking at the time that it drafted the statute.

The statute has created enormous confusion in the lower courts. For the first ten years or so, relatively little harm was created, but then, as cartel enforcement in the US increased, and there was then increased follow-on private litigation involving international cartels in US courts, mischief began to appear.

There were three principal Court of Appeal's decisions over the last four or five years that created this confusion. The first and from the point of view of a defence counsel, most encouraging was the Fifth Circuit opinion coming out of the heavy lift barge cartel, known as Statoil.[5] The Fifth Circuit said, we read the FTAIA to say that jurisdiction is available to foreign plaintiffs for foreign harm only when those plaintiffs can show that their harm is inexorably linked to the harm that has occurred in the US.

There then proceeded shortly thereafter to be two other Court of Appeals decisions.

First, and somewhat unfortunate because of the very complicated facts on the case, the *Kruman* decision[6] in the Second Circuit—which arises out of the Sotheby's and Christie's price fixing arrangement—read FTAIA much more broadly. Without getting into the details of the statutory issue, it comes down to the question of whether 'a' means 'the'. The Second Circuit says 'a' means 'a' and therefore any time that the foreign plaintiff can point to the existence of a claim by somebody that there was a US effect, the foreign plaintiff may bring his or her claim in the US court, regardless of whether his particular claim is directly related to the harm on US commerce.

The DC Circuit effectively adopted the *Kruman* test in the *Empagran* case—which grows out of the vitamins cartel—and opened the doors, arguably, to very broad extra territorial jurisdiction for foreign plaintiffs as long as there is some nexus to the US at all.

The Supreme Court, because of the split between the Fifth and Second in the DC Circuits granted certiorari and I think a lot of us had hoped that the Court would clarify this dispute between the circuits. Initially, when the decision came out in June, there was euphoria among the defence counsel, because you take the opinion and you thumb through it and you see

---

[5] *Statoil ASA Den Norske Stats Oljeselsteap As v Heeremac Vof*, 241 F3d 420 (5th Cir 2001).

[6] *Kruman v Christie's International Plc*, 284 F 3d 384 (2d Cir 2002).

'reversed' and that was good and you read through it and it seemed to say that *Kruman* was rejected, the DC Circuit's opinion was rejected, and they decided favourably to Statoil and that all looked wonderful.

Then you go back and read it again more closely—the euphoria fades into concern and then, ultimately, disappointment. Because Justice Breyer is struggling, I think, with a variety of factors that underlie the question of extra territorial jurisdiction of the antitrust laws in the US, he has written an opinion that I fear resolves very little, except on the margins. What he has done is written an opinion that says 'Foreign plaintiffs whose harm is independent of the harm that occurs in the US, do not have the ability to bring the case in the US'.

The problem is this: Let us take the vitamins cartel: The vitamins cartel is an international cartel where the agreement was to raise prices world-wide. The argument has been made by the foreign plaintiffs in that case effectively as follows: In order to maintain higher prices in the US, you have to raise prices in let's say Ecuador, otherwise arbitrage will occur and the US customers will simply buy a product in Ecuador and ship it in to the US. So, therefore, the harm to the Ecuadorian purchaser, who has paid a higher price is inextrably linked to the US harm on the market.

That is the argument that is being made on remand in *Empagran*. It is an argument that is fairly compelling under a reading of much of Justice Breyer's opinion, particularly the last section of it. It will be interesting to see how this will play out in the DC Circuit and an opinion is expected probably by the end of the year, although that Court can be sometimes slow in reaching decisions. But that will be the key case, I believe, on where we are headed here.

There is some good news. Kevin mentioned the worst news there is, which is a District Court opinion entitled MM Global Services, which involves a resale price maintenance case in India, which is really quite puzzling on a whole host of levels. It is also puzzling because it was released a week after the Second Circuit released the first—and most encouraging—of the post-*Empagran* decisions in a case that I was involved in called *Sniada v Bank Austria*[7] which, to paraphrase Judge Posner, is a sad excuse for an antitrust case. It involves an individual American who traveled to Europe and exchanged intra-European currencies—Francs for Deutchmarks—and alleges that he was charged a supra-competitive fee by the banks as a result of the Lombard Group and other agreements. He alleges that he was suffi-ciently harmed that he ought to have a right to sue in US courts for the

---

[7] *Sniada v Bank Austria*, 378 F3d 210 (2d Cir 2004).

harms that the Austrian and German banks cost him when he exchanged currencies at their banks.

The Second Circuit, following *Kruman,* had actually reversed a District Court opinion that had thrown out that case. On remand after *Empagran,* the Second Circuit said, 'No, that was a mistake. The District Judge was right. This is a poor excuse for an antitrust case and after *Empagran,* this case cannot survive.' The Second Circuit has some very nice useful language where it says the Supreme Court decision in *Empagran* endorses the District Judge's prescient view of the FTAIA, that Sniado must allege that his European conspiracy effect on domestic commerce gave rise to his claim.

That would be very nice language that others can use, but it is a broad reading, I think, of *Empagran.* Indeed, I don't think that is actually completely consistent what Justice Breyer said, and I suspect that lots of District Courts will find lots of large loopholes in this notion of what constitutes 'independence' from the US effects. I predict there will be a lot of confusion on this.

One could read—and, indeed, there are sections of Justice Breyer's opinion that do read—like a plea to Congress to fix this statute and perhaps that may eventually happen, although I would not hold my breath for that to occur. As Kevin said, there is the Modernisation Commission. In some senses that the existence of that Commission, which will take up this issue in part, may in fact freeze Congress even longer than it might have otherwise. There is also the possibility that this gets taken back up to the Supreme Court, either perhaps in *Empagran* itself, or in some future case, when confusion continues to reign.

But this is a 'stay-tuned' issue, because this one is far from resolved, and I do not believe that I can tell my clients, and I do not believe that those of you in private practise here can tell your clients, that this is an issue with a clear resolution going forward.

So the question of the extra territorial reach of the US antitrust laws, I think remains largely open, other than for purely foreign cases. Clearly cases that have little or no viable claim for having an impact on the US are dead, but except for that narrow category of cases, the rest remains to be seen, and, so, do stay tuned, because this is an area for much future development.

SIR CHRISTOPHER BELLAMY

Thank you very much James. Confusion obviously goes a bit deeper than the difference between [the pronunciation of] vitamins and vitamins. We will see how that develops.

Jean François Bellis is one of the older statesmen of European Competition

Law and International Trade Law generally. He is going to give us his perspective on this—particularly from the point of view of German experience.

JEAN FRANÇOIS BELLIS

When listening to your presentation, I realized that I may be perhaps the only beneficiary in this room of the US extra-territorial jurisdiction. A few months ago, I received a letter from a US law firm informing me that I was a member of a class of victims of Christie's, because I had bought a small painting at Christie's in Milan many years ago. I thought maybe after this I will be able to retire, but when I read the letter, I realized that my share of damages was provisionally estimated at $92, but would in any case, not be less than $20! I am still waiting for the money, and when I receive the cheque, I will have it framed—I will not cash it!

This is not really the subject which I wanted to cover this morning! I wanted to bring a continental/European perspective basically focusing on Germany. I think it is in Germany that probably the most interesting problems in the field of competition litigation have occurred.

Interesting problems because of the cases, which have been dealt with by German courts, and also interesting because of what is coming—the Seventh Amendment to German cartel law, which contains some interesting provisions, which I think have no equivalent in any other system.

First let me deal with the existing cases. Basically, there are two lines of cases, which both deal with vitamins. This is the German 'wing' of the vitamins case. All in all, five judgments were issued but three of them were issued at the same time by one court in Mainz, which took a very restrictive position and basically held that plaintiffs had no standing to bring actions for damages for competition law infringements based on a very special notion of German law. Under German law, certain laws are regarded as only pursuing public interest goals. Other laws are considered as also protecting private interests and it is only if a law is in the latter class that an action for damages could be brought in case of infringement. The Mainz court basically decided that competition law was not meant to protect private interests, or at least not those private interests which were involved in the case.

There was another judgment by a District Court in Mannheim, which basically took the same line and in addition, held that there was no damage in this case because the damage had been passed on to the next level of purchasers. Substantively, there was no ground for granting damages.

Then came in April this year a very interesting judgment from the Court of Dortmund. This judgment is under appeal. I think a Court of Appeal decision is expected by mid-2005 and in the judgment the Court took a very different line. It considered that private parties could claim damages: in other words, competition law was meant to protect private interests.

As far as the assessment of the damage and also the passing on issue are concerned, the Court adopted a very clever approach. It did not dismiss the notion that passing on could be a defence, but it held that it was for the defendant to prove that passing on had occurred. The Court found that the defendant had not really established that passing on had taken place, so the defence was dismissed. The damage was assessed on the basis of what had happened to vitamin prices after the termination of the cartel. The Court basically relied on the Commission decision, which had found that after the end of the cartel, prices had declined by 15–50 per cent. The Court took an average figure of the decline and awarded damages on this basis. The damages which were awarded in this case were in the order of 1.6 million Euro. This is, I think, the most significant damage award for a competition law infringement in Continental Europe so far. Of course, it remains to be seen what will happen to this case when it is decided by the Court of Appeal.

In addition to this, I think it is very interesting also to know that there is a draft amendment of the German cartel law, which is being discussed. This amendment would make it clear that the notion that competition law does not protect the private interest should, of course, disappear. Also the amendment would indicate that the profit made by the parties to the cartel could be a factor in awarding damages. Moreover, there would be a very interesting provision that would allow associations representing the public interest to make claims for a share of the profit which was unlawfully earned by the cartel participants, but then that share of the profit would not end up in their pocket. It would be paid to the state. In other words, associations would basically sue the cartel participants for a share of the profit on behalf of the state. As far as the assessment of damages is concerned, the amendment would make it clear that this assessment can be an approximation. It need not be absolutely precise.

On passing-on, initially it has been envisaged to exclude the passing-on defence, but in the final text, which was presented, it was left to the courts to decide whether passing on should be accepted as a defence, or not.

I think these are very interesting problems which have no equivalent in other Member States. Of course, there have been cases elsewhere, for instance, in France where damages were awarded for a competition law infringement. Otherwise you hear about threatened litigation, but very few actual actions. Germany and the UK are at the forefront of competition litigation in Europe.

SIR CHRISTOPHER BELLAMY

The possibility of an association suing for some part of the profit, but the profit then going to the state—why would anybody want to bring such an action? Is it the public authorities—hospitals or local authorities?

JEAN FRANÇOIS BELLIS

Well, it would be associations representing the general interest. It would be more like a public interest association, something which is not so uncommon in Germany. You have a lot of litigation in Germany, for example, in the field of unfair competition law, which is brought by associations of that type. So basically, associations of busy-bodies!!

PAUL LOMAS

I discovered I share a common experience with Jean François Bellis in that I too have received a letter from the lawyers in the *Sotheby's/Christie's* cartel, which is particularly ironic because I negotiated the settlement, and because of that I can share a piece of information with you in relation to Monsieur Bellis. He tells us that he is entitled to $92 dollars back. He is either a seller at Christie's, or if he were a buyer, he has bought an enormous amount!

JEAN FRANÇOIS BELLIS

I deny!

PAUL LOMAS

Moving swiftly on, I volunteered to look a little bit at a particular manifestation of the international aspects of private damages actions in relation to cartels and looking at them essentially within the European environment.

That is clearly relevant for two particular reasons. It is a trite point that these type of operations are intrinsically international in a single market, and it is also the case, I think, that modernization, which we haven't spoken about very much this morning, which is something of a relief in that it has been spoken about a great deal elsewhere, does, I think, skew the playing field a little bit in that area. Not so much in a case of pure cartel actions, but in another form of infringement, where there is an Article 81(3) possibility, then forum shopping becomes an extremely interesting prospect. Therefore, I think it throws into sharp relief, the ability for plaintiffs to choose their defendant to choose their jurisdiction.

The case that is most relevant on that is probably *Provimi*, a case in which one of my partners acted for the defendants, so we have views on the case. Again, pausing, it is a case when exemplary damages were run as a claim, although not actually litigated, as a throw-back to a conversation earlier this morning.

It is a decision of Mr Justice Aitkens in the Commercial Court, which of course probably wouldn't even occur now—it would probably be in the Chancery Division. A couple of introductory points. First of all, it is a cartel case. It is the vitamins cartel, it's Roche, etc, so the factual backdrop is not helpful to the defendants, and the decisions that have already been taken against them on liability meant that the case was very constrained.

Secondly, it was a decision on strike-out application. It went on appeal, but without going into details, the appeal will not be proceeding, and Sir Christopher Bellamy has the undeniable pleasure of a second set of damages claims coming before him at the moment. This means, of course, that as a strike-out the matter was being looked at very much on the question whether the points were arguable, the facts being assumed, and the court concluded in most cases that they were and the case should go ahead.

It introduced quite an interesting test within the court. The test was being applied, which to my mind was a relatively new one, was whether or not either party had very much the better of the argument. That was the test that was applied. There may actually be a very honest appraisal by the judge, because I suspect very much the better of the argument is probably the test that is usually applied!

I won't spend too long on the facts, because they become insanely complicated due to the trading relationships. Not only between the Roche and Aventis groups of companies, but the various parties that were buying vitamins from them. They were buying from or trading with a variety of different subsidiaries. The issues essentially related as to whether the claims could be pursued against various of the subsidiaries in the jurisdictional environment that applied at the time.

The case looked at four issues. The difficulty was that some of the plaintiffs had not traded with, or had any commercial contact whatsoever with some of the defendants. The question then came up as to whether they were entitled to pursue those claims.

The first issue that came up was in a sense, where is the underlying infringement. Part of the judgment is taken up with looking at whether you can actually look at the anti-competitive agreement as operating within the groups of companies so that the subsidiaries were effectively participating in it. I think the Court came analytically to the entirely correct conclusion in the light of cases like *Viho* that the single economic unity theory holds good and you can't look at the relationships between the subsidiaries.

What you can look at however, is that a broad Community-wide definition of an undertaking and if you come to the conclusion that this infringing behaviour between two undertakings, then a third party is entitled to pursue it's rights against any of the subsidiaries that were involved in implementing that anti-competitive agreement. Regardless of whether or not they were involved in forming the agreement, whether or not they even had any knowledge of it—if they were simply applying pricing directives coming from people further up the organisational chain who had been infringing.

That, of course, opens the door to very wide forum shopping in the sense of putting all subsidiaries involved in implementing a pricing agreement into the firing line.

There was then a separate issue that was looked at in relation to jurisdiction and whether or not it was actually possible to bring some of these cases before the English tribunals. The court took a fairly robust approach to Article 6 of Regulation 44[8]—the one saying that you can be joined into a case brought against a defendant in the jurisdiction in which they are domiciled, if there is a sufficiently close connection, such is expeditious effectively in the interest of expediency and avoids the risk of irreconcilable decisions and other jurisdictions.

Here, I think, we see an interesting impact of modernisation. Again, not so applicable in a cartel case, but if we look at a lesser infringement, I think it must be said that there is an increased risk of irreconcilable decisions where Article 81(3) is likely to be deployed in multiple cases across Europe. So the impact of that, I think, is to go for a fairly inclusive interpretation of Article 6 on jurisdictional grounds.

Moving on, there was a short debate on causation, where the court effectively decided that it was not surprising that there would be a single price line applied within an organization, and that the loss was suffered by virtue of the cartel applying those price lines, and it didn't want to delve into detailed causation arguments.

---

[8] Council Regulation (EC) No 44/2001 of 20 Dec 2000 on jurisdiction and the recognition and enforcement of judgments in civil and commercial matters, OJ L12/1 (16/01/2001).

The fourth point that was considered was the role of the exclusive jurisdiction clauses. That is relevant because the purchasers were buying on standard terms from the various subsidiaries and there was both a French and a German and a Swiss exclusive jurisdiction clause in the standard terms. In each case of course, the defendants pleaded those exclusive jurisdiction clauses as a way of restricting litigation back to other jurisdictions, as they were entitled to do under Article 23 of Regulation 44.

The Court took a very traditional approach to the analysis of this, sighting the wonderfully named *Hugo Trumpy*[9] case frequently, and looked at whether or not the exclusive jurisdiction clause was within the scope of Article 23 very much as a matter of Community law interpreting the Regulation and then delved down into domestic law to identify the scope of the clause once it's validity had been established.

That was where they hit the difficulties because in each case under Swiss, German, and French law, they held that the scope of the exclusion clause wasn't wide enough to debar the UK or English jurisdiction. It is quite a complicated analysis going through with the benefit of expert interpretation advice from foreign lawyers, the application of each one of those clauses, but the judge was obviously persuaded by things like general duties of good faith under civil law systems and the fact that this was a deliberate act and therefore, arguably outside the scope of what parties had intended to deal with in their exclusive jurisdiction clause.

So in that case, the clauses failed on every count and the litigation was due to go ahead in the UK. As a broad approximation, I think we would say that *Provimi* encourages forum shopping, which poses the question of what can companies do to control that process, if anything.

There are two suggestions that I will venture and leave with you, although I don't think they are particularly clean solutions. One was one that we actually did look at very closely in *Sotheby's/Christie's*, because everybody who deals with the auction house, although they don't always admit it, is dealing on their standard terms and conditions which contain exclusion clauses, some of which, I am about to redraft in the light of some of these cases.

This was an issue that went away because of the settlement of the *Kruman* litigation and the Bellis benefit cheque, but this was an issue that was going to be quite relevant because those clauses were much stronger than the ones that applied in the vitamins case and English law generally favours an interpretation relation to those exclusion clauses. I think English canons of

[9] C-159/97 *Trasporti Castelletti Spedizioni Internazionali SpA v Hugo Trumpy SpA* ECR [1999] I-1597, [1999] ILPr 492.

interpretation would be more generous to those exclusion clauses, than perhaps French, Swiss or German. In particular in a German case, the exclusion cause referred the case to a court that didn't have a jurisdiction to consider competition matters, which was a little unhelpful.

So I think, it is possible to do things with appropriately drafted exclusion causes still, but they will have to be very, very clear as to the breadth of potential alleged infringements that are to be submitted to the designated court. So clear, as to perhaps raise a question on the mind of the counter-party, as to why it has to be that wide.

Also, I think, if it is to be effective, it has got to look at all claims raised by the purchaser of the goods, in relation to the goods, rather than arising out of the contractual relationship to the vendor. That may, in certain circumstances, give you the right as the parent company to persuade your subsidiary to enforce that exclusion clause against the counter-party.

You do then hit the interesting case of *Taylor and Grovit,* of course. Mr Grovit who has contributed so fulsomely to jurisprudence in a number of areas, who runs the Exchange Bureaus 'Checkpoint' and a number of others. *Taylor and Grovit* was decided earlier this year and made a point on anti-missile missiles on anti-suit injunctions, making the point that you can't make an application to a new court effectively to prevent the fresh litigation being conducted elsewhere because under the regulation, the courts have a comity and you should expect the newly-seized court to take and apply the convention against it's own jurisdiction, rather than go into the original court and asking for an injunction against the parties from pursuing that litigation. So there is a *Taylor and Grovit* risk, I think, with the exclusion causes.

The second point, which we have developed on occasions is arbitration. Elisabeth Morony referred earlier to arbitration. I think some of the difficulties associated particularly with modernisation in the context of arbitration have yet to be explored, but that is of course outside the scope of the regulation, and is possible that a well drafted exclusion clause, particularly in the light of a case called *Excel against Owen Corning*—from a couple of years back, would take a very strong and purposive approach to an arbitration clause and may assist in controlling the risk that way.

MICHAEL BOWSHER

I focus on the consequences that might arise from judicial decisions in different jurisdictions of the Community touching on the competition law analysis of the same or similar facts. This is not necessarily a situation in which judgment is being sought on the same claim twice. Rather in a competition law context, as already alluded to by Paul, the validity of an agreement may be put in issue more than once in different jurisdictions in relation to different claims.

This topic may be of particular concern in light of the need to achieve some sort of consistency in the contractual area. It is probably a much more pressing issue in Article 81 litigation than in Article 82 issues. Those who are nostalgic for the days of the negative clearance or the Article 81(3) decision that gave one security for many years will be rooting around for some equivalent today. The only message I draw from this short survey of the new multi-jurisdictional litigation environment is that we are certainly denied certainty in this field. In the notes I explore how one might try to obtain such security.

The headings in my notes start with the straightforward jurisdictional situation under Regulation 44/2001. A judgment from one Member State has to be recognized in another Member State unless such recognition is manifestly contrary to public policy in the Member State in which recognition is sought. Some of course have wondered whether or not the court of one Member State is entitled to as it were reject what is perceived to be an erroneous decision of another Member State. At the very least, that would be a very difficult course for a national court to take following the decision in 2000 in the *Renault* case,[10] which made it pretty clear that that is almost impossible. Presumably, though, if a national court made it plain that it was wilfully ignoring the application of EC competition law, it might be that one could simply ignore the cross-application of a judgment from one jurisdiction to the next.

The more pressing problem arises in the situation in which there is a debt action in one proceedings and a pan-European multi-jurisdictional contract has been found to be valid in those proceedings, but you are faced with the prospect of a decision of a national court in another Member State that might want to find that your network of agreements is invalid. This would create a substantial commercial difficulty for those trying to operate major distribution networks. It is a topic which has not been addressed in the case law in any detail, and we are left to speculate on what the answer might be from general principles of private international law. We have an uneven or barely developed system of competition law litigation in so many Member States, so these cross-jurisdictional points do not often arise. In principle, though, the different effects produced by interactions between 25 Member States' different legal systems will create a variety of approaches to this

---

[10] C-38/98 *Regie Nationale des Usines Renault SA v Maxicar SpA* [2000] ECR I-2973, [2000] ECDR 415

practical problem. In the time available I take only an Anglo-centric view concerning the possible estoppel effects of a foreign judgment in England.

Issue preclusion. Issue preclusion is obviously related to *res judicata*. It is an extended version of res judicata estoppel as set out in my notes. Its purpose is not to achieve certainty. Its purpose is to protect individuals from vexatious litigation and to bring a finality to litigation. Within the domestic context, it is clear that where a judicial decision has determined the outcome on a particular factual issue and that same issue arises in the new proceedings, the earlier finding on that issue will be treated as binding as a matter of evidence if that finding was necessary and fundamental to the first decision. In any debt action in which validity under Article 81 is raised as an issue, the determination of validity or invalidity of the contract must be such a necessary and fundamental finding.

There is conceptually no particular difficulty with the application of issue estoppel on a cross-jurisdictional basis. It is a rule of evidence in which I found at least one reference that I put in the notes to a decision in 1678 of an English court applying by issue the finding of a court in what is now Italy. In principle, therefore, there is no difficulty with an English court saying that the fact of invalidity has been decided. It seems in principle that any decision under Article 81(1)/81(2)/81(3) relating to the validity of a contract, is a decision that would apply across the community just on a natural reading of 81(1).

As I set out further in my note, the security may be illusory. Is it in fact possible for there ever to be a finding that is the same under Article 81 in national litigation, given the potentially transient nature of that finding of validity? I do not propose to consider here the effect of the decision in *Passmore v Morland*, as to which there are strongly held views. However, if one looks at the Article 81(3) guidelines,[11] paragraphs 44 and 45, it is clear from that that if those guidelines represent the law, a large number of agreements do indeed benefit or suffer from changing validity situations over time.

The guidelines explain why some agreements will not have this temporal transience and some agreements will. However, certainly in regard to those agreements defined in the guidelines as being subject to changes in validity from day to day it seems likely to be impossible for any Member State Court to be able to say the decision that was given last week on a different debt action, relating to circumstances at a different time, is in fact the same issue that has to resolve regarding validity in its judgment. If that is right,

---

[11] *Communication from the Commission—Notice—Guidelines on the application of Article 81(3) of the Treaty Official Journal* C 101 pages 97-118 , 27.04.2004.

there is no possibility for free movement of judgements on this topic and the consequences for the certainty of the agreements are interesting.

At the end of the note, I then go on to consider what one might want to do if some additional certainty is sought. Paul Lomas in an article earlier this year noted that of course for a few agreements you could repackage your joint venture agreement as a concentration and go for certainty that way.

The only other route, which people have suggested is the option of going for declaratory relief, but again, I do not see how an English judge is ever going to give a declaration that this judgement is valid today and is still going to be valid in five years time, akin to the sort of decision that one used to get from the Commission under Article 81(3). I do not see how we are going to get that declaration from the court when the court is going to be faced with the same transient voidance problem, and the person arguing for non-validity will simply say that you can't give that declaration beyond today because you do not know what facts will be relied upon in a year's time to show that the situation has changed.

So there we are, the consequence of this multi-jurisdictional framework is, I would suggest, that there can be no constancy, or very little constancy, in the determination of Article 81 validity issues. Please read my notes.

Sir Christopher Bellamy

Thank you very much indeed Michael. I think we now have the chance for a little bit of audience participation, if you would like to participate. Just glancing around, it seems to me that Elisabeth Morony and Aidan Robertson have actually gone off to do a bit of private enforcement. But Kevin Grady and Subarta Bhattacharjee are still here, so I was wondering if people would like to ask questions either for this panel, or for those two previous speakers.

John Peysner (*Nottingham Law School*)

I am not suggesting that we want to open the flood gates on private enforcement, but it is extremely important that we get some cases up and running in this jurisdiction, otherwise it is going to be a complete damp squid, and the policy will suffer. There are two very important problems that we have to get over.

One is the fact that claimants bringing actions in this jurisdiction face big cost penalties that have been talked about, and secondly that the lawyers bringing actions—not for big business to big business, but say for small business to big business or individual citizens to big business—simply don't have the reward that you can get in the States with the contingency fee system. As Elisabeth said earlier on, our conditional fee system is completely ridiculous and simply doesn't give enough reward.

I think there are two possible ways forward. One is to develop the jurisprudence of pre-empting cost capping. In other words, if you are bringing a claim, your costs are guaranteed in advance if you lose the case, and secondly, to look at some developments in Canada. In Ontario they have a system there where if you wish to bring a class action claim and there have been some competition action cases there, you can get protection against costs; you can get help with your disbursements, and your lawyer can proceed under a contingency fee in a class action setting. That means a number of cases have started off and have been successful. I think we need to start looking at those sorts of ideas.

SIR CHRISTOPHER BELLAMY

Any comments on that?

DONALD BAKER (*Washington, DC*)

The statute of monopolies provided the successful plaintiff with treble damages and double costs and it would seem to me if you were trying to encourage more litigation, but not go the American way, which not even the Americans are in favour of, at least we won't publicly recommend early in the day, is to have a situation where the courts could award a successful plaintiff, double costs because the court found there may be a case for an injunction or something, was particularly meritorious.

PAUL LOMAS

I was talking about this with Jean François Bellis earlier. I think it is true that predictions of a flood of civil litigation have always been ill founded, but I suspect that it is also true that there is steady underlying growth in it. Sir Christopher's tribunal is going to see quite a lot of good solid compensation claims coming through because the structure is for it and there are more coming through before the Chancery Courts, so I wouldn't be too pessimistic from that perspective about the prospects of private sector enforcement, and the UK rules on group actions are steadily evolving, albeit slowly, so I wouldn't be quite as pessimistic as that.

MICHAEL BOWSHER

Let me just pick up one last point on that, which is simply that in all areas of commercial litigation even if there is a steady growth in litigation, there is the countervailing factor which is probably stronger in diminishing the number of decisions that we are getting in any area and that is mediation. Elisabeth said earlier that most cases settle. I suspect that proportionately, more cases are settling of the small batch that are starting, even more are settling now because more and more will end in mediation.

GEORGE PERETZ (*Monckton Chambers*)

I wanted to make a point about interim relief applications, which I think are still a problem area in this jurisdiction. Essentially for three reasons.

One is that as far as enforcement through the public authorities is concerned, principally through the OFT, certainly in urgent cases, it is simply unrealistic for a variety of bureaucratic and legal reasons for the OFT to move as fast as is sometimes necessary. Elisabeth referred to a case, and it's not an untypical case where one is looking for relief by the middle of next week, and that is just not ever going to be within the OFT's possible timescale.

If one is then looking at seeking interim relief in the ordinary courts, one has of course, two critical difficulties. One is the need to give a cross-undertaking in damages, which understandably is pretty frightening—certainly to a small plaintiff and the second difficulty, which is a consequence of our current constitutional arrangements, that one will find oneself in the Chancery division in front of a duty judge, who if one is unlucky, is a great specialist in the law of real property, but is not as up on competition law as one would like when one has very little time in which to educate him or her.

SIR CHRISTOPHER BELLAMY

Perhaps I could just make, as it were from the Chair, one or two comments on some of those topics. From the point of view of the Competition Appeals Tribunal, the issue of costs is a particularly worrying one and in general in English litigation, costs although extremely important to parties, tends to be the least well-argued and the least detailed argued part of the case, and is very often dealt with more or less on the hoof right at the end. All I can say on this—all it would be appropriate to say—is that we haven't yet approached the question of what the right approach to costs is in damages jurisdiction. But our judgements on costs so far in jurisdiction controlling decisions of the administrative authorities have been extremely guarded, and I think you may find there is quite a lot of room for argument as to what the right approach is even if it's a private enforcement matter.

There is, I think, some case law and at least some practice that the cross-undertaking in damages is ultimately a matter of discretion for the judge, and there are clearly arguments that need to be raised at some point, in terms of the small firm against the large firm, and the public interest in seeing competition law properly enforced, as to what the right approach in civil litigation is as regards the cross-undertaking in damages. That is a very important issue that is floating around, and one which one would hope at some stage is properly addressed in the context of civil litigation.

As far as the judges of the transfer decision are concerned, they are actively engaged in training programmes of various kinds, and I would very much hope that you don't come across a real property specialist who has never heard of competition law, or at least not very often. I am sure you will find that in general they will become increasingly on top of these things as time goes on.

Peter Roth QC (*Monckton Chambers*)

It is a question for Jean François Bellis and a comment on these very interesting German developments. I don't think you mentioned, and I wanted to ask, if you know what has happened. I believe there was a proposal in the new German law that would make decisions of other national competition authorities—not just the Bundeskartellamt and the European Commission—binding decisions in the German courts, which seemed to me a very interesting idea and of huge potential significance. I don't know if that has been adopted. That is the first point.

The other is a comment on the Dortmund case where damages were awarded, albeit under appeal. One of the striking features of that case is that no economic experts were used. The judge took that fairly clear and simple and perhaps commendable and it has huge costs consequences to the bringing of these cases because one of the great problems in this jurisdiction when we look across at other Continental European jurisdictions, is the level of costs that English litigation involves. The moment the potential for forum shopping as Paul has discussed emerges that comes into play, and we really do need to address our costs and the way we deal with them in England, and possibly occasionally we have a slightly excessive use of experts.

Jean François Bellis

Yes, and these are two interesting questions. Concerning the first question, yes this in this draft amendment to the German cartel law there is indeed a provision to the effect that the German Courts should take into account decisions by the Commission and national Competition Authorities as to establishing the existence of an infringement. So this would basically make it a necessity for plaintiffs to basically reinvent the wheel and to prove the existence of dominance, definition of the market, etc, so that would make the plaintiff's task much easier.

Concerning your second comment about the quantification of the damage, yes, in fact the plaintiff lawyer in the Dortmund case declared publicly this statement here calculating quantum as tricky. We looked at prices at the end of the cartel and put them in relation. So that is all they did, and it worked. Of course, all this may indeed sound unscientific, but I think there is a major problem in any attempt at quantifying damages in a cartel case. How can one know what level of prices would have been in the absence of a cartel. I am sure that for every economist that proves that the prices would have been much, much lower, it can find ten who will prove to us that the opposite is true. So may be this very pragmatic German approach after all, is not so bad.

But in many cases, however, it won't work because you have that the termination of the cartel does not bring about any noticeable change in pricing levels. In this case it just happened, there was a very significant drop in prices. Maybe coincidental, but that was convenient.

SIR CHRISTOPHER BELLAMY

What I would say I think, I would make two comments. One is, it seems to me highly desirable that the courts over time develop rules of thumb or presumptions that enable one to adopt a fairly broad brush approach to these things without the necessity of trying to examine in excessive detail what the exact quantum of damages is. I think, you'll find considerable judicial reluctance to go down the route of enormously complicated assessments where a commonsense solution, however broad brush and however much rough justice may present itself. That is one comment.

The other comment as a sort of cautionary comment, at one stage in a previous part of my career, I had the slightly unusual job of actually operating as having responsibility for taxing costs in cases brought at European level from various different jurisdictions and working out what on a European basis, would be a fair recovery of costs for the lawyers of the winning side. It was not always an easy task because the British costs were always at least four times everybody else's costs, and if London is to be in the future a significant centre for this kind of litigation, that is an aspect that needs to be thought about by somebody.

However, I think unless there are particular questions that anyone is burning to ask on the topics we have already discussed, it is probably time to move on to our last panel.

Cross-Border Effects of Judicial Determination of Article 81(2)EC (In)validity of Contract

Michael Bowsher*

In this paper I address the impact that a determination by a court or arbitral tribunal in one jurisdiction as to the impact of the Article 81(1) prohibition on a contract may have on subsequent proceedings in another jurisdiction.[1]

These remarks start with Article 34 of Council Regulation (EC) No 44/2001 on jurisdiction and the recognition and enforcement of judgments in civil and commercial matters. This provides as follows:

A judgment shall not be recognised:
1. if such recognition is manifestly contrary to public policy in the Member State in which recognition is sought;
2. ...
3. if it is irreconcilable with a judgment given in a dispute between the same parties in the Member State in which recognition is sought;
4. if it is irreconcilable with an earlier judgment given in another Member State or in a third State involving the same cause of action and between the same parties, provided that the earlier judgment fulfils the conditions necessary for its recognition in the Member State addressed.

The application of this provision in the context of a contractual dispute regarding the validity of the relevant contract raises a number of issues that are important for the consistent and uniform application of competition law in the EC, and for the achievement of certainty in parties' commercial relations.

A similar limitation on enforcement of arbitral awards under the New York Convention is provided for in Article V.2 as follows:

* FCIArb Chartered Arbitrator, CEDR Accredited Mediator.
[1] Certain aspects of this note are significantly affected by a decision handed down by the Court of Appeal after this note was delivered: *Sun Life Assurance Company of Canada, American Phoenix Life and Reassurance, Phoenix Home Life Mutual Insurance v Lincoln National* [2004] EWCA Civ 1660, 10 Dec 2004. Parts of this note have been adjusted accordingly.

Recognition and enforcement of an arbitral award may also be refused if the competent authority in the country where recognition and enforcement is sought finds that:

(a) the subject matter of the difference is not capable of settlement by arbitration under the law of that country; or

(b) the recognition or enforcement of the award would be contrary to the public policy of that country.

I. UNIVERSAL APPLICATION OF JUDGMENT ON VALIDITY OF CONTRACT, REGARDLESS OF INCORRECT APPLICATION OF COMPETITION LAW BY COURTS IN ANOTHER JURISDICTION

In Case C-38/98, *Régie nationale des usines Renault SA v Maxicar SpA and Orazario Formento*[2] the European Court of Justice considered the application of the analogous provision to Regulation 34(1) in the Brussels Convention.[3] This decision was made in response to a preliminary reference by an Italian court that was called upon to enforce a judgment of a French court. The Italian court was concerned that the judgment of French court ought not to be enforced as it was based on an erroneous application of EC competition law.

The effect of the decision was that a judgment would be enforced even where it appeared to be based upon such errors. It was said that refusal to enforce the judgment of another Member State could only be envisaged where recognition or enforcement of the judgment would be at variance to an unacceptable degree with the legal order of the State in which enforcement is sought inasmuch as it infringes a fundamental principle of the latter State. The infringement would have to constitute a manifest breach of a rule of law regarded as essential in the legal order of the State in which enforcement is sought or of a right recognized as being fundamental within that legal order. The fact that the decision might be based upon errors of application of EC competition law would not constitute a manifest breach of a rule of law regarded as essential in the legal order of the State in which enforcement is sought.

II. EFFECT OF DETERMINATION OF COMPETITION LAW ISSUE IN SEPARATE DISPUTE UNDER SAME CONTRACT

Regulation 44/2001 provides a legislative basis for the universal application of the determination of a particular dispute in which competition law invalidity was an issue. It does not address the impact that any finding as to the

---

[2] [2000] ECR I-2973.
[3] This provision was in similar terms without the word 'manifestly'.

validity of the contract in this case may have in subsequent litigation under the same contract (or even under another contract that is part of the same contractual network). Plainly a number of causes of action could arise concerning the same agreement, and given the different bases for jurisdiction that arise under Regulation 44/2001,[4] there may for most 'cross-border' contracts be at least two if not more possible jurisdictions in which proceedings could be brought depending, for instance, on which party commenced the proceedings.

Many of these problems can be avoided by a well-drafted exclusive jurisdiction clause. It may not, however, be possible to make this provision. Even where exclusive jurisdiction is conferred on courts of a particular jurisdiction, or there is a mandatory arbitration clause, other related agreements to which the same competition law issue applies may have different jurisdiction provisions. Further, in some cases it is an inevitable consequence of compliance with competition law requirements that the disputes under a contract cannot be limited to one jurisdiction. For instance the current motor vehicle block exemption appears to provide for arbitration[5] of certain disputes, without prejudice to the courts' jurisdiction.

III. ISSUE PRECLUSION/ISSUE ESTOPPEL

Is it possible, therefore, for Article 81 issues to be relitigated in different Member States, in, say, two separate debt actions in different Member States arising under the same agreement? In principle each debt action would raise a separate cause of action and ought properly to be brought in different national courts. Inherent in both claims, however would be the allegation that the contract was valid and the judgment would either find or assume that it was, or was not, valid. If Article 81 (2) were pleaded as a defence to the claim, the claimant might, for instance, seek to rely upon Article 81 (3) in both proceedings. The Article 81(3) issue might then be decided differently in the two sets of proceedings and an agreement purporting to be valid across the Community might become valid in some Member States and not in others.

If however there had already been a judgment for the claimant in one jurisdiction in which the contract was expressly found to be prohibited, would Article 34 of Regulation 44/2001 apply so that a judgment on a different claim, that took a different view of the validity issue would be refused recognition. Recognition might be refused because it was irreconcilable

---

[4] eg, domicile of defendant (Art 2); Place of performance of the obligation in question (Art 5 (1)).

[5] Or mediation in the Spanish text.

with a judgment given in a dispute between the same parties in the Member State in which recognition is sought or with an earlier judgment given in another Member State or in a third State involving the same cause of action and between the same parties?

A matter of greater practical importance probably concerns whether in a second claim for performance of the contract the earlier decision on validity in another jurisdiction would be treated as giving rise to an issue estoppel or *res judicata* estoppel so that the issue would be treated as already determined? Clearly, the certainty of contracts would be greatly enhanced if a finding of validity could, or would normally have such a binding effect.

Typically the questions whether a particular contract falls within the Article 81(1) prohibition or benefits from the Article 81(3) exception will be matters that are incidental issues raised as just one issue in a dispute regarding performance of the contract. When proceedings are brought in another jurisdiction on the basis of a different claim, the question of validity or invalidity of the agreement may be raised again.

It appears from Korah & O'Sullivan, *Distribution Agreements under the EC Competition Rules*[6] that while Denis O'Sullivan argues for the community-wide effect of a judgment conferring an individual exemption, Professor Korah regards her co-author's views along these lines as 'far-fetched'. If a finding of individual exemption cannot be treated as just another judgment under Regulation 44/2001, the great utility of the system of recognition and enforcement of judgments in the Community would be significantly undermined and an opportunity for forum shopping in competition law issues would be opened up. This runs contrary to the essential scheme under Articles 27–29 of the Regulation 44/2001 that there should normally be only one decision on any particular cause of action anywhere in the Community.

The estoppel doctrines referred to above are concerned not with achievement of the goal of contractual certainty, but with the achievement of finality[7] and the protection of parties from vexatious litigation.[8]

In order to consider whether the impact of a finding or validity or invalidity on the subsequent proceedings it is necessary to consider the content of the finding of the original finding, and then determine whether either

---

[6] 2002 edn, 257.

[7] *Interest reipublicae ut sit finis litum.*

[8] *Nemo debet bis vexari pro una et eadem causa.* The more extended doctrine of *res iudicata* often referred to as the rule in *Henderson v Henderson* is more a rule of policy intended to limit the demands on judicial resources. It is probably not, for instance, applicable in arbitration.

Article 34 of Regulation 44/2001 above, or general considerations of issue preclusion would mean that any subsequent decision in another jurisdiction would have to follow the same decision on validity (or invalidity).

The analysis of the effect of a judgment in one Member State on the validity of a contract in precluding that issue from being relitigated in another raises a number of difficult questions of private international law.[9] Long before the Brussels Convention, however, English courts have been prepared to give effect to foreign decisions by operation of *res iudicata* estoppel.[10] In particular, it is still open to debate whether the preclusive effect of the first judgment is to be assessed by reference to the law of the Member State in which it was given or by reference to the law of the State in which it is relied upon to preclude relitigation.

Indeed in English courts it might not even be relevant whether the Article 81 issues were raised in the earlier dispute as the courts retain a discretion (under *Henderson v Henderson*) to prevent any issue from being litigated if it could and should have been raised in earlier litigation.

IV. APPLICATION OF *RES JUDICATA*

There must be the following elements for a *res judicata* estoppel to succeed in an English court.

- A judicial decision
- That has been pronounced
- Taken by a tribunal with jurisdiction
- Where the decision was a final decision on the merits
- And the decision determined the same issue as that raised in the later litigation
- The parties to the later litigation were either parties to the earlier litigation or their privies.

Issue estoppel in English law is an extension of the same doctrine[11] to determinations of matters that are necessary and fundamental to the final

---

[9] See Barnett, 'Res Judicata, Estoppel and Foreign Judgments' ch 7.

[10] *Cottington's Case* (1678) cited in 2 Swan 326, per Lord Nottingham LC:
'It is against the law of nations not to give credit to the judgment and sentences of foreign countries, till they be reversed by the law, and according to the form, of those countries wherein they were given. For what right hath one kingdom to reverse the judgment of another? And how can we refuse to let a sentence take place until it be reversed? And what confusion would follow in Christendom, if they should serve us so abroad, and give no credit to our sentences.'

[11] *Thoday v Thoday* [1964] p 181; cited in *Thrasyvoulou* [1990] 2 AC 273. See also the decision of the Court of Appeal *Sun Life v Lincoln National* (ibid) paras 38 to 47 in judgment of Mance LJ, and the shorter judgments of Longmore LJ and Jacob LJ.

determination in the judgment.[12] Validity of a contract is likely to be such an issue in a claim for performance or breach. It is well established that issue estoppel can be based on foreign judgments in English law[13] but the courts will exercise caution as to whether the issue has been decided in the decision, or whether the judgment was made in default of appearance. Principal concerns are that it may be difficult to be certain that the foreign judgment addresses the same issue as that before the Court, and that the foreign judgment addresses that issue on a final and conclusive basis. The Court may also be concerned that a party might have allowed a default judgment to be made against it simply because it would have been unduly onerous to fight the proceedings in the other jurisdiction.

By contrast with that last consideration, English courts are prepared to find that reargument of a particular issue is precluded by an earlier foreign judgment in which the issue was not raised, but could and should have been raised.[14] This is an application of the *Henderson v Henderson* doctrine to foreign proceedings and places a considerable burden on the English court to establish whether in the context of the foreign court's procedure the issue could, and more particularly should have been raised. The application of this doctrine is open to a number of forceful objections.[15]

V. DID THE DECISION DETERMINE THE SAME ISSUE? THE CONTENT OF THE DECISION

It is a necessary condition for an estoppel that the question in the second proceedings be the same as that decided or covered by the first.

Assuming for these purposes that the issue was contested in the first proceedings (as different factors apply to default judgments, and judgments given without the issue being considered), any finding of validity or invalidity under EC law is clearly intended to apply across the Community, at least for the purposes of that judgment.

For instance, if an English court is called upon to consider the validity of an agreement, it may be contended before the Court that it is not valid because it has anti-competitive effect in only part of the EU, whether that be in another jurisdiction of the United Kingdom, or in the Baltic states. The English court might have to consider whether any part of the agreement could be severed to remain in force in some or all of those geographic

---

[12] As to what constitutes a necessary and fundamental matter for this purpose, see the decision of the Court of Appeal in *Sun Life v Lincoln National* (ibid).

[13] *Carl Zeiss (no 2)* [1967] 1 AC 853.

[14] *Kok Hoong v Leong Cheong Kweng Mines Ltd* [1964] AC 993.

[15] See Barnett.

markets in which there was no anti-competitive effect, but the decision on validity under either Article 81(1) or 81(3) must, given the language of those provisions, be applicable to the entire Community[16] (subject to issues of severance). This must be the case for a number of reasons.

- This is the only possible reading of Articles 81(1) or 81(3). For instance, Article 81(3) cannot be read as referring to benefits to consumers in one Member State, for example.
- If it were otherwise, national courts would be entitled or required to limit their decisions to their own geographic markets leading, potentially, to partitioning of markets where, for example distribution systems were valid in one Member State (or part of it) and not valid in another.
- Any other interpretation would be entirely inconsistent with the purpose of the Regulation 44/2001 as set out in the *Renault* decision discussed above. Right or wrong, decisions on competition law are of universal application.

There may, however, be other reasons why the judgment in the first case considered a different question. To put the point simply, the fact that two judgments relate to different points in time may mean that they apply to two different sets of facts. The facts relating to the validity issue and perhaps the outcome on this issue may have altered. This is because of the temporal limits that appear to be placed on the application of the decision on (in)validity. Paragraphs 44 and 45 of the Guidelines on the application of Article 81(3) of the Treaty are relevant here (and are also relevant to Article 81(1)).[17]

> The assessment of restrictive agreements under Article 81(3) is made within the actual context within which they occur and on the basis of the facts existing at any given point in time. The assessment is sensitive to material changes in the facts. The exception rule of Article 81(3) applies as long as the four conditions are fulfilled and ceases to apply when that is no longer the case . . .

> In some cases the restrictive agreement is an irreversible event. Once the restrictive agreement has been implemented the *ex ante* situation cannot be re-established. In such cases the assessment must be made exclusively on the basis of the facts pertaining at the time of implementation . . . However

---

[16] I do not for these purposes consider the important questions as to how an English court might address the application of Art 81(1), or Art 81(3) with regard to a market in a part of the EU beyond its jurisdiction.

[17] As acknowledged in the footnote to the following passage from those guidelines,
> 'the prohibition of Article 81(1) also only applies as long as the agreement has a restrictive object or restrictive effects'.

Note also the reference in that footnote to the Commission Decision in *TPS*.

the prohibition of Article 81 may apply to other parts of the agreement in respect of which the issue or irreversibility does not arise...Article 81 may apply to this part of the agreement if due to subsequent market developments the agreement becomes restrictive of competition and does not (any longer) satisfy the conditions of Article 81(3) . . .

These guidelines may represent a development, and improvement upon the effect of the controversial decision of the Court of Appeal in *Passmore v Morland*.[18] It had been suggested by some that the concept of 'transient voidness' as suggested in that decision involved a serious departure from English and Community law,[19] albeit that English precedent for transient illegality can be found.[20] Whatever the merits of this debate, it is clear from the above guidelines that a finding of (in)validity may not be fixed in stone.

Surprisingly, therefore, it seems that the limits on the application, at least in an English court, of the judgment of another national court by way of issue estoppel may be limited by reason not of the geographical jurisdiction of the courts, but by the different points of time to which the decisions relate.

Thus, if the decision of another national court of a Member State has made a finding of contractual (in)validity on EC competition law grounds, that is determinative of the identical question of validity that arises in an English court, that court ought not to seek to consider the question again but should treat itself as bound by issue estoppel. However, the utility of this proposition may be limited in many cases by the limited time frame to which the original decision relates.

VI. IMPACT ON DISPUTES BETWEEN DIFFERENT PARTIES FROM THOSE IN FIRST DISPUTE

Recent authority may provide grounds for an extension of the application of an issue estoppel from a dispute between, say, A and B to another dispute on a related contract between B and C. The decision of Court of Appeal (reversing the decision of Toulson J) in *Lincoln National Life Insurance Co v Sun Life Assurance Co of Canada, American Phoenix Life and Reassurance Co and Phoenix Home Life Mutual Insurance Co*[21] is an important decision concerning the application of *res iudicata* in arbitration, and in disputes between different parties. The case concerned an arbitration award in a dispute between X and Y and its relevance in a subsequent sepa-

---

[18] [1999] EuLR 501.
[19] As set out in *Shell v Lostock Garages* [1976] 1 WLR 1187.
[20] *Group Josi Re v Walbrook Ins.* [1996] 1 WLR 1152 in which it was found that a previously illegal contract gained retrospective legality by subsequent legislation.
[21] [2004] EWCA Civ 1660.

rate arbitration between X and Z in which the legal position between X and Y was a relevant issue. As explained by Longmore LJ, the decision in that case is only binding insofar as it decided that the relevant decision in the first arbitration did not by its nature create an issue estoppel, or have any other binding effect (for instance by way of obiter dictum) in the second arbitration. Nonetheless the decision of all three lords justices, and in particular Mance LJ, considered in some detail the earlier case law. Detailed analysis of that decision falls beyond the scope of these remarks, but it seems from that decision that there may still be some cases, in litigation rather than in arbitration, in which a court would regard it as fair that a decision against B in the case involving A may be treated as binding against B, again, in a subsequent dispute with a different party, C.

On the basis of this decision, though, it seems highly unlikely that, for instance, a finding of invalidity against the manufacturer/seller in a network of vertical agreements in respect of one agreement in one jurisdiction could preclude reargument of that issue in another jurisdiction. Even if the first decision could be said to encompass the same finding of validity or invalidity regarding the entire network of agreements it seems unlikely, at least in English courts, that the judgment would be applied in this way.

VII. DECLARATORY RELIEF

In English procedure, a judgment as to contractual (in)validity over a period might be obtained by way of declaration. A claim for a declaration of (in)validity could be sought as part of the relief claimed in a claim for performance or breach, but it could also be claimed in separate proceedings limited only to the claim for a declaration.

The grant of a declaration is, however, a discretionary remedy even if the proposition that one or other party seeks to have 'declared' is correct. No party has an entitlement to any declaration.

Those seeking the certainty and security of an individual exemption, or a negative clearance for a period in respect of a 'difficult' agreement, might consider a claim for a declaration of validity over a particular period, or a series of alternative periods of varying lengths as one of the few means of achieving this. Are there any circumstances in which a judge of the Chancery Division would grant such declaratory relief? Certainly while *Passmore v Morland*[22] remains good law it is hard to see how any English judge could grant such relief, but if the effect of that decision can be modified so that it is consistent with the Article 81(3) guidelines there may be

---

[22] [1999] All ER 1005, Court of Appeal.

circumstances in which such a declaration can be given, just as such declarations have been given regarding the validity of restrictive covenants.

One objection to this course would be, however, that if the parties to an agreement are seeking guidance from the court, they may not disagree as to the validity of the agreement. In those circumstances it seems likely that the court will decline to grant the relief sought on the basis that the dispute as at that point 'theoretical', or that in practical terms the full arguments for invalidity may not be being canvassed before the Court.

At the very least, the value of such declaratory relief in other jurisdictions might be limited as it could be said with some force that a declaration given in a contrived 'dispute' ought not to have the issue preclusion effect of a contested decision—for the same practical reasons that the arguments for invalidity might be deployed with greater force if one party were seriously contending for that outcome.

Panel 3—Agency Perspectives on Private Enforcement

SIR CHRISTOPHER BELLAMY

Ladies and gentlemen, our last panel is the agency perspective on private enforcement and in addition to, as it were, the home team that I won't need to introduce at all, we are particularly privileged today to have Don Baker, former Head of the Justice Department now in private practice, who also taught at Cornell, one of the most experienced and distinguished people in the world on this kind of topic, and also Suzanne Legault, Assistant Deputy Commissioner, Legislative Affairs Division in the Competition Bureau, Canada, with again, the Canadian perspective.

I will, if I may, give pride of place to our visitors, rather than calling on the home team, who I am sure would anyway, wish to say as little as possible. So I think without more ado, Don, perhaps I could ask you to lead this panel off.

DONALD BAKER

It's a great pleasure to be here with such an outstanding group under such a distinguished Chairman. I have during my career worked on all sides of the street, I think. In private practice, I bought some private cases, and I have defended others. Back when I was with the Government I worried about some private cases and took occasional joy in others. I have also been an arbitrator and counsel in several arbitrations in which antitrust disputes were central issues.

It seemed to me, as I tried to think about this important issue of potential conflict between what the Government does, or can do, and what private parties do, or can do, I realized that there are really three kinds of private cases and each category raises.

One category is the follow-on case, which has already been referred to several times. The second is the private case that is brought when the Government has been approached but explicitly declined to act. And the third category is what we might call the independent case, for a lack of a better name.

Now, in follow-on cases, you start off with the fact that private treble damage remedies generally increase public deterrence and so in many ways they are going to be the least controversial. Indeed in the United States, I think, you would say that mandatory treble damages in straight cartel cases is not controversial in the bar. It becomes more controversial when you start adding mandatory treble damages in joint venture cases, in distributor cases, and in monopolization cases. Of course, the mandatory trebling tends to cause the plaintiff's counsel to try to bring all kinds of common law tort and unfair competition cases as antitrust cases because then they get automatic treble damages if successful.

I think it is generally a good idea to have treble damages on top of fines for criminal violations such as price-fixing, bid-rigging, and market allocations. Right now, we may have a window in which it is a particularly important idea. As you probably know, the Supreme Court in a case called *Blakely*[1] has just tossed out the State sentencing guidelines and has just heard argument in a case in which throwing out the Federal sensing guidelines seems a high probability.

What the court has said is the Constitutional right of trial by jury means that a judge cannot increase the fine, except on the basis of a jury verdict. The present antitrust law which applies to all past conduct, including major things like the vitamins cartel, has a maximum fine of $10m, but this is going increase to $100m for conduct going forward, as Kevin said. Because of the $10m limit, the Government has been using an alternative sentencing standard—which allows fines up to twice the gain or twice the loss of the thing.

Well, talk about something that is difficult. Imagine proving to a criminal standard, beyond a reasonable doubt, twice the gain or twice the loss. I think, we will have a period in which the Government, which has become rather used to collecting $100m fines, is going to be collecting more $10m fines, and meanwhile the private treble damage cases are going to be an important part of reminding companies and counsel that antitrust cartel activities are risky stuff. Basically, that is the situation.

The one conflict issue on follow on cases concerns the Government's amnesty program. Somebody comes in and blows the whistle on the cartel and gets amnesty, but then when the follow-on private cases are filed, it is jointly and several liable with everyone else without any right of contribution. This chilling reality was brought home as a big issue in a very recent vitamins case involving Mitsui, the Japanese trading company. Their subsidiary Bioproducts was the whistle blower in a case where I was defending someone else. Mitsui said, 'we weren't involved'. The jury in the District of Columbia didn't agree with them on that, so they were held liable for $150m of treble damages in this case based on joint and several

---

[1] *Blakely v Washington* No 02–1632. Argued 23 Mar 2004—Decided 24 June 2004.

liability, even though they had apparently participated in their subsidiary's decision to seek amnesty.

I think that this Mitsui result was a big catalyst for including amnesty applicants in this new antitrust bill that recently passed Congress—which essentially says that the amnesty applicant will only be subject to single damages, and won't be subject to joint and several liability. Interestingly Congress has pre-empted state law on that, so you cannot bring a state law claim against the amnesty applicant for more than single damages.

I think the amnesty situation in Europe is inevitably much weaker than in the United States because eliminating the perceived risk of jail is an important incentive in the US amnesty programme. I think this is an issue that people designing public sanctions and private remedies in Europe have to think about.

I just want to say one last thing about follow-on cases. It seems to me—and I am sure Vincent, you will say whatever you can that is diplomatic—I think, the new UK system of allowing private plaintiffs to go to the Competition Appeals Tribunal in a follow-on case, is going to generate a lot of effort to get OFT to bring cases. Since you are subject, unlike the American authorities, to an appeal from your failure to bring a case, I think we are going to see some very interesting litigation, by private parties trying to push OFT because they see so much advantage in being able to bring follow-on cases in the CAT.

The next category of cases is where the Government has declined to act, after being invited by complainant(s) to do so. Now this was very much a goal of Congress when it set up the original treble damage system in 1890. Members were afraid that the Government would be too timid, when faced with these entrenched and reviled trusts and cartels. So you look at the history, and private actions were seen as a way to fill the gap. This is what they wanted. They provided treble damages because they wanted private cases when that the Attorney General declined to act.

Now there are some, of course, wonderfully famous examples of such cases, some of which are known quite well over here. One is *Minorco v Consolidated Goldfields*[2] where both the British authorities and the American authorities declined to block this hostile merger attempt, but Goldfields sued and the District Court in New York in the Second Circuit Court of Appeals blocked the merger, even though the biggest effects were elsewhere in the world.

---

[2] *Minorco and Consolidated Gold Fields plc*: a report on the merger situation Cm 587, 2.2.89, Competition Commission <http://www.competition-commission.org.uk/rep_pub/reports/1989/index.htm>.

Let me give you a reverse side of this. This was actually a case that my firm brought. We have a major nationwide newspaper chain called Gannett which publishes USA Today and dozens of local newspapers. They already controlled the morning newspaper in Honolulu—the largest newspaper in Hawaii—and they had a joint venture with the afternoon newspaper that operated a joint publishing plant.

Gannett agreed to pay a huge price to the afternoon paper's owner to buy out their interest in the publishing plant, thus making sure that there would be no place to publish an afternoon newspaper. On behalf of a Hawaii citizen's group, we went to the Justice Department during the Clinton Administration, and they simply didn't want to take this issue on. The State Attorney-General and our citizens group ('Citizens to Save the Star Bulletin') brought an injunction suit, and prevailed—and so there are still two newspapers in Honolulu, which there wouldn't otherwise have been. It was a particularly heart-warming victory because it involves media and preserving choice in news sources. , it is certainly a case that I will go to my grave feeling better about myself for having worked hard and won!

The third category consists of cases that are independent from any requested enforcement action or inaction. I want to combine a point that you made, Sir Christopher, and a point that Kevin made. You made the point that a judge looks at this and says 'Jeez, this is an awful thin case' and he then says 'You know, it is a pretty good basis for a summary judgement motion' and so grants a summary judgment motion rather than sit through a trial of a weak case. As Kevin says, those are the kinds of cases can make bad law—creating appellate decisions that come back to haunt the Government in later years.

One of the worst examples, which I cited in my outline, was a case called *Gordon v the New York Stock Exchange*.[3] It concerned a general area, where we in the Justice Department had devoted a lot of resources to both administrative proceedings and even litigation. The *Gordon* case then got to the Supreme Court came up on summary judgement. I am not going to say what I think about the contingency-fee lawyering for the plaintiffs, but it wasn't very energetic or good. So now the case goes up to the Supreme Court—rather than in the dustbin where it belonged. We had little choice but to weigh in. Thus we ended up with the Justice Department on one side, supporting the plaintiff's argument that the Stock Exchange was not exempt from the antitrust laws, and the Securities & Exchange Commission supporting the Stock Exchange on the other side. At the time we had worked so hard to have real factual records in the cases we were pursuing

---

[3] *Gordon v New York Stock Exchange*, 422 US 659 (1975).

against the Exchange, but the Supreme Court ended up ruling on an important point of law in a case where there was no record of competitive effects or anything else. The Supreme Court ultimately ruled that the Exchange enjoyed a broad antitrust exemption so long as the SEC was purporting to regulate it. It was a bitter disappointment to those of us in the Justice Department who had worked for six years developing how the Stock Exchange cartel worked and wasn't necessary to effective markets. (Fortunately, in the end, we prevailed—but in Congress rather than in the courts.)

On the reverse side, it is possible to find some private antitrust cases that have triggered useful opportunities for the Justice Department. One of my favourites is a case called *Carter v AT&T*,[4] cited in the materials, which I also worked on. This arose back in the 1960s when all the telephone companies in the world, including BT, monopolized the terminal equipment that we had in our houses and offices to make telephone calls and send information.

Along came this picturesque guy from Texas who filed an antitrust boycott suit in US District Court, charging the telephone companies with boycotting independent sources of terminal equipment. Mr Carter was a consumer who wanted to use his homemade piece of equipment to call from out on his oil rig in the Gulf of Mexico. The District Court dismissed the case and the Fifth Circuit Court of Appeal said that, 'This is really an issue for the Federal Communications Commission.' Mr Carter's case thus got pushed from Texas to the Commission in Washington, but with the Fifth Circuit encouraging the Commission to do something. So they held an evidentiary proceeding and the Antitrust Division of the Justice Department came in as amicus and helped persuade the Commission to get rid of the telephone companies' odious restrictions in a famous decision called *Carterfone*. Thus Carter's rather parochial boycott case set in motion a chain of events that opened up the market to consumer-owned telephone equipment. I This probably wouldn't have happened—at least for a while—but for that private case.

There is thus some good news and some bad news on private litigation in the US—and sometimes there is even no news from the United States.

SIR CHRISTOPHER BELLAMY

No news is good news, come on! Thank you very much indeed Don. Suzanne Legault.

---

[4] *Carter v AT&T*, 365 F 2d 486 (5th Cir 1966 *cert den'd*, 385 US (1967).

Suzanne Legault

Thank you very much. It is really my pleasure being here today, and I guess speaking from an agency perspective, given that I have a Canadian colleague in the room, I will start with stating that the views I'm going to express are entirely my own, and not those of the Canadian Competition Bureau.

I have been at the OECD this week and Sir Christopher yesterday was speaking on private enforcement issues. I think it is fair to say that I have certainly learned a lot in terms of what's going on in Europe in relation to the balance between public and private enforcement. It is certainly a very lively debate, and I think that these exercises in comparative law are very helpful. However, I think they are only meaningful if one truly understands the intricacies of each legal and judicial system. In that respect, I guess in order to make my comments meaningful today about what is going on in Canada, I think it is helpful to understand a little bit about how the Competition Act[5] functions in Canada.

Although it started historically by being only a criminal statute, it has evolved since then, and we had major reforms both in 1976 and 1986, which has lead to us having a criminal regime for cartels, predatory pricing and these types of behaviour. These cases go to regular criminal courts, and these are courts of inherent jurisdiction.

We also have a civil regime, which deals with cases of abuse of dominance, tied selling, refusal to deal, other types of vertical restraints, which all go to quasi-judicial expert tribunal, which is composed of a Federal Court Judge, but also with two lay members.

The reason I am mentioning this, is because the way that Canada has looked at striking the right balance between private and public enforcement is that we very much have adopted a 'tailored approach'. I say a 'tailored approach' in the sense that we don't believe that there is 'one size that fits all' for all types of anti-competitive practices. I think that many of the speakers have addressed this by saying that 'well in terms of achieving the optimal deterrence level, the people consider that in cartel cases, it's ok probably to have private actions with treble damages as they have in the States'. But such a scheme might not be the optimal balance between private and public enforcement in cases of vertical restraints or abuse of domi-nance.

So what are we doing in Canada? Well, Subrata earlier approached the issue of Section 36, so we have under our Competition Act a specific right for

---

[5] Competition Act RSC 1985 c C-34 as amended.

private action for criminal cases. So that's fine. It has usually been used in follow-on cases dealing with cartel cases. There are facilitating devices in follow-on as one would want to have in trying to encourage private enforcement in competition situations, mainly because they are so hard to prove. It is so hard to gather the necessary evidence to make your case.

But what does that mean in practice, this facilitating device that we have in Section 36 of our Act? Well, maybe we have an issue with the substantive provision that underlies these types of action. Canada has been trying to reform its cartel provision, mainly because it has a very difficult competition test attached to it, which one has to establish beyond reasonable doubt. The undue lessening of competition, which means that you have to establish the competitive effects on each of the markets affected by the cartel's behaviour.

So that means that from the public enforcement perspective, very few cases have been brought forward by the Competition Bureau that have led to a fully litigated case. Most of the cases settle and they are mostly a result of immunity applications. But what does that mean for the private litigant? That means that the record of proceeding is very skimpy. So the prima facie facilitating device in terms of bringing a case forward under Section 36 does not mean a lot in Canadian law, I think at this stage. It is probably in part the reason why so many cartel cases do settle before going to trial.

Then the Competition Bureau is limited in terms of the confidentiality rules, in terms of what it can give to private litigants, in terms of information that it has collected as part of its investigation. So it makes matters even more difficult.

In conjunction with that we have, I guess most of you are familiar with the fact that in Canada we have a Federal system, so we have provincial governments, which have their own provincial legislation, and we have a Constitution that basically divides powers between both. So that causes other types of issues in terms of private enforcement. The gentleman over there mentioned that in Ontario we have the ability to bring class actions. Well, that exists also in Quebec and in British Columbia, but it doesn't exist to my knowledge in the other provinces of Canada, and it is very much something that is part of a provincial legislation.

We also don't have a very well developed plaintiff's bar in Canada. The other thing we don't have is that we don't have a very well organised consumer's association's movement in Canada. We have one that is quite active in the Province of Quebec, but anywhere else in Canada, it is not a very strong voice any more, and you would think that these types of organization would actually boost private enforcement.

So there is a lot of movement to be had there. I think it is evolving. I think, time will tell. I think those class action proceedings that are emerging now are probably going to be helpful in terms of developing private enforcement in Canada.

Aside from that, what we have done is since 2002 and Subrata alluded to this earlier, we have the ability now under our legislation for private litigants to bring a case directly to the Competition Tribunal, for a few vertical restraints types of practices.

The reason why these were put into the Act is mostly because these types of practices, tend to be more localised in nature. It is not that they don't have affected competition, it is that they don't tend to have an impact nationally on competition, so therefore, they would tend to be very low on the priority range of the public agency.

When that went to Parliament, and there were many studies before that, but when that went to Parliament, there was a big fear of the crocodile in the sense that unleashing private litigation and strategic litigation in Canada. As a result of that, we have had a lot of safeguards that were put in place as part of this regime to prevent strategic litigation.

So for one thing, the private applicants must obtain leave; the Commissioner must not be on inquiry already; there must not have been a settlement in the case; so there is no duplicity of the actions in these types of cases. The Commissioner of Competition has the right to intervene in these types of cases; if there are situations where the Competition Bureau would consider there are competition issues that must be brought to bear before the Tribunal. However, in this particular type of scheme, there are no damages, so the remedies that are available to the private applicants are only a cease and desist order type of remedy. So it is fairly limited.

That is essentially the landscape in Canada in terms of what's going on with private enforcement. But there is a lot that is evolving and for these private rights of access to the Tribunal so far, we have had, I believe, and Subrata, correct me if I am wrong, but I think there are about only nine applications—several of which are linked, essentially raising the same types of issues. This is in two years time, and we have only been to the stage of interlocutory issues. So, more to be had in terms of development, and there are several reforms that are on the horizon, which I will address later.

SIR CHRISTOPHER BELLAMY

Thank you very much indeed Suzanne. Let's see if there is anything the OFT has anything it would like to add to that!

VINCENT SMITH

On the balance between public and private enforcement. I think, the only thing that I would like to say, is that, and again it is a very personal remark, At least from a UK perspective, in my view public enforcement is there to punish and to deter, and private enforcement is there to compensate. I think that we must keep those two principles in mind, when deciding how to get the balance correct.

Just on the second point, if I may, on the potential clashes between the private enforcement and the goals of public enforcement, I think there are clashes but there are also some complements.

The three clashes I would like to raise in the UK context are in relation to disclosure and confidentiality, where the regimes for private litigation and for public enforcement are very different. Clearly there are rules of court which, require disclosure of more or less everything at certain points in private litigation. Part 9 of the Enterprise Act[6] applies to us, the OFT, to prevent us from disclosing anything, at least until a fairly advanced stage of an infringement proceeding. I suggest there might be a risk that people might bring private actions in order to get disclosure from parties to public infringement proceedings, which they wouldn't be able to get otherwise, because it would be prevented under the Enterprise Act.

The second clash is possibly in relation to the position of third parties. Here I am thinking in particular of the rules as to standing. Certainly in relation to judicial review, the rule as to standing seems to me to be increasingly wide in the Administrative Court, and I suggest that it is not impossible that the same kind of rules might apply in private antitrust actions. Clearly there are cost penalties for interveners in private litigation. The same doesn't apply to public litigation, and I would be concerned if the same broad rules on standing were applied in public enforcement actions that might apply in private actions. Given that more people are likely to come along and knock on our door, it would slow us down significantly.

The third clash relates to timing. Clearly, there is an issue where a private action is brought in parallel with an ongoing OFT or other public investigation. The courts have generally been willing, I understand, to allow applications to stay the private action pending the outcome of the public investigation. Clearly, that raises issues in particular for private applicants. Interest on damages will run from the date of the tortious act. If our investigation is unavoidably prolonged, that means that interest will be running

---

[6] UK Enterprise Act 2002.

for possibly quite a long period—several years conceivably. Compound interest at the judgment rate is not a small amount.

Then there is the issue which has been raised by other people earlier about the cross-undertaking as to damages, which is often asked for of a plaintiff in a private action, and which would also continue to run for the same period. Clearly these are issues, which would be in our mind when we are progressing a case, but it is not something, I would suggest, which we could allow to skew our priorities in investigating public enforcement matters.

As I said, there are also some complements. First of all, private enforcement action, particularly when carried on in parallel, does raise the profile of a public investigation. As an example of that, I would take the current litigation via the NHS against various supplies of generic drugs, which is also being carried on parallel with a potential investigation into criminal offences by the Serious Fraud Office. As has been raised by a number of people, the binding effect of OFT infringement decisions on the addressees is an important point here. Clearly the question of what the effect of an OFT decision is on people who are not addressees of them, is an open question. The Court of Appeal's judgement in the *Crehan* case[7] may very well influence courts to take more account of the findings of fact, which are beyond the reach of appeal in our decisions, even in relation to parties who are not actually the direct addressees of our decisions.

And finally, on a complementary basis, I think it is a very good thing that it is likely, in my view, that most private damages claims will be brought before the Competition Appeal Tribunal and that will enable there to be at least a degree of coherence between the principles applied to public enforcement, particularly in relation to issues such as confidentiality, timing and so forth, and in private claims. That is a distinct advantage of the British system over, in particular, the American system where private enforcement could be brought more or less at any time, in a more or less guerilla way to slow people down. I think that that particular innovation that we have invented is a good one.

SIR CHRISTOPHER BELLAMY

Thank you very much indeed Vincent. Peter Freeman, Deputy Chairman, Competition Commission.

---

[7] *Crehan v Inntrepreneur Pub Company (CPC)* [2004] EWCA Civ 637, judgment on 21 May 2004.

PETER FREEMAN

Well, hello everybody. I think the Chairman has already said about as much as what I want to say. I want to say nothing at all really. Indeed, I thought, I could get away with discussing for five minutes the difference between a policy and a perspective, because I could safely say we have no policy on private enforcement. Indeed, anybody who knows anything about the history of the Commission would regard the whole idea of the Commission having a policy on such a matter as novel, if not heroic.

Do we have a perspective? Well, on the basis that a perspective is something like 'Well, how does it look to us?', I suppose I can tentatively make a few very superficial observations. The first one is absolutely blindingly obvious, which is we do not as the Competition Commission initiate cases. We have two main relevant jurisdictions; mergers and markets. We take cases as referred to us. So there is no question of our position being that of 'Government failing to intervene' or 'Government not taking a case'—we take cases referred to us.

I would draw a distinction in relation to the market side between private interests and private enforcement. Private enforcement has a very, very peripheral role for us, but when we conduct an enquiry into a market, we take private interests into account very fundamentally. There aren't any market inquiry reports under the Enterprise Act yet to peruse, but if you look at the recent monopoly enquiries under the Fair Trading Act,[8] you will see that private interests played a very big part in the appreciation there.

So I would draw that distinction. Of course, we don't make findings under Article 81 or Article 82 or under the Competition Act, so those findings that we make in relation to market investigations are not formally binding on anybody. But we are quite thorough, and we do disclose in our reports a very large number of facts, and we make judgments on those facts to some extent. That is bound, in our view, to have some effect on possible follow-on action by people who are affected.

I seem to remember from a previous existence (I can't remember which hat I was wearing) but there was a flurry of activity after the SME banking report by the Competition Commission as to whether the facts there disclosed gave rise to a cause of action under Chapter II. That is just an example of the sort of thing that could happen.

I suppose we don't have any power to order compensation, taking up Vincent's point, but some of our remedies in a sense are quasi compen-

---

[8] UK Fair Frading Act 1973, c 41.

satory. We have the power to adjust contracts. That could be regarded as compensatory, but we can't say 'This person has suffered this loss, whether it's $92 or some other more significant amount, and therefore they should be compensated.' That I think is very much in the private enforcement field.

One brief point about merger control, just touched on by Donald Baker. Again, this is purely a tentative view, but I think our perception is that in the UK we have a merger-control system operated through the public authorities. You can like it, or you can not like it, but it is there. One of the ways in which it operates is by sending signals through decided cases and through guidance to enable operators in the market to plan their actions and policies in the future. I think that is one area that might possibly be less easy to operate if there was a proliferation of private actions, banning mergers, interrupting mergers, holding mergers up. I think the whole question of guidance would then become much more problematic.

SIR CHRISTOPHER BELLAMY

Are there questions from the Floor on any of the topics that we have discussed during the morning?

DR ALAN RILEY (*Nottingham Law School*)

I am just taking up Vincent's point about taking up public enforcement and the relationship between public enforcement and private enforcement and what potentially the antitrust agencies, be it the OFT, or the European Commission or other national competition authorities across Europe could do to help private enforcement.

One suggestion I would make is perhaps to introduce the concept of 'kindly drafting'. If the Office of Fair Trading, or the European Commission or other agencies could perhaps kindly draft their prohibition decisions, when dealing with cartels. If you do have all the information about the over-charges; if you do have all the information about the full scope of the damage—please put it in the decision. You are going to make life a lot easier for the plaintiffs, who want to subsequently bring their actions. You will save a huge amount of cost, effort and time on discovery, and you will make it much easier for the plaintiffs overall. And what is more, in terms of not doing anything particularly dodgy or slightly off the mark as regards the OFT being a public enforcement agency surely, because if you take the Commission's own fining Notice, one of the bases for the calculation of the fine is in part the actual level of the damage inflicted by the cartel, the level that is gained, and putting all that in a decision is perfectly reasonable as part of your overall calculation of the fine you are going to impose.

So what I am suggesting please, is 'kindly drafting'.

Dr Irwin Stelzer (*Irwin Stelzer Associates*)

I have a question for Mr Smith. I have the impression, listening to you, that you are rather annoyed about the whole process of private enforcement. In fact you have said you distinguish between deterrence and so on, in other words that you are very eager to preserve your own monopoly in this area, and perhaps I missed the point where you were explaining the virtues you saw in private enforcement. I would agree with the previous speaker. I think the point you made, stems from the point I am making, that they are not very eager to help private enforcement, because it just can't be sloppy writing all the time that leaves out the information that somebody would need in private enforcement, so I wonder if I have got it right, and if I haven't, would you be good enough to explain why you might favour some competition from the private sector.

Dr Alan Riley

Can I make a small intervention. It occurs to me that you want to take this just a little further. What you could potentially do is link additional carrots for the leniency applicant, so that you have something equivalent to single damages, or a lower level of damages to the leniency applicant in return for emphasizing in the Leniency Notice, that you want as much information as possible in relation to the damage inflicted by the cartel. I mean, there are lots of ways you could twist this to encourage that evidence to appear on your table and then put it into the decision.

Sir Christopher Bellamy

Now you have an avalanche of questions. I am going to just add to the avalanche. You don't have to answer this particular question. In considering a leniency application, or in drafting leniency rules, what part, if any, should the willingness of the applicant for leniency to pay damages play?

Jean François Bellis

On this issue, I would like to refer to a case with which our Chairman is certainly very familiar. The *Akzo* case in which the fact that Akzo compensated the complainant, it was taken into account by the Commission in stating the level of the fine, so that is one way of making sure that public enforcement also assists private enforcement.

VINCENT SMITH

I think the main point is Irwin's point. What is the actual purpose of private enforcement, and should we have a monopoly on making sure the consumers get their money back if they have been the victims of anti-competitive behaviour, to which the answer is self-evidently 'no'.

The difficulties I have and the reservations I have about it, in a relatively under-developed regime such as ours, and bear in mind we don't have one hundred years of jurisprudence on this, is that the cross-over between public enforcement and private enforcement and the procedural difficulties that that gives rise to have not yet been fully thought out, and they need to be. My reticence is one of caution, rather than one of principle, I think.

As to the 'kindly drafting' point, yes of course we will, if we can, but it is very difficult often to get the evidence to show what the loss was. I am looking at a couple of cartel cases now where some of the potential addressees of the infringement decision can't even tell me what their relevant turnover in the relevant market in the relevant period is—let alone what the prices might have been. So actually getting the evidence together, even for us, is not straightforward, and I can well believe that private plaintiffs have an even worse time of it.

To take the point that you made, Sir Christopher about consideration of leniency, and the question of whether or not, as a condition of leniency, we might wish to ask the parties whether they are willing to pay compensation. I think that given that the payment of compensation, would, it seems to me, necessarily imply some admission that there had been an infringement and that is not currently a condition of our leniency application, I don't think we would do that. But what I think we might want to do, even though it is not in our penalties guidance, is suggest that if the parties voluntarily undertook to compensate customers and consumers for the loss they have suffered, we might take that as a mitigating factor. A mitigating factor in setting the amount of fine. Of course, I seem to recall there is actually some precedent for this because I think it happened in the *British Leyland* case in the early 1980s and the *Unipart* case,[9] I seem to recall.

---

[9] *Unipart Group Ltd v O2 (UK) Ltd (formerly BT Cellnet Ltd)*(CA (Civ Div)) Court of Appeal (Civil Division), 30 July 2004, [2004] EWCA Civ 1034, (2004) 148 SJLB 1119.

So that may be a way forward, and I certainly wouldn't rule that out, although as I say, it certainly is not clear in our guidance. But of course guidance can be amended if necessary.

DONALD BAKER

I just wanted to point out briefly that there is a real conflict here between the public authority and the private interests in the plea or settlement process. In a court-centered system, the Government is faced with actually having to prove itscase beyond a reasonable doubt in court, This is clearly burdensome and ties up limited agency resources iif there has been no agreement with the parties to plead and pay fines. So the prosecutors would, if possible, like a deal rather than a trial—which would clearly be true of Canada and the United States, and I gather UK as well. In my experience, the negotiation that goes on over the plea is driven by the private consequences. Consequently one may go into the Justice Department and say 'We would be willing to plead to a felony, provided the charged period of the cartel is no more than thirteen months.' This happens because whatever ends up in the indictment filed with the guilty plea becomes prima facie evidence in the follow-on private cases. In Canada you have these wonderful 'statements of agreed facts'—which, as far as I can tell from my experience involved, facts that I never knew about, let alone agreed to. I am sure that these 'agreed facts' are not only featured, in follow-on Canadian privated litigation, but they are now a regular and significant part of US litigation in international cases.

The Canadian statements of fact are wonderful stuff for plaintiffs, and the likely defendants who are negotiating with the Canadian agency are going to worry about the collateral consequences in the US courts at least.

SUZANNE LEGAULT

From the Canadian perspective, in terms of sharing information we have collected, there have been some cases, where we have an exception in our confidentiality provisions in Canada that says that the Competition Bureau can share information if it is necessary for the enforcement of the Act. There has been some decision that I think, and Subrata mentions it in his paper, whereby the Court has indicated that sharing the information in the private case was part of the enforcement and therefore, covered by the confidentiality exception under our Act. So that is something quite interesting.

In terms of drafting these types of settlements, I think in cartel cases, we cannot escape the fact that these are done in an international context now, and the consequences in one jurisdiction will have huge consequences in other jurisdictions, especially in light of the situation in the US. Treble damages are certainly one of the key considerations of any settlement discussions in Canada, and you know, when you look at all of these things in the grand scheme of things, you have to consider the cost to the economy as a whole of a protracted litigation as opposed to a settlement. These are the types of consideration that do bear in the balance of public and private enforcements. These are the kinds of things that we have to consider.

In Canada, we do have the possibility, in criminal cases, because we are before courts of inherent jurisdiction, to have restitutionary awards as part of our cartel cases or any of the cases on the criminal side, which is a very interesting remedy.

On the civil side, we actually have a proposal for reform in certain circumstances to also equip our tribunal with the ability to issue these restitutionary awards, which the tribunal would be able to award at the same time that they render a decision. So the benefit is that there is no necessity for a separate civil action in order for parties to be compensated. That is an interesting remedy that adds to the study of the appropriate balance into all of this discussion.

PETER FREEMAN

I agree with a lot of what's been said by many of the contributors, but just specifically on the 'kindly drafting' point, I do think the Competition Commission, whilst not undertaking to do this in any particular case, is in a more favourable position perhaps than the Office of Fair Trading to elaborate on some points of detail in market enquiry reports. That may be an area where 'kindly drafting' is easier to do than in a focused decision, where you have to limit yourselves to the reasons for the decision, otherwise, you are susceptible to review.

DR VELJANOVSKI (*Case Associates*)

I am not sure that it would be useful for private action in one sense because breach of statutory duty is as old as the common law itself, but if one recasts the problem more in terms of administrative versus judicial resolution or determination, I think it does broaden the scope because we have in another area seen considerable concern about the quality of administrative decisions through the European Commission's decisions on antitrust merger decisions. One would go to a public enforcement system because of this evidentiary problem. In one sense that is too hard to collect the information, and it is inefficient to have just pure private enforcement, the economies of scale to enforcement, but the other side of the coin is that if there is a monopoly enforcer, then of course you have inefficiency in determining the cases, and so you have recourse to judicial appeal. Judges have in some sense shown themselves more sensitive to the evidentiary burden than the administrative agencies have.

So the question is if one looks at it as judicial versus administrative, rather than public versus private, then you might see a different sort of depology? evolving.

VINCENT SMITH

Can I first say that I think the distinction that you are trying to draw is possibly rather illusory, certainly so far as infringement decisions under the Competition Act are concerned. They are all or almost all appealed and so therefore, in fact the resolution is judicial and at least until the appeal has run out and judgement has been given, there is no resolution.

As to the inefficiencies of a monopoly enforcer, yes there is an economic theory which says that all monopolies are inefficient, and I suppose that applies to public enforcement as much as any other area. I think that I therefore repeat again, what I said to Dr Irwin Stelzer about this. My concern is not one of principle. Clearly, as a matter of principle, a monopoly enforcer is not a good thing. But my concern is one of practicalities and they do need to be thought through carefully before we rush in and have too much 'uncontrol' of the cross-cutting processes on single cases.

SIR CHRISTOPHER BELLAMY

For the Chairman's closing remarks I will just make three very quick points on the balance between private enforcement and public enforcement and how one does it.

First point. There is a great deal of pent up energy in the private side as it were and unleashing that energy or facilitating its proper direction is an interesting way of thinking about how competition law should be made effective.

There is at the same time, with the best will in the world, a finite amount of public money that will be available to the public enforcement authorities. In some ways it is a bit like other aspects of the public service. There will never be enough money for the public enforcers to enforce everything that they want to enforce. So they need, of course, to make policy choices.

Second point arising out of the first point. The policy choice that needs to be made, it may very well be that the public enforcer feels that in terms of policy they need to choose cases that have a major impact on the economy—high profile cases in some sense or other 'important' cases, there are of course in competition law many cases that may not meet that such criteria, which involves smaller or medium-sized firms or smaller competitors or whatever, and those kinds of cases may well be the very cases that find it most difficult to bring cases in the civil courts because they are small firms, because they haven't got the money, because they can't afford to instruct the lawyers, or because they don't know what the law is, or because they can't afford the cross-undertaking in damages.

The question I would just ask, without having any view one way or the other, as to what the answer is, is whether there is a sort of gap in the system at that level, where there is a constituency and possibly quite an important constituency that has not been thought about which is the constituency that is slightly below the interest level of the public enforcer but not really able to afford private enforcement.

The third point, which I think picks up something that Suzanne was saying about Canada and the association of the private parties with the criminal proceedings in Canada. Of course, it is well established and this may well be the origin, I don't know Suzanne, in many civil law systems when you have got a public enforcement, certainly in terms of a public prosecution. The civil parties are there, and they simply, as it were immediately follow-on without the need to bring separate proceedings. Indeed we have in our normal criminal jurisdiction anyway, all kinds of ancillary proceedings for ordering compensation and so forth, which is rather similar, and it may be again that when one needs to think about ways of making all these different procedures flow in some more uniform channel, rather than getting meshed in procedural mosaic that dates from another time and another system when these sorts of problems did not arise. I just throw that point out as a final point.

PART TWO

Merger Conference
6 December 2004

Panel 1—ECN and Case Referrals

Chair: Dr John Fingleton, Irish Competition Authority

Speakers:
  Professor Abel Mateus, *Portuguese Competition Authority*
  Edith Müller, *BundesKartellamt*
  John Schmidt, *Shearman & Sterling LLP*

PROFESSOR ABEL MATEUS

Ladies and Gentlemen it is a great honour to address this distinguished audience on a topic related to the recent modernization in European Competition Law. This modernization effort at a European level has seen a complete overhaul of the competition rules within Articles 81 and 82, but also in the field of merger control: a new EC Merger Regulation, a new Implementing Regulation, and a Notice on Case Allocation.

Importantly, accompanying this effort is the creation of the European Competition Network (ECN), that has come into effect on 1 May, and that has a crucial role to play in the coordination and cooperation of the European Competition Authorities—now increased with the enlargement of the European Union to ten new members since that date.

The ECN is already a known and central player in the antitrust field, and it might also increase its role significantly in the merger field, where it currently provides a means of secure official communication between the Commission and Member States, and vice versa.

In fact, a centrepiece of the modernization package is the issue of case allocation between the European Competition Authorities, as there are several mechanisms for the referral of cases available to both the Authorities and now the parties themselves. The clarification of these rules is important for legal certainty.

I will examine these in turn, and go through the experience of the newly created Autoridade da Concorrencia (AdC) of Portugal as appropriate—in particular as regards so called pre-notification requests for mergers.

Overall, I must say that the system is working rather satisfactorily, as the increase in referrals shows. Up to now there were two case referrals from the Commission to National Authorities and about 14 cases from the Authorities to the Commission. This is important for undertakings, which have seen a substantial reduction in paperwork need or notification, under the principle of one stop shop. There are however, still some areas that may need further work, that I will detail later.

I. CASE ALLOCATION: WHY IS IT IMPORTANT?

The question of which authority deals with a given case has quite important consequences for the undertakings or companies and also for the Member States that may be involved. Not only will the resources employed be different but they may also prove more or less costly depending on where and to how many authorities a case has to be notified.

Among other things this is because the EC Merger Regulation is based on the concept of exclusive jurisdiction: that is to say, a merger is to be reviewed either at the Community level or at the national level. There is no such thing as a parallelism of jurisdictions.

In addition, the Commission and national competition authorities do not apply the same substantive and procedural rules. Whilst the Commission reviews mergers falling within its own jurisdiction on the basis of the EC Merger Regulation, the national competition authorities apply their respective national legislation to mergers falling within their jurisdiction.

The main question that underlies case allocation between the European Commission and the Member States is: who is best placed to deal with the case?

II. COMMUNITY DIMENSION

Community jurisdiction in the field of merger control is defined by the application of turnover thresholds contained in the EC Merger Regulation. This financial criteria provides an objective division of jurisdiction between the Community and Member States, and should they be met, indicate that the Commission is the more appropriate authority. In such cases there is a 'one-stop shop' for the competition analysis of mergers with a cross-border impact, instead of a multitude of potential filings within the EU.

On the other hand, in certain transactions it is a Member State that is best placed to deal with the case as it may particularly affect, from a competition viewpoint, the market in that Member State.

III. THE MECHANISMS

There is therefore a certain flexibility in the rules and these have been increased in the EC Merger Regulation, which retains the Articles 9 and 22 mechanisms as post-notification referrals, but the new Regulation has an innovative system of pre-notification referrals—whereby the parties themselves may decide they would rather request a notification at the European level, or at the level of the different member states. Thus far, the problem of forum shopping that has been a concern of many of the persons responsible of the ECN has not so far materialized.

All these mechanisms of referral must be as efficient as possible in order to avoid multiple notifications of a given operation, and this requires consultation and information sharing between Authorities, always with strict regard for professional secrecy obligations, as provided for in Article 17 of the EC Merger Regulation.

Let me just point out that, in what concerns all of the mechanisms described below, *silence*, by either the Commission or Member State(s), is to be assumed as concurrence.

IV. PRE-NOTIFICATION MECHANISMS

The pre-notification referral mechanisms have given parties a right of initiative in the determination of case allocation between the Commission and Member States. Here the parties to the transaction file a Form RS with the Commission, who then endeavours to send these to the relevant Member States via the ECN secure network. This mechanism may only be applicable if no notification within the European Union has been made.

Referrals may be of two types: (i) either it involves a transaction without community dimension but which complies with the merger jurisdiction of at least three Member States and that the parties wish to notify to the Commission, or (ii) a transaction with a community dimension may significantly affect competition in a distinct market within a Member State and therefore the notification that the parties submit should be analysed at national level.

Since 1 May there have been 14 reasoned submissions requesting a one-stop shop notification at the Commission. Of the submissions made only two have resulted in vetoes by Member States, which impede the referral taking place.

In effect, in practice this has meant that the Member States involved are in constant contact via the European Competition Network (ECN) regarding potential veto decisions by other Member States, as all it takes is one Member State to be set on refusing the referral that this will not take place. I think that Member States have used vetoes sparingly and responsibly. For instance, small countries may have an incentive to use the veto power more often in order to make a point on their concerns been taking more forcefully.

As you know, the ECA is a forum that was founded only recently in 2001, but that serves as an unofficial mechanism for cooperation between European Economic Area (EEA) members.

The AdC has been very much involved in these referral requests, as it has thus far examined four cases, in such distinct sectors as the automobile sector, agricultural sector and the printing plates. Internally, these have been treated like any other notification made under the Portuguese Competition Law, involving the same level of resources and analysis, even if limited by the 15-day time limit for decision.

When doing so, our case handlers profited from the AdC being an integral part of the ECA initiative regarding referrals, which is currently being prepared by the Multi-jurisdictional Mergers Working Group. This Group has been discussing general, non-binding, principles on the application of such referrals, in order to achieve consistency of application and increased legal certainty to the parties to the concentration.

These principles have served as inspiration to our application of Article 4(5), but we have taken into account that every situation is unique, and each merger operation has its particular circumstances that must be duly considered.

Namely the AdC has considered: whether there is a national market where the concentration has its main competition impact and that it can reasonably expect to be in a good position to analyse the case, or whether on the other hand, the Commission is best placed to analyse a merger with true cross-border impact.

V. POST NOTIFICATION REFERRALS

A. Article 9

As was the case already in the previous EC Merger Regulation, the current legal framework also provides a post-merger notification system, whereby the initiative lies with the authorities to which the operation has been notified.

In the case of Article 9 of the Regulation, where the operation has a Community dimension and has been notified with the Commission, the Member States may request for a merger to be referred to it.

The basic legal criteria that may underlie such a request is whether the operation may threaten to significantly affect competition within a distinct market in that Member State, or more basically if it affects a market within a Member State that is not a substantial part of the common market.

Ultimately the Commission has discretion whether to accept the request, even if this is not an unlimited discretion.

Again underlying the whole referral system is the effectiveness of the merger control and who is best placed to deal with a given transaction, always considering the 'one stop shop' principle.

Thus far the AdC has not yet made such a request, although we do undertake internal procedures in order to closely follow notifications made to the Commission that may meet the legal criteria mentioned. In fact the parties themselves normally take the first step and inform us that they will be notifying in Brussels and will often request meetings and explain the deal. We cooperate with them closely as well as with the Commission, not only at the possible referral phase, but also later, during the proceedings, should we decide not to request a referral.

B. Article 22

Article 22 sets the opposite mechanism envisaged in Article 9. It basically states that Member State(s) can request a referral to the Commission of a merger, with no Community dimension and, therefore notified nationally.

The basic legal criteria are that the merger affects trade between Member States and it threatens to significantly affect competition within the requesting Member State(s) territory.

Again, as in Article 9, the Commission has discretion on whether to accept the referral from Member State(s). If it does so, the parties might have to submit a Form CO notification to Commission.

Within the European Competition Authorities' Network, the AdC has developed strong contacts, in particular when a multiple-notification merger has been notified with it.

A frequent exchange of correspondence with all other European NCA's enables us to keep informed and to decide to request a referral, to join a referral from other Member State(s), or to oppose a referral requested by other Member State(s). In so far as I can recall, the AdC has only experienced one Article 22 referral.

Let me now refer some points for further reflection . . .

C. Points for further improvement

1. The theory of referrals is obviously related with the theory of case allocation within the ECN. In order to further clarify and add legal certainty

we think that an effects-based theory should clarify certain rules. For example if an undertaking has sales of less than 25 per cent of the total in cross-border markets, it should be considered a strictly national market. Furthermore, if only an undertaking has more than 25 per cent of its sales in a given market should it be considered as a relevant national market.

Similarly, if an undertaking in a given country acquires assets of another undertaking of another country, but all the effects are circumscribed to a given national market, then it should be the respective Authority to review that case.

2. National Competition Authorities have very different statutes and operate within very different political and institutional frameworks. For example in some countries merger decisions can be overturned by Ministers of Economy, and in one case they are decided by the Council of Ministers. In difficult cases would the Commission be willing to refer those mergers to these Authorities?

3. National legislations still have different criteria for analysing mergers, mainly dominant and SLC tests. As practice develops, forum shopping could start to exploit those differences, which will open cracks in the enforcement of competition law. Both points 2 and 3 should be addressed, like in monetary integration and statutes of the national central banks, of a certain minimum set of institutional rules that national legislation should respect, within the context of a protocol to the Treaties.

VI. CONCLUSION

Ladies and Gentlemen, I hope that these explanations will give you a sense of the importance that the Portuguese Competition Authority, and I am sure all competition authorities in Europe attach to the principles so dear to undertakings of the one stop shop, but also to the effectiveness of merger control. In this role of case allocation, communication with all the players is vital, between the Member States as between themselves, between these and the Commission, but also with the parties involved in a concentration operation. The ECN plays a vital role in all the latter of these, and further deepening of our cooperation will certainly contribute to building the single market.

JOHN FINGLETON

Thank you very much. You answered a question that I was going to put to you, which I also think I asked here last year about referrals from the Commission to Member States, whether it would depend on the involvement of Ministers in the decision-making. That will be something to watch as we go forward, as to whether there is a different rule in countries like the UK where ministers have been moved from merger decisions and countries like France and Portugal, where there is still a political involvement in decision-making.

We are now turning to Edith who is going to continue the description of how the system works, but from an operational prospective.

EDITH MÜLLER

Thank you John. Good morning ladies and gentlemen. Before I briefly start with my presentation, let me thank you and let me express my thanks to both John Schmidt and Philip Marsden for inviting me to take part in this conference. I feel very honoured.

First let me start with my resumé, which is unusual but I will do it for clarity's sake. From our point of view, having been in the business for quite some time, I believe that the new referral system involves new opportunities for all parties involved, meaning undertakings, as well as Member States and the Commission. I will explain later on what these opportunities are. I think there is no doubt that not every single question as regards referrals has been solved. But what is most important from our point of view, and I'm very happy to say so, is that cooperation between the various players when it comes to referrals has dramatically improved and become much more intensive.

When I talk about cooperation, I refer not only to contacts between the Commission and the Member States, but also to discussions among Member States. The new referral system creates additional incentives for co-operation and we hope that they will lead to a division of labour on a partnership level between all the agencies involved together with, of course, the undertakings.

I will now give you a short overview about the most important things from a practitioner's point of view.

I would like to ask you to bear in mind what it is we wanted to achieve when, during last year's merger review, we actually worked on the system of referrals. I will give you a hierarchy of priorities: We wanted obviously to (1) protect competition by (2) the authority most suited to deal with the given concentration and (3) without creating undue burden on undertakings.

I must stress that this is, from my point of view, a list of priorities because protection of competition is the main goal that we want to reach.

What has been achieved? I believe the main point to be the decentralization of the right to initiate a request for referral. Under the old regime, it was a Member State's right to request a referral in either direction. Now in Article 4(4) and 4(5) there are referrals, which can be initiated by the undertakings. Moreover, the Commission has the right to invite Member States to refer a case to it, or to ask for a referral. Member States' rights mainly remain the same.

It is a question whether it is now easier to ask for a referral under Article 9. Some people tend to say it is easier, because of a new material criterion. I am rather doubtful about that, I must admit.

The applicability of Article 22 has certainly been improved. I think all of us who have ever worked on an Article 22 case, know that this Article has been very difficult to understand—to make it work was practically impossible. It needed a lot of goodwill from all sides to actually try and make it work. But now, the new Article 22 has improved dramatically.

We see the introduction of referrals prior to notification. I am going to dwell on this later on. What we have also experienced is additional flexibility.

Let me hint at what we have not achieved. Unfortunately we have no uniform material criterion for a referral which can be found in all the referral provisions. In Article 4(4), the criterion is that the concentration 'may significantly affect' competition. In Article 9, the concentration has to 'threaten to affect significantly' competition. In Article 22, we have the criteria that the concentration 'affects trade between Member States and threatens to significantly affect' competition and in Article 4(5) actually you are looking in vain if you want to see a material criterion. There is nothing in it; the criterion is only that the concentration is 'capable of being reviewed under national competition laws of at least three Member States'.

I am not sure whether we could have found one material criterion for referrals, but three different ones and one missing is probably too many.

There was a chance to reduce multiple filings even more than is now possible in that there are no partial referrals under Article 4(5). If a Member States blocks a referral-request under Article 4(5), via its right to veto, the concentration is not referred to the Commission; not even to the parts of those Member States who actually agree to refer the case. I call that missing a chance for further reducing multiple filings.

One could argue about simplicity. I suppose most people would say the new system does not really look simple. But then again, what seems to be very difficult and very complex after half a year of practice seems to work amazingly well. So I put a question mark after simplicity when I wonder whether we have achieved it. After all it has to be borne in mind that there was some pressure to reach flexibility, simplicity, speed and legal certainty simultaneously and I suppose that most of us know it is very difficult to maximize all of these goals at the same time. You can only try to optimize them.

What the whole referral system actually requires is a lot of communication. I am concentrating on Article 4(5) referrals, because that is the overwhelming majority of referrals we have seen recently.

I have to draw on my German experience. I am not familiar with the internal proceedings of the OFT, so forgive me for drawing on my own practice.

Communication with undertakings taking part in the concentration: We do talk with undertakings that ask for a referral to the Commission. However, there is Form RS, which stands for 'reasoned submission' as you know, and most of the questions should be answered by fully filling in Form RS. Being of a confidential nature, the concentration cannot be reviewed by the National Competition Authority by asking third parties. So we depend on the information we have received from the parties. That makes communication with undertakings a bit sensitive. We can't give too much of an opinion, we cannot indicate whether we are willing or not to refer, on informal talks before we have actually seen the form RS and verified to our best efforts the information contained therein.

What we do give guidance on is the question on whether we are capable of review. That is a rather formal question, but it is very basic to the question, 'Can we veto? Can we refer a case?'. Consequently, we do talk to undertakings, in particular if they have questions as to whether we want any additional information in the Form RS.

We have to talk quite a lot internally to decide whether we refer or not. Having received Form RS, we start an internal procedure whereby staff that have been involved in last year's merger review have a look into the individual Form RS. Then the whole case is sent to our branch departments responsible for the industry at hand to have a look into the market. Once we have taken an initial opinion, we have a whole hierarchy to get our proposal through

Then of course, there is also communication with the other Member States, and with the Commission. Generally that is informal and we use the merger mailbox, which has recently been introduced by the Commission. I must say that we are very grateful for it. It is a secure line of communication and helpful to spread things around to other Member States. It is very useful, but, and I want to stress this issue here because I know it is always a concern, of course, we can not exchange business secrets. This is obvious, really.

With the Commission, we communicate very informally as well. Normally we get a note from the Commission saying that they have looked into the Form RS and whatever they found out to point our attention to. If there are questions of mutual interest, we set up telephone conferences on an ad hoc basis to see whether somebody has a particular insight into the market and how it works. Then again, there are the guidelines. I know you are all familiar with the Commission's guideline on case allocation. National Competition Authorities are also working on the ECA Principles. I suppose most of you are familiar with the ECA—the European Competition Authorities, where the working group on multijurisdictional filing is currently drafting a new version of the ECA Principles for referrals from Member States to the Commission.

I will be very brief on Article 22 and Article 9. Regarding Article 22, time limits seem to be much clearer now and much more workable. We do still have some questions about what is meant by 'If no notification is required'? and the notification having been 'otherwise made known' to a National Competition Authority. But these are questions we have also had under the old Article 22. Now, once a Member State has requested a referral, other Member States do have the chance to join in, which is an improvement. And there is another need for communication. All national time limits where Member States are working on the same concentration are suspended once a Member State has requested a referral to the Commission involving this particular concentration. This means, obviously, if you are one day before taking a final decision and another National Competition Authority asks for a referral of that very concentration to the Commission, you can not decide. Your proceedings are blocked. So there is obviously a mutual interest in communication in that point of referrals.

Article 9 is probably the provision, which has been changed the least. We have seen only one referral according to Article 9 under the new regime and that was Spanish. Due to my lack of Spanish, I couldn't get much information out of it yet.

It is doubtful whether we will see many Article 4(4) referrals. I will stop here but if there are any questions, I will be happy to answer them.

Thank you very much for your attention.

JOHN SCHMIDT

Starting with my conclusions, I actually agree with quite a lot of what Edith has said. The text of Article 9 obviously has not changed very much. Its application has evolved and the text has caught up with the application. Therefore, I would expect Article 9 to work in very much the same way as it has been working in the past. As for Article 22, I think there has been a very significant improvement as to the way the Article will work in future, which should bring with it a substantial reduction of the timeline.

I have a couple of raised eyebrows left for Article 4—one each for Article 4(4) and 4(5). The main reasons why I would not be advising my clients to rush into filling in the form RS in relation to Article 4(4) is purely the timing issue. I do not believe that Article 4(4) gives any timing advantages—quite the opposite. On Article 4(5) I believe that the veto right of an individual Member State to block the entire reference is a great disincentive for any party to use that process. If we look at the numbers of cases—there have only been some ten cases—I think being vetoed in two (ie 20 per cent) is not insignificant. In merger cases timing is usually one of the foremost issues and for those cases I suspect Article 4(5) will only rarely be used.

I. THE RATIONALE FOR REFERENCES

To start with, let me briefly go back, to the rationale of references. This has evolved since the early days of the ECMR. Its primary purpose has evolved into a mechanism for redressing the failure of the secondary thresholds to capture those mergers that fall below the primary thresholds but which still have a 'Community dimension' in the non-technical sense. The Commission and the NCAs sought to introduce a sufficient amount of flexibility that would allow the authorities to sit together and to reallocate the cases to the most appropriate authority.

II. GUIDING PRINCIPLES

In order to achieve this flexibility, the Commission has formulated its Case Allocation Notice[1] which is based on three guiding principles.

The main principle is flexibility. We are promised a lot of flexibility on the part of the authorities in order to achieve the main aim of allocating the case to the most appropriate authority. The principle of flexibility is, however, subject to two caveats. Certainly from a practitioner's perspective these are two very important caveats.

The first one is the one stop shop: fragmentation of a case should be avoided. The second one is legal certainty: one should only depart from the original authority with the original jurisdiction, for very compelling reasons.

---

[1] Commission Notice on Case Referral in respect of Concentrations <http://www.europa. eu.int/comm/competition/mergers/legislation/consultation/case_allocation_tru.pdf>.

When you read the guidelines you will see that a lot of time and space is spent on the topic of flexibility. I believe that a lot more space could have been devoted to the caveats—the one stop shop and what constitutes a compelling reason for allocating the cases, or not allocating the cases.

III. WHAT DO THE PARTIES WANT FROM THE MERGER PROCESS?

Apart from receiving a clearance, of course, the two most important things that merging parties look for in the merger process is (i) certainty, and (ii) speed. Sometimes speed is more important than certainty and sometimes the priorities are reversed.

Very often you hear from the Commission and NCAs a fear that the parties' main interest may be forum shopping; that they want to go to the authority that gives them the easiest ride. In my experience, that is not really on the parties' agenda. Obviously, they want a clearance, but in complicated cases with significant substantive issues I would expect those issues to be dealt with relatively similarly, be it at national level or before the Commission. So I do not think that the fear of forum shopping is one that the authorities should be concerned with.[2]

IV. WHAT DO THEY GET?

Let me now turn to what the parties get out of the new process (here I am primarily looking at Article 4(4) and 4(5) processes). Under the old ECMR they got a very clear, very speedy process, fixed timetables and clear jurisdictional divide. There was a risk of an Article 9 process, but in terms of timing, that risk translates into range of an additional period of review of between two to six weeks. You had an additional two weeks if a request was made and was ultimately rejected, so you had Phase I extended by two weeks. You had an additional maximum of six weeks if the Commission decided to refer a case at the end of Phase I from which point the national timelines started.

By using Article 4(4) as a means to manage that timing risk, you would have to engage in a process that takes some four to five weeks. So in order to remove a risk of an extension of two to six weeks, you need to take on board a process that takes four to five weeks to determine that issue. I think that is the principal reason why merging parties will not be using Article 4(4) to any significant degree. In most cases the parties will be better off by notifying to the Commission and taking a risk on Article 9.

---

[2] Is it not curious that particularly competition authorities are afraid of competition from other authorities or regimes? Wouldn't the possibility for parties to arbitrage between competition systems create an incentive for those authorities to apply the rules uniformly?

Turning to Article 4(5), I think the picture changes quite significantly: with the old ECMR an Article 22 reference involved a process of at least two months, probably around three months from the date of notification to the NCA in order to receive (an Article 22) Phase I clearance. For a Phase II process, the review took significantly more, seven months, probably a year, probably over a year. Article 4(5) now provides for a mechanism that will result in a decision on whether a reference should made within three to four weeks. This will be the main selling point for Article 4(5), given the time it takes to prepare national filings and the varying national review periods.

The drawback, as I said at the beginning, is the fact that any single Member State can veto the whole process. If there is a significant danger of a veto, again the parties might as well just notify at national level especially if a Phase I clearance can be expected.

V. REMAINING CERTAINTY ISSUES

There are also a number of certainty issues where the guidelines are very unclear on the Commission's (and NCA's) likely thinking.

It is quite clear from the guidelines that if the geographic market is less than a Member State, the NCA will be best placed to look at the case. If the geographic market is wider than a Member State, the Commission is best placed to look at the case.

However, there is still a distinct lack of clarity where the geographic market is national. If any one Member State is affected it is pretty clear, in my view, that the NCA should have jurisdiction. If multiple Member States are affected, I believe that the Commission would almost invariably be best placed to review that case. The guidelines however try to keep all the doors open, suggesting 'a considerable margin of discretion' on the part of the authorities, particularly on the part of the Commission. As this touches issues of due process, I believe that further clarification would be helpful. Such clarification can come through the cases, but virtually no information on Article 4 cases is published. You are lucky to find out the number of reference requests that have been made. As the final decision is published on the Commission's or the NCA's website, it is possible to see whether a case was referred, but the reasons for making or not making a reference remain clouded in mystery.

VI. OTHER ISSUES

I have also identified a number of other interesting issues, some purely practical and some more theoretic, which I will discuss in no particular order of preference.

First, can you make neutral requests? The ECMR and the Form RS do not provide for neutral requests. In many cases, the parties do not mind which authority reviews the case, but in some cases, it may be important to force that decision upfront. The way the Form RS is currently drafted, you have to argue in favour of a reference, even if you may not want a reference after all, or even if you are agnostic about a reference.

The second issue is confidentiality. As I said already, I believe there is too much secrecy surrounding the entire Article 4 process. The Commission is quite keen to point out that you could have a confidential Article 4 process (ie where the transaction is still secret) but I am not entirely sure that I could persuade many clients to engage in an Article 4 process where the form RS is circulated to 25 Member States. Particularly in public bids, I do not see that as a viable option. At any rate, once a transaction has become public there is no reason not to publish the Article 4 decision (subject to business secrets) in the same way that Article 6 decisions are published (for which there is equally no legal requirement).

The third issue is the old chestnut of whether you can have an Article 22 reference in a situation where the national merger thresholds are not exceeded. I was quite interested to read in Edith's paper that the Bundeskartellamt would not be looking to request referrals under these circumstances—although there are not very many mergers that are not caught by the German thresholds.

It is still a live issue in jurisdictions where the thresholds are very much higher and where there is a real likelihood that mergers with substantive issues fall below the thresholds.

The fourth issue is a very interesting procedural point on the appealability of Article 4(4) decisions to refer. In *Philips v Commission*[3] the court confirmed that third party competitors had standing to challenge an Article 9 reference. The reason essentially was that such a reference effectively precluded third parties from benefiting from an EC review and from potentially challenging a merger before the European Court.[4] In the context of Article 4(4), the issue of standing becomes mingled with due process issues. As I said earlier, the Article 4(4) process does not provide for the Commission taking third party views on the question of a reference and does not provide for publication of the decision once it is adopted. Given that a third party has the right to appeal a decision where the process does not even envisage giving them an opportunity to make their views known

---

[3] T-112/02 *Royal Philips Electronics NV v Commission*, Judgment 3 Apr 2003.
[4] Note: So a third party would not have standing to challenge a decision not to refer, or an Art 4(5) decision.

should stand them in good stead if they want to challenge a decision to refer in court. There is also the wider point of whether such a confidential Article 4(4) process is *per se* incompatible with the general principles, such as the right to a hearing.

In any event this looks like quite an interesting new tool in a complainant's toolbox.

JOHN FINGLETON

Thank you very much John, that has given us some food for thought there. And I now want to open up this discussion to the room and if there are questions if people will identify themselves, before they speak.

JOANNA McDWYER (*FIPRA UK*)

I have a question about how the ECMR works on case referrals. I am not sure whether you will be able to comment or not, but perhaps it is a question I can follow up later in the day with some people from the Commission. What I am interested in is as a national authority, what is the discussion and debate between the Commission and a National Competition Authority in terms of a reference, where there is a request that comes from a national authority for a case which has been notified to Brussels.

The other thing, which I would be interested in, is how does the process work within the Commission? Obviously case teams working on merger notifications would clearly be involved in the discussion that takes place between national authorities and the European Commission, but I would suppose that perhaps the unit which deals with strategic support for mergers which was set up earlier this year might be involved but I would assume also that the Legal Service gets involved.

I wondered if it was possible to comment on any of that.

EDITH MÜLLER

OK. I'll take the first part of your question. I feel a bit incompetent if that's the right word, to talk about the second part of it, as that refers to internal Commission procedures, which I am not familiar with.

When it comes to referrals I must say that from my experience there hardly is a case, in which the Commission and the National Competition Authorities as well as parties (at least in Germany), were not aware of the fact that there is an issue for referral in it. Normally, discussions start on a confidential level long before that concentration is notified, and the process usually starts with companies coming in to talk to the Commission and to see us at the Bundeskartellamt. We very often get a draft notification which is discussed with the Commission and with the case team at the Bundeskartellamt. We have a fairly good idea whether we are willing to ask for a referral or not, and obviously there will be telephone calls between the Commission and the case team in Germany and vice versa. However, there is no formal procedure because every case is unique and has its particular issues. But I should like to stress again that I don't think that a company has ever been surprised by the decision to request a referral.

JOHN FINGLETON

That is very helpful. I think in Ireland we have twice considered an Article 9 request and the first time it was the ministry at the time which made it, and it seemed to stop the deal from going ahead and the parties withdrew from the transaction.

The second occasion, we didn't make the request in the end, but it raised a lot of issues about how we interacted publicly with the company, because obviously the decision whether or not to bring it back to Ireland, or even whether we requested it, could have implications on things like stock prices and so forth. I think that what we found was that we needed to think through our own public procedures and internal procedures for that more carefully, and I suspect that that is going to be something that Member States' Competition Authorities would naturally do once they go through one of these.

But I am going to ask Carles Esteva Mosso, who is the new head of the Policy Unit at the Commission and who we are happy to have here today, just to answer the second part of Joanna's question.

CARLES ESTEVA MOSSO (*European Commission*)

OK. Let me profit from the opportunity also to give a very factual contribution to the debate and the latest statistics on referrals. We have got two 4(4) successful requests and 14 4(5) requests. Of these 14, two have been settled and one is still pending, which means we have in fact had 11 cases on the 4(5). If you compare this figure with the total number of cases that we have dealt with under the new Merger Regulation, this represents around 10 per cent of these cases, so clearly a quite satisfactory figure. I would say that the fears that the Form RS would be too burdensome and that the parties would be discouraged by the length of this process for the moment are not confirmed by the facts. I think this 10 per cent is a good figure and in these 11 cases in seven months, they compare very favourably with three joint referrals by Member States on Article 22 in 13 years.

Then we may not have eliminated the problem of multiple notifications, but I think we have made a better step towards it. And to reply to your question about internal procedures, well the contact point for the parties should always remain the case team. It is the case team who will be dealing with the parties and with Member States on the specific case, but certainly the policy unit, which has among other functions to ensure consistency and to keep the relationship with Member States, will internally be involved, but parties may not always be aware of this.

MONICA KOHOLA (*Le Boeuff, Lamb, Greene & MacRae*)

My question is this. I was wondering whether any of the speakers could give their opinion on what is meant in Article 4(5) on 'capable of being reviewed'.

CHRIS BRIGHT (*Shearman and Sterling LLP*)

Going back to Article 9, I was interested in the comments about political influence and also Edith's comment that nothing much had changed in Article 9. I think certainly I had had the perception that the removal of the strong threshold that the Member State had to show that there was a significant risk of creating or strengthening a dominant position would have some impact on the number of Article 9 requests. The new words say simply, I think, 'Significantly affect competition', or something like that, which is pretty vague. It could be positive, it could be negative, it could be all sorts of things. The question really is, is there any expectation that Member States will ask for referrals back in cases where there aren't any real really major concerns about competition. It may be in some Member States the deal is significant, simply because of the nature of the bidder for instance, for a company that may be no significant competition issue really, but people may be concerned about that.

The second point was in relation to political influence. If you look at the Article 9 referrals back there that have been historically, there are some that stand out I suppose, from an advisers point of view, that look as if there has been some tactical play and people have benefited from the Article 9 referral back. Take one, for instance, which people probably don't really focus on much, the *Arca Covena* reference back to Norway, which was, I think, probably most illustrative of the situation because it was a case where a notification had been made to Brussels, the Commission had cut up rough and said 'No, you can't do it'. It was withdrawn, renotified, an Article 9 request came and the Norwegian authority approved the case.

Is there a political issue in Norway? I don't know. It is possible that a small Member State has very different concepts of thresholds for anticompetitive effects, because of the nature of the market. Just how much concern I suppose is there about that, and if Carles wants to comment on it, is the Commission at all taking that sort of thing into account, when it is thinking about Article 9?

Philippe Chappatte (*Slaughter and May*)

While we have the benefit of our representatives of the National Competition Authorities here, it would be very interesting to hear from them, when they are likely to exercise their veto powers, in relation to 4(5) requests. We have had the statistics, we have had a lot of encouragement from Carles Esteva Mosso, that we should be using 4(5). What we are not quite clear about as practitioners is whether we should be advising our clients to make 4(5) applications because there is a little bit of uncertainty as to how the NCAs are going to exercise that power of veto. What we hope to hear, of course, is that the NCAs will be very restrained in their discretion to exercise their veto. Thank you.

Abel Mateus

Well, two or three points on the questions. The first one regards the criteria of 'substantial lessening of competition' in merger analysis. As you know, there are several countries that still use the dominance criteria. This duality may raise problems in the future within the ECN and in the perspective of harmonization of legislation. Although, from the practical point of view, and from the cases we undertake in my country, most of the cases would lead to the same conclusion with both criteria, except for the joint dominance problem.

In terms of arbitrating among the fora, like notifying the Commission or the National Authorities, I see some problems. Without referring to specifics, in a recent case, the notifying firms expected the National Authority to be tough on the case, exactly the opposite of the case you referred to in Norway, so they went over to the Commission thinking the Commission would be easier. Fortunately, the approachs were quite coincident in the end. But it is up to the different authorities to apply the law as strictly as possible, and to define the level playing field.

In terms of the veto that each of the authorities can use. From my perspective, my authority would be using very, very sparingly, the veto, only in the very exceptional cases and I don't see any special link between cases and markets.

JOHN FINGLETON

Where might you use a veto, even if it is sparingly?

ABEL MATEUS

It would be only a case where it is really significant in part of the national market that we do have some major concerns that we are not sure might be taken into account by the other Member States or the Commission. There might be specific aspects to my country in terms of the dynamics of competition in particular markets.

JOHN FINGLETON

When would Germany and the Bundeskartellamt exercise a veto here?

EDITH MÜLLER

I cannot speak for all of my colleagues at the Bundeskartellamt and I must add that it is not only the Bundeskartellamt which has to agree, it is also the Federal Ministry, so I apologize for probably not giving you as clear an answer as you possibly wish for. All I can say is that I think we would be very much inclined to exercise our right to veto a request for referral not only in rather obvious cases in which our national or sub-national markets are concerned, but also if we realize that information submitted in Form RS is misleading or wrong or incomplete. Such behaviour is nothing that should be seen as positive. A problem is that the Commission does send to us incomplete Forms RS and thus starts our very short deadline to verify the information contained therein. If we realize that the information is misleading or wrong or incomplete, I think that would be a very good reason for us to want to look into the concentration.

I apologise for being so direct about it, but as the Commission has laid down that they will forward any form RS to the Member States, and upon our questioning this practice, told us 'Well, if you are not satisfied, you can veto', I am most willing to do so if that is the only way to get the information we need, and which is valuable and correct. I am saying so very deliberately here. If there are any questions about the information that has to be submitted, the Bundeskartellamt will be more than willing to enter into discussions with the companies involved before they submit their form RS. This Form RS is the only means of information for Member States to decide whether they give up their jurisdiction. I think it is our duty to look into a potential referral case in much detail to be sure of what we are doing.

JOHN SCHMIDT

Can I comment as a follow-on question to Edith? Would you be prepared in Article 4(5) pre-notification discussions to give an indication to the parties on the likelihood of you using the veto before you have actually received the formal notification?

EDITH MÜLLER

We haven't discussed that within our offices, but there might be a chance that for somebody listening very carefully, this person might get an idea.

JOHN FINGLETON

I hope you are all listening very carefully to that coded message! This is an interesting discussion, but we are going to have to draw to a close. I will answer Philippe Chappatte's question on Article 9 because it fell through the sieve there. I think from our perspective, the great difficulty in using Article 9 was the question of almost having to make a finding on dominance before we have the information to do it. We interpreted Article 9 as being in our view based on the information we had at that point in time and there was a sense of acrobatics about that that was unsatisfactory, and I think that the new test won't increase the set of Article 9 references, but will actually in a way that doesn't involve the authority convoluting itself with language and make it possible to make Article 9 requests. I wouldn't expect to see an increase there.

On the question of vetos, I think our third ever merger notification under our new law two years ago was the third ever successful Article 22 reference. And I think the Member State competition values are more frustrated by the inability to make Article 22 requests, than by the desire to veto, so I think that in the overall scale of things, we are going to see much more of that type of referral to Brussels. I think on the question of vetos, in the early days you may see some vetos, but I think countries will obviously want to avoid having a reputation for being the country that is the unique country that is always vetoing things, I think the thing to watch on both of these is the difference between large and small Member States. I think small Member States like Ireland and Portugal, are probably very concerned about being ignored about something that is very important within a very small part of the Union, 2 per cent or 3 per cent of GDP and would be quite a few Member States each, and concerned that Brussels won't maybe pick up something that might be very important locally. Whereas for large Member States I think very different issues apply when looking at whether to refer cases back and forward and I think that sensitivity to that issue about those people making referrals are probably very useful and also to watch it as a trend.

So I think, in conclusion, there was an almost disturbing degree of consensus on some issues and certainly people thought that Article 22 was a good thing; Article 9, possibly improved, maybe a little bit more uncertainty at the margins about it, and Article 4(4) and 4(5), Carles Esteva Mosso has told us are working extremely well. But I think that as I said in the answer, it is possibly too early to make a definite conclusion and there is probably room, Philip Marsden, for discussing this again next year and maybe more focussed around Article 4 at that stage and how that is working one year on, but I think I found this very informative, and thank you very much to our three speakers for their preparation and to those people who asked questions.

Panel 2—Devil's Advocate Panels

Chair: Chris Bright, *Shearman & Sterling LLP*

Speakers:
   Philippe Chappatte, *Slaughter & May*
   Carles Esteva Mosso, *European Commission*

CARLES ESTEVA MOSSO

Some of the most relevant reforms introduced during our recent merger review are related to the decision making process within the Commission. These reforms did not require an amendment of the ECMR, or to be detailed in a Notice, and therefore may be less visible than the changes introduced in the areas of substantive assessment or procedures. Their impact, however, is not less relevant.

The goal of these internal reforms was to ensure that the decision making process within the Commission would allow for a real confrontation of points of view before a major decision in a particular case is adopted. Merger control is not a science; with the same set of relevant facts, there is scope for different opinions as to the final direction of a case assessment. It is, therefore, particularly important that the team assessing the case is confronted with different views and that the final decision makers are aware of these different views and can benefit from a healthy debate before taking position.

The case team will obviously be confronted with the views of the parties and of other market operators—customers, suppliers, competitors—that intervene in the investigation or from whom information is requested. As you are aware, several reforms have been introduced in our procedure to ensure that the case team can benefit from these views and, in particular, to give to the parties the opportunity to develop their position throughout the procedure. I will not develop these reforms in detail, but let me simply refer to the possibility for the parties to request a state of play meeting at different moments of the investigation, to confront complainants in the so-called triangular meetings or to have access to key documents at an early stage of the investigation. All these reforms have been detailed in the Best Practices for merger investigations, a document that can be found and downloaded in DG COMPs website.

Another important point of view that has been incorporated into the decision making process is the opinion of the Chief Economist. As you are aware, this is a reform that originates in the merger review, but has a wider impact, because the Chief Economist is also active in the areas of antitrust and State Aids. For relevant cases in all these areas the Chief economist provides an independent view to the decision makers. And, while his team interacts with the case team and contributes to the investigation, in particular when there are quantitative assessment issues, at the end of the process the Chief Economist is free to consider whether the relevant standards to sustain an objection from an economic point of view have been met by the case team.

What are the results up to now of this system? I consider them highly positive. Not only in terms of the contribution of the Chief Economist in individual cases, but also on the general change of culture that his role is generating. The fact that the Chief Economist is involved in the analysis of cases has certainly encouraged the reflection and debate on the economic soundness of the theories of harm at earlier stages of the procedure than before, which certainly benefits the investigation and the decision process. Policy debates also benefit greatly from his insights.

Let me move now to the main subject of this discussion—the peer review panels. This reform also develops the concept that I have outlined before: to ensure that there is an open confrontation of ideas, this time between the case team and a group of peers, before a major decision—it could be a statement of objections, or a final decision—is adopted. The discussion will focus both on the factual elements of the case and on the legal and economic reasoning.

The objective of the panel process is dual. On the one hand, it provides an opportunity to the case team to identify the weaknesses of the case and try to remedy them where possible, and on the other, it provides different reasoned points of view to the management that has to take a final decision.

How does the system work in practice? First, it is the Director General who decides in which cases there should be a panel. He could decide on his own initiative or at the request of the Commissioner, but several members of the management of DG COMP, such as the Policy Director, the Chief Economist or the Director in charge of the case could suggest it.

Panels are very resource consuming; we have to be selective. But in principle, the idea is that major Article 82 cases and major second phase merger cases will be the subject of a panel. This is, though, a flexible rule and will depend on the importance of the issues raised by each case. Panels are probably less necessary for cartel cases where the nature of the issues to be discussed is totally different. But it is not excluded that in certain cases, a panel can take place also in relation to an Article 81 case.

The Director General, once he has decided to have a panel in a particular case, will appoint the Scrutiny Officer. He or she is a head of a unit, who will have the responsibility to ensure that the scrutiny works smoothly, who will chair the panel meeting and at the end will draft a report summarising what happened in this panel. Normally the Scrutiny Officer is the Head of the Scrutiny Unit in the Policy Directorate, but any other Head of Unit of this Directorate could also be appointed as a Scrutiny Officer.

The Director General also appoints what we call the 'fresh pair of eyes' team, which is composed of a Head of Unit or case manager and several other officials that will review the case in detail. The composition of the 'fresh pair of eyes' team attempts to secure a diversity of skills and points of view. A sector specialist is normally appointed (for merger cases, for instance, there is normally someone dealing with antitrust cases in the relevant sector), and the team normally includes both lawyers and economists. As soon as the team is appointed, they will be relieved for a certain period of their normal tasks. They will be allowed to focus on reviewing the case file.

In practice, the process starts with a meeting between the 'fresh pair of eyes' and the case team, where the timing of the review will be discussed and the most relevant documents of the case will be exchanged, (but in any case the reviewing team has full access to the file). If there would be problems in this process, the Scrutiny Officer is there to resolve them.

The most important step of this process is what we call 'the panel'. This is a long meeting—it could take half a day, a full day, or in some cases it has even been extended to a second day—where the case team meets the 'fresh pair of eyes' team and all aspects of the case are discussed in great detail. Normally the meeting is prepared with an agenda, which is drafted by the 'fresh pair of eyes' team, which includes all the issues they would like to discuss. For each issue there is a brief presentation by the case team, followed by questions by the 'fresh pair of eyes', and finally questions by other people participating in 'the panel'.

Who participate in this panel? Well, apart from the case team and the peer-review team, the Hearing Officer, the Chief Economist, a member of the Cabinet, a member of the Policy Directorate, and also members of other Commission departments that are relevant for the case in question.

At the end of this long discussion, the Scrutiny Officer will draft a report, which will describe the main points discussed and opinions expressed. The report will make it clear on which issues there is agreement between the case team and the 'fresh pair of eyes' team, and in relation to which ones there is a disagreement. This report is submitted to the Director General.

Once a proposal for a decision is made by the Director General to the Commissioner, a copy of the report will also be attached.

This means that the Commissioner, before taking a decision on a proposal from DG Competition, will know what issues were discussed at 'the panel' and what were the different views or alternatives discussed. When the Director General meets with the Commissioner to discuss the issue both the 'fresh pair of eyes' and the Scrutiny Officer will normally be present and they will be able to develop their points of view orally.

What is our experience in applying this system for more than one year? I will not discuss individual cases, because this is an internal process, but I can give you a general view. We have organized between 15 and 20 panels this year, not all in merger cases, some in antitrust, and we have also started to apply this procedure in relation to state aid cases.

In some of the cases, but few of them, there has been full agreement between the case team and the 'fresh pair of eyes' team. What is most common is that the 'fresh pair of eyes' team identifies some weaknesses or some point of disagreement. The consequence of these may be different in the area of mergers than in the area of antitrust. In mergers, due to the deadlines, in the short time remaining after a panel it will be normally difficult to resolve the shortcomings identified. The outcome is likely to be the abandonment of a numberof objections, or even of the whole case, which would lead to a clearance decision.

In the area of antitrust, normally there is another possibility. The panel discussion could lead, like in mergers, to the abandonment of an objection or to a clearance decision, but the case team may also try to remedy the shortcomings identified. For instance, the case team can launch a new round of requests for information to find new factual evidence the panellists had considered important to support the case. This could even require the adoption of a supplementary statement of objections afterwards.

The conclusion is quite positive after one year of experience. I think the system works. It has worked in relation to individual cases, but again I think it has contributed to change somehow the culture of DG Competition. Case teams view the assessment of a case more and more as an open process where different points of view have to be integrated, and where the common goal is to reach a sound and solid decision that can withstand judicial scrutiny. I think this process has also contributed to ensure that the management is confronted with the different options that merger investigations can lead to and has to take explicit and reasoned choices. Overall, our decision making process is of better quality and should, logically, lead to improved results.

I think I will stop here. I realize that I have been rather positive as to the functioning of all these reforms. You may not have expected me to take a different line. Maybe I am a bit biased—I contributed to the design of all this—but I honestly think it is working quite well. I am very open, however, to hear opposite views that point to things that are not working. This is a process which is not finished. We will continue to try and improve it and any criticism and suggestions for improvement will certainly be welcome.

CHRIS BRIGHT

Well Carles, thanks for a very thorough review of the changes and Philippe may have some suggestions.

PHILIPPE CHAPPATTE

Thank you very much Philip Marsden for inviting me to speak and to contribute to this panel and to talk about panels.

The peer review panel is clothed in secrecy. What is it? What is it called? Sometimes it is called a peer review panel. Sometimes the 'devils advocate' panel. Sometimes the decision 'scrutiny' panel. Sometimes a 'fresh pair of eyes'.

What is the role of this panel? There's a lot of confusion about what this panel is there to do. Is the primary purpose of the panel a confrontation of views or the identification of weaknesses in the case, and assisting the case team to fill in the holes? If the panel is there as part of the Commission's internal quality control to come out with the best quality statement of objections, then that is a fundamentally different role to a 'devils advocate' panel at the end of the process. I will come back to that.

When does it meet? This is shrouded in secrecy. Many calls are made to the Head of the Decision Scrutiny panel to find out when it meets in practice and who are its members? Its members are also shrouded in secrecy. You can't find out, even if you are reasonably well-informed. Even its conclusions are shrouded in secrecy.

Now, all this may not be a problem, but we have to decide one fundamental issue, which is: what is its role?

I think there is still a bit of schizophrenia on the part of the EU Commission in the merger field as to what the peer review panel's role is. Is it the internal quality panel that is there to get the best statement of objections out? Or is it a check and balance at the end of the procedure? When you have the panel is critical because if the purpose of the panel is to help the case team develop the best statement of objections, then you have got to logically have the meeting of the panel prior to the statement of objections being issued.

If, however, the fundamental role of the panel is a check and balance in the system so as to help the Commissioner come up with a balanced view of the issues at the end of the procedure having read the statement of objections, having read the response, having had access to the file, having attended all the hearings. If that's the case, then the panel has got to take place after the oral hearing.

Now, we are talking about mergers here. We are not talking about Articles 81 or 82 cases, when there is loads of time, and you can maybe have both a panel pre oral hearing and a panel after the oral hearing. In a merger case, there is only time for one panel. In the aftermath of the *Airtours* decision[1] and the other decisions of the Court, the role of the panel should be a check and balance—that is certainly the role of the panel envisaged by Commissioner Monti when he first publicly introduced the concept of the panel.

I find that quite hard to reconcile with the current standing instructions from the Commissioner that in merger cases the panel should take place before the statement of objections is issued.

The procedural rules and best practice guidelines, but more importantly, the introduction of a panel and the Chief Economist have been put forward as the new checks and balances within the system by Commissioner Monti. The problem with the Chief Economist is that his staff are going to be an integral part of the case team. Whatever their reporting lines are, they are going to be, in effect, trying to develop the case and trying to establish the best possible statement of objections, and indeed that is my experience of the Chief Economist's unit. They participate in meetings as part of the case team and are part of the case team.

We in fact rely heavily on the peer review panel, or the 'devils advocate' panel, or the decision 'scrutiny' panel as a real check and balance where the issues can be properly addressed, the pros and cons, the strengths and merits of the official statement of objections and the answers given by the parties. Therefore, it is fundamental that it should take place after the oral hearing. It should come right at the end of the procedure and it should be the last meeting effectively of the services of the Commission where they meet together and discuss the merits of the case.

In the two cases I participated in, where the panel has been held it has

---

[1] T-342/99 *Airtours plc v Commission* Judgment of 6 June 2002.

certainly had a material effect on the outcome of the case. The panels were held after the oral hearing. But in one case, we had to fight quite hard to get the panel to take place after the oral hearing, because certainly until very recently, the panels were taking place before the statement of objections were issued in merger cases.

I think that is the key point about the panel, which is fundamental to the Monti reforms. I understand from Oliver Guerent that the standing instructions are being changed and that in merger review cases now panels will invariably take place after the oral hearing. But I would certainly like to hear from Carles (Estava Mosso) confirmation that this is the case.

CHRIS BRIGHT

Carles, do you want to have a quick go at that?

CARLES ESTEVA MOSSO

Yes. Three comments.

First of all, the official name, if you want it, is peer review panel. This is how it appears in our documents.

Secondly, about secrecy. I don't think this is a secret instrument. I think I have been quite open in explaining to you how it works and operates. But it is clearly an internal one. The role is to facilitate the Commission in taking better decisions.

The panel members are not there to represent the views of the parties in front of the case team. I understand that the parties may have an interest in contacting them. This is not their role. As I have explained in my presentation when I referred to the 'Best practices for merger investigations', the parties will have now ample opportunities to make their views well known to the case team. These views will also be known by the panelists, that have access to the file and can also attend the hearing. The parties are normally much better placed to defending themselves, presenting their own arguments, than relying for this defence on panel members. The goal of the panel members is to provide the case team with a fresh view on the facts, maybe an alternative view on what a competition authority could do. Then in certain cases, they will want to see that the case team has good answers to what the parties are arguing, but in other cases, the panel will not follow at all the arguments of the parties.

Finally, when panels are taking place? Even if we had some basic instructions, I think in this first year we are all learning by doing and we have tried different configurations. As Philippe said, in some cases, the panel took place before the statement of objections, in some others it took place before the final decision was adopted.

I think there are advantages and disadvantages in any configuration. If you do it before the statement of objections and the panel concludes that the statement of objections is not sound, you may avoid a lot of costs and efforts for the Commission and the parties, in terms of having to argue the case in an oral hearing, or discussing remedies, to find at the end that the objections were not sound enough.

If you do it at the end, of course, then you have a role to facilitate the final decision making by the Commissioner, because the panel will present the final views on not only the objections, but probably also on the replies by the parties or even on remedies.

We have also had in one case a combination of both. There was a panel before the statement of objections, but the panel members were requested after the hearing to look at the replies by the parties, and the market test and to provide their opinion also to the Commissioner. This may be also a good system, but certainly has a high cost in terms of involvement of officials because it basically means that two teams are kept in parallel for a long part of the investigation, and this was one of the things that we wanted to avoid under the new system.

PHILIPPE CHAPPATTE

So we will see a change?

CARLES ESTEVA MOSSO

We may see a change, but it will not be a radical one. The current practice will naturally evolve and it could well be that the peer review ends up taking place after the hearing in many cases.

CHRIS BRIGHT

OK. I think one of the interesting things to observe would be I suppose that a change from what we assume these panels will be, which are restraining influences, to see if there are any occasions where they become encouraging influences to the case team. But with that, are there any questions out there?

PETER-CARLO LEHRELL (*FIPRA International*)

I have just two short questions for Carles. One is if a panel's function is of the type that Philippe describes at the end, a check and balance, of course you want it to be as independent and stand alone as possible, which is always a question mark, if it's drawn from people internally, so do you include on that panel any representatives from the Member States, such as the rapporteur of the case from the Advisory Committee. That is my first question.

The second question. You mentioned very briefly triangular meetings. Now this to me is a very nebulous concept. It is the only type of meeting I have never actually in person participated in. So I have some questions on it. If you have a merger case with three or four complainants, do they all come to this triangular meeting, and let's assume that they all have roughly equal weight and their arguments might have too. Do they all come to it? Or do you have them individually for each one? Who attends those triangular meetings? Presumably the case team, of course will. Somebody from the Chief Economist's. Somebody from the Scrutiny Panel I would imagine? Legal services as well? Again, the rapporteur from the country concerned? What exactly are the triangular meetings? They have sometimes been mistakenly referred to, I think, as being mini-oral hearings. I don't know whether other people in the room have attended them, and I would love to know more about the experience as to who is actually there.

CHRIS BRIGHT

Shall we gather a few questions. Before we go to Joannna, we will let someone from a different organization have a chance. John Davies at the front here.

JOHN DAVIES (*Freshfields*)

I would like to make two observations which I think may sound rather odd coming from a practitioner, because I think I am going to be quite supportive of the Commission. First of all on secrecy, I think if the panel is going to work effectively and you are not going to have difficulties with timing, I think the panel members are going to have to remain secret. I have been involved in one situation where Philippe has already talked in parallel—and we have been trying to identify who the panel members were and the Commission was unusually secretive, but I think that must be right, because otherwise people like Philippe, people like myself, people like Peter-Carlo, will desperately try to get at those panel members, and I think that is not consistent with a peer review concept.

The second observation is about triangular meetings. Again, I haven't had experience of that, but I was in favour of that concept at the time of the review, and I think that again, the Commission should be very forceful with third parties, and of course, we've all been on both sides of the fence, but I think the Commission needs to be forceful and oblige those meetings, even if they don't want to. I am sure they will be rather reticent. Perhaps there is some message, that if they are not prepared to stand up and have their views heard and tested, then the Commission is going to draw the obvious conclusions.

LUIS GOMEZ (*Baker and MacKenzie*)

I had a quick question for Carles which in fact goes back to the previous discussion we were having in the context of referral requests and I am wondering in the new era of transparency, etc, and access to key documents, we have heard in the last session about the merger mailbox and the increasing communication between the Commission and Member States, and I am wondering whether you think there is an issue there in terms of as the fluidity inflexibility of communication increases, how are you ensuring transparency of those communications with the parties. And if you think that is an issue, for example, there may be complaints that are articulated to Member States authorities which don't necessarily come through in the formal paperwork. Do you think there is an issue there? And if so, how do you think transparency is best served?

CARLES ESTEVA MOSSO

Well, I will try to go to the different questions in order.

Representative of Member States attending the panels? This is something that we have not tried yet, but certainly something worth discussing. My first reaction, however, would be that Member States attending the Advisory Committee have a consultative role on the final proposal by the Commission and that involving them in the internal deliberations of the Commission may not fit too well with this role.

As to triangular meetings. It is not always the complainant who is opposed to having these meetings. We have had several cases where the parties are the ones that prefer not to be confronted by the complainants at the early stages of an investigation. Then, in view that we can clearly not oblige any one to take part in these panels, we have to find a way to convince them that the process is in their interest. Of course, we could take a very harsh line towards possible complainants and say that unless you stand by your complaint publicly, in a triangular meeting, we are not taking it into account. But this may also discourage complaints or concerns that may be of relevance for us. Some complainants may not be prepared to make their position openly at very early stages of a procedure, before knowing whether the Commission will really take on the case, and I think there are some legitimate confidentiality concerns that have to be taken into account.

As to who is present in these triangular meetings. Normally the case team, the complainants, the parties. If there are several complainants, they could all be there or only one of them could be there. I think the benefits would still be worth it if only one of them is there.

CHRIS BRIGHT

Well I for one think we should be hugely encouraged by what has happened over the last few years. If we go back to conferences such as this even three years ago, we were all wailing and gnashing our teeth about the Commission's internal procedures and things have moved on hugely. It is encouraging also to hear from Carles to some extent that this is a period of experimentation, and that the system is still fluid and capable of evolving further. So the focus in effect may turn to some Member States I suspect, as we go forward and the level of decision scrutiny within some of the Member State organizations.

Panel 3—Remedies

Chair: Professor Paul Geroski, *Competition Commission*

Speakers:
    Goetz Drauz, *European Commission*
    Simon Priddis, *Office of Fair Trading*
    Dale Collins, *Shearman & Sterling LLP*

PROFESSOR PAUL GEROSKI

This is the final session of the morning on merger remedies. It is a session that I for one have been looking forward to for quite a while. Not least because of the panel that has been assembled to enlighten you on this subject. I was in a conference last week in Edinburgh on human rights law, intellectual property law and competition law and every speaker and every intervener started with a caveat that they knew nothing about any of the three types of law. Actually, I was the only person there for whom this was true.

As a display of modesty, it was overwhelming and totally unwarranted. In this case, our three speakers aren't going to be able to get away with this nonsense. They are all very distinguished people who know exactly what they are talking about.

Our first speaker is going to be Simon Priddis, who is the Director of Mergers at the Office of Fair Trading. Our second speaker is going to be Goetz Drauz, who is Deputy Director General in charge of mergers at the European Commission, and our third speaker is going to be Dale Collins, who I am told specializes in the defence of mergers and acquisitions, whatever this means!

All three speakers have very kindly agreed to keep the number of insights down to no more than 25, which they are going to deliver in no more time than ten minutes. That should leave all of us possibly as much as half an hour for discussion and much more important, it should get us to lunch on time.

That's it. Simon do you want to start us off please?

SIMON PRIDDIS

Thank you very much Paul. Good morning everybody. As Paul said, we are going to try to stick to about ten minutes each. I hope all of you have a copy of my slides, because what I would like to do is go through them relatively quickly, and then perhaps leave some of the more substantive points for free discussion afterwards. I should of course commence with the usual disclaimer that these views are my own and are not necessarily those of the OFT.

That said, what I thought I would try to do this morning is cover basically three points. First of all, a few thoughts on remedy design, and in particular how that relates to the incentives to the merging parties and the outcomes that we are looking for from competition. Secondly, a few thoughts on implementation of remedies and the process by which we go about doing that. Thirdly, some concluding thoughts on enforcement and in particular, monitoring.

Let me kick off with remedy design. There are four basic points that I would like to make. The first point is basic, but I think it is worth repeating. The remedy must flow from the theory of harm in the case. It is an extremely basic point, a bit like teaching a grandmother to suck eggs, but I think it is worth repeating.

It is important for a couple of reasons. First if you are a competition authority looking for a remedy, you need to make sure your remedy is directly related to the theory of harm you come up with, or else your remedy will not be effective.

And secondly, if you are the merging parties proposing the remedy, you want to make sure the remedy you propose goes directly to the theory of harm being advanced by the Competition Authority, or else there is a reasonable prospect the authority will say this just doesn't do the job.

Now that's all very straight forward and very simple, but it takes me directly to my second point, which is what is the aim of a merger remedy? The OFT's view is that the aim of a merger remedy is to restore or preserve effective competition. What do we mean by competition? Well, our guidelines say we mean 'process of rivalry' by which firms compete with each other to win customers, to win business. It is that process of rivalry that delivers benefits for consumers in the form of lower prices, or better products or greater choice.

So we always start off with the premise that the remedy that we look for must be effective in restoring the competitive process to the extent that it is substantially lessened by the merger. It is only once we have addressed those questions of effectiveness that we then go on to think about questions such as proportionality. There is, I think, sometimes a reversal of those points in the analytical process. The authorities think about proportionality first and then effectiveness afterwards. The OFT's policy line is you think about effectiveness first. If you don't get over effectiveness, you don't get to proportionality.

Thinking about how those points work in the OFT process, it is probably true to say that it does give us something of, what I would call, a first phase bias. I think that arises in two ways. First of all, because we are a first phase authority, we have something of the comfort of saying we have to be absolutely certain that this remedy works. Because if we're not, we can send the case to the Competition Commission and ask them to take a longer look at it. That does give us something of a luxury.

But the second point, which is linked to that, is that there is of course an information asymmetry in thinking about the remedy, especially in the first phase process, where we do not have as much time as a second phase regulator to look at the remedy and think about it. That means that we do take quite a hard line in thinking about first phase remedies and thinking about how they work.

Put differently, if there are any doubts about the effectiveness of a remedy, we will resolve them in favour of consumers, rather than in favour of the merging parties. I think that fits in very well to the overall remit of the Office of Fair Trading as essentially a consumer protection organisation. Our role is to make markets work well for consumers.

As I say, that gives us something of a first phase bias, and it leads to our preference for the sorts of remedies we look at. Clearly we prefer structural remedies over behavioural remedies because the degree of certainty that one can place on a structural remedy working is generally greater than the sort of certainty that you can place on a behavioural remedy.

Of course, it is perfectly true that you may get different answers to these questions whether you look at the first phase in merger review or second phase in a merger review. This is because the differences in time and investigatory resources between the first phase of UK merger review may lead to different conclusions. This is where the OFT comes out as a first phase regulator.

We are often asked whether this policy view leads to different conclusions in respect of completed and anticipated mergers because, of course, as you all know, in the UK it is perfectly permissible for the merging parties to close the transaction ahead of clearance from either the OFT or the Competition Commission. So in many cases, the transactions we are looking at for remedies are completed cases. Again, our starting point is that it doesn't make any fundamental difference to the analytical framework. The questions one has to ask oneself are the same.

Obviously the introduction in the Enterprise Act of hold-separate undertakings during the first process does facilitate the remedies process a little more. We have been able in a number of tricky cases to ask the parties to completed mergers to hold separate the merging businesses until we have been able to conclude our merger review. In a couple of cases, those transactions have gone to the Competition Commission which has continued the hold-separate undertakings until the conclusion of its review of the transaction.

The third point I wanted to make is a little more detailed. When thinking about a remedy's design, I think we are all as competition authorities getting smarter about the incentives that remedies give rise to and how they relate to the theory of harm.

It comes back a little bit to the point that I started with. Remedy design needs to be consistent with the theory of harm. So for example, the theory of harm identified by the competition authority might relate to high barriers to entry, making it difficult for a new firm to enter the market place. The remedy might therefore seek to lower those barriers to entry in some way. To craft an effective remedy in this context, you have to think about what findings you have reached as to why entry barriers are high, how long it would take firms to enter, and thus how long a remedy might need to exist for.

A good example of this is the *IMS Health* case[1] where the design of the remedy was to lower barriers to entry to the identified market. But if you look at the assessment in the competition section and you look at the remedy, you will see that the periods of time anticipated for entry to occur in the competition assessment section are identical to the remedy. There is a clear match-up between what the European Commission then thought of as the incentives on the merging parties with the remedy that they went for.

But this incentive point isn't confined to behavioural undertakings. It is also a point in structural remedies. So for example, even in divestment sales, we often have to think very closely about the incentives for the acquiring company, ie. the company that is acquiring the business to be divested, to actually operate the business as an effective competitor in the same market. In the *iSOFT/Torex* merger,[2] that is a question we are still looking at at the moment. Given the narrowness of the finding of SLC in that case, there are difficult questions to be answered in thinking about the effectiveness of the remedy. There isn't much time for a competitor to come into the markets concerned there and compete. That means you have to think very carefully about how strongly a new entrant would compete with iSOFT in the market after the divestment.

---

[1] C-418/01 *IMS Health v NDC Health GmbH & Co KG* Judgment 29 Apr 2004.
[2] <http://www.oft.gov.uk/News/Press+releases/2004/56-04.htm>.

One area of developing thinking as to ways in which you can solve these incentive problems, is to use arbitration or other sorts of adjudicatory mechanisms to try to set the right incentives. The Competition Commission in one case, *Carlton and Granada*,[3] used a variant on an adjudicatory mechanism to try to solve some of the incentive problems. The European Commission did likewise in *GE/Instrumentarium*[4] as a way of trying to square what the merged entities incentives' might be to try to derail the remedy with what the acquirer of the divested assets might need to do in order to compete, and with preventing the acquirer from free-riding on the merged entity's investments. There are some interesting questions for us to develop there.

Of course, my final point is enforcement. Enforcement is a key principle. If you can't enforce the remedy, it is basically not worth accepting because you can't make it work. And the merging parties have no incentive to try to make it work because you can't enforce it. But we will come back to that in a moment.

Let me work very quickly through implementation. I need only make a couple of points on this slide I think. This basically sets out factually what the process now is in the UK for negotiating, monitoring and implementing undertakings.

Perhaps I can skip straight to the last point, which is on trustees and hold-separate undertakings. I have already alluded to the importance of the hold-separate undertakings. I think trustee provision is an area where the OFT and the Competition Commission are still developing their practice and it is an area where we are pushing forward quite aggressively. For example, we have used trustee provisions to sell a business in the *Sibelco* case;[5] the CC included them in *P&O/Stena*.[6] We are also now starting to use trustees almost as monitors as well to see how well the businesses are being operated, to see whether the merging parties are sticking to undertakings, and indeed to ensure that the businesses are being held separate in the way that we envisaged.

On enforcement itself, structural remedies are obviously quite straight forward. The idea is to sell the business. I know Goetz is going to talk a little bit more about how you actually define asset packages, and the risks that are involved in that, so I won't spend very much time on this. I can come back to this topic later perhaps in response to questions.

[3] Proposed merger of Carlton Communications Plc and Granada Plc, 11 Feb 2003 <http://www.oft.gov.uk/business/mergers+fta/advice/clearances+and+referrals/carlton.htm>.
[4] Case No COMP/ M3083 *GE/Instrumentarium* 02/09/2003.
[5] SCR-Sibelco SA/Fife Silica Sands/Fife Silica Resources, 04/07/01 <http://www.competition-commission.org.uk/rep_pub/reports/2001/fulltext/455c1.pdf>.
[6] Stena AB/P&O, 06.02.04, <http://www.competition-commission.org.uk/inquiries/completed/2004/stena/index.htm>.

What I would like to spend a last couple of moments on is enforcement of behavioural remedies. Enforcement of behavioural remedies is of course extremely difficult as a starting point. Before talking about it in more detail, there is just one point that is worth mentioning and that is to go back to where I started, thinking about the competitive process; why we have remedies in merger cases. Sometimes behavioural remedies can actually deliver for us the outcomes that you would expect the competitive process to deliver and, in those rare cases, it is worthwhile thinking about what a behavioural undertaking might actually do to deliver the competitive outcome. So for example, in cases like *Coloplast*[7] and *Ivax*,[8] you see on the one hand the Competition Commission and on the other hand, the OFT, accepting a price cap remedy. But these price caps were accepted in quite specific circumstances: where there is a regulatory structure; where it is essentially one price that is being set. But of course, these sorts of remedies are often accepted at the expense of competition as a process, and that in itself, in the OFT's view, is a reason for rejection of these sorts of remedies as undertakings in lieu. I have cited there the *Knauf*[9] and *Emap/ABI*[10] cases, which are both still ongoing.

Monitoring is difficult, often because it is time intensive and costly. The cost of this sort of third party monitoring is something that we are all still investigating. But one point worth picking up is conflicts. It can be difficult in some of these cases to identify a suitable third party trustee or a monitor to supervise behavioural undertakings. This may be because obvious candidates are too closely connected with existing markets participants to be sufficiently independent. That is an issue that we are working through in a couple of cases at the moment—*Dräger*[11] and *Scotrail*.[12] As to costs, the only good example is the *British Aerospace/Marconi* case from some years ago, where there is a very extensive system of monitoring that turned out to be extremely costly.

Perhaps I could just move on to some concluding thoughts, Paul, so others can speak. On remedies, our learning is still growing rapidly and that will

---

[7] Coloplast A/S and SSL International plc, 14.06.02, <http://www.competition-commission.org.uk/rep_pub/reports/2002/fulltext/467c1.pdf>.

[8] *Ivax International GmbH/ 3M Company* 09/01/04 and <http://www.oft.gov.uk/News/Press+releases/2004/04-04.htm>.

[9] Knauf Insulation Limited / Superglass Insulation Limited, 01.12.04, <http://www.competition-commission.org.uk/inquiries/completed/2004/superglass/index.htm>.

[10] *Emap/ABI* 10/11/04 <http://www.competition-commission.org.uk/press_rel/latest/2004/nov/pdf/66-04.pdf>.

[11] Dräger Medical AG & Co KgaA / Air-Shields, 19.05.04, <http://www.competition-commission.org.uk/inquiries/completed/2004/dragair/index.htm>.

[12] Firstgroup plc/ Scotrail, 28.06.04, <http://www.competition-commission.org.uk/inquiries/completed/2004/first/index.htm>.

of course, continue. Particularly on things like how to monitor some of these behavioural undertakings. I think it is quite clear that the OFT has a tough approach in policy terms to things like undertakings in lieu, both as to design, implementation, and enforcement and that will continue. One thing we are working on developing more is how to go about some of the more intensive monitoring. Both of behavioural undertakings, but also of structural undertakings to ensure that they have actually worked and that the market is developing in the way that either we, the OFT, or the Competition Commission have predicted in its findings.

GOETZ DRAUZ

I am going to start with some statistics. The first slide shows the number of cases involving remedies has very dramatically increased since 1996, but also decreased again. This slide shows you that the remedy intensity quite well correlates with the overall increase in the number of merger cases in the years after 1996 and with increased complexity of competition concerns.

The pink line here represents the number of remedy cases, with a peak, which you all remember probably in 2000, which was the most intensive year accounting alone for 40 remedy cases and two outright prohibitions on the left scale. The blue line shows the overall number of modifications and decisions over the years since the entry into force of the Merger Regulation. It peaks again in the year 2000. The slide also shows that over the years some 4–10 per cent of merger cases involved remedies or prohibitions, except again for the year 2000, in which the complexity I would say of the mergers led to a peak of 12 per cent.

In the year of 2004 until the end of October, we have had twelve clearance decisions with remedies out of a total of 184 cases, and if you look at the year end, we will have probably some 245 cases involving 18 remedy clearances. So there is a clear trend to re-establish around the last year.

Statistics, which I shall present in the coming slides, are based on an in-house stock-taking of some 250 remedies in 84 decisions in the years 1998 to 2000. As you can see from this slide, roughly two-thirds of the 255 remedies were divestments, either of stand-alone businesses of individual assets or shares in companies.

You will see that the number of individual asset cases is relatively high and is one of the points which we may have to critically review. Fourteen per cent of those cases are concerned with licensing of, or assignment of, IP rights, which arguably are also structural remedies. There are only 2 per cent of access remedies, and some 24 per cent of what is called here 'other remedies' which is all kinds of remedies, but I would say mostly of a behavioural type or complementary type to more structural remedies.

Now the majority of remedies concerned the manufacturing sector. The next biggest one was in transport, storage and communication (13 per cent); electricity (6 per cent); financial intermediation banking insurance (4 per cent); and only 2 per cent of all remedies in those years were in the sector of wholesale and retail trait. If you look at similar figures in the US, they are much higher on the last point—maybe ten times higher. This could reflect maybe that the higher concentration level in distribution in the US and also to some extent that this often concerns local issues, local markets where National Competition Authorities are obviously more active.

Forty per cent of remedies concerned consumer goods and services; 60 per cent business to business. In this slide the cases are sorted around competition concerns, distinguishing between horizontal, vertical and conglomerate concerns, and I think this slide should also have to alleviate, if it still exists, concerns of our American friends, which we see here that conglomerate concerns are also in Europe only a very small issue as well.

Now here you see, quite expectedly, single dominance 90 per cent; collective dominance 10 per cent. Now let me briefly make some reflection on findings of our remedies study, which centres mostly on divestment remedies, and I am using here the typology of risks identified in the UK Competition Commission's draft consultation guidelines on the application of divestiture remedies in merger enquiries.

Just to stress something Simon has said already. The starting point for all effective remedies or all remedy discussions is, of course, to clearly define the theory of competitive harm.

Only when you have done that you can really start to think about the remedy. This does not mean that companies can not think about remedies if they have good reason to expect the competition concerns arriving during the procedure. Also Simon has talked about the structural/ behaviour issue. It is quite clear that competition authorities are rather sceptical about behavioural remedies. Probably the best place is in vertical or conglomerate cases, when it is concerned with access to key inputs. For example, network, or the conditions surrounding those exits.

The other weak point of behavioural remedies is of course the need to monitor those during their lifetime. Something which is very unpopular with competition authorities.

So the divestitures of course are the most common ones of the structural remedies and our study shows very clearly that the single and most important reason why divestitures have not always worked successfully in the past is either because companies have divested the weaker part of the combined businesses, which of course is quite natural in a way, or it was a kind of carve-out or the famous mix and match remedy by putting together certain assets coming from the purchaser and the target company.

The sum of our experience shows that it is much more successful to divest an existing business entity, and it is equally important that all tangible assets, as well as rights to critical intangible assets, are included in the divestiture package.

So for example, if the problem is if the market requires an installed customer base to operate on an effective scale, the assets divested should either include the installed base of customers or quickly enable the purchaser to obtain an installed customer base. You have always also to think that there is an important asymmetry of information between the Commission or the agency on the one hand, and the parties on the other hand, because the parties know their business, they know the market, of course, much better than we do. There is obviously a natural incentive on the parties to explore it, this asymmetric information, as much as possible. Of course our counter element is the market test, which we try to bring in third party information.

Now let me spend a few moments on something, which I would call a very European problem which often occurs even in large and world-wide mergers. Many parties combine businesses which affect a large number of products in a substantial number of Member States. This especially happens in cases like pharmaceuticals or crop protection products cases.

For example, *Bayer Aventis*[13] which is in the area of protection, we had about 100 product markets, problems with the remedy, to say if the case should be settled for example in phase 1. There were problems for tomato fungicides in Portugal, for example, or wheat in Greece, or tomatoes in Austria. So of course, if there is a problem in a relatively small market, that can mean at the same time that the business in that country is not substantial enough to support a viable business, or if you go on a more European scale by combining businesses in various countries, this could lead to an unproportionate effect, or could even, which is also a concern for competition authorities, could reduce the efficiency of the operation itself.

Then of course, this is very much a nightmare to agencies and to lawyers, and I think some of you here in the room know what I am talking about.

---

[13] Case No COMP/ M 2547—*Bayer/Aventis Crop Science*, 17/04/2002. <http://www.europa.eu.int/comm/competition/mergers/cases/decisions/m2547_en.pdf>.

But in some of those cases it might be better not to insist ultimately on a remedy at all if this remedy is too small, or exceptionally to look for some rather behavioural solution.

In the past the use of up-front crown-jewel provisions was probably the most significant difference between the US practice and the European practice. The European Commission has only insisted up-front, crown-jewel, or alternative solutions when there were significant doubts on the viability of the business to be divested. But I have the feeling that US practice is moving closer to the European approach.

On timing, in the old days, the Commission seemed to accept other divestiture periods of around 12 months. We have now become more realistic. Closer to the US on the other side, we have a standard starting point of three to six months with a possibility for regulation.

This slide—I will not go into it. It only shows the importance of detail in remedy discussion. For example this relates to hold-separate provisions.

Then after the viability issue, the single other big problem is of course, to find the right purchaser. As I said, parties have an incentive to choose a weak competitor, which is understandable to some extent, but why then may you ask does the Commission allow the parties to choose the purchaser in the first place? I think there are three reasons for that.

First, if parties are selling a really good valuable business, then of course, they have an interest in getting a good price as well, for example through an auction process. Secondly, for the agency to select a purchaser would of course be some kind of industrial policy which I think would not be a good solution, so what is our alternative? The alternative is to define in a very clear way the purchaser's criteria, which need to be there, experience, resources and most importantly I would say, the incentive of the purchaser to compete effectively and in the long term. This means for example, we would want to see a business plan. We will grill the candidates in individual discussions. And again, here I would stress the importance of detail.

To conclude, our remedy study is foreseen to be published in the first quarter of 2005. This should lead in our view to a large discussion with Member States, with the business, with the legal community and including also the US agencies, which we think is quite important, and should ultimately lead on a European level to a refinement of our Remedies Notice.

DALE COLLINS

Notwithstanding Paul's introduction, I do have an apology to make to all of you. I am somewhat misplaced on this panel. The reason for that is although I actually do a lot of merger work, I only represent pro-competitive mergers and merger remedies presume that there is anticompetitive harm. Since my deals don't have that, I am a little misplaced here. But that is notwithstanding the fact that several of the deals that we have already talked about, like the *GE/Instrumentarium* deal[14] and the *Bayer Aventis* deal, I happen to be the counsel for the seller's side.

I do observe the process and let me give you somewhat of a practitioner's perspective, but it is going to be a little different slant than probably what you are expecting. I am going to try to look at negotiated undertakings.

I am going to ask the question, basically, what is the nature of the bargain between the parties. That is the enforcement agency on one hand and the parties on the other. In particular, I am going to look at it from a practitioner's perspective to try to understand what exactly is the objective of the enforcement agency in order to determine how I position in those very few cases where, of course, the deals are anticompetitive, but my clients sometimes decide that expediency is a better force than dollars and decide they are going to negotiate.

So, this is the way I look at it. I think this is really a process of decision making under uncertainty. When you have uncertainty in a decision making process, there are two kinds of areas that you want to look at and this is the fundamental question for the agencies I think.

One is what you might call an under-inclusiveness area. That is where you fail to fully remediate an anticompetitive merger. So what happens is you don't get all the remedy you really need so the merger goes through or there may be a problem with your remedy and as a result of that some anticompetitive harm results from the transaction. That is an under-inclusiveness merger, for an under-inclusiveness area.

Then there are over-inclusiveness areas and this is where you basically stop a deal that is not anticompetitive or was remediable or you over-enforce in some way. That is you get too much. When you have that, you have a loss in efficiency gain that otherwise would have resulted from the merger or at least there is the prospect of that.

So you have over-inclusiveness areas and under-inclusiveness areas and the way that the agencies I think finally determine in the first instance on how they are going to negotiate for relief depends very heavily on their view of what are the social costs of those two kinds of areas.

---

[14] Case No COMP/ M3083 *GE/Instrumentarium* 2 Sept 2003.

In particular, if you think about this, the balance on those areas are going to depend on the likelihood and the magnitude in the first instance on what the anticompetitive harm is on the one hand, and on the other hand what the potential efficiency gain from an unrestructured merger is.

I am going to focus on the efficiency gain side than the anticompetitive harm, because I find as a practical matter, it is very difficult to convince enforcement agencies, at least when you are at the bargaining table, that there is significant uncertainty in many cases whether or not the deals that they think are anticompetitive are actually going to result in an anticompetitive effect.

I will say as a quick aside that one of the favourite things I used to do in the early nineties when Anne Bingaman was the Assistant to the Attorney General in charge of the Antitrust Division. She used to stand up at almost every speech and almost complain about the enforcement policy of the Reagan administration with respect to mergers. I was the Deputy Assistant Attorney General at the beginning part of the Reagan administration. She said we would let all sorts of mergers go through that were anticompetitive. I was at a number of these conferences where Anne was speaking and I would always ask her; at least for the first three she said this, 'well you know there is no statute of limitations in the United States on the enforcement against anticompetitive mergers. There is no clearance in the US. The Hart-Scott Rodino Act does not provide for any immunity to a deal that is anticompetitive. You can come after it any time, so if you think there are anticompetitive mergers that were passed in the Reagan administration, then why didn't you go after them now, or at least tell us what they were.' And after at least the third conference, I noticed that Anne stopped making that statement.

So there is this prospect that there are deals that are anticompetitive when the agencies think they are; but like I say, I'm not going to focus on that. I'm going to focus on the efficiency gain.

If you are the agency and you think that the efficiency gain is small, then if you over-enforce, there is no foregone efficiency gain. Consequently the areas that result from over-inclusiveness that are demanding too much really don't have a social cost to them and that leaves you in one direction of demanding a lot.

That is what we saw in I think the mid- to late 1990s, particularly at the Federal State Commission when Bob McCosty was the Chairman of the Commission. I think Bob had a very hostile view towards efficiencies, although he had great press on it because he modified the merger guidelines in the United States to include explicitly, or more explicitly, an efficiency

section; but if you really understood what Bob was doing with that efficiency section, he essentially gutted the efficiency's defence enforcement
process. So what they would do is they would insist upon, for example. For
some of these there are some good reasons behind it, but they would insist
more on the divestitures of on-going businesses, they were highly sceptical
towards mix 'n' match solutions. They looked very carefully at things like
whether there were adequate distribution and were indeed going to the
divestiture buyer and they hardly ever accepted relief that was the type to
say ease of entry relief. That is where you would divest assets in order to
eliminate a barrier to entry and basically allow entry to take care of what
you thought was the competitive problem.

There was also a high degree of scepticism. At least this emerged in the
1999 staff report on the buyer's assessments. That is the divestiture buyer's
assessments. So the agency was basically saying 'well we really don't trust
the buyers that much to tell us whether or not the solutions are going to
work, where we, the agencies are going to determine that on our own'. I
always have these questions of why did the agencies think they are going to
determine better than the buyers did. That is a curious question, but I will
leave that one right now unaddressed.

There was a heavy bias at the Federal Trade Commission towards upfront
buyers. There was also an emphasis on what they call 'crown-jewel provisions'. These are where you basically have one set of assets that you have
to divest initially, but if you fail to do so, then you have to divest usually a
super set of those assets, or at least something that is much more burdensome to the combined parties.

The Federal Trade Commission likes to say that they use the Crown-Jewel
provision in order to eliminate the uncertainty of whether or not the divestiture was actually workable. Those of us in practice thought that it had very
little to do with it and what they were really doing was using this as a club
in order to ensure that the divestitures that were originally negotiated as the
step one divestitures were actually accomplished quickly. Predictably as
they tighten the time periods which start off literally between a year to eighteen months after the consent decree was signed and they tried to tighten
that down to somewhere between 60 and 90 days. They thought these
crown-jewel provisions were extremely helpful in getting the parties to
actually focus on those divestitures in a hurry.

They also put in things like monitoring trustees and clean sweeps, which is
the whole idea that if you were trading up, if you had an anticompetitive
deal that you could get rid of, if you have smaller markets here than the
acquiring party than the target had, what they like to see is a clean sweep.
That is, you sold the smaller entity, but you sold it in its entirety. You didn't

carve out a piece of it and sell it, even though if you had bought the piece by itself that would have been OK.

That is what we saw in the 1990s. Now I will tell you really quickly. People ask me in a lot of big discussions in the United States 'Do enforcement policies change with administrations?' By and large the answer is that is no they don't. But in the United States there have been three big changes I think between the Clinton administration and the Bush administration. The first one was that there is much less emphasis now on civil non-merger cases, particularly dominance cases. The Clinton administration brought a number of those and they lost almost all of them in court.

There is a lot less emphasis now on non-horizontal theories of anticompetitive harm, particularly in mergers and the third big change is, I think, on merger remedies. Most of the restrictive practices I think that came into being with the Pitofsky administration at the Federal Trade Commission now, at least the Justice Department had gone, and I think that they have been mitigated substantially I think at the Federal Trade Commission, and my guess is that we will see more than that with the new Chairman, but that is purely a private prediction. I don't think that Deborah Platt Majoras has really said anything on this. But she comes from a Justice Department background, so it is more likely that she is going to push things in the direction of the Justice Department which cuts back on most of the things I have just talked about.

I think what you will see is that there will be some emphasis, but less of an emphasis on the divestiture of ongoing businesses. I think there will be much more credit, given the buyers, although they'll be checked out.

We clearly have seen, and this was even true during the late 1990s, the Justice Department did not demand up front buyers like the Federal Trade Commissioner did. The Justice Department has never liked the Crown-jewel provisions and you see those very rarely in any of the consent decrees by either agency today, monitoring trustees are falling off. Justice Department never liked those. They used them occasionally and I think we have seen far fewer of them at the Federal Trade Commissions during the last couple of years than we saw in the late 1990s.

I also don't think that you are going to see the same emphasis on clean sweeps. This is an area where I think there has been a big pendulum swing in the United States. Back to much more accepting relief, if you will. You think the consignments in the ideas of what you need in order to get effective relief. I mean, all of those are still present in the United States. This deal of having to identify the anticompetitive harm and active fashion of remedy, I mean it addresses the harm. The whole question is what do you do at the edges? How much do you believe that the remedy that you fashion is actually going to work, or for that matter, be implemented.

I think what we are going to see in the US is that the agencies are going to be more accepting that things are going to actually work.

I only have two more minutes left, so let me ask this question. Why did the agencies or at least the Federal Trade Commission, in the 1990s think that things were going so badly when the Justice Department didn't think it was going so badly and now I think both agencies are saying 'Well, it wasn't going nearly as badly as they thought in the late 1990s'.

Let me give you two reasons perhaps. One is, I think, the 1999 divestiture study by the FTC, which was the basis for a lot of the much more restrictive views. I think I asked the wrong question in many ways. This goes back to my notion of the uncertainties associated with the anticompetitive harm. I will then ask a different question, which is whether or not the markets in which they thought the divestiture remedies weren't working actually had become anticompetitive as a result of the deal. I think that they would have found in many, if not most, of those cases purely an intuition, that in fact those markets did not become more anticompetitive and to that extent the relief either worked or it was unnecessary and consequently demanding more out of the relief in the social benefit. That is number one.

Number two, and my last point, is that there is a fascinating institutional reason why there is this difference. It's a purely consistent difference between the Justice Department and the FTC and for people to think about the structure of their agencies, this is something to think about. At the FTC there is a specialized division, a section called the Compliance Section, that deals with compliance of consent decrees, particularly merger consent decrees. At the Antitrust Division, there isn't one. So the Compliance Division at the FTC has an institutional interest and not only monitoring what is going on, but I would suspect they are finding that there are problems. Whereas there is no such institutional entity at the Justice Department and I think quite frankly, probably it steps the other way. They have an institutional interest of not finding problems with the consent decrees that they have taken in the past and perhaps they don't.

So anyway, let me stop there and turn back to Paul.

ALEX POTTER (*Freshfields*)

My question about one aspect goes to describe the purchaser risk. It relates to financial buyers as acceptable purchasers in remedy cases. I think my own experience is that there is, at least at the Commission level, not so much as a presumption against, but at least a scepticism about, financial buyers as being acceptable purchasers in these circumstances. Earlier this year, I was on a case where in fact the Commission did approve a financial buyer as a purchaser, but not until it had asked some fairly close questions about the buyer's intentions. Questions which could just as easily been proposed to a traditional industrial buyer. So my question is to both Goetz and Simon, is there a scepticism about these sorts of buyers and if so, in these days when so much transactional activity is driven by private equity houses, in any event, whether that's appropriate? Thank you.

GOETZ DRAUZ

I wouldn't say there is a general scepticism to financial buyers, I think it very much depends on the kind of situation, which you have. I give you a recent example where this issue was discussed in great detail. It was the *Alcan/Pechiney* case[15] where ultimately the divested business consisted of an alternative package of whole world-wide roll equipment. This was a remedy where the product, which is divested is some kind in between the pre-product and the finished product, and we came to the conclusion that being successful in this kind of intermediate area you need to have a very strong knowledge about how the business works, and a very strong incentive in this case to become a real competitor, and therefore we basically describe the purchaser criteria as more or less excluding financial buyers which we would have expected to act in the market probably from the incentive, rather as a follower in the market, rather than be an active competitor.

You may have seen that Alcan has chosen the third kind of remedy, which was neither of the original two European packages, but rather put the whole world-wide role business together in that company and is going to divest it to their own shareholders. Now this is a different solution. First of all, the business is world-wide and secondly, the shareholder base will probably guarantee that this much larger business is developing an independent life.

SIMON PRIDDIS

Just a couple of quick points. Alex, I think I share all the points that Goetz has made. We don't have any institutional view that financial buyers are necessarily less attractive. I think in a number of cases, we have looked at transactions where the proposed buyer was a financial buyer and we didn't

---

[15] Case No COMP/ M3225 *Alcan/ Pechiney(II)* 29/09/2003, OJ C204, 29 Aug 2003.

come to that analysis with the view in mind that they face greater obstacles to approve more than a trade buyer might.

I think the sorts of questions that we ask ourselves are very similar to the questions you would ask yourself in relation to a trade buyer. First of all, what are the proposals of the financial buyer to run the business? How did they propose to do it? What sort of expertise do they have? What sort of management do they plan to put in place? Do they plan to retain any existing management of the business? How strong a competitor do we think that they will be?

A key part of understanding that is to look at what the particular investment strategy is of that financial buyer. If the financial buyer comes to us with a well worked out business plan, it shows how they intend to run the business, how they intend that it will compete and what they think that their plan is for actually realising their investment in that business, then that goes a very long way towards show that they are a credible buyer. I think the circumstances in which we might be more concerned about a financial buyer are where the investment strategy and the business plan looks much more like a break up plan just to realize the actual value of the assets on the books rather than actually running the business as a going concern. But that is the sort of thing we would expect to get at by looking at the firm, the business plan for the divested assets and the overall investment strategy of the financial buyer.

DALE COLLINS

Just quickly in the United States, at least since the mid-1980s, there have been a number of divestitures made to financial buyers. As far as I am aware, there has been no real concern expressed on the party enforcement agencies. There are two characteristics that are important.

One is that in almost all of these cases, when the purely financial buyer took on the management, usually with heavy financial incentives, that management would stay. And number two the business plan of the financial buyer was not to flip the business in a short period of time. Particularly in businesses where R & D and the like, long term investments are necessary, if you have got a financial buyer who is just going to buy in and basically wants to flip it in two years, I think the agencies are extremely sceptical.

PAUL GEROSKI

What I might do is accumulate two or three questions and give the three speakers a last shot at the audience.

TOM HOEHN (*Price WaterhouseCoopers*)

The question about the buyer assessment. It is often forgotten that there is also a separate transaction document and the question is, is there a separate review of the purchaser, as well as the transaction documents, and is that made very clear to the businesses and their legal advisers?

In connection with that, one problem is there are often in SPAs non-compete agreements to protect the purchaser to facilitate them setting up in a particular market if they are not already present. So what is the attitude— I am interested in the UK and in Europe as well as the US—on the appropriate lengths of these non-compete agreements?

ALAN HOFFMAN (*Alcatel Legal Department*)

I noticed Goetz you had a slight mention of transfer of IP rights, and I was just curious if that has been successful or if you have cases in which it is not very practical to divest companies or production assets?

JOHN DAVIES (*Freshfields*)

I wonder if I might be a bit cheeky. The underlying comment or message from Dale is that the US has become less interventionist and that is something that I hadn't heard before, but I would like to hear the response of the Europeans on the panel to that message, particularly as, of course, the European policy is now well established in terms of the number of things that were mentioned, for example, trustee monitoring and so forth. The UK is going that way and becoming more detailed. Particularly in the context of my experience what tends to happen when you have a transatlantic merger negotiation, you end up with the lowest common denominator—the one that satisfies all the regulators. In the past, I have had experience of having to add things to European remedies in order to fit, as Goetz will remember from one situation, the US model and it sounds like maybe we are going the other way?

DAMIEN LEVIE (*European Commission*)

I have been part of that remedy study project and reviewed quite a few decisions of the Commission on the remedy, and what its name was and sometimes the aim of the remedy was just to remove the overlap. At least in the final decision, I was wondering how explicit should agencies be in stating the aim of remedies?

ALISDAIR BALFOUR, *Freshfields*

A question for Simon. You mentioned proportionality as an issue for considering undertakings in lieu. Do you think that parties should be concerned about over-delivering in terms of offering too much, and, if you do think that's a concern, do you think it's appropriate if the parties are prepared to give a remedy package, the agency should be able to say 'no that's too much!'? Do you believe that the UK regime gives narrower scope for the parties in that regard than the EC?

PAUL GEROSKI

OK, I'll let the three speakers make a couple of final observations each taking in the questions and each other's comments. Maybe we should go in reverse order. Dale?

DALE COLLINS

Just real quick. Let me just run through the questions. There are clear answers I think in the United States to all of these. First of all, as far as the separate review of buyers and transaction documents, that that has been explicit in US practice for probably the last twenty years and explicit that they are done separately, completely separately. Or at least, I think completely, but that's not quite right. You know, what the nature of the transaction is going to be reviewed in addition to whether or not the buyer itself is acceptable. Almost all remedies in the United States are on horizontal mergers and usually the selling party, the combined party, is going to stay in the business, so you have hardly ever seen non-compete transaction documents in the problematic area.

There are other things going with the package that do not deal with the problem area, then you can see a non-compete there, but as far as the problem areas are concerned, you just don't see them.

On the transfer of IP rights, this has been one of the thorniest issues in the United States. The biggest case that the Justice Department or the FTC, actually this is an FTC case, brought had to do with what was basically strategic behaviour on the part of the combined firm and failing to live up with its obligations and licensing technology; that is not the *Boston Scientific Cybus* case. I will leave the question as to whether or not Europe is going to be more restrictive than the United States going forward to the other panels.

How explicit is the agency in stating the aim of the remedies? The United States agencies are explicit, but they are explicit in, I think, a relatively meaningless way. That is, they say the purpose of the remedy is to alleviate the threatened anti-competitive harm and they just identify what the harm is by saying the merger is going to be anticompetitive in a certain market if it goes through unrestructured.

And what if the parties offer too much? This is an interesting thing in the United States. The Justice Department in particular and also the FTC, at least in their public pronouncements, are saying that they will not accept the remedies that are offered by the parties unless they are convinced that there is an anticompetitive harm that the remedies actually solved. This is going to be a huge problem if they really stick with that in contested take-overs.

GOETZ DRAUZ

First may one word be to Tom's point about the length of non-compete obligations. I think if they had all needed it, they should be as short as possible. On treatment of IP rights instead of divestiture of production assets and other things, well I think this depends on the case at hand, especially whether the emphasis really to enter that market lies on having access to IP rights or not. It may also depend on whether the merger has already some production facilities. So I think it can not be answered in a very general way, but there are certainly cases where the divestiture of the IP right is really the essence of what you will need to enter the market.

On the John Davies point, I think this was the point to be considered by the parties themselves. I think it is to the extent that they are frank and open, discussing with both agencies and we have often the impression that companies are not telling exactly the same story in Washington they tend to tell the EU, which I think is not a good story actually because almost in all cases this is somehow discovered in the discussions between the two agencies and it is therefore not a good strategy.

It is also what you have said all the time, but is still not very popular, that is to make sure that the timing of the operation, and therefore the timing of the remedies discussion, is more or less taking place in parallel, because then you can avoid to some extent that we could have one agency which was first then the second one thought they had to go a bit higher to make it a bit more expensive, to show that they are there as well. I think that this is not a very good policy. It may be human to some extent, but again, I think you have quite a strong influence on your side to avoid this happening.

Finally, the question whether the aim of the remedy should be defined either in a decision or remedy itself. I think this brings us back to the initial point that one has to be very clear about the harm which the operation may create. This harm is to be defined in a very clear way in the decision and by consequence I think the aim of the remedy should also be defined quite clearly.

If you bring these two things in close connection, then you will also avoid the problem that Dale mentioned a moment ago, that companies may offer too much, or initially too much, and are stuck with it. The policy of the European Commission clearly is, for a couple of years I would say, that if an initial remedy was proposed which goes too far, or the competition concern is not confirmed in the later investigation, then our policy is to clearly give back that unnecessary remedy.

SIMON PRIDDIS

As to whether we look at the transaction documents in making the buyer assessment, Tom's question—the answer is simply, yes we do. We look at both the buyer assessment, we will look at the transaction documents, we will look at the allocation of the purchaser price to various elements of the deal and we will take those things into account in looking at the length of non-compete agreement as well. The starting point for the OFT in thinking about non-competes is broadly the same as the European Commission's Remedies Notice. But one has to take each case on its facts.

As for the transfer of intellectual property rights, we are perfectly willing to think about that as a remedy. I think our general approach is that as a remedy it is difficult to make it work effectively. First, because it is difficult to be certain that you are going to be able to transfer the IP rights to a firm that will use them, and it is difficult to incentivise a firm to use them in the right way.

It comes back to one of the points that I was alluding to earlier. Using things like adjudication mechanisms, or arbitration mechanisms, to try to create the right incentives both for the divesting party, but also for the party that is taking on the IP rights.

Is the UK becoming more detailed in its merger undertakings? Well, yes it is, quite clearly. Will we get to a point where we are more restricted than the US? I don't think so. I think I understood Dale's point to be that the US are moving back in the same way that we are moving forward, if you like. I do not think we will cross in the middle. I think we will reach a point of perfect equilibrium.

How explicit do you have to be in setting out why you have accepted a remedy and why it works? I think the simple answer is that you have to be very explicit. It is all very well to have people like Goetz and myself sitting here and explaining all these principles, but if we do not then explain in merger decisions how we apply those principles, I think the comments we make here today are seriously undermined.

The final question on over-delivery, should we accept the first undertaking if it is proposed, even if we think it goes too far? That is an extremely difficult question. I am aware of only one case I think in which we expressed a general concern that the remedy might go too far. As you know, we did in that case reject the undertaking, but I think it was only one of a variety of reasons as to why we were uncertain that the remedy actually fixed the problem. This goes back to the very point that I started with. You have to be sure that the remedy flows from the theory of harm. In that particular case there was great difficulty in identifying exactly whether the merger would be anticompetitive and how the theory of harm would play out. So there were great risks in accepting an undertaking in lieu, not just because the scope of it might be too broad, but also because it might have just not have been needed at all.

So taken on its own, I suspect it is a reason we would probably would not rely on alone, but in a broader case where it is difficult to identify precisely the scope of the competition problem. We say on our guidance that a remedy to be clear cut. Certainly questions about Type 1 and Type 2 error that Dale posed are one of the issues that we will factor into that analysis.

PAUL GEROSKI

I am going to close this session, but not the topic. I think we all know that this is an important topic and that all the agencies, including the Competition Commission, take this topic very seriously. We don't know as much as we ought to know about which remedies work well in what circumstances and we have many minefields in the process of finding the right remedy and we still don't know how to get through all of them. It is a topic that is going to run and run and so it should. I know that the Competition Commission is doing a study in the effectiveness of remedies. Goetz Drauz has been talking about what the DG Competition is doing, and I know other agencies are doing much the same. We will come back to this.

Panel 4—Vertical and Conglomerate Mergers

Chair: Damien Levie, *European Commission, DG-Enterprise*

Speakers:
Andrea Lofaro, *RBB Economics*
Paul Lugard, *Philips*
Guillaume Loriot, *European Commission, DG Competition*

DAMIEN LEVIE

Good afternoon. If you have come to a panel to hear how the Commission will treat the mergers in its common guidelines, you have come to the right panel. How efficiency should be treated, how the court will decide the predictions of the panels on the oncoming judgement of *GE/ Honeywell*[1]— maybe this will be discussed today, raised by you or raised by the panellists.

We have great speakers to address these issues. Andrea Lofaro will start presenting economic aspects of these mergers. Andrea works in consultancy, has a PhD from the University of Florence and I suggest, Andrea, that you start with your presentation.

ANDREA LOFARO

My presentation will highlight a number of differences between horizontal mergers and non-horizontal mergers. I will also draw extensively on the results of a study that we have recently conducted for DG Enterprise on the efficiency enhancing effects of non-horizontal mergers.

Let me give you a very brief overview of the presentation.

I will start by describing some basic differences between horizontal and non-horizontal mergers. Horizontal mergers eliminate a direct competitive constraint between the parties and this may give rise to a price increase. On the other hand, non-horizontal mergers normally involve complementary goods and therefore the prediction is that the merger will be pro-competitive. This does not imply that all non-horizontal mergers are pro-competitive. It is a well-established principle in economic theory that these mergers can actually give rise to anticompetitive effects.

---

[1] Case No COMP/M 2220 *General Electric/Honeywell*, 3 July 2001 and Case T-209/01, *Honeywell v Commission*; Case T-210/01, *General Electric v Commission*.

I will then move on to the role of efficiencies and again I will highlight a number of differences between horizontal and non-horizontal mergers. Finally I will set out a proposed framework for the assessment of non-horizontal mergers. Because of the differences that I have highlighted throughout the presentation it is going to be significantly different from the framework that is used for the assessment of horizontal mergers.

So, let's start from the difference between horizontal and non-horizontal mergers. Horizontal mergers involve producers of substitutable goods. A and B are substitutable products if increasing the price of A gives rise to a decrease in the demand for product A and an increase in the demand for product B. So B exerts a competitive constraint on the price of product A. This in turn implies that a merger between A and B removes a competitive constraint and therefore there is a general prediction that these horizontal mergers can give rise to a price increase.

On the other hand non-horizontal mergers do not involve substitutable products but normally involve complementary products. A and B are complementary products if an increase in the price of A gives rise to a decrease in the demand for product A and also of product B. So in this case, there is no direct competitive constraint that is exerted by product B on product A. So there is no general prediction that these mergers give rise to a price increase. Actually, the prediction is that these mergers give rise to a price decrease. Why is that? Because pre-merger, there is no incentive to decrease the price of A and boost sales of product B. However, post-merger A and B belong to the same company, and therefore there is an incentive to decrease prices. That is why the general prediction is that these mergers are pro-competitive.

Does this mean that these mergers are always pro-competitive? The traditional Chicago School claimed that that was the case—always pro-competitive. But more recent developments in economic theory have clearly shown that these mergers can give rise to anti-competitive effects.

For example, in conglomerate mergers, the typical concern is that a firm that enjoys a position of market power in a certain market may be able to leverage that market power into another market. It can do that, for example, by engaging in tying or bundling. Bundling occurs when the firm sells the two products in a bundle at a discount. Tying occurs for example when the firm makes its products incompatible with those of the remaining competitors. Bundling and tying concerns have been raised in several recent cases; Paul will describe a few of these.

With vertical mergers, the concern is often that the merged firm will deny access of an input to rival downstream suppliers. Alternatively, it could make that input incompatible with the products of suppliers in the downstream market.

There is an extensive economic literature on the possible anti-competitive effects to which conglomerate and vertical mergers may give rise: it is impossible to summarise all the available literature here. However, the typical chain of predictions goes as follows.

The first element of the chain of predictions is that the post-merger firm will have an incentive to engage in tying (or deny access to its products). Why would it do that? Because as you may remember, I said that these mergers give an incentive to reduce prices: in order to appropriate fully of the benefits of this price reduction the post-merger firm may have an incentive to engage in tying, or make its products incompatible with those of its rivals.

The second element of the chain of predictions is that rival suppliers should be unable to respond. This means that rival suppliers should be unable to merge (or create a selling consortium) which would replicate the offer put forward by the merged entity.

The third element is that rivals should be weakened. What I mean here is that rival firms will likely lose sales, which is not a problem per se. However, a problem would arise to the extent that rival firms may be unable to finance investment in the development of new products in the future. Indeed, this may in turn lead to their marginalisation in the long term and possibly to their exit.

The final element is that customer interests would be harmed because prices will tend to go up after exit has taken place. Crucially, there should be no threat of re-entry by those firms that have left or by new firms.

The above chain of predictions is clearly very speculative but, as recent developments in the economic literature have shown, it can not be ruled out on an a priori basis. The chain of predictions needs however to be tested rigorously against the facts of the industry.

Moving on to the role of efficiencies, again I would like to draw a distinction between horizontal and non-horizontal mergers. In a horizontal merger we said that the concern is that the merger eliminates a direct competitive constraint that the firms exert on one another. However, once the competitive concern has been identified, and an increase in price has been estimated, it is possible that efficiencies may counter-balance this price increase. So it is possible, for example that the merger will give rise to a decrease in the marginal cost of production. The post-merger entity will have an incentive to pass that reduction in the marginal cost through to the consumers and this could more than offset the increase in price that was predicted due to the elimination of the direct competitive constraint.

The above discussion has two implications.

First, efficiencies are clearly separated from the anticompetitive effect. One needs first to identify the anticompetitive effects and then possibly look at countervailing efficiencies. You don't need to look at efficiencies unless you have identified an anticompetitive effect.

Secondly, to the extent that an anticompetitive effect has been identified, a high burden of proof is placed on the parties to demonstrate that the merger will give rise to efficiencies that will offset the price increase. Importantly, it is relatively unusual that a merger will give rise to a significant reduction in the marginal cost. More often these mergers actually give rise to more dynamic benefits, such as fixed costs savings. This may explain why the Commission has traditionally placed a high burden of proof on the parties. Indeed, to the extent that a clear anticompetitive effect has been identified, one will normally be expected to have to do a lot of work to prove that the efficiencies would counter-balance the price effect.

The story is totally different in non-horizontal mergers. As discussed, the direct effect of non-horizontal mergers is a decrease in price and not an increase in price. However, efficiencies, as noted before, may under certain circumstances, be the source of anticompetitive foreclosure.

So what are the implications? One implication is that the assessment of efficiencies can not be separated from the overall competitive assessment. So we don't have—like in a horizontal merger—the analysis of the anticompetitive effects first and then the analysis of the pro-competitive effects, because in a non-horizontal setting the pro-competitive effects may actually be the source of the anticompetitive foreclosure concern.

Another implication is that, as exclusionary effects can only arise in rare circumstances, the same high burden of proof that is placed on the parties in a horizontal merger to prove efficiencies, should be put on the Commission to demonstrate the anticompetitive effects.

The above considerations imply that the framework for assessing non-horizontal mergers should be quite different from the framework that is typically used to assess horizontal mergers. The framework can be divided in five steps.

Step one, which coincides with horizontal mergers, requires the identification of the relevant market. This is very important: unless one can identify a position of dominance in one of the markets involved in the transaction, it is extremely unlikely that the merger will give rise to anticompetitive foreclosure.

Step two: evaluate efficiencies. That was the final step in a horizontal merger. In a non-horizontal merger, it becomes fundamental to assess efficiencies straight away because in some cases efficiencies could be the very source of the anticompetitive effect.

Step three: identify a theory of anticompetitive harm. This requires the identification of a number of conditions that have to be satisfied in order for foreclosure to arise.

Step four: test whether those conditions apply or not. So it is crucial to test the theory that was identified in step three critically against the facts of the industry. If the facts do not support the theory, then the theory should be rejected.

Step five: identify whether competition between the remaining suppliers is sufficient to prevent a price increase. In other words, if foreclosure is likely to take place; so if some of the suppliers will likely be foreclosed, it becomes relevant to analyse whether competition between the remaining suppliers will be strong enough to prevent a price increase. If that is the case, the merger is not anticompetitive, if competition between the remaining suppliers is not enough, then the merger is anticompetitive.

DAMIEN LEVIE

Thank you, Andrea. Now I will give the floor to Paul Lugard, who studied in The Netherlands, was in private practice until 1995 and has been with Philips since 1995 in the Antitrust Law Department. Paul, you have the floor.

PAUL LUGARD

Good afternoon. For those of you who share with me a slightly cynical view on life, and perhaps also on competition policy, I propose to you the following quote by an economist, Mr Liebeler, who was not particularly fond of lawyers and for the subject of this afternoon, vertical mergers and conglomerate mergers, I suggest to you a variation of what Liebeler said in 1982 which is 'It is a curious tribute to the ingenuity of economists, to take a relatively simple problem and make a mess like this out of it'. I will stand to be corrected on that one.

Very briefly, we will probably be discussing the *Tetra Laval* case[2] and also *GE/Honeywell*[3] later on, but I would like first to focus on a number of other cases which have come to the forefront lately, then move to the role

---

[2] Case T-5/02, *Tetra Laval BV v Commission*, [2002] ECR II-4381.
[3] See n 1.

of efficiencies in vertical and conglomerate mergers, and finally I would like to reflect on what perhaps should be in the future guidelines that the Commission is intending to issue.

You will see that the first three cases I had in mind all concern conglomerate cases. They all concern medical equipment a hospital needs to monitor and to treat patients when they are ill, and I will start with the *GE/ Instrumentarium*[4] case, which was a case about anaesthesia products, which were produced by Instrumentarium and patient monitors. Patient monitors are needed to monitor the patient's condition and both products are complementary in the sense that doctors need both products to monitor patients and to treat them.

In *GE/Instrumentarium*, there was a concern that a significant position of market power of Instrumentarium in the field of anaesthesia machines would lead to a situation whereby the merged entity would make it very difficult for rival suppliers of patient monitors to supply those products and that the merger entity would thereby foreclose competition on the market for patient monitors. In this case the Commission also identified a number of horizontal concerns, which were subsequently solved by a divestment of an entity, but much more interesting in this case is the vertical issue. Again, as I said, Instrumentarium had a significant market share in the anaesthesia machine market 30–40 per cent on the European scale, but up to 70 per cent in certain Member States.

The concern was that the combined entity would post-merger refuse interface between anaesthesia machines outpatient monitors and would favour GE's own patient monitors. That prompted the Commission to accept a commitment which consisted of an interface arrangement enabling third party monitor suppliers to interface their equipment with GE's anaesthesia equipment. What is interesting in this case, is that the analysis that the Commission used to arrive at the vertical concerns is quite elementary, and basic. You would think that what has lead the Commission to impose those commitments are simply high market shares in the anaesthesia machine market, without any calculation or quantification of the likely negative effects on competition. Moreover, those market shares were not extremely high, they were in the range of 40–60 per cent, but certainly not per se indicative of a dominant position.

Secondly, there was a concern regarding the technical nature of the products. It appeared very simple to devise anaesthesia machines in such a way that they would only work with certain patient monitors, namely those of

---

[4] Case No COMP/ M3083, *General Electric/Instrumentarium* 2 Sept 2003.

GE. There was some indication that GE intended to leverage its position from the anaesthesia market into the patient monitoring market and that basically was it. All in all, it strikes me that the reasons for the Commission to arrive at interface commitments are at first glance somewhat meagre. What you would have expected is a sort of calculation of why it would have been more beneficial for the merged entity to foreclose others, rather than to continue supplying the two products at the same time, thereby benefiting from customer demand for both products.

Lets then move to the *Siemens/Draeger* case,[5] which, by the way, concerned similar effects. It also involved an anaesthesia machine producer combined with a patient monitor manufacturer. Also in that case, the Commission accepted interface commitments, but there I believe the economic framework is even less clear because the combined entities market shares in patient monitors were even lower than those in the *GE/Instrumentarium* case.

Now, it may be that the *Siemens/Draeger* case, which actually was decided prior to the *GE/Instrumentarium* case, has influenced the Commission's decision in the *GE/ Instrumentarium* case, in the sense that once the parties in *Siemens/Draeger* had agreed to accept to interface arrangement it may have been very difficult for practical reasons for *GE/Instrumentarium* to refuse a similar set of interface commitments. But again, the economic analysis is not very clear.

A much better decision I believe is the third case—the *GE/Amersham* case,[6] which included complementary products, pharmaceuticals, which are used in combination with diagnostic imaging equipment. The Commission conducted an in-depth investigation of whether the merged company would have an incentive and ability to engage in tying and bundling and technical tying, and here the analysis is much more convincing. The Commission, in the end comes to the conclusion that despite very high market shares, both in the diagnostic imaging equipment markets and in the markets for the pharmaceuticals that work together with these machines, the potential for competitive harm is not present. Why not? Customers will not accept it. I do think that the part of the decision on dominance is questionable— that is a clearly a weak part of the decision. But the Commission also concludes that rivals have effective means to counter the possible foreclosure concerns. Therefore, all in all, I think the *GE/Amersham* clearance decision is quite convincing.

5 Case No COMP/M 2861 *Siemens/Draegerwerk* /JV 30 Apr 2003.
6 Case No COMP/M 3304 *General Electric/Amersham*, 21 Apr 2004.

Fourthly, a case which is pending, the *Microsoft/Time Warner/ ContentGuard* case.[7] Very briefly, it concerns a case in which ContentGuard, that owns patents for digital rights management, is acquired by Microsoft and Time Warner. The IPRs that are owned by ContentGuard are used and are necessary for rival DRM solutions, and the issue here is: will the merger change the incentive of ContentGuard to freely license its IPRs for DRM solutions? Again, the transaction is pending—but you may think that this would be an interesting case. Some of the issues in this case are very similar to the ones discussed in the *Microsoft* case,[8] which is pending with the Court of First Instance.

Let me now come back to what Andrea just mentioned. Efficiencies are very important. It is universally accepted that non-horizontal mergers bring about efficiencies, particularly dynamic efficiencies. It is also true that those efficiencies are very difficult to quantify. What we have is a set of horizontal guidelines,[9] which set out the general framework for the evaluation of efficiencies, but it is only a very basic framework. We also have the Notice on the application of Article 81(3),[10] which clearly spells out what type of efficiencies may be involved in vertical restraints. Again, those efficiencies are very similar to the ones that occur in vertical mergers.

But the big problem with the Notice on Article 81(3) is that it is very difficult to apply. The analytical framework is as such convincing, but I think that most of you would agree that convincingly arguing efficiencies under the Article 81(3) Notice is a very difficult task.

So the question is: What should be done? Should the Commission issue guidelines, and if so, what should be included in those guidelines? The aim for guidelines would of course be very simple. We would like to have a clear unambiguous framework of analysis. We would look for a framework of analysis which applies to input foreclosure, customer foreclosure, and conglomerate cases, and then within the framework of conglomerate cases, we would like to see something on tying and bundling. The Commission should, I think, identify exactly what the theory of harm is for each of those categories.

At a very minimum, I think the Commission should be instructed under the guidelines to indicate exactly how much market power is needed for companies to engage in anti-competitive conduct. It would not be sufficient

---

[7] Case No COMP/M 3445 *Microsoft/Tiem Warner/ContentGuard/* JV, 25 Aug 2004.

[8] Case T-201/04 *Microsoft v Commission*, judgment 22 Dec 2004.

[9] Guidelines on the assessment of horizontal mergers under the Council Regulation on the control of concentrations between undertakings OJ C 31/03 5–18, 5 Feb 2004.

[10] Communication from the Commission—Notice—Guidelines on the application of Art 81(3) of the Treaty, Official Journal C 101, 27 Apr 2004, 97–118.

to simply indicate whether anticompetitive effects can only occur if there is market power. I also believe that some of the economic models only work if there is near monopoly. If that is the case, then that should be explained in the guidelines.

Very importantly, the Guidelines would have to discuss the relevance of the nature and structure of competition in potentially foreclosed markets. Which types of companies must be foreclosed before anti-competitive effects are likely to occur? Should that category be confined to companies which are equally efficient or also companies which are less efficient than the merging parties? It would also be interesting to see how the Commission evaluates the commitment of the merged entity to an anticompetitive strategy, and very importantly—this is an issue that came up in the *GE/Honeywell* case[11] and also in the *GE/Amersham* case—what would in the case at hand be an effective counter-strategy that would defeat anti-competitive conduct of the merging firm? There is some ambiguity on the condition of marginalization. How long would it take for companies to be marginalized and what exactly would be meant by marginalization in the first place? The same would apply to buyer power.

That only is the negative side, ie questions that relate to possible anti-competitive effects, but there should equally have to be a framework for the evaluation of efficiencies in the Guidelines. The ones that Andrea just mentioned are clearly very important, and what I am a little bit afraid of is that the future guidelines would not sufficiently instruct the Commission to come up and to show anticompetitive effects and at the same time instruct the merging parties to fully substantiate efficiencies. In that case the future Guidelines would be overinclusive. So in that sense, it is important to make sure that future guidelines would be very balanced. They should require the Commission to set out clearly what anticompetitive effects may be expected, and they should ideally instruct merging parties to come forward with efficiencies, but not put the burden of proof too high. So that would be my personal wish list.

Now coming back briefly to Mr Liebeler, I think that vertical and conglomerate mergers do raise difficult issues. Those issues are a fact of life. They are not 'invented' by economists, and the challenge for the Commission is to come up with a framework of analysis that would be both supported by economic doctrine and is practical and useful in practice.

[11] See n 1.

DAMIEN LEVIE

Thank you Paul for this very interesting presentation. Now comes Guillaume Loriot. Guillaume studied law in Paris, London, and Bruges and worked for a law firm at the European Court of First Instance for five years. He was assistant to Judge Vilaras and then joined the Commission in 2002, where he is currently a member of the Merger Policy and Strategic Support Unit of DG Comp. He has been working on merger cases and on the horizontal merger guidelines. He is a member of the group on non-horizontal mergers.

GUILLAUME LORIOT ('Vertical and conglomerate mergers: Some considerations relevant to enforcement guidelines')

The purpose of my presentation is to raise several issues that would have to be considered when drafting Enforcement Guidelines on vertical, and more generally non-horizontal, mergers, if we ultimately do so.

Let me first emphasize that, at the moment, there is no decision to have such guidelines. That decision will be for Mrs Kroes to take in due time. Meanwhile, we have been reflecting inside DG-Comp on what we should do, but of course there are open issues, that may have an influence on the content of such guidelines.

The first question that I would like to discuss is whether we should oppose, as it sometimes suggested, the framework for analysis for non-horizontal mergers and horizontal mergers (I). Then I would like to mention some of the important issues that are currently being raised before the Community Courts and that may have to be addressed after the Court's rulings (II). Finally I would like to briefly deal with what should be, and what could be the objectives of non-horizontal merger guidelines (III).

I. FRAMEWORK FOR ANALYSIS: SHOULD THE ANALYTICAL FRAMEWORK FOR NON-HORIZONTAL MERGERS AND FOR HORIZONTAL MERGERS BE SYSTEMATICALLY OPPOSED?

As to the first question, the purpose here is not for me to deny the specifics of non-horizontal mergers, whether they are vertical or conglomerate, but rather to examine the following issue: should we systematically consider that, on the one hand, there are bad mergers, which are systematically considered to be the 'horizontal mergers', whereas, on the other hand, non-horizontal mergers should benefit from the assumption that they bring about efficiencies and are therefore good for competition?

One of the questions that it raises is also whether there should be a higher burden of proof when assessing non-horizontal effects. For instance, it was suggested before that we should have a kind of different *sequential* analysis and therefore first analyse efficiencies before coming to the analysis of the anticompetitive concerns.

Several elements suggest that there should not be a systematic opposition between the analytical frameworks of horizontal mergers and of non-horizontal mergers.

• Unilateral/Coordinated effects

The first one is that, when analysing a horizontal or a non-horizontal merger, it always at the end boils down to one question—ie whether there will be an increase in market power because of either unilateral effects or coordinated effects, irrespective of whether it is a horizontal or a non-horizontal merger.

Of course there are different types of analysis to be made, but ultimately, in a non-horizontal merger, you also look at whether there is a unilateral effect. A unilateral effect would occur in a non-horizontal merger if products of rivals would no longer be considered post-merger as attractive substitutes as they were pre-merger, thereby enhancing or creating market power for the benefit of the merged entity. As you know, when assessing horizontal mergers, our analysis also aims at identifying the existence of such unilateral effects.Both types of mergers may also lead to coordinated effects in different circumstances, but that is also the other types of broad anticompetitive harm that we would have to consider.

So in that perspective, I would say that there is not so much difference in the type of aim that we are pursuing as an agency. We are looking at whether the merger would change the ability and the incentives of the merged entity in a sense that it would end up with a significant market power, which would be detrimental to competition, ie to consumers.

• In practice, most problematic non-horizontal mergers are 'multidimensional'

The second element I tend to observe is that in practice, the distinction between horizontal and non-horizontal mergers is somewhat artificial, because most problematic non-horizontal mergers have also horizontal effects, and each of these horizontal, vertical or conglomerate effects may have an influence on the other. In essence, the creation of market power on one market as a result of horizontal effects may also have some significant consequences when assessing the vertical effects of the merger.

Of course one lesson from the *Tetra Laval* judgement,[12] and it is also contained in other judgments, is that the Commission should always look at each of the effects resulting from the merger, whether they are horizontal, conglomerate and vertical. That was an obiter dictum which was very clear in the judgment and which is also very useful. It must also be added that we are faced with the same procedural constraints in all cases. In practice we have one month to identify whether we have serious doubts and a few weeks to raise potential concerns. In this context, it is quite difficult to envisage that the competition assessments of non-horizontal and horizontal mergers should be conducted under two distinct analytical frameworks.

- No positive or negative presumptions in the ECMR

I would add that the EC Merger Regulation does not contain any positive or negative presumption with regard to mergers, whether they are horizontal, vertical or conglomerate. I don't want to anticipate on the debate that President Vesterdorf may have later on with you, but in my mind at least, and it is of course strictly personal, there is nothing that says that we should be more lenient to some particular kinds of mergers. Either we have strong concerns or we don't have any strong concerns and, at the end, our test is whether there will be a significant increase in market power.

- Need for a practical and consistent framework for analysis

Finally, when considering the framework for enforcement guidelines, in my mind we have always to follow—whatever the type of merger—the same kind of sequence. We have to identify the possible theories of harm in light of the facts and of the evidence that is put to us.

In my personal experience, it is difficult to assume from the start that there are pro-competitive efficiencies in a particular type of mergers. My recent experience is that, although you can be dealing with a vertical merger, the parties do not come with any allegation that there would be efficiencies. Even if they were making the argument, it is highly difficult for us to assume that, only because it is a vertical case, it is good for competition.

In practice, I tend to consider that in all cases, whether there are horizontal or vertical or conglomerate, we need an integrated approach where we assess whether there is a harm to competition considering the efficiencies that are likely to be brought about by the parties.

---

[12] Case T-5/02, *Tetra Laval BV v Commission*, [2002] ECR II-4381 and Case T-80/02, *Tetra Laval BV v Commission*, [2002] ECR II-4519.

II. PENDING CASES BEFORE THE COMMUNITY COURTS: WHAT ARE THE ISSUES RAISED AS REGARDS NON-HORIZONTAL MERGERS?

The other set of questions that are open when considering whether we need, and if so, how we should draft, enforcement guidelines are the issues raised by the cases before the ECJ and the Tribunal.

- Structural/behavioural effects

I think one of the important issues raised by the *Tetra Laval* judgment is the general distinction that is made in the judgment between structural and behavioural effects. There is a paragraph in the judgment, which tends to consider that a merger may have structural effects in the sense that they arise directly from the merger—that is the wording of the judgment— whereas it can also have behavioural effects, which would occur if the merged entity, already dominant on market A, engages in certain practices in order to achieve dominance on market B. Of course, it has to be borne in mind that the judgment only makes that distinction in order to assess whether dominance on a neighbouring market will be achieved or strengthened thanks to the dominant position that the merged entity already enjoyed pre-merger on another market. Once it has been established that dominance would be achieved, the judgment does not suggest that the Commission should also assess the type of conduct that the merged entity would adopt. This being said, when you read that judgment, you may get the impression that, according to the CFI non-horizontal (conglomerate) mergers mostly produce behavioural effects with some kind of practices that may be caught under Article 82 EC. In essence, horizontal mergers would tend to have a kind of straightforward effect, which is more structural and more direct, whereas, in a non-horizontal (conglomerate) merger, the merged entity may need to adopt a certain conduct in order to achieve dominance on a neighbouring market, which can be more difficult to predict.[13]

That distinction may really be difficult to make in practice and I do not agree with the idea raised by some that anticompetitive effects resulting from non-horizontal mergers should be seen as 'behavioural' rather than structural.

For example, in vertical mergers, one of the concerns that we may have is the fact that the supplier upstream will have full access to information on the costs of the downstream firm that is competing with the merged entity. And we may have a particularly strong concern when the input that is supplied represents a substantial proportion of the overall costs of the

---

[13] Of course, the judgment of the CFI also envisages the possibility that a conglomerate merger produces immediate structural effects.

downstream firm. That is a kind of straightforward concern that may occur in some cases, and it is hard for me to consider that it is a 'behavioural' effect. If such a distinction were to apply, it would rather be a structural effect which may allow the merged entity to achieve dominance on the neighbouring market.

I can also take the example of conglomerate mergers involving the sale of complementary goods to a single group of customers. In my mind, although it is a feature common to various conglomerate mergers, it is an issue which is more structural than behavioural.

- Assessment of behavioural effects under Article 82

Now of course, the real question is whether or not, when drafting guidelines, and if this distinction is maintained, we should distinguish accordingly the type of effects which we consider would raise concerns when assessing non-horizontal mergers.

This issue is very relevant of course, because if you have to consider that only behavioural effects would allow the merged entity to achieve dominance in a neighbouring market then you may have to assess them under Article 82, if we follow the line in *Tetra Laval*. If so, the next question would be: what should be our standard? Should it be a prima facia assessment, or should we rely mainly on past cases or on the experience that we got in previous Article 82 Commission decisions. Besides, what should the Commission focus on? Should it focus on the legal disincentives for firms to engage in Article 82 practices, or should we rather focus on the risk of detection of such illegal practices by competing firms or by national authorities?

These are important issues in practice. Since the *Tetra Laval* judgment there were indeed some cases where we have been considering that type of issue and we have tried, without knowing the outcome of the judgments before the courts, to be as cautious as possible. Sometimes it may be easy to assess whether there is of timely detection by competitors or by agencies, but in other cases it may be much more difficult. That is something that we may have to elaborate on, I guess, when considering whether we need non-horizontal guidelines.

In this context, there is also an obvious link to be made with the need for Article 82 guidelines. There is a reflection on the approach that we should take, but of course if our reflection is to have less of a per se approach with respect to Article 82, it would have a clear impact on our assessment under our non-horizontal merger guidelines.

- Time dimension

Another issue that is relevant when assessing vertical mergers (in particular if one has to make this distinction between structural and behavioural effects) is the time dimension that we are allowed to look at. In *Tetra Laval*, it is admitted by the Court that we should have some flexible timeframe. The Commission does not have to look only at the immediate effects of a merger, but also at its effects 'in the relatively near future'. It is quite important, especially with respect to non-horizontal mergers.

III. OBJECTIVES: WHAT SHOULD BE THE OBJECTIVES OF NON-HORIZONTAL
   MERGER GUIDELINES ?

Finally, when considering what should be the objectives for vertical and conglomerate merger guidelines, we should bear in mind that there are two types of constraints. On the one hand, we want legal certainty as Paul said. I think it is in the interest of everyone—the agency, but also the firms—to have guidelines that are as clear as possible. But of course, in practice, I tend to observe that there are many evolving economic theories, and it can be very difficult to be exhaustive when setting out the various type of competitive harm that may arise as a result of non-horizontal mergers. The US guidelines for example did not, at the time of their drafting, set out the 'Raising Rivals' Costs' theory when addressing input foreclosure. So, besides legal certainty, you also need some flexibility.

Bearing in mind these two contradicting constraints, I would tend to consider that there are two possibilities for us. Either we try to develop guidelines that identify all the structural conditions which are more likely to raise concerns or we adopt a more realistic approach in which we try to be clear as to the types of theories of harm that may arise, but we remain flexible as to the type of circumstances that would trigger the application of these theories.

DAMIEN LEVIE

Thank you Guillaume. I think there are many interesting issues which you have discussed, and somewhere personally I heard different opinions. One is on the treatment of efficiencies in various types of mergers. It would be interesting to hear, Andrea, on whether we need to change the section of the horizontal merger guidelines, at least at European level to deal with efficiencies and non-horizontal mergers.

The second issue I saw is the standard of harm. You talked about the speculative chain of prediction, whether that raises a higher level of a standard of harm or not. Guillaume, I think, expressed a slightly different opinion. Finally, whether we are at a stage to adopt guidelines that can be predictable, clear, and are economically sound. Maybe you want to react, and I will give the floor to the audience.

ANDREA LOFARO

Starting from the guidelines on non-horizontal mergers, I am definitely in favour of that. Indeed, while it is true that it would be impossible to produce guidelines which can summarize all the theories of vertical foreclosure that have been developed over the last 15 years, it would definitely be useful to have guidelines setting out a framework for the assessment of these mergers.

In particular it is possible, I believe, to set out a number of conditions that need to be satisfied in order for non-horizontal mergers to give rise to anti-competitive concerns. It seems to me that authorities have focused too much in the past on one condition, ie the incentive that the parties may have post-merger to engage in bundling or vertical foreclosure and so on. While this is clearly relevant, I think that competition authorities should focus heavily also on testing whether other firms would be able to replicate the same strategy that will may potentially be adopted by the merged parties. In other words, a lot of emphasis seems to have been placed in past cases in testing the incentive that the post-merger entity will have to engage in bundling or tying and not enough emphasis has been placed in testing whether other firms would be able to replicate, whether they would be able to do the same thing, basically.

Regarding the question of whether the horizontal merger guidelines should be changed to accommodate for differences in the nature of the efficiencies brought about by non-horizontal mergers, I think the answer should be 'no' because the two things are too different. As noted earlier, the Commission has traditionally adopted a sceptical stance on the role of efficiencies in horizontal mergers. This is caused by the fact that the assessment of efficiencies takes place after a very well-defined anticompetitive effect has been demonstrated, and therefore, it may be legitimate for the Commission to be sceptical about the horizontal efficiencies to which the merger could give rise. However, the same sceptical stance is certainly not appropriate for vertical mergers because these mergers are inherently pro-competitive.

I also wanted to address Guillaume's point on presumption. When I talked about the presumption of non-horizontal mergers being pro-competitive, I did not refer to a legal presumption, I just talked about the general effect to which these types of mergers give rise. I think there is a general agreement among economists that horizontal mergers may potentially give rise to a price increase. I don't subscribe to the theory that all horizontal mergers give rise to a price increase unless one can prove efficiencies, but it is certainly true that there is an upward pressure on prices that may result from horizontal mergers due to the elimination of a competitive constraint. But to the extent that there is an upward pressure on prices arising from horizontal mergers, it is also true that there is a downward pressure on prices that arises from non-horizontal mergers, certainly not an upward pressure.

I also wanted to address Paul's point on Article 81(3). I totally agree with his point that it is unfortunate that the Commission has adopted the same framework to analyse horizontal and vertical restrictions. As Paul said, vertical restrictions are unlikely to give rise to efficiencies that imply a reduction in marginal costs. Very often they give rise to an improvement in the quality of products, they eliminate free riding, they eliminate investment hold-up problems and it is difficult to quantify the effect that these efficiencies will have on price and, therefore, it is very difficult to verify whether these efficiencies will more than offset the potential anticompetitive effects of these restrictions.

DAMIEN LEVIE

Thank you. I will ask the panellists whether they would have a tendency of predicting whether the CFI or the Court would decide in the conglomerate—or just call them—merger cases that are pending in *GE/Honeywell*[14] and *Tetra Laval*.[15] Does anyone want to say a word on this?

GUILLAUME LORIOT

I wouldn't like to make any predictions but one of the questions that I tend to ask myself in the *GE/Honeywell* case is whether the CFI would limit itself to consider the horizontal issues that were very real in that case, because it could stop there, if it is favourable to the Commission. Or whether it would conduct a full analysis on the vertical and conglomerate issues, and I think that whatever the result—as a Commission official, I would prefer one type of result—but I think it would be beneficial to everyone to have a kind of extensive judgment on that issue, so that we can go forward and debate further, but at least tackle the issue in a clear-cut way.

With the *Tetra/ Sidal* appeal I have no prediction at all.

[14] See n 1.   [15] See n 11.

PAUL LUGARD

In contrast to some of you in the audience, I have not been involved in a *GE/Honeywell* case, so I am completely free to speak about that case, I think. When I look at conglomerate cases, I ask myself sometimes: well, this sounds very nice, but will foreclosure actually happen? To me, the mechanism is often very clear, but I sometimes have difficulties in deciding how real the problem is, and some of these issues also come up in the *GE/Honeywell* case. For example, I find it a bit difficult to see why all these competitors of GE and Honeywell don't have any effective counter strategies. These are big companies, and the part of the decision dealing with counter strategies is a bit, I wouldn't say thin, and I am sure that the Commission has looked at these cases very carefully, but I have difficulties in accepting that none of these competitors are able to adopt effective counter measures. I also think that the decision might be a little bit static in term of market definition.

For example, if you look over the last 20 or 30 years at the market for aircraft engines, then you see a lot of fluctuation in market shares. That is perhaps not completely reflected in the decision. At least I don't see any real analysis of that specific effect, so I fully agree with Guillaume that it would be very interesting to see a comprehensive analysis by the Court of the case.

ANDREA LOFARO

I also don't know the facts of this case, but what I find interesting is the difference in the issues to which the two merger cases gave rise and how these have been dealt with by the Commission.

In *GE/Honeywell*, the products were clearly complementary. On the one hand we have GE's engines and on the other Honeywell's avionic systems. So these two are complementary products and therefore the first element of the chain of prediction described above whereby the parties may have an incentive to offer the two products in a bundle at a discount is potentially legitimate. Clearly, the overall anti-competitive theory would have to be tested against the facts.

In *Tetra Laval/Sidel* the situation is different because the products produced by the two parties were actually substitutes—not substitutable enough to be included in the same market, but they were still substitutes. We have Tetra on the one hand, which is the leading supplier in the carton packaging market, and Sidel on the other, which is the leading supplier in the equipment for the production of PET bottles. These two products are clearly substitutable and therefore the starting point of the Commission's exclusionary theory that the post merger entity would have an incentive to engage in bundling and discounting is less clear because as these products are substitute and not complements, if there is an incentive to change prices, that incentive has to be to increase prices post-merger and not to decrease prices and offer discounts.

Incidentally, the Commission also put forward a more straightforward horizontal concern, but this plays a less important role in the analysis than the conglomerate effect, which for the above reasons I find less convincing than the theory considered in the *GE/Honeywell* case.

DAMIEN LEVIE

I have another question for Paul Lugard. In your experience, is it much more difficult, or just more difficult, for a competitor to complain about a merger, which you would call conglomerate or vertical, compared to just a horizontal merger?

PAUL LUGARD

Some people would argue that the Commission listens more to competitors than looks at competition in general. I don't think that's true. I think it is difficult for a complainant to attack, or to successfully complain, about a conglomerate or vertical merger. In my experience, the Commission might be interested in a good story and a good story might bring you perhaps to the second phase if that's what you want, but that is certainly not sufficient. So I would say, yes, it is very difficult to successfully complain about conglomerate mergers, precisely because the net anticompetitive effects are very difficult to establish and if the Commission really wants to go to the bottom of the case, it would also have to look at the efficiencies, so it would have to balance somehow, these two effects, and that I think, makes it very difficult for complainants.

There are practical issues as well. Ideally you would like to have a lot of data that shows a potential competitive effect, but it all depends on the type of market and the type of activities your client is engaged in, whether that data is available. In the *GE/Instrumentarium* case,[16] the markets and the behaviour of the most important market players were quite well documented, which allowed for some quantification of the potential horizontal and vertical effects, but I would think that those cases are the exception, rather than the rule.

[16] See n 4.

There is another practical issue, which is the Commission's practice of bringing the merging parties and complainants together in triangular meetings. In practise there may be many companies that might be willing to complain but that may be hesitant to step forward, knowing that they would have to defend their case in triangular meetings.

So, all in all, I think it is quite complicated to successfully complain about a non-horizontal merger case; it is much more difficult than a horizontal case.

DAMIEN LEVIE

A question to the other two panellists. Is that sound from a policy point of view? Guillaume, for example, what Andrea said about the speculative chain of prediction that logical consequences will by definition almost be much more difficult to complain about as to bring forward a case against a merger.

ANDREA LOFARO

My impression is that traditionally it was probably easier to complain about a non-horizontal merger than a horizontal merger. The reason for this I think is that there are so many theories of anticompetitive foreclosure that it would have been quite easy to identify one theory that could potentially apply to a certain case. Moreover, the Commission did not always test those theories rigorously against the facts, and that is perhaps why maybe it was easier to complain about non-horizontal mergers than about horizontal mergers.

That said, I believe that this has now changed especially after the Court has made it clear that the Commission needs to test theories of anticompetitive harm more rigorously against the facts. I believe things have changed quite dramatically over the last two/three years.

GUILLAUME LORIOT

My impression is that in the field of horizontal mergers the Commission has refined a lot its assessment in particular through the horizontal merger guidelines.[17] Now we tend to be more focused on the type of competition we are looking at, the type of products, the type of markets—you know the bidding markets for example, as in the *GE/Instrumentarium* case where we have conducted a very extensive analysis of how competition effectively

---

[17] Guidelines on the assessment of horizontal mergers under the Council Regulation on the control of concentrations between undertakings, OJ C 31, 5 Feb 2004, 5–18.

takes place on the market, rather than to focus only on the overlap and the structural change on the market.

So my impression is that for horizontal mergers it may be more difficult than before for complainants to put forward sound complaints whereas for non-horizontal mergers, of course, there are a whole variety of effects. It may be more difficult to identify them. At least we know what type of story we are looking at and complainants tend to have a good story there. Then, the burden of proof is high on us and will remain so; so that's where the change is, I think.

DAMIEN LEVIE

Thank you. Any comment or question from the audience? Any concluding comments from the panellists, before we hand over the floor to a more distinguished panel.

LEON FIELDS (*Oxera Consulting Ltd*)

I think there is a difference in terms of the underlying economics in some areas that is actually quite new, but that doesn't mean that we shouldn't necessarily try and take those conditions and the theory of harm as it is; if certain pre-conditions are there then you are more likely to get problems regarding the effects of the mergers. So the theory of tying or bundling in all these areas are recent developments, but isn't that inevitable because that is how we got away from Chicago School all those years ago in terms of looking at how effects which weren't part of the established theory at the time.

ANDREA LOFARO

I think that a lot of progress has been made over the last few years and to go back on the guidelines point, a lot of established principles and conditions, which is what I think you are saying, can be incorporated in guidelines. So, guidelines that attempt to incorporate all the existing theories are clearly not feasible, but it is certainly possible to incorporate many established principles that have been clearly set out by recent developments in economic theory.

GUILLAUME LORIOT

I would share that position. I mean we have to find a structural framework in terms of likely concerns that the Commission would raise in certain specific situations without being exhaustive. I don't think it is completely possible, but I think we have enough experience now. Maybe we have to wait for the Court judgements, but we have enough experience in order to set out clearly what would be the principles and what would be the likely conditions for us to act.

Panel 5—Standard of Proof in Merger Cases

Chair: Nicholas Green QC, *Brick Court Chambers*

Speakers:
Judge Bo Vesterdorf, *President, Court of First Instance*
John Bodrug, *Davies Ward Phillips & Vineberg*

NICHOLAS GREEN

Well ladies and gentlemen, welcome to the second session this afternoon. I was interested to hear in the first session discussions of such topics as the speculative chain of prediction and the Advocate General's opinion in *Tetra Laval*[1] where he has expressed the view that grey mergers should not be prohibited.

Our first speaker this afternoon is someone who has to grapple on a day-by-day basis with the evidential questions. For him, it would not be so much a matter of theory as sifting through the evidence to decide the crucial answer for the rest of us—yes or no.

Judge Bo Vesterdorf was a member of the CFI from 1989 and has been President for the last six years. He has, as everybody knows, presided over many of the most pivotal antitrust cases and has therefore grappled with the issue for this afternoon, which is standard of proof in merger cases. So without more, I will turn to our first speaker this afternoon, Judge Bo Vesterdorf.

JUDGE BO VESTERDORF

Thank you very much Nicholas. Ladies and Gentlemen, it was a particular pleasure for me to be invited to speak on this topic—standard of proof—this afternoon. For one simple reason, it gave me occasion for the first time in many years to sit down with some of my *référendaires* and try to reflect, in more abstract terms, on what we had been doing for years and years in these cases. How do we in fact appreciate what the Commission does? What are the standards that the Commission must meet? What are the standards that my own Court must meet? That was a particularly interesting exercise I can assure you.

---

[1] T-5/02 *Tetra Laval AB v Commission* [2002] ECR II-4381.

I have been dealing with these competition cases, merger cases, now for almost 15 years in the Court of First Instance. Some of the cases have been easier than others, some haven't been easy at all, and in some of them we may have got down to the right and correct judgment, in some of them, perhaps, we haven't.

One of the cases that you have been discussing this afternoon, which is of major interest for our topic, is of course the *Tetra Laval* case,[2] in which I myself was Judge Rapporteur. You will, no doubt, be aware that this case is currently pending, on appeal, before the Court of Justice. The judgment is expected for February of next year. The ECJ has taken more than one year to deliver it and to consider the case, which may be an indication that they take that topic very seriously. Indeed, the case raises very interesting questions as to what is the standard of review that is to be expected from the Court of First Instance and whether the Court of First Instance, in that particular case, respected its role in the system of judicial review?

The topic, of course, is particularly interesting and has led to heated debate since the Commission's unfortunate experience in the year 2002 to face annulment judgments in three high profile merger cases. These cases are *Airtours*, *Schneider*[3] and *Tetra Laval*. The year after in *Babyliss*[4] and *Philips*,[5] the CFI had to annul those two decisions. This period was perhaps seen as somewhat a shocking experience for those who so far had the experience that merger cases had a tendency to get approved by the CFI without major problems.

We had those three high profile cases in 2002; we had in 2003 a number of other cases that were less high profile, probably because they didn't lead to the same kind of result and I won't mention all of them, but just briefly we had *Petrolessence*[6], *Moser v Commission*,[7] *Verband der freien Rohrwerke v Commission*[8] and so on. And of course, we have some pending cases. We have I think about 16 pending cases before my own Court and the Court of Justice. Some of them are awaited with impatience, not only by you, but also by my own Court, because if you are excited about the judgment,

---

[2] Joint cases C-12-13/03P *Tetra Laval AB v Commission* (judgment expected early 2005).

[3] Case T-310/01, *Schneider Electric SA v Commission*, [2002] ECR II-4071 ('*Schneider*') regarding the Commission's Art 8(3) prohibition and case T/77/02, *Schneider Electric SA v Commission* [2002] ECR II-4519 regarding the Commission's Art 8(4) divestiture decision.

[4] Case T-114/02, *BaByliss SA v Commission*, [2003] ECR II-1279.

[5] Case T-119/02, *Royal Philips NV v Commission*, [2003] ECR II-1433.

[6] Case T-342/00, *Petrolessence and SG2R v Commission*, [2003] ECR II-1161.

[7] Case C-170/02P, *Schluesselverlag JS Moser and others v Commission*, an appeal against the Order of the CFI in Case T-3/02, *Schluesselverlag JS Moser and others v Commission*, [2003] ECR II-1473.

[8] Case T-374/00, *Verband der freien Rohrwerke eV v Commission* [2003] ECR II-2275.

certainly and particularly in *Tetra Laval*, so is my own Court. This is the case in which our legal review test that we applied in my own Court will be examined and scrutinised by the Court of Justice to see if we did our job correctly, or if we, as the Commission has claimed, did go beyond our limits of legal review: in fact, as alleged by the Commission, more or less substituted our own opinion for that of the Commission.

Before I go into my analysis of these various problems, just let me put the things into perspective by quoting the Commission press release when it appealed the *Tetra Laval* case. Just an excerpt from that press release; I quote 'The CFI has imposed a disproportionate standard of proof for merger prohibition decisions. As a result, it has upset the balance between the interests of the merging parties and the protection of consumers, which is provided for in the Merger Regulation. In this respect, the CFI has also exceeded its role, which is to review the administrative decision of the Commission for clear errors of fact or reasoning and not to substitute its view of the case for that of the Commission'.[9]

This is the criticism raised against the *Tetra Leval* case and I am extremely interested to see what the Court of Justice is going to say in that respect. Because if the Commission's appreciation and their grounds of appeal are accepted by the Court of Justice, it is a fact that the work of my own Court will be easier. We will not have to go that far into the examination of the case. We will have to withdraw or step back and of course, make life a little easier for us perhaps.

If on the other hand, the Court of Justice were to confirm our judgement by and large, or completely, it would mean that we will go on doing exactly what we did in *Schneider*, in *Airtours*[10] and what we did in *Tetra Laval*. That means the relatively tight control of facts, application of the law to the facts, followed by an examination of of the Commission's appreciation of a merger as decided by the Commission.

I think we should for the discussion for this afternoon distinguish between two things. First we have to distinguish between what is the standard of proof, and what is the standard of legal review. Standard of proof is traditionally defined as the amount of evidence, which a plaintiff or a prosecution authority in a criminal case must present in a trial in order to win. In other words, the standard of proof is the threshold that must be met before an adjudicator decides that a point is proven in law.

---

[9] Commission Press Release of 20 Dec 2002, IP/02/1952, 'Commission appeals CFI ruling on *Tetra Laval*/Sidel to the European Court of Justice'.
[10] Case T-342/99, *Airtours plc v Commission*, [2002] ECR II-2585.

I think we can distinguish between two main standards of proof, depending on whether the case is a civil case or a criminal case.

Criminal cases I think are decided, at least in all the civilized countries in the Western world, with a standard of proof beyond reasonable doubt. This is a very high standard which requires that the case be proven to the point that the adjudicator, the jury or the judge, has no reasonable doubt that the crime was indeed committed by the defendant.

In civil cases, on the other hand, a much lower standard of proof is normally used—that of 'balance of probabilities', also known as the 'preponderance of evidence'. This generally means that a party will win if he can show that it is more likely than not that his contentions are true.

Now does there exist between these two different levels of standard of proof—the criminal level of standard of proof or civil law standard of proof—any other standard of proof? In my opinion, we can and we will find in fact that there are some variations in between. Some standard of proof which will be higher than the simple civil law standard of proof, but not as high as the criminal law standard of proof, but there may be cases where we will get fairly close to what is normally the standard of proof in criminal law cases.

There is in particular another, third standard of proof, which is in fact what I think we use and most courts in administrative law use, which is the standard of proof or test known as 'manifest error of appreciation'. These are three words which you will find generally in the judgments by my own Court and by the Court of Justice when we review the legality of Commission decisions. At some point in time, in the reasoning, you will find these words a 'manifest error of appreciation'. Has that been proven? Or has it not been proven? Have we found that there is a manifest error of appreciation in some respect?

This is the classical standard of proof, or the 'standard of review', that we use in the case law and in the cases before the Court of Justice and that should indeed be reclassified not as a standard of proof, but really a standard of judicial control. Indeed, it is a standard used when reviewing the legality of the administration's decisions and not when deciding a case on the merits. This is the limit to which we must go and no further than that when reviewing the legality of Commission decisions.

If we now turn from this slightly theoretical distinction between the various standards of proof or the standard of legal control, I think we could say that the standard of proof is the test which is incumbent upon the Commission. That is why they must meet a certain standard of proof.

What is the standard of proof inherent in the Merger Regulation? That is a topic that I will come back to later on.

As I said this should be distinguished from the standard of legal review which is what is expected of the Court of Justice and the Court of First Instance when reviewing the legality of the Commission's decisions: what is it that we can do? In this regard we need to take as a starting point that the whole system has been built around the concept that it is for the Commission and only for the Commission, as an administrative authority, to examine these cases and adjudicate them on the merits once they are notified to the Commission. When we are talking about merger cases (when they are notified to the Commission) it is for the Commission in the first instance to verify whether or not there are problems with regard to the Merger Regulation. In that respect, it is for the Commission once it has to take the final decision to apply a certain standard of proof and it is for the parties before the Commission to provide the Commission with the necessary evidence, and if not possible, the Commission has to go out and find the evidence necessary through a market investigation.

Once the Commission has taken the decision, it follows clearly from, first of all, Article 230 EC and then from the Merger Regulation, that these administrative decisions are subject to appeal before the Community courts, first before my own court, and then, on appeal, on points of law, to the Court of Justice.

It is in this respect that we need to examine and we will examine this afternoon, what is the standard of legal review and at the end of my intervention I will turn to the standard of proof incumbent upon the Commission when it is deciding the case under the Merger Regulation.

As regards the standard of legal review, which is the subject of the case before the Court of Justice in *Tetra Laval*, did we or did we not go beyond what we could do in those cases and in particular the *Tetra Laval* case. I think it is quite clear and I will not go into all the details about the case law. You will see that in my paper there is a large—long-winded perhaps—explanation of what is the state of the case law, suffice it simply to say that we will use in practice, and it is my firm conviction that we do and do only use in practice, the classic test of 'manifest error of appreciation', when we regard the economic assessment of the case. We will simply verify if the Commission's economic assessment is or is not tainted by any manifest error of appreciation.

I quote from the *Portland* case '[The] examination by the Community judicature of the complex economic assessments made by the Commission must necessarily be confined to verifying whether the rules on procedure and on the statement of reasons have been complied with, whether the facts have been accurately stated and whether there has been any manifest error of appraisal or misuse of powers'.[11]

Now this is very well put forward as the framework within which we examine the Commission's decision. What does it mean in practice in real terms when we get a case before us? We all know that a case presented by the Commission will obviously present a certain amount of facts. Things which according to the Commission are the facts of the case. The decision will also present the Commission's legal reasoning, the legal criteria that the Commission will apply when assessing these facts. The Commission will then, after having assessed the facts and found existence of a certain number of facts, try to infer from those facts what will be the outcome, what would be the result of the merger case before the Commission. Will it or will it not, lead to negative competitive effects on the market in question?

What will the Court of First Instance do? The first question we will put to ourselves as Judge arbiters—and later on when we sit in Chambers discussing the case, before and after the court hearings—is 'Has the Commission got the primary facts correct, or haven't they?'

Of course the applicant before the Court will very often claim that the Commission on this and that point, or on several points, regarding the primary facts haven't got it right. So this is the first task when we sit down. There the control by the Court is a full-fledged control. There is absolutely no margin of appreciation left to the Commission. If the Commission states as a fact in a particular case that the companies in question have presently today, these and these market shares, we are going to check on the basis of the evidence if that is the case, or if that is not the case. If we find it is the case, ok, we will then go on to further facts of interest. What are the positions of the other competitors out on the market? What are their factual situations? What are the products they produce? What are their market shares?

Those are facts on which the Commission must build in order to be able to appreciate what is going to happen in the future. Those facts will be verified to the very letter.

So primary facts will be examined and examined closely. It's full control.

Regarding the legal criteria the Commission will then apply to those facts, on that point it is clearly for the Community judges to define those criteria and decide if those criteria are the relevant criteria and legal criteria, and if

---

[11] Joined Cases C-204/00 P, C-205/00 P, C-211/00 P, C-213/00 P, C-217/00 P and C-219/00 P, *Aalborg Portland and Others v Commission*, not yet published in the ECR, point 279

they have been applied to the facts in that particular case. So it is for the judge to have these legal criteria set out in the Commission's decision. Are they the relevant, pertinent, decisive legal criteria? That is our job and there is no margin of appreciation in that respect.

The third thing that we would have to assess and go into is obviously then, once we have the facts, once we have the legal criteria set up, that is the prospective analysis, what is then going to happen? It is in this respect that we need to address or apply the normal tests saying that we need simply to appreciate whether the Commission in that respect has committed any manifest error of appreciation. In other words, do the reasons, which the Commission presents in its decision, ensure an end result that is plausible on the basis of the facts, and on the basis of the legal criteria to be applied? Do they present themselves as coherent, cogent, and reasonable at the end of the day? Is it that something a reasonable person could arrive at on the basis of the facts?

In the various cases, in the *Schneider* case and *Tetra Laval* and *Airtours*, we have been applying the tests, I think, that I have indicated, examination of the primary facts, legal principles and then control of the Commission's appreciation.

On the appreciation point, in these three high profile cases, this is where the Court found that there were errors and manifest errors in the reasoning and the reasons given by the Commission, partly on the basis of errors with respect to the factual situation and partly as to the legal principles to be applied to the facts.

I think it is interesting to see in the opinion by Advocate General Tizzano in the *Tetra Laval* case, the opinion which has been handed down a short while ago, that he acknowledged the intensity of control that the Court of First Instance exercised in the *Tetra Laval* case, as regards the facts; I think it is useful to quote here that he said that

> With regard to the findings of fact, the review is clearly more intense, in that the issue is to verify objectively and materially the accuracy of certain facts and the correctness of the conclusions drawn in order to establish whether certain known facts make it possible to prove the existence of other facts to be ascertained . . .[12]

However, when we get to the point which, I think, is for the Commission probably the most troubling aspect of the negative merger decision taken by my Court, this is the fact that the Commission believes that we went too far

---

[12] *Tetra Laval* Opinion, point 86.

when reviewing the activity of prospective economic analysis made by the Commission, the economic assessment, what would happen in the future? The Commission, if you remember, said that the Court of First Instance in fact had substituted itself for the Commission in a number of points in particular in the *Tetra Laval* case.

This is obviously worrying. I think we should nevertheless not forget that already when we started out one of the very first and important merger cases decided by the Court of Justice was the *Kali and Salz*[13] judgment, in which the Court said

> the basic provisions of [the old Merger Regulation], in particular Article 2 thereof, confer on the Commission a certain discretion, especially with respect to assessments of an economic nature . . . Consequently, review by the Community judicature of the exercise of that discretion, which is essential for defining the rules on concentrations, must take account of the discretionary margin implicit in the provisions of an economic nature which form part of the rules on concentrations.[14]

What is the manifest error of appreciation? Now that is a very hard thing to determine except in a concrete case, because we need to go back and look into the facts, look into the reasons given by the Commission, all the premises which build up to the final result of the Commission's decision. I don't think one can really go any further than to say this: if on the basis of the correct facts and the correct legal principles to be applied, two reasonable persons could reach on the basis of the same facts and the same legal principles to be applied two different results and both of these results would seem fairly convincing in their argumentation leading up to the result, if that were to be the case, I think my Court and the Court of Justice would then easily and without hesitation accept that the Commission has chosen one of these two different results because both of them were plausible results on the basis of the fact and the legal criteria to be applied. In other words, in such a situation my own Court, and certainly myself, would never say that, even though I might favour solution A, and therefore not decide as the Commission had decided, if the Commission decided B on the basis of reasonable argumentation, then that is what must be respected. That is the margin of appreciation that the Commission must enjoy, so that if at the end of the day it falls down on B, and it might as well fall down on A, it is for the Commission to decide whether it prefers B or A, as long as its argumentation and motivation for that result is sufficiently clear and is not tainted by manifest errors of appreciation.

---

[13] Joined Cases C-68/94 and C-30/95, *France and Others v Commission*, [1998] ECR I-1375.
[14] *Kali and Salz*, points 223-4.

One problem that was also mentioned by one of the speakers in the earlier panel is a particularly difficult problem for the merger cases. At least I found it myself fairly difficult in the *Tetra Laval* case. That is the case in which the Commission does not find that the merger in question creates immediately a certain situation, but when the Commission fears and has reason to fear that within a certain time frame it will generate negative effects for competition. You will remember in the *Tetra Leval* case the Commission found that with time that Tetra Laval by leveraging into the PET (plastic packaging equipment) market might end up in a situation where they might harm the competitors considerably, resulting in anticompetitive effects.

One of the problems in that case is how far into the future can such a decision reasonably reach? Are we talking two/five/ten/fifteen years? In the *Tetra Laval* case the Commission said that it predicted that within a time frame of around five years from finding the facts of the case, there would be such negative effects and that, therefore, the merger had to be prohibited. I think you will find that my own Court in that decision found that the length of the time frame used by the Commission is not in itself a problem. The only problem is that the further we go out into the realm of uncertainties, the more necessary it is to convince the court by other means that the negative effects are indeed plausible. This is why I think we applied the word 'particularly convincing' or persuasive arguments. It seems right to ask for 'particularly convincing' evidence when you are predicting events for five years or more, and I think the logic of the judgement is simply to say that unless we ask for a very convincing explanation, it would be far too easy to say that in five years time it is going to happen like this. Many things can happen in the meantime; so many things that all predictions can at the end of the day be fairly useless.

Now let me turn to the question of the standard of proof before the Commission. As I said at the beginning, we have to distinguish between the standard of legal review, which I repeat is a standard of control of legality of the Commission's decisions: control of procedural requirements, control of the facts of the case, correct application of the law and no misuse of powers. That is what we will verify. That is the test under Article 230 EC.

As regards this standard, my own opinion, obviously, is that we have not gone beyond what we should, but that remains to be seen once the judgement of Court of Justice is handed down in *Tetra Laval*.

Turning now to the standard of proof inherent in the Regulation, ie what is the level, or the amount of proof that the Commission itself must have before it can decide one way or another. We have to bear in mind that under the Merger Regulation the Commission has to take a decision, either in

Phase 1 or Phase 2. It has to decide that either this merger must be prohibited, because it will provoke those negative effects, or it must decide that the merger must be cleared. It can not just say 'well, we don't really know, but we'll just let it fly like that'. That can not be done, unlike the situation in the US prosecutorial system. In the EC system, the Commission cannot leave the case and let it drop and that's it. The Commission has to decide one way or the other and has to adopt a written and reasoned decision.

So one of the problems the Commission has to face is that if the standard of proof, in order to prohibit a merger is set relatively high, the amount of evidence that the Commission has to have, before it can prohibit the merger, must also be fairly high.

The second question is: must the same level or amount of evidence be present before the Commission can clear a merger? If the standard of proof for prohibitions is way beyond 50 per cent that this merger will generate considerably negative effects for the competition in the future, is it the same level of proof the Commission must have in order to clear a merger?

This would have the bizarre result that the Commission might find itself in the situation where it couldn't find that it has sufficient evidence to prohibit or to clear. We are not up at around a 60 per cent chance that we will have negative effects and therefore we will not prohibit. But on the other hand, must I also then have 60 per cent chances in order to clear the merger? In my example, the chances of the merger not having anticompetitive effects would be less than 50 per cent. Can the Commission clear the merger even though it believes there is less than a 50 per cent possibility that the merger is compatible with the common market? A 60 per cent standard of proof for both prohibitions and clearances would thus make it impossible for the Commission, because it will be faced with cases in a greay zone where it does not have sufficient evidence to reach 60 per cent either way. That is something which is clearly undesirable and impossible to have as a result. Nevertheless some might claim that our case law is indeed as hard on the Commission in clearance decisions as in prohibition decisions

Such a situation would be fairly impossible. I think therefore the standard of proof can not be one and the same standard. The only thing I think one can reasonably say is probably what Advocate General Tizzano said in the *Tetra Laval* case, that you must have such evidence that you are convinced that it is very likely either that the merger will produce some negative results (and then it must be prohibited) or it is likely that it will not produce such negative results.

What is in between those two standards? I think the answer must simply be that we will have to wait and see. We can not put the Commission in the impossible situation of having to prove at exactly the same (high) level. Therefore I think—that is also what you can read out of Advocate General Tizzano's opinion—if the Commission is sufficiently in doubt as to the negative consequences, it should be reticent, hesitant to prohibit. It should probably rather clear the merger, even though it has doubts in that respect, as long as those doubts are not just as high as the doubts as to the negative effect. In other words, I think that one should perhaps (and that can be read out in the *Tetra Laval* judgment) keep in mind that it is for businesses in principle to organise themselves, and it is for businesses to do that freely of course within the framework of the legislation. As such, one should perhaps be a bit more hesitant to prohibit than to clear mergers, particularly since even if you clear, and it would later appear that you should in fact have prohibited, there are still means at our disposal, at the Commission's disposal, to deal with companies which abuse the power that they have gotten through the merger. So I think at the end of the day, from my own point of view, the level of standard of proof to prohibit must be that you can demonstrate that it is very likely that the merger in question will provoke some negative consequences. In such cases, you should prohibit, in other cases you should rather clear. But that is a very personal observation there. We will have to wait and see in future cases if we can prove that that is the correct test.

Now what I have said is not binding on my Court. I should have said that at the beginning, but at least it explains what I think myself are the correct tests. I distinguish between the legal review test, which is one—and clear, ie the 'manifest error' test—and the level of the standard of proof, ie the test inherent in the Merger Regulation itself, which is slightly more difficult to define.

NICHOLAS GREEN

I'd like to thank Judge Vesterdorf. His comments on the topic are of immense importance—not just to the way the Commission enforces the Merger Regulation, but also to us lawyers advising on such transactions, and indeed in front of the Court.

Our next speaker will provide a point of comparison. You will know that Canada had antitrust law early in the last century in the Combines Investigation Act. John Bodrug has practised very extensively in Canada, in Toronto for the last 15 years in all aspects of civil and indeed criminal competition law. He was one of Global Competition Law's 'top 45, under 45' recently, of world-wide antitrust lawyers and we are delighted that he has crossed the Atlantic to give us some form of comparative analysis. John, thank you.

JOHN BODRUG

Thanks very much. I appreciate the opportunity to be here today. What I thought I would talk about in general is the exacting review of government agencies' cases in mergers, such as the trilogy of CFI decisions in 2002, which is not unique to the EU. I am going to comment on a few selected cases in both the US and Canada in which tribunals and courts have applied very exacting standards in the face of evidence that the enforcement agencies undoubtedly felt was very strong and might normally have been considered a basis for a successful case by government agencies.

In passing, I can't resist talking about some Canadian cases in which the merging parties would have very much appreciated the presence on the panel of Judge Vesterdorf for a more exacting standard of review than the Tribunal applied in Canada.

I am going to review some of the types of evidence that have been accepted and not accepted by the courts and tribunals and draw some generalisations from that.

First, I would like to make a couple of points. Most cases obviously do not make it to the full litigation stage and, from a practical point of view, there is a different standard that applies for the types of evidence that are necessary to persuade a regulator not to challenge a merger, or for the types of evidence that the regulators might rely on as a basis for a negotiated settlement that parties in many cases accept because of timing considerations and a desire to get the deal done.

In fact, I think you could expect that close call types of cases are going to be the only ones that make it to full litigation, as neither side is going to be inclined to devote the time, resources and expenses to full litigation over a case which they don't think they have a strong chance of winning. In other words, when both sides think they have a strong case, there is likely to be a compelling story on both sides and a close call for the adjudicator.

If the presumption is generally in favour of legality, then you would expect the regulators to be losing a good number of the cases in this area, because only the tough ones are going to be litigated, and generally the bias would be in favour of letting them go through. So we should resist the temptation to keep a score card of how many cases they win and how many they lose.

I don't need to review the EU cases, but I am going to be referring to a number of US cases that some people might not be familiar with.

The first ones are cases in which the US antitrust authorities brought an action and were not successful in their challenge. Two of them were decided just this year. The *Arch Coal* case[15] was a coal mine merger in which the Court denied the FTC's motion for a preliminary injunction. In the second case, *Dairy Farmers of America*[16] (DFA), DFA had interests in two competing milk processors which were principal competitors of each other. The Court issued a summary judgment for DFA. The *Oracle/Peoplesoft* merger[17] is another recent case dealing with enterprise software where the Court dismissed the Government's challenge. And going a few years back, *SunGard Data Systems/Comdisco*[18] involved computer recovery services, in which again the Court declined to issue an injunction. I will also comment briefly on the *Staples/Office Depot* case[19] in which the Government did succeed.

I will comment briefly as well on a few Canadian cases including *Superior Propane*,[20] which is better known for the application of the efficiency defence. In that case, it was relatively easy for the Government to establish a substantial lessening of competition.

The first factor or type of evidence that I would like to discuss is customer preferences. In the *Superior Propane* case the Canadian Competition Bureau had a fairly easy time establishing a market for national coordination of propane supply because it led evidence that some customers preferred to deal with one source of supply across the country, as opposed to several sources in different regions. In contrast to courts in some other cases, the Canadian Competition Tribunal didn't require any evidence of cost analysis or any kind of backup to the customer preferences.

In *Oracle/Peoplesoft*, for example, the Government led fairly extensive evidence from a number of customers, including reports from their consultants, indicating that they had a real preference for high function software provided by the merging parties and one other firm. Some of these customers were quite sophisticated. They included senior representatives from Daimler Chrysler, Pepsi, the State of North Dakota and Greyhound Lines. Each of them said that they would not switch to anybody outside this group of three firms, even for a 10 per cent price increase. The Court was not persuaded on that point, notwithstanding this evidence, because the

---

[15] *Federal Trade Commission v Arch Coal, Inc; State of Missouri v Arch Coal, Inc (District of Columbia, Civil* Nos 04-534 & 04-535; DC Circuit, Nos 04-5291 and 04-7120).

[16] *United States and Commonwealth of Kentucky v Dairy Farmers of America, Inc and Southern Belle Dairy Co, LLC* (Eastern District of Kentucky, London Division, Civil No 03-206).

[17] *United States v Oracle Corporation* (Northern District of California, Civil No 04-807).

[18] *United States v SunGard Data Systems, Inc*, Civ Action No 01-2196 (DDC).

[19] *FTC v Staples, Inc*, 970 F Supp 1066 (DDC 1997).

[20] *Canada (Commissioner of Competition) v Superior Propane Inc* (2000), 7 CPR (4th) 385 (Competition Tribunal).

judge said that, for these sophisticated customers to have reached that conclusion he would expect some analysis of the costs of using some of the wider group of firms which had not exactly the same software but offered a similar set of features and capability in combination, or which didn't have quite the same reputation but nevertheless had similar products.

In the words of the Court, unsubstantiated customer apprehensions are not a substitute for hard evidence and what customers do is more persuasive than what they say. However, a fundamental point was that Oracle had its own evidence that other large customers, including the United States Department of Justice itself, had used firms others than the three the DOJ was asserting in this case were a market unto themselves.

Similarly, in the *Arch Coal* case the Government led evidence that the utility customers which purchased coal were quite concerned about this transaction. Again, however, the Court discounted the evidence of customer concerns, citing a text by Areeda[21] to the effect that the subjective testimony of customers is the least reliable evidence. That comment seems quite harsh to me and not accurate on a practical basis.

Finally, in *Sungard* both sides filed over 50 customer statements on whether they were or were not willing to switch to suppliers outside the Government's alleged market in the event of a small but significant increase in price. The Court there found that it was faced with evidence on both sides, so it did not have enough evidence to find one way or the other, which amounted to a finding against the Government, given its burden of proof.

I think the point is that while customer complaints are certainly a necessary precondition to any successful challenge by the Government authorities, it is not sufficient to meet the burden of proof to just have some competing customer statements. There has got to be some evidence beyond just the stated preference of the customers to back up their expressed willingness to either switch or not switch in a particular case.

Another key factor in contested cases is internal corporate documents. It is hard to imagine a contested case without at least some bad documents. The real question is what does it take for those bad documents to be fatal.

The *Southam* case in Canada involved an acquisition by Southam, which owned both the daily newspapers in the City of Vancouver.[22] It was effectively buying most of the community newspapers in the area. The Competition Bureau pointed to evidence, including internal documents and

---

[21] *FTC v Arch Coal*, 329F Supp 2d 109 at 145, citing 2A Areeda, et al, *Antitrust Law*, 538b, at 239.
[22] *Canada (Director of Investigation and Research) v Southam Inc* [1995] 3 FC 557 (CA) and [1997] 1 SCR 748.

a study by a consultant prepared for Southam, indicating that the daily papers were losing business to the community papers and the community papers were a competitive threat. There was some fairly colourful language about how the community newspapers were 'eating our lunch'.

Notwithstanding that evidence, the Tribunal found that the internal documents themselves were not enough to demonstrate that the two types of newspapers were in the same market. The Tribunal held that there was a need to show that the substitution or the movement was more than one way—more than just from the daily papers to the community papers. The Tribunal also found that such one-way movement was not a reaction to a change in price, but more of a change directed towards a different type of advertising, notwithstanding that physically both daily and community newspapers carried the same type of relevant advertising (multiple product and price print ads). The community newspapers were qualitatively different because they had denser coverage over a smaller area, as opposed to the daily papers which were covering a much wider area, but less densely.

This case went all the way up to the Supreme Court of Canada, which commented with regard to the internal documents to the effect that, just because a company thinks something is so, does not make it so, and a belief by a company does not establish that belief as a legal fact.

I am going to digress a little on this case because it directly involves the issue of the standard of review. This aspect of the decision was appealed to the Federal Court of Appeal. The Federal Court of Appeal held that the Tribunal had erred in requiring evidence of price sensitivity and held that, as a matter of law, the two types of newspapers were in the same market because they were functionally substitutable and there was evidence from corporate documents of inter-industry competition between daily and community newspapers. So the Court found a legal error by the Tribunal, overturned that part of the decision, and sent the case back to the Tribunal.

But on further appeal to the Supreme Court of Canada, the Court held that the market definition test was a question of mixed fact and law and that no factor should be given decisive sway. The Court further decided that it was not unreasonable for the Tribunal to find as it did in looking for price sensitivity before it found two products to be in the same market.

The standard that the Supreme Court adopted was one of reasonableness. The Court commented further that the reasonableness of a decision is based on whether, first, there is any basis in the evidence for the finding, second, whether the finding is contrary to the overwhelming weight of the evidence, third, whether there is a contradiction in the premises of the evidence, and fourth, whether an invalid inference has been drawn from the evidence. It was quite clear from the Supreme Court's decision that the Court itself would have found differently if it had been the trier of first instance. However, the Court determined that the Tribunal's decision was not unreasonable and let the Tribunal's decision stand.

Southam is an interesting comparison to the *Tetra Laval* case[23] where some documents were put forward about Tetra's internal assessment that the merger gave rise to an opportunity to take a leading position in the relevant market. The CFI made a similar comment that, just because Tetra believed such a dominant position was possible, didn't mean that was the case.

I think that is an appropriate result because, particularly in this day and age, companies generate a lot of documents and not all of them necessarily reflect considered views. I think it is appropriate for courts to recognize this. At the same time, it is often difficult to defend isolated documents that may be presented in the context of a court proceeding several years later.

In my experience, one category of documents that is becoming more and more significant is win/loss analyses in which companies provide or make records of jobs or accounts that they have won and lost and whom they have won them from or lost them to.

In the *Oracle* case, the Court signalled that win/loss documents could be given a very significant weight. One of the issues there was whether a company called Lawson was in the market with SAP, Oracle and Peoplesoft. The Court gave significant weight to Peoplesoft's win/loss reports which showed that Lawson had competed 27 times for enterprise customers, which was not far off the number of times that SAP and Oracle showed up in the reports. This was in contrast to the evidence of some of the witnesses who were called by the Government, claiming that Lawson was not in the relevant market. The judge somewhat graphically described this 'Lawson amnesia' on the part of such witnesses and put these documents forward as evidence that these witnesses had forgotten about the significance of Lawson.

Win/loss reports were also very significant in the *SunGard* case where they showed that the parties had lost more business to customers who were internalising their protection of computer data than to all of the other external competitors combined. An example of perhaps more decisive internal corporate documents was the *Staples/Office Depot* case where the parties' planning documents referred to office supply superstores, and not other types of office supply retailers, as their competitors. The internal documents also described markets which had only one superstore as 'non-competitive'.

---

[23] Joint cases C-12-13/03P *Tetra Laval AB v Commission* (judgment expected early 2005).

One more proposition I would suggest is that it is more difficult to demonstrate a product market in a product continuum. In the *Oracle* case, the Court had a lot of difficulty accepting the Government's proposed market definition, in part because its terminology was not common in the industry and was not widely recognised. The Court talked about the need to have articulable product market boundaries and commented that it is not enough to just show that there is something different between the parties' products. In fact, Oracle argued successfully that there has to be a break in the chain of a product continuum in order to identify and prove separate markets within the continuum.

Again, *SunGard* is another good example. Computer recovery systems fall on a continuum of different types of products that each meet a range of recovery time objectives. The Court said it was difficult to pigeonhole a group of services along this continuum of what it considered to be a nebulous product market into traditional antitrust principles since the customers had a very wide range of needs, and there was a wide range of available options.

The *SunGard* Court contrasted this type of product market to markets that involve discrete items like pens, baby food and loose leaf tobacco. Things you can pick up and touch and which are quite different from one another are easier to place in distinct relevant product markets for competition law purposes.

Another factor that has a significant influence on the standard of proof is the state of the market before the merger. In a number of cases, the Canadian Competition Tribunal has made a statement to the effect that, if the pre-merger market is highly uncompetitive, then almost any lessening of competition will be considered to be substantial, which is part of our test.

In the *Airtours* case[24] there are indications that the presumption of a competitive pre-merger market, or at least the absence of evidence that the market was anticompetitive before the merger, put a real focus on demonstrating what the merger changed in the marketplace.

Similarly in the *Arch Coal* case the merging parties' ability to demonstrate that the market was competitive before the merger undermined the Government's theory of post-merger coordination.

On the other hand, and this may be a bit of an anomaly, in the *Dairy Farmers* case, the merging parties had previously pleaded guilty to a bid-rigging scheme, but that wasn't enough to support the Government's contention of likely post-merger co-ordination in that market.

---

[24] Case T-342/99, *Airtours plc v Commission* [2002] ECR II-2585.

One practical factor is the presence of significant remaining competitors in the market. In the *Oracle* case, once the Court found that Microsoft was in the market as one of the other competitors beyond the three that the Government was trying to put forward as the market, it became very tough for the Department of Justice to demonstrate that the merger was anticompetitive. I guess it could almost be a legal principle that if you can demonstrate that Microsoft is one of your competitors then it is going to be tough to prove that your merger is anticompetitive.

Similarly in the *Schneider* case[25] the fact that ABB, Siemens and GE were among the competitors in a number of the national markets was a significant factor in the CFI annulling the EC's decision to block that merger.

A number of the cases that I have been referring to involved instances where the parties took some action before the court hearing to try to fix some of the problems that had been identified. In the *Arch Coal* case the parties had entered into an agreement to sell one of the coal mines acquired in the merger, and the Court took that into account in its analysis. In the *Tetra Laval* case the commitments put forward by the parties were accepted by the CFI for the purpose of its analysis. In the *Dairy Farmers* case, which I find curious, the Court took into account a conversion by DFA of voting shares in one of the two milk processors to non-voting shares, even though the conversion took place after the Government filed its challenge. DFA had a 50 per cent voting interest in each of the two main competitors. It converted one of those interests into a non-voting interest and entered into some contractual restrictions that limited the information flow to DFA. The Court analysed the transaction in that framework. I find this curious because it seems to me that, in the absence of an order or some Government consent decree, the parties could very easily have amended their contracts and changed the situation after the fact.

To wrap it up, I would make three points. First, the close scrutiny and sceptical analysis of the Government's position is not confined to the EU. We have seen close scrutiny on both sides of the Atlantic. Given that litigated cases are likely going to be close cases, we are going to see mixed success on the Government's part.

Secondly, generally speaking, I think the Government is going to have a better chance of success if its theory and evidence are more concrete to the extent that it is alleging product markets comprised of discrete articles, rather than product continuums, or to the extent that the case is based on

---

[25] Case T-310/01, *Schneider Electric SA v Commission* [2002] ECR II-4071 ('*Schneider*') regarding the Commission's Art 8(3) prohibition and case T/77/02, *Schneider Electric SA v Commission*, [2002] ECR II 4519 regarding the Commission's Art 8(4) divestiture decision.

control theories, as opposed to theories of influence. As well, unilateral power theories rather than collective dominance theories are likely more concrete and easier to prove.

Actual past conduct will be stronger evidence to meet the standard of proof than speculation by customers or others. Finally, where the market is already uncompetitive, it is going to be easier for the Government to make the case for a merger's likely adverse competitive effects.

NICHOLAS GREEN

John, thank you very much indeed. That is an extremely interesting presentation of comparative analysis. It demonstrates that judges quite rightly, the world over, are sceptical of the evidential skills of regulators. I am going to throw the floor immediately open to questions to either of the speakers.

DOUGLAS LAHNBORG (*Slaughter and May*)

I have a question for Judge Vesterdorf. There has been I think a major shift towards focus on facts since your three judgements where you have ruled on the Commission's decisions. As a practitioner, I certainly welcome that. I think you are less likely to be faced with some nouvelle theories on competitive harm, shall we say.

I find your description on how you assess the cases very interesting and you focus on primary facts. You say there is no marginal error for the Commission in relation to those primary facts. My question is exactly, what are those facts? No doubt they are highly relevant for the case. If you could give some concrete examples, that would be great.

JUDGE BO VESTERDORF

What are primary facts when we look into the cases? A primary fact would be 'what are the products in question'? I will be clear about what products we are talking about. Which products from the parties to the merger and which products from the other party? What is the present situation on the market as to market shares of this company, the other company and the third party's competitors out there. That is what we would call primary facts. It may well be that there will be litigation as to what are other primary facts. The Commission claimed that that is the market share and that of that company. It would be contested by the applicant who will have to verify it, and normally we would say that there is no margin of appreciation. Of course, if you think of the question is it the primary fact to be dominant or not? That is not necessarily something we would call primary fact because that will have to be deduced from a number of factors which are primary facts, such as the present situation in the market, in the product markets and geographic markets in question. These are what we would call primary facts and the other primary facts are who did what more precisely in the past.

What does the contract say more precisely? Who acquired what and what parts of the other companies? What are the functions of the merging parties, the various parties to the merger? All the things that we normally see in the beginning of the decision of the Commission, where they try to describe what the situation is today? What is this company about? Where are they active on the market? What kind of activity are they doing? What is the other party to the merger doing? What are the other companies' positions on the market?

Those are what we would call primary facts. This is where we need proof. When the Commission claims something, it must be clear that this is a fact. But once you go from the primary facts to assessing what is the market power of those companies on the relevant markets, that is an inference from a number of facts and this is at a point where we will certainly leave a certain discretion to the Commission, because it depends on the overall appreciation of all the relevant facts.

LUKE FROEB, *Federal Trade Commission*

I have a question for both the panellists. There was a question raised about customer testimony and whether it was representative of the customer population. What would both of you think about a formal scientific survey conducted by an independent marketing firm of the customers asking them what were the alternatives, or what would they do in response to a price effect? Would you consider that to be a good alternative to a kind of haphazard affidavit war that parties often get involved in?

JOHN BODRUG

I think that's an interesting idea, but I can just imagine the fight over the terms of reference for that survey. In the absence of agreement between the regulator and the parties, the tribunal or the court would be asked to rule on the validity of the underlying assumptions, and it may be difficult in such a survey to achieve the level of detail that the court appeared to seek from customer testimony in the *Oracle* case.

JUDGE BO VESTERDORF

That is something that we have seen in practice, in various types of cases.

Not only merger cases, but also in other competition cases. The parties have tried particularly in Article 82 cases, to convince us by presenting to us surveys done by individual third parties.

The problem is normally that the survey has been commissioned by somebody who is not necessarily the Commission, or if it is the Commission that has proceeded to some kind of independent survey it is not necessarily something that would be appropriate for the other parties, therefore contesting the conditions under which the survey was performed, the questions asked, the appreciation and so on. But we will look into all kinds of evidence that will be presented before us, all kinds of evidence. The only thing is that it has to convince us at the end of the day that the Commission could reasonably on the basis of those elements arrive at a certain result. And perhaps, in that context when I say 'convince the judge of something', much has been said about the *Tetra Laval* case, and in a certain part of the *Airtours* case, when we talk about 'convincing evidence'. I mean if the Court was supposed to decide on the basis of 'unconvincing evidence' we would be slightly surprised; we would normally say that we would need at least to be convinced that the evidence before us is sufficient to lead to a certain appreciation. So 'convincing evidence' is just another way of describing the fact that that party has succeeded in proving before us that their decision is the correct decision.

DAVID LAWSKY

May I ask you about comparative transparency? In the US—I don't know about Canada, maybe you can help us—with the exception of business secrets, all briefs are open, filings are open, evidence is open, verbatim transcripts are available. People argue that this gives private parties rights to check the consistency of government arguments and, more appropriately, to look and judge the judgments either way of what you do in the courts; the public can do that. Here you have a very different tradition. You have a tradition where hearings are open, the report of the hearing is available, but there is no transcript of the hearing and all written briefs are closed. I guess I'm asking if this continues to be a good idea and why?

JUDGE BO VESTERDORF

What we *do* have in our courts: you have a court hearing, you have a report of the hearing: that's what you hear, that's what you get, the result of those two elements at the end of the day. We think that that is preferable and necessary, not only and not least because, in many of these cases the briefs from the two parties, primarily from the companies involved, very often have to give information to the Court which is confidential information vis-à-vis third parties. So for that reason we would never accept it if the application presented to the Court were to be made public nor if the defence made by the Commission were to be made public. You have the decision which is contested and you have our judgment at the end of the day, and you can attend the Court hearing. I don't see any prospect of us changing that model of thinking in the future. One point of difference completely from our way of dealing with these cases and the way they deal with it, at least in the US, and to some extent in the UK, is that we don't know of the procedure of disclosure; this formal way of providing evidence. That's not something that we know about, to the extent that the parties can go and ask for disclosure by the other parties. What we will do—which is perhaps different from many of the national courts in Europe—is that the Community judges exercise a much more active role in the instruction of the case, in the examination and preparation of the case, which is why we often send to the parties before the court hearing a number of written questions—to the Commission, to the applicants, to the intervening bodies—asking them for concrete responses, either written or orally during the hearing, on specific points either of fact or of law or about various other elements. We also ask for the production of documents from the Commission and from the other parties if it is necessary in our opinion to appreciate and to judge the case in the correct way. This may be an approach perhaps not as effective, in the view of some, as what we call the purely adversarial procedure but I think it works reasonably well.

JOHN BODRUG

Briefly, the actual tribunal proceedings in Canada are pretty much open and all of the filings get put on the record, subject to confidentiality concerns, and in camera portions of the hearings. I think it works quite well at the end of the day in getting enough on the public record so that one can appreciate the factors that went into the decision. Obviously, from the parties' perspective there is more of their business laid open than they would prefer, but I don't think that there is any way to avoid that. A more pressing problem in Canada is—on just the Competition Bureau review level—anything up to a fully contested case is really not very transparent at all: the Bureau discloses less and less than they used to. Even consent proceedings in Canada are now just an agreement that is literally rubber-stamped by the Tribunal. We have moved away from even the Government having to file statements of material facts and explanations of how the remedy addresses the problem. That came about because the Competition Bureau lost a couple of consent cases where the Tribunal was not satisfied that the proposed remedies met the test of coherency or that they achieved their stated objectives.

JUDGE BO VESTERDORF

Perhaps one further comment on your question: you'll note—at least that is what we are often criticized about—and that is the length of our judgments. We do in fact take great pains in trying to explain extensively the motivation for the judgment, for the result, and why and on what basis and recalling what sort of considerations we had in arriving at the result of our judgment. This is why our judgments are as long as they are. We are, on top of that, of course, under the control of the Court of Justice.

My second observation in that respect: I think something for the future is still not possible, that is the fact we always pronounce our judgements as if all of the judges were in agreement as to the result. There is no dissenting opinion, that is not possible under the law, which is the case in many other countries. However, this may be useful when you have a court decision which is subject to appeal to a higher court. It might be useful for parties to know if this is a judgement on which all the five judges are uniformly in agreement, or whether it is really a 3:2 judgment. Or, if we have a three-judge composition, is it a unanimous judgment or a 2:1 judgment. That would be useful both for the parties and for the Commission to know: is this a unanimous decision, or is it not?

It is not something that we can do, and I am, perhaps, slightly disappointing those who might wish for it, but I do not see it happening, in the near future at least, simply because it has never been the tradition of the Court of Justice. Traditions are there to break from time to time, but whether I will see it in my lifetime, that is another question.

NICHOLAS GREEN

On the basis that everybody I can see is still awake, I am going to break my promise to the organizer, and I am going to allow two more very quick questions.

CARLES ESTEVA MOSSO (*European Commission*)

I do not want to reopen the debate that we have in front of the Court on the standard of proof, but nevertheless, let me ask a question to President Vesterdorf. On the policy implications that he suggested as standard of proof, merger control is about probabilities, rather than about certainties. Therefore if the standard is higher for one outcome in prohibitions, that for another outcome clearances in the long term, what will it be is favouring one type of errors in relation to another type of errors. That more mergers at the end will be cleared that were actually anticompetitive than the opposite. I wonder whether there is a good policy reason to favour this type of outcome. You have, I think, hinted at one that these would get it wrong and a merger that is anticompetitive would be cleared, we could always use other instruments, like Article 82. I think that would apply to some types of vertical or conglomerate mergers, but certainly would not be effective to prevent a merger leading to unilateral effects. It would be very difficult to prove excessive prices, and probably you would not even have dominance there.

Is there any other policy consideration that would plead in favour of favouring one outcome in relation to the other one—that would be my question.

JUDGE BO VESTERDORF

Now let me state clearly that you are right. I should have said earlier that, in my view, in the Merger Regulation there is no clear basis for claiming that there is a presumption either for legality or for illegality, for the one way or the other. What is clear is that the Commission must positively either find that the merger is to be cleared or that it should be prohibited.

What I said earlier, however, is that, in my own view, unless the Commission finds on the basis of the facts and its appreciation that this merger is very likely to lead to significant lessening of competition—unless it finds this—I think that normally one should say in that case 'we will clear it'. On the odd risk from time to time that you would have been clearing something that at the end of the day perhaps leads to some kind of lessening of competition, perhaps not very much lessening, if it was sufficiently important, one might use other remedies ex post. For example, if abuses occur, then the Commission can use Article 82 EC.

No, there are no other political reasons behind it. It is not even a political reason on my side, but simply a statement of fact. I think the Commission needs to feel certain *itself* that this is very likely to happen before it prohibits. If it finds it very likely, it should prohibit. If that is not the case, it should normally not take that decision, simply because then the intervention in the freedom of activity on the market is too large to accept simply on the basis that something is just likely. That is, in my view, the approach the Commission should have at the end of the day.

CLAUDIA BERG (*Linklaters*)

Individuals and companies, including merging parties, have a right to effective judicial protection. Do you think the right to effective judicial protection is a factor that mitigates in favour of actually a very tight standard of legal review, including perhaps the application of the law to the facts, as you described earlier?

JUDGE BO VESTERDORF

I think that the idea when it was decided to set up my own Court in 1988, with effect from 1989, was precisely to make sure that companies out there were to be assured that they had a court to which they could address themselves, which would deal with and decide on the basis of real examination of the facts of the case. Because it was a general perception, at least in those days in the 1980s, that the Court of Justice was on to such a workload that it simply couldn't do anything of this sort. It even kind of admitted that itself setting up this Court, so you should expect from our Court a thorough examination. This is what we are there for. Examining the facts, examining the law, but leaving the Commission a margin of discretion as to the economic assessments of the case.

Effectively if you could get that from our Court this should normally assure companies out there that if they feel convinced that the Commission's decision is wrong, they have somewhere to go. The problem for you companies out there today is probably that you have to wait far too long before you get a judgement from the Court, even though we have the expedited procedure, which we have only used on three or four occasions in merger cases, and which we will be very much at pains to use in the future because we are simply so overworked. This is a major problem. But when another big merger case comes in, if it is sufficiently important or urgent, we will just have to find the ways and means of doing it and thereby ensuring the legal protection that companies feel they need.

NICHOLAS GREEN

Ladies and gentlemen, thank you. If one extends one's time limit in Judge Vesterdorf's Court presently he turns the translation off. I am very grateful to both of them for having exceeded their time limit today.

Panel 6—Use (and abuse?) of Economic Evidence

Chair: Simon Bishop, *RBB Economics*

Speakers:
  Benoit Durand, *European Commission*
  Luke Froeb, *Federal Trade Commission*
  John Davies, *Competition Commission*

SIMON BISHOP

This is the last session of today and it is populated exclusively by economists, so it is therefore the most interesting session of the day. I think the fact that given that it is the last session and there are still a large number of people in the room, is in fact testimony that economics is playing an increasing role in competition law certainly on both sides of the Atlantic.

Today we have three economists from competition authorities. We have Luke Froeb, who is Director of the Bureau of Economics of the Federal Trade Commission, ie, the Chief Economist. Luke before that was an academic at Vanderbilt University, but before that he actually worked in the Department of Justice and is therefore very well qualified.

We have Benoit Durand from the Chief Economist team. He also has external experience before joining European Commission. Finally we have John Davies who is at the UK Competition Commission and again he had external experience in consulting before joining the Competition Commission.

BENOIT DURAND

Thank you Simon. Let me start this presentation with actually a quote from now ex-Commissioner, Mario Monti, who said in his last speech before leaving office on 28 October 2004, though he actually stayed longer than he thought, 'A major trend of this mandate has been to ensure that competition policy is fully compatible with economic learning.'[1] There is clearly, and this is undisputed, a growing use of economics in antitrust and merger control within the European Union. This can be seen in the activities of

---

[1] Speech by Mario Monti European Commissioner for Competition Policy, 'A reformed competition policy: achievements and challenges for the future', Center for European Reform, Brussels, 28 Oct 2004 SPEECH/04/477.

antitrust agencies in Europe, whether at DG-Competition or in many National Competition Authorities.

The growing use of economics is the result of a shift from what we call form-based rules to effect-based analysis. What does that mean? In the not so distant past, in some areas of antitrust, decisions were based on simple and clear rules. A priori there is nothing wrong with maximizing transparency of antitrust enforcement, this helps strengthen legal certainty. However, many of the simple rules were just too simplistic with potentially a high risk for false-positives. Today, competition policy is moving to a decision making process based on facts and the assessment of effects or likely effects.

I think there are several reasons behind this trend and I am going to at least cite three of them. First, there is a growing need to justify the benefits of competition policy in the political arena. I am just going to take one example. In the context of merger control, industrial policy considerations may come into the picture. As an enforcer you must explain why merger control has to be strict and effective. That is, you must demonstrate what the benefits to consumers are that justify prohibiting or altering a transaction. The term 'European champion' is becoming more and more fashionable, and this adds pressure on the regulator to explain to the politician and to citizens, why effective merger control is beneficial to society. And the use of economic analysis to assess the likely detrimental effect on consumer welfare of a merger should be helpful in that context.

The second reason that I think is important to explain the growing use of economics is the impact of the European Courts. There is no need to dwell on this aspect as we had ample discussions in the previous panel on the effect of the Court on the decision-making of DG-Competition. But the impact has been mostly felt in the field of merger control, where the Court has clearly addressed the need to increase the use of economic evidence.

Thirdly, there is also a growing need to work more closely with other jurisdictions, most notably with the federal antitrust agencies of the United States. More and more merger and acquisitions are notified on both sides on the Atlantic. Dominant firms are active both in the US and in Europe, and their conduct is scrutinised by antitrust agencies on both sides of the Atlantic. Although Europeans and Americans have different legal traditions, and even different appreciation of antitrust laws, economics can be a common language between the two sides. Increased communication and understanding help reduce the potential for contradictory decisions, and the use of economics plays a key part in making this work.

In my view, these three reasons are now part of what explains the growing trend for the use of economics in antitrust and merger control.

The shift to effect-based analysis is still resisted by some. We often hear 'economists will tell you whatever you want to hear; what we need are just clear and simple rules'. The first part of this assertion is simply not true. I am not saying this because I am an economist; I am saying this because a good economic analysis should follow established principles and scientifically proven methodologies. There is a high level of rigour associated with a good economic analysis. In principle, economists just don't say whatever they want to please their clients. There is a danger that some economists may abuse their position, but I think the rigorous application of economic thinking is a constraint to which the profession abides. Another related issue is that non-economists do not always understand what economists say. Economists need to communicate better and more effectively with non-economists and that is probably what this panel is all about. Often issuing guidelines help clarify the rule of enforcement, and what type of economic analysis the parties should expect.

The second assertion that I often hear is 'effects-based analysis is just too demanding'. It would be a circumvented way of raising the standard of proof. Again, I don't think that that is quite right. I think that form-based and effect-based are just different ways of tackling anti-competitive conduct. But it is not clear to me why form-based rules would be more effective, because less demanding than an effect-based analysis. Actually if you think a bit about some of the actual rules in antitrust, they do not always make a whole lot of sense from an economic perspective. But I am not going to debate that here. But worse, it is not even clear that actually form-based rules are very effective in deterring and catching anti-competitive conducts. If you take the *AKZO*[2]*'s* rules on predatory pricing, they are basically relying on the accounting books of the dominant company. A predation case is based solely on accounting evidence. First, it is not obvious to me that antitrust agencies are capable to decipher the accounting rules of a company to show that prices are set below cost. This makes me wonder about our ability to bring a case if all our analysis is based this tedious and difficult exercise. And secondly, I can't help asking where is the economics in all of that?

The growing use of economics in competition work has emerged in many policy documents of the Commission. For example, in the field of Article 81, the vertical guidelines[3] were issued a few years ago; more recently a new

---

[2] Case C-62/86 *AKZO Chemie BV v Commission* [1991] ECR I-3359, [1993] 5 CMLR 215.

[3] Commission notice—Guidelines on Vertical Restraints, *Official Journal C 291*, 13 Oct 2000, 1–44.

version of the TTBER[4] has seen the light. In the field of merger control, a recent change in the Merger Regulation established a new test, which was accompanied with the horizontal merger guidelines.[5] Finally, and for the future it is well known that DG Comp is currently reviewing its policy on Article 82.

So parallel to the growing use of economics, we have observed that competition authorities in Europe have acquired additional economic resources. This is certainly true in the U.K. At DG Competition the most important event in that respect was the creation in the summer of 2003 of the Chief Economist Office and the Chief Competition Economist's position. An academic has been appointed as the Chief Economist, Professor Lars-Hendrik Röller, and working under his direction is a small team of PhD economists. There are also a handful of PhD economists working within DG Comp who are not part of the Chief Economist Office. In terms of economic resources, there is a clear effort here to acquire the right human capital to perform the economic analysis.

What I am going to talk about now is the role of the Chief Economist Team. Actually there will be a paper by Lars-Hendrik Röller on the one year anniversary of the Chief Economist Office. Actually it is more than one year now, but he has been very busy. So I am drawing a bit on his paper here.

Just for you to know, we have different functions at DG Comp all related to the use of economics in competition policy or cases. First of all, one very important function is the support role of the team in various investigations. Members of the Chief Economist Office get involved in the more complex cases. This means that the economist assigned to the case helps the case team develop a coherent theory of harm. I am not saying that people at DG Comp could not establish an economically sound theory of harm before, but the economist provides an additional economic element that strengthens the analysis. When it comes to the use of empirical analysis, the economists also play a crucial role. It is very important that everyone involved in a case, whether on our side or on the parties' side, employ the proper method with sufficient rigour to empirically identify the effect of the conduct at issue, or the lack thereof.

The economists from the Chief Economist Office are embedded in the case team. However these economists report directly to the Chief Economist. We have a strange animal because economists do depend also on the Director

---

[4] Commission Regulation (EC) No 772/2004 on 27 Apr 2004 on the application of Art 8193 of the Treaty to categories of technology transfer agreements, *Offical Journal* L 123, 27 Apr 2004, 11–17.

[5] Guidelines on the assessment of horizontal mergers under the Council Regulation on the control of concentrations between undertakings, *Offical Journal* C 31, 5 Feb 2004, 5–18.

General. At the end of the day, the Chief Economist has a special position. He is a full member of DG Competition, yet he assists to the regular meetings with the Commissioner, where he can provide his opinion. Finally, the Chief Economist may provide a final advice that would be available to the College of Commissioners. But this depends on whether any economist from the Chief Economist has been involved in the case at issue, which is a decision that belongs to the Director General.

This was a brief description of the institutional environment in which the Chief Economist Office operates in the context of antitrust, merger and even state-aid investigations. Another aspect of the activities of the Chief Economist Office that is important is its involvement in policy discussion within DG Competition. The Chief Economist Office is currently involved in the Article 82 Review, and the Non-Horizontal Merger guidelines that Guillaume referred to in a previous panel. In addition, members of the team write internal notes to various services to actually provide an economic opinion on various competition policy matters. In sum the Chief Economist Office participates in the internal debate of DG Comp.

I am going to finish this presentation with the ways forward. I foresee at least two issues that will need to be addressed in the future to at least reduce the risk of abuse of economic evidence. Because the title was use and abuse and I haven't talked about abuse yet. But to abuse, you need first to use, and that is a recent development.

The growing use of economic evidence is undisputed. But it is not clear that DG Comp has presently all the resources to actually handle it all. I believe that there are still too few competition economists working for DG Comp, and the Commission will have to eventually address this issue, especially that of recruiting a sufficient number of qualified competition economists and econometricians to actually handle the growing use of economic evidence. Maybe DG Comp should take the example of the UK agencies that have been very active in recruiting economists in the last few years. Without enough specialised manpower in the economic field the risk that economic evidence gets abused in both direction is still present.

There is another concern. Effects-based analysis requires the collection of market data and information. In terms of investigating power, it is not so clear that DG Comp has all the tools necessary to retrieve the relevant information to build a case. It has been our experience that companies have been very reluctant to actually provide the data necessary to perform a good economic analysis. If you don't have the proper information, it is going to be very difficult to make an informed decision, and even more so to actually predict the likely effect of the conduct at issue. This might not be true for merger control because the merging companies usually have an incentive to provide all the information that will expedite the process, but it is definitely true in the context of Articles 81 and 82 investigation where often companies have a tendency to drag their feet. This issue will have also to be addressed if we want to continue moving towards this effect based analysis.

Luke Froeb

I want to open by saying that my remarks reflect only my own opinions, not necessarily those of the FTC, nor any of its Commissioners. I also want to thank Simon and BIICL for organizing this very interesting conference.

The United States is very different. The FTC has 75 PhD economists who report to me. There is an economics memo on every case that goes up to the Federal Trade Commission—this is the same for the Department of Justice. So you have economists as part of the case team working with the attorneys, but the economists also write a separate economics memo that goes straight up to the Commissioners. And I screen it, but I screen it for economic content. I don't care about legal content, in fact if the economists opine about the law or address issues of law, I will send the memo back down and say 'economists do economics; attorneys do law'.

So we may get memos that sometimes disagree as to conclusions, but the analysis is always different. We give them economic, not legal, analysis and that is very different than EC practice.

Having said that, it is always reassuring to come over and find out that the problems on this side of the Atlantic are exactly the same as those in the US. We struggle with the exact same issues that you struggle with. Some of the talks earlier in the vertical session and the merger session and Benoit's comments show this clearly.

We both face the same movement away from form-based analysis to effect-based analysis as Benoit indicated. Just a couple of years ago our Supreme Court legalized resale price maintenance. Basically, it said it wasn't per se illegal, but rather, one had to determine the effects of it. We viewed that as a huge victory.

Increasingly, the problem facing economists is how to draw inferences from the facts in a case about the effects of challenged behaviour—about whether it is anticompetitive. I like to use a simple taxonomy that place most of what we do into one of two categories. We draw inference from what I call 'experiments' and use what I call 'theory-based inference'. The nomenclature is not precise, but it will become clear what I mean with a couple of examples.

How do you determine effects? The natural experiment method says 'Let's find a natural experiment that mimics the effect of a merger or vertical restraint.'

By comparing a control group to an experimental group you can learn something about the merger or vertical constraint. The questions for the parties and for the courts and the decision makers are first, did you hold everything else constant or could some other change be responsible for the observed effect?; and second, how well does the experiment mimic the merger or vertical restraint?

An example, this is a relatively recent development in the United States, we have just brought a consummated merger case. The control group is the pre-merger period, and the experimental period is the post-merger period and you ask: did price increase? Did quantity decrease? Did quality change? You have to ask these questions and the big question is change compared to what? That is a rough natural experiment, so you might like to control for a demand shock or cost shocks that could have affected price, and so you use control areas, control cities, control markets, that weren't subject to the merger effect. There is jargon for this and I think you are going to see a lot more of it: it is called 'differences in differences'. One difference is between the pre and post merger periods, the other difference is between control and experimental markets.

This slide illustrates the natural experiment we constructed for the Marathon—Ashland joint venture in gasoline.

We had a 4 to 3 merger in that market. We looked at the price in Louisville before the merger and after the merger and we measured the price in Louisville relative to three control cities.

In the graph, we don't see much effect of the merger. There is a little spike here and a little spike here, but these are well within any kind of confidence interval you would draw for these data. The variance is so big that you cannot really see a merger effect.

Merger follow-ups, post mortems, are a very important part of our mandate as we try to figure out exactly what happened to determine whether we are in fact making correct enforcement decisions, that is, decisions that enhance consumer welfare. We all practice antitrust but does anybody actually see if it works?

It is an embarrassing question. We should do more of it.

The other kind of inference that you can use is theory-based inference, where you postulate a pro-competitive theory and an anticompetitive theory and see which theory best explains the evidence. A merger stimulation is an extreme example of this approach. In a merger simulation, we write down the model of price competition and then we estimate demand to measure the substitution between the merging firms' products. If the brands are close substitutes, you get a bigger merger effect. If they are not very close substitutes, you get a smaller merger effect.

The key thing about the theory-based inference for merger analysis is that there is a mapping from the facts of the case with the evidence which is how close the substitutes they are to. The policy question 'will this merger raise prices significantly?' becomes a question about demand substitution. Parties can raise questions about the evidence or about the theory that maps the evidence to the anticompetitive inference. There is no such mapping in the theory of vertical control, vertical restraints or abuse of dominance.

Let me talk about vertical restraints just very briefly and then I will finish up with some conclusions.

There is a growing body of evidence that vertical restraints reduce price, and induce the provision of demand–increasing activities by retailers.

Here are some examples. In the United States we have 50 different states each with their own laws. Now some states mandate that oil refineries can't own their own retail outlets. These are called vertical divorcement laws. We look at states with and without the vertical divorcement laws and try to hold everything else constant. When we do this, we find that the gasoline prices are about 3 cents a gallon higher in states that have these vertical divorcement laws. This is consistent with the theory that vertical restraints solve the double mark-up problem that was spoken about in the vertical session. There is also a nice natural experiment in the UK: following the beer orders—prices went up for beer.

What about using theory based inference to assess the effects of vertical restraints. The problem with following the same kind of inferential reasoning as we do in horizontal, is that there is no clear mapping from the facts of the case to the outcome for vertical restraints. Vertical theory hasn't given us that to date. There are many so-called 'post-Chicago' vertical theories, although I dislike the term, but these are only possibility theories. Vertical restraints can soften horizontal competition or make entry more difficult.

But there are also pro-competitive theories. And the problem is that you cannot tell them apart. Theory does not give us a way to distinguish the pro- from the anti-competitive outcomes and that is a problem when you are using theory-based inferences to determine the effects of a vertical restraint.

So what's an economist to do? If you are moving towards an effects-based legal standard, we can either search for screens to allow you to distinguish vertical restraints that have pro-competitive effects from those with anti-competitive effects. We heard a lot about conditions under which vertical restraints are necessary to harm competition. But necessary conditions don't tell us what is likely to happen. An example of that is pre-existing market power; an increase in market power in one market in order to leverage that market power of the second market. That is a necessary condition for the leveraging in theory.

But that is also a necessary condition for the elimination of the double marginalisation problem. If you have market power in one market, and you extend it to another market, another complementary market, a necessary condition for the elimination of double mark-up problem is market power. The more market power I have the bigger the efficiency I get from vertical integration.

So this tells me that the search for screens that are going to work in any but a few well-specified cases. So what are we going to do if we move towards an effect-based analysis of vertical restraints? Well, I have just one answer. Let's take a lesson from the empirical comments and look for good natural experiments. We can't use theory based inference, but we can use natural experiments.

Let's compare markets with a restraint and markets without a restraint. Let's compare and try to hold everything else constant.

There are two questions that immediately rise. How well does the natural experiment mimic the effects of the restraint of interest and did we hold everything else constant? Those are the evidentiary standards that the courts and the decision-makers should be concerned about.

Let me just say one more thing. The European Commission has been much more successful than the United States in exporting its antitrust regime around the world. The reasons for that are many, but the US law is itself very brief and there is a body of case law that supports the interpretation of the brief statutes. It is very difficult to export case law. Instead, they are importing the EC antitrust laws, because these laws actually tell you what is legal and what is not. But ironically, as we move towards a similar effects-based analysis, I predict it is going to become more difficult to export the EC antitrust laws.

So in that sense, it is really important that we export these laws responsibly. You have all heard this growing body of evidence that good government matters—that legal regimes, the ability to enforce contracts, encourage the movement of assets to higher valued uses, which is the wealth-creating engine of capitalism. Since our biggest and most valuable assets are companies, we have to be careful that newly developed economies, who are so eager to enjoy the benefits of capitalism, are not hindered by our laws.

JOHN DAVIES

My topic is the same as the other two speakers: the uses and abuses of economic evidence. I think that I have a problem with this title, in that I don't really know what it means. I don't know what 'economic evidence' means. I had a look around the Internet and discovered that the *Aberdeen Journals* case[6] in front of the Competition Appeal Tribunal made a lot of reference to 'economic evidence': particularly with reference to not accepting it and to accepting 'non-economic evidence' instead. But it seems to me that all they were really talking about there was statistics.

I would interpret 'economic evidence' as meaning the use of economics more generally in merger control. Even that is not a straightforward definition, because there is no really useful and generally good definition of 'economics'. I am not sure there is one of law either, but there certainly isn't one of economics.

If you look in the first-year economics textbooks, they will tell you that economics is the study of 'optimum allocation of scarce resources', or they might refer to something about the theory of choice. My work certainly doesn't seem to me to have anything to do with 'the optimal allocation of scarce resources'. To my mind there has only ever been one definition of economics that is sort of both sensible and also useful and true, and that was one from Jacob Viner about 50 years ago when he said 'Economics is what economists do.' So that is what I propose to talk about.

Defined like that, there is a lot of economics about at the CC these days. As we were saying this morning, our Chairman is an economist; our previous Chairman was also an economist. Among the forty or so Members of the CC, we once estimated that we had twelve economists. I don't want to talk too much about those Members, partly because those economists occupy a very wide range of different economics backgrounds from people who are economists by any definition—such as Paul Klemperer or Paul Geroski—to people who took an economics degree, but no longer particularly regard themselves as economists. But the other reason for not focusing on them is that they don't necessary regard themselves as being the economist on the group, any more than other Members act as the lawyer on the group, or the accountant on the group—they tend to just act as generalists within the group.

---

[6] Case No 1005/1/1/01 and Case No 1009/1/1/02 *Aberdeen Journals Ltd v The Office of Fair Trading*, 18 Sept 2003, [2003] CAT 21.

So let me talk about the CC staff instead. Among the staff, using my definition of economics, there is certainly a lot more economics than there used to be. It took 23 years for the MMC to get round to appointing its first staff economist in 1971, according to Stephen Wilks' splendid book, which I would recommend to all of you, which is great in all respects, except the title which is out of date: it is called *In the Public Interest.*[7] We still act in the public interest, of course, but it is no longer the official test.

So in 1971, one economist. Twenty-seven years later, in 1998, according to the same book, there were six economists. We are now six years on from that. As you probably know, the CC has grown. Generally the staff numbers have increased over those six years from 78 staff in 1998 to round about 150 today—approximately doubling in size. So of course, that number will have increased from six staff economists.

As of last Wednesday, when our newest recruit arrived there were 21 economists in the CC staff economists group and we are recruiting. By summer 2005, there may be 25 economists. And it is worse because there are three or four more economists elsewhere in the organization not actually under the control of the economics group. Finally, this year in 2004, we set up a panel of four academic advisers, to bring in from time-to-time, should we need them to advise us on particular aspects of economics.

So there has been a huge expansion of economics capacity. We have an economics capability in the CC that is totally different from the sort of court-based systems that we have been hearing a lot about.

All of the staff in the economists' team, apart from one or two temporary staff, are highly qualified. They have all got Masters degrees, about half of them PhDs, which is about the same as you will find in competition-specialising consultancies in the UK. They are the right sort of economists: they are competition specialists. When we recruit, we look for expertise in either industrial organization, or in econometrics, or preferably in both and we get them. In other words, these people are not rotated from general Government service, although many of the best of them do indeed have a public sector background.

As well, we have recruited staff in the last couple of years from academia, or from specialist competition economics consultancies: from NERA, from Lexecon, from Frontier Economics (not from RBB Economics—yet!). But most of all, we take some of the best Masters course graduates around and we train them up.

---

[7] Stephen Wilks 'In the public interest: competition policy and the Monopolies and Mergers Commission' (Manchester University Press Manchester 1999).

Has it made any difference? If it has, is it just an arms race? I think that is possibly something that we can discuss among the panel. For now let me put in a little bit of context by comparing to other groups. We have got 21 economists in the economics team, there are three other groups of so-called specialists who do most of the analysis on mergers cases—accountants, business advisers and lawyers. There are 11 accountants, 10 business advisers, one who is an economist anyway and—I am afraid—just nine lawyers.

So I have two conclusions to draw today. First, when you are talking to the Competition Commission, you are talking, to a greater extent than ever before, to economists. Not exclusively—and we are not in the majority—but more people that you are talking to are economists than come from other professional backgrounds and that has to affect the way that *we* behave and the way that we behave *towards parties* that come before us.

This means for example, that we would expect to see (and if we don't see it, we will calculate it ourselves) significance levels for any sort of statistical evidence that is put in front of us. So if we get a graph that is supposedly showing some sort of relationship between two variables, we will say 'what is the statistical significance of that relationship?'. We would expect to get an answer. Of course, you can send us the data and we will do it for you, but then you lose control of the process and lawyers tend to prefer not to do that.

Secondly, we ourselves have a lot of economics capability. I don't think people will necessary have seen the full effect of that yet. I think it goes across our three types of inquiry: market inquiries, regulatory inquiries and mergers. I don't want to talk about market inquiries because there haven't been any completed yet under the Enterprise Act. Regulatory inquiries— there haven't been any for some time. On mergers, it seems to me that we haven't yet fully used that capability. Some of the cases we have had this year perhaps haven't been terribly amenable to it—the data has not always been available. But also we are still learning to use this capability effectively and I think the parties to enquiries are still adjusting to the fact that the CC has much more economics capability than it used to.

I think you can expect to see an increase in the amount of technical analysis on merger inquiries, but most of all I think a lot of what economists do is not hard-core economics, but just a way of thinking. If I can quote John Maynard Keynes 'The theory of economics does not furnish a body of settled conclusions immediately applicable to policy. It is a method, rather than a doctrine. An apparatus of the mind, a technique of thinking, which helps its possessors to draw correct conclusions.'

We are in a totally different position from the European Commission and from what happened in America before, in that we are not moving from form based to effects based merger control. We have always had effect-based merger control, but the effect is question used to be upon 'the public interest'. Now it is upon competition. So we are moving to a more precise economic definition of the effects and there is more potential for technical economic analysis in a case.

I want to finish by thinking about two potential problems that might occur in the future. The first is that we fail to make use of these techniques. This has occasionally happened in the past. People put things into the CC or to other Competition Authorities who then say 'Oh, I don't want to think about this. This is much too complicated'. I don't think that should happen. It is essential that we don't lack the capability to deal with whatever the parties wish to send, no matter how complex and that we also have the willingness to engage over those arguments.

Secondly, I think there is another danger, which is that if we become technocrats, we could lose the benefits that we get from having our members. and the benefit of having a very open process in which the parties themselves get direct access to the Commission. What we must avoid at all costs, I think, is what you might call 'contracting out' where it ends up just being a technical debate between two teams of specialists with no real connection to the people who are really interested in the case. The parties—the parties that you represent—are the ones whose business interests are directly affected and, on the CC side, the members themselves who are the ones who have to put their reputations on the line in order to judge the merger.

How can we avoid these pitfalls? Well we have to be able to have a debate on economics during the process. It is not clear to me that hearings are necessarily the best forum for that. Paper exchanges work well, but in merger cases in particular there may not be time for that. I personally think that it would be interesting to explore more the use of direct contact between staff at the CC and economic specialists from the parties, in order to have an economics debate in an atmosphere that perhaps is not as charged as a hearing. But I think we haven't yet got the answer to how we are going to deal with the increasing potential technicality of merger control, while retaining the virtues of the UK system and that might make a good topic for discussion.

SIMON BISHOP

I am in the unusual position of actually putting questions to competition authorities, so I am just going to have two questions and then throw it open to the floor. The first one is something which John has just raised. How should authorities respond to the economic evidence submitted to it? In particular, how do you go about deciding whether this is a good submission or a bad economics submission?

John Davies

I think the most important thing with any economic submission is to be able to debate it and in order to debate it you have got to be able to reproduce it. This is particularly true of empirical analysis. (Also in a way with the theory: we have got to be able to think about how any cited papers affect the question that is actually on the table.) But with empirical analysis, I think the best thing is if the CC economists can reproduce it. If for some reason that is deemed impossible, perhaps because there is some huge database which is just impossible to transfer, then at the very least, it should be possible to ask questions of it: 'suppose you had done this differently, suppose you have done that differently, what would be the effects on the outcome?'

I was thinking about this the other day. John Fingleton was talking about the role of expert witnesses, and we just don't use economists as expert witnesses. We might take expert witnesses from other disciplines who come along and say 'because I am an expert in this, this is what I say and so therefore, you should believe it', but with economists, we always say: prove it.

So I think we want to have the ability to continue to say 'prove it' and to test and to probe. And that just reinforces the need for a submission to be the *start* of a process, rather than to be some sort of self-contained answer in itself.

Luke Froeb

We don't accept empirical evidence at the FTC unless we can reproduce it. We demand all the code and the data that generated the evidence or we don't look at it. That is absolutely critical. If you give us an economic argument, the benefit of economics is that it makes you put your arguments on the table where everybody can see them and object to them and you see exactly how you get from the facts of the case to the conclusion—that it is either anticompetitive or pro-competitive. You can examine each of the links of logic, be it the theory or the evidence that goes into the theory to reach the inference about the effects of it. So if we can't reproduce the analysis, we just don't listen to it.

Benoit Durand

I just want to add one thing. I thoroughly agree with what John and Luke just said. But actually I will say that interestingly enough in the Commission, we go even further than this because we actually let the parties look at what we do. That is not very common. You are not going to go to DoJ or FTC and ask them what is it you are doing. Please give me your program code and your data. That is not going to happen.

Interestingly, we actually did this and we let economists—actually, Simon on one occasion—come on site, come to the Commission and look at what the economists at DG Comp have done. So what I think we are playing the game of transparency, we like the parties to also play that game and give us their analysis, and I think at the end of the day, this is the best way to proceed because ultimately the debate will probably lead to the correct inferences.

SIMON BISHOP

My second and final question is what would you say to lawyers and officials who doubt the value of economics in competition law?

LUKE FROEB

We fought that battle in the 1980s and we won.

The US laws are very brief. They just outlaw everything that's anticompetitive and they have changed radically in interpretation over the years. What's anti-competitive? You ask an economist and he will tell you himself. It is absolutely critical.

JOHN DAVIES

Yes, I think I agree. One of the things that came up in my Internet search for definitions of economics bizarrely was 'economics is inevitable'. I just think that what merger control does in an effect-based regime, as we have always had in the UK, *is* economics. It was economics before the Enterprise Act as well. There is going to be an economic assessment of the merger. If that is done by people who are not economists, then they may not realise that they are doing economics, but probably they are.

So the economics is going to be done by someone and the question of whether it is done by an economist is perhaps secondary. That is a serious point. Economics is a way of thinking. It does seem to me that some of the more expert lawyers around do have that way of thinking. For them it would be a question of the degree to which they actually wanted to do that themselves or to contract it out. But economics is going to happen in the merger control, there is no doubt about that.

BENOIT DURAND

Just a quick comment on your very biased question—before, economic submissions at the Commission would go to the bin. Then, they used to ask the economists to give them three reasons to kill that economic analysis. Now we are trying to tell people who don't believe in economics that it is very helpful. Economics is going to help you to bring cases and bring a good case when we have a very strong economic theory of harm. I think it is very important at the agencies that economists actually play that role. To convince the legal community that actually we are not here to kill cases, and not to say whatever you are doing is wrong, but actually to help them bring cases, make the case more convincing and if we do that, we will win that battle and I think we will.

SIMON BISHOP

There is a rare occurrence of three economists agreeing. Let me throw it open to the floor for questions.

ANNE RILEY (*Shell*)

What are you going to do as economists to persuade businesses leaders, as opposed to just their legal advisers? Economics is the way to go in antitrust terms, because it is quite often as an in-house lawyer a bit of an uphill struggle to persuade our clients to use economists. Of course I am convinced, but what are you going to do to get my bosses convinced?

BENOIT DURAND

Actually, I think this is a very relevant question and actually this is going to be your job because it is really surprising sometimes how reluctant these companies are to apply economic analysis in antitrust proceedings. I have had first hand experience of that. I think by being at these antitrust authorities and by saying well you need to submit economic analysis because we are going to do economic analysis, then they will have to realize that it is not by lobbying that they are going to get off the hook but by actually performing the real analysis, the economic analysis, to convince the agencies that actually they have no case and their merger is pro-competitive. I think this is going to be more your job than ours!

LUKE FROEB

I think that is partially a reflection on the irresponsible behaviour of some of the economists. There is a principal-agent problem between any consultant and any economist. The economists know a lot more about what they can do and they will run off if you don't rein them in. We see that in cases where people spend hundreds and thousands of hours estimating demand and it's not getting any better estimates and you just have to pull the plug at some point. I think one of the things you can do to your economists is to ask them before they go off on a binge, 'What are you trying to do? And let's suppose you knew it. Suppose you didn't have to estimate demands. Suppose you knew what demand was. How would that help me?'. So start at the end and work back. Put some discipline on your economists.

As attorneys hiring economists, you have got to communicate with your economists. Don't let them run a-muck.

JOHN DAVIES

I agree with all of that and it just points out from the other side the problems that I was talking about. Economics, even in its most technical form, somehow has to be fully integrated into the process and the essentials of it need to be appreciated by people whose interests are at stake—and those are typically not the economists!

Our Chairman is fond of saying that one of the virtues of the Competition Commission is that when parties walk into a hearing room and they have got the Chief Executive or maybe a Finance Director or someone like that, then facing them across the tables are the members of the Competition Commission: they see people who look rather like themselves. I think that is an important virtue of the system and we must not lose that as we become more technically competent. And I think that is a challenge for both sides. So yes, I think that's your problem!

LIAM COLLEY (*Price Waterhouse, Coopers*)

A question for Luke really. Luke, I had the pleasure of listening to you speak twice in the last four days. You haven't spoken very much about merger simulation, which is an area I know that you are very familiar with. I just wanted to ask you a question about merger simulation and the efficiency defence where as you know, on this side of the Atlantic, there is an allegedly new found acceptance in theory of these arguments. It seems to me that the merger simulation techniques, their key strengths really is that they allow you to answer the question 'Have I got enough efficiencies?' so there are a whole bunch of questions around merger specificity and whether efficiencies will be passed on, so on and so forth. You will still be left with the question 'Have I got enough?' It seems to me that simulation really is quantitatively the only show in town. So can I just ask as an observation, questions arising from that, I would be very interested to hear your perspective on, in a sense, who is winning on your side of the Atlantic, in terms of the lawyers and the economists? If the courts are continuing to be sceptical, what is happening below the water-line at the authorities in terms of efficiencies and how are these arguments playing out and how is merger simulation being used and is there wide-spread use of it by the authorities by indeed by merging parties?

LUKE FROEB

In the States, that is a very good point. I don't want to leave you with a statement that gives some kind of impression that economists run the show. One of my colleagues, Bobby Willig, says that never before has economics been as important as it is right now, but never have economists been as unimportant as they are right now. That is because the attorneys are able to develop and articulate the economic arguments by themselves, without the use of an economist.

One area where I think there is a lot of potential to be had is that the question is really 'How do you do cost–benefit analysis for the mergers, unless you can show what the merger is going to do, what is it going to take to off-set the effects of the merger in terms of efficiencies? Unless you can do that kind of balancing, there is no way to judge whether or not the efficiencies are sufficient. My former boss, Tim Muris, who knows a lot about economics, says 'I have never seen a close balancing case. I have never seen a close case'. Although in the United States, the FTC recently blocked the baby food merger. In the United States, there were three firms in the market: one giant firm, and two small ones. The two small ones wanted to merge. One had a good factory and one had the good recipes so there was a natural obvious way to take account of the account of the synergies, but it was a 3 to 2 merger and the FTC blocked it. Since we blocked it, the smaller firm has lost ten points of its shares, the larger company has gained ten points of market shares. That is the kind of post-mortem to do regularly to figure out if we are doing the right thing. We have this conceit that dictates that we know what is going on, but do we really? We are often asked a lot to help other countries to develop their antitrust laws and to avoid being the ugly Americans telling them this is what you're to do we just tell them the process. Whatever you do, set up a feedback mechanism so that you can check on whether your decisions were good—what happened? Did you make the right decisions? Following up on our enforcement decisions is a large part of the mission at the FTC and that gasoline retrospective that I showed you was part of our mandate. Let's go back and look at the specific cases.

That's our kind of answer to the transparency question. We are not as transparent as the EC is on every case, but we are transparent in trying to provide data and to go back and look at cases where we think the natural experiment is a good one, where we can learn something from the outcome, we do publish it.

Efficiencies are one of these areas where there is the chicken and egg problem. Nobody comes in with efficiencies defences because they believe we don't take them seriously, we don't know how to evaluate them, we don't know how to balance them, and so they don't come in with them and so we don't see them, so we don't.

So it's a problem and we're actually trying to figure out how best to address that. Whether it is post-mortems like 'Let's look at what happened on the *Heinz/Beech-Nut* case.[8] Did we do the right thing? Or non-traditional efficiencies. When I was in private practice, before I came to the FTC, I worked on the *Chex/General Mills* merger.[9] General Mills is the large ready-to-eat cereal manufacturers in the US, bought the four letters C-H-E-X. They didn't want the recipe, they didn't want the production equipment. They just wanted the four letters. Because they were a better brand manager than Ralston, who sold Four Letters to General Mills for $300 million.

The rationale was 'Hey, we're a better brand manager. We brought out Cheerios. We brought out Honey Nut Cheerios. We can do the same thing for Chex. So they claimed that they were going to be able to realize all these post-merger efficiencies and they did. They bought out the brands. They brought out Honey Nut Chex. All these brand extensions. How do we take into account that kind of efficiency? It is a very interesting, difficult question. It is an open question and we are actively trying to figure out the answer. We don't have the answer.

BENOIT DURAND

About merger simulation. At least from our end, we have used it sparely, on very few occasions. Of late I can name at least one big merger, the French case *Lagadère/VUO*, in which the merger simulation was actually conducted by two outside economic consultants, Jérôme Foncel and Marc Ivaldi. The experience was relatively helpful but not the whole case was based on that merger simulation. There were many other aspects of the cases that were problematic, but at least for some of the competition problems that were identified, the merger simulation was very helpful at least in

[8] *FTC v Heinz HJ Co* No 00-5362, US DC Circuit Court of Appeals, Decided 27 Apr 1001.
[9] File No 961 0101 *In the Matter of General Mills, Inc.* FTC Decision of 26 Dec 1992 <http://vvv.ftc.gov/os/1996/12/genermil.pdf>.

identifying the competitive constraint. The exercise also helped figure out what would be the appropriate remedies.

So we included the simulation results in the decision, but I would like to emphasize that this was certainly not the only evidence that the Commission used in its decision. I think you should not expect decisions from the Commission to be based only merger simulation. I would really doubt that.

GERALD FITZGERALD (*McCann Fitzgerald*)

Would the economist like to say what they see as the role of the lawyer?

BENOIT DURAND

You should ask my colleagues. First of all, we are so few that we still need lawyers, but that is obviously not an answer to your question. The lawyers are still very important. Obviously competition policy is legally grounded and we need to work hand in hand with the lawyers. It is not that the economists are taking over and pushing the lawyers to the side. I don't view it in this way.

LUKE FROEB

In the US, the economists have won the war and the lawyers win the battles. If you look at any individual case, it is still the attorneys who dominate. For example, if you look at the case memos. Because of the way the Federal Trade Commission is organized, we have to write opening memos and closing memos, so we have a fairly complete documentation about what the lawyers recommended and what the economists recommended and what happened. By and large, when there is disagreement the lawyers typically win. So that is what I mean when I say the lawyers still win the battle.

But the economists help them organize evidence, help them present the evidence, make sure the arguments are correct. Going back to what Bobby Willig said, I think the attorneys are getting incredibly sophisticated in terms of articulating economic arguments and if you can articulate good economic arguments, maybe you don't need economists.

JOHN DAVIES

Various CC lawyers in the audience seem to be fixing me with a steely stare, so I won't suggest what they should be doing. On the parties' side, in the UK we haven't suddenly moved from form-based to effects-based. As far as the CC is concerned, even under the Enterprise Act, there has never been an enormous amount of really legal argument, because we don't put much weight on precedent. There are only so many times you can debate the meaning of the word 'substantial'.

But what lawyers do, and what they have always done, is martial the evidence. I don't like this distinction I started with between 'economic' evidence and all the other evidence: there is only evidence. Good and bad economics is the same as good and bad evidence. When something is bad economics and something is bad evidence, it is usually for the same reasons. It might be rather harder for a non-technical person to see why the bad economics is bad evidence, but it is usually for the same sort of reasons that any other piece of evidence would be bad evidence. I think that lawyers try to sort that out on behalf of their clients, and I think they should continue to do so.

Standard of Proof in Merger Cases: Reflections in the Light of Recent Case Law of the Community Courts

Judge Bo Vesterdorf*

I. INTRODUCTION

Recent litigation in the field of merger control has brought the standard of proof issue not only into the spotlight of Community law but even outside the esoterical world, which we Community lawyers inhabit, into the mainstream press.[1] A string of merger judgments in 2002 has, thanks to the accidents of the litigation calendar, seen the Court of First Instance (CFI) annulling, one after the other, three high-profile Commission merger prohibition decisions in the cases of *Airtours v Commission*,[2] *Schneider Electric v Commission*[3] and *Tetra Laval v Commission*,[4] as well as one Commission authorization decision in the case of *Lagardère and Canal+ v Commission*.[5]

Less high-profile, in terms of press coverage, but equally intensive merger litigation continued unabated in 2003, when the CFI and the European Court of Justice (ECJ)[6] delivered no fewer than seven merger judgments in

---

* President of the Court of First Instance of the European Communities. The views expressed are entirely personal and do not necessarily reflect the views of the CFI; they endeavour to set out reflections on the law as it stands on 1 Dec 2004. I would like to thank Kyriakos Fountoukakos, *référendaire* in my chambers, for his assistance with the preparation of this paper. This is a slightly edited version of an address given at the Third Annual Merger Control Conference organized by the British Institute of International and Comparative Law, London, 6 Dec 2004.

[1] See, eg, P Meller 'Court Ruling Muddies Merger Scene in Europe', *The New York Times*, 26 May 2004, available at <http://www.nytimes.com>; D Dombey 'Monti Given Small comfort over Tetra', *Financial Times*, 26 May 2004, available at <http://www.ft.com>; D Lawsky 'Week of Tests for EU in European High Court', 23 May 2004, available at <http://www.forbes.com/newswire/2004/05/23/ rtr1381344.html>.

[2] Case T-342/99, *Airtours plc v Commission* [2002] ECR II-2585 (henceforth *Airtours*).

[3] Case T-310/01, *Schneider Electric SA v Commission* [2002] ECR II-4071 (henceforth *Schneider*) regarding the Commission's Art 8(3) prohibition and case T-77/02, *Schneider Electric SA v Commission* [2002] ECR II-4519 regarding the Commission's Art 8(4) divestiture decision.

[4] Case T-5/02, *Tetra Laval BV v Commission* [2002] ECR II-4381 regarding the Commission's Art 8(3) prohibition (henceforth *Tetra Laval*) and Case T-80/02, *Tetra Laval BV v Commission* [2002] ECR II-4519 regarding the Commission's Art 8(4) divestiture decision.

[5] Case T-251/00, *Lagardère SCA and Canal+ v Commission* [2002] ECR II-4825.

[6] Hereinafter references to both the ECJ and the CFI will be to the 'Community judicature', 'Community courts' or simply 'Courts'.

the cases of *BaByliss v Commission*,[7] *Philips v Commission*,[8] *Petrolessence and SG2R v Commission*,[9] *ARD v Commission*,[10] *Moser v Commission*,[11] *Verband der freien Rohrwerke eV v Com- mission*[12] and *Cableuropa v Commission*.[13] 2004 saw the hearings in *GE/Honeywell*,[14] the delivery of Advocate General Tizzano's Opinion in the *Tetra Laval* appeal,[15] and the CFI's judgment in *MCI v Commission*[16] which annulled the Commission's prohibition decision. The CFI's judgment in *GE/Honeywell* and the ECJ's judgment in *Tetra Laval* are still pending and are, no doubt, widely anticipated by anyone remotely interested in this area of the law.

In the 2002 annulments in *Airtours*, *Schneider* and *Tetra Laval*, the CFI engaged in what has been called severe criticism of the Commission's analysis, stating, for instance in *Schneider*, that 'the errors, omissions and inconsistencies . . . in the Commission's analysis [were] of undoubted gravity'[17] so as to 'deprive of probative value the economic assessment of the impact of the concentration which forms the basis for the contested declaration of incompatibility'.[18]

In the light of those judgments, legal commentators have been debating whether the CFI has intensified its judicial control and has raised the standard of proof required before the Commission can lawfully prohibit a merger.[19] The importance of having a clear standard of proof is of course

---

[7] Case T-114/02, *BaByliss SA v Commission* [2003] ECR II-1279 (henceforth *BaByliss*).

[8] Case T-119/02, *Royal Philips NV v Commission* [2003] ECR II-1433 (henceforth *Philips*).

[9] Case T-342/00, *Petrolessence and SG2R v Commission* [2003] ECR II-1161 (henceforth *Petrolessence*).

[10] Case T-158/00, *ARD v Commission*, judgment of 30 Sept 2003, not yet published in the ECR.

[11] Case C–170/02P, *Schluesselverlag J.S. Moser and others v Commission*, an appeal against the Order of the CFI in Case T-3/02, *Schluesselverlag JS Moser and others v Commission* [2003] ECR II-1473.

[12] Case T-374/00, *Verband der freien Rohrwerke eV v Commission* [2003] ECR II-2275.

[13] Cases T-346/02 and T-347/02, *Cableuropa and others v Commission*, judgment of 30 Sept 2003, not yet published in the ECR.

[14] Case T-209/01, *Honeywell v Commission*; Case T-210/01, *General Electric v Commission*. For the sake of completeness, note that 2004 also saw the delivery of the ECJ's judgment in Case C-42/01, *Portugal v Commission*, not yet published in the ECR, concerning a Commission decision under Art 21(3) of Merger Regulation.

[15] Case C-12/03P, *Tetra Laval BV v Commission*, Opinion delivered on 25 May 2004 (henceforth *Tetra Laval Opinion*).

[16] Case T-310/00, *MCI v Commission*, judgment of 28 Sept 2004.

[17] *Schneider*, point 404.   [18] ibid, point 411.

[19] See the following articles discussing this issue: D Bailey 'Standard of Proof in EC Merger Proceedings: A Common Law Perspective' (2003) 40 Common Market Law Review 845–88; E de la Serre and J Peyre 'Le contrôle du juge communautaire sur les décisions d'incompatibilité en matière de contrôle des concentrations: quelques perspectives ouvertes par les arrêts Schneider et Tetra Laval' (2003) 3 JCP, Cahiers de Droit de l'Entreprise, 1–8; E Coulon 'Le nouveau droit communautaire des concentrations: Le rôle du juge', *Chambre de Commerce*

undeniable. The Commission has actually appealed against the CFI's judgment in *Tetra Laval* on precisely this point in order to receive further guidance from the ECJ.

Turning to an analysis of the issue, let us first put the significance of the whole debate into context by quoting from the Commission's press release on the occasion of its appeal in *Tetra Laval*.[20] The Commission considers that the CFI's judgment in *Tetra Laval* 'raises problems of legal principle concerning several aspects of the work of the Commission in the field of merger control'.

In particular, the Commission believes that:

> the CFI has imposed a disproportionate standard of proof for merger prohibition decisions. As a result, it has upset the balance between the interests of the merging parties and the protection of consumers, which is provided for in the Merger Regulation. In this respect, the CFI has also exceeded its role, which is to review the administrative decision of the Commission for clear errors of fact or reasoning, and not to substitute its view of the case for that of the Commission.

The remainder of this paper contains personal reflections on this highly controversial and interesting issue. The precise issue is still pending adjudication by the ECJ in the *Tetra Laval* case[21] and, therefore, the following comments have to take into account this particular situation. To begin, we will address the definition of standard of proof and standard of judicial review and then go straight into the Community judicature's role in reviewing Commission merger decisions. The conclusion consists of personal reflections on the appropriate standard of proof in merger cases. We will not be looking at issues relating to types and treatment of evidence, eg internal documents of the parties, expert evidence etc, used in litigation before the Community courts.

Internationale, Paris, 20 Nov 2003; S Kim, A Vallery, and D Waters 'Judicial Review of Mergers' (2005) The European Antitrust Review; J Swift 'Judicial Control of Competition Decisions in the UK and the EU', Competition Commission Autumn Lecture, September 2004, available at <http://www.competition-commission.org.uk>; M Siragusa 'Judicial Review of Competition Decisions under EC Law', Competition Commission Autumn Lecture, Sept 2004, available at <http://www.competition-commission.org.uk>; M Collins 'The Burden and Standard of Proof in Competition Litigation and Problems of Judicial Evaluation' [2004] ERA Forum, 2004–1; B Vesterdorf 'Certain Reflections on Recent Judgments Reviewing Commission Merger Control Decisions' in M Hoskins and W Robinson (eds) *A True European: Essays for Judge David Edwards* (Hart Publishing Oxford 2004).

[20] Commission press release of 20 Dec 2002, IP/02/1952, 'Commission Appeals CFI ruling on *Tetra Laval*/Sidel to the European Court of Justice'.

[21] The judgments in Cases C-12/03P and C-13/03P, *Tetra Laval BV v Commission*, are expected to be delivered in early 2005.

II. WHAT IS MEANT BY 'STANDARD OF PROOF' AND 'STANDARD OF JUDICIAL
REVIEW'?

It is useful to begin with some definitions. What is normally meant by standard of proof is: 'the amount of evidence which a plaintiff (or prosecuting attorney, in a criminal case) must present in a trial in order to win'.[22] In other words, the standard of proof is the threshold that must be met before an adjudicator decides that a point is proven in law.[23]

In national legal systems, notably in the common law systems, different cases require different standards of proof depending on what is at stake. Broadly, we can distinguish between two main standards of proof depending on whether a case is civil or criminal.[24]

In criminal cases, the standard of 'beyond reasonable doubt' is used: this is a very high standard which requires that a case be proven to the point that the adjudicator of the case (eg a jury) has no reasonable doubt that the crime was indeed committed by the defendant.

In civil cases, a much lower standard of proof is used, that of 'balance of probabilities' (also known as 'preponderance of the evidence'): this standard generally means that a party will win if he can show that it is more likely than not (ie there is at least a 51% possibility) that his contentions are true.[25]

Between the civil standard of 'balance of probabilities' and the criminal standard of 'beyond reasonable doubt', a multitude of in-between standards are conceivable.[26] In particular, we note that the civil standard of

---

[22] Quotation from 'Lectric Law Library's Lexicon', US on-line legal dictionary, available at <http://www.lectlaw.com/def2/s217.htm>.

[23] A related but distinct concept is that of the 'burden of proof', ie who has to prove what. In principle, under the Merger Regulation, it is for the Commission to prove that a merger is or is not compatible with the common market. However, the burden may be reduced or shift where there are certain presumptions or where it is up to the notifying parties to produce certain information in their possession such as information relating to efficiencies. In addition, it is to be noted that, in litigation before the Community courts, in principle, it is the applicant who bears the burden to prove that his case is well founded. On the distinction between standard and burden of proof see also Bailey above n 19, 849–50.

[24] See the recent judgment of the UK Competition Appeals Tribunal (CAT) in case 1001/1/1/01, *Napp Pharmaceuticals v Director General of Fair Trading*, available at <http://www.catribunal. org.uk> (henceforth *Napp*) at para 107, where the CAT, after reviewing English case-law in this field, found that 'under the law of England and Wales there are only two standards of proof, the criminal standard and the civil standard; there is no intermediate standard'. However, the CAT went on to say that '[w]ithin the civil standard . . . the more serious the allegation, the more cogent should the evidence be before the court concludes that the allegation is established on the preponderance of probability' (*Napp*, point 107).

[25] See <http://www.lectlaw.com/def2/s217.htm>.

[26] Indeed an express reference to a 'standard of high probability but less than the standard of proof in criminal matters' has been made by Webster J in the case of Sheirson *Kehman Hutton v Maclaine Watson* [1989] 3 CMLR 249.

balance of probabilities is sufficiently flexible so that its intensity can vary depending on the interests at stake.[27]

There is a third well-known standard: the standard of 'reasonableness' or 'manifest error': this is the classic judicial review standard used in administrative cases. Under this standard, a tribunal reviewing the legality of a decision taken by an administrative body will allow the administration a margin of discretion and will only annul the decision if it is 'unreasonable' or, in other words, if it is based on 'manifest errors of appreciation'. In English law, the classic test is the so-called 'Wednesbury unreasonableness' test, which is shorthand for an act or decision which is so unreasonable as to be an act or decision which no person or tribunal properly instructed and taking account of all but only relevant considerations could do or make.[28]

This third standard is, in our view, a standard of judicial review and not strictly speaking a standard of proof to be used when deciding on the merits of a case. Indeed, 'standard of review' is a different concept to that of 'standard of proof'. Standard of review is the standard that a reviewing tribunal or appellate court applies when reviewing the legality of a decision of an administrative body or lower tribunal. Another term which can be used to denote 'standard of review' is 'judicial control' (*contrôle juridictionnel*). A standard of review, as the term literally indicates, is therefore a standard used to review another person's decision; it cannot be a standard by which to decide a case at first instance on the merits or *de novo* on appeal.

It is therefore theoretically feasible to imagine that a particular statute obliges an administrative body to decide on a given case according to the high standard of 'beyond reasonable doubt' and then allows judicial review of that first instance decision by a tribunal according to a 'reasonableness' or 'manifest error' standard. In such a scenario, the administrative body, at first instance, would have to decide, on the merits, whether the case before it had been proven beyond a reasonable doubt. The reviewing tribunal, on appeal, would have to decide whether the administrative body's decision to conclude that the matter was proven beyond a reasonable doubt was a 'reasonable' decision not vitiated by any 'manifest errors of appreciation'.

---

[27] See *Napp*, point 107. The CAT further held that, since cases under the UK Competition Act involving penalties are serious matters, it follows that strong and convincing evidence will be required before infringements of the Ch I and Ch II prohibitions (the Art 81 and 82 EC equivalents) can be found to be proved, even to the civil standard.

[28] Quoted recently by the Court of Appeal in *OFT and other v IBA Health Limited* [2004] EWCA Civ 142, point 58. The role of a tribunal exercising judicial review has been defined as follows: 'It is important to remember always that this is judicial review of, and not an appeal against, the judge's decision. We can only intervene if persuaded that his decision was perverse, or that there was some failure to have regard to material considerations or that account was taken of immaterial considerations or that there was some material misdirection.' *R v Crown Court ex p MacDonald* [1999] WLR 841, 855 A–B.

Transposing this distinction to the field of EC merger control, the standard of proof is the standard inherent in the test enshrined in Article 2 of the Merger Regulation, ie the standard that is incumbent upon the Commission before it can adopt a lawful decision under the Merger Regulation. It is the standard that the College of Commissioners ought to have in mind on the day they adopt a decision authorizing or prohibiting a merger under the Merger Regulation. By contrast, the standard of review is the standard that the CFI ought to apply when it reviews the legality of the Commission's decision on appeal.

The above theoretical distinction between the standard of proof and the standard of judicial review has never been addressed explicitly in the Community courts' case law except, to a certain extent, recently in Advocate General Tizzano's Opinion in *Tetra Laval*. In this Opinion, the Advocate General makes a rather clear distinction between the standard of proof incumbent on the Commission before that institution can prohibit a merger under the Merger Regulation and the standard of judicial review, or, in other words, the role and bounds of judicial review which the CFI must respect when reviewing the legality of the Commission's decisions.[29]

Despite this theoretical distinction, it has to be acknowledged that the standard of proof and standard of review are, albeit different concepts, so closely linked as to become inseparable.[30] Thus, when a court applies a manifest error standard of review, it is inevitable that the standard of proof incumbent on the administration, whatever that may be, becomes much easier to meet, as the administration is allowed a significant margin of discretion in reaching decisions. Still, the intensity of judicial control, even under a classic judicial review standard, will fluctuate depending on the underlying standard of proof required by the administrative body having taken the decision on the merits, the context of the case, the complexity of the issues raised and so on.[31]

Given the uncertainty surrounding in particular the standard of proof issue, our focus is more on the standard of review and the role of the Community

---

[29] See *Tetra Laval* Opinion, points 71–89. In particular, AG Tizzano referred to the need to assess whether or not 'the Court of First Instance committed an error of law in applying *too rigorous a judicial review* or in claiming *a standard of proof too high* for decisions prohibiting mergers' (emphasis added). The appropriate standard of proof is then discussed by the learned AG in points 72–81, followed by a discussion of the bounds of judicial review in points 82–9.

[30] On this point, see Bailey above n 19, 850.

[31] That standards of judicial review fluctuate according to context is trite in English case law. See, eg, the judgment of the Competition Appeals Tribunal in Case 1023/4/1/03, *IBA Health Ltd v OFT*, point 219, quoting previous case law to the effect that 'the actual application of the orthodox principles of judicial review will of course vary according to the subject matter of the case' or 'in law context is everything'.

courts in reviewing Commission merger decisions than on the standard of proof inherent in the Merger Regulation. However, the following are personal reflections as to what the appropriate standard of proof in the Merger Regulation should be in the light of the features of that Regulation which will be discussed further below.

III. JUDICIAL REVIEW OF MERGER DECISIONS

A. An administrative system of merger control

When discussing issues such as the standard of proof and of judicial review, the first thing to bear in mind is that the EC Merger Regulation[32] establishes an administrative system of merger control. Unlike the system in the US and some Member States (eg Sweden), the EC merger control system is not a judicial system of control whereby the competition agencies act as prosecutors. This has important implications on the role of the Community courts and the standard of review they ought to apply.

In adopting the Merger Regulation, the Community legislator has entrusted the Community's executive body, the Commission, with the task of reviewing mergers falling within the scope of the Merger Regulation and of taking all the decisions necessary to establish whether or not such mergers are compatible with the common market.[33] The Merger Regulation establishes an *ex ante* system of administrative control with mandatory notifications of all concentrations with a Community dimension before their implementation. There are severe penalties for failure to notify and for unauthorized implementation of a merger.

The Regulation lays down precise procedures and imposes strict time limits within which the Commission must adopt its decisions. Roughly, the Commission has only slightly more than one month in order to decide whether a merger ought to be cleared in Phase I or whether to proceed to an in-depth Phase II investigation. In Phase II, the Commission has an additional period of about four months within which it must adopt a final decision authorizing or prohibiting the merger in question.

Under the Merger Regulation, the Commission enjoys wide powers of investigation and inspection, and significant enforcement powers such as

---

[32] Council Regulation (EC) No 139/2004 of 20 Jan 2004 on the control of concentrations between undertakings, OJ [2004] L 24, 1 (the 'new Merger Regulation'), replacing Council Regulation (EEC) No 4064/89 of 21 Dec 1989 on the control of concentrations between undertakings (OJ 1989 L 395, p. 1; corrigendum in OJ 1990 L 257, 13) (the 'old Merger Regulation'). References to the 'Merger Regulation' are to cover both the old and new Merger Regulation, and will be used in areas where no material changes have been made by the new Merger Regulation.

[33] See Recital 35 of the new Merger Regulation.

the imposition of fines and periodic penalties and powers to restore effective competition by ordering the undoing of a prohibited merger deal.

It is clear that the Community legislator has entrusted the Commission with the exclusive jurisdiction of taking those complex decisions in order to further the Community's policy in this field, which is a crucial cornerstone of the objective of undistorted competition enshrined in the EC Treaty and, thus, of paramount importance to the European economy as a whole.

B. Judicial review as part of the administrative system of merger control

The Commission's powers are not, however, unchecked. Far from it. Indeed, the Merger Regulation contains specific provisions on judicial review, the role of the Community courts and the procedure to be followed in case of annulment of a Commission decision. Pursuant to Article 21(2) of the Merger Regulation, the Commission's exclusive jurisdiction in the field of merger control is expressly 'subject to review by the Court of Justice'. In addition, Article 16 of the Merger Regulation provides the Community judicature with unlimited jurisdiction to review decisions under the Merger Regulation imposing fines on undertakings or persons. Article 10(5) of the Merger Regulation governs the procedure to be followed in case of annulment of a Commission decision by the Community judicature. In brief, the case is remitted to the Commission for re-examination on the merits in the light of current market conditions.[34]

Even in the absence of express provisions in the Merger Regulation, the Community courts' jurisdiction to review the legality of the Commission's decisions in the field of mergers derives directly from Article 230 EC, which gives them competence to review the legality of acts adopted by the institutions, including the Commission, and which allows any natural or legal person to seek the annulment of a Commission decision which is addressed to that person or is of direct and individual concern to it.

The Community courts' case law has sufficiently clarified which acts of the Commission under the Merger Regulation can be challenged and who is entitled to bring such challenges. A detailed analysis of those conditions is beyond the scope of this article. Suffice it to say that the case law has effectively extended the scope of judicial review in the field of mergers both *rationed material* (what acts can be attacked) and *rationed personae* (who can attack). All decisions producing binding legal effects such as to affect the interests of an applicant by bringing about a distinct change in his legal

---

[34] Art 10(5) was amended in the recent merger review. The original provision left doubts as to the procedure to be followed, in particular regarding time limits and whether re-examination ought to take place on the basis of current market conditions.

position are acts which may be the subject of an action for annulment under Article 230 EC.[35] In the merger field, these include (and the list is not exhaustive) final decisions authorizing or prohibiting mergers under Article 6 and 8 of the Merger Regulation, final decisions ordering the undoing of a merger under Article 8(4) and decisions referring concentrations to the Member States under Article 9.[36] As regards who can attack such decisions, the Community courts' case law has clarified that, apart from the parties to a merger, which will always have standing to bring an action, competitors of the parties will also be entitled to attack a decision which affects them directly and individually.[37]

C. The courts' role is one of review of legality—not re-examination on the merits

The role of the Community courts in the EC system of merger control is one of restricted and not full jurisdiction (except, as noted earlier, in the case of decisions imposing fines). It is classic judicial review and not re-examination of a case on the merits. This is in conformity with Article 230 EC which provides for limited grounds of review and with the division of power between the Community administration (the Commission) and judicature (the ECJ and the CFI). This is settled case law and is a fundamental principle of the institutional balance provided for in the EC Treaty. We are in full agreement with Advocate General Tisane that:

> The rules on the division of powers between the Commission and the Community judicature, which are fundamental to the Community institutional system, do not . . . allow the judicature to go further, and . . . to enter into the merits of the Commission's complex economic assessments or to substitute its own point of view for that of the institution.[38]

D. What standard of review does the CFI apply?

Turning now to the heart of the matter, what type of control does the CFI exercise within those bounds of review and what standard of proof does it require the Commission to meet under the Merger Regulation? Only one thing is entirely clear in the standard of review debate: that neither the

---

[35] This is established in the case law of the Community courts. See, eg Case T-125/97, *Coca-Cola v Commission* [2000] ECR II-1733, point 77 and the previous case-law cited therein.

[36] For the 'attackability' of referral decisions under Art 9 of the Merger Regulation, see *Philips*, points 267–308. For referral decisions under Art 22 see Case T-346/02 and T-347/02, *Cableuropa SA and others v Commission*, judgment of 30 Sept 2003.

[37] See, eg, Case T-3/93, *Air France v Commission* [1994] ECR II-121.

[38] *Tetra Laval* Opinion, point 89.

Merger Regulation nor the Treaty, contains any direct or indirect reference as to the appropriate standard of proof or standard of judicial review in the field of merger control. The Merger Regulation and the EC Treaty are simply silent on this matter.

So how are the Commission and the judges to know what standard of proof or of review should be applicable? Taking into account previous case law in the field of competition, the particular nature of the administrative system of merger control established by the Merger Regulation and the bounds of judicial review just outlined, the Community courts have carefully crafted an appropriate standard of judicial review over decisions taken in the field of mergers which respects institutional balance but also provides for effective control of the legality of the Commission's decisions.

The classic formulation of this standard of judicial review was well established in the competition field before being transposed to the more particular field of merger control. The classic formulation is to be found in the ECJ's judgment in the Aalborg Portland case, a case under Article 81 EC:

> Examination by the Community judicature of the complex economic assessments made by the Commission must necessarily be confined to verifying whether the rules on procedure and on the statement of reasons have been complied with, whether the facts have been accurately stated and whether there has been any manifest error of appraisal or misuse of powers.[39]

This formulation is also repeatedly used by the Community courts in the field of merger control.[40]

As the quote indicates, the intensity of control varies depending on whether the Courts are reviewing, on the one hand, the correctness of facts or the correct application of the law (full control) and, on the other, the correctness of the Commission's appreciation of complex economic matters (restrained control). This distinction was expressly acknowledged by Advocate General Tizzano in his Opinion in *Tetra Laval*.[41]

---

[39] Joined Cases C-204/00 P, C-205/00 P, C-211/00 P, C-213/00 P, C-217/00 P and C-219/00 P, *Aalborg Portland and Others v Commission*, not yet published in the ECR, point 279 (emphasis added). To the same effect, see Case C-42/84, *Remia and Others v Commission* [1985] ECR 2545, para 34, and Joined Cases C-142/84 and C-156/84, *BAT and Reynolds v Commission* [1987] ECR 4487, para 62.

[40] See recently, *Petrolessence*, point 101.

[41] *Tetra Laval* Opinion, point 85.

E. Full control of law—it is the Courts' prerogative to interpret community law

As regards matters of law, the Community courts exercise full jurisdictional control. Indeed, it is for the Community courts to provide the definitive interpretation of Community law, be it Treaty provisions or secondary legal provisions such as those contained in the Merger Regulation, and this goes for both procedural and substantive legal provisions. The Community courts interpret the law and then check whether the Commission has applied the correct legal principles in the case under examination. There is no margin of appreciation left to the Commission in this respect as to what are the legal criteria to apply.

Some further examples of the Community courts' control of the correct application of procedural and substantive legal rules may also be instructive. First, as regards procedure, the Community courts have consistently held that respect of the rights of defence is a fundamental right of Community law which must be respected in any contentious administrative procedure even in the absence of specific provisions in the legislation. (Of course, the Merger Regulation does contain specific provisions guaranteeing the right to be heard and access to the file for notifying parties, and provides more limited rights to third parties involved in the administrative procedure.)[42]

Two examples from the *Tetra Laval* and *Schneider* cases show how the CFI exercises rigorous control with respect to procedural aspects. In *Tetra Laval*, the CFI dealt with a plea raised by the applicant that the Commission had infringed its rights of defence by not providing it with full access to the file, in particular to responses received during the market investigation of the commitments. The Commission had only provided access to non-confidential summaries of those responses, claiming that this was necessary to protect respondents from possible retaliation by Tetra. The CFI referred to settled case law underlining that 'breach [of the rights of the defence] in the procedure prior to the adoption of the decision can, in principle, cause the decision to be annulled'.[43] In relation to access to the file, such infringement is proven where it 'established that the non-disclosure of the documents in question might have influenced the course of the procedure and the content of the decision to the applicant's detriment'.[44]

---

[42] See Art 18 of the new Merger Regulation. See also Arts 11–18 of Commission Regulation (EC) No 802/2004 implementing Council Regulation (EC) No 139/2004, [2004] OJ L133, 1 (the 'Implementing Regulation').

[43] *Tetra Laval*, point 89, quoting case *Hercules Chemicals v Commission*, paras 76 and 77.

[44] *Tetra Laval*, points 89 and 90. See also cases quoted therein: Case T-36/91, *ICI v Commission* [1995] ECR II-1847, point 78; Joined Cases T-305/94, T-306/94, T-307/94, T-

The CFI went on to interpret the relevant provisions governing access to the file under the old Merger Regulation (Article 18(1)).[45]

> Although the short deadlines in the second phase of a merger procedure may, for practical reasons and especially when many requests for confidentiality have been received, give grounds for drawing up non-confidential summaries, the Commission is still obliged to give valid reasons for a blanket refusal to allow access to the responses to a market investigation concerning the commitments offered by a person concerned.[46]

Having established the legal criteria applicable, the CFI went on to examine whether the Commission had indeed applied them in the case in question and found that the Commission was justified in providing Tetra with only non-confidential summaries. The CFI therefore concluded that 'the Commission's decision to allow Tetra access only to the non-confidential summaries of the responses to the market investigation did not infringe Tetra's rights of defence'.[47]

In *Schneider*, the CFI was faced with the question of whether the Commission's Statement of Objections (SO) contained all the grounds on which the Commission had ultimately relied in its final prohibition decision. This is a fundamental aspect of the rights of defence as the purpose of the SO is to enable the parties to know the objections against them and to be able to provide their views (and possible solutions in the form of remedies) on those objections.[48] The CFI found that it was 'not apparent on reading the statement of objections that it dealt with sufficient clarity or precision with the strengthening of Schneider's position vis-à-vis French distributors of low-voltage' and concluded that, through this omission, the Commission had infringed the applicant's rights of defence by basing its prohibition decision on elements that were not clearly included in the SO.[49] Consequently, the Decision was found to be 'vitiated by an infringement of the rights of defence'[50] and was annulled.

As regards interpretation of substantive provisions, the CFI may be faced with questions of interpretation of legal provisions such as the legal criteria

---

313/94, T-314/94, T-315/94, T-316/94, T-318/94, T-325/94, T-328/94, T-329/94, and T-335/94, *Limburgse Vinyl Maatschappij and Others v Commission* [1999] ECR II-931, point 1021; and *Endemol v Commission*, point 87.

[45] As well as Art 17 of the old Implementing Regulation (Commission Regulation (EC) No 447/98 of 1 Mar 1998 on the notifications, time limits and hearings provided for in Council Regulation (EEC) No 4064/89 on the control of concentrations between undertakings, OJ [1998] L61, 1).

[46] *Tetra Laval*, point 105.   [47] ibid, *Laval*, point 117.
[48] *Schneider*, points 440–2.   [49] ibid, point 445.
[50] ibid, point 462.

determining jurisdiction or the correct legal interpretation of Article 2 of the Merger Regulation itself. Regarding the latter, the CFI may be faced with a situation where the Commission is invoking a theory not previously addressed in the case law, which requires that the pertinence of the criteria used by the Commission in order to appreciate the competitive effects of a concentration be established as legal criteria. Two examples from *Tetra Laval* and *Airtours* will help illustrate this point.

In *Tetra Laval*, in interpreting Article 2(3) of the old Merger Regulation, the CFI set out the legal criteria which ought to apply before the Commission can take into account future conduct by an undertaking which may lead to the creation or strengthening of a dominant position. The CFI interpreted the law as it saw fit and held that the Commission must take into account the extent to which the economic incentives to engage in anticompetitive practices would be reduced, or even eliminated, by the illegality of the conduct in question, the likelihood of its detection, action taken against it by the competent authorities, both at Community and national level, and the financial penalties which could ensue from such action. Since the Commission did not carry out any such assessment in the contested decision, but merely referred to the economic incentives of the merged entity to engage in anticompetitive practices, the CFI rejected those parts of the Commission's conclusions which were predicated on, what would in all likelihood, constitute illegal conduct and especially conduct likely to violate Article 82 EC.[51]

In *Airtours*, the CFI interpreted Article 2(3) of the Regulation with regard to the concept of 'collective dominance'. It held that there were a number of conditions (briefly, market transparency, the existence of a deviation mechanism and absence of reaction by customers and competitors) which the Commission must prove are met before a conclusion can be reached that the merger would lead to the creation of such a collective dominant position.[52]

These extensive quotations from those recent judgments of the CFI illustrate the point made earlier that, in matters of interpreting the law, the CFI (rightly) exercises full jurisdictional control. Interpretation of the law is the prerogative of the Community judicature and is an area where there is no reference to 'manifest errors' on the part of the Commission. The CFI simply checks whether or not the Commission applied correctly the law as interpreted by the Community courts.

Once the CFI has controlled the legality of the criteria applied by the Commission, it controls the application of those criteria to the case in

---

[51] *Tetra Laval*, points 159–62.   [52] *Airtours*, point 62.

question. It is then that the CFI checks the correctness of the facts on which the Commission based its analysis and the Commission's analysis itself.

F. Full control of the correctness of facts

To use a relatively well-known quote, 'Facts are stubborn things. And whatever may be our wishes, our inclinations or the dictates of our passions, they cannot alter the state of the facts and evidence.'[53] It is important, at this point, to stress that, even though the Commission's analysis in the field of merger control is by its very nature prospective and focuses on predictions as to whether the merger will or will not result in anticompetitive effects in the future, this prospective analysis cannot be carried out in a vacuum. It must be based on present facts and solid evidence.

Thus, in any merger case, the Commission, before it can take a decision either to approve a merger following its notification (Phase I) or to move to a full Phase 2 examination and final decision in respect thereof, needs first to ascertain and base its assessment of that merger, and of its potential effects on competition, on already existing material facts. These include the present position and market shares of the undertakings in question on one or more precisely defined and analysed relevant product or service market,[54] as well as the present position and market shares of competing undertakings and the likely capacity of the merged entity's actual or potential suppliers or customers to resist any future nefarious conduct on its part. The Commission must secondly, having ascertained such primary facts, evaluate the likely effects of the merger on the competitive situation on the market(s) concerned. This is where the Commission performs a complex economic assessment by trying to ascertain whether or not the merger will have significant anticompetitive effects on the markets concerned.

Control of facts by the CFI is intensive and, again, in this field there is no room for discretion on the part of the Commission. This is inherent in the nature of a control of the accuracy of facts. Either a fact is correct or it is not. It is important to recall that the CFI was created in part because there was the need for a court of first instance to review comprehensively and rigorously the factually complex decisions that the Commission adopts in the field of competition.

In his Opinion in *Tetra Laval*, Advocate General Tizzano acknowledged this intensity of the control of facts by the CFI as being correct. He stated:

---

[53] The quote has been attributed to John Adams, the 2nd President of the United States.

[54] It is to be noted, however, that market definition is a complex task for which the Commission is allowed the appropriate margin of appreciation.

With regard to the findings of fact, the review is clearly more intense, in that the issue is to verify objectively and materially the accuracy of certain facts and the correctness of the conclusions drawn in order to establish whether certain known facts make it possible to prove the existence of other facts to be ascertained.[55]

In the recent merger judgments in *Airtours*, *Schneider*, *Tetra* and *BaByliss*, which resulted in annulment of the Commission's decisions, the CFI did not shy away from examining closely, and without restraint, whether the Commission had got the core material facts right.

At this point, an example of the CFI's control of the correctness of the facts underlying a Commission decision would be useful: the CFI's rejection, in *Airtours*, of the Commission's analysis of the significance of what it perceived would be the moderate growth of the relevant British short-haul, package-holiday market. Having requested production of the market 'study' to which the Commission referred in its decision in partial justification of this conclusion, the CFI found that it comprised a single page extract prepared at an unknown date.[56] On examination, the CFI observed that it was 'apparent from a cursory examination of that document that the Commission's reading of it was inaccurate',[57] the author actually having emphasised the massive growth in the market in the previous 20 years! The Commission was therefore 'not entitled to conclude that market development was characterised by low growth, which was, in this instance, a factor conducive to the creation of a collective dominant positions'.[58]

This example demonstrates that it is essential for the CFI carefully to review the facts presented as material by the Commission, as well as the direct factual inferences drawn therefrom, if effective judicial control of the latter's merger decisions is to be a reality.

A small parenthesis is necessary at this point. A distinction exists between law, facts, and assessment or appreciation of facts which merits further discussion. It is indeed a distinction that is not always easy to make, but one which it is necessary to make nevertheless.[59] Is, for example, an estimation of growth of a given market a matter of fact or appreciation of facts? The issue must be decided on a case-by-case basis depending on the precise context. It seems to me, however, that whenever an issue involves a complex assessment which may lead two reasonable persons to disagree as to the

---

[55] *Tetra Laval* Opinion, point 86.   [56] *Airtours*, point 129.
[57] ibid, point 130.   [58] ibid, point 133.
[59] The Competition Appeal Tribunal has recently had to face this precise question in its judgment providing reasons on refusing permission to appeal in Case 1001/1/1/01, *Napp Pharmaceutical Holdings Limited v Director General of Fair Trading*, available at <http://www.catribunal.org>. See in particular points 26–35.

conclusion to be drawn, we are not in the realm of pure fact but in the realm of appreciation of facts, where a margin of appreciation ought to be left to the Commission as the institution entrusted with making those complex assessments.

G. Restrained (but effective) control of complex economic assessments

We now turn to perhaps the most controversial aspect of the Community courts' control of Commission decisions in the field of mergers: the control of the Commission's complex economic assessments under the Merger Regulation. It is this area which allows for most disagreement as to whether a given merger is or is not compatible with the common market. Once the legal criteria and correctness of the facts underpinning a merger decision are established by the Courts, there is considerable scope for divergence in considering whether, on the basis of those criteria and facts, the merger will or will not result in significant anticompetitive effects.

Merger control predictions are not a precise science and, while industrial economics is highly developed as an academic discipline, application of economic theories and models in concrete cases remains an area fraught with difficulty and uncertainty (one is reminded here of the often quoted GB Shaw aphorism: 'if all the economists were laid end to end, they'd never reach a conclusion!').

Given these complexities and uncertainties, and by contrast to control of facts and law discussed above, judicial control of complex economic assessments by the Community is, and ought to be, restrained. It is based on the manifest error standard which respects the Commission's margin of appreciation and the division of powers between the Commission and the Community judicature.

The classic formulation of that standard has been enunciated by the ECJ in the *Kali and Salz* judgment.[60] The ECJ held that:

> the basic provisions of [the old Merger Regulation], in particular Article 2 thereof, confer on the Commission a certain discretion, especially with respect to assessments of an economic nature . . . Consequently, review by the Community judicature of the exercise of that discretion, which is essential for defining the rules on concentrations, must take account of the discretionary margin implicit in the provisions of an economic nature which form part of the rules on concentrations.[61]

[60] Joined Cases C-68/94 and C-30/95, *France and Others v Commission* [1998] ECR I-1375 (henceforth *Kali and Salz*).
[61] *Kali and Salz*, points 223–4.

This formulation which was first used by the ECJ in *Kali and Salz* has become the classic standard for judicial control in the field of mergers, having been consistently repeated by the CFI in its recent merger judgments.[62]

> This means in particular, as the CFI stated clearly in Petrolessence, that the control exercised by the Community judicature must observe the bounds of permissible judicial review, ie it 'must be limited to ensuring compliance with the rules of procedure and the statement of reasons, as well as the substantive accuracy of the facts, the absence of manifest errors of assessment and of any misuse of power'; the CFI must in particular not 'substitute its own economic assessment for that of the Commission'.[63]

However, this standard does not mean in practice that the Commission's discretion is unfettered. One is bound to agree with Advocate General Tizzano that:

> the fact that the Commission enjoys broad discretion in assessing whether or not a concentration is compatible with the common market does certainly not mean that it does not have in any case to base its conviction on *solid elements* gathered in the course of a *thorough and painstaking investigation* or that it is not required to give a full statement of reasons for its decision, disclosing the various passages of logical argument supporting the decision. The Commission . . . is bound to examine the relevant market carefully; to base its assessment on elements which reflect the facts as they really are, which are not plainly insignificant and which support the conclusions drawn from them, and on adequate reasoning; and to take into consideration all relevant factors.[64]

Where the evidence, which the CFI must scrutinise closely, does not reasonably support the conclusions drawn from it, the CFI must find that the Commission has committed a manifest error of appreciation.

The term 'manifest' allows for certain flexibility in the Courts' control. We quote once more Advocate General Tizzano in *Tetra Laval* in order to make the point that the manifest error standard permits effective control of the Commission's appreciation of facts in merger cases.

---

[62] The formulation is used, eg, in cases: T-102/96, *Gencor v Commission* [1999] ECR II-753, points 164–5 ('*Gencor*'); T-221/95, *Endemol v Commission* [1999] ECR II-1299, point 106; T-22/97, *Kesko v Commission* [1999] ECR II-3775, point 142; *Airtours*, point 64; *Tetra Laval*, point 119; T-374/00, *Verband der freien Rohrwerke eV and others v Commission*, point 105.

[63] Point 101, emphasis added.

[64] *Tetra Laval Opinion*, point 87 (emphasis added).

[The Kali and Salz test] make[s] it possible for the Community judicature to exercise an adequate review. Without entering into the merits of the Commission's assessments, it can in particular ascertain whether the factual information on which such assessments are based is accurate and whether the conclusions drawn as to fact are correct; whether the Commission undertook a thorough and painstaking investigation, and in particular whether it carefully inquired into and took sufficiently into consideration all the relevant factors; and whether the various passages in the reasoning developed by the Commission in order to arrive at its conclusions in respect of the compatibility or otherwise of a concentration with the common market satisfy requirements of logic, coherence and appropriateness.[65]

H. Standard of proof incumbent on the commission/evidence required by the CFI

Control of the Commission's appreciation is also intrinsically linked with the standard of proof incumbent on that institution before it can lawfully decide to authorize or prohibit a given merger. A distinction was made earlier between 'standard of review' (or 'standard of judicial control') on the one hand and 'standard of proof' on the other. In exercising judicial control over the Commission's assessment on the compatibility of a merger with the common market, the Community courts require the Commission to produce enough evidence as to meet a 'requisite legal standard'. The precise nature of the 'requisite legal standard' is by no means clear in the Courts' jurisprudence, the courts making frequent use of this very conveniently imprecise term.

This question of the standard of proof ('the requisite legal standard') can in essence be distinguished from that of the standard of judicial control by thinking in terms of the following question: how much evidence is required before the Commission can prohibit (or authorize) a merger under the Merger Regulation?

Consider that in a given case the CFI exercises its full jurisdictional control as to the legal criteria applied by the Commission and the correctness of the facts, and finds that the Commission, indeed, applied the correct legal criteria and that all the facts contained in its decision are also correct. The question may, however, still arise as to whether the evidence contained in the decision suffices to reach the conclusion that the merger is incompatible (or compatible) with the common market. In other words, is the Commission's conclusion about the compatibility of the merger with the common market

---

[65] ibid, point 88.

one that meets the requisite legal standard? This begs the question of how certain the Commission is required to be. Should it be asked to conclude that it is merely probable, very probable or absolutely certain that the merger will or will not lead to significant anti-competitive effects?[66]

The Courts' case law gives certain indications as to the level of certainty incumbent on the Commission and the amount and type of evidence required to achieve that level of certainty. In *Kali and Salz*, the ECJ referred to the need for a 'sufficiently cogent and consistent body of evidence'.[67] The ECJ also held that the merger's effects must be assessed with 'a sufficient degree of probability' and for that the Commission must rely on 'a rigorous analysis'.[68]

In *Airtours*, the CFI thought it was incumbent on the Commission to produce 'convincing' and 'cogent' evidence.[69] In *Tetra Laval*, the CFI, in the light of the fact that 'the anticipated dominant position would emerge only after a certain lapse of time', required that the Commission's analysis be 'particularly plausible'.[70] The CFI also criticized certain elements of the Commission's analysis as being 'not really very convincing', given that the Commission had not, in the view of the CFI, based its conclusions on a '*prudent analysis* of the independent studies or on a *solid, coherent body of evidence* obtained by it through its market investigation'.[71]

The CFI also indicated that 'in a prospective analysis of the effects of a conglomerate-type merger transaction', the Commission must prove that, in the relatively near future, a dominant position would be created or strengthened 'in all likelihood'.[72] As regards the strengthening of Tetra's dominant position in carton, the CFI concluded that, 'on the basis of the evidence relied on in the contested decision', it was not possible to conclude that such strengthening would indeed take place 'with the certainty required to justify the prohibition of a merger'.[73]

In *Philips*, which involved the examination of a Commission decision to refer a case to the French authorities under Article 9 of the old Merger Regulation, the CFI stated that the referral must be refused if 'on the basis of a body of precise and coherent evidence' it is clear that the referral would not safeguard effective competition.

---

[66] The Merger Regulation remains silent but such a standard may implicitly be read into Art 2 of the Regulation. The Article would thus read: 'A concentration which would [certainly/very likely/likely] impede effective competition . . . shall be declared incompatible with the common market.'

[67] *Kali and Salz*, point 228.

[68] ibid, point 246.

[69] *Airtours*, points 63 and 294.

[70] *Tetra Laval*, point 162.

[71] ibid, point 212, emphasis added.

[72] ibid, point 153.

[73] ibid, point 324.

In *BaByliss*, the CFI remarked that, for the Commission to lawfully accept commitments in Phase I in order to authorize a merger, they must be 'sufficient to rule out clearly any serious doubt'.[74] In addition, if commitments are not provided, the Commission's analysis must 'rule out any serious doubts in respect of each of the geographical markets for which it did not impose commitments'.[75]

More recently, in *MCI v Commission*, the CFI, faced with the question whether the Commission was correct to conclude that the parties had not abandoned the notified merger agreement and hence entitled to adopt a decision prohibiting the merger, concluded that the Commission's allegation was 'not founded on any evidence capable of proving it to the required legal standard'.[76]

Two broad questions arise from the above statements made by the CFI in these recent judgments. First, do they reveal an (unjustified) increase in the intensity of judicial control, and secondly, do they reveal any change in the standard of proof required, in particular a heightened standard for prohibition decisions?

I. Change in the intensity of control?

First, regarding the debate in the media and academic circles that these recent judgments reveal an increased intensity in judicial control and heightening of the requisite legal standard.[77] The charge that the CFI has adopted a new approach to reviewing substantive Commission merger decisions must be categorically rejected. It has, rather, adjusted the normal approach to reviewing Commission competition decisions so as to take account of the peculiarities of all merger cases and, above all, the peculiarities of each merger case that it has to review.

In those recent judgments, the CFI has adhered to the established judicial review standard of, first, fully controlling the correctness of the facts and the legal criteria applied, and then assessing whether the Commission committed manifest errors of appreciation. Indeed, in its judgment in *Tetra Laval*, the CFI refers to the 'manifest error' standard at least 11 times.

---

[74] *BaByliss*, point 169.   [75] ibid, point 314.   [76] *MCI*, point 90.
[77] See, eg, articles cited in n 19 and also: Thouvenin 'L'arrêt *Airtours* du 6 juin 2002: l'irruption du juge dans le contrôle des concentrations entre entreprises' [2002] Revue du Marché commun et de l'Union européenne 482; Vilmart 'La remise en cause par le TPICE de la notion de position dominante collective' [2002] *Semaine juridique* 1209; Stroux 'Collective Dominance under the Merger Regulation: a Serious Evidentiary Reprimand for the Commission' (2002) 27 European Law Review 736; Nikpay and Houwen 'Tour de Force or a Little Local Turbulence? A Heretical View on the *Airtours* Judgment' [2003] European Competition Law Review 193.

In its appeal against the *Tetra Laval* judgment, the Commission claims, however, that the CFI, although ostensibly accepting the principle of a certain margin of appreciation for the Commission as regards its economic assessments, has nevertheless in reality failed to respect that margin and, in so doing, allegedly raised the level of proof required. The Commission contends that the test effectively applied is no longer whether the applicant has established that the Commission has committed a manifest error of appreciation in the contested decision but whether it has cast sufficient doubts regarding the convincing nature of the Commission's case. In effect, the Commission would appear to be contending that the CFI has effectively substituted its own appreciation for that of the Commission regarding the likely effects of the merger on competition on the markets concerned.[78]

In his recent Opinion in that case, Advocate General Tizzano recommends the dismissal of the appeal, even though he agrees with the Commission that in certain respects (in particular the assessment of the growth of the PET market for liquid dairy products) the CFI overstepped the permissible bounds of judicial review by substituting its own view for that of the Commission.[79] As this case is still pending for adjudication by the ECJ, it is not possible to pass further comment on it. The ECJ's judgments will, it seems, be given in early 2005, most likely in February 2005.

My impression, as one of the judges responsible for *Gencor* and the *Schneider* cases, as judge-rapporteur (almost all third parties interested in the matter seem already to be aware of this formally undisclosed fact) in the *Tetra Laval* cases and as a very interested reader of the judgments in *Airtours*, *BaByliss/Philips* and *Petrolessence*, is that, with the possible exception of *Petrolessence*, the CFI has simply been more exacting latterly than it arguably was previously when applying the well-established principles referred to above. These cases also show that the margin of appreciation allowed to the Commission, and hence the intensity of judicial control, is clearly a function of the degree of discretion involved.

Thus, where the Commission's assessment is based upon inferences drawn from primary facts, a more limited discretion will be allowed (in other words, it may be easier for the Community courts to control whether the Commission's assessment was manifestly erroneous or not), while a greater margin will be allowed to pure economic assessments.[80]

---

[78] For a more detailed summary of the pleas in law advanced by the Commission in its appeals, see the *Tetra Laval* Opinion and the notice regarding the appeals published at OJ 2003 C 70, 3 and 5 respectively.

[79] See, eg, *Tetra Laval* Opinion, points 93–94.

[80] I should perhaps note here that there is a debate as to whether the two limbs of the test enshrined in Art 2 of the old Merger Regulation (dominance and significant impediment to effective competition) entail a different margin of discretion. The argument is that dominance

Likewise, in areas where the Merger Regulation itself provides a large margin of manoeuvre to the Commission, the Courts will exercise a more limited control. This arises mainly in areas where the Commission enjoys genuine discretion as to whether or not to act in a certain way, such as decisions refusing to refer cases to national authorities, where, even where the relevant legal criteria are met, the Commission retains significant discretion on deciding whether to refer a case (Article 9(1) states that the Commission 'may' do so).[81] Another such area is that under Article 8(4) of the Merger Regulation, which allows the Commission to adopt the necessary decisions to restore effective competition.[82] Finally, the Commission also should enjoy a wide margin of appreciation in deciding modalities relating to

being a more established concept in law entails a stricter control by the Community judicature whereas assessments under the second limb fall squarely within the realm of pure economic assessment where the Commission ought to enjoy a wider margin of discretion.

The recent changes made to the substantive test in the Merger Regulation beg the question as to whether the Commission will enjoy wider discretion under the new Merger Regulation than under the old.

I do not want to delve into the differences between the old and new tests. This would be an interesting topic in its own right (perhaps for a future conference organised by the BIICL!). Allow me, however, to make a few comments on the nature of the substantive test which may have some bearing on the appropriate standard of proof under the Merger Regulation.

Arguably, the concept of 'significant impediment to effective competition' is one that appears to be more open to interpretation than the more established notion of a dominant position. It is, however, a matter of time before the concept is sufficiently clarified and the Commission's Horizontal Guidelines, as well as the limited case law which refers to this limb of the test, minimise the uncertainties involved to the greatest extent possible. Both the assessment of whether a merger creates or strengthens a dominant position and the assessment of whether a merger significantly impedes effective competition involve the appreciation of complex economic factors and therefore entail a certain margin of discretion on the part of the institution making this appreciation. Whether one or the other test is applied should, therefore, not have any particular bearing on the standard of proof involved.

[81] Art 9 is a good example of this distinction between areas where the text of the Merger Regulation allows the Commission discretion and areas where it imposes a duty on that institution. According to Art 9(3), if the Commission finds that the legal criteria enunciated in the first paragraph of that provision (distinct geographic market and threat to competition in that market) are met, it has a choice: it can either keep the case (Art 9(3)(a)) or it can refer the case to the national authorities (Art 9(3)(b)). If, however, the Commission finds that the legal criteria are not met, it does not have discretion. It must ('shall') refuse the referral and deal itself with the case (Art 9(3), second subparagraph). Control by the Community judicature of the correct interpretation and application of the legal criteria is more intense, whereas control of the Commission's discretion ought, by implication, to be more limited.

[82] See Case T-50/02, *Tetra Laval v Commission*, concerning the Commission's decision to order the dissolution of the merger between Tetra and Sidel pursuant to Art 8(4) of the old Merger Regulation. It is to be noted that Art 8(4) of the new Merger Regulation contains a more precise test which makes clear that full dissolution of the merger is required following a prohibition. For an article discussing the changes made to Art 8(4) see the following paper: Kyriakos Fountoukakos 'Unscrambling the Eggs: Dissolution Orders under Art 8(4) of the Merger Regulation' DG Competition Newsletter, Spring 2004 issue, available at <http://europa.eu.int/comm/competition/ publications/cpn/cpn2004_1.pdf>.

commitments or in the conduct of its investigation, eg what questions to ask or what deadlines to impose in Article 11 requests for information.[83]

J. Varied intensity of control according to the novelty of the theory put forward

The *Airtours* and *Tetra Laval* cases also illustrate that the scope of the margin of assessment should be a function of the novelty and/or controversial or contested nature of the economic theory or data upon which the Commission bases its assessment.[84]

Thus, in *Airtours*, the CFI observes that

> the *prospective analysis* which the Commission has to carry out in its review of concentrations *involving collective dominance* calls for *close examination* in particular of the circumstances which, in each individual case, are relevant for assessing the effects of the concentration on competition in the reference market . . . where the Com- mission takes the view that a merger should be prohibited because it will create a situation of collective dominance, it is incumbent upon it to produce *convincing evidence* thereof.[85]

In *Tetra Laval*, the CFI held that

> since the effects of a conglomerate-type merger are generally considered to be neutral, or even beneficial, for competition on the markets concerned, as is recognised in the present case by the economic writings cited in the analyses annexed to the parties' written pleadings, the proof of anticompetitive conglomerate effects of such a merger calls for a *precise examination*, supported by *convincing evidence*, of the circumstances which allegedly produce those effects.[86]

---

[83] In *Schneider*, the CFI agreed that the Commission had acted correctly by requesting the parties to the concentration to provide it with a large amount of information and imposing a short deadline for their response thus suspending the relevant deadlines for the adoption of a final Decision until the requested information was provided. See *Schneider*, points 94–113.

[84] This is logical, even if exactly the same standard of proof is applied, the point being that it is much easier to prove things that are inherently more likely to happen than those that are not. The point is illustrated successfully by Bailey at 853, quoting the apt example of Lord Hoffmann in *Rehman* that it would require more convincing evidence to conclude that it was more likely than not that the sighting of an animal in a park was a lion than it would to satisfy the same standard of probability that the animal was a dog. *Secretary of State for Home Department v. Rehman* [2002] 3 WLR 877 at 895.

[85] *Airtours*, point 63 (emphasis added).

[86] *Tetra Laval*, point 155 (emphasis added).

Similarly, in *Tetra Laval*, the fact that the dominant position would only allegedly emerge after a certain lapse of time was a factor which called for '*particularly plausible*' analysis.[87]

By contrast, certain elements may reduce the burden of proof that the Commission has to discharge. For example, very high market shares may create a presumption or inference of a dominant position and may be sufficient to prove the existence of dominance in the absence of countervailing factors. Thus, in *Schneider*, it was relatively easy to convince the CFI that, in the absence of remedies, a dominant position would be created or strengthened in France, given the high market shares of the parties in that national market and the limited constraining power of their competitors.[88, 89]

When, on the other hand, new theories advanced by the Commission in the context of the exercise of its merger control function are contested before the Community judicature, it is the duty and responsibility of the CFI to ensure effective judicial review by scrutinising closely the convincing nature of the evidence relied upon in the contested decision in support of such theories. In so doing the CFI has correctly taken its lead from the approach adopted by the ECJ itself in *Kali and Salz*, where, having recalled the Commission's margin of assessment, the ECJ had little hesitation in annulling the Commission decision once it detected 'flaws' affecting the economic assessment carried out by the latter.

I do not see the controversy of using terms such as 'convincing evidence' in the recent judgments of the CFI. When the CFI states that the Commission has not proved a claim to a sufficient legal standard or to the absence of 'convincing evidence', it is quite clear that the CFI means that, having regard to primary facts and the direct inferences made therefrom, the particular prospective positive or negative analysis of the Commission at issue is so uncertain as to amount to, or form part of what amounts overall to, a manifest error of appreciation. There is no difference of any substance between this approach and that of the ECJ, upon which it is

[87] ibid, point 162 (emphasis added).

[88] See *Schneider*, points 415–16, where the CFI stated that 'In the light of the factual findings in the Decision, it is impossible not to subscribe to the Commission's conclusion that the proposed transaction will create or strengthen on the French markets, where each of the notifying parties was already very strong, a dominant position . . . It is clear from the Decision that the Schneider-Legrand group has, on each of the French markets affected, market shares which are indicative of dominance or of a strengthened dominant position, given the weak market presence and thinly spread market shares of its main competitors . . .'

[89] Such an approach was also explicitly admitted as permissible by the CAT in *Napp*, where the Tribunal, discussing the appropriate standard of proof and concluding that it should be the balance of probabilities, held that 'in discharging the burden of proof the administration could rely on inferences or presumptions that would, in the absence of any countervailing indications, normally flow from a given set of facts, for example that dominance may be inferred from very high market shares . . .' (*Napp*, point 110).

based, in *Kali and Salz*. No one, including the Commission, would require that the Community courts base their analysis on evidence that is not convincing!

K. Does the case law reveal what the precise standard of proof is?

Finally, let us look again at what the precise standard of proof (as opposed to the standard of review) under the Merger Regulation may be. The comments made above show one thing clearly: that whilst the nature of judicial control is by now well established (it is, as we have seen, a judicial review type of control, with full control of facts and law and limited control of complex assessments), the case law of the Community courts does not reveal, with any degree of clarity, whether the standard of proof incumbent upon the Commission is one of balance of probabilities, beyond reasonable doubt or any other intermediate standard.

The quotations from the recent merger judgments recited above give some indications as to the standard the CFI has in mind. The CFI requires that matters be proven on the basis of a consistent and cogent body of evidence, that the evidence be convincing and that novel theories predicting effects in the future be particularly plausible. In *Tetra Laval* in particular, the CFI was rather clear that the Commission must prove that the merger will result in anticompetitive effects 'in all likelihood'.

Advocate General Tizzano has addressed this point for the first time in EC case law.[90] He concludes that the nature of merger analysis (entailing complex evaluations based on criteria open to question such as economic ones) necessarily mean that the Commission cannot be required to establish 'with absolute certainty' that a merger would lead to significant anticompetitive effects. He thinks, instead, that the Commission should be persuaded that the merger would 'very probably' have such effects.[91]

The Advocate General does not agree with the Commission that such a standard (which appears to be much higher than a normal standard of balance of probabilities) is contrary to the nature of Articles 2(2) and 2(3) of the Merger Regulation, which the Commission believes impose an identical standard for clearance and prohibition decisions. According to the Advocate General, there will inevitably be some cases where it is not possible to prove either that the merger will 'very probably' lead to significant anticompetitive effects or that it 'very probably' will *not* lead to such effects. Those will be cases where the ultimate conclusion is a 'close call'. In such cases, the Advocate General believes, the Commission should authorize the transaction.

---

[90] *Tetra Laval* Opinion, points 72–81.   [91] ibid, point 74.

The Advocate General uses two main arguments to support this conclusion:

(i) Article 10(6) of the Merger Regulation (which stipulates that, if the Commission does not act within the requisite deadline, the merger is deemed to be authorized) indicates that there is a presumption for authorization; in other words

> it has been thought preferable to run the risk of authorizing a transaction incompatible with the common market, rather than the risk of prohibiting one that is compatible, so unjustifiably restraining the parties' freedom of economic activity.[92]

(ii) it is preferable to have a presumption of authorization since, if an anticompetitive merger is authorized, any distortions of competition can be corrected *ex post* by making use of Article 82 EC.[93]

L. Reflections on the appropriate standard of proof for merger decisions

The ECJ will hopefully shed more light into this rather obscure issue in its forthcoming judgment in *Tetra Laval*. It is futile to speculate about the outcome of the judgment on this point, but again some personal reflections might be instructive.

First, the previous case law contains helpful indications but does not expressly deal with the issue of the standard of proof. The Community Courts have dealt with approximately 30 merger cases and have delivered judgments dealing with a wide range of issues under the Merger Regulation, such as jurisdiction, referrals, the Commission's powers of investigation, the Commission's powers for ordering dissolution of a merger, the acceptance or rejection of commitments, and, of course, the correctness of the Commission's assessment under Article 2 of the Merger Regulation in both authorization and prohibition decisions and involving classic horizontal mergers, collective dominance, vertical and conglomerate effects. In this decade of merger control, the CFI has annulled four clearance decisions (in the cases of *Kali and Salz*, *RJB Mining*, *Canal+ Lagardère* and *BaByliss*), four prohibition decisions (in the cases of *Airtours*, *Schneider*, *Tetra Laval*, and *MCI*) and two decisions ordering divestitures under Article 8(4) (in the cases of *Schneider* and *Tetra Laval*).

These judgments do not reveal a clear standard of proof or significant differences as to the standard incumbent on the Commission depending on whether the decision is an authorization, a prohibition or a referral.

---

[92] ibid, point 79.   [93] ibid, point 81.

However, as regards judicial review, the Community courts have consistently applied the classic 'manifest error' standard. This standard has permitted them to exercise their judicial review function effectively. The Community courts have not shied away from annulling decisions whenever they have found errors in law, procedural infringements or manifest errors in the Commission's appreciation.

Secondly, the nature of merger control and analysis must be taken into account in the discussion surrounding the standard of proof. Unlike cases under Articles 81 and 82 EC, which relate to past infringements and involve severe penalties of a quasi-criminal nature, merger control is by its very nature administrative[94] and forward-looking. Analyses of the future effects of a merger on the market are by their very nature highly complex and involve the appreciation of a multitude of data that the Commission collects in wide-ranging investigations involving a large number of responses by competitors, customers and suppliers, independent studies, studies produced for the purposes of the analysis and so on. In addition, the Merger Regulation imposes strict and relatively short time limits within which the Commission must reach a decision.

This inherently complex and forward-looking nature of merger control as well as the time constraints imposed by the Merger Regulation militate against an excessively high standard of proof such as the one used in criminal cases, as such a standard would be almost impossible to meet in practice. No administrative body or judge could conclude with certainty that a given transaction would or would not lead to significant anticompetitive effects 'beyond reasonable doubt'.

Thirdly, there are arguments to support both sides in the debate as to whether the whole scheme of the Regulation contains a general presumption of lawfulness for mergers.[95] On the one hand, owning and buying property and engaging in economic activity is a fundamental right which

---

[94] It is interesting to note that the recent overhaul of the UK's competition regime created two different standards for anti-trust and merger cases. Anti-trust infringements are dealt with, on appeal, by the CAT on a full re-examination on the merits; the relevant legislation being silent on the standard of proof, the CAT has decided, in *Napp*, to apply a civil balance of probabilities requiring strong and compelling evidence (see *Napp*, point 109).

By contrast, with regard to mergers, the Enterprise Act 2002 s 120 specifically provides for a 'judicial review standard'. At s 120(4) it provides: 'In determining such an application [for review of a decision by the OFT], the Competition Appeals Tribunal shall apply the same principles as would be applied by a court on an application for judicial review'. The fact that the ordinary standard of judicial review ought to apply in review of OFT merger decision by the CAT was confirmed by the Court of Appeal in *OFT and other v IBA Health Limited* [2004] EWCA Civ 142, judgment of 19 Feb 2004, points 50–64.

It is also interesting to note that, in the US, courts decide on merger cases at first instance on a full examination on the merits using the civil standard of balance of probabilities.

[95] See Bailey above n 19, at 882 ff.

should be limited only in exceptional circumstances.[96] On the other hand, exercise of property rights is not unlimited, but it is subject to the competition rules of the EC Treaty. Article 3(1)(g) EC establishes 'undistorted competition' as one of the fundamental objectives of the Community. And merger activity may be caught by Articles 81 and 82 EC even in the absence of a specific legal instrument such as the Merger Regulation.[97]

The Regulation does not contain any express presumption of unlawfulness in any of its provisions,[98] but nor does it contain any express presumption of lawfulness for all mergers either. Recital 32 to the Merger Regulation, provides an indication for a possible presumption of lawfulness only for a specific category of mergers, those which, by reason of the limited market share of the undertakings concerned, namely a share of less than 25 per cent, are not liable to impede effective competition. Given this express provision, it is by no means clear that the intention of the Community legislator was that all mergers ought to be presumed lawful. On the contrary, one has to bear in mind that the Merger Regulation does not allow parties to implement their merger deals, having Community dimension, without prior express authorization by the Commission except in limited circumstances,[99] and Article 7(5) specifically makes the validity of such merger transactions dependent on an authorization decision.

Finally, it is not clear whether, as a matter of merger policy, the legislator considered it preferable to make a type II error (authorizing an anticompetitive merger) than a type I error (prohibiting a benign merger). Making a type II error (authorizing an anticompetitive merger) may be more costly and detrimental to the European economy as a whole and to European consumers than making a type I error (prohibiting a benign merger), which affects directly mainly the parties to a merger transaction.[100] On the other

---

[96] Art 295 EC provides that the Member States' system of property ownership is unaffected by the Treaty. Arts 16 and 17 of the Charter of Fundamental Rights affirm the right to conduct business and own property.

[97] See Recitals 6 and 7 of the new Merger Regulation. See also Case C-142/84, *BAT and Reynolds v Commission* [1987] ECR 4487, points 37–9 for the principle that Art 81 EC could apply to the acquisition of minority shareholdings, and case C-6/72, *Continental Can v Commission* [1973] 215 for the principle that an acquisition leading to the strengthening of a dominant position may be caught by Art 82 EC.

[98] See in this respect the Opinion of Advocate General Tesauro in *Kali and Salz*, point 7, where he states that 'It is also significant that the regulation raises no presumptions of unlawfulness connected with the market shares held by the undertakings and no mathematical criteria that can be used for the appraisal, in contrast to other antitrust legislation.'

[99] Art 7(1) of the Merger Regulation provides for a stand-still obligation, ie parties cannot implement a merger transaction before receiving an authorization by the Commission. Some limited exceptions to this principle with regard to stock exchange transactions are provided in Art 7(2).

[100] Unless it can be shown that the merger entails clear efficiencies which would benefit consumers.

hand, in case of prohibition, the merger would be killed forever, whereas in case of authorization, if competition problems later arise, they can be controlled by the Commission *ex post* through recourse to Article 82 EC.[101, 102] This provision is particularly apt to control situations where the Commission fears anticompetitive effects based on behaviour by the merger company that would fall squarely within Article 82 EC, such as leveraging or tying.

Fourthly, the symmetrical nature of Article 2 of the Merger Regulation, the system of positive decisions established in that Regulation and strong indications in the case law that the Community courts are equally demanding in the required standard of proof in both authorization and prohibition decisions are elements that militate in favour of a flexible standard which would allow effective control by the Community judicature of both authorization and prohibition decisions.

What is meant by 'symmetrical nature' and 'positive decisions'? Articles 2(2) and 2(3) of the Merger Regulation (the symmetrical nature has not changed in the new Merger Regulation even though the test itself has) are indeed linguistically perfectly symmetrical, simply stating that a concentration which leads to anticompetitive effects shall be prohibited whereas a concentration that does not lead to such anticompetitive effects shall be authorized.

In addition, the provisions of the Regulation on the basis of which the Commission adopts substantive final decisions on the compatibility of a concentration with the common market, ie Article 6 and Article 8(1)–(3) of the Regulation do not allow the Commission to express 'doubts'. This is only allowed at the end of a Phase I investigation as grounds to open an in-depth Phase II investigation.[103] On the contrary, when a final decision is adopted, eg pursuant to Article 8, the Commission must positively find that the criterion in Article 2(2) or 2(3) is satisfied and then must declare the concentration compatible or incompatible with the common market. A positive decision by the Commission is envisaged in every single case. Article 8 does *not* say: 'If the Commission finds that a merger creates significant anticompetitive effects, it shall declare it incompatible with the common market, *otherwise* it shall declare it compatible.' It asks the Commission to positively find that the merger will or will not lead to significant anticompetitive effects.

---

[101] See Advocate General Tizzano's Opinion in *Tetra Laval*, point 81.

[102] It is not always clear that Art 82 EC could be used to prevent anti-competitive behaviour following the authorization of a merger as many pricing decisions or other behaviour by the undertakings concerned may not fall within the scope of that provision or may be extremely difficult to detect.

[103] Art 6(1)(c) of the Merger Regulation.

Article 10(6) of the Merger Regulation, which falls under the heading 'Time Limits for Initiating Proceedings and for Decisions', may be considered as leaning towards a presumption of lawfulness in situations of inaction or even of uncertainty as to the effects of a merger, as AG Tizzano was prepared to hold in *Tetra Laval*. However, it may also be considered not so much as a presumption of lawfulness but as a provision designed to ensure the administrative efficiency of the EC system of merger control, ie that the Commission takes decisions within pre-determined and legally binding deadlines and that failure to act by the Commission cannot benefit that institution but can benefit the parties that introduced a valid demand in accordance with the provisions of the Regulation.[104] If seen in this way, Article 10(6) would be not a presumption of lawfulness but a penalty for inaction. It could not, therefore, easily be applied by analogy as a general principle of lawfulness along the lines of 'where in doubt, clear' to situations where the Commission has actually acted by adopting a decision (albeit one in the grey area of certainty).

The Merger Regulation thus establishes a system of positive declarations by the administrative authority in every single case falling within its scope without clear presumptions of authorization or prohibition.[105] As a consequence, not only the Commission's prohibition decisions but also authorization decisions may be attacked before the Community courts. An appropriate standard of proof should therefore permit effective scrutiny of both those types of decision by the Community judicature especially given that private parties cannot attack merger decisions in national courts. If a presumption for authorization were accepted as a feature of the Regulation, with a correspondingly high standard for prohibitions and a much lower standard for authorizations, effective scrutiny of authorization decisions by the Community judicature could be jeopardized.

Consider this. Say that the standard of 'very probable' should be taken to mean a probability of more than 60 per cent. Imagine that in a given case the Commission believes that the merger is likely to lead to significant anti-competitive effects but that the probability of this happening is only 51–60

---

[104] A similar penalty for failure to act within a deadline is also included in Art 9(5) of the new Merger Regulation (and the other provisions dealing with referrals of cases to and from Member States), which stipulates that where the Commission has not taken a decision to refer the case to a requesting Member State within a relevant deadline, it is deemed that it has decided to refer the case. This cannot be taken as a presumption that mergers fall within national jurisdiction but as an application of the principle of good administration and that inaction should not benefit the party that has failed to act.

[105] This is unlike the system in the US, where the agencies act as prosecutors and where they enjoy significant prosecutorial discretion. In a prosecutorial system, the prosecutor need only close the file without adopting any positive declaration on the compatibility of the merger with the relevant legislation.

per cent and therefore it decides to authorize the merger. This would lead to the rather absurd result that the Commission authorizes the merger even though it believes there are more probabilities that consumers will be harmed than not.

Still, if the Community courts require a symmetrical standard which is equally very high for both prohibitions and authorizations (as it appears from the annulment of authorization decisions such as *Kali and Salz* and more recently *BaByliss*), there would certainly be, as AG Tizzano concluded, a number of cases falling into such a grey zone where matters cannot be proved to a high standard either way. This would be an odd situation. The standard must therefore allow for a certain degree of flexibility in such cases.

This debate can become quite philosophical and may not be determinative of what precise standard of proof is most appropriate under the Merger Regulation. As a concluding remark, it should be stressed that Recitals 4 and 5 to the Merger Regulation make clear that, whilst corporate reorganization in the form of mergers is to be welcomed, it should be ensured that such reorganization does not result in lasting damage to competition. This is to be achieved by establishing a Community system of merger control. A fine balancing act must therefore be performed in each and every case. The Commission must decide, on the elements before it, whether a concentration is likely to lead to anticompetitive effects or not.

While the above analysis unveils elements supporting both arguments, overall a slight inclination towards authorizing mergers in cases of significant doubts, uncertainty or inaction is in-built in the EC system of merger control. The balance has to tip one way or the other at the end of the Commission's review, when the College of Commissioners sits round a table in the *Berleymont* and decides what to do with a given merger case. In cases that are 'too close to call' the benefit of the doubt should lean towards authorization of the merger in question, especially where the alleged anti-competitive effects are too remote or of a nature that allows effective *ex post* correction using Article 82 EC.

Prohibiting a transaction between two companies is a far-reaching measure which requires the Commission to be certain at a relatively high standard (more than just 51 per cent) that the merger in question is likely to result in significant anticompetitive effects. The degree of likelihood need not be established at a precise level—indeed, over-refinements of standards of proof are a futile exercise—but it would appear that something more than a pure balance of probabilities standard but most certainly something less than a criminal standard ought to apply.

The Commission, under the judicial control of the Courts, would have to decide that it was satisfied at a high degree whether the concentration would be likely to result in significant anticompetitive effects and would have to prove that its conclusion was based on a body of solid, cogent and convincing evidence and not vitiated by any errors of fact, law or manifest errors of appreciation.

It is worth stressing again that this concerns the actual standard of proof incumbent on the Commission. As regards the standard of review, given that the Courts' role in the EC system of merger control is one of review of legality of Commission decisions and not of re-examination on the merits, the Courts would necessarily need to apply a judicial review, 'manifest error' type of standard when reviewing Commission decisions. However, the distinction between standard of review and standard of proof should be borne in mind. The intensity of judicial control, even under a classic judicial review standard, will fluctuate depending on the underlying standard of proof/legal test that ought to be met by the administrative body having taken the decision on the merits, the context of the case, the complexity of the issues raised and so on.[106]

The Courts' role is precisely to control effectively the limits of the Commission's discretion in deciding whether such significant anticompetitive effects are likely to take place or not. In performing this role, the Courts too should bear in mind that, despite being administrative in nature, a prohibition decision interferes materially with the parties' right to engage in commercial transactions. As a result, review by the Courts of such decisions may be more intense and exacting given that the interests at stake are much higher.[107]

The Courts' control has been and should continue to be intense and effective. If the Commission presents a case for or against a merger (and/or commitments offered by the parties thereto) in a contested decision in

---

[106] See above n 30.

[107] The approach of adopting a standard of balance of probabilities tailored to the precise context of competition infringements has been adopted by the Competition Appeals Tribunal in *Napp*. The CAT thought that while a civil standard ought to apply to proceedings under the Act, 'but that standard is to be applied bearing in mind that infringements of the Act are serious matters attracting severe financial penalties. It is for the Director to satisfy [the CAT] in each case, on the basis of strong and compelling evidence, taking into account of the seriousness of what is alleged, that the infringement is duly proved, the undertaking being entitled to the presumption of innocence and to any reasonable doubt there may be' (*Napp*, point 109). See also *Case R v Department for Education and Employment, ex p Begpie* [2000] 1 WLR 1115, 1130B, where Laws stated: 'Fairness and reasonableness (and their contraries) are objective concepts: otherwise there would be no public law, of if there were it would be palm tree justice. But each is a spectrum, not a single point, and they shade into one another. It is now well established that the Wednesbury principle itself constitutes a sliding scale of review, more or less intrusive according to the nature and gravity of what is a stake.'

which, for example, it has clearly overlooked, underestimated or exaggerated the relevant economic data, drawn unconvincing, in the sense of implausible, direct inferences from primary material facts or adopted an erroneous approach to assessing the material facts, such failings may, depending on their cumulative effect in the context of the circumstances of the case viewed as a whole, suffice to constitute, for the purpose of the CFI's review of the relevant overall economic analysis, a manifest error of assessment. On the other hand, if no such (or very few or insignificant such) errors are found, then the CFI, even if it would not itself have subscribed to the Commission's economic assessment of the foreseeable effects of the merger and/or the adequacy of the commitments offered, should uphold the Commission's findings.

IV. CONCLUDING REMARKS

In conclusion, both the CFI and the ECJ have discharged the burden imposed on them by the EC Treaty to review carefully the legality of the Commission's decisions in the field of mergers and not to shy away from engaging in close scrutiny of the facts and economic data underpinning those decisions.

The high-profile annulments of 2002—the Commission's *annus horibilis* as far as merger decisions go—changed dramatically the landscape of judicial review of merger control decisions. This was not because of a new or heightened legal standard of proof, but because the careful and exacting scrutiny of the Commission's decisions by the CFI acted, and continues to act, as a strong reminder that, in our administrative system of merger control, the Commission is not prosecutor, judge and jury.

Private parties are increasingly willing to challenge the Commission's decisions before the CFI. Of the 48 merger cases lodged with the Community judicature to date, more than 20 date after 2001. There are currently no fewer than 16 merger cases pending before the Community courts, touching upon all aspects of merger control.[108]

---

[108] Case T-209/01, *Honeywell v Commission*; Case T-210/01, *General Electric v Commission*; Case T-282/02, *Cementbouw Handel v Commission*; Cases T-48/03 and T-351/03, *Schneider Electric v Commission*; Case T-145/03, *Festival Crociere v Commission*; Case T-163/03, *Scania v Commission*; Case T-212/03, *My Travel Group plc v Commission*; Case T-269/03, *Socratec v Commission*; Case T-350/03, *Ampere Strompool v Commission*; Case T-443/03, *Retecal Sociedad v Commission*; Case T-48/04, *Wireless Business Solutions*; Case T-177/04, *EasyJet Airline v Commission*; Case T-248/04, *Scania v Commission*; Case T-279/04, *Editions Odile Jacob v Commission*; Cases C-12/03 P and C-13/03 P, *Tetra Laval v Commission*.

Judicial review has an important role to play in the EC system of merger control. Future judgments in this field, under the provisions of the new Merger Regulation, will continue to clarify the law, provide guidance and, above all, ensure that the administration's actions in this important area of the law remain subject to effective checks and balances.

PART THREE

Transatlantic Antitrust Dialogue
Conference
9–10 May 2005

Transatlantic Antitrust Dialogue

Philip Marsden

Welcome all of you to London and to the British Institute's Trans-Atlantic Antitrust Dialogue. I was on a run this morning by the river and I thought on a day like this you really see London at its very best and I hope you will think that of the British Institute after today and tomorrow.

In a way, the British Institute is a bit like London. It is steeped in tradition, but it is very vibrant and varied. Competition law is only a small part of what we do at the Institute, but I am very proud to be part of that. Today outside it is brisk and bright and while the weather might be changeable, I hope that we have worked hard enough to ensure the quality is consistent and high during this event and that the dialogue remains brisk and bright throughout.

This is our Fifth Annual Trans-Atlantic Antitrust Dialogue, and I would like to thank our organizing committee, our sponsors, and our speakers for contributing, as always, to a very stimulating programme. We always aspire to attract a very high or senior level of delegate, because that way we benefit as well from your comments. The proceedings are being recorded for publication in our annual *Current Competition Law Yearbook*, and so I do ask that if members of the audience are asking a question, please identify yourself as that would be very helpful for our transcribers.

This year we have taken on board several suggestions that have been made to us in past years. For example, I have cut the size of the panels and I have extended the time available for them to speak, to make sure that they can therefore have a more detailed and more involved discussion from which we can all benefit. We have also tried to emphasize the truly transatlantic nature of antitrust in a comparative manner, as befitting the Institute's mandate. So in that sense, we are not just focusing on EU and US issues, we are focusing on issues that are of relevance to many countries and also that is reflected somewhat in our speakers and the identities of many of the delegates and indeed the officials who are here from various countries throughout Eastern Europe, Brazil, Argentina, Mexico, Canada and elsewhere.

This conference today and tomorrow is the showcase of our competition programme at the Institute. We also have an annual competition litigation conference in October and an annual merger control conference in December and we have practitioner workshops throughout the year. We also have formed, as many of you will be aware, a Competition Law Forum which involves, in a slightly more private sense, a group of experts, officials, economists, lawyers and industry experts who meet on a quarterly basis to discuss issues of pressing policy and submit papers to governments and to the European Commission in that regard.

Most of what we do here is not just to put on events obviously, but to try to stimulate our research and our publications programme, so that we can thereby have some form of multiplier effect, so people can understand more about what we are doing and benefit from our discussions. Just a word briefly about our research programme, because we don't necessarily publicize it all that much, in the last year our little competition team at the Institute has completed quite a lengthy study on international enforcement cooperation, specifically between 'developed' country regimes, and 'developing' country regimes. This was sponsored by the European Commission. We presented that report in Brussels last week at a meeting with officials from the Commission, from UNCTAD and from the WTO.

We also did a very large study on exclusionary business practices in developing countries that was commissioned by UNCTAD in Geneva. Our own research and policy programme in the last few months has focused primarily on reform of Article 82 and in that regard we have had meetings with the OFT, we have had Competition Law Forum meetings in Brussels and next week we go to Bonn to meet with the Bundeskartellamt to discuss varying approaches to abuse of market power in Europe.

Three weeks ago, we were training national judges in competition law, as part of a European Commission tender. We did this in Brussels. We had 38 national judges, from 14 different Member States and I was very pleased to have been able to be part of a programme which benefited from the expert membership we have at the Institute. We had economists, practitioners and barristers able to offer their own insights to the national judges about the pressing nature of the work that is starting to move towards them as a result of modernization last year.

Finally, just a brief word about membership. You will have heard this from me before, but just briefly. We are the British Institute of International and Comparative Law. It says *British* there, but that does not mean that we receive any funding from Her Majesty's Government. It says *Institute* there, but that does not mean, despite the fact that we are housed in Russell Square, that we are part of any of the universities, and so we don't receive any University funding. The majority of our revenue stream comes primarily from membership and I do encourage you to join the Institute as an individual or corporate member. It entitles you to an annual subscription to the *International and Comparative Law Quarterly*, which is worth the value of the subscription in itself, but also considerable savings on events like this and also access to non-competition-law-related events. We have a very stimulating research programme at the Institute relating to public international law, tort law, company law, data protection, regulation generally and, of course, competition law and European law.

So I encourage you to join. The Competition Law Programme of the Institute may seem on the face of it to be just me and the Junior Fellow, but that is not at all the way I view it. I view it as consisting of all of the members of BIICL who are active in this area: all of you in particular who devote your expertise and your time to helping us with the projects we are doing, and that is why we are able to accomplish what seems to be so much.

Anyway, I am grateful for you coming today. I encourage you, as I say, to join the Institute and to get more involved in our programme. I am always looking for new ideas and new ways to expand the programme and I am very pleased now to launch the Conference and to begin with our first panel, which concerns, of course, a very pressing issue, an issue that is related to many areas of competition law, but in particular, in my view, to the review of Article 82 and of course in some ways the Lisbon Agenda and the innovation and competitiveness of European business. I am very grateful to one of the members of our organizing Committee, Pat Treacy, from Bristows, who is convening this panel and who is chairing now.

Panel 1—Competition Policy and Intellectual Property: What is the Right Balance?

PAT TREACY

Good morning. I have to say it is a great honour for me to have been asked to chair this panel this morning, particularly with such distinguished panel members who I hope will lead us through what will be an interactive debate about the way in which competition law and policy and intellectual property law and policy interact. I think it is fair to say that for the first five years of the 21st century, this has been one of the big questions for competition lawyers and antitrust lawyers and for that reason I am delighted that this morning we have managed to pull together people from both sides of the Atlantic. We have regulators; we have someone from industry; we have someone who is generally a regulator but is taking a little sabbatical at the moment. So we have a fine array of people to lead us through the problems that arise from the tension, at least in the short term, between the policy goals of competition law and those of intellectual property law.

I think that one of the reasons why this panel is particularly strong is that we are going to look at a whole range of the ways in which these two policies interact. There has been a great tendency, I think because of the case law, certainly on this side of the Atlantic, to look at the inter-relationship between intellectual property law and competition law only in one fairly narrow focus, which is the issue of compulsory licensing. Certainly, it won't come as any surprise as we have Jean-Yves here from Microsoft, that that will be one of the issues that we will look at this morning, but it won't be the only one. There are a number of other areas in which the inter-relationship between these two policies is absolutely critical, both in practice for industry and in theory for law-makers, law enforcers and regulators. So we are looking not just at the issue of compulsory licensing, but also in a broader sense at the theoretical relationship between the two policies. Also at some of the ways in which other issues have come to the fore, for example in the United States. Alden Abbott will talk a little bit about the way in which patents, intellectual property rights and antitrust policy have clashed in the field of patent litigation and in particular in settlement agreements relating to patent litigation. That is not an issue that has traditionally caused much of a stir on this side of the Atlantic and perhaps some would wish that it wouldn't and that we should just be quiet and not raise it, but

I think it does raise some very interesting theoretical and policy issues that sometimes don't get looked at so much in Europe.

So I think without any more ado I will hand over to the first of our very distinguished panel members, who is Alden Abbott. He is an Associate Director of Policy and Coordination at the Bureau of Competition at the FTC, but he has very kindly agreed to leave Washington for a few months and is at All Souls in Oxford, taking a brief sabbatical which I understand he is enjoying quite a lot, and I can understand why, particularly at this time of year.

Alden is going to introduce a few thoughts on the correct balance between intellectual property law and antitrust policy from a primarily US perspective.

ALDEN ABBOTT

Thank you very much, Pat. And before I proceed, I have to give you the standard disclaimer of all Government representatives that the views expressed are my own and do not necessarily represent the views of the Federal Trade Commission, or any Federal Trade Commissioner, or for that matter, any of my colleagues at All Souls College, Oxford.

It has become a truism that intellectual property law and antitrust law can be harmonized. This relationship has a long history. One can look at the history of certainly the United States' interaction over the last century between the courts and the patent agency and the treatment of patents. The treatment has gone in cycles and I would say certainly throughout a good part of the mid-twentieth century really from the 1940s through to the 1970s there was certainly, in the antitrust community, great suspicion of patents, because they were viewed as monopolies, State-granted monopolies. Hence the Antitrust Division argued that almost any restrictive licensing scheme—the famous or infamous nine no-nos—should be treated as if it were per se illegal and would be prosecuted. That was based really on a sort of a matter of faith: 'well this is a monopolist and anything that the patentee does is an extension of the monopoly and somehow therefore it's bad', and didn't really involve a lot of economic analysis or indeed policy analysis. Then I think most, but not all, of you know that policy was changed dramatically in the early 1980s, and I think based on appreciation of work that really dated back to the 1950s in American law schools, in the University of Chicago and then Bowman at Yale did a lot of work on licensing. They said: 'Look there are lots of reasons why firms may want to license restrictively, there are all sorts of efficiency explanations'.

So out go the nine no-nos. Subsequently, a sort of more sophisticated—or so we Americans think—rule of reason developed, that was well encapsulated in the 1995 Antitrust Guidelines on Intellectual Property, jointly issued by the Justice Department and the Federal Trade Commission. I don't remember if Judge Wood was still at the Antitrust Division; I think she was, at the time they were released. Very frankly, I think those guidelines have been widely cited and noted. I think to some extent—my personal view again—they help inform the guidelines accompanying the Technology Transfer Block Exemption revision, but there are some differences.

So I think there is a growing appreciation for how one should apply a rule of reason in that area. There are other areas, however, of relationship between antitrust law and patent law that are quite unsettled. As Pat mentioned, one of these has to do with settlement of litigation. But before getting into that topic, I am going to address another topic also very briefly: *ex ante* negotiations by standard-setting organizations.

Most of you should also be aware that the Federal Trade Commission and the Justice Department, with input from the Patent and Trademark Office, and with input from some foreign commentators as well I might add, held hearings on the relationship between intellectual property, specifically patent policy, and really thought patents were a big enough topic to focus on in the 2001–2002 hearings on patents and antitrust.

The basic conclusion of those hearings really was that there are a lot of patent rights that are certainly important, no question about it . . . and they are property rights. There is a big issue about many patents being issued which as it turns out empirically we see are being struck down. There are higher costs involved in issuing some patents. That led the FTC, speaking as an independent agency, to recommend that the Patent Trademark Office in Congress consider some statutory administrative law changes, to sort of strengthen review, post-grant review, of patents, to enhance the application of standard legal terminology and the standards of a patent law itself, such as obviousness, which sometimes had been honoured in the breach, we felt. Those recommendations certainly got a lot of attention and the FTC now is holding some additional follow-up sessions, culminating in June in Washington, in which it is hearing more about representatives in affected industries and what they have to say about the recommendations.

There are parts of the hearings dealing with specific antitrust law issues, including licensing, but excluding settlements, but specific antitrust topics were actually not discussed in that report. I will not say anything more about that. So the FTC's report really was more about a sort of legal policy to reform the patent system—some patent lawyers might have said, what does the FTC know about this? However, actually the Patent and Trademark Office and a number of patent attorneys with whom we work, said a lot of recommendations were well-founded and indeed I think the American Intellectual Property Law Association, for example, is generally supportive of at least some of the recommendations, such as the strengthening of post-grant review.

So what does this tell us about antitrust? Well, we will get to that in a moment when I talk about settlements. It shouldn't derogate from the fact that the patent right is a property right, but it may tell us something interesting when we look at the nature of settlements.

First, let me briefly talk about standard-setting negotiations. Now, as many of you know, the FTC is currently in administrative litigation, and obviously all I can say is look at the complaints underlying the administrative litigation. These two litigations aren't finished. But the two matters of so-called *Rambus* and *Unocal*[1] matters are both involving alleged 'hold-ups' in standard setting. What do we mean by 'hold-ups'? That is a hypothetical situation. In the *Rambus* case where you have a standard-setting organization which has specific rules and those rules are either ignored or through deception are manipulated, so that the company participating in the standard-setting causes the organization to adopt, or allows the organization to adopt, the standard which reads upon its patent at the time the standard has been developed, and the other parties don't believe or know about the patent and don't think it is going to be invoked, and after the fact it is invoked. It is sort of what is called an *ex-post* hold-up and that has consequences if sunk costs have been absorbed by firms in order to adapt to the standard.

What do we have to say about that? One issue raised in the 2001–2 hearings was what about negotiations on price among the members of the standard-setting organization prior to the final development of the standard? Would that raise antitrust problems? I think the classic simple answer is that it sounds like price-fixing. We know the first thing antitrust counsellors tell their clients is 'Don't talk about prices'.

However, I think there is a strong argument, an argument made by some of the commentators at our hearings, that really applies to sort of a rule of reason analysis: if you view intellectual property as an input into a sort of an efficiency-creating standard and standards have substantial benefits that may reduce transaction costs, they may reduce production costs when companies compete around the standard. There are dangers that standards

---

[1] For the text of the Rambus and Unocal complaints, respectively, see *In the Matter of Rambus, Inc.*, Docket No 9302 (18 June 2002) ('Rambus Complaint'), *available at* <http://www.ftc.gov/os/2002/06/ rambuscmp.htm>; *In the Matter of Union Oil Company of California*, Docket No 9305 (4 Mar 2003) ('Unocal Complaint'), *available at* <http://www.ftc.gov/os/2003/03/unocalcmp.htm>.

may be used to exclude potential competition, but nevertheless, if a standard may reduce cost, it may reflect efficiency. So firms are developing an efficient standard. But if they decide one thing that may deter us from developing this standard is the possibility of hold-up, might it be reasonable for us to negotiate with potential purveyors of input, intellectual property inputs, of the standard to allow us to take into account the potential costs of competing intellectual property rights in devising the standards? Even say by improving the sort of flow of information about what patents are out there, who is supplying them and under what terms they would be supplied if a standard is developed. That is potentially quite efficient. There is a term of art, some people wonder what it means, out there: 'reasonable and non-discriminatory', a sort of RAND standard for pricing patent licensing. It is possible that firms might say well, we can agree on some sort of RAND license term without fixing the prices or affecting the prices or output of downstream products. Just trying to fix the potential cost of an input into a broader production process covered by the standard is ok if, but for this agreement, we would not be able to develop the standard; under those circumstances, there is a strong argument that the rule of reason could apply. It still obviously is a source of concern to counsellors and it may well be that standard-setting organizations would say 'Well that's all well and good', but certainly in the United States and now in Europe, we face private litigation. We don't want to take the risk, and that's fine. But I think that a sophisticated understanding, just as the *BMI*[2] case taught us, is required: not all price-fixing is price-fixing. I think what you have to look at is the discussion of something that looks like price, but is part of a broader efficiency-enhancing project. Is it no broader than necessary to achieve the efficiencies? Does it have no effect on downstream product or service markets? If it doesn't, and if the two efficiencies are being engendered, then that is a good reason to think that antitrust risk might not be all that high.

Now let me leave this interesting topic—and of course our administrative litigation remains to be resolved—and deal with another matter in litigation at the FTC: exclusion payments made in settlement of patent litigation.

Let me tell you what I mean by exclusion payments. The proper role of antitrust in evaluating patent settlement agreements has come to the forefront in a number of courts, with recent challenges brought by State Attorneys General, the FTC, and private litigants to patent settlements in the pharmaceutical area. Exact terms of the settlement agreements vary, but they shared a common feature of requiring a payment from a brand name drug manufacturer to a generic drug manufacturer in exchange for a promise by the generic company to refrain from marketing the product for

---

[2] *Broadcast Music, Inc. v Columbia Broadcasting System*, 441 US 1, 8–9 (1979).

some time, and that has been referred to by some of us as exclusion payment. So the analysis of whether such a payment tends to restrict competition and decrease output and violate the antitrust laws, must view the agreement we argue—I think some of us at the FTC—from that point in time in which the parties enter the agreement. At that time, if the outcome of litigation is uncertain and the purpose of the settlement is to eliminate that uncertainty, the agreement ensures that competition will be delayed. For example, a payment from a branded drug manufacturer, to a potential generic entrant, in exchange for ending the litigation, in setting generic entry for a future date, can be characterized as the brand's payment to eliminate the chance that the generic company will win litigation, or otherwise market its product at an earlier date.

Now you might say, 'Isn't that the patent property right, isn't it the right to exclude?' Yes, but . . . and I will explain what I mean. The statutory presumption of patent validity is a procedural device, allocating the burden of proof to an accused infringer who seeks to demonstrate the patent's invalidity in patent litigation. It shouldn't be understood to alter antitrust's traditional approach to the uncertain outcome of litigation at the time of the settlement agreement. There is a history of courts striking down collusive settlements in the patent area, not involving a specific reverse payment. There is nothing novel about that.

Now studies show that a large share of patents are found invalid in litigation and, furthermore, even holders of valid patents frequently have their patents found not to have been infringed, and that's key. It is not as if you are saying, 'Here we have a property right. We can use it and delay entry to this market until the patent expires'. It may well be that the party accused of patent infringement is not infringing. Some simple analogy: if you think of patents as property, the fact that you own a house and some surrounding property and you are accusing someone of trespassing, doesn't mean a person is actually trespassing. Despite the fact that you have that right to use that property, you are still constrained by other laws: you can't use your house to enter into an agreement with your competitors to fix prices, or to engage in other violations of law, or you couldn't agree with a neighbouring property-holder, as I say, to collude, to exclude potential entrants, say by buying up all the property in a particular area. So that is a simplistic analogy, some would say, but it points out that patent rights are like other property rights; they are constrained by the operation of the other laws, and we should remember that.

Antitrust analysis of payments to a potential competitor to delay entering the market is straightforward: such a payment purchases insurance that eliminates the risk of potential competition and is presumptively anticompetitive. As the Supreme Court has said: 'The antitrust laws are as much violated by the prevention of competition as by its destruction'. The fact that the potential competitor's status is uncertain in no way changes the analysis, for antitrust law condemns agreements to prevent competition, even when a potential entrant's prospects for successful entry are not assured. A leading antitrust treatise simply articulates the principle: 'The law does not condone the purchase of protection from uncertain competition any more than it condones the elimination of actual competition'.[3] So, as a matter of economics, agreements to delay on certain competition clearly are anti-competitive and harm consumers. Delaying potential competition harms consumers in exactly the same way that destroying existing competition does, though discounted by the probability of entry. Consumers are always better off at the possibility of competitive entry and lower prices than with the certainty of no entry, or some guaranteed lesser amount of competition.

Reflecting this economic reality, courts have long recognized that even agreements to delay uncertain competition have anticompetitive effects and using famous language from *Chicago Board of Trade*,[4] talking about the rule of reason, that one should focus on a restraint of fact, actual or probable, and an agreement to settle is not unilateral action by a patent holder: it is an agreement between parties; it is not unilateral action. Because a reduction in uncertain competition itself is an anti-competitive effect, proving what would have happened, absent the restraint, is not an element of an antitrust action. So even if subsequent events meant the likely effects of the agreement would not have materialised—let's assume for example, the potential entrant's plant had burnt down, failed to obtain regulatory approval or some other reason—that would not alter the conclusion that when an anticompetitive agreement was entered into it was likely to cause substantial harm.

Let's assume two gas stations enter into a price-fixing agreement. They think because of some zoning or other law, no gas stations are going to be able to enter. They fix prices; the zoning law changes the next month. All sorts of entrants come in. The price-fixing agreement is nugatory. It is quickly undermined. Does that mean that although it didn't really have effects that the price-fixing agreement was insulated? Absolutely not. You have to look at the expected effects of the agreement at the time it is entered into. There are anticompetitive agreements that later on, because of some unexpected circumstances, turn out not to harm consumers, but that does-n't mean one should let those agreements off the hook, because you can't

---

[3] XII Phillip E. Areeda, Herbert Hovenkamp *Antitrust Law* 2030b at 175 (1999).
[4] *Chicago Board of Trade v The United States*, 246 US 231, 238 (1918).

just wait saying, 'Well this agreement may or may not harm consumers, it doesn't have any efficiencies, or we are going to let it go by on the possibility that it doesn't cause harm.'

Now the DC Circuit's opinion in the *Microsoft*[5] case illustrates the importance of this policy. I know we have a colleague from Microsoft on the panel, but this has nothing to do with Microsoft as a company. It is a broader issue of applying the rule of reason here under section 2 of the Sherman Act, which hadn't happened before and that is still controversial and of course, I am talking about section 1 issues; it is not a section 2 issue. The DC Circuit confirmed that impeding nascent entry, instead of actual competition, is a fully cognizable anticompetitive effect; it rejected Microsoft's argument that the Government did not establish a causal link between Microsoft's foreclosure, Netscape and Java distribution channels and the maintenance of Microsoft's monopoly. It could infer causation, even when exclusionary conduct is aimed at nascent competitive technologies. Admittedly in the former case there is evidence, certainly in as much as nascent threats are merely potential substitutes, but the underlying proof problem is the same. Neither the plaintiffs, nor the court, can confidently reconstruct the product's hypothetical technological development in the world absent the development's exclusionary conduct. In short it was not the Government's burden to establish what would have happened in a hypothetical 'but for' world. As I say, what everyone thinks as to whether it should be a balancing test under section 2 of the Sherman Act, we are here dealing with section 1 of the Sherman Act. Clearly you do weigh costs and benefits in looking at the effects of conduct.

Now, applying these general principles to exclusion payments demonstrates, I would argue, that they can be anticompetitive; in the settlement of pharmaceutical patent litigation, an exclusion payment effectively is a temporal market allocation arrangement under which the brand company retains its sales for several years and shares its profits with a potential generic entrant, which in turn refrains from selling its competing product. Here a potential generic entrant clearly constitutes a threat to a brand company. Now, I am not going to go into the specifics of the *Schering-Plough* case,[6] which is the litigation that involves one of these so-called reverse payments—exclusion payments—I have described. There is a petition for a rehearing en banc, filed by the Federal Trade Commission a couple of weeks ago, before the 6th Circuit. Those of you who are interested can read the petition on the Commission's website.

---

[5] *United States v Microsoft Corporation*, 253 F.3d 34, 79-80 (DC Cir 2001).
[6] *Schering-Plough Corp v FTC*, 2005 WL 528439 (11th Cir 2005).

I will just leave you with a closing thought that I think of in looking at patents and the underlying themes: patents are important property rights and as our 1995 IP Guideline said, they are not monopolies, they are property rights. In certain circumstances, they may confer monopoly power; in other circumstances they may not. But like other forms of property, patterns can not be used to advance an anticompetitive agreement. Use of a patent to advance the anticompetitive agreement extends beyond a proper sphere of those property rights just as use of one's house to enter into a price-fixing agreement, or a combination of plots of land, as part of an anticompetitive scheme, violates the law, even though you are dealing with people who have genuine property right interests at stake.

So I would say that the FTC should not be viewed as anti-patent. Quite to the contrary, I think patents are very important, but we think antitrust law principles, like other statutory principles, have to remain available to be applied and the invocation of the term 'patent right' should not be sufficient in itself to stop more careful, reasoned analysis.

PAT TREACY

Thank you very much Alden for that very thought-provoking discussion. Now we turn to Jean-Yves Art, who is the Director of Competition Law at Microsoft for Europe, the Middle East and Africa. He is based in Brussels, so we are delighted that he has been able to make time, in what is undoubtedly a very busy time for him, to come over and speak to us today. Before he joined Microsoft, Jean-Yves was in private practice, and prior to that he spent several years at the Court of Justice clerking. He is also a Professor at the College of Europe, so I think you will agree that there is no-one better placed to talk to us today about the effects of compulsory licensing and whether or not there should be compulsory licensing of intellectual property rights mandated by the antitrust and competition laws.

JEAN-YVES ART

Thank you very much Pat. If you look at the title of my presentation—'An Exception in Need of Limiting Principles'—I am sure it sounds funny to many antitrust lawyers and I have to say that I certainly do not pretend to be as bright and as inspiring a competition lawyer as the most famous professor who wrote an article having a title which is very similar to that one on essential facilities in the US.[7]

---

[7] See Philip Areeda 'Essential Facilities: An Epithet in Need of Limiting Principles' 58 Antitrust Law Journal 841.

In fact, the idea of this title came to my mind because I was thinking that the legal theories which are involved in compulsory licensing, the type of issues and also the dangers that compulsory licensing is raising and the type of response that refusal to license IP rights and compulsory licensing may call for: those issues are pretty similar to the ones that were contemplated in this article and they seem to me to warrant at least a nod to this article. But again, I am certainly not pretending to be as inspiring as the professor who wrote the famous original article on essential facilities.

'An exception in need of limiting principles'. Why? Because the EU case law makes it clear that refusal to license IP rights is the right of the IP owner; it is a principle. A refusal to license in principle is not a violation of antitrust law. But in exceptional circumstances, it can be. If you look at the case law which has developed over the past close to twenty years now, since 1988, you realize that the scope of the exception has progressively broadened and it seems to me that it is important to know where we are going. Where are we going? Where are we going to put a limit to the broadening of the exception, because today it seems to me that we are close to changing the exception and the principle and that is what I would like to discuss, to show to you and to provide at the end maybe some thoughts of where we could find the limit to this broadening of the exception.

The first major case that dealt with the refusal to grant an IP licence is *Volvo*.[8] It is a case which dates back to 1988. In that case, Volvo—and the same happened with Renault,[9] the French automobile manufacturer—refused to grant a licence for the manufacture of spare parts to independent repairers. The spare parts incorporated a product design and Volvo and Renault both relied on the IP rights and the protective design to refuse to grant a license. The question was whether this refusal amounted to a violation of EU antitrust law. The Court responded at the time that as a rule an IP owner is fully entitled to refuse to grant a licence. This is really part of the substance of its exclusive right as an IP owner. As an IP owner, you have an exclusive right and because you have this exclusive right, which is granted within a certain scope, for a certain period of time, as long as you have this exclusive right, you are fully entitled to refuse to license. That is the principle. However, the Court added, there are certain circumstances in which the refusal to grant a licence, or more generally the exercise of the exclusive right, can give rise to abusive conduct. The Court gave as examples the fixing of prices of the spare parts at an excessive price; discrimination in the supply of spare parts to independent repairers; limitation in the volume of spare parts that is put on the market; discontinuation of the production of spare parts that consumers still need.

---

[8] Case 238/87 [1988] ECR 6211, [1989] 4 CMLR 122.
[9] Case 53/87 [1988] ECR 6039, [1990] 4 CMLR 265.

So what clearly appears from this ruling is that first the principle is that the IP owner is fully entitled to refuse to grant a licence to the IP; it has an exclusive right and it's entitled to refuse to grant a licence to third parties. The second thing which appears is that refusal to grant a licence may give rise to an abuse in the secondary market, the market for spare parts. This is an abuse which is caught by Article 82. It's exclusive pricing, limitation of production, discrimination. All this appearing in the secondary market where the IP right can be exercised.

That was *Volvo* (1988). Then ten years later, in fact in 1998, the Court was called upon to render a judgment in the *Magill* case[10] and six years later in the *IMS Health* case.[11] In the two cases, the Court took the same approach and laid down the same principle. In both cases, the Court restated *Volvo* and *Renault*, highlighting the difference between the principle and the exception. In principle the IP right-holder has an exclusive right and it is part of the substance of this exclusive right for the IP holder to be entitled to refuse to grant a licence to third parties. That is the substance of the right, which has been granted to the IP right-holder by national IP law. So that is a full right, exclusive: you are entitled to refuse to license. However, just as in *Volvo*, in some exceptional circumstances, the exercise of the exclusive right may involve abusive conduct. Whereas in *Renault* and *Volvo* it was clear that the abusive conduct was a clear-cut abuse under Article 82 in the secondary market, in *Magill*, as well as in *IMS Health*, the Court has started to somewhat broaden the scope of the exception or going in a direction which opened the scope for a broadening of the exception.

In both *Magill* and *IMS Health*, the Court said that there are essentially four circumstances which need to be cumulatively met in order for a refusal to grant a licence to amount to an abuse of a dominant position, to amount to an abuse contrary to Article 82.

The first condition is that the copyright-protected material, the asset which is protected by the IP right, must be indispensable in order to conduct business in a secondary market, so it must be in a sense an 'essential facility'. That is something which would be made clear by the Court in *IMS Health* where the Court expressly refers to another case, which is the case in which I think for the first time the term 'essential facility' was used: *Oscar Bronner*.[12] The Court made the link between *IMS Health* and *Oscar Bronner* and said you can have as an abuse the exercise of the exclusive right, of an IP order: the refusal to grant a right to third parties may amount

---

[10] *RTE and ITP v Commission* (Cases C-241/91P, etc) [1995] ECR I-797, [1995] 4 CMLR 718.
[11] *IMS Health v NDC Health* (Case C418/01) [2004] ECR I-5039, [2004] 4 CMLR 28, [2004] ECDR 23.
[12] *Oscar Bronner v Mediaprint* (Case C7/97) [1998] ECR I7791.

to an abuse. The first condition provided that the asset which is protected by the IP right be an essential facility which is indispensable to conduct an activity in a secondary market.

The second condition is that—and it is a condition which is closely linked, and I think in my view, it is identical to the very first one—the refusal to grant a licence risks eliminating competition, eliminating all competition in the secondary market; to the extent that the IP-protected asset is indispensable in order to conduct business, an out-right refusal to grant a licence if it's a non-discriminatory refusal, if it's applied to all applicants, such a refusal would eliminate all competition in the secondary market. So the two conditions are very closely linked to each other.

The third condition—and it is here that the exception seems to broaden somewhat compared to *Volvo*—is that the refusal to grant a licence must prevent the emergence of a new product in the secondary market, a new product for which there is potential consumer demand. In the *Magill* case this new product was a comprehensive TV guide, for which it was established there was potential consumer demand. Consumers no longer needed to go and buy weekly or daily newspapers in order to have the weekly or daily TV programmes by TV channel. They could buy a comprehensive TV guide. So the refusal to grant a licence over the copyright on the TV programmes prevented the appearance of a new product, the comprehensive TV guide, for which there was potential consumer demand.

I am saying that in adopting this decision the courts have broadened the scope of *Volvo*, although to prevent the emergence of a new product for which there is a potential consumer demand is also an abuse which fits under Article 82 (b) of the Treaty: the limitation of production, limitation of market, limitation of technical progress, to the detriment, to the prejudice of consumers. So, to some extent, we are still within the scope of *Volvo*, but because you move from something which are clear-cut abuses—predatory pricing, discrimination, discontinuation of supply—to another type of abuse which is much vaguer: the limitation of markets; the limitation of technical progress to the detriment of consumers; because you move to that part of Article 82, you open the scope to a broader exception than the one that was set in *Volvo*.

And the fourth condition which the Court imposed in *Magill* and which it repeated in *IMS Health* is that the refusal to supply goes beyond what is necessary in order to protect the essential function of the IP right. What the Court said in that respect in *Magill* is that it would have been possible for Magill to license its copyright over TV programmes to the producer of a weekly TV guide and still to ensure the commercial viability of its activity as not only the TV station, but also as a publisher of its own proprietary

TV guide. That is how the Court explained in that case in *Magill* that the refusal to license went beyond what was necessary in order to safeguard and to protect the essential function of the copyright. It was still possible for Magill, as the Court said, but there is not much explanation of the judgment on that point, it was absolutely possible for Magill to license its copyrighted material TV programmes to a publisher of a comprehensive TV guide and still ensure the commercial viability of its own proprietary TV guide. Again, that is a statement and there is no further explanation or demonstration on this point in *Magill*.

I am not going to spend time on *IMS Health* and the reason is that *IMS Health* is essentially a restatement of *Magill* with the same conditions being imposed: the IP protected material asset for the service; this IP protected material must be an essential facility; it must be indispensable in order to conduct business in a secondary market—that is a reference to *Oscar Bronner*. If you have alternative means of doing business, even if they are more onerous, even if it is more cumbersome to go through those alternative means, then a refusal to grant a licence is something which is acceptable under EU antitrust law. The IP protected asset must be *indispensable* in order to conduct business in the secondary market. Second condition: the refusal to license prevents the emergence of a new product for which there is potential consumer demand. It is the same condition as in *Magill* for the weekly TV guide. In *IMS Health* the condition is also applied to the production of a new data-gathering database by those providers of services to the pharmaceutical companies. So preventing the emergence of a new product for which there is potential consumer demand—the same condition will be used in the case *Ladbroke*[13] where it is used to explain why the refusal to grant a licence is not an abuse under Article 82. There was no prevention of the emergence of a new product and the IP right was not indispensable in order to conduct business in a secondary market in *Ladbroke*. The third condition that was restated by the Court in *IMS Health* is the same as the one which was indicated in *Magill*. The refusal to license isn't justified because it goes beyond what is necessary in order to protect the essential function of the IP right.

So the three conditions: If you look at all the cases together of *Volvo*, *Magill* and *IMS*, the three elements that appear there are that the IP right licence is an essential facility indispensable to conduct business in a secondary market and the refusal to grant a licence goes beyond what is necessary in order to protect the essential function of the IP right. The second element is based on statements made in both *Magill* and *IMS*, but without much explanation in the judgments on how a compulsory licence protects the

---

[13] *Ladbroke* (Case T-504/93) [19977] ECR II-923, [1997] 5 CMLR 309.

essential function of the IP right. And the third condition, which antitrust lawyers will see easily, is that the refusal to grant a licence is the cause of the abuse in the secondary market. The abuse being either excessive pricing, because you have a monopoly and you have excessive pricing; discrimination; discontinuation of supplier from the consumers, or as in *Magill* and *IMS*, a lack of development—effectively you do not give a licence; that your refusal to licence the IP right to third parties, even competitors, is going to prevent the emergence of new products for which there is consumer demand.

So that was the scope defined by *Volvo*, *Magill*, and *IMS*.

I turn now to *Microsoft*.[14] I am sure you will have noticed that for the first preceding three slides, the title was 'The Principle and the Exception'. *Microsoft*: the question is whether there is a principle or an exception. Where is the principle? Where is the exception?

In *Microsoft*, the part of the case which deals with the refusal to license IP rights—and let me say that by way of introduction, the Commission challenges the issue whether the materials which were requested by third parties, SunMicroSystems and others, about whether those materials are protected by IP rights. I think that today there is no longer any significant dispute as to whether they are IP rights that protect those materials and let's say that for the sake of this presentation, let's assume that they are IP rights. Otherwise, the *Microsoft* case would have nothing to do with this presentation.

Let's assume that they are IP rights. Copyrights and several patents are involved and are protecting the technology which is embedded in the communication protocols. I am not going to go into details of the technique on server communications, I can reassure you. I am going to stay on the principles. So in *Microsoft*, the question was whether the refusal to supply copyright and patent-protected material technology—which was to be implemented in directly completing products in other server operating systems, competing directly with Microsoft server operating systems, the Windows server operating system—whether this amounted to an abuse. The Commission, as you know, found an abuse despite a number of factors which set this case very much aside from the case law as I summarized it in the previous slide—*Volvo*, *Magill*, and *IMS*. The first condition of *Volvo*, *Magill*, and *IMS* is that the copyright-protected material must be indispensable. It must be an essential facility, indispensable to conduct business. What we are saying in the case is that there are other means available to

---

[14] Commission decision of 24 Mar 2004, COMP/37.792. *Microsoft Corp v Commission* (Case T-201/04 R) [2005] 4 CMLR 18.

ensure inter-operability and to ensure inter-operability between the different server operating systems. So the access to the copyright-protected and the patent-protected material is not really indispensable. Yes, it is more cumbersome. Yes, it is more onerous. Yes, it is more difficult. It may be more difficult to implement those other means, but other people are doing this; other vendors of server operating systems are doing this. The best proof that it is not indispensable is that there are competing vendors of server operating systems that are entering the market these days and that are growing, succeeding in the market and they do not have access to the material which Microsoft should have provided to third parties, to this copyright-protected or patent-protected material. They do not have access to this. They nevertheless continue to enter the market and to grow into that market. That is a fact which is established.

I would like to concentrate on the other two conditions which were set out in *Magill* and *IMS Health*. Remember that in *Magill* and *IMS Health,* as I indicated, the refusal to grant a licence is the cause of an abuse in the secondary market. The abuse in *IMS Health* and *Magill* was that because the IP right-holder prevented, or had refused to grant, a licence, potential competitors were not in a position to develop new products for which there was potential demand. As I said at the time, we entered there into the scope of Article 82(b) of the Treaty; Article 82(b) characterizes an abuse as the limitation of production, limitation of market, limitation of technical progress to the prejudice of consumers. That was *IMS Health, Magill* and in this case, *Microsoft*, the Commission does not show that the refusal to grant a licence on copyright and patent, the refusal to supply this technology—the communication protocols—prevents the emergence of a new product for which there is consumer demand. The Commission does not show that the refusal to grant a licence goes beyond what is necessary in order to protect essential function of those IP rights. In particular, it does not go beyond what is necessary in order to protect Microsoft's incentives to innovate. The two conditions are merged in fact in the Commission's decision in a balancing test which the Commission does between the impact of a compulsory licence of copyright on the incentives to innovate by Microsoft, if Microsoft is forced to give a licence to its copyright and to its patent; what is going to be the impact of this compulsory licensing obligation on Microsoft's incentives to innovate? What is going to be the impact of the grant of the licence on the incentives to innovate of third parties? The Commission says, in order to determine whether there is an abuse under Article 82(b), 'Let's look at the consequences and the impact of an obligation to license'. Will this obligation to license contribute to a limitation of production, of markets, of technical progress to the detriment of users, or not? And the Commission in the decision says, again in my view without any explanation, without any clear assessment, without any supporting facts supporting that analysis, the Commission says that if you balance the impact of the compulsory license on the incentives to innovate of Microsoft and third parties, other vendors of operating systems, the balance leans towards those competitors. The balance leans towards a compulsory licensing. Therefore, the fact that Microsoft refuses to grant a licence amounts to an abuse under Article 82(b) because it limits production, or it limits technical progress to the detriment of users. That is how I read this decision, and I think that that is a fair reading of this decision, trying to give much sense to part of the decision.

I am not going to spend a lot of time to advocate Microsoft's position on this. I think what is really important is to see that we have gone from a statement in *Volvo* (1988), where it was very clear that the refusal to grant a licence could be abusive only if this refusal caused or involved an abuse in the secondary market: a clear-cut abuse which is caused by the refusal to license.

We go to *IMS Health* and *Magill* and there is there a broadening of the scope of the exception. What is the abuse? The abuse can be the limitation of markets or the prevention of the emergence of a new product. And now we are at *Microsoft*, what is the abuse? Well the abuse is in the balancing interest that you have to do between the incentives to innovate of Microsoft and third parties, a balancing interest which is, in my view, a theoretical principle which lacks in the decision, any supporting facts, any supporting basis, any supporting analysis, any structural test. There is no indication given to any body and, in particular, the IP right-holder, on what it is supposed to do in order to determine whether refusal to license its IP right may be abusive or not.

I would like at the end for the remaining two minutes to give what I think could be some thoughts and again I am not saying that this is the principle. This is not the limiting principle to the exercise of copyright, but some thoughts on how we can look for a limiting principle. I must say, I am going to give those thoughts from the perspective of EU law. I frankly do not know, and I would be very interested to hear what the American colleagues in this room have to say about what could be the US law. My knowledge of US law on compulsory licensing is that today there are judgments that go in different directions and those judgments if my understanding is correct pre-date the *Trinko*[15] judgment, and I frankly do not know whether the *Trinko* judgment would have an impact on the direction that we would take between these two alternatives under US law. But if you look at this from

---

[15] *Verizon Communications Inc v Law Offices of Curtis v Trinko, LLP*, 540 US 398 (2004).

the viewpoint of EU law, with the case law that exists, I think there are some elements that a limiting principle should enforce.

The first one is that the IP right is an essential facility. It must be indispensable to conduct business. The second condition is that access to the IP right must be indispensable in order to remedy an abuse in the secondary market. There must be an abuse in the secondary market and access to the IP right must be indispensable in order to remedy this abuse. That is a principle of proportionality. If there are other remedies that are available, such as in the software industry the right to decompile under Article 6 of the Software Directive, if there are other remedies which are available and that could be used in order to avoid compulsory licensing, and still remedy the abuse that exists in the secondary market, this other remedy should be used. That is the last condition. If you have a less intrusive remedy, which can be either from an IP law perspective, or from an antitrust law prospective, I think that preference should be given to this alternative remedy rather than compulsory licensing which is a major encroachment on the rights of the IP order, a major encroachment on the rights of the IP holder and also a major disincentive to innovate.

So these are a few thoughts on where we could go in order to find the limiting principle. Essential facilities; causal link between the exercise of the IP right and the abuse; protection of the essential function of the IP right; the compulsory licensing should not affect the essential function of the IP right; and, the last condition, there should be no less intrusive remedy than compulsory licensing, either from IP law, such as a right to decompile, or from an antitrust law perspective. Remember the abuses in *Volvo*? The abuses in *Volvo* were predatory pricing, discrimination, discontinuation of production—these are not infringements or abuses that require compulsory licensing. Predatory pricing can be corrected by an obligation to increase prices; that is something which has been done in other cases involving predatory pricing. Discrimination is an order not to discriminate. There is no need to force the IP right-holder to give a licence in order to correct those abuses. So again, a compulsory licensing order is a remedy which seems appropriate only in those conditions where there is no other less intrusive remedy which is available, either under IP law, or under antitrust law.

PAT TREACY

Thank you very much Jean-Yves. That was extremely interesting. One of the issues which seems to have formed a theme through both of those presentations so far is the extent to which competition law, antitrust law, can intervene to protect or to encourage nascent competition. Now those of my colleagues who are patent lawyers would say that of course the whole point of having a patent is to stop *all* competition within the scope of your patent, nascent, actual or otherwise. So I do wonder whether it is a question that perhaps some IP rights are too broad, whether it is the fact that competition law is too bold, and I think that perhaps Steven is a man who may be able to give us some theoretical answers to the correct balance between those two.

Steven Preece is a Principal Case Officer at the Office of Fair Trading. He has had a deep interest in issues of competition law and intellectual property for a long time, and in fact he has a Masters in competition law and intellectual property, so I think that he is well positioned to sum up some of the issues that come out of what we have heard so far and try and lead us into a question time when you can give your views.

Steven Preece

Thanks very much, Pat. Now as you can tell by my accent, I am a British civil servant and as a result of which British civil servants, like their American counterparts, do speak with some caution in such a vulnerable venue such as this and I would say that the views I express are entirely personal and do not necessarily represent those of the Office of Fair Trading. Let me add also though that the views that I do express and the questions I raise do come from looking at things through the lens of experience in a competition authority and they may well be very different from colleagues who were patent and copyright lawyers and copyright specialists.

I feel slightly daunted as well because it is kind of like coming on after The Beatles. Having had two very distinguished speakers in their fields speaking very knowledgably and very interestingly on such critical topics and I am going to try and raise a framework for discussion and some questions perhaps leading to some of the areas that they have discussed as well. In particular, as Pat said, one of the very interesting issues which arises time and time again now, is the question of whether intellectual property law is 'becoming overprotective'. If so, if it is becoming overprotective, or has been overprotective, is antitrust intervention an appropriate means of curing those problems on a case-by-case basis? And those are some of the questions I am going to explore right now and I very much value the input also of other panellists and yourselves as well, because there is no easy answer to this question and I don't think the answer is going to come very quickly either. I think it has to be done against a broader framework of differing views.

The starting point, of course, is that, as we have heard from our two prior speakers, IPRs are exclusionary by nature. Why are they exclusionary? What they are doing is that they are preventing appropriation or indeed misappropriation and free-riding on the innovation or the creativity of the inventor or the author. Those of the examples of patents and copyrights are the two main areas. Obviously there are other areas such as registered designs and database rights. Now, the objective of that lawful exclusion in my view is to enhance producer welfare. What that means to say is that the benefits that the producer has over and above after simply being in the market, just pricing at a very basic level simply covering its costs. What that lawful exclusion does by enhancing producer welfare, or creating an incentive of producer welfare, is it creates an incentive to innovate and create. So what we have is the potential for charging what economists call monopoly rents, in other words super-competitive prices. That, as we have heard from Alden, and I certainly share the view and many others in European competition law would share that view, is that the potential is only a potential, it is not guaranteed. Other goods or services may well act as a competitive discipline in respect of the work or the patented invention. Why do we have that potential for exclusion or potential for monopoly rents? The answer is to enhance long-term consumer welfare benefits. This creates what economists call sometimes dynamic efficiency. It is creating an incentive for innovation. The public knows about an invention. The public knows about a work. It doesn't simply stay in the vaults in the creator's offices. So that is sort of an elementary economic framework. There is an element of trade-off there. The consumer benefits from this limited period of enhanced producer welfare.

Which brings us to the question of 'overprotective IPRs'. I will use that term in quotes, because I am not going to say definitively today that IPRs in some cases are overprotective. I am going to raise the question as to the circumstances in which they may be. But, if the analysis that I have offered initially about essentially the consumer producer welfare trade-off as an incentive for IPRs is correct, then it would follow in my view that IPRs become overprotective when the long-term consumer welfare detriment exceeds what is necessary for the producer welfare incentive. In other words, the consumer is in the long-term being harmed by the existence—and the exercise for that matter—of that intellectual property right over and above any sort of necessary producer welfare incentive in order to enter that market.

Now Alden has spoken about the FTC DOJ hearings in Washington that took place about two years ago and one of the very interesting reports is by the FTC on just looking at the balance between competition antitrust law and patent law and policy. I don't want to speak too much on this one, because Alden is considerably more knowledgeable in this area than I am and I think his views will have far more credibility. But nevertheless, one of the interesting points in there, I think, relates to post-grant challenges and also the opportunity for challenges during the examination period before the US patent office. In my view, I think the overprotection at least on this side of the Atlantic is probably less likely to occur because obviously we do have quite a high standard of novelty and inventive step which is involved. Now the FTC report does address those issues and does call for some reform in the USA on that, but to a large extent it seems as if some of the problems that may be identified by the Federal Trade Commission arising from the hearings relates to procedural matters such as opposition proceedings before the US patent office and furthermore post-grant opposition. Now to a large degree in my view, I think that is actually quite well taken care of under the European Patent Convention system, the opposition proceedings on a certain limited basis before the European Patent Office in Munich, but also before the UK Patent Office as well. There are considerable, probably more generous, UK grounds for third party intervention and opposition there as well and as we all know, we can always, obviously if you have a lot of money, you can go to the High Court just across the road there and seek a declaration of invalidity of the relevant patent.

Perhaps more problematic, and I think it is very interesting that the cases that we have heard about today in European competition law concern copyright, is what I myself would call windfall copyrights. These are copyrights which may arise over a 'protected work' as a result of activities incidental to the copyright proprietor. They embody a very low level of creativity and the exercise of that windfall copyright prevents new product markets from emerging or otherwise creating efficiencies. For example, it just creates higher costs owing to licensing and again there is that consumer welfare detriment. Now this may in particular arise in circumstances when the windfall copyright, so to speak, is concerned with protecting the idea or the method of presentation of the data. Now a very distinguished commentator such as Ian Forrester QC has commented on this. In fact Mr Forrester testified before the hearings in Washington DC two years ago before the Federal Trade Commission and the Department of Justice and he presented a very interesting paper referring to *Magill*[16] and *IMS*,[17] as those were the big cases at the time—this precedes *Microsoft*[18]—as cases of European competition law correcting what he called 'aberrant national copyright law'. Now I don't want to necessarily offer a view to say that the copyright subsisting in those cases was actually a case of *aberrant* national copyright law. Nevertheless, I do think that it does raise an interesting question as to

---

[16] *Magill* (n 9).   [17] *IMS* (n 10).   [18] *Microsoft* (n 13).

whether there is any potential for a copyright law, for example—windfall copyright law is what I call it—to heal thyself.

Now in this sense it is very interesting to have colleagues from the States here because part of the reason why I would suggest you don't see cases like *Magill* and *IMS* in the United States is, for all that we hear about *Trinko*[19] and the very interesting and very economically analytical US law in refusal to supply, the reality is that in US law it is very unlikely that these cases would concern works in which copyright was deemed to subsist. For example, in *IMS*, or should I say *Magill* and possibly *IMS*, it is unlikely that the subject matter at issue would actually be protected by copyright law. This has been addressed in the leading cases in US copyright law. The leading case is *Feist Bureau Publications*.[20] In *Feist* what had happened was that in rural Kansas you had a telephone company who published its own telephone directory. You had another telephone directory publisher who specialized in telephone directories. They came along and said 'We are going to do a comprehensive telephone guide for this market'. They said to Rural Telephone Services: 'Please can we have a licence of your copyright?' It was understood at that point in time in US copyright law that that sort of work would be protected. RTS said no. Then Feist, the publisher, went ahead and did it anyway and ended up going to the Federal Court system under the US Copyright Act of 1976. It went to the US Supreme Court and Justice O'Connor, writing for an essentially unanimous court, said that originality is the *sine qua non* of copyright and that certainly in the US law there is a constitutional requirement of originality and originality in that context was understood to require some element of creativity.

Now this, certainly in United Kingdom and Canadian copyright law, is a concept which has been definitively rejected by the courts. Going quite far back to the *University of London Press* case[21] back in 1916 when Mr Justice Peterson referred to 'skill, labour and judgment' and with that he refers to the concept of literary work as something that is protectable. Whereas originality in United Kingdom and, as I say, Canadian copyright law, for example, simply means that the work originates with the author; it is not a copy. In those sort of circumstances, you can see then why in the Republic of Ireland, which has a copyright law essentially based on and very similar to the United Kingdom copyright law, you have copyright subsisting in something so really prosaic as television listings. I would probably bet a little bit of money that if I went before a US Federal Court, following the *Feist* judgment, I would not be successful in trying to establish that copyright would

---

[19] *Trinko* (n 14).
[20] *Feist Publications, Inc v Rural Tel Service Co.* 499 US 340 (1991).
[21] [1916] 2 Ch 601.

subsist in those works. So in the United States, I think you have seen the case of copyright law heal thyself because the United States Supreme Court in 1991 recognised that there are certain consumer welfare detriments which may potentially arise from copyrights subsisting in works of extremely low creativity. That is being fed into the originality requirement. Certainly that is a stand that is widely viewed and many people would argue that the *Feist* judgment in the United States must be understood by reference to Article 1, section 8, clause 8 of the US Constitution, which is the famous copyright and patents clause which is a constitutional mandate to Congress to create copyright law and patent law, which certainly in the UK we don't have here.

Another interesting issue of copyright law heal thyself in the US is a much broader concept of what we call the 'merger doctrine'. The famous case of *Baker v Selden*,[22] which is a 19th century case under very early US copyright law, dealt with the situation in which the proposition is of course that copyright law does not protect the idea, it protects the expression of the idea. What you had is a system of essentially a presentation of a method of accounting; somebody copied that. The courts in the United States also held that the expression of the idea in this case is merged with the idea itself. So in that case, the copyright proprietor was prevented then from preventing somebody else from utilizing that system. Now query, and I am not saying this is the case, query in relation to *IMS*. Did we actually have a situation in which what was really being protected—admittedly by harmonized law under the database directive, again a work of very low originality in German law—was the method of presentation involving the 1860 Brick Structure. If that was the case, then again a broader scope of the merger doctrine, as embodied in the US copyright law, may well then serve to correct that. I can't speculate upon the operation of any merger doctrine in German copyright law, which was the relevant copyright law, but what it would say is that in the UK we do have much narrower concepts of the merger doctrine. We have been slightly more generous I think to copyright proprietors in seeing ways out of saying the merger of the idea and expression has not been there and one of the leading cases on that is Mr Justice Jacob in *IBCOS and Computer Associates*.[23]

So query that. I certainly will not be suggesting now in this forum that we absolutely need to have a higher standard of originality for example in UK copyright law or indeed that the Merger Doctrine should be broadened. But I do raise the question as to whether if that is the case in some of the cases such as *IMS* and *Magill*, that that might have been an appropriate way of

---

[22] 101 US 99 (1880).
[23] *Ibcos Computers Ltd v Barclay's Mercantile Highland Finance* [1994] FSR 275.

correcting that. That is one option. If there is overprotective copyright law, or any form of IP law—to a large degree other forms of IP laws, such as registered designs and patent law, do have compulsory licensing provisions. Now certainly, at least at the relevant time in UK-registered design law, we have heard about the *Volvo* case in 1998 at that point in time, under the Registered Designs Act in 1949 there certainly was a compulsory licensing process, which again query: would that actually have been relevant to the analysis of the Court? It is not on the face of the record itself, but is an underlying concept. We all know the Patents Act 1977—there are very important compulsory licensing provisions as well, which would correct if you like consumer welfare detriments arising from the non-exercise of the patent monopoly. That is the question, should intellectual property law heal itself? In which case, what I would say is the means by which it is doing so is expanding the scope of the public domain. It is ensuring a fairly rich public domain, by which no royalty stream would come to the intellectual property law proprietor.

The other alternative, what some people might advocate, is antitrust law intervention. We have heard a great deal about it today—very articulately about compulsory licensing. In other words, the competition law authorities are intervening in some sense to compel a licence to be granted in cases in which they see that there are sub-optimal levels of productivity and consumer welfare in secondary markets. That is an option. It has been exercised on a number of occasions now in EU competition law. It doesn't really have as strong a counterpart in the US. Now, it is a very interesting opportunity. One of the limitations I would say that we want to bear in mind of course is that antitrust law by definition is an *ex post* form of intervention. In other words, we at the Office of Fair Trading, European Commission, and the national courts now under modernization *have had* a complaint; they have looked at it, and taken a certain course of corrective action. By definition if you like, the harm may well occur; sometimes we can prevent the harm, but in other cases, the harm has occurred. Furthermore, it is selective. We only get a certain number of complaints every year. We can only act on a certain number of complaints every year. So what it does suggest is that not every case where there is a situation of overprotective copyright or other forms of IPRs, which can appropriately be corrected by antitrust law intervention, is only going to deal with that particular case. Certainly we have heard Jean-Yves say that yes there are dynamic efficiency implications for that sort of intervention in a sense by which pretty soon a market may look at the probability of competition law intervention in doing its cost benefit analysis, but for the most part again it is limited to very specific circumstances. So is it better for a limited form of intervention in exceptional circumstances? The exceptional circumstances we have heard about, and I certainly don't think I would be controversial in saying that I think expanding the scope of exceptional circumstances is something that can not be rushed into; competition authorities must be absolutely certain as to why they are doing that and the benefits which will ensue to the economy as a result of doing so.

That is an opportunity, but is that desirable owing to the, as I say, the *ex post facto* and limited nature of competition law intervention or is it more appropriate for example that substantive intellectual property law corrects itself in terms of consumer welfare analysis? I don't know if there is a best way forward. I think it may be the case that there is one better way forward and this is something I think which is a great deal of interest and I would certainly welcome the views of other panellists and yourselves on this as to which you think is the better way forward. Now in doing so, of course, both in terms of intellectual property law correcting overprotection and/or competition law from time to time to be absolutely necessary in exceptional circumstances you must bear in mind the requirements imposed by TRIPS: Trade-Related Aspects of Intellectual Property Rights agreement of the WTO. Article 13, for example, in respect of copyright sets out a three-part test which limits the scope of limitation of those rights. So any sort of analysis we do must be taken against that.

PAT TREACY

Thank you very much Steven. Well we have heard quite a round-up of the issues that are currently at the forefront of people's minds in relation to the balance between intellectual property law and competition law and policy, so I think what I would like to do now is to hear some thoughts from the audience, from you who have been listening to this.

VALENTINE KORAH

There are a wonderful load of issues that have been raised, but I would like to confine myself to *IMS* and Jean-Yves' contribution.

I have great difficulty with *IMS*.[24] Of course it was decided a month after the *Microsoft*[25] decision and it said that the special circumstances must be those in *Magill*[26] if the conduct was to be abusive. But if that's true then what about *Volvo*?[27] How is a spare front wing panel to a car to be a new product? Because it is blue or the car is green? It is absolutely inconsistent with the *Volvo* set of special circumstances and there is no discussion at any point as to the policy.

---

[24] *IMS* (n 10).   [25] *Microsoft* (n 13).
[26] *Magill* (n 9).   [27] *Volvo* (n 7).

Another change is that *IMS* excludes all competition on the market. The early cases on refusal to supply goods or services were excluding all competition on the part of the *complainant* and why have we switched to all competition for *anyone*? I don't want the essential facilities doctrine expanded. I think it should be used in very rare cases. I don't think this is a good way for reconciling it. Supposing you really do need my product. Perhaps I invested when there was public finance available. Then in those circumstances, I might want to use the essential facilities doctrine, but the monopolies could avoid me by licensing someone, one who is not very aggressive. So that seems to me to be a very silly change and with no policy explanation.

It was however I think right on the third novelty—that it didn't require there to be actual sales to the secondary market. The best case in this area, I think, is the Australian one of *Queensland Wire v Broken Hill Propriety*,[28] where the refusal to supply a component except at the price it was selling for the total product was treated as a constructive refusal to supply. The High Court, the Australian Supreme Court, said contrary to the Court of Appeal, that the fact that there was no market downstream was actually not true. There was a *potential* market. That seems to me that on that point *IMS* was right because it is much worse not to supply at all, than not on a margin squeeze.

JEAN-YVES ART

I would like to comment especially on the very first point that you made about the inconsistency between *IMS Health* and *Volvo*. It goes to a point which has been raised by President Vesterdorf in the interim measures case, which was brought by Microsoft. The question which he raised in that case is whether the conditions which are laid down in *IMS Health* and *Magill* are sufficient and necessary. Although I have much difficulty in deciding when the conditions are sufficient and when they are necessary, it is clear at least from *IMS Health* that what the court said, that for an abuse to exist, for refusal to license to constitute an abuse, it is sufficient to have several conditions. I think that the question put by President Versterdorf also refers to *Volvo*. You do not have an abuse *only when* there is prevention of emergence of the new product; you can have an abuse when the refusal to license may be contrary to Article 82, when there are other abuses in the secondary market such as in the *Volvo* case.

I think the main point which I would like to make in this respect is that you at least need to show, and to be absolutely definitely convinced, that the

[28] (1989) 167 CLR 177.

refusal to license causes an abuse in the secondary market. It was probably the case in *Magill*. It may also have been the case in *IMS Health*, although the effects there are less certain than in *Magill*. In *Magill* it was quite clear that there was prevention of emergence of a new product which was demanded by consumers. In the *Microsoft* case, for me it is really a question mark. I think that you could agree with the principle of the balancing of interest but if you have an indication of how to measure the interest to innovate of the IP right-holder, how to measure the interest to innovate of the vendors or the prospective licensees, how to balance the two and you have a clear-cut balance leaning in one direction, rather than the other, you could, in those circumstances, maybe say yes there is an abuse under Article 82(b) of the Treaty: limitation of technical progress. You might assert this case. Then you also have to show that this limitation of technical progress is to the detriment of consumers—which is not obvious in the case of operating systems. Maybe the users want to have a harmonized, a consistent computing system and not to have the variety. So the fact that you do not have innovation does not necessarily lead to a prejudice of the consumer, at least in certain markets, in certain circumstances.

So when you say that *IMS Health* is not consistent with *Volvo*, I agree with you, it is clearly not consistent but they *do* all go in the same direction: that you have to show an abuse in the secondary market.

PAT TREACY

Alden would you like to comment?

ALDEN ABBOTT

Obviously it is a topic of some interest. I think obviously and I will say more about it now. The *Verizon v Trinko*[29] case and the question of essential facilities—I don't want to get into the specifics, certainly of the *Microsoft*[30] case or licensing—I would just point out that the Supreme Court avoided the issue in *Trinko* really; as a footnote that noted that the Supreme Court has never recognized the essential facilities doctrine. Some lower courts have. The Supreme Court studiously avoided the opportunity to say there is no essential facilities doctrine. Certainly, it also studiously avoided saying too much about monopoly leverage, although again I think it is implicit in that decision. There was some doubt about the doctrine, so given the unsettled nature of the doctrine, I had better not say more.

---

[29] *Verizon Communications Inc v Law Offices of Curtis V Trinko, LLP*, 540 US 398 (2004).
[30] *Microsoft* (n 13).

THOMAS VINJE

Firstly I would like to compliment Jean-Yves on a very interesting and stimulating presentation.

I will take a short moment to address the preliminary question which Jean-Yves raised, which is whether the *Microsoft*[31] case actually involves any intellectual property issues. I would suggest that it doesn't. Indeed, Jean-Yves raised patent and copyright and with respect to patents, Microsoft has raised four patents that it has and one application and says that it intends to apply for quite a number of other patents. I think we can probably discard the applications it intends to make because I don't think the court would regard that as sufficient to demonstrate much of anything. With respect to the existing patents, as Mr Abbott said, it is one thing to say that one has a patent and another to say that someone else infringes it, but that doesn't necessarily make it so. Indeed in our view, the interface specifications that the Commission has required to be disclosed can clearly be implemented by competitors without infringing any of Microsoft's patents. So there is no compulsory licence of patents involved in the case. Secondly, with respect to the copyright, it is important to recall that the Commission's decision does not require the disclosure of any source code. It requires only the disclosure of interface specifications. The specifications are descriptions of the principles and methods for inter-operation which underlie the interface code; they are merely the principles and the methods. None of the Microsoft source code will be disclosed, so therefore none of it can be implemented in competitor's products. Also, none of the specifications themselves will find their way into competitor's products. Not one single line will. Only the principles and methods will be implemented. So I would suggest that there simply cannot be any copyright infringement. So there is no copyright license involved. Trade secrets was not mentioned, so I won't mention it either, but we could have an interesting discussion on that front.

With respect to if we assume there is a compulsory licence involved, whether the Commission's decision meets the *IMS Health* and *Magill* criteria, or indeed Jean-Yves's criteria himself, I would suggest that it quite easily meets those criteria. First with respect to the indispensability to compete. Let's remember what we are talking about here. We are talking about a company that has a 95 per cent market share on the desktop operating system market. Let's remember what work group server operating systems do. They inter-operate with and basically provide services to desktop computers. So I think it is fairly clear that if you are a consumer of a server operating system, it is going to be rather significant to you whether the

[31] ibid.

work group server operating system you are considering purchasing can inter-operate with your desktop computers. So the proposition that it is indispensable to be able to compete in the work group server operating system market, to be able to inter-operate with the desktop computers, should not be a rather surprising thing. The proposition that there is entry into this market and that others are thriving in the work observer operating system market, I must say in my view, is incorrect. There is of course some success by Linnt in some server markets, but not in this server operating system market, not in the work observer operating system market as defined by the Commission.

Secondly, to take Jean-Yves's second criterion, is access to the intellectual property indispensable to remedy the abuse? Indeed it certainly is, and I think the Commission has fully demonstrated that and frankly I must say I found it rather disingenuous to suggest that decompilation could conceivably be an alternative. It simply is not even close to that.

Thirdly, with respect as to whether the Commission's approach preserves the essential function of intellectual property, just as was the case in *Magill*, as you mentioned Jean-Yves, I don't think Microsoft is going to have any trouble continuing to do what it does with respect to providing interfaces to its desktop operating systems; I don't see how there can be any change to its incentives to achieve such inter-operability and indeed innovate with respect to the kind of inter-operability that it provides. So to say that that is the essential central function of whatever rights Microsoft might have strikes me as rather far fetched.

Finally, whether there is, with respect to Jean-Yves' fourth criteria, a less intrusive remedy, I think it follows from the things that I have already said that the interface specifications being indispensable and there being no alternative for them means simply that there is no less intrusive remedy. The only way for the abuse to be remedied is for the interface specifications to be made available.

Pat Treacy

I think perhaps we ought to move away from the specificities of the *Microsoft* case, because I think the Court of Justice is probably better placed to deal with those issues than we are here today. Does anybody have a more general comment on issues not related specifically to *Microsoft*?

Tim Cowen

Just as a sort of more general point. Reflecting on the title of the discussion today—'What is the right balance between competition policy and intellectual property?'—the question really I have is that this is a horribly difficult problem if the organization of antitrust authorities doesn't involve deep understanding of the industries that they are looking at. You can look at almost any industry and you could take, whether it is the *Microsoft* case, or many others, the challenge of forcing of access to property rights can undermine the incentive to develop the intellectual property rights in the first place. Normally the defence case, if you like.

Then there is the challenger's case that says I need these rights because they are an essential facility or a component that is essential to the production or the innovation of the downstream activity. The question really for me is how does an authority that doesn't understand the market place—because they are simply not organized to look at markets over time; they look at markets on a case-by-case basis—how do those balances get struck? So the question raised is what is the right balance? My question is what is the process? Or have we properly organized ourselves so that the process by which we achieve the right balance, whatever that might be, have we organized ourselves in a way that is sufficient to do that, because I am not sure that we have?

Steven Preece

I am not sure that I share the view that, at least in the UK experience, we have regulators who don't actually understand the markets that they are regulating. We certainly have the advantage in the UK under the Competition Act of having a number of what we call concurrent regulators who are specialist regulators in their fields in addition to the Office of Fair Trading. So in the telecommunications industry, for example, we have Ofcom. They don't just do *ex post facto* cases. What they also do is they do market studies. They look at the profile of the market. There are people dedicated just to looking at specific markets. So speaking from the UK point of view, as a starting point, I just wouldn't share the views that there is not a lot of understanding about the specialist markets. Furthermore, even at the Office of Fair Trading, when we look at a case, first of all we have specialized branches within the office, who are dedicated; there are a number of people here from specialist units within the Office of Fair Trading and they have been in the field for some years. Often they come in with experience from the field and they look at the market pretty closely.

Now I'm not going to speak with the specific issue of compulsory licensing of intellectual property rights within these fields, but what I would say is that when you see regulatory intervention in the UK, or non-intervention as the case may be, it is as a result of quite a bit of detailed analysis of that market.

So as I say, I can't speak for my US counterparts, but I would also observe that the US have specialist regulators, such as the Federal Communications Commission, as well, who I think really look at those markets.

ALDEN ABBOTT

I just have one comment. I think, certainly in the view of some people in the competition agencies in the US, they would think that other agencies, eg the FCC, have specific statutory duties, but there is sometimes a concern when other agencies end up sort of second-guessing the decisions made by the antitrust enforcers and there is one school of thinking for example, that statutes should be clarified. For example, clarification to make sure that you don't have another agency which doesn't have a sort of expertise in doing competition analysis, technically proficient though it may be, trying to replicate a competition analysis. Sector regulators are really important and expertise is very important, but on the other hand, I think my personal view is competition or antitrust analysis should remain in the hands of the antitrust agencies.

TIM COWEN

Perhaps I should say that in my position as General Counsel of BT's Global Services Division, we are operating in about 170 countries worldwide and just to give you a couple of pointers to what we might think.

I am not surprised, first of all, that Ofcom here in the UK, when it became a competition body, inheriting the position it had previously existed of being a telecoms regulator, launched a strategic review. There is obviously an implication and I think there are some clear statements made by Ofcom about the previous decisions and what they called a 'cat's cradle' or some such of interest that had occurred over ten years or so that wasn't properly in line with what it's thinking is likely to be in the future; so I think there is some inherent criticism there.

I am not suggesting that that is a non-constructive criticism. I think that this is a very difficult area. I am not going to confine my comments to the UK. If you look at the position in the US, where you have concurrent regulation in the communications industry, to the position taken by the antitrust authorities, part of the difficulty there is a constitutional difference, and if you look at the *Trinko*[32] case, if you look at the original AT&T break-up between a long-distance company and a series of local access companies in 1984, the original concern was that the FCC's regulation in the 1984 case

---

[32] *Trinko* (n 14).

was insufficient to address the antitrust remedy. So I would say that that is a very good example of things like telecoms taskforce as it exists within the DOJ today and an example of its necessity, because it wasn't being addressed by the regulatory regime. The *Trinko* case actually provides an example of perhaps the opposite being true.

There are many cases worldwide where regulators are perceived to understand the industry, but perhaps not understand the antitrust issues and there is a separation between them. I think this is becoming the case, not just in the communications industry—there are many other areas: water, gas, electricity, specific systems of regulation, often at national level, that don't address the antitrust issues which are often more of an economic concern where national regulation, or industry specific regulation, is either inconsistent with or incompatible with antitrust. I just wanted to bring that out as a matter of current concern. I know it is something the European Commission is looking at.

The Right Balance of Competition Policy and Intellectual Property Law: A Federal Trade Commission Perspective

Alden F Abbott, Suzanne Michel,
and Armando Irizarry*

I. INTRODUCTION

Historically, the policies underlying antitrust law and intellectual property ('IP') law[1] were often seen as being in conflict, with IP law being viewed as designed to 'promote' monopolies and antitrust being designed to 'combat' them.[2] More recently, it has been recognized that these two legal regimes, properly understood, seek to promote innovation and the general welfare, albeit through two somewhat different mechanisms—IP law by protecting the property rights interests of (and thus financial returns to) inventors, antitrust law by combating restrictions on the competitive process that may harm consumers and slow innovation. As a 2003 Federal Trade Commission ('FTC') report on the interrelationship of competition and patent law explained,[3] enlightened public policy aimed at promoting inno-

---

* Alden F Abbott is Associate Director for Policy and Coordination, Bureau of Competition, Federal Trade Commission, Washington, DC Ms Michel and Mr Irizarry serve within the Office of Policy and Coordination as Chief Counsel for Intellectual Property and Counsel for Intellectual Property, respectively. The views expressed below are their own and do not necessarily represent the views of the Federal Trade Commission or any Federal Trade Commissioner. Mr Abbott prepared the final version of this paper during the spring of 2005 while on sabbatical at All Souls College, Oxford.

[1] We use the terms 'antitrust law' and 'competition law' interchangeably in this article, although the 'competition laws' may be deemed to go beyond the antitrust laws to encompass as well all other legal rules that promote market processes. Thus, 'competition policy' refers to the fully panoply of legal institutions that promote reliance on markets, rather than government, to guide the use of society's resources. Although 'intellectual property law' encompasses a variety of legal schemes (including, for example, patent, trademark, copyright, and trade secret law), this article focuses on patent law, that branch of intellectual property law that creates general federal statutory incentives for innovation. Patent law historically has been viewed as being in great tension with competition law.

[2] This stereotypical generalization was never entirely accurate; patents typically do not confer monopoly power in an economic sense, and in the past (prior to the injection of economic analysis into competition policy), antitrust law often did more to create artificial impediments to efficient business transactions than to correct 'monopolistic' interferences with efficient market transactions.

[3] See Federal Trade Commission *To Promote Innovation: The Proper Balance of Competition and Patent Law and Policy* (Oct 2003), ('FTC Competition-Patent Report'), available at <http://www.ftc.gov/os/2003/10/innovationrpt.pdf>.

vation and welfare[4] requires that an appropriate balance be struck between these two legal regimes.

This article explores the appropriate balance between patent and IP law in the context of two contentious IP-antitrust topics. After providing a background discussion of patent law characteristics that are crucial to informed antitrust analysis, we turn specifically to (1) the treatment of *ex ante* price-related negotiations in standard-setting organizations; and (2) the analysis of exclusion payments made in the settlement of patent litigation. We conclude with a few general comments about the implications of our analysis for the patent-antitrust interface.

II. THE NATURE OF PATENT LAW: IMPLICATIONS FOR INNOVATION AND WELFARE

Patent law is a utilitarian set of property rules that derives legitimacy to the extent it promotes innovation and welfare.[5] Thus, the patent law system is not sacrosanct; aspects of patent law that undermine these goals are properly subject to reform. Indeed, the heavier role of government in shaping the contours of patent rules as compared to other property rules strongly suggests that patent law may be, relatively speaking, a rather socially inefficient form of property protection.[6]

---

[4] The term 'innovation' refers in this article to economic growth (encompassing both increases in the quantity and improvements in the quality of output) that is brought forth by technological change. The term 'welfare' is used herein to refer to 'total surplus,' that is, the difference between the value (measured in a unit of account, such as a currency) of goods or services produced in a market and the costs of producing those goods or services. Total surplus is divided between 'consumers' surplus' (the aggregate difference between consumers' willingness to pay for the output of the market and what they are charged) and 'producers' surplus' (profits plus 'Ricardian rents,' the return to a scarce productive asset apart from profits). For a good recent summary of these concepts, see W Ross Thomas and Ralph A Winter 'The Efficiency Defense in Merger Law: Economic Foundations and Recent Canadian Developments' (2005) 72 Antitrust LJ 471, 473–4. I will not delve into the policy debate as to whether antitrust law should promote 'total surplus maximization' or 'consumer welfare maximization'; as a practical matter, under most circumstances, policies that advance total surplus maximization generally are consistent with the maximization of consumers' surplus.

[5] This conclusion follows from the words of the patent and copyright clause of Art I, Section [????] of the US Constitution, which seeks 'To promote the Progress of Science and useful Arts, by securing for limited Times to Authors and Inventors the exclusive Right to their respective Writings and Discoveries'. Thus property interests flowing from patent grants (arguably unlike certain other property rights) would not seem to be accorded the dignity of 'natural rights' that merit protection regardless of their utility in advancing science and technology.

[6] Significantly, Landes and Posner, two leading market-oriented proponents of strong property rights, have argued that '[e]quating intellectual property rights to physical property rights overlooks the much greater governmental involvement in the former domain than in the latter . . . . Government is continuously involved in the creation of intellectual property rights through the issuance of patents, copyrights and trademarks. Skeptics of government should hesitate to extend a presumption of efficiency to a process by which government grants rights

Hearings on competition policy and the patent system organized by the FTC and the Justice Department, held in 2001 and 2002, support this implication. Evaluating the implications of those Hearings, the FTC Competition-Patent Report[7] found that 'questionable patents' (patents that are likely invalid or that contain claims that are likely overly broad) are a significant concern and can harm innovation. More precisely, the Report concluded that questionable patents (1) may directly deter third parties from undertaking innovative research due to litigation risks and costs; and (2) may create licensing difficulties that substantially raise transaction costs and deter agreements that disseminate the fruits of innovation.[8] To deal with these problems, the Report urged specific patent law reforms designed to improve patent quality and minimize the anticompetitive costs of the patent system.[9]

Antitrust law is not designed to 'step into the breach' created by faulty patent rules. The fact that certain 'bad patents' exist does not mean that antitrust may be used as a sword to attack the statutorily guaranteed right to exclude that flows from legitimate patents. But the problematic nature of certain patents does suggest that antitrust analysis should not shy away from closely scrutinizing transactions involving patent questions, if those transactions hold out the possibility of extending market power beyond the legitimate scope of the property right a patent generates. The 'legitimate

to exclude competition with the holders of the rights.' William M Landes and Richard A Posner *The Political Economy of Intellectual Property Law* 23–24 (2004), available at <http://www.aei-brookings.org/admin/authorpdfs/page.php?id=985>.

[7] FTC Report (n 4).

[8] Licensing difficulties include 'defensive patenting' by third parties in response to questionable patents. As patents proliferate, the costly 'stacking' of royalty claims on multiple patents looms increasingly serious. The 'patent thickets' that result from such activities raise the costs of agreements among technology developers and thereby retard contractual arrangements aimed at increasing the flow of innovation.

[9] That the proliferation of patents (documented in the Report) raises concerns should not be read to suggest that 'mass patenting' by corporations has no possible efficiency explanations. One scholar, Paul J Heald of the University of Georgia Law School, has argued that patenting may: (1) reduce information costs to firms, by allowing them to assemble a portfolio of rights that signals information about themselves more cheaply than by other means; (2) prevent other firms from obtaining technological inputs necessary to the first firm's production; (3) reduce the cost of monitoring team production (patent output may be a useful, albeit imperfect, measure of the contribution of individual team members); and (4) effectively partition information assets (patent assets can readily be transferred under a liability regime that does not require the transferee to enter into costly protective agreements and that creates statutory 'gap filler' rules). Paul J Heald, 'A Transaction Costs Theory of Patent Law,' available at <http://papers.ssrn.com/sol3/papers.cfm?abstract_id=385841> (posted Apr 2003) (forthcoming in (2005) 66 Ohio State LJ). Heald's theory suggests that patent law may be seen as a cost-reducing title recordation system that promotes the efficient transfer of information assets. Although this theory may be interesting, it lacks much empirical support at this time; in contrast, the FTC Competition-Patent Report refers to substantial testimony documenting the costs of patent proliferation. Future empirical work may shed light on the extent to which industry-specific patent proliferation is more beneficial than harmful.

scope' question properly may take account of the fact that patents may be deemed 'probabilistic' property rights;[10] the complexity of patent claims often creates ambiguity as to whether particular third party activity may properly be blocked by the patent, which may only be resolved by litigation.[11] As discussed below, antitrust enforcers may properly take into account these peculiar attributes of the patent system in weighing the wisdom of proposed interventions; an antitrust challenge does not undermine a patent-created property right, if the patentee's claims as to the nature and breadth of the right are inaccurate.[12] In fact, according less legal respect to illegitimate invocations of patent rights may implicitly enhance the value of well-founded patent invocations, thereby actually enhancing patents' ability to drive innovation.

III. *EX ANTE* PRICE-RELATED NEGOTIATIONS BY STANDARD-SETTING ORGANIZATIONS

Before we turn to the specific questions raised by potential *ex ante* price-related negotiations, a background discussion of standards setting, and of recent FTC cases alleging standards setting abuses, is in order.

A. Background on Standards

Standards have been defined succinctly as 'any set of technical specifications that either provides or is intended to provide a common design for a product or process.'[13] Standards have been in existence since the early days of civilization.[14] They are promulgated by governments,[15] by private

---

[10] This point has been made by Professor Carl Shapiro. Carl Shapiro *Antitrust Limits to Patent Settlements* (2003) 34 Rand J Econ 391, 407–8.

[11] Obviously, the scope of property rights other than patents may be less than certain, but, in general, there is far less uncertainty about the coverage of such rights—particularly rights to tangible property. For example, the right to possess an automobile is merely a question of who holds title, and the extent of the rights covering a plot of land turns on relatively straightforward questions, such as the existence and location of an easement or a boundary line. The boundaries of a complex, patent-protected industrial process or processes may be far less clear.

[12] Whether the patent was issued erroneously because it did not meet the statutory standards for patentability is a separate issue, best resolved through patent reforms that improve patent accuracy by, for example, facilitating simple post-grant appeals. As already discussed, antitrust authorities are not well-positioned to cure the problem of 'bad patents.' Of course, if a court or an administrative body strikes down a patent, property rights-based objections to antitrust enforcement are eliminated.

[13] Mark A Lemley 'Intellectual Property Rights and Standard Setting Organizations' (2002) 90 Cal L Rev 1889, 1896.

[14] Maureen A Breitenberg 'The ABC's of Standards-related Activities in the United States,' NISTIR 6014, at 4 (1987) (citing American Standards Association 'Through History with Standards,' in Rowen Glie (ed) *Speaking of Standards* (1972)), available at <http://ts.nist.gov/ts/htdocs/210/ncsci/primer.htm> (hereinafter 'Breitenberg').

[15] Governments may develop their own standards or endorse and adopt private standards through the passage of laws or regulations.

groups, or arise from their spontaneous acceptance by consumers. In the United States, private standard-setting organizations, ('SSOs') as we now know them, began to appear in the latter part of the 19th century, in the midst of the industrial revolution.[16] Catastrophic events have also helped create awareness about the need for standards. For example, in 1904, a great blaze destroyed much of the city of Baltimore because the hoses brought by the fire engines that came from outside the city did not fit the city's hydrants. This led to the standardization of hydrants and hose couplings.[17] Similar circumstances led to the creation of hundreds of private SSOs which have promulgated thousands of standards that have improved our daily life, promoted efficiencies and innovation in industry, and facilitated trade among nations. The adoption of standards may be particularly important in markets with 'network effects' (where the utility of the network rises as parties are added to it) and global interconnections, such as information technology and telecommunications. Thus, the techno-logical revolution that we are experiencing in these markets has benefited from, and resulted in, significant standard-setting activity.[18]

Standards are classified as de facto or de jure. A de facto standard is adopted through the self-interested actions of market participants. A clas-sic example of a de facto standard is the Microsoft operating system, which became a standard simply because of widespread consumer demand and use, and not because it was mandated by government regulation or adopted or endorsed by a private SSO. A de jure standard may be mandated by government authority, or it may be 'highly recommended' (in the sense that it is widely adopted and used in the market, and failure of a business to adopt it will likely result in a significant competitive disadvantage).[19]

B. Benefits and Drawbacks of Standards

It is widely recognized that the development and adoption of standards

---

[16] For example, the American Society of Mechanical Engineers ('ASME') was founded in 1880; the origins of the Institute of Electrical and Electronics Engineers ('IEEE') can be traced back to 1884; the American Society for Testing and Materials ('ASTM') can be traced back to 1898.

[17] Breitenberg at 4.

[18] See Janice M. Mueller 'Symposium: Patent System Reform: Patent Misuse Through the Capture of Industry Standards' (2003) 17 Berkeley Tech LJ 623, 631–2; See Marc Hansen et al, 'Disclosure and Negotiation of Licensing Terms Prior to Adoption of Industry Standards: Preventing another Patent Ambush?' (2003) Eur Competition L Rev; Robert A Skitol 'Concerted Buying Power: Its Potential for Addressing the Patent Holdup Problem in Standard Setting' (2005) 72 Antitrust LJ No 2, 727, 730 (explaining that the patent holdup problem 'arises from the interaction of (1) proliferating patents generally and (2) proliferating needs for standards to enable interoperability among both competing and complementary products seeking to exploit new technologies').

[19] Mueller (n 19) at 633 (referring to highly recommended standards as 'consensual').

provide valuable economic benefits. Standardization lowers the cost of products, which benefits consumers if the cost savings are passed on to them by the product manufacturer. Standardization allows much-desired interoperability among products and services in network markets.[20] For example, standardization allows users of computer technology to create their systems using products and parts from different companies, such as a Dell CPU, a Hewlett-Packard printer, and a Brother fax machine. Standardization also eliminates 'standards wars' in the market and their associated costs to both firms and consumers.[21]

There are also drawbacks associated with standards. Standards may deny consumers, to some extent, the benefits derived from competition.[22] Competition drives competitors to innovate to make a better product or develop a better solution for the consumer's needs. The use of standards may dull this drive. Standards may also result in higher prices to consumers if the standard is encumbered with royalty-bearing patent rights. Another drawback of standards is that superior technologies may be excluded or shunned from the market because an inferior standard is mandatory or reigns as a standard due to the 'tipping' effect or simply very strong consumer demand.[23]

C. Holdups In Private Standards-Setting—the Rambus Case

The problem of patent holdups is illustrated by the FTC's recent *Rambus* and *Unocal* investigations. *Rambus* is an example of an alleged holdup in a private SSO; *Unocal* illustrates an alleged hold-up in a governmental regu-

---

[20] Lemley (n 14) 1896–7 (discussing network markets).

[21] For example, during the 1980s VCR war between Beta and VHS technology for the de facto standard in home videocassette recording technology, the losers of the war had to reinvest in this technology by buying a VHS player. Their Beta-formatted cassettes also lost substantial value.

[22] SSO participants will continue to compete in downstream product and service markets throughout the standard-setting process. Ideally, after development and acceptance of an efficient standard, this competition will continue, but at a reduced social cost (competitors will no longer face uncertainty about what standard to employ in production, and consumers will no longer run the risk that they are buying a product embodying a 'loser' standard that will soon be superseded). There is some risk, however, that welfare would have been greater absent an SSO-developed standard, if competition among standards had yielded a de facto standard superior (in welfare terms) to the SSO-developed standard. This is, however, basically a theoretical concern; there generally is no way to determine that the absence of an SSO standard would have yielded this superior result. Another serious competitive concern, which is beyond the scope of this article, is that collusion among members of an SSO may lead to development of a standard that favors their product design and excludes potentially more efficient technologies employed by firms outside the association that dominates the standard-setting body. See *Allied Tube & Conduit Corp v Indian Head*, 486 US 492 (1988) (makers of steel conduit 'packed' SSO meeting with its agents and thereby obtained SSO decision disapproving plastic conduit for building construction).

[23] Lemley (n 14) at 1897 (discussing tipping effect).

latory standard-setting process. In both cases, it is alleged that deceptive private behaviour undermined standard-setting activities, thereby allowing market power to be exercised to the detriment of firms using the standards and of ultimate consumers. In June 2005, the FTC and Unocal announced a proposed settlement of the *Unocal* case.[24]

In 2002 the FTC issued a complaint against Rambus Inc—a computer chip technology provider—charging Rambus with violating federal antitrust laws by engaging in anticompetitive acts and practices that served to deceive the JEDEC[25] Solid State Technology Association ('JEDEC'), a private SSO, into adopting a standard that JEDEC had no reason to believe was encumbered with Rambus's patents. The complaint charged that Rambus's conduct harmed competition and consumers.

According to the complaint, JEDEC develops and issues technical standards for use throughout the semiconductor industry. JEDEC endeavours to promote free competition among industry participants by not 'giving a competitive advantage to any manufacturer, [or] excluding competitors from the market'.[26] Toward this end, JEDEC seeks to ensure that if patented technologies are incorporated into its standards, these technologies 'will be available to be licensed on royalty-free or otherwise reasonable and non-discriminatory (ie 'RAND') terms'.[27]

One of the technologies for which JEDEC developed and issued standards was a common form of computer memory chip known as SDRAM.[28] SDRAM chips are used in a wide variety of products, including computers, fax machines, printers, and video game equipment. Rambus participated in

---

[24] For purposes of the following discussion, the allegations set forth in the initial Rambus and Unocal administrative complaints are treated as accurate. The ultimate disposition of these allegations in the Rambus matter rests upon the final results of ongoing administrative litigation. For the text of the Rambus and Unocal complaints, respectively, see *In the Matter of Rambus, Inc*, Docket No 9302 (18 June 2002) ('Rambus Complaint'), available at <http://www.ftc.gov/os/2002/06/rambuscmp.htm>, *In the Matter of Union Oil Company of California*, Docket No 9305 (4 Mar 2003) ('Unocal Complaint'), available at <http://www.ftc.gov/os/2003/03/unocalcmp.htm>. On 10 June 2005, the FTC announced a settlement of the Unocal matter in connection with the settlement of Chevron Corporation's proposed acquisition of Unocal. As noted below in the text following discussion of the Rambus matter, this settlement will prevent future competitive harm from the Unocal patent 'holdup' by precluding Unocal from enforcing the reformulated gasoline patents in question. See FTC Press Release *Dual Consent Orders Resolve Competitive Concerns About Chevron's $18 Billion Purchase of Unocal, FTC's 2003 Complaint Against Unocal* (10 June 2005), available at <http://www.ftc.gov/opa/2005/06/chevronunocal.htm>. See also *In the Matter of Union Oil Company of California*, Docket No 9305 (10 June 2005) (Agreement Containing Consent Order), available at <http://www.ftc.giov/os/adipro/d9305/050610agreement9305.pdf>.

[25] 'JEDEC' is an acronym for Joint Electron Device Engineering Council.

[26] Rambus Complaint at para 19.

[27] ibid para 20.

[28] SDRAM is an acronym for synchronous dynamic random access memory.

JEDEC's SDRAM-related work for more than four years without ever making it known to JEDEC or its members that Rambus was actively seeking to develop patents that covered technologies proposed for—and ultimately adopted—in the SDRAM-related standards. Specifically, the complaint alleged that:

> Rambus's very participation in JEDEC, coupled with its failure to make required patent-related disclosures, conveyed a materially false and misleading impression—namely, that JEDEC, by incorporating into its SDRAM standards technologies openly discussed and considered during Rambus's tenure in the organization, was not at risk of adopting standards that Rambus could later claim to infringe upon its patents.[29]

The FTC alleged that Rambus's conduct caused or threatened to cause substantial harm to competition and consumers because it allowed Rambus to assert patent rights against—and to obtain substantial royalties from—memory manufacturers producing products in compliance with the relevant standards. In addition, Rambus's conduct allegedly threatened or resulted in other anticompetitive effects, including increases in the price of SDRAM chips and other products incorporating or using SDRAM technology, decreased incentives to produce the SDRAM memory chips, decreased incentives to participate in JEDEC and other SSOs, and decreased reliance or willingness to rely—both within and outside the computer memory industry—on standards set by industry SSOs.

D. Holdups in a Governmental Setting—the Unocal Case

The *Unocal* investigation concerned conduct by the Union Oil Company of California ('Unocal') before the California Air Resources Board ('CARB'), a department of the California Environmental Protection Agency. According to the FTC's complaint:

> CARB's mission is to protect the health, welfare, and ecological resources of California through the effective and efficient reduction of air pollutants, while recognizing and considering the effects of its actions on the California economy. CARB fulfills this mandate by, among other things, setting and enforcing standards for low emissions, reformulated gasoline.[30]

The FTC complaint issued against Unocal alleges that, in the early 1990s, CARB embarked in rulemaking proceedings to promulgate specifications

---

[29] Rambus Complaint at para 71.   [30] Unocal Complaint at para 16.

for low emissions, reformulated gasoline ('RFG'). CARB relied on industry, including Unocal, to provide the information it needed for these proceedings. Unocal allegedly misrepresented to CARB that certain information it provided to CARB related to RFG was non-proprietary and in the public domain when in fact Unocal had applied for a patent that would enable Unocal to charge substantial royalties if the information was used by CARB. The complaint alleged that these statements by Unocal to CARB were materially false and misleading. CARB did use the information in its rulemaking, which resulted in standards for 'summer-time' RFG. The California refining industry spent billions of dollars to reconfigure refineries to produce RFG in compliance with the standards mandated by CARB, thus effectively locking in to the production of this gasoline.

After the industry was locked in, Unocal began enforcing its patent rights through licensing and litigation.[31] Unocal prevailed in its private infringement actions and obtained judgments requiring the major refiners producing CARB to pay 5.75 cents per gallon of RFG, a not insignificant amount. Unocal's own expert estimated that approximately 90 per cent of this royalty would likely be passed to consumers through higher retail gasoline prices.

The FTC alleged that Unocal's misrepresentations harmed competition and allowed Unocal to obtain monopoly power over the technology to produce and supply RFG. Had Unocal not engaged in such conduct, the FTC contended that CARB would not have adopted RFG regulations that substantially overlapped with Unocal's patent rights, or the terms on which Unocal could enforce its patent rights would have been substantially different.

On 10 June 2005, the FTC announced two consent orders that would resolve the competitive concerns arising from the Unocal investigation and from the proposed acquisition of Unocal by Chevron Corporation. Under the terms of the orders, Chevron's acquisition was allowed to proceed, subject to the requirement that Unocal would stop enforcing its reformulated gasoline patents that were the subject of the FTC's technology market monopolization complaint. This settlement will resolve the problem of competitive harm arising from Unocal's 'patent hold-up'.

E. Can SSO participants negotiate licensing terms and royalties ex ante?

The SSOs' concerns that *ex ante* royalty negotiations may expose them to antitrust liability may have precluded SSOs from allowing such negotiations

---

[31] Unocal eventually received five patents related to RFG.

among the patent-holder and SSO participants. The concern arises because participants in a standard-setting process are usually competitors, and SSOs—under whose auspices the standard-setting processes occur—may fear that *ex ante* negotiations will be deemed illegal price fixing or acts of 'monopsonization' (the creation of a monopsony single buyer of technology inputs).

Such concerns are ill-founded, given the state of modern antitrust analysis. A legitimate SSO (as opposed to a sham organization organized to mask a cartel) is properly viewed as a welfare-enhancing joint venture aimed at jointly bringing forth an output—a standard—that yields benefits to industry and, ultimately, consumers (see previous discussion of benefits of standards). Even legitimate joint ventures, of course, may engage in collateral conduct that is anticompetitive and not reasonably related to joint venture efficiencies. Nevertheless, as explained further below, *ex ante* price-related negotiations by SSOs, properly analysed, are not collateral anticompetitive conduct.

In the United States, antitrust liability and the legality of agreements among competitors are determined by analysing the agreements under two rules: the per se rule and the rule of reason.[32]

---

[32] Federal Trade Commission and US Department of Justice, *Antitrust Guidelines for Collaboration Among Competitors* (2000), at § 1.2 (hereinafter 'Joint Venture Guidelines'). Application of rule of reason analysis under the Guidelines to *ex ante* negotiations is set forth below in the text accompanying nn 42–4 and 46–7. The antitrust analysis applied to agreements among competitors is described in somewhat more 'contemporary' language in the discussion preceding the evaluation of exclusion payments made in settlements, see nn 59–64.. Both strands of analysis, however, embody essentially the same approach, and, properly applied, should produce the same results. Given the fact that SSO price-related negotiations might at first blush (albeit incorrectly) appear to involve the traditional per se rule, I found it useful to employ the slightly more traditional analysis in discussing *ex ante* negotiations.

In its 2003 *Polygram* opinion, the FTC eschewed the binary 'per se' and 'rule of reason' categories, in favor of a more nuanced approach in which conduct among competitors would be evaluated along a spectrum and a multi-step framework would be followed to guide analysis. Specifically, in evaluating an allegedly collusive horizontal agreement, *Polygram* indicates that an antitrust assessment should proceed as follows: (1) ask first if the agreement is 'inherently suspect' (behavior that past judicial experience and current economic learning have shown to warrant summary condemnation) (if it is not inherently suspect, full rule of reason treatment is warranted); (2) if it is inherently suspect, then defendant can avoid summary condemnation only by articulating a legitimate justification that is cognizable (consistent with the goal of antitrust law to further competition) and plausible (cannot be rejected without extensive factual inquiry) (if defendant does not articulate such a justification then the case is over); (3) if defendant does articulate a cognizable and plausible justification, then plaintiff must make a more detailed showing that the restraints are indeed likely, in the particular context, to harm competition; and (4) if plaintiff has not met its burden of persuasion on the first step (agreement inherently suspect) or one of the next two (either no justification or actual anticompetitive effects almost certain), then one goes to a full rule of reason test. For the FTC's *Polygram* opinion, see *In the Matter of Polygram Holding, Inc et al*, FTC Docket No 9298 (24 July 2003), available at <http://www.ftc.gov/os/2003/07/polygramopinion.pdf>. The United

The per se rule applies to agreements that 'are so likely to harm competition and to have no significant pro-competitive benefit that they do not warrant the time and expense required for particularized inquiry into their effects.'[33] Agreements that are deemed per se illegal include:

> Agreements of a type that always or almost always tends to raise price or reduce output . . . . Typically these are agreements not to compete on price or output. Types of agreements that have been held per se illegal include agreements among competitors to fix prices or output, rig bids, or share or divide markets by allocating customers, suppliers, territories or lines of commerce.[34]

The only category of per se illegal conduct under which *ex ante* negotiations of royalties conceivably might fall is price fixing.[35] It could be said that when a patent-holder[36] and an SSO participant negotiate a royalty payment they are fixing a price of a product component. As we will explain below, however, fixing a price in this context should not be characterized as illegal 'price-fixing' as that conduct is contemplated by the antitrust laws.[37] 'As generally used in the antitrust field, "price fixing" is a shorthand way of describing certain categories of business behavior to which the per se rule

States Court of Appeals for the District of Columbia Circuit affirmed the FTC's decision and endorsed the FTC's *Polygram* methodology in *Polygram Holding, Inc v FTC*, 2005 US App LEXIS 14931 (DC Cir 2005) ('*Polygram Holding*'). A rough and ready application of the *Polygram* framework might suggest that *ex ante* price related negotiations (1) are inherently suspect, but (2) have a cognizable and plausible efficiency justification, and (3) cannot be shown on detailed examination to be likely to harm competition, and (4) generally should pass muster under a full rule of reason analysis. Nevertheless, although the FTC's *Polygram* opinion advances an enlightened and structured methodology for analyzing agreements among competitors, that methodology has not yet been endorsed by courts other than the DC Circuit (and the DC Circuit's opinion did not hold that the *Polygram* methodology was the *only* acceptable mode of s.1 analysis). Accordingly, in the main text following this note, we employ the more traditional antitrust framework for evaluating agreements among competitors in order to assess the legality of *ex ante* price-related negotiations involving SSOs.

[33] Joint Venture Guidelines at §1.2.

[34] ibid (footnotes omitted).

[35] The *ex ante* negotiations on which we focus are price-related negotiations (usually regarding royalties) with respect to patents that might arguably relate to the future implementation by producers of a standard under consideration by the SSO. *Ex ante* negotiations that are not reasonably related to the development of an SSO standard—but, instead, relate to downstream product markets that will employ the standard—are still illegal. Thus, for example, *ex ante* negotiations on fixing outputs or 'shar[ing] or divid[ing] markets by allocating customers, suppliers, territories or lines of commerce' for products made according to a standard would be illegal, whether conducted inside or outside an SSO.

[36] It is assumed that the patent-holder is also a participant in the SSO's standard-setting process. We do not address the situation where a patent-holder that does not participate in the SSO's standard-setting process holds up the industry after the standard is adopted.

[37] *Broadcast Music, Inc v Columbia Broadcasting System*, 441 US 1, 8–9 (1979) (explaining that price fixing under the antitrust laws means something different than the literal meaning of fixing a price) (hereinafter *BMI*).

has been held applicable. . . . Literalness [of the term 'price fixing'] is overly simplistic and often overbroad.'[38]

Should the per se rule apply to *ex ante* negotiations in SSOs? It should not, for several reasons. First, the per se rule applies to agreements and practices that are 'so plainly anticompetitive, . . . so often lack[ing] . . . any redeeming virtue, . . . that they are conclusively presumed illegal without further examination under the rule of reason generally applied in Sherman Act cases.'[39] That is not the case with *ex ante* negotiations in SSOs. Those negotiations have procompetitive effects. *Ex ante* negotiations provide for more evenly balanced negotiating conditions than ex post negotiations, ie negotiations that take place after adoption of the standard by the SSO. In ex post negotiations the patent holder has superior bargaining power over those who want to license the patents—because the standard covered by the patents already has been adopted and many industry members have 'locked into' the standard (absorbed standard-specific sunk costs, such as building facilities to standard). This superior bargaining power allows the patent-holder to command supracompetitive royalties. With *ex ante* negotiations the patent-holder does not have such a bargaining advantage—because the standard covered by the patent has not yet been adopted, the industry has not locked into the standard, and the SSO participants negotiating the licence with the patent holder (who ultimately determine whether the standard will be adopted) have the option of switching to another alternative if the negotiations fail due to the patent holder's unreasonable royalty demands. (In other words, *ex ante* negotiations facilitate competition among technologies that are inputs into future standards-based products and services; a bar on *ex ante* negotiations may sacrifice this competitive efficiency.) These are cognizable pro-competitive effects that should suffice to preclude *ex ante* negotiations from being per se unlawful.

Secondly, the per se rule is applied after courts have had 'considerable experience' with the business relationship under scrutiny.[40] That is not the case here. The general practice of SSOs has been to discourage or prohibit *ex ante* negotiations for fear of antitrust liability. Antitrust enforcers and courts have seldom, if ever, had occasion to evaluate *ex ante* royalty negotiations. Thus, there is no 'considerable experience' with *ex ante* negotiations.

Having disposed of the argument that *ex ante* price-related negotiations are per se illegal, we briefly assess them under the antitrust 'rule of reason'. The rule of reason applies to:

---

[38] *BMI*, 441 US at 9.   [39] ibid at 8.   [40] ibid at 9.

'[a]greements not challenged as per se illegal . . . to determine their over-all competitive effect. These include agreements of a type that might be considered per se illegal, provided they are reasonably related to, and reasonably necessary to achieve procompetitive benefits from, an efficiency-enhancing integration of economic activity.'[41]

In applying the rule of reason, we turn to the Joint Venture Guidelines jointly released by the FTC and the US Department of Justice in 2000. According to the Guidelines, the central question in a rule of reason analysis:

'is whether the relevant agreement likely harms competition by increasing the ability or incentive profitably to raise price above or reduce output, quality, service, or innovation below what likely would prevail in the absence of the relevant agreement.'[42]

There are close similarities between the benefits that the Joint Venture Guidelines recognize flow from competitor collaborations and those that flow from *ex ante* negotiations in SSOs. As the Guidelines state:

The Agencies recognize that consumers may benefit from competitor collaborations in a variety of ways. For example, a competitor collaboration may enable participants to offer goods or services that are cheaper, more valuable to consumers, or brought to market faster than would be possible absent the collaboration. A collaboration may allow its participants to better use existing assets, or may provide incentives for them to make output-enhancing investments that would not occur absent the collaboration. The potential efficiencies from competitor collaborations may be achieved through a variety of contractual arrangements including joint ventures, trade or professional associations, licensing arrangements, or strategic alliances.[43]

These benefits substantially overlap the benefits, discussed below, that SSOs provide. Furthermore, note that the competitor collaborations contemplated by the guidelines include trade or professional associations, which include some SSOs. For example, the IEEE is a trade association of electrical engineers and related professions that is very active in setting standards in several industries, including information technology and communications.[44]

---

[41] Joint Venture Guidelines at § 1.2.   [42] ibid.   [43] ibid at § 2.1.
[44] A discussion of the IEEE's standard-setting work may be found on its web site, <http://www.ieee.org/portal/site>.

The Joint Venture Guidelines also contemplate that competitor collaborations may engender anticompetitive harms through a variety of mechanisms.[45]

> Among other things, agreements [among competitor collaborators] may limit independent decision making or combine the control of or financial interests in production, key assets, or decisions regarding price, output, or other competitively sensitive variables, or may otherwise reduce the participants' ability or incentive to compete independently.
>
> Competitor collaborations also may facilitate explicit or tacit collusion through facilitating practices such as the exchange or disclosure of competitively sensitive information or through increased market concentration. Such collusion may involve the relevant market in which the collaboration operates or another market in which the participants in the collaboration are actual or potential competitors.[46]

The narrowly circumscribed conduct of patent-holders and SSO participants negotiating *ex ante* does not create the potential for most of these anticompetitive harms. For example, *ex ante* negotiations do not require that the parties combine financial interests or key assets, nor does it include decisions regarding the price at which a product or service is offered in the market. Furthermore, when parties negotiating *ex ante* agree to reasonable terms, their ability or incentive to compete independently should not be compromised. *Ex ante* negotiations could be problematic if they facilitated collusion with respect to products or services produced by SSO members, but that concern would not arise as long as the negotiations did not involve the exchange of information relating to those products or services (and legitimate negotiations over licensing terms with patentees would not require such an information exchange). In short, the Joint Venture Guidelines Analysis suggests that legitimate *ex ante* negotiations, properly structured, clearly would pass antitrust muster under the rule of reason.

One final potential antitrust critique of *ex ante* negotiations remains, namely, that joint *ex ante* negotiations would give an SSO collective monopsony power over patentees' technology, yielding harm to competition (under this theory, the joint negotiations would be deemed a vehicle for monopsonization). Careful analysis, however, reveals that this antitrust concern is misplaced. Classical monopsony concerns arise when: (1) the monopsonist purchaser of a competitively supplied input pays a less than socially optimal amount for the input; and (2) leading the sellers to restrict their supply to less than the socially optimal amount. The monopsonist

---

[45] Joint Venture Guidelines at § 2.2.   [46] ibid.

purchaser in turn enjoys monopoly power downstream over the final product that embodies the input, and ultimate consumers are harmed due to an artificial restriction of final product output (which is sold at an inefficiently high price). Under this scenario, antitrust enforcers are well justified in acting to prevent the monopsony behaviour.

This 'harmful monopsony' scenario, however, is unlikely to pose a problem for *ex ante* price-related SSO negotiations. First, to the extent different SSOs compete to purchase particular technology rights, any one SSO engaged in collective price negotiations cannot exercise monopsony power. Secondly, purveyors of technology rights that face SSOs are unlikely to be perfect competitors; they may enjoy some negotiating leverage vis-à-vis an SSO or SSOs. Thirdly, intellectual property is not a tangible product sold in divisible units whose output can harmfully be restricted in the short run; at most, an SSO may be able to capture some rents that otherwise would have been retained by the patent-holder. Although theoretically possible, it is questionable to what extent this redistribution of rents away from certain patentees (assuming it occurs) will diminish future incentives to do research that spurs innovation. Some patentees would only sacrifice 'excessive pure rents' that are above the level necessary to spur optimal innovation levels. As discussed in the FTC Competition-Patent Report, many patents make marginal contributions (at best) to innovation, some are of questionable validity, and many may be asserted in an overly broad fashion; to the extent that excessively broad assertion is curbed *ex ante* , companies that utilize an SSO's output (a standard) may pay lower royalties and thereby free up funds for innovative research of their own.[47] Furthermore, to the extent that SSO members themselves hold patents (which is often the case), they would not have an incentive to pose onerous terms that in turn could be turned against them as patentees in future *ex ante* negotiating cycles. In sum, not only is a 'monopsony-induced reduction in innovation' story unlikely to arise from *ex ante* price negotiations, there is good reason to believe that such negotiations, by reducing costly hold-ups and litigation, may create a climate that is more congenial to innovation. This reinforces the notion that antitrust analysis, properly applied, should not create obstacles to SSOs' *ex ante* price arrangements with patent-holders.

---

[47] The concerns about patent quality, and the notion that patents are 'uncertain' or 'probabilistic' property rights, noted earlier, may serve as 'trump cards' that reinforce the inclination against antitrust challenges to legitimate *ex ante* negotiations.

IV. EXCLUSION PAYMENTS MADE IN THE SETTLEMENT OF PATENT LITIGATION

A. Overview

The great majority of patent disputes settle before trial[48] and the great majority of those settlements are pro-competitive.[49] A settlement can save public and private resources that would otherwise be consumed by litigation, and it can provide certainty that will encourage business investment.[50] Many settlements contribute to marketplace competition because they result in a licence or cross-licence that allows the accused infringer to market or continue marketing its product.[51] Moreover, a cross-licence may provide a pro-competitive benefit by eliminating the problem of 'blocking patents' that potentially could prevent both parties from bringing their products to market.[52]

Courts generally favour settlements as an efficient means to avoid litigation,[53] but these public policy considerations do not mean that all settlements are presumptively efficient regardless of the cost. Because the patentee and accused infringer may be horizontal competitors or potential competitors when they enter the settlement agreement, the agreement may attract antitrust scrutiny if, for instance, the parties agree to allocate markets or fix prices as a part of the settlement.[54] The issue of the proper role of antitrust in evaluating patent settlement agreements has come to the forefront of US law with the recent challenges, brought by the FTC, the attorneys general of the individual states, and private litigants, to patent

---

[48] Mark A. Lemley 'Rational Ignorance at the Patent Office' (2001) 95 Nw UL Rev 1495, 1501.

[49] We refer to an agreement among competitors that furthers efficiency and enhances consumer welfare as procompetitive. We refer to an agreement that does not plausibly further efficiency and harms consumers as anticompetitive. See, eg, *Federal Trade Commission v. Indiana Federation of Dentist*, 476 US 447, 459 (1986) (hereinafter *IFD*).

[50] *In the Matter of Schering-Plough Corp.*, Dkt. No. 9297 (Opinion of the Commission) (18 Dec 2003), at 37, available at <http://www.ftc.gov/os/adjpro/d9297/031218commissionopinion.pdf> (hereinafter FTC Schering Op).

[51] Willard K Tom and Joshua A Newberg 'Antitrust and Intellectual Property: From Separate Spheres to Unified Field' (1997) 66 Antitrust LJ 167, 174–75; Federal Trade Commission & United States Dept of Justice *Antitrust Guidelines for the Licensing of Intellectual Property* at § 2.3 (1995) (discussing the procompetitive benefits of licensing), available at <http://www.usdog.gov/atr/public/guidelines/ipguide.pdf> [hereinafter IP Licensing Guidelines]; see also Robert J Hoerner *Antitrust Pitfalls in Patent Litigation Settlement Agreements* (1998) 8 Fed Circuit BJ 113, 115 (patent settlement agreements will be analyzed similarly to patent licensing agreements).

[52] IP Licensing Guidelines (n 52) at § 5.5 ('Settlements involving the cross-licensing of intellectual property rights can be an efficient means to avoid litigation and, in general, courts favour such settlements.').

[53] eg *Aro Corp v Allied Witan Co*, 531 F.2d1368, 1372 (6th Cir 1976) ('Public policy strongly favours settlement of disputes without litigation. Settlement is of particular value in patent litigation, the nature of which is often inordinately complex and time consuming.')

[54] *United States v Masonite Corp*, 316 US 265 (1942).

settlements in the pharmaceutical arena. The exact terms of the settlement agreements at issue in these cases vary, but they share the common feature of requiring a payment from a brand-name drug manufacturer (the patentee) to a generic drug manufacturer (the accused infringer) in exchange for a promise by the generic company to refrain from marketing its product for some time. We will term the payment from the brand-name company to the generic an 'exclusion payment'.

The courts that have undertaken an antitrust analysis of these agreements have varied in their approach and conclusions. One court of appeals found an interim settlement agreement that included an exclusion payment to constitute a per se antitrust violation.[55] Another court, overturning an FTC decision, found an agreement between Schering-Plough and Upsher-Smith to be legal, in part because the exclusion payment fell within the exclusionary power of Schering's patent.[56] Commentators also have varied in their analysis.[57] In this section, we set forth our thoughts on how to approach the antitrust analysis of these agreements in a manner that considers the nature of the patent property right and the exclusionary power of the patent at issue in the dispute. Our prior comments about the probabilistic nature of patent rights will help inform our application of antitrust analysis to this area.

Settlement agreements including exclusion payments are horizontal restraints that violate the antitrust laws if they 'unreasonably' limit competition.[58] To assess the reasonableness of a horizontal restraint, courts begin by asking whether the conduct appears to be a practice that would 'always or almost always tend to restrict competition and decrease output', or instead is 'designed to increase economic efficiency and render markets more, rather than less, competitive'.[59] Horizontal restraints are evaluated along an analytical continuum in which a challenged practice is examined

[55] *In re Cardizem CD Antitrust Litig*, 332 F.3d 896 (6th Cir 2003).

[56] *Schering-Plough Corp v FTC*, 402 F.3d 1056 (11th Cir 2005); see also, *Valley Drug Co v Geneva Pharmaceuticals, Inc*, 344 F.3d 1294 (11th Cir 2003). In our view, jurisprudence in this area is far from settled. Accordingly, we will not delve into the details of particular cases brought by the FTC and other plaintiffs in this area, but, rather, will focus on more general principles that inform the evaluation of settlement agreements including exclusion payments.

[57] *Contrast* Herbert Hovenkamp, Mark Lemley and Mark Janis 'Anticompetitive Settlement of Intellectual Property Disputes' (2003) 87 Minn L Rev 1719, 1759 (arguing that a payment from a patentee to an infringement defendant for the latter's exit from the market is presumptively unlawful), with Daniel A Crane 'Exit Payments in Settlement of Patent Infringement Lawsuits: Antitrust Rules and Economic Implications' (2002) 54 Fla L Rev 747 (arguing that exclusion payments should be permitted when the likelihood of success of the patentee's infringement suit is high).

[58] *State Oil Co v Khan*, 522 US 3, 10 (1997) ('Although the Sherman Act, by its terms, prohibits every agreement in 'restraint of trade', this Court has long recognized that Congress intended to outlaw only unreasonable restraints').

[59] *BMI*, 441 US at 19–20.

in the detail necessary to understand its competitive effect.[60] Although it is true that 'when there is an agreement not to compete in terms of price or output, "no elaborate industry analysis is required to demonstrate the anti-competitive character of such an agreement"',[61] it remains necessary to consider whether the parties offer plausible and cognizable efficiency justifications for the agreement in determining the extent of the inquiry required.[62] A horizontal restraint may have legitimate pro-competitive efficiencies when it creates a new product or improves the operation of the market, for example.[63] In evaluating whether a settlement including an exclusion payment is anticompetitive because it 'tends to restrict competition and decrease output', we consider the likely effects of the agreement and any plausible, cognizable, efficiency justifications.

B. Assessing Uncertain Litigation Outcomes

The analysis of the competitive effects of a settlement including an exclusion payment must view the agreement from the point in time at which the parties entered the agreement.[64] At that point in time, the outcome of the patent litigation is uncertain. Indeed, the very purpose of the settlement is to eliminate that uncertainty. The payment from a branded drug manufacturer to a potential generic entrant in exchange for ending the litigation and setting generic entry for a future date can be characterized as the brand's payment to eliminate the chance that the generic company will win the litigation or otherwise market its product at an earlier date.[65] There is no

---

[60] See *California Dental Association v FTC*, 526 US 756, 781 (1999) ('What is required . . . is an enquiry meet for the case, looking to the circumstances, details, and logic of a restraint.') [hereinafter, *CDA*]; see also, *In re PolyGram Holding, Inc* slip op [???]at 22 (discussing development of a continuum of analysis in the jurisprudence of horizontal restraints).

[61] *NCAA v Bd. Regents Okla Univ*, 468 U.S. 85, 109 (1984) (quoting *National Society of Professional Engineers v United States*, 435 US 679, 692 (1978)).

[62] *CDA*, 526 US at 774–78; see also, *PolyGram Holding*, 2005 US App Lexis 14931 (approving the FTC's analysis that if it is obvious (based upon economic learning and market experience) that a restraint of trade likely impairs competition, then it is presumed unlawful and will lead to liability, unless the defendant: (1) gives a reason the restraint is unlikely to harm consumers; or (2) identifies some pro-competitive benefit that plausibly offsets the likely harm to competition).

[63] *NCAA*, 468 US 101–3.

[64] *Valley Drug*, 355 F.3d at 1306 (citing *SCM Corp v Xerox Corp*, 645 F.2d 1195, 1207 (2d Cir 1981)). Were this not the case, intervening events, such as the potential entrant's plant burning down, would absolve parties that had entered clearly anticompetitive agreements not to compete from antitrust liability. Evidence of the actual effects of an agreement may be highly probative of an agreement's likely affect on competition when entered, however. See ABA Section of Antitrust Law, *Antitrust Law Developments* p 877 (5th edn 2002) (collecting cases). For instance, evidence of the effect of actual generic entry on prices and market share is highly probative of the competitive conditions the parties preempted through an agreement to delay generic entry.

[65] The market structure in which generic entry occurs creates an incentive for the parties to

dispute among the courts and commentators who have examined these agreements that this is a fair characterization of the exclusion payment. The disputes centre on whether such agreements are anticompetitive or whether they are within the scope of the patentee's exclusionary right.[66]

It is incorrect to begin an examination of the likely effect of an agreement including an exclusion payment from the premise that the patentee could exclude all competitors for the term of the patent. There is no certainty that a court will find that an accused product actually infringes—a matter on which the patentee has the burden of proof.[67] In fact, accused infringers frequently win litigation by demonstrating that they do not infringe the asserted patent. In 2003, of 339 written judicial decision addressing infringement, courts found the patent not infringed 75 per cent of the time.[68] A more optimistic study still shows patentees losing litigation 42 per cent of the time.[69]

Moreover, the fact that a patent has been issued by the Patent & Trademark Office ('PTO') is no guarantee that the courts will uphold its validity, despite the statutory presumption of validity.[70] 'The validity of a patent is always subject to plenary challenge on its merits. A court may invalidate a patent on any substantive ground, whether or not that ground was considered by the patent examiner.'[71] Empirical studies have demonstrated that courts invalidate nearly half of all issued patents litigated to judgment on validity issues. A study examining nearly all written, final validity decisions by either the district courts or the US Court of Appeal for the Federal Circuit during the eight-year period from 1989 to 1996 found that 46 per

delay generic entry even when that entry is uncertain to occur. Because generic drugs sell for less than their branded counterparts, generic entry causes the branded company to lose more in profits than the generic company earns, with the difference accruing as consumer savings. A brand company could pay a generic to delay market entry more than the generic would earn by entering, and still be better off than if it faced competition. FTC Schering Op 21–22.

[66] eg *Schering-Plough Corp*, 2005 WL 528439 at *15 ('By entering into the settlement agreements, Schering realized the full potential of its infringement suit—a determination that the '743 patent was valid and that ESI and Upsher would not infringe the patent in the future'.); Marc Schildkraut 'Patent-Splitting Settlements and the Reverse Payment Fallacy' (2004) 71 Antitrust LJ 1033, 1047–50 (acknowledging the loss of uncertain competition from settlements including exclusion payments).

[67] In patent litigations, the patentee bears the burden of proving that the accused product infringes its patent by a preponderance of evidence. *Envirotech Corp v Al George, Inc*, 730 F.2d 753, 758 (Fed Cir 1984).

[68] Patstats, US Patent Litigation Statistics, University of Houston Law Center, available at <http://www.patstats.org/2003.html>.

[69] Kimberly A Moore 'Judges, Juries, and Patent Cases-An Empirical Peek Inside the Black Box' (2000) 99 Mich L Rev 365, 385.

[70] 35 USC § 282 ('A patent shall be presumed valid.').

[71] *Magnivision, Inc v Bonneau Co.*, 115 F.3d 95, 960 (Fed Cir 1997); 35 USC § 282 ('A patent shall be presumed valid,' but, '[i]nvalidity of the patent' shall be a defense in any patent suit.).

cent of patents challenged in litigation were found to be invalid.[72] A more recent survey found that in 2003, of 201 judicial decisions addressing validity, 58 per cent found the patent invalid.[73] The presumption of validity is simply a procedural device for allocating the burden of proof to an accused infringer who seeks to demonstrate a patent's invalidity in patent litigation.[74] 'The presumption has no separate evidentiary value.'[75] It should not be understood to alter antitrust law's approach to the uncertain outcome of the litigation at the time of the settlement agreement.

The FTC's survey of patent litigation in the pharmaceutical industry between brand-name drug manufacturers, as patentees, and generic drug manufacturers as accused infringers, parallels these trends. Of 30 cases resolving patent litigation between a brand-name drug manufacturer and the first generic company to file an application to sell a generic version of the drug at issue between 1992 and 2002, the generic applicant prevailed by proving either the invalidity of the patent or non-infringement 73 per cent of the time.[76]

The exclusion payments themselves demonstrate the uncertainty of the litigation. One commentator has noted that the willingness of the brand company patentee to make the very large payments at issue in most of these cases indicates significant doubts about the validity of the patent or the strength of the infringement claim. 'A firm willing to pay roughly $75 million per year to keep an alleged infringer out of the market when a successful preliminary injunction would have done the same thing for the cost of obtaining the injunction indicates that the prospects for a preliminary injunction were very poor'.[77] Others have recognized that the size of an exclusion payment is proportional to the strength of the generic applicant's case.[78] In other words, 'the less likely the patentee is to win, the more it is willing to pay a generic to stay out of the market'.[79] According to one

[72] John R Allison and Mark A Lemley 'Empirical Evidence on the Validity of Litigated Patents' (1998) 26 AIPLA Q J 185, 205–6.

[73] Patstats, US Patent Litigation Statistics, University of Houston Law Center, available at <http://www.patstats.org/2003.html>.

[74] *Stratoflex, Inc v Aeroquip Corp*, 713 F.2d 1530, 1534 (Fed Cir 1983).

[75] *WL Gore & Associates Inc v Garlock Inc* 721 F.2d 1540, 1553 (Fed Cir 1983).

[76] *Generic Drug Entry Prior to Patent Expiration: An FTC Study* pp 15–16 (Jul. 2002), available at <http://www.ftc.gov/os/2002/07/genericdrugstudy.pdf> [hereinafter FTC Generic Drug Study].

[77] Herbert Hovenkamp 'Sensible Antitrust Rules for Pharmaceutical Competition' (2004) 39 USFL Rev 11, 28.

[78] Thomas F. Cotter 'Refining the 'Presumptive Illegality' Approach to Settlements of Patent Disputes Involving Reverse Payments' (2003) 87 Minn L Rev 1789, 1808–9; Crane (n 58) at 774 ('The 'directional flow' of the settlement payment, therefore, will be affected by the probability of the plaintiff's lawsuit succeeding.').

[79] Hovenkamp et al (n 58) at 1758 (discussing this feature of Cotter and Crane's arguments).

model, if the patentee has a 25 per cent chance of losing, it will be willing to pay up to 25 per cent of the value of its monopoly to exclude its competitors without a trial.[80] The accuracy of the model's numbers is not important, but this feature of exclusion payments nicely illustrates their nature as the purchase of 'insurance' against potential competition.[81] The greater the risk of competition, the higher the premium paid to avoid the risk.

C. A Payment to Eliminate Uncertain Competition can be Anticompetitive

Thus, the market structure in which generic entry occurs and the uncertainties inherent in patent litigation demonstrate that the purpose and effect of an agreement between brand and generic pharmaceutical companies containing an exclusion payment may be to delay potential, albeit uncertain, competition. An agreement that purchases 'insurance' that eliminates the risk of potential competition is likely to harm competition, absent any countervailing, pro-competitive efficiencies. As the Supreme Court has said, '[t]he anti-trust laws are as much violated by the prevention of competition as by its destruction'.[82] The fact that the potential competitor's status is uncertain in no way changes the analysis, for antitrust law condemns agreements to prevent competition even when a potential entrant's prospects for successful entry are not assured.[83] A leading antitrust treatise succinctly articulates the principle: 'the law does not condone the purchase of protection from uncertain competition any more than it condones the elimination of actual competition'.[84]

As a matter of economics, agreements to prevent uncertain competition clearly are anticompetitive and harm consumers, absent significant efficiencies. Preventing potential competition causes harm to consumers in a manner similar to that caused by destroying existing competition, though

---

[80] Cotter (n 79), at 1806.

[81] *In re Ciprofloxacin Hydrochloride Antitrust Litigation*, 2005 WL 736605 at *17 (EDNY 2005) ('Plaintiffs' point is well-taken that the greater the chance a court would hold the patent invalid, the higher the likelihood that the patentee will seek to salvage a patent by settling with an exclusion payment.'); see George L Priest 'Cartels and Patent License Arrangements' (1977) 20 J L& Econ 309, 327 (arguing that rational patentees won't reduce the royalty below zero unless they are cartelizing and industry).

[82] *United States v Griffith*, 334 US 100, 107 68 S Ct 941 (1948), overruled on other grounds, *Copperweld Corp v Independence Tube Corp* 467 US 752, 104 S Ct 2731 (1984).

[83] eg *Blackburn v Sweeney*, 53 F.3d 825 (7th Cir 1995) (unlawful for attorneys to agree not to advertise in one another's cities); *Engine Specialties, Inc v Bombardier Ltd*, 605 F.2d 1 (1st Cir 1979) (unlawful for maker of snowmobiles and maker of minicycles to agree that the former would not enter the latter's market); but see, Schildkraut (n 67) at 1049 ('[u]ncertain competition analysis is a substantial depature from the traditional civil burdens of proof').

[84] XII Phillip E Areeda, Herbert Hovenkamp *Antitrust Law* ¶ 2030b at 175 (1999) (hereinafter '*Areeda & Hovenkamp*').

discounted by the probability of entry. Consumers are always better off with the possibility of competitive entry and lower prices than they are with the certainty of no entry. Reflecting this economic reality the courts have long recognized that even agreements to delay uncertain competition have anticompetitive effects. Since *Chicago Board of Trade v United States*,[85] the rule of reason inquiry has focused on the restraint's 'effect, actual or probable'.

Because the reduction in uncertain competition itself is sufficient to demonstrate an anticompetitive effect, proving what would have happened absent the restraint is not an element of an antitrust action.[86] Even if subsequent events meant the likely effects of the agreement would not have materialized—for example, because the potential entrant's plant had burned down, it failed to obtain necessary regulatory approvals, or for some other reason—that would not alter the conclusion that when the agreement was entered into, it was likely to cause substantial competitive harm.[87]

The DC Circuit's opinion in *United States v Microsoft Corporation*[88] illustrates the importance of this policy for antitrust law. Applying the rule of reason under section 2 of the Sherman Act, the DC Circuit confirmed that impeding 'nascent' rather than actual competition is a fully cognizable anticompetitive effect. Rejecting Microsoft's argument that the Government did not establish a causal link between Microsoft's foreclosure of Netscape's and Java's distribution channels and the maintenance of Microsoft's monopoly, the Court held that it could infer causation even when the exclusionary conduct is aimed at nascent competitive technologies. 'Admittedly, in the former case there is added uncertainty, inasmuch as nascent threats are merely *potential* substitutes. But the underlying proof problem is the same—neither plaintiffs nor the court can confidently reconstruct a product's hypothetical technological development in a world absent the defendant's exclusionary conduct.'[89] It was not the Government's burden to

---

[85] 246 US 231, 238 (1918). Uncertainty about the time of entry may influence a plaintiff's ability to prove damages but does not alter the analysis of liability. See, eg, *United States v Microsoft Corp* 253 F.3d 34, 79–80 (DC Ci. 2001) (per curiam) (distinguishing liability and remedy); *Andrx v Biovail*, 256 F.3d at 806, 808 (holding plaintiff need establish only threat of injury to have standing for injunctive relief); *Microbix Biosys Inc v BioWhittaker, Inc*, 172 F. Supp. 2d 680, 694–95 (D Md 2000) (distinguishing damages inquiry from assessment of competitive effects for purposes of assessing liability under rule of reason), *aff'd on other grounds*, [????]2001 WL 603416 (4th Cir 4 June 2001).

[86] *IFD*, 476 US 461-2.

[87] See, eg, *Microbix*, 172 F Supp 2d at 694–5 (an exclusive supply agreement that created a barrier to competition at the time it was entered into could be condemned under the rule of reason, even though subsequent action by the FDA made it impossible for the target of the exclusionary conduct to enter the market.

[88] 253 F.3d 34 (DC Cir 2001) (*per curium*).

[89] ibid at 79 (emphasis in original).

establish a 'but for' world—to show that Java or Netscape would have become viable substitutes for Microsoft's operating system. Rather, the central question was whether 'as a general matter the exclusion of nascent threats is the type of conduct that is reasonably capable of contributing significantly to a defendant's continued monopoly power' and whether the potential entrants constituted nascent threats at the time the conduct was undertaken. As the Court recognized, 'it would be inimical to the purpose of the Sherman Act to allow monopolists free reign to squash nascent, albeit unproven, competitors at will . . . '[90]

D. *Exclusion Payments Made in the Settlement of Pharmaceutical Patent Litigation Can Harm Competition*

Applying these principles to exclusion payments made in the settlement of pharmaceutical patent litigation demonstrates that such agreements can be anticompetitive. A settlement of pharmaceutical patent litigation containing an exclusion payment effectively is a temporal market allocation arrangement, under which the brand company retains its sales for several years and shares its profits with the potential generic entrant, which, in return, refrains from selling its competing product. Here, just as in *Microsoft*, a potential generic entrant clearly constitutes a threat to a brand company.[91]

The uncertainty about whether the generic ultimately would have prevailed in the patent case does not undermine the likely anticompetitive effects of the settlements including exclusion payments. It clearly would be anticompetitive for an incumbent to pay a potential generic rival to defer entry until a specific date in the future, even if the generic's ability to obtain FDA approval was uncertain. From an economic point of view, there is no reason to treat uncertainty due to patent litigation any differently. Although some patents that are litigated through trial will be found valid and infringed, the anticompetitive harm stems from the settlement's elimination of any chance that the market will be competitive before the agreed-to generic entry date.[92] As one commentator has explained, '[t]he very fact of that uncertainty [that the patentee may win the patent litigation] suggests that exclu-

---

[90] ibid.

[91] A delay in generic entry undisputedly delays consumer access to a lower-priced drug product. An agreement to delay or prevent generic entry, if proven, provides direct evidence of anticompetitive effects that makes a conventional product market analysis unnecessary. IFD, 476 US at 461 ('the finding of actual, sustained adverse effects on competition. . . is legally sufficient to support a finding that the challenged restraint was unreasonable even in the absence of elaborate market analysis') (footnotes omitted); see also, Eric L Cramer and Daniel Berger 'The Superiority of Direct Proof of Monopoly Power and Anticompetitive Effects in Antitrust Cases Involving Delayed Entry of Generic Drugs' (2004) 39 USFL Rev 81.

[92] Hovenkamp (n 58) at 1759 n 176.

sion payments are anticompetitive—that on average such agreements exclude at least some generics that in fact had a legal right to compete.'[93]

There is no basis for the assertion that to demonstrate the anticompetitive effect of agreements containing exclusion payments, it is necessary to show that other factors, including the loss of the patent litigation, would not have prevented generic entry in any event. Just as Microsoft's exclusionary conduct provided less competition in an expected sense, so too can agreements containing exclusion payments. Given the obvious effect that large payments to stay off the market have on a generic firm's decision about when to enter, the challenged agreements are 'likely enough to disrupt the proper functioning of the price-setting mechanism of the market' that they may be deemed anticompetitive even without proof that they actually 'resulted in higher prices. . . than would occur in [the conduct's] absence',[94] based on proof that the generic would have entered the market earlier absent the payment. Indeed, as the Court of Appeals observed in *Microsoft*, to rest antitrust liability on a requirement that plaintiffs 'reconstruct the hypothetical marketplace' absent the challenged conduct would merely encourage 'more and earlier anticompetitive action'.[95]

Moreover, there is no need to consider the outcome of the litigation because antitrust law distinguishes between effects achieved unilaterally and those achieved concertedly. A price-fixing agreement is unlawful even if a party could have raised prices unilaterally.[96] A patentee's proving infringement in litigation and its paying a potential entrant to withdraw its challenge are fundamentally different. Therefore, what a brand-name company might have been able to achieve unilaterally (excluding the generic by winning the patent suit) is no defence to its entering an agreement to pay its competitor not to compete.

An often-cited concurrence in *United States v Singer Manufacturing Co* discusses this point. Justice White found a *separate* antitrust violation in 'the *collusive termination of a Patent Office interference proceeding* pursuant to an agreement between Singer and [its Swiss competitor]'.[97] The parties entered the agreement, wrote Justice White, 'to help one another *to secure as broad a patent monopoly as possible*, invalidity considerations

---

[93] ibid at 1758; Keith Leffler and Cristofer Leffler, 'Efficiency Trade-offs in Patent Litigation Settlements: Analysis Gone Astray?' (2004) 39 USFL Rev 33, 53 ('it is anticompetitive for an incumbent manufacturer to enter into an agreement to eliminate potential competition, based on the probability that the competition would in fact have occurred').

[94] *IFD*, 476 US 461–2.

[95] 253 F.3d at 79.

[96] *Lee Moore Oil Co v Union Oil Co* 599 F.2d 1299, 1302 (4th Cir 1979) ('the fact that [the defendant] might have caused the same damages' by unilateral conduct is 'irrelevant').

[97] 374 US 174, 197 (1963) (White J concurring) (emphasis added).

notwithstanding'.[98] Justice White pointed out that 'the desire to secure broad claims in a patent may well be unexceptional—*when purely unilateral action is involved,*' but does not justify the collusive agreement to terminate a PTO interference proceeding.[99] Thus, that a branded company *might have* won its patent litigations and therefore *unilaterally* precluded the generic from entering the market does not justify paying off that competitor to *guarantee* that it remains off the market.

Of course, the antitrust analysis of these agreements must also consider whether they generate any cognizable pro-competitive efficiencies. In its *Schering* decision, the FTC acknowledged hypothetical situations in which the effect of a payment from a brand to generic company would be pro-competitive because it would hasten generic entry, such as that of the 'cash-strapped generic'.[100] However, neither the FTC, nor any court that has examined these agreements, has found the existence of facts sufficient to support such a situation. Moreover, unlike many patent settlements, an agreement based on an exclusion payment is typically devoid of the kind of efficiencies that can result, for example, when owners combine their conflicting intellectual property so as to produce a product that otherwise would not exist, or when a patent-holder and a new entrant compromise and allow the new entrant to come to market in exchange for compensation to the patent-holder.[101] For that reason, we will continue our analysis of agreements containing exclusion payments assuming that they present no cognizable pro-competitive efficiencies, but recognizing that that determination is fact-specific.[102]

E. The Nature of a Patentee's Right to Exclude

In spite of the economic and antitrust analysis demonstrating that exclusion payments not having legitimate efficiency explanations can be anticompetitive because they purchase protection from potential, albeit uncertain, competition, some courts and commentators have asserted that such agreements must be allowed as falling within the patentee's right to exclude its

---

[98] ibid (White J concurring) (emphasis added).

[99] 374 US at 199 (emphasis added).

[100] FTC Schering Op 38–9.

[101] See IP Licensing Guidelines at § 3.4 (1995) ('To determine whether a particular restraint in a licensing arrangement is given per se or rule of reason treatment, the Agencies will assess whether the restraint in question can be expected to contribute to an efficiency-enhancing integration of economic activity').

[102] For a response dismissing additional proposed hypothetical and generalized procompetitive justifications for settlements including exclusion payments, see Hebert Hovenkamp, Mark D Janis and Mark A Lemley 'Balancing Ease and Accuracy in Assessing Pharmaceutical Exclusion Payments' (2004) 88 Minn L Rev 712, 714–18.

competitors.[103] We believe this assertion misinterprets the nature of the patent right.

A patent grants a patentee a statutory right to 'exclude others from using, offering for sale, or selling the invention throughout the United States . . . '[104] Thus, the patent system 'embodies a carefully crafted bargain for encouraging the creation and disclosure of new, useful, and non-obvious advances in technology and design in return for the exclusive right to practice the invention for a period of years'.[105] Patent policy provides relatively short-term limits on competition because of its judgment that those limits will provide greater incentives to innovate over the long run and increase social welfare by that means.[106]

1. The Right to Exclude Must Be Exercised Consistent with Other Laws

The Patent Act and controlling case law has established two methods by which a patentee may exercise its right to exclude. It may seek and obtain an injunction from a court or it may persuade the accused infringer unilaterally to decide to accede to the patent.[107] Pursuant to the Patent Act, a patentee may seek, and a court may grant, 'injunctions in accordance with the principles of equity to prevent the violation of any right secured by patent, on such terms as the court deems reasonable.'[108] The justification for the use of permanent injunctions in patent cases arises from the constitutional and statutory bases for the right to exclude, as well as a patent's status as personal property.[109] It is important to note that before obtaining a court-awarded permanent injunction, the patentee must win its patent case by proving infringement and warding off any challenges to the validity of its patent. When a patentee exercises its right to exclude by obtaining

---

[103] *Schering-Plough Corp* 2005 WL 528439; see also, *Valley Drug Co* 344 F.3d 1294; Crane, (n 58, arguing that exclusion payments should be permitted when the likelihood of success of the patentee's infringement suit is high).

[104] 35 USC § 154(a)(1). The basis for that statutory right is found in Art I, s 8, Clause 8 of the US Constitution, which gives Congress the power '[t]o promote the Progress of Science and useful Arts, by securing for limited Times to Authors and Inventors the exclusive Right to their respective Writings and Discoveries.'

[105] *Bonito Boats, Inc v Thunder Craft Boats, Inc* 489 US 141, 150–1 (1988).

[106] See, eg, Robert P Merges et al, *Intellectual Property in the New Technological Age* (3rd edn 2003) 13.

[107] In addition, the patentee may license the patent and obtain compensation for the use of its property, rather than exclude all infringers. *Fromson v Western Litho Plate and Supply Co* 853 F.2d 1568, 1576 (Fed Cir 1988) ('In a normal [patent licensing] negotiation, the potential licensee has three basic choices: forego all use of the invention; pay an agreed royalty; infringe the patent and risk litigation.')

[108] 35 USC § 283.

[109] *Richardson v Suzuki Motor Co,* 868 F.2d 1226, 1247 (Fed Cir 1989) ('[i]nfringement having been established, it is contrary to the laws of property, of which the patent law partakes, to deny the patentee's right to exclude others from use of his property.').

a permanent injunction, it obtains that exclusion through the merits of its patent case and the strength of it patent—what we will call the patent's 'exclusionary power'.

If a patentee has not yet won its patent litigation, but wishes to exclude an accused infringer for the course of the litigation, the Patent Act supplies but one means for accomplishing that goal. The patentee must seek a preliminary injunction from the court, pursuant to 35 USC § 283. In considering whether to award a preliminary injunction, a court considers (1) the patentee's likelihood of success on the merits; (2) irreparable harm caused to the parties by granting or denying the injunction; (3) the balance of hardships; and (4) the possible impact of an injunction on the public interest.[110] If a patentee succeeds in obtaining a preliminary injunction, it does so through the strength of its patent case and the demonstrated exclusionary power of the patent.

The Patent Act also makes clear that a patentee may exercise its right to exclude by a means other than obtaining an injunction—by unilaterally and unconditionally refusing to license its patent.[111] If a competitor chooses to exit or refrain from entering the market in the face of that refusal, it is unilaterally acceding to the strength of the patent arguments and the exclusionary power of the patent.

Thus, a patentee has the right to try to exclude allegedly infringing products by instituting a lawsuit—or even by merely threatening a lawsuit. 'The heart of [a patentee's] legal monopoly is the right *to invoke the State's power* to prevent others from utilizing his discovery without his consent'.[112] When it asserts its patent and threatens a lawsuit, the patentee can hope that the strength of its patent allegation convinces the accused infringer to accede and unilaterally decide to exit the market. Alternatively, if the accused infringer views the patent allegation as sufficiently weak to warrant continuing with the accused activity, the patentee's recourse for exercising its right to exclude is to institute litigation and invoke the State's power through a judicially granted injunction. Neither path guarantees success for the patentee. As both economists and legal scholars have remarked, 'a patent is not a right to exclude, but rather a right to *try* to exclude'.[113]

Patent law's right to exclude is not unfettered or free to be exercised by means outside this paradigm, in any manner the patentee sees fit. A patent confers a property right: 'The right to exclude recognized in a patent is but

---

[110] See eg *Hybritech Inc v Abbott Laboratories*, 849 F.2d 1446, 1451–58 (Fed Cir 1988).
[111] 35 USC § 271(d).
[112] *Zenith Radio Corp v Hazeltine Research, Inc* 395 US 100, 135 (1969) (emphasis added).
[113] Hovencamp et al (n 58) at 1761; Shapiro (n 11) at 395.

the essence of the concept of property.'[114] Indeed, the Patent Act grants patents 'the attributes of personal property'.[115] The antitrust agencies also view patents as they do real property.[116] Just as the use of real property is constrained by other legal regimes, so too is a patentee's use of its intellectual property. A patentee must exercise its property right—its right to exclude—in a manner that is consistent with other laws: 'Patents are property, and entitled to the same rights and sanctions as other property.'[117] Nowhere does the Patent Act suggest otherwise. On the contrary, as the Supreme Court has explained, '[s]ince patents are privileges restrictive of a free economy, the rights which Congress has attached to them must be strictly construed so as not to derogate from the general law beyond the necessary requirements of the patent statute.'[118]

For that reason, the 'self-help' of exclusion through means that violate other laws, including the antitrust laws, cannot be justified later through a showing that the patentee could have won patent litigation (assuming such a showing were possible).[119] No one would argue that by making an unproven accusation of patent infringement, a patentee becomes entitled to the 'self-help' remedy of confiscating the accused product in order to exclude it from the market. Confiscation violates other laws and is simply not a component of the patentee's exclusionary right, even if it does eventually prove infringement and the validity of its patent in court. The patentee obtained exclusion through the confiscation, not the exclusionary power of the patent.

Likewise, the patentee's legitimate exercise of its right to exclude by either invoking state action and obtaining an injunction or obtaining the accused infringer's unilateral decision to acquiesce to the strength of the patent is entirely different from a patent-holder's decision to buy off a potential challenger by an agreement to share supra-competitive returns, as occurs in the settlement of pharmaceutical patent litigation. When the patentee obtains exclusion through the 'self-help' remedy of paying an accused infringer to exit or not enter the market it obtains that exclusion through the power of the payment, not the exclusionary power of the patent. Purchasing a horizontal competitor's exclusion from the market violates the antitrust laws and nothing in the patent laws condones it. On the contrary, courts have long held that a patentee 'cannot extend his statutory [patent] grant by

---

[114] *Richardson*, 868 F.2d at 1247.
[115] 35 USC § 261.
[116] IP Licensing Guidelines (n 52) at §§ 2.0, 2.1.
[117] *Continental Paper Bag Co v Eastern Paper Bag Co* 210 US 405, 425 (1908).
[118] *Masonite Corp*, 316 US at 280.
[119] Defenders of exclusion payments have not pointed to any authority holding otherwise, other than a facile reference to the patentee's statutory right to exclude at 35 USC § 154.

contract or agreement.'[120] A settlement, such as those including an exclusion payment, may be unlawful if the patent-holder obtains 'protection from competition which the patent law, unaided by restrictive agreements, does not afford'.[121]

2. The Patent and not a Payment must Provide Exclusion Resulting from the Agreement

An attempt to justify exclusion payments entered in these pharmaceutical patent settlement cases on the grounds that antitrust law allows other agreements that would be illegal absent the assertion of the patent, misses the point that in those cases the source of the exclusion remains the exclusionary power of the patent rather than a payment. For example, a horizontal geographic market allocation would normally be a per se antitrust violation.[122] However, the Patent Act explicitly provides that a patentee may grant a licence to a limited territory, allowing it to establish a geographic market allocation.[123] In the face of the patentee's assertion of its patent rights, through litigation or otherwise, the licensee/accused infringer secedes territory to the patentee based on its assessment of the probability that the patent might exclude it completely, ie the patent's exclusionary power at the time of the agreement. Were the licensee to secede that territory not because of the merits of the patentee's infringement allegations, but because the patentee offered it a payment to do, the antitrust analysis of the agreement would change dramatically. The same principles apply to other 'market-allocations' allowed in patent licences, such as field-of-use restrictions and production limits.[124] The ability to impose such limitations is within the 'exclusionary right' of the patent-owner because the patentee licenses only some portion of its bundle of property rights included within the patent grant. The licensee accepts limited competition due to the patent's strength. The antitrust analysis will differ depending on whether the licensee agreed to the market-allocation in recognition of the exclusionary power of the patent or, as revealed by an examination of the agreement and the market structure in which it arises, because, as revealed by the

---

[120] *Masonite Corp.*, 316 US 265; see also *Singer*, 374 US at 196–97; *United States v Line Material Co* 333 US 287, 308 (1948); *Ethyl Gasoline Corp v United States*, 309 US 436, 456 (1940).

[121] *Masonite Corp*, 316 US at 279.

[122] XII *Areeda and Hovencamp* ¶ 2030 (1999) (noting that naked market division agreements are unlawful per se).

[123] 35 USC § 261.

[124] *B Braun Med v Abbott Labs*, 124 F.3d 1419, 1429 (Fed Cir 1997) (discussing field-of-use restrictions); *Atari Games Corp v Nintendo of Am Inc* 897 F.2d 1572, 1578 (Fed Cir 1990) (upholding quantity limitations in a patent licence).

agreement and the market structure in which it arises, the licensee was paid by the patentee to do so.[125]

These concepts are most easily understood in the context of a patent licensing negotiation. Those negotiations are conducted under a cloud of threatened, potential litigation. If the negotiation fails, the parties will likely become entangled in patent litigation.[126] For that reason, the terms of the licence are driven, at least in part, by the probability that the patentee could win the litigation by proving infringement and surviving a validity challenge.[127] A patentee's power to exclude accused infringers or to dictate the terms under which they may enter the market is never absolute and never described by the patentee's unilateral views of its patent coverage until it obtains a final, successful court judgment on validity and infringement. Until that time, the exclusionary power of the patent is tempered by the statistically high probability that either the patentee will fail to prove infringement or that the accused infringer will demonstrate invalidity.[128] Indeed, as explained above, generic drug manufacturers defeat charges of patent infringement 73 per cent of the time.[129] Thus, until a patentee has obtained a final, unappealable decision of validity and infringement, it is simply incorrect to accept the patentee's infringement allegations as describing the exclusionary power of its patent.[130] A brand pharmaceutical

---

[125] We are not advocating an analysis based on an examination of the parties' subjective thought process. Rather, as described in Pt II above, an examination of the agreement in the context of the market structure of the relevant industry should reveal the source of the exclusion, as it does in the pharmaceutical patent settlement matters. As a practical matter, there may be circumstances in which it is difficult to discern whether the source of the exclusion is the patent or a payment, but the exclusion payments made in the context of brand/generic pharmaceutical patent litigation do not appear to present that difficulty, for the reasons described above.

[126] 'In a normal negotiation, the potential licensee has three basic choices: forego all use of the invention; pay an agreed royalty; infringe the patent and risk litigation.' *Fromson v Western Litho Plate and Supply Co* 853 F.2d 1568, 1576 (Fed Cir 1988) (a patent license is a waiver by the patentee of its right to sue for infringement).

[127] See eg Michael J Meurer 'The Settlement of Patent Litigation,' (1989) 20 RAND Journal of Economics, 77, 77–79 (to avoid the threat of having its patent invalidated, a patentee will often settle a dispute by licensing the patent exchange for royalty payments; the terms of the license depend, in part, on the probability of the patentee prevailing in litigation.). Jean O Lanjouw and Josh Lerner '*The Enforcement of Intellectual Property Rights: A Survey of the Empirical Literature,*' NBER Working Paper Series, Working Paper 6296, 1–4, 19 (1997), available at <http://www.nber.org/papers/w6296> (the likelihood that the patentee will win the patent litigation increases the value of the patent).

[128] *A Patent System for the 21st Century,* National Academies' Board on Science, Technology and Economic Policy, 46–62 (2004), available at <http://www.nap.edu/html/patentsystem> (discussing the patent invalidity rate and the factors affecting the issuance of invalid patents).

[129] FTC Generic Drug Study 15–16.

[130] Errors in granting patent rights may be expected; as previously noted, Professor Landes and Judge Posner have cautioned against an expansive view of intellectual property rights inefficiencies involved in the process of their creation. See Landes and Posner (n 7), 23–4.

company's payment to a potential generic entrant cannot be justified by the exclusionary power of the patent simply because the brand accused the generic of patent infringement.

If the parties settle or avoid litigation by agreeing to a patent licence, the stronger the patentee's validity and infringement arguments, and the higher the probability that it will win the threatened litigation, the more advantageous the terms it can negotiate.[131] The licensee/accused infringer accepts a degree of limitation on its ability to compete freely in the market in proportion to its view of the patent merits and the probabilistic outcome of litigation. That degree of limitation reflects the exclusionary power of the patent. If the licensee/accused infringer seeks a licence of limited geographic territory, the territory might be smaller or larger depending on the perceived strength of the patent. Analogously, the breadth of a field of use licence, the life-span of the license and the royalty paid can all vary depending on the parties' views of the probable outcome of potential litigation. One economist has described patent rights as 'probabilistic' for this reason.[132]

An accused infringer/licensee might also agree to refrain from marketing its product for an agreed length of time in acknowledgement of patent's exclusionary power. While such an agreement would be per se antitrust violation absent the patent dispute, antitrust allows it when the accused infringer's acquiescence and decision to refrain from competing for the agreed length of time is driven by views on the probable outcome of patent litigation, which determines the patent's exclusionary power at the time of the agreement. However, if the agreement is structured so that the patentee obtains some portion of its exclusion through a payment, even if some portion is also arguably obtained through the power of the patent, the agreement raises antitrust concerns.[133]

The Commission's consideration of the Schering/Upsher agreement illustrates this point. The Commission began its consideration of the exclusionary power of Schering's patent with the simple but fundamental principle that, short of a final court judgment on the issue, the parties' collective expectation of the outcome of their litigation—as reflected in a genuine, arms-length settlement—represents the most accurate assessment of the

---

[131] Jean O Lanjouw and Josh Lerner 'The Enforcement of Intellectual Property Rights: A Survey of the Empirical Literature,' NBER Working Paper Series, Working Paper 6296, 1–4, 19 (1997), available at <http://www.nber.org/papers/w6296> (the likelihood that the patentee will win the patent litigation increases the value of the patent).

[132] Shapiro (n 11) pp 407–8.

[133] O'Rourke and Brodley explain that a payment from the brand to the generic distorts the generics incentives to negotiate for the earliest entry date possible. Maureen A O'Rourke and Joseph F Brodley 'An Incentives Approach to Patent Settlements: A Commentary on Hovenkamp, Janis and Lemley' (2003) 87 Minn L Rev 1767, 1786.

subject patent's exclusionary power. The parties' litigations in this case would have fixed only the time of entry of the alleged infringers, because no money damages were at issue.[134] Therefore, *a hypothetical no-payment compromise* on the entry date would most accurately reflect their collectively expected outcome of litigation—ie the exclusionary power of Schering's patent—and would not be illegal.[135]

Thus, any payment provision in the settlement agreements—beyond the expected savings in litigation costs[136]—will affect the compromise entry date in one direction or another: a payment from the alleged infringer to the patent holder, ie a royalty, would be made to gain an earlier entry than a compromise on the date alone. A payment of this kind is unremarkable and indisputably within the limits of a patent's exclusionary power. A payment in the opposite direction, however—an exclusion payment—purchases a *later* time of entry than a compromise on the date alone. A patentee would not make a substantial payment if it believed it could exclude the competition for that period solely on the basis of its patent.[137] This much more unusual form of payment raises serious antitrust concerns because its effect is to *extend* the patent-holder's exclusivity beyond the exclusionary power of it patent and harm consumers by delaying the entry of low-cost generic drugs.[138]

In conclusion, as a leading article discussing pharmaceutical patent settlements explains, the right to exclude granted by a patent does not absolve exclusion payments from antitrust scrutiny:

> The legitimate exclusion value of a pharmaceutical patent is the power it actually conveys over competition, which is in turn a function of the scope of the patent and its chance of being held valid. What the pharmaceutical patentees who agree to exclusion payments seek is something

---

[134] This is common in the context of patent litigation under the Hatch-Waxman Act because the alleged infringer there (ie the ANDA applicant) need not enter the market in order to challenge the referenced patent. *See Mylan Pharms Inc v Shalala*, 81 F Supp 2d 30, 32 (DDC 2000) (filing of ANDA with Paragraph IV Certification 'automatically creates a cause of action for patent infringement').

[135] FTC Schering op 25–6; See also Hovenkamp et al (n 58) at 1762.

[136] The expected savings in the cost of litigation represent merely the transaction costs of litigation versus settlement and, therefore, do not affect the substantive merits of the dispute (ie the expected outcome of litigation). See Hovenkamp (n 58) at 1750–51; FTC Schering op 37, n 67.

[137] Phillip E. Areeda, Herbert Hovenkamp, *Antitrust Law,* ¶ 2046 pp 349–50 (2004 Supp).

[138] *See Andrx Pharms*, 256 F.3d at 809 (patentee's payment to alleged infringer may strongly suggest an anticompetitive agreement). Those antitrust concerns could be addressed by legitimate efficiency explanations, such as those acknowledged by the FTC in its Schering opinion. FTC Schering op at X[????].

more—a guaranteed insulation from competition, without the risk that the patent is held invalid. IP policy does not offer such a guarantee, and does not immunize from antitrust scrutiny those who seek it by entering into agreements that exclude potential competitors.[139]

3. The Right to Exclude Is Neither Unbounded nor Unconditional

Patent policy does not establish the type of unbounded and unconditional 'right to exclude' for patentees that those who defend exclusion payments as within the patent grant must invoke. Furthermore, the courts and Congress have incorporated strands of competition policy into patent policy and allowed antitrust concerns to limit the use of the patent right so that patent policy extends beyond a pure incentive model to include some limitations on the right to exclude that cautions against allowing exclusion payments.[140]

For instance, the Patent Act does not establish a patentee's right to exclude even proven infringers as absolute and unyielding. The statute requires that a court consider the equities when deciding whether to grant an injunction. The equitable factors considered include: (i) whether the patentee would face irreparable injury if the injunction did not issue; (ii) whether the patentee has an adequate remedy at law; (iii) whether granting an injunction is in the public interest; and (iv) whether the balance of hardships favours an injunction.[141] No one factor is dispositive, and a court need not give all factors equal weight.[142] The equitable factors considered in patent cases are the same as those that courts consider when deciding whether to grant an injunction in non-patent cases.[143] Although it is a 'general rule that an injunction will issue when infringement has been adjudged, absent a sound reason for denying it',[144] courts have deemed the 'principles of equity' to allow denial of a permanent injunction

---

[139] Hovenkamp et al (n 58) pp 1761–2.

[140] See Daniel J Gifford 'Antitrust's Troubled Relations with Intellectual Property' (2003) 87 Minn L Rev 1695, 1705–10 .

[141] See, eg, *Boehringer Ingelheim Vetmedica Inc v Schering-Plough Corp* 106 F Supp 2d 696, 700–1 (D NJ 2000); *Odetics, Inc v Storage Technology Corp*, 14 F Supp 2d 785, 794-7 (ED Va 1998).

[142] See *Boehringer Ingelheim Vetmedica*, 106 F Supp 2d at 701.

[143] See, eg, *Weinberger v Romero-Barcelo*, 456 US 305, 312 (1982), cited in *Odetics, Inc*, 14 F Supp 2d at 794.

[144] *Richardson*, 868 F.2d at 1247; see eg Donald S Chisum et al *Principles of Patent Law: Cases and Materials* 1342 (3rd edn 2004) ('Regardless of the justification, for more than two hundred years, the result has almost always been that, after there has been a final determination of infringement, the prevailing patent owner will be granted an injunction that permanently enjoins the adjudicated infringer from infringing the patent in suit').

after a final judgment of infringement,[145] stays of an injunction pending appeal,[146] and delayed injunctions to allow time for the adoption of comparable, non-infringing devices.[147]

Moreover, patent policy limits a patentee's exclusionary right to the scope of the patent claims.[148] In the *Motion Picture Patents* case, the Supreme Court refused to enforce a licence in which a patentee sought to limit the use of its patented film projectors to only those non-patented films authorized by the patentee. One might argue that the patentee's statutory right to exclude gave it authority to design any condition on which it would license, but the Court rejected that view of the exclusionary right, holding that nothing in the patent law gives a patentee the right to condition the use of a patented invention with goods selected by the patentee.[149] Because that right is not within the patentee's bundle of rights, the tying condition must be judged by the general law, including the antitrust law.[150] Congress has recognized that the patent right to exclude does not allow a patentee having market power to tie sales of a commodity item to a patent licence.[151] 'Patent law creates a system of economic incentives designed to

---

[145] *City of Milwaukee v Activated Sludge, Inc* 69 F.2d 577, 593 (7th Cir 1934) (injunction seeking to close sewage plant denied due to public health concern); *Nerney v New York, NH & HR Co*, 83 F.2d 409, 410-11 (2d Cir 1936) (injunction seeking to close railroad denied).

[146] See, eg, *Pall Corp v Micron Separations, Inc* 792 F Supp 1298, 1328 (D Mass 1992) (granting a partial stay of injunction pending appeal to ensure the availability of certain medical supplies to third parties).

[147] See, eg, Shiley, *Inc v Bentley Lab* 601 F Supp 964, 969–71 (CD Ca 1985) (providing for a six-month transition period with royalties to facilitate patient care before the injunction becomes effective); *Johns Hopkins University v CellPro*, 1997 US Dist Lexis 24162 (D De 1997) (granting a partial stay of injunction, and certain fees during the stay, until approval of patentee's licensed medical devices by the FDA); *Moxness Products, Inc v Xomed, Inc* 7 USPQ2D 1877 (MD Fl 1988) (granting a stay of four months, with royalties, to allow health care providers to switch to other devices); *Schneider (Europe) AG v SciMed Life Sys, Inc* 852 F Supp 813, 850–1, 861–2 (D Mn 1994) (providing for a one year transition period, with royalties, to allow health care providers to switch to other medical devices); *Eolas Technologies Inc v Microsoft Corp*, 70 USPQ2D 1939 (ND Ill 2004) (allowing Microsoft a lead time of 17 weeks to develop non-infringing products; and staying the injunction pending appeal to ensure an orderly progression from the use of infringing features to non-infringing features without disruption to computer systems and capabilities that would greatly inconvenience the public).

[148] See, eg, *Mallinckrodt, Inc v Medipart, Inc* 976 F.2d 700 (Fed Cir 1992).

[149] *Motion Picture Patents Co v Universal Film Mfg Co* 243 US 502, 518 (1917).

[150] Anticompetitive tying is prohibited by section 3 of the Clayton Act, 15 USC § 14. Although tying arrangement may result in anticompetitive effects that would be condemned by antitrust law, such arrangements can also result in significant efficiencies and procompetitive benefits. Dennis W Carlton and Jeffrey M Perloff *Modern Industrial Organization* (3rd ed 2000) 303–4. The US Antitrust agencies consider both the anticompetitive effects and the efficiencies attributable to a tying arrangement. IP Licensing Guidelines at § 5.3; see also, Tom & Newberg (n 52) at 210–15 (discussing the procompetitive benefits of tying arrangements).

[151] 35 USC § 271(d)(5) (A patent owner will not be guilty of patent misuse for having ('conditioned the license of any rights to the patent or the sale of the patented product on the acquisition of a licence to rights in another patent or purchase of a separate product, unless,

foster invention, but the incentive structure of patent law is not be augmented by leveraging the power of the patent.'[152]

Competition policy, like patent policy, also directly limits the use of patent rights. For example, some patent rights, clearly within the bundle of a patentee's property rights are, nevertheless, limited by the antitrust laws in the same sense as the analogous real property rights. A patentee may assign or exclusively license its patent in the same way that an owner of real property may sell or lease its property. The patent laws expressly allows for exclusive licenses and assignments of patent rights.[153] In spite of this, section 7 of the Clayton Act[154] prohibits assignments and exclusive patent licenses that harm competition by overly concentrating a market just as it prohibits acquisitions of real property under those circumstances.[155]

In sum, exclusion payments provide 'a powerful inducement to abandon competition.'[156] By paying a generic to not enter until an agreed-upon date, a brand induces the generic to accept what the force of its patent alone would not—foregoing their patent challenges and staying off the market until the agreed-upon dates, several years into the future. An argument that such behavior falls within the patentee's exclusionary right expands that right in way that is unwarranted by either patent policy or competition policy's relationship to patents.

F. Policy Issues Surrounding Pharmaceutical Patent Settlements

Some courts and commentators have argued that settlements including exclusion payments should be allowed on policy grounds, because prohibiting them would chill litigation settlements and undermine the value of a patent's incentive to innovate. As explained below, both fears are unwarranted. Rather, Hatch-Waxman's goal of encouraging generic entry and patent policy's goal of awarding an exclusionary right commensurate with the inventive contribution both caution against allowing exclusion payments.

in view of the circumstances, the patent owner has market power in the relevant market for the patent or patented product on which the licence or sale is conditioned.').

[152] Gifford (n 141) at 1709.

[153] 35 USC § 261.

[154] 15 USC § 18.

[155] 1 Hovenkamp et al *IP and Antitrust: An Analysis of Antitrust Principles Applied to Intellectual Property Law*, § 14.2b1.

[156] *Masonite Corp* 316 US at 281.

1. Prohibiting Exclusion Payments will not Chill Patent Settlements

As the US antitrust enforcement agencies have recognized, the general policy of the law has been to encourage settlements.[157] Therefore, some have worried that finding antitrust liability for patent settlements including exclusion payments will chill settlement activity.[158] Empirical data shows this fear is unwarranted.

Preventing a brand-name drug company and its potential generic competitors from settling on terms including an exclusion payment not supported by efficiency justifications would not prevent them from using any number of other methods of reaching settlement. For example, a generic company may pay for the right to enter by taking an immediate license, in which case it would be buying the right to compete instead of being paid not to compete, or the parties could split the patent life without a payment that purchases additional protection from competition.

To mitigate the possibility that brand-name and generic drug manufacturers might enter patent settlement agreements that could harm consumers, the FTC Generic Drug Study recommended that Congress pass legislation to require brand-name companies and generic applicants to provide copies of certain agreements to the Federal Trade Commission and the Department of Justice. Congress passed the Medicare Modernization Act, containing such a provision in December 2003.[159] As a result of that legislation, during fiscal year 2004, drug manufacturers filed 14 agreements with the FTC that resolved patent infringement litigation. None of these included a payment from the brand to the generic manufacturer in exchange for the generic's agreement not to market its product.[160]

Those data, indicating that 14 pharmaceutical patent litigation settlements were entered in a single year, fiscal year 2004, as compared to the 27 settlements entered between 1992 and 2002, suggest that a perceived prohibition on exclusion payments in settlements has not deterred parties from finding alternative, acceptable means to reach a settlement agreement. Moreover, of

---

[157] *Standard Oil Co (Indiana) v United States*, 283 US 163, 171 (1931); Federal Trade Commission & United States Dept of Justice, *Antitrust Guidelines for the Licensing of Intellectual Property* at § 5.5 (1995) ('Settlements involving the cross-licensing of intellectual property rights can be an efficient means to avoid litigation and, in general, courts favour such settlements'), available at <http://www.usdog.gov/atr/public/guidelines/ipguide.pdf>.

[158] See *Schering-Plough Corp.*, 2005 WL 528439 at *16.

[159] See s 1112 of the Medicare Prescription Drug, Improvement, and Modernization Act of 2003, Title XI, Access to Affordable Pharmaceuticals, PL 108–73, 117 Stat 2066 (8 Dec 2003). For information on the types of agreements that must be filed, see 'Pharmaceutical Agreement Filing Requirements,' at <http://www.ftc.gov/os/2004/01/040106pharmrules.pdf>.

[160] For a summary of all agreements filed in FY 2004, see <http://www.ftc.gov/os/2004/01/40106pharmrules.pdf>.

20 final patent settlements between brand-name companies and first generic applicants identified by the FTC Generic Drug Study, only nine included exclusion payments. Although settlements containing exclusion payments were prevalent in the pharmaceutical industry during this time, by no means were they the only mechanism used to achieve settlements.[161] Thus, data from both the FTC Generic Drug Study and the agency's recent review of pharmaceutical patent litigation settlements indicates that condemnation of allegedly unjustified exclusion payments has not chilled settlement activity. The settlements filed with the Commission in 2004, after the Commission's Schering decision, show that legitimate patent settlements continue to take place without hindrance from the Commission decision.

2. Revisiting the Merits of the Patent Litigation in the Antitrust Analysis Would Discourage Settlements

Some have argued that the exclusionary power of the patent can be properly assessed by a plenary trial on the issues of patent validity and infringement.[162] This approach views the exclusionary power of the patent in any given situation as binary rather than probabilistic—either the patent is valid and covers the accused product, or it is not. This approach presumes that if the patent is valid and covers the accused product, patent policy allows the patentee to exclude the accused product from the market through means that would otherwise violate the antitrust laws, such as direct payment or market allocation. If the later review of the patent issues demonstrates either the patent's invalidity or non-infringement, the antitrust analysis need not consider the patent's exclusionary power and the agreement may violate the law.[163]

Such an approach disserves patentees and accused infringers equally, for they can never perform a satisfactory antitrust analysis of a settlement agreement as of the time they enter it, and obtain the predictability and certainty that the settlement was meant to convey. The antitrust analysis will depend on a later court's view of the patent merits.[164] The parties have simply traded the uncertainty of the outcome of the patent litigation, based

---

[161] FTC Generic Drug Study 27–35. The remaining two settlements do not fit into any of these three categories.

[162] Crane (n 58, arguing that exclusion payments should be permitted when the likelihood of success of the patentee's infringement suit is high).

[163] See Schildkraudt (n 67) at 1041.

[164] The later court's review of the patent merits will be undermined by the fact of the settlement, which changed the incentives of the generic from wishing to defeat the patent to supporting it in the interest of preserving the settlement. O'Rourke and Brodley (n 134) at 1786.

on the patent merits, for the uncertainty of the outcome of the antitrust litigation, based again on the patent merits.[165]

If the antitrust court were to find the patent valid and infringed, virtually any settlement into which the parties might enter, short of exclusion following the patent's expiration or of products falling outside the claim scope, could be deemed pro-competitive compared to continuing litigation, and, therefore, legal. On the other hand, if the antitrust court were to find the patent invalid or not infringed, a settlement that restrained the accused infringer in any way, as certainly most settlements would, would be deemed anticompetitive compared to continuing litigation and, therefore, illegal. The better approach, and the one that provides more respect for the patentee's exclusionary right, considers the exclusionary power of the patent, based on the parties' collective views on the probability of the outcome of the actual or anticipated patent litigation at the time of the agreement.

3. Prohibiting Exclusion Payments is Consistent with Patent Policy

Some have worried that prohibiting exclusion payments would lessen the value of the patent and undermine the patent system's incentive to innovate.[166] This concern misunderstands that exclusion payments actually distort the patent system's incentive structure by allowing the patentee rights not granted by Congress.

Patent policy provides that the exclusionary power of the patent is proportionate to the inventor's contribution to his field. If a patented invention is truly revolutionary compared to the prior art, the patent claims are much more likely to be found novel and non-obvious over the prior art than are claims reciting only a minor distinction. Moreover, the claims protecting a pioneering invention will be interpreted broadly to cover a wide range of possibly infringing products as compared to claims protecting a minor improvement.[167] Thus, patent policy intends that claim scope and strength will be governed by the extent of the inventive contribution. That policy encourages greater leaps of technological innovation.[168] It would be contrary to that fundamental policy of patent law to allow a patentee to supplement the exclusionary power of its patent with exclusion payments. Such payments give the patentee a degree of market control that its inven-

---

[165] See *Valley Drug*, 344 F.3d at 1308 ('Patent litigation is too complex and the results too uncertain for parties to accurately forecast whether enforcing the exclusionary right through settlement will expose them to treble damages if the patent immunity were destroyed by the mere invalidity of the patent.').

[166] *Valley Drug Co* 344 F.3d at 1311 n 27.

[166] *Augustine Med Inc v Gaymar Indus Inc* 181 F.3d 1291 (Fed Cir 1999).

[167] See Edmund W Kitch 'The Nature and Function of the Patent System' (1977) 20 JL & Econ 265 (discussing the economic incentive for 'patent mining' provided by broad patents).

tive contribution could not provide and distort the patent system's incentive structure as established by Congress.

By enacting the patent laws, 'Congress has implicitly balanced the trade-off between the static efficiency of competition and the low prices against the dynamic efficiency of increased incentives to seek patentable innovations. A proper economic welfare analysis of patent rights must take as given the patent rules specified by Congress with the presumption that those rules properly and correctly balance static and dynamic efficiency.'[169] A rule that allows a patentee to pay a competitor to not compete based solely on an untested allegation of patent infringement reaches beyond the 'right to exclude' granted by Congress in the Patent Act and disrupts that balance.

4. Exclusion Payments Undermine the Policies of the Hatch–Waxman Act

Congress intended the Hatch–Waxman Act to increase the flow of generic pharmaceuticals into the marketplace and the purpose and effect of exclusion payments is to stymie that flow. In the Hatch–Waxman Act, Congress struck a carefully considered balance between maintaining the incentives for innovation of new drug products and promoting significantly lower-priced generic drugs. [170] Important elements in this balance were provisions that made it easier and more lucrative for generics to challenge the validity and scope of pharmaceutical patents. The brand company patentee and the generic challenger typically litigate the patent issues before a generic enters the market.[171] Most importantly, the statute provides a powerful incentive to generics to challenge weak and narrow patents in the form of a 180-day marketing exclusivity awarded to the first generic company to take on that challenge.[172] The principal goal of these provisions is to encourage generic drug manufacturers to challenge weak or narrow patents and enter the market as soon as possible.

Some have justified exclusion payments in the settlement of pharmaceutical patent litigation as 'a natural by-product of the Hatch–Waxman process.'[173] This rationale turns the Hatch–Waxman process on it head by interpreting provisions designed to *promote* patent challenges by generics to

---

[169] Leffler and Leffler (n 94) at 34–5.
[170] See HR Rep No 98-857(I), pp 14–15 (1984), reprinted in 1984 USCCAN 2647–8.
[171] See 35 USC § 271(e)(2).
[172] 21 USC § 355(j)(5)(B)(iv); Medicare Prescription Drug, Improvement, and Modernization Act of 2003, Pub L No 108–73, § 1102, 117 Stat 2461–3 (2003) [hereinafter MMA].
[173] *Schering-Plough Corp*, 2005 WL 528439 at *16 (quoting *In re Ciprofloxacin Hydrochloride Antitrust Litigation*, 261 F Supp 2d 188, 251 (EDNY 2003)).

justify payments to *avoid* patent challenges.[174] Congress recognized that exclusion payments undermine the policies of the Hatch–Waxman Act when it passed the 2003 Medicare amendments to Hatch–Waxman, which require that patent litigation settlement agreements between brand and generic companies be reported to the antitrust agencies.[175] As the legislative history for that provision states, 'the industry has recently witnessed the creation of pacts between big pharmaceutical firms and makers of generic versions of brand name drugs that are intended to keep lower-cost drugs off the market. Agreeing with smaller rivals to delay or limit competition is an abuse of the Hatch–Waxman law that was intended to promote generic alternatives.'[176] Thus, properly understood, exclusion payments can undermine broad Congressional purposes, something the 2003 amendments to the Hatch–Waxman Act recognize.

G. Summary

A careful examination of some recent pharmaceutical patent litigation settlement agreements conducted within the context of the market structure in which generic entry would occur reveals that payments from the brand-name drug company to a potential generic entrant are payments made to insure that generic entry will not occur until an agreed-upon date. By examining the Patent Act and other aspects of patent policy, we have shown that the right to 'buy-off' a potential competitor that one has only accused of infringement does not fall within a patentee's right to exclude. We have also explained how the prevention of potential, albeit uncertain competition can be anticompetitive. Both principles are critical in the proper antitrust analysis of patent settlement agreements containing exclusion payments.

V. GENERAL CONCLUSIONS

The patent-antitrust interface is and will remain one of the most complicated areas of competition policy analysis. In recent decades American antitrust commendably has overcome its traditional hostility to patent rights and recognized that patent law, like antitrust law, is a powerful tool for promoting welfare. Nevertheless, it would be wrong to exalt patent law over other forms of property—as is the case of other property law schemes, patent law must remain fully within the reach of antitrust law, to prevent anticompetitive restrictions that harm welfare. Indeed, because a lack of

---

[174] Marcy Lobanoff, Comment, 'Anticompetive Agreements Cloaked as "Settlements" Thwart the Purposes of the Hatch-Waxman Act' (2001) 50 Emory LJ 1331.
[175] MMA §§ 1111–17.
[176] S Rep No 107–67, at 4 (2002).

competitive vigor discourages the dynamic economic rivalry that encourages business experimentation, largely exempting patent-related arrangements from antitrust scrutiny would retard, rather than encourage, the innovation that the Patent Act seeks to achieve.

Taking into account these considerations, we have explored two contentious topics that implicate patent and competition policy, the treatment of *ex ante* price-related negotiations involving SSOs and patent holders, and patent litigation settlements involving 'exclusion payments' by patentees. As we have show, allowing *ex ante* negotiations does not undermine patent rights holders—it merely restrains patentees from receiving excessive and economically inefficient returns due to ex post 'hold-ups.' Moreover, barring anticompetitive exclusion payments in settlement negotiations does not discourage efficient settlements, it merely prevents collusive bargains that delay entry and harm consumer welfare. In reaching these conclusions, we took due note of the peculiar characteristics of patent property rights, namely the fact that they are more 'probabilistic' in nature than other property rights.

This analysis does not derogate from the dignity of patent rights—it merely reflects the careful, issue-specific evaluation that is required to ensure that an appropriate balance is struck in jointly applying the antitrust and patent laws. In these and other areas at the patent-antitrust interface, a careful balancing of antitrust and patent considerations should yield outcomes that promote consumer welfare and innovation, consistent with the general policy goals of both legal regimes. These observations, we maintain, are general principles that apply not just within the United States, but to the antitrust and patent systems of other nations as well.

Panel 2—The Rights of Complainants and Third Parties (Cartels, 82, Mergers): Getting the Balance Right

PHILIP MARSDEN

Welcome back everyone for the second session, on the rights of complainants and third parties in a range of areas and getting the balance right. You can see the theme that this conference is having.

I am very pleased that chairing our second panel is indeed a former hearing officer, which is very important for this particular panel's discussion. Joseph Gilchrist is also a senior adviser at FIPRA now who comes with a wealth of experience from his many years at the European Commission. I am very grateful to him for chairing this panel.

JOSEPH GILCHRIST

Thank you Philip for that very kind introduction. The discussion of this panel is entitled 'Rights of Complainants and Third Parties—Getting the Balance Right'. We started off by asking the previous panel what is the right balance and we now go over to the real practitioners who will show you how you get it right.

We have three panellists. First Serge Durande, who is the current Senior Hearing Officer at the European Commission. Before joining the Commission in 1975 he was a legal eagle in the university world and since joining the Commission he has had seven different jobs in DG IV/Competition. I am delighted that he has not been mobile outside that august DG and he has therefore in fact broken very elegantly another Commission policy. Nicholas French is a partner in Freshfields and I think needs no introduction. He has written very extensively and the list of his cases probably makes you jealous. Finally, we have Julian Maitland Walker, who is an entrepreneur, as well as being a lawyer, in the sense that he had the courage to leave the big boys in competition law in the City of London and establish his own niche competition legal firm, basing himself in the West Country. He has worked for a long time with Clifford Chance in Brussels, and he has also been editor of the European Competition Law Journal.

So I don't think you can have three more experienced people to discuss this topic. We are going to start with Serge Durande, to put the functions of complainants and third parties from the point of view of the Commission and administering the system.

SERGE DURANDE

Thank you, Joe. It isn't quite right saying that I haven't moved, because I have left DG Competition three years ago, but it is true that I have had seven different jobs in the place.

OK, what can I tell you in these few minutes as an overview? When I was first asked to participate in this panel, I was interested in the title: 'Rights of Complainants and Third Parties—Getting the Balance Right'. It is interesting, if only because complainants and third parties often provide an invaluable input into a case, but at the same time I have heard that there was a need for some clarification before getting into the technicalities, because the issue can not be taken in isolation. It seems to me that at least three parameters have to be mentioned in order to put the issue in perspective.

First, the question of the purpose of competition law. It is about putting into place the framework for sound competition. In essence, it is there to defend competition in the marketplace. It is not there to defend competitors from competition in the marketplace.

Secondly, one has to consider the responsibilities of the institutions, the Commission, or the tribunal and also the court. Also their perspective may be somewhat different. The Commission's responsibility is to make the investigation, take a view on the questions and the arguments and take a decision to act, or not to act. Whatever it does, its decision to act or not to act is appealable in Luxembourg. As far as we are concerned, this means that the law and the practice of the Commission have to put in place a system which is fair. It has to allow due process to work properly. But then one finds that in the view of the regulators, in applying the law and the case law, due process works somewhat differently according to each category of actors in a case. This is the very interesting question. Why is that so?

I think the third remark follows from this. Running the risk of stating the obvious, I would say that complainants and third parties only exist in a case because you have parties in the first place. The parties are at the core of the case, before the others who are in a way peripheral. If I take an example, the Commission condemns an undertaking for an abuse of dominant position; the ones who have suffered from the abuse are the competitors and ultimately the consumers because competition did not work properly. Whilst the benefit from the abuse is for a dominant undertaking, it is also the one which damages competition, the one which will have to change its commercial policy and also in all likelihood will have to pay the fine.

What are the rights of these different groups, under the law and the case law? Well, it is relatively easy. As far as rights of defence are concerned, only the parties have them because they are the only ones who have been confronted with objections of the Commission. As far as the right to be heard is concerned, one has to consider whether it is a right to be heard in writing or orally.

Parties to a case have a complete right. There is no discretion for the Commission. They have access to the entire file, with a few exceptions, which are very limited in fact. On the contrary, for the complainants and the third parties there are margins of discretion for the Commission. The complainants have two rights, as you know, under the law. One is to receive a non-confidential version of the Statement of Objections, if that complaint has led to a case, and provide their points of view on the objections of the Commission. The other is to be informed through a motivated decision of the reasons why the Commission may not pursue their case. And the third parties have fewer rights. They have to demonstrate enough interest to be informed in writing of the nature and the purpose of the case. This is the law.

The differentiation is understandable when reading the 'whereas' of Regulation 773. Whereas Number 5 simply says that complainants are a fundamental source of information; they can be closely associated to the proceedings. Therefore, it appears that complainants and third parties: (a) do not have rights of defence; and (b) benefit from some form of a right to be heard. And the criticism on their side is, of course, the perception that they have too few opportunities to take the debate in a specific direction. However, I doubt that this would nowadays be entirely the right picture. I believe that the European courts in particular have conferred a substantial role on them and the Commission is no longer the sole master of the procedure. Its discretionary power has been progressively reduced by the courts. The courts have indeed corrected a number of short comings and the third parties will inevitably benefit from the latest jurisprudential developments.

If I take for instance, the last *Tetra Laval* case,[1] amongst many other things what the court tells the Commission is: a) they are in the hands of the tribunal as far as the facts are concerned and their appreciation; and b) that the standard of proof is raising constantly, even more for mergers than for antitrust cases. I believe this is fair enough. Because a merger analysis is in anticipation there can be no direct evidence nor direct proof of what is quite often a theoretical construction. Therefore, says the Court, the demonstration needs to be entirely convincing, even more than in a classical antitrust

---

[1] *Tetra Laval v Commission* (Case C-12/03 P, judgment of 15 Feb 2005), not yet reported in the ECR.

case. I put it to you that as a result—because the Commission is under a duty to understand perfectly the facts and the economics of a given case—it will rely more and more on the contribution of those who are on the market, who know the market better and these are the complainants and the third parties. So we have a balanced situation.

Although the intensity of the rights of complainants and third parties is different from the one of the parties, it can only be raising in such a jurisprudential context. They will continue to enjoy a softer right to be heard than one of the defendants, because their right is not the expression of a fundamental right. Their involvement in a case will continue to serve primarily the purpose of the procedure, more than their direct own interest, but they will be heard more and more, particularly through the market test. As far as their own interest is concerned as opposed to developing competition law, they have also been tremendously helped by the courts. The courts have identified a number of obligations which have been laid down on the Commission.

Let's look at the complainants. Following a number of cases, reaffirmed a number of times, particularly recently in *Atlantic Container Line*,[2] the Commission, it is for sure, may not be obliged to pursue every complaint, but it has to exercise a duty of vigilance. It also has to investigate the facts submitted by the complainant. Then the strongest right which the complainant hears is when his complaint is being rejected. What it really means in this case is that the Commission believes that the competition situation submitted by the complainant either is not a problem of competition law or is a problem which the Commission will not investigate further, because this can be done better at a national level, or because it is allowed to set priorities in the public interest. As you know, this triggers a number of rights for the complainants. The right to receive an Article 7 letter, which I will call maybe a 'reverse Statement of Objections'. I say reverse, because the Statement of Objections says why a case will be investigated, why it is being investigated. This Article 7 letter will state why it is not. They also have a right to challenge the decision rejecting the complaint. This is because following the *Delimitis*[3] case in 1991, fourteen years ago already. It has therefore been established that the fundamental mission of the Commission is about the implementation of competition law and that it is entitled to define its priorities

To conclude, I would say a few words about the notion of balance, getting the balance right. This is not such an easy concept. I see a balance in front

---

[2] Joined Cases T-191/98, T-212/98, T-213/98, and T-214/98, judgment of 30 Sept 2003 (not yet published in European Court Reports).
[3] *Delimitis v Henninger Bräu* (Case C-234/89) [1991] ECR I-935, [1992] 5 CMLR 210.

of all the courts; the judges have ponder the facts of the case and decide on their influence on the legal issues. The Commission also makes a balance of the same kind under the control of the courts. I make often a balance between the necessity to disclose confidential information and the right to the protection of confidential information.

There are other questions of balance—there are many of them. One, fundamental: the standard of proof. It is about balancing the evidence available. Against a test which has to be met before a case can be considered to be proven in law. This test is becoming more and more demanding in the recent case law. We come from a standard of proof of balance of probabilities where one can take a view on the legal issue when the facts of the case are established at say 51 per cent, to a new system, closer to the standard of beyond reasonable doubt, which is dear to the hearts of criminalists. In fact there are many things to balance in competition cases.

As to what the right balance should be on the extent to which complainants and third parties would interfere in the investigation or contribute to it, I would limit myself to the fundamentals. I would say nowadays, they do not lead the investigation, they accompany it; they may be tremendously useful, but their rights are of a procedural nature; they are not the expression of fundamental rights; they don't have rights of defence and I believe that this is the right balance. Although I recognize that they may feel sometimes that they are somewhat instrumental and they may be looking for more, I do not think that they should shape the debate. Nevertheless, I am convinced that they will carry more and more weight.

JOE GILCHRIST

Thank you very much Serge for that very succinct overview, both of the problems that this subject raises, but also I think very interestingly, on how you tackle those problems. Serge in his post as Hearing Officer is the first port of call for complainants and third parties. If he doesn't let the thing go further, as he said, a decision could be challenged in the court, but it is not likely to be.

NICHOLAS FRENCH

I was invited to join this panel following my involvement representing Pepsi Co. in relation to the Commission's investigation into Article 82 activities relating to Coca-Cola.[4] I was asked to share with you some of my thoughts and experiences of rights of defence, or rights of complainants, or lack of

---

[4] Commission decision of 26 June 2005, Case COMP/39.116/B-2.

rights of complainants as the case may be in the context of Article 9 Commitment Decisions settling Article 81 and 82 investigations.

For the non-Europeans among us, just by way of a little bit of background, Article 9 of Regulation 1 formalizes the Commission's pre-existing ability to settle Article 81 and 82 investigations. But Article 9 is important. It allows the Commission to terminate an investigation upon the companies concerned giving, and the Commission receiving, binding specific commitments which remove the Commission's competition concerns that are set out in its preliminary assessment. Now, that is very significant. For the Commission it enables cases to be settled quickly; it increases the ease and effectiveness, I expect, with which the Commission will be able to enforce the commitments that have been given to the Commission. For the companies being investigated I think it is very important too. It permits the possibility to settle an investigation prior to the issue of the Statement of Objections which, as Serge said, would ordinarily be given in a non-confidential form to complainants. Critically, an Article 9 decision does not conclude whether there has been an infringement of Article 81 or 82. For third parties including complainants the procedure, I think, does enhance transparency. In particular, it allows for the involvement of third parties in the market testing of the commitments before they are adopted in an Article 9 decision.

Just briefly as a matter of process, before an Article 9 decision is adopted the Commission issues an initiation of proceedings. That is followed by the Commission issuing a preliminary assessment to the companies being investigated only. That is followed by the company's concerned giving draft commitments to the Commission with a view to satisfying the concern set out in the Commission's preliminary assessment, followed by a period of market testing, and then the commitments being accepted by the Commission in the form of an Article 9 decision.

Now there are a number of cases as many of you know where Article 9 decisions have either been taken, or are now in the course of being taken. There is one, the *Bundesliga* case,[5] which an Article 9 decision was issued in January and half a dozen more which have been through a market testing phase, and there are more in the pipeline. One of those cases, the one which I was involved in, related to an investigation being launched as a result of a number of complaints from third parties. That is what I would like to share with you: my observations in terms of the rights of the complainant in the context of that case.

---

[5] Commission decision of 19 Jan 2005, Case COMP/C.2/37.214, OJ L 134/46, 27/5/2005.

I am going to focus on three issues and I will be very brief, but would be happy to expand in questions afterwards.

One is the impact of the lack of access to the preliminary assessment, even in a non-confidential form. The complainant doesn't see the Commission's thinking in the preliminary assessment.

The second is the impact of the commitments decision on the complainant's ability to bring follow-on actions in national courts. I question how that sits with the encouragement of private enforcement of competition law generally.

Third, I want to express some observations on the hurdles facing complainants trying to enforce a commitment's decision, to the extent that they have been breached in front of national courts.

So turning to my first point: the impact of the lack of access to the Commission's preliminary assessment. I struggle to see why the Commission does not share the preliminary assessment with complainants and other third parties. To my mind, although I understand the preliminary assessment is a briefer document than the Statement of Objections, it fulfils much the same role as a Statement of Objections and, as we have said, the Statement of Objections in non-confidential form is shared with complainants and other interested third parties. In *BAT and Reynolds*,[6] for example, the Commission described the Statement of Objections as a preparatory document containing assessments which are purely provisional in nature. It seems to me that a preliminary assessment is much the same document, even if it is briefer. But Regulation 1 and the implementing regulation are not clear as to what happens to the preliminary assessment with third parties, but the practice as far as I've seen it is that it is not shared. Does it matter? I think it does. I think if a complainant has been instrumental in launching a case or giving the Commission sufficient evidence to bring a case and, as Serge said, it is often the case that complainants have an important role in bringing evidence to the Commission's attention, then I think just like when a complainant sees a copy of the Statement of Objections before any final decision, I think it would be useful for a complainant to be able to see a copy of the preliminary assessment. Also it would be useful in order to understand the Commission's thinking in relation to the commitments that it eventually accepts. The question also as to whether it might be helpful to the Commission: it would certainly be something that complainants I think would like in terms of being able to assist in the way in which the commitments are put together and comment more

---

[6] *BAT and Reynolds v Commission* (Joined Cases 142/84 and 156/84) [1987] ECR 4487, [1988] 4 CMLR 24.

fully when the market testing takes place. Finally, which is my next point, it would be helpful, I think, in the context of private damages actions for complainants to be granted access to a copy of the preliminary assessment. So that is my second point.

What is the impact of a commitments decision on a complainant's ability to bring follow-on actions in national courts? As we know, infringement decisions bind national courts and can be relied upon where follow-on actions are available, such as in the UK. Understandably, a commitments decision, which doesn't carry with it or include a statement as to whether or not there has been infringement, can not be relied on in the same way. There is no finding of an infringement and I think that is right. However, if a complainant or any other third party wishes to bring a follow-on action the Commission's thinking as to where it got to before it accepts the commitments, I think, would be useful as some sort of starting point in the pleadings as to developing the case in front of a national court. The weight of that preliminary assessment I think is a moot point, but I think it is quite interesting in the Commission's facts, or the published memorandum, of its thinking preliminary assessment, where it says that 'while the addressee of a commitment decision does not receive a prohibition decision with the consequent negative publicity for a violation of antitrust rules, neither does it get the Commission's blessing, since the Commission decision is a substitute for a prohibition decision and not an exemption decision'. I think that is quite forceful in terms of what the Commission thinks, and maybe it's changed its mind, but in terms of the type of weight the Commission would give to the preliminary assessment . . . my observation then is that arguably it would be easier and helpful for a third party to have a copy of the preliminary assessment if it is going to bring follow-on actions. Would it not be more consistent with the Commission's general policy of encouraging private actions to give the complainants a copy of the preliminary assessment?

My final point is on enforcement of commitment decisions in national courts. The companies concerned give their commitments to the Commission. The Commission in my experience has expressed a hope, an expectation, that complainants and other third parties will bring actions before national courts to ensure that commitments where they are infringed are abided by. Now the Commission is certainly best placed to respond to breaches of the commitment, since it has got the power to impose significant fines, and it can also reopen proceedings if the commitments are breached. But, as I said, the Commission appears to be looking to third parties also to back-up or to replace the Commission in some circumstances, by bringing actions in national courts. According to the Commission, national courts must enforce the commitments by any means provided for national courts, including the adoption of interim measures. That suggests that Article 9 commitments have direct effect possibly, or it certainly seems to be suggesting that it creates enforcement rights for third parties in national courts. It also suggests that national courts aren't only competent to enforce commitments but they are obliged to ensure an effective remedy is provided to the plaintiff. I think it is very questionable that commitments decisions give rights to third parties, complainants in these cases. I think in practice, a national court may very well make a preliminary reference before deciding that it can enforce an Article 9 commitments decision.

So we come back to a situation where I think the reality will be that the Commission will have to be the body which enforces the commitments. Certainly it is looking for decentralization of enforcement, which I think is a good aim, but I think in the context of Article 9 commitments, I can't see that that is going to happen very quickly.

Joe Gilchrist

Thank you very much Nicholas. We have had two interesting bits setting opposite views. Serge gave us the Commission's philosophy in this matter and Nicholas has now taken a very practical but forward looking view of the problems raised by modernization, because I think one of the problems perhaps which you will have in considering this is that the Commission has had just over a year in applying this new system so there aren't as many precedents perhaps as we would like to discuss at this point.

Nevertheless, I think in the discussion we will probably go into that in more detail. Our final panellist is Julian Maitland Walker and he has the floor.

Julian Maitland Walker

I want to address a slightly different aspect of this subject, and that is to look at the issue from the perspective of third parties, seeking a competition law remedy to a wrong which they believe they have suffered. Therefore, to look not so much at the procedural aspects which the previous speakers have addressed, but rather look at it from the point of view of complainants. My practice tends to be acting for complainants in relation to particular cases. In fact I act for Crehan in the *Crehan Inntrepeneur* case,[7] which has been such an important case and is a continuing case, dealing with these particular issues. It is relevant of course, in the context of

---

[7] *Crehan v Inntrepreneur Pub Co* [2003] 27 EG 128. See also *Courage v Crehan* (Case C-453/99) [2001] ECR I-6297, [2001] 5 CMLR 28.

modernization and I know this afternoon we are going to be looking in more detail of modernization. My position on modernization is that it seems to have been implemented very effectively. It seems to be very useful in a procedural way, in expanding enforcement throughout the Member States; I have great hopes that because there are going to be more regulators looking at infringements there should be more potential for regulatory intervention and a greater chance that anti-competitive infringements will be investigated properly and anti-competitive practices will be discouraged. That is what everybody wants modernization to achieve. But the position, at least from the perspective of complainants, in my perspective at any rate, is that there is nothing yet which we have seen which suggests that their position is going to be improved. Now in the context of complainants, I would go further and say there is a real fear that I have that the position of complainants, the potential for complainants to get their complaints addressed by the regulators, is actually likely to become more difficult in the future than it has been in the past.

Now in the limited time available to me, I want to really focus on two issues. One is to deal with my perception of that increased reluctance on the part of regulators to take up complaints and the second aspect is to look at civil enforcement as an alternative and where we are in relation to that and perhaps also to suggest that, in the light of the *Crehan* experience, what I at least hope that the Commission's green paper on this issue will contain when it is published later on this year.

I will deal first of all with the investigation of complaints. We have heard from Serge that where a complaint is made to the Commission in this particular case the Commission now has a discretion as to whether or not to pursue the complaint. Of course it has a responsibility to pursue infringements and from that point of view Serge quite properly stresses the importance of complainants and their complaints in bringing to light anti-competitive infringements. But the Commission's interest of course, as Serge has mentioned, is not to protect the interests of the competitors but to protect the interests of competition. My view is that you cannot protect the interests of competition without protecting the interests of competitors. If you have a complainant competitor raising an issue with a regulatory authority then that competitor has an interest, and I believe a right, to expect the regulating authority to pursue the complaint if it is valid. It is not sufficient in my view for the regulator to say 'You have got a remedy elsewhere. It is more appropriate for this particular matter to be dealt with at a local level' or to say that 'I'm sorry but we are so busy with so many other cases which are much more important than yours. Go away!'

Now, that latter point of course is understandable. One accepts that regulators have limited resources; they can't do everything. But the solution to that problem, I don't believe, is simply to walk away from those problems. I think it is damaging to the whole principle of enforcement of competition law. My concern is that modernization emphasizes the devolution of responsibility away from the Commission to the national competition authorities and also, and more seriously perhaps, the national competition authorities themselves seem to be adopting the same approach and saying 'We have priorities. We have too much on our plate at the moment. Your case in the scheme of things is really not very important. Go to the national courts.' Now, of course, it is true that complainants can go to the national courts, but as I shall be illustrating in a minute and I am sure you all know, it is extremely difficult to pursue competition cases in the national courts. It is a nightmare pursuing cases in the national courts. Think about *Crehan*. Mr Crehan, a licensee of two pubs in Staines, thrown out of business because of anticompetitive practices. Twelve years have past. We have had six preliminary issues in the national court. We have had one reference to the European Court of Justice and we still don't know the answer. We have a hearing in the House of Lords next year and hopefully there will not be yet another reference, but that is possible still. It could see us, at least me, out to retirement this case. Of course one can see immediate personal benefits in that, but that is not the object of the exercise. If the Commission is serious about the need to increase the enforcement at a private level of competition law there has to be a realistic option to do so. Sadly, we haven't reached that position at the moment.

Going back to the point about complainants—I would like to deal with that first. A couple of cases I have had recently give rise to concern about this tendency to simply take a view to prioritize and to really dismiss cases notwithstanding that they illustrate a prima facie infringement of competition law. Two examples I would like to mention very briefly.

One involves the Commission where I acted for a distributor of automotive paints who had his distribution agreement in the UK cancelled, terminated. There was evidence that the reason for this, although one couldn't prove it directly, the reason for this is that he was buying this particular paint at much cheaper prices, a third of the cost of the paint in continental Europe. There was evidence of this massive differential in price between the UK and the rest of Europe for this particular company and yet, surprisingly, there was hardly any parallel trade. Now, you might ask why. I would have thought a regulator would say, 'Well, that's very interesting. Three times the price in the UK and yet there is no demand to buy the product in the UK from France or Germany or wherever and import it into the UK.' That coupled with the evidence as to the termination of the distribution agreement and the fact that these products were traceable seems to me to suggest at least a reasonable argument that there was some export ban going on. Unfortunately, although the European Commission accepted that there was evidence that there was a ban on exports implicit in the overall distribution structure they felt that it wasn't something they were able to deal with and that we had a remedy in the local courts. Now the problem was that my client couldn't afford to take the matter to the national court. Not surprisingly, given the experience of *Crehan* and the millions of pounds in legal costs that that case has involved, he was left without a remedy. I would say that Article 7 as an approach—the right to demand that the Commission give a statement of its reasons and a potential for an appeal to the Court of First Instance—really doesn't take you very far. Two or three years more delay and you don't get a remedy. So it really isn't of much help.

The second case actually involves the Office of Fair Trading. This was the first case I have come across where the Office of Fair Trading was not interested in a case which if ever there was a slam dunk, was this: a situation where a client wanted to build a circuit for a particular sport, a minority sport admittedly in the UK, in a particular geographical location; in order to be able to set up this circuit, the client had to join the Association, the Sports Association, which provided the sports and set up leagues and so on; the sporting body comprised the existing operators of these circuits within the UK, all of them; the decision as to whether or not to admit my client goes to that sporting association, one of them decides that because the circuit is a little bit too close to his circuit and will compete with the existing circuit, he opposes it and so the application is chucked out. We even have a letter from the member of the association concerned, saying 'I don't want X in this particular area, some 15–20 miles away, because I am worried about competition.' We present those facts to the Office of Fair Trading. The Office of Fair Trading look at it and they say that first of all they try to present an argument that perhaps it's not a very easy case, but on appeal and I mean that informally, the view comes back, 'Well we are really very busy with lots of cases. We have lots of demands on our time and on our resources. This sport is a minority sport. It is not terribly interesting. We have to spend a lot of time on more important things like horse racing and football so I am sorry but you can always go to the national court.' Now this sport isn't tiddly-winks. It isn't an amateur sport. In fact, Sky TV spends rather a lot of money each year putting it on TV. It may be a minority sport today but it's not necessarily going to be a minority sport in the future. By allowing an organization to operate a cartel of that nature, to restrict entry into that business and after all sport these days is a business, seems to me to be contrary to the objectives of the law, competition law, and contrary to the responsibilities of the regulator concerned.

It does a lot of damage rejecting complaints of that type. It is not just that the complainant suffers, because the complainant then has the option either to spend a fortune in litigation, or to drop the case altogether, but it also gives the wrong signal to business in general and to the organizations that are responsible for the anti-competitive practices. Because in both the cases I have mentioned and normally the regulator would be required to ask some questions before it decides not to proceed with a particular case, what it does is that it gives the impression to the other side in this dispute that somehow their anticompetitive practices are justified. First of all, that encourages them to continue their anticompetitive activity and secondly, it makes litigation even more difficult, because of course once we issue our claim the other side will say, 'You went to the Office of Fair Trading; you went to the Commission and you got nowhere. They rejected it. That is evidence that your case lacks substance.' So that is the kind of double-bind which a complaint can result in if it's not sufficiently important to grab the attention of the OFT or the European Commission and be taken up by them. I don't want to see that ethos develop, least of all in a situation where we have so many difficulties in trying to seek private enforcement to the courts.

I would now like to move on to that issue, namely the question of private enforcement and to look at *Crehan*.

Very quickly in relation to *Crehan*, what I wanted to say and I have already mentioned how long it has taken to bring that case to court and how much it has cost and of course the green paper that is shortly to come out will address many issues. What I would like to do, if I may, is just to put forward a shopping list of points which I would like to see in any regulation which the Commission might introduce in order to deal with or facilitate private enforcement. The issue really is that I think there must be a European regulation which covers private enforcement. The Ashurst report last year, produced for the Commission, demonstrates what a chaotic system we have throughout Europe in terms of private enforcement; if we are serious about private enforcement we must do something to harmonize the rules and to make it easier for private enforcement to happen.

Causation is an important issue and was an important issue in the context of *Crehan*. The issue in *Crehan* was that the English court decided that Mr Crehan had suffered the wrong kind of damage. Now we need to have a sufficiently robust system of enforcement in the European Union such that any infringement of the competition rules should give rise to a remedy in damages for any loss suffered as a result and not get involved in some formalistic interpretation of what kind of damage and whether the damage matches the actual type of breach involved in the infringement itself.

We need to deal with the situation in relation to costs. Mr Crehan's case has only been able to be pursued because he was legally aided. Legal Aid is no longer available in the UK for commercial cases and I don't think it would be available in any other Member State. Mr Crehan's case has cost millions. The downside risk—not only does a litigator have the prospect of having to pay for very expensive competition law litigation, but also has to accept the downside risk of having to pay the other side's costs if he loses. Those issues need to be addressed if we want to have effective enforcement at a private level.

An idea: how about the Commission setting up a Legal Aid System such that occurs in the CFI or the European Court of Justice? How about using these four billion euros of fines which the Commission have generated since 1999 to provide at least some legal aid for deserving cases where there is a competition issue, which for one reason or another, a regulator cannot address?

Finally, I would like to mention rights of appeal. It seems to me that it would be very sensible that in addition to trying to streamline, coordinate, and harmonize the procedures in competition cases across the European Community, there ought to be a right of appeal to an equivalent body to the CFI, but dealing just with competition cases. I think the Competition Appeals Tribunal in this country has been very successful and its role could be expanded to focus on competition matters. It is such a specialized field it merits a special tribunal to deal with it. If we have one appeal body, a European Competition Appeals Tribunal, it would make the system more efficient. It would make decision-making more uniform. It would also take a bit of the heat off the CFI, which maybe would mean that the timetable for hearings before the CFI would be improved.

JOE GILCHRIST

We have now had three very interesting presentations, each emphasizing slightly different, but very important, aspects of our subject. I think the very practical suggestions that Julian has made could be considered but I suspect the Member States would not like to see the fines, which are not only sources for the Commission but unfortunately go to the Member States, they would not like to see those used for financing more competition cases. However, we shall see.

What I propose now is that we allow our three panellists to comment on the contributions of their colleagues and then we will throw the debate and discussion open to the floor. Serge, I know has some points on Article 9.

SERGE DURANDE

These two contributions are helpful. One limited comment on Article 9. Limited because Article 9 is something specific. The legislator has wanted Article 9. It is in the regulation. It has to be made workable, but it would be very wrong if one would think that this will be the recipe to solve all of the issues. Certainly not. As a matter of principle, Article 9 should not be made use of when you have crystal clear cases of violation of competition law. When would the Commission take Article 9 decisions in principle? That becomes a consideration of expediency. It would be faster and it would be less burdensome for the Commission and for the parties. Fine.

Then the query is, and the struggle to comprehend is, why the Commission would not give access to the preliminary assessment; when in a classical case, ie an Article 7 decision, it would give access to the Statement of Objections? I think there are differences, important differences, between a Statement of Objections and a preliminary assessment. It is true they are both preliminary, but a preliminary assessment for Article 9 does not constitute the basis for the rejection of a complaint; it does not. A Statement of Objections would constitute the basis of a rejection, and this is the reason why the complainants would have access to it. Secondly, it is different from a statement of objections because an Article 9 decision would be more a negotiated decision. I don't really fancy the concept of negotiation between public authorities and private parties, but one has to face the facts and the reality. There is much more negotiation in Article 9 decisions than in any other one. So it is an invitation therefore. There is something of an invitation to negotiate in a preliminary assessment, which you do not have in a Statement of Objections. Statement of Objections: this is the reason why the Commission is willing to do this case and here are the introductions to the competition law. Now the picture is completely different in Article 9 because it is clear from the law that there will be no straightforward denomination of an infringement. The infringement will not be established. It is a different animal. It is something completely new. It is not either the equivalent of something which concludes in a consent decree in the United States. As far as I know, in a consent decree, there is a judge looking at the matter. Another difference, another feature. If one considers that Article 9 is a preliminary assessment, when you send it to the parties, you don't know whether you will conclude the case with an Article 9 decision, or an Article 7. You don't know, at this stage. It depends on the outcome of the investigation/negotiation.

So, it may very well be the case that this preliminary assessment does not work. You then go the classical path of the Statement of Objections and it appears that this was part of the investigation after all. It is an established rule, established law, that the parties do not have access to the investigation file, unless and until the Commission has come to a Statement of Objections.

I agree with you, of course, that it would be useful for the complainant. It would be useful for private enforcement. Yes, of course. It would be helpful for the Commission. Yes, indeed! But now it comes to my mind that although I am pretty convinced that there will be no right for the complainants to get the preliminary assessment, I am not sure that the Commission would not actually hand it over if it thought that it was in the interest of the investigation, under, of course, non-confidential version. But why not?

The second issue which was more fundamental, more interesting in a way, is about modernization. This is very, very critical indeed. But I think the view which was stressed was rather pessimistic. It was a bit like describing a situation where you had lazy European regulators handing the case over to lazy national regulators, handing it over to the national judge, and then you get stuck. I was just waiting for you to conclude that in all likelihood the national judge would send a request to Luxembourg because it was a European case and it would raise difficulties. We are laughing, but it is a very serious matter, of course.

You may have been unlucky with two recent cases, but I can assure you, having had so many years in DG Competition before, that each and every case team in this place is looking, not desperately, but is looking for the good complaint. The good complaint is the one which really paves the way for a decision which is helpful for competition, developing competition policy and, of course, which brings as much help as one can think for the investigation. There aren't that many good complaints. There are some, but not many. I can think of many bad complaints. I have seen a number of them. You have genuine complaints and you have complaints which are not that genuine. You have complainants who are fishing for information. It happens. You have complainants who will swamp you with dozens of cases which are not that interesting for developing competition law.

I just wonder, your first case, was it by any chance in the pharmaceutical industry?

JULIAN MAITLAND WALKER

No, but I know about those. I didn't mention those. I could have spent some time talking about those as well.

SERGE DURANDE

Yes, indeed. Because then the consumer is not the buyer. The price is fixed by national authorities, national health services, and competition doesn't work properly. Of course, you would not have eager case teams to receive these complaints.

But it is very fundamental nevertheless that the case teams at the Commission and, of course, in the national authorities, would investigate these companies. I am somewhat surprised and disappointed listening to what you said because not that long ago I have taken action myself as Head of Unit two times on the basis of a postcard, as a basic complaint. This has led to investigations and decisions and so on. So the idea that the competition authorities are not willing to act to me is novel. This would be a bad surprise. I don't know whether it is, but maybe you have been unlucky.

Now on the private enforcement side, I would agree with virtually everything you say. Indeed there should be a European regulation to harmonize this and make it workable. Indeed. But what is it after all? Is it procedural or is it substance, the question of damages? You know how the thing has developed over time. There has been an agreement between the Member States on the substance. It is easy enough to agree on the substance but, surprisingly enough, impossible to agree on the procedures, on the rules of the game; impossible so far. So we will see. We have to make it work but I am not that pessimistic; I am genuinely convinced that this modernization thing is something which will bring lots of new developments. I don't think one should look at this from the start in such a pessimistic way. As for your shopping list, did you pass your shopping list to the Commission?

JULIAN MAITLAND WALKER

No.

SERGE DURANDE

You should. It would be taken with a good deal of interest.

JOE GILCHRIST

Thank you Serge for that very clear explanation of the Commission's position. Nicholas: your comments.

NICHOLAS FRENCH

Serge, thank you very much. I think it is interesting that the Commission sees the preliminary assessment as an invitation to negotiate rather than the Commission's position that it has got to after maybe a few years of investigation. I can see that it could be. It wasn't my understanding that that was what the document was supposed to do. What I would say is that if you do end up with an Article 9 decision then the complainant hasn't seen the Commission's reasoning behind its decision and [its?] decision to accept specific commitments. If you have had a third party that has been heavily involved then I think that third party, by virtue of that, has had, if you call it that, its rights circumscribed somewhat from being able to fully participate in getting a resolution as it would have hoped for.

I am interested to hear that the preliminary assessment might be given to some complainants in certain cases. Again, that comes more down to the discretion that has been a theme of your talk at the beginning, but third parties and complainants may benefit from certain discretions. I feel that more is needed than a discretion here. I still think that the preliminary assessment ought to be handed over, partly because of the follow-on actions that I was talking about.

Julian's talk was very interesting. I agree with Serge that harmonization would be a good thing. Everybody who read the Ashurst report for the Commission, I think, was very interested to see how little there is and still how difficult it can be in practice to bring actions. I think there is an awful lot to be done there, and I look forward to the Commission's green paper at the end of the year. I think that is when it is due.

JULIAN MAITLAND WALKER

Just one very quick point on Serge's comments and that is, of course I accept that the Office of Fair Trading and the Commission officials do their best to pursue complaints that are consistent with developing their policy, but to me the role of the Commission or the OFT or any other regulator is not just to take interesting 'sexy' complaints in the jargon which develop policy; the role is, I would have thought, to take up complaints and where there is a clear case of infringement to act upon it, and not to try to pass that responsibility down the line.

STEVEN PREECE

Thanks very much. My question is for Nicholas French, concerning the preliminary assessment issue under Article 9 commitments cases. I can certainly see the point as far as the preliminary assessment being sent to an undertaking, outlining the Commission's concerns, how you in terms of private litigation may wish to have access to that, but would you not agree that it is the case that in England and Wales, and I can't really comment upon jurisdictions in Northern Ireland and Scotland, but we have a very powerful tool in the civil procedural rules called Standard Disclosure, which is in my view, considerably more powerful in some cases than just obtaining things from the European Commission, in so far as the preliminary assessment sent by the European Commission is in the possession of an undertaking subject, or I should say a person subject, to the civil procedural rules in England and Wales. Then you would have a very strong case for saying that is relevant to the civil proceedings in which you are engaged. There is the added bonus that confidentiality deletions are considerably more circumscribed under statutory disclosure. I am just wondering, would you not agree that at least within England and Wales that would be a relevant concern to addressing some of the concerns about obtaining the preliminary assessment?

NICHOLAS FRENCH

That is a very important point and here certainly you would have access to the document by virtue of that procedure. I don't know whether that is the case everywhere. I think from the perspective even of a complainant in England and Wales the value of having something early on to inform yourself as to whether you are going to bring an action has benefit, rather than spending more money to go down the route that you are talking about. So it is more a question I think in this country of timing, but I agree there are ways in which you can get at it during the procedure.

MICHAEL HUTCHINGS

I would like to build on a number of points, particularly those raised by Julian. I think there is a problem not just of how complaints are dealt with, but the fact that for many people, making a complaint is itself a problem. I am thinking particularly about suppliers and customers, rather than about competitors. It is alright if you have got a company with the, not to put too fine a point on it, the balls of Pepsi Cola, taking an action against Coca Cola. But in most cases you have got a vertical problem and whichever end of the supply chain you are in you are just not prepared to put your head above the parapet. Now that is a problem, I think, in a lot of competition cases and I don't know how the authorities are planning to get around that, because I think it is not so much a problem of how you deal with complaints when they come in, it is a question of actually making sure those complaints get a voice.

The second point is on the point that Julian made about court cases, particularly in this country, and the cost issue. That, as I understand it, is what happened in one case brought by the Federation of Wholesale Distributors against the Office of Fair Trading, who had cleared a merger between Tesco and a group called Adminstore Ltd. They lodged the complaint; they lodged the case, at the CAT. As I understand it, as soon as the third party intervened, that being Tesco, they shied off that case and immediately withdrew it, because they could contain their own costs, but it was the fear of having to actually pay the third party costs, which would potentially be enormous. Now I think that is another problem with complainants generally, in all types of cases. That you are often facing a very substantial multinational large company, which has almost unlimited resources to fund cases and the complainants often do not.

The third related point is that I think the voice that is in an extraordinary way absent in so many cases is the voice that fundamentally ought to be present in every case. That is the consumer. I don't think we have cracked the problem of making sure that consumers in the broad sense, not just buyers of the goods and services, but the consumer interest more generally, is properly heard. I don't know the solution to that, but I quite like Julian's suggestion of using a very small proportion of the funds available from fines to fund a way of getting that voice heard. Whether as *amicus curiae* or in some other way, I don't know, but I think that is a problem both in the UK, at national level and at European level.

Peter Carlo Lehrell

I just have one point on the preliminary assessments. There was one case just very recently which we were involved with where we found ourselves negotiating, or discussing things, not just with the Commission, but also with the third parties. In fact, there were four complainants, one of which represented seven more, so we obviously were talking more to that side. I find it interesting that you feel that you should be able to rely on that document in a possibility of damages, because it really was very loose and gave, if you like, the parties an opportunity to respond to something that had been initiated, if you like, by the complainants. It was a first chance to put the house a little bit in order, rather than going through a full scale Statement of Objections case and so on and so forth, which was successful in that incident.

Not much has been said about mergers, but one small plea to add to the shopping list to Serge Durande, is to make things more transparent. One way also to make things more transparent to all third parties below vertical, up/down, left/right, or indeed consumers, is for the Commission perhaps to think about making the actual questions it asks throughout the system available. In Article 11, it is more accessible earlier on, also of course to the actual parties, but also if there is a line of questioning, that that is somehow put on record: these sorts of questions have been asked to suppliers; these sorts of questions have been asked to consumers. I don't know; I am just opening it up as a thought.

ORIT DAYAGI-EPSTEIN

Regarding good complaints and interesting complaints, I think this is a decision of that administrative authority whether a complaint is a good one, or whether it is interesting. So I think one of the points is to have a monitoring process. How to monitor the decision of that administrative authority? How did that administrative authority decide? What is a good complaint? What is interesting for priorities? I think it should be open for the complainants to challenge the administrative authority's decision. On the other hand, it should be done in-house: having invested resources in trying to develop all kinds of systems; trying to see whether their graduation and whether their priorities are the right ones, whether we really tackle the consumer's problem and other problems in the market.

The other thing is regarding the right to complain. I think perhaps we should regard it as a fundamental right, substantive right, and not as a procedural one. Because otherwise, this is the right to give right to the people; in a way give them a voice. I think it may affect the way we treat complaints and the way perhaps the administrative authority may take a more active role.

If it is not a good complaint, what can we do? Should we ask particular questions and try to see whether there is something behind it, or just kind of write a closure letter saying you haven't brought enough proof or evidence to support your case. Because sometimes especially consumers and small businesses and consumers, they don't know how to make a compelling claim. We need to help them in a way. So this is the other side, kind of educating how to make a good complaint.

The third point is to have a database of the various complaints that we receive. Some of them are competition issues. Some of them are more appropriate to have, for instance, to be considered under the consumer protection law. But if we have two systems that have a good dialogue between them I think we may be able to identify all kinds of structural problems in the market and to the benefit of the end consumers eventually.

JOSEPH GILCHRIST

Thank you. I think we will pass forward to the panel now. As so many of the questions are a way in which complaints are dealt with, I think Serge, you may start.

SERGE DURANDE

The last question—what is a good complaint?—of course can not be answered *in abstracto*. But there have been so many, I mean thousands, of complaints which were inexploitable, that I think in the new regulation there is a proviso that the complainant must fill in the formulae and explain in details what it is about, because very often we simply don't know. So it would be the beginning. If somebody comes to you and raises a question which has been already answered ten times, in principle you don't take it as a very interesting situation to investigate because it has already been answered in the past. The right to complain: of course, everybody has the right to complain. To telephone and write letters, fill in the forms—it is a fundamental right. The right to complain is not disputed.

Now the issue of putting Article 11 letters on the web goes against the principle that the investigation is not open and transparent because you are at the preliminary stage. You simply do not know at this point in time what the outcome will be. You may damage the company's reputation, or the company's interest, simply by putting it in a too transparent a way, that you are investigating this and this and that. I am not saying that, on a given case, the Head of Unit concerned would not get in touch with the complainants and generally explain to him where he is and what he is doing. He may not hand over the questions but he may very well get himself understood as to what the questions really mean.

I am somewhat concerned that I have heard too many people talking of the costs and this is new to me. Maybe this was not considered in the modernization. The Commission was a cheap way of getting justice between the parties. If it is true that the costs would rise because the procedures would be more national and so on then this would really be bad news for the enforcement of the competition rules. If the developments are such that it is limited to the multinationals, who have unlimited resources, then it would really be bad news. I don't know. I don't have an answer to that and I don't believe that attributing the fines to European funds to generate more complaints and so on is the answer to it.

NICHOLAS FRENCH

Peter, yes I would like to respond to your comments. I think you said that you always understood that the preliminary assessment was an invitation to negotiate. The Regulation 1 and the Procedure Regulation say nothing about what this document is supposed to be or not to be. There was a very interesting article by John Temple Lang, just after Regulation 1 came in, when he suggested that it would be as full as a Statement of Objections; the concept of a preliminary assessment not being known to date in the European institutions. So it may be that the practice is that the Commission is using it as an invitation to negotiate. Whether that was the intention at the outset, I am not so sure. I question is it right that that is the practice that has been adopted? Not only from the perspective of a complainant, but also query from the perspective of the company under investigation.

JULIAN MAITLAND WALKER

Just a few quick points. I think in relation to the point that Michael raised about putting a head above the parapet, I think it is a serious difficulty and I have had several cases where the complainant is extremely unhappy at even being identified, and of course the Commission would not normally accept a complaint in circumstances where the complainant can not be named to the alleged infringement, so I think there is a problem there and I am not quite sure what the solution is, unless the Commission could be persuaded to pursue the case on its own initiative without having to identify the complainant.

But I think there are a whole range of difficulties in a situation where the regulator has a discretion which allows it to simply duck out of investigating a complaint even though there is clear evidence of infringement. I think there is a problem in saying that we think we have other priorities or that it is not sufficiently interesting for us at this time. I think there has to be a point at which the regulator must pursue an investigation if the evidence is clear. To put it another way, I think if it is going to be rejected, it should not only be on those criteria, but there should be a proper addressing of the realities of alternative remedies. Is it possible on those facts for the case to be pursued in a national court? You can't just say it as a throw-away line. I have had several cases where it just hasn't been possible because there are all sorts of jurisdictional issues. For example, the infringement arose in France; the loss is experienced in the UK. Can you imagine the jurisdictional difficulties of bringing proceedings in a national court to deal with that particular problem?

I think, finally, the downside risk is a serious factor and a serious inhibitor to proceedings in this country, because if you get, in the case that Michael identified, a very substantial company coming in as a third party, you know there is the risk that you might have to pay their costs if you lose. That can discourage proceedings and maybe one of the other things to add to my shopping list is that we should adopt the US-type approach in costs not normally being awarded against the complainant in an antitrust suit.

Panel 3—Keynote Speech by R Hewitt Pate (followed by Panel Discussion on Antitrust Modernization)

PHILIP MARSDEN

Let me welcome Hewitt Pate, the Assistant Attorney General from the US Department of Justice (Antitrust Division) back to London for our conference. He has been a stalwart supporter of our conference and has come over for the past three years and we are also very pleased that he was able to join us at one of our Competition Law Forum meetings in Brussels in March to join our panel on abuse of dominance. Hew's colleagues are also here in the room. They have come to many of our Competition Law Forum meetings and conferences and we really do appreciate the support that Hew and his colleagues at Justice have shown us at the Institute.

HEWITT PATE

Philip, thanks very much. It is great to be here, as you said, for the third time. I love coming to BIICL, not just because it is in London which is a city that I enjoy visiting, but because the quality of the discussion in the programmes I really think has grown and grown and you have put together a terrific fixture on the annual competition programme year.

It has been a great year, I think, for the Trans-Atlantic competition law cooperative relationship. We have Neelie Kroes installed as the new Commissioner in Europe. Cooperation continues to be very good between the DOJ and the Federal Trade Commission and our colleagues at the Commission. We have had John Vickers knighted; now Sir John Vickers. It is nice to have friends become knights from the competition community and that is terrific!

I have brought along a newsletter we have put out for those of you who have an interest in our activities generally. I am still more or less on the same track that I have been three times in a row in these meetings talking about our hierarchy of antitrust enforcement. Focusing first on cartel enforcement: I think the figures have shown that we have been producing some very good results there and we have new legislation in place, on a speedier pace than Kevin Grady predicted when he was commenting on it as the Head of the ABA Antitrust Section, but legislation that provides for stiffer penalties and also provides for de-trebling civil damages liability for firms that come in under our amnesty programme, which we think will help keep our unique tort system from getting in the way of cartel enforcement both here and abroad. I think international cooperation on the cartel front just continues to grow and grow. We have new legislation recently in Japan, in Australia, changes to increase the utility of amnesty programmes in other jurisdictions and so that is a topic I always like to begin with.

On the merger front, we have continued to do the best job we can of applying economic thinking to mergers and to make appropriate calls and to litigate if necessary. Certainly the big story for the past year in the United States has been one that did not have a happy ending for the US Justice Department: the *Oracle* case.[1] Greg Werden will be speaking on that and on some aspects of unilateral effects analysis. But have no fear, we are undaunted and continue on what we think is a very sound path of merger enforcement and that will, and does, include continuing to pay attention to customers who believe they are being harmed by mergers that they believe reduce competition.

Finally, on the unilateral conduct front, there will be a lot of debate here. We are continuing in our efforts to try to improve US antitrust law in the context of non-cartel section 1 offences and section 2 monopolization offences by trying to advocate objective transparent standards that can guide the businesses who are required to obey the law.

This afternoon Philip asked if I would make some remarks on recommendations that I recently sent to the Antitrust Modernization Commission in the United States. This is a Commission that was put in place by Congress. It has a three-year life span. It has an appropriation for some level of permanent staff and also is getting assistance both from the Federal Trade Commission and the DOJ in terms of help from economists and from lawyers in trying to look at whether there are ways the US antitrust system could be improved. So I will talk a little bit about that. There are obviously some issues that I have brought up that could equally apply to the modernization that is ongoing in the EC and hopefully that will spark some discussion. Then as Philip mentioned I will leave some time for questions on any topic that might interest you.

This speech outlines the letter that I have sent to the Modernization Commission and sets forth the topics that I suggested for study. As you know, in our system an official administration proposal for legislation goes through a process run by our office of management and budget. Nothing that I am going to be talking about today represents an official administra-

---

[1] *United States v Oracle*, Inc, 331 F Supp 2d 1098 (ND Cal 2004).

tion legislative proposal. Rather what this represents are some ideas that I personally sent to the Commission with a view that it might be helpful as they try to select topics for study.

Let me talk first about the idea of more empirical study of antitrust enforcement. This is a topic that gets a lot of attention in conferences, or has gotten more attention in conferences, but gets a good deal of resistance in the official antitrust community. I think that that resistance may not come to serve those of us who support vigorous antitrust enforcement very well. There has been, for example, a relatively recent article by Professor Crandle [??] questioning whether antitrust enforcement really can be shown to provide any benefits to consumers or to our economies. No-one questions whether it provides benefits to lawyers who sell their time by the hour, or to economists who do the same, but questioning whether there really is any benefit from what we are engaged in. I don't find that a particularly difficult question myself. I think if you look only at combating cartels and also at the clear way in which having effective antitrust enforcement can displace the perceived political need for more regulation and prevent the political cycle from spewing forth a new regulatory agency every eight to twelve years, well you have got tremendous public benefit right there before you go any further.

Nonetheless, I don't think it does for those of us who are involved in antitrust enforcement simply to say that we had better not engage in empirical study because it is too difficult or we are afraid of what it might show. I think that leaves the field entirely to people who may not have the same level of sympathy with antitrust enforcement. So I have suggested to the Commission, not that they themselves undertake a mammoth study, but that it would be well for them to try to approach respected economists and others including people who don't make their money in the antitrust business and try to figure out what metrics might be applied to determine what level of benefit cartel enforcement is providing, to what degree merger enforcement can be shown to provide a public benefit, and to let the study unfold over a period of time. But not necessarily in a backward-looking way. I think studies that try to go back and look at past enforcement are always going to be subject to the claim that the person doing the study has cherry-picked the cases to be studied. I think that is, nonetheless, a useful thing to do. Our Federal Trade Commission is doing it. I know the Competition Commission is involved in some very important work in that regard and I have spoken with Paul Geroski about that and I am hoping to get the benefit of it. But my proposal to the Modernization Commission is for something different. It is for a group of experts to agree on what benchmarks might shed light on the benefits of antitrust enforcement and then to identify how cases might be sampled going forward and have such a steady run for some amount of time. I can't report that I am particularly optimistic that the Commission is going to take up this idea and there seems to be a good deal of resistance to it. That being the case, we are looking at the Antitrust Division and at ways in which we can follow the lead of the Competition Commission here and try to do a bit more along the line of empirical research. Fred Jenny and the Competition Committee at the OECD are going to be having a program along this line coming up in a few months and so whether the Modernization Commission takes this up or not I think empirical study is something that could benefit this enterprise in which we are all involved.

Next, this will come as no surprise to those of you who followed the American competition law scene for any length of time: the Robinson–Patman Act frequently comes in for criticism by those who think that antitrust law ought to be based on improving efficiency and demonstrated benefits to consumers. The Federal Trade Commission, I am very happy to say, has primary authority for enforcing the Robinson–Patman Act and I am also pleased to say that they have *not* done a particularly vigorous job of using government authority to enforce that Act for quite some time. That is because those of us who have taken a look at it believe that the frequent result of applying the Robinson–Patman Act's prohibition on discriminatory discounting by manufacturers to its customers primarily can end up being anti-consumer. If discounting is prohibited, if it is going to be the subject of a price discrimination suit, what we may end up with is higher prices all around. So the letter I sent to the Commission raises the question whether the Commission ought to study the repeal of this Act and whether an Act that right now is producing only private treble damages litigation really can at this stage seem to be justified without providing stronger consumer benefits. I do keep going back on the Trans-Atlantic note. I remember being at a conference a couple of years ago at which the European speakers were somewhat apologetic about the degree of which pricing and distribution regulations proceed over here on a per se basis and the suggestion was made that 'Well, I know you have moved beyond all that in the United States'. But I always say: 'Remember the Robinson–Patman Act, we are not really all that different in some ways if you look at that statute'.

Civil fines for Federal Government Sherman Act cases, what do I mean by that? The United States Government does not have the authority to seek fines for misconduct in civil Sherman Act cases. When we intervene civilly in a case really the most that we can seek in a government action is an *injunction* to prevent future misconduct. So the question I am raising here is whether in some circumstances that leaves us without the deterrent tools that we really might need. I have in mind a couple of cases that have occurred during my tenure. One, the so-called *Alternative Newspapers*[2] case, another one called the *Mathworks*[3] case which you could read more about on our website, but on those cases what we alleged to have occurred was essentially a take-out agreement. An agreement among or between two or three competitors in the *Alternative Newspapers* case swapped the Cleveland market paper for the Los Angeles market paper, leaving the two parties to that deal as the exclusive alternative News Weekly in each of those markets and leaving them without competition. Likewise in the *Mathworks* case, there was a take-out agreement that would leave the market with one competitor. When we intervene in a case like that we can seek to unwind the transaction but because we are left without fines as a potential remedy and because the transaction has only occurred recently there is no prospect of private litigation imposing damages and the question I am raising is whether that can leave parties too ready to just sort of take a flyer and see whether perhaps this transaction escapes notice and leaves them in a position of benefiting from the absence of competition. So the recommendation I made is that the Commission might study whether in conjunction with adjusting the private litigation system we have in the United States one thing that ought to be considered is giving the Government the authority to seek fines.

Now the flipside of this for me occurs in non-cartel Sherman Act cases, particularly those involving section 2 of the Sherman Act. The question I am raising is whether we are really well served by a system that is so heavily weighted towards private treble damages as the mechanism for enforcement. Certainly with respect to section 2 of our Sherman Act, similar to the standards applied over here under Article 82, these cases are highly dependent on the facts, they can be highly controversial in terms of the appropriate theories and the appropriate economic analysis, and the problem that it raises is that a company may well not realize until after it has been the subject of an enforcement action that it has violated section 2 in the first place. Those of you who have heard me speak here before know that I believe perhaps that, if not the single biggest, one critical under-appreciated difference between the American and European systems of competition law enforcement is the fact that we have this private treble-damages system. That requires Government enforcers, such as myself, to be very careful about what we do under these headings because we know that any case we bring is likely to spawn, perhaps not identical cases, but cases in which theories we advance may be stretched somewhat beyond what the

---

[2] *United States v Village Voice*, Civil Action No 1:03CV0164. Case settled 27 Jan 2003. See <http://www.usdoj.gov/atr/public/press_releases/2003/200670.htm>.

[3] *United States v Mathworks Inc* Civil Action No 02-888-A. Case settled 15 Aug 2002. See <http://www.usdoj.gov/atr/public/press_releases/2002/200164.htm>.

Government would believe is appropriate and then litigated before general-ist judges and juries in our system. The question I raise here is whether the Commission should study changes to the system: whether damages should be automatically trebled, whether they should be paid in every instance to the plaintiff, but the general question is whether we really have the right balance of enforcement tools in the United States with the terrifically heavy weighting we place on post-hoc treble damages litigation.

Antitrust immunities and exemptions are a popular topic for the division. We historically spend a lot of our competition advocacy time opposing immunities and exemptions to the antitrust laws. A recent example of that, we have a somewhat, shall I say, different view from our Securities and Exchange Commission, about the degree of which SEC oversight ought to displace antitrust scrutiny of activities in financial markets. But three of the immunities (under the Shipping Act, the Export Trading Company Act, and the Webb–Pomerene Act) are certainly ones that I hear about frequently in international conferences, or at least two of them are. The point I think the Commission needs to consider is how our global leadership really is affected when we speak to enforcers in other markets when they are able to turn around and point out that our law provides for specific statutory exemptions for cartels, as long as they are export cartels. I guess I would have to admit that this part of my letter to the Commission did not receive a unanimously friendly response on Capital Hill. This may well be one of the least likely areas for the Commission to actually take up. Nonetheless, I think it is important that we at the DOJ keep hanging in there in terms of trying to push back what is going to remain, I am sure, the constant call for more immunities and exemptions to the antitrust laws from those who would be favoured by those exemptions.

State enforcement of federal antitrust laws was a subject that got a lot of attention around the time of our settlement of the *Microsoft* case.[4] As you know, under our system, each of our 50/53 states, depending on how you look at it, is entitled to bring antitrust actions under our federal antitrust law, and in addition they are entitled to have a state antitrust law, that may or may not be identical in its requirements to the federal law. In some cases, this is a great thing. I have constantly applauded the efforts of state attor-neys general, to detect local price-fixing activity, local anticompetitive activ-ity. The Federal Government certainly can not be in every market and in that respect a cooperative relationship can be very valuable. On the other hand, I think it is fair to question whether there is a great deal of added value in, for example, a multi-state or an international merger, in having

---

[4] *United States v Microsoft Corp* 147 F.3d 935 (DC Cir 1998); *United States v Microsoft Corp* 87 F Supp 2d 30 (DDC2000), 253 F.3d 34 (CA DC 2001) (No 03-5030).

theoretically at least, 53 or 54 independent decision-makers who might review it. Certainly there are serious issues of cost and duplication and as we move to a more and more global competition arena the problems this raises just in terms of a coherent system of review in my mind deserve to be considered.

An area that has been occupying me a good bit lately is our so-called 'state action' doctrine. We have had relatively less experience in the United States than in Europe with state monopolies and with direct state involvement in our markets, so I don't want to over-blow this point. On the other hand, I think we would do well in the United States to reconsider the degree to which state action immunity is available for action which leaves markets uncompetitive in ways that the market has no prospect of remedying. We can agree or disagree about how vigorous an enforcement programme we need in the unilateral conduct context; we can agree or disagree about how quickly the market may or may not correct the Oracle PeopleSoft merger's loss of competition, but if a state legislator, if a government body moves in and outlaws competition, that is something that the market is simply never going to be able to correct. Under a body of cases stemming from *Parker v Brown*,[5] our Supreme Court, relying on federalism principles, has set up a system by which if a state legislator validly enacts a provision that eliminates competition, or if a state regulatory body does so in a way that is appropriately supervised, that is the end of the story. There is no federal antitrust scrutiny for that activity and the elimination of competition is permanent.

To give you an example of that, we are right now engaged in some competition advocacy, trying to counter an effort that is being undertaken by the real estate industry in the United States. Real estate agents in the United States typically represent sellers and obtain a commission for their activities. Six per cent seems to have been the traditional commission level, but in recent years what we have seen grow up are so-called fixed fee discount brokers, menu-driven services. These have a variety of names, but what they do for example, is to allow a consumer to say 'I'd like to go to the discount firm and obtain simply a multiple listing service, an MLS Computer Listing of my house and perhaps get a yard sign'. But the consumer might say 'I really don't need the full range of services, nor do I want to pay the traditional full commission'. Well what we have seen in the US is that a variety of real estate associations have, with some degree of success, begun approaching the state legislators in the United States to say that this is just unprofessional for a real estate professional to hold themselves out to the public and not provide the full range of services. Surely the

---

[5] *Parker v Brown*, 317 US 341 (1943).

better thing to do is to pass a law saying that each and every real estate professional who participates in the buying and selling of real estate must offer in every transaction the full range of professional services, presumably for the traditional full fee. If and when those provisions become law, that essentially eliminates these new models of service which allow consumers to choose whether they want to get a more limited range of assistance at a lower price. There is nothing wrong with the idea of consumer protection and full disclosure. Certainly a state has a legitimate interest in making sure that consumers aren't misled as to what they are getting. But this is one instance where we have been very active on the competition advocacy front because once a statute has passed that outlaws competition there really isn't any prospect that the market can fix it.

So the recommendation here is simply that the Commission should study whether the *Parker* doctrine might be cabined to try to avert any competitive harm. Certainly it has its purposes. There are situations in which, again certainly under our tort system, you would not want to see a legitimate state governmental programme made subject to post hoc litigation in certain circumstances. If you want to get the full balance on this, as Alden Abbott can certainly tell you, the Federal Trade Commission website has an excellent report on this point that was put together under the leadership of Tim Muris when he was at the Commission.[6] So we at the FTC are going to keep trying to work on the question of limiting the degree to which the state action doctrine damages competition.

Indirect purchaser liability: A little bit less of a fundamental point, but one that has been important in the United States. The Supreme Court, in a case called *Illinois Brick*[7] some years back, held that indirect purchasers are not proper plaintiffs to seek to recover damages for violation of the antitrust laws. In the wake of that *Illinois Brick* decision, a number of states passed so-called *Illinois Brick* Repealer Statutes that would say: 'No, we disagree. Under our state law, we want the rule to be different from what the federal law is and so under our state antitrust law the same indirect purchasers who were disallowed from bringing a federal action may bring a state cause of action'. I think there is broad agreement that the current situation is one that doesn't make a great deal of sense, in terms of permitting multiple recoveries. For example, if the direct purchasers are answerable and pay damages for the antitrust violation in the first instance you have double, or multiple, recovery issues if indirect purchasers in a number of states can then come behind and bring an additional action. So there are a number of proposals that have been made. The suggestion I made to the Commission

---

[6] See <http://www.ftc.gov/os/2003/09/stateactionreport.pdf>.
[7] *Illinois Brick Co v Illinois*, 431 US 720 (1977).

is that they should study whether the best course isn't to simply respect as a matter of national policy the result the Supreme Court reached in *Illinois Brick*. That would mean pre-emption of the state laws which allow for interactive purchaser recovery. Professor Hovenkamp had a somewhat different proposal. He would say, let's have a federal law that pre-empts the variety of state laws but then leaves in place the possibility federally for an indirect purchaser recovery, but eliminating the possibility of double, or multiple, recovery. This is an area where reasonable folks could differ as to which of these approaches makes the most sense, but where I think there is some broad agreement that the current patchwork system doesn't make a lot of sense.

I guess finally, and not surprisingly, in writing to the Commission I said 'Look, don't go trying to change the fundamental language of the Sherman Act'. Again, those of you who have heard me here know that I think the common law method of developing competition law doctrine, which allows new economic thinking to be incorporated without having our legislature and all the pressures to which it can be subject embarked on a legislated rewrite, is a good system that on balance has worked quite well. So I am quite clear in thinking the Commission would be better off not trying to rewrite the fundamental language of the Sherman Act. Just looking at the cost that would be involved in the years and years of litigation trying to interpret what the new language might mean without the margins would out-weigh in my judgment any predictable benefit that could come from that sort of task. So my concluding point to the Commission is that basically the Sherman Act has served us well for a long time, and should be left alone.

So those are some of the recommendations contained in my letter to the Modernization Commission; we certainly have a few minutes left before we turn to the panel, so I am happy to take questions on this topic or any other.

BERT FOER

Taking on the real estate industry I think is a terrific idea. It is the kind of idea we were talking about earlier today that can help rally consumers to understand the benefits and the need for the antitrust laws, something that in the US and also in Europe is I think sorely lacking. So I want to compliment you on making that a priority and we will do our best to provide you with some public support, as I think this is something we can all build with.

HEWITT PATE

Well, when Bert Foer from the AAI says I am doing the right thing on an initiative it may be time for me to just jump out of the window and run down the street. You know I do think it is important and I have no particular axe to grind with the real estate industry. I have used and happily paid the full commission to full service realtors in the past and I suspect I will in the future. But in the United States we have had a tremendous increase in real estate prices and absent new forms of competition that means presumably a tremendous increase in compensation to real estate agents for the same amount of work; it just seems to me we are in a situation where the last thing we need is legislation that would outlaw competition in this field.

KEVIN GRADY

Hew, earlier this morning there was a discussion about the relationship between competition laws and intellectual property and this is an area I know that you have been pretty much involved with, both before you assumed your position and since. One of the things that those of us in the US have been curiously watching is when the joint report is supposed to come out on the IP hearings that were held a little over two years ago, I think; while using the old cliché about 'Waiting for Godot' is probably overused, any predictions at all when we might see something?

HEWITT PATE

So, did you want to know when it was supposed to come out or when it is going to come out?

KEVIN GRADY

I know when it was supposed to come out!

HEWITT PATE

You know, it is one of those things that we continue to work on with our colleagues at the Federal Trade Commission and it is a difficult project. There is a lot going on in the law there. We have had Tim Muris depart and then frankly, it didn't get out by the time Tim left. Debbie Majoras, our new Chairman of the Federal Trade Commission has been busy with other things, but she and I have talked about it. It is something that remains an active project that I know she very much wants to get out, as do I. It has taken a lot longer than we thought, but I know I can't give you a date because I have learnt my lesson on that. I have given people dates for this report and it hasn't been forthcoming, but it is a project that we are going to continue to work on and we are going to produce.

MICHAEL HUTCHINGS

You mentioned the Robinson-Patman Act, which is a subject that comes up quite often in discussion over here. You say it has perverse results, but presumably when it was enacted it was thought to be able to cure other perverse results. I would be interested in your reflections because of course the whole subject of sales below cost and discriminatory pricing is a subject for debate in a number of jurisdictions in Europe at the moment.

HEWITT PATE

Well, by saying 'meant to cure perverse results' this is not a question where economic thinking of one era was thought to have made things more efficient in one fashion, or to better protect consumers in one fashion, and then sort of time has passed it by. The Robinson–Patman Act was passed very overtly to protect competitors, not to protect competition, to protect distributors from price differentials from manufacturers as a small business protection statute. It remains on the books; it is a valid law. The point I have made: I wonder whether there isn't as much change in primary conduct in the United States as a result of private enforcement of the Robinson–Patman Act as there may be here through official government actions by regulators and enforcers, who by definition can only reach a smaller number of cases each year. But the statute is a validly enacted statute that will continue to be a font of litigation in the United States as long as it is on the books because there are interests who are protected by the statute and who appropriately seek to take advantage of it.

The question that we continue to raise is whether it makes any sense judged in light of the rationale that we rely on for competition law enforcement because it is very clearly based on a different set of premises.

BRIAN MCHENRY

Just listening to your presentation, it struck me that in quite a few areas, the parallel universe or universes of the UK in Europe might have been able to contribute towards your evidence. Did you cite the examples of the modernization regulation or the European experience over state action doctrine or over civil fines in your evidence to the Commission?

HEWITT PATE

Well, I didn't present evidence to the Commission. I do think in my letter I pointed out that as Europe is trying to grapple with this fundamental question of how to coordinate merger review, for example, and how to appropriately allocate cases as between the Commission and the national authorities, that it was high time we do this in the United States with our system.

I am not sure what the experience over here is going to demonstrate. We watch it with interest. In some ways, you know again, I think of mergers. You have the prospect of an allocation that will prevent duplicative review by having appropriate cases taken up in Brussels. On the other hand, you are potentially about to witness a big decentralization of decision-making, particularly if private litigation is going to be emphasized as a way forward.

So yes, I think in that one context, I did cite it, but not in terms of evidence to the Commission that it is going to tell it what to do, but to the point that we had better be looking out for this in Europe. Those interested in competition are doing a pretty good job of raising fundamental issues for discussion at least.

STEVEN PREECE

It is interesting what you are saying about possible pre-emption of state anti-*Illinois Brick*[8] laws; and you are saying that there is a general degree of consensus that that probably is a good thing. Does that consensus include the antitrust bar? I am just wondering to what extent you might actually see the antitrust bar then going lobbying Congress, maybe under the guise of states rights, or something like that, to avoid legislative pre-emption.

HEWITT PATE

Let me be clear. I think there is a consensus that it is not an optimal result to have a federal rule that precludes indirect purchaser liability and then a selection of states with the opposite rule and no mechanism to eliminate double or multiple recovery. But there is not any consensus at all as to which way that ought to be fixed. I have made a proposal to study following the *Illinois Brick*[9] rule as a national model. Professor Hovenkamp as I mentioned says 'Let's federalize a rule that allows for indirect purchasing cases, but get the counting right.' Of course there are plenty of folks who benefit from having a system that is not quite as well thought out as that and so nothing that I put in this letter is meant to represent my prediction as to even what the Antitrust Modernization Commission may come out with in a report, much less that it would actually be the subject of successful legislator reference.

[8] ibid.   [9] ibid.

MARGARET BLOOM

Hew, you mentioned that the fact that you can get treble damages in the US is one reason why the agencies and presumably also the courts have narrowed the application of section 2 of the Sherman Act. Now in Europe, does this drive to encourage private actions probably only for single damages—we don't know whether you can get exemplary damages in some Member States—do you think that is an added reason why in Europe we should be more cautious about the application of Article 82 and how widely it's applied? Should we, therefore, if we are going to have the courts taking Article 82 cases, possibly follow-on cases with private actions, should that make us pretty cautious about how widely we apply Article 82?

HEWITT PATE

It is a good question. On that topic, I often say be careful what you ask for—you might get it. But you are a long way in any jurisdiction over here from what we have in our federal and state tort system in the United States. Private antitrust litigation is an important part of the enforcement system in the United States. This is one reason why the antitrust laws are respected to the degree they are.

As for Article 82, section 2, I don't want to over-blow that either. I think there is something of a substantive difference that would remain regardless of the enforcement system. I think we are to some degree more comfortable with the idea that competition is going to displace firms, is going to completely up-end the markets and we think that we get a great deal of economic vibrancy and terrific results from that system. I think in Europe generally there is more of a concern about displacement of competitors and a little bit of suspicion of markets that is not present in the United States. But I do think nonetheless that the enforcement system is very important to understanding the systems. I think courts never say this but it must be that some of the caution in US decisions is driven by the knowledge on the part of judges that private law suits can occur without any oversight or ability to predict how long or how expensive litigation may be for those involved. I guess the point I would make is that you could probably get along with a very restrained view of section 2, Article 82-type liability in the United States with the system that we have, or you can get along with a somewhat more aggressive enforcement scheme, although I would frequently caution you that you are better off to be more trusting of markets. But you can get along as long as you don't have this leveraged private treble damage sort of enforcement scheme. But, if in Europe you decide to go with the European substantive rules and you adopt American rules of enforcement in terms of private litigation and recovery, you could just shut the whole place down if you go that way. So the combination I think may be one you should be cautious about. Again, you are not anywhere near where we are at this point.

So that's it and we're going to turn to the panel.

PROFESSOR DAVID EDWARD

Thank you very much for starting that off. Now the plan for the rest of the session is we start with Don Baker who is going to talk about private claims for damages and injunctions. John Temple Lang will then comment on that. Maybe Hew may want to come in when he's heard those two. Then we switch and John Temple Lang will talk about state measures restricting competition and Don will comment on that.

DON BAKER

I am delighted to be here. What I would say just in general before I start talking about the damage things is this. Your letter and your suggestions include a lot of useful ideas and of course what happens is then we all ignore those and go on and talk about the things we might disagree with.

The Robinson–Patman Act which you mentioned: I had to study it and how it was enacted. It was enacted because the wholesale grocers were afraid that the supermarkets were going to eliminate the wholesale grocery function. Meanwhile, the retail druggists got vertical price-fixing through, and it was all in that period of people in the depression failing and like, going under. When I was Assistant Attorney General we issued a big thick report asking for this and all I got was a lot of political hot water when the Democrats came back to power. Similarly I think that going after these exemptions is a very good idea, but these industry-specific exemptions like the Shipping Act represent a sort of monument to narrow communities' political power and they can be very hard to break. So, as I looked at the recommendations, I wanted to think about them both in terms of their practicality. Are they serious things that might be enacted despite their correctness?

On the question of private remedies, I think you are asking the right questions but maybe not giving the right answers. The whole idea of mandatory treble damages for everything from a cartel case to a sophisticated joint venture rule doesn't make any sense at all. We did copy it from the British Statute of Monopolies of 1623, but it still doesn't make any sense. Of course, people over here abandoned it anyway. But, I don't think that one quickly goes; so I think that de-trebling damages in non-cartel cases is a good idea. But I think the idea of just completely eliminating private liability in section 2 kinds of cases, first of all is a serious non-starter and, secondly, I am not sure it is a good idea. Obviously there are two kinds of section 2 cases. One type involves follow-on cases from the Government. So, the Government brings a case and prevails; the people who have been injured—it seems to me—they have a reasonable basis for going forward and obtaining damages. Much as they would do in the UK, in the Competition Appeal Tribunal or the High Court. So I think we started off with the right thing, but gone too narrowly. One would quickly say, and I am sort of picking up on Hew's last comment, the risk of you being overwhelmed by US-style private litigation is virtually nothing. If you are worrying about that, you ought to worry about something else.

We haven't talked much about cost rules. But if you wanted to change the American private litigation scene fundamentally, probably all you would do is ask Congress to enact the English cost rule, whereby the losing party has to pay. As you know in our system, we have a one-way bounty system in which the plaintiff, if successful, recovers costs. The defendant, if he prevails, doesn't get costs. I would point out, and I think it was mentioned once this morning, that the *Crehan*[10] case is essentially being litigated because it is by Legal Aid under the US cost rule. In other words, if ultimately the Legal Aid in *Creehan* prevail they will get costs. But Courage won't get costs if they ultimately prevail. The cost issue is an important one for you to think about as you and our colleagues in Brussels try to develop a basis for going forward.

At that point, I want to turn to indirect purchasers in *Illinois Brick*.[11] This is a subject that I feel particularly strongly about, because I argued that for the Government. In the *Illinois Brick* case, as Hew says, the US Supreme Court held that indirect purchasers had no standing to sue. They did it because in another case called *Hanover Shoe*,[12] they had held that the defendant could not raise a passing on defence. So they left the situation in which the first purchaser could recover the full amount. The Justice Department's position in that case, which I also argued, was that we ought to allow indirect purchasers to sue, and we ought to use the procedures that were available under the federal rules of civil procedure to try to consolidate those cases so that they can get the direct and indirect claims in. Instead of which we got this political circus which Hew is talking about which I think very few thoughtful people think is a good thing and it may

---

[10] *Courage v Crehan* (Case C-453/99) [2001] ECR I-6297 [2001] All ER (EC) 886.
[11] *Illinois Brick* (n 7).
[12] *Hanover Shoe, Inc v United Shoe Machine Corp* 392 US 481 (1968).

be mollified by the recent class action legislation which may enable defendants in class actions for indirect purchasers to bring them into the federal system and then consolidate them.

I think any system that doesn't at least provide the opportunity for indirect purchasers to recover is a political non-starter and it is really wholly inconsistent with modern tort law, with *Donoghue v Stevenson*[13] in this country, and *McPherson v Buick*[14] in the United States, where we got away from the notion that you had to have privity with the defendants. I think anyone who is foreseeably injured and can prove it should be able to come in. But I think the Modernization Commission should look at whether we need special rules for consolidation, so that you end up with essentially a two-stage proceeding in which the first stage is recovering the over-charge from the cartel and the second stage is more or less like an interpleader proceeding, where over-charge is allocated. I think that's something that's worth giving serious thought to.

I will say for whatever it is worth, that the working group in Brussels at the Commission is spending a lot of time thinking about this problem.

JOHN TEMPLE LANG

I have four points to make in connection with private claims for damages. The first one concerns all the supposed difficulties that I have been told exist for any private plaintiff.

Most of these difficulties boil down to two fairly simple problems. The first is that the community law on who can recover and what it can recover for is not at all clear. The second is the rule that, as Don mentioned, the loser pays both lots of costs. That, combined with the very high cost of litigation in this country and in some other countries in Europe, means that plaintiffs are very cautious about bringing proceedings and tend inevitably to settle cases that they have brought, if they have the courage to bring them at all. So that is the fundamental reason, and not problems about self-incrimination and discovery and so on, why there is so little litigation in Europe of this kind. If that is broadly right, then we are not going to see an outbreak of private claims for damages no matter how much the Commission may try to encourage them, until the law is clarified by community measure. That is, I think inevitably, a couple of years off. But we do need such a regulation or a directive if we are going to get anywhere. That is the first point.

My second point, however, is to say that something is going to happen in

---

[13] *Donoghue v Stevenson* [1932] AC 562.
[14] *McPherson v Buick*, 217 NY 382 (1916).

the meantime. Public authorities, and in particular local authorities, are going to start making claims for compensation in price-fixing and bid-rigging cases. If they do not, local government auditors and the Controller and Auditor General in this country are going to ask why they didn't. Taxpayers, once they wake up to the problem, will also want to know why claims were not made. Judges would be much more sympathetic to claims by local and national authorities for compensation in this sort of situation than they seem to be so far to ordinary private claims.

There are several ways in which this could be facilitated. One obvious one is that public authorities ought to have at least nationwide databases, and preferably community-wide databases, for all the bids for public contracts that are being made in the last couple of years. That would facilitate checking up on price-fixing. It would enable you to identify rotation, taking it in turn to bid for each contract successfully. That would be an obvious way of making certain that public authorities do in fact detect, with the aid of the Office of Fair Trading if necessary, price-fixing and the like. Another suggestion, which was made years ago by the Office of Fair Trading, was that all public contracts should have a clause in them saying that if the successful contracting party is found subsequently to have engaged in price-fixing or bid-rigging, the liquidated damages would be X per cent of the value of the contract. Pretty difficult if you are representing a company to say that: 'Of course we wouldn't get involved in price-fixing and therefore we couldn't possibly agree to a clause of that kind', but if there was a clause of that kind, in the standard local authority contract, and if the liquidated damages was 10 per cent or 15 per cent, it would have a very salutary effect indeed. What is more, just in case there is anyone here from the OFT here who is listening to this idea, the cost saving to the tax-payer would pay for doubling, or tripling, of the staff of the OFT overnight!

My third point concerns indirect purchasers—the *Illinois Brick*[15] problem that Don was talking about. That is not, I think, an insoluble problem even today under current European Union law. You can solve the problem if you can identify most or all of the indirect purchasers. They ought to be able to identify all of the direct purchasers and the whole lot of you sue together as joint plaintiffs. The defendant can't say that he doesn't know how the money is going to be allocated between the plaintiffs. That is not the defendant's business. If you can prove the amount by which the price was increased, you should be able to arrive at some sort of modus operandi for splitting up the spoils after you have won the case. It seems to me that that is a workable way of handling this, even without any law reform of any kind.

---

[15] *Illinois Brick* (n 7).

My fourth point concerns a suggestion made by a very distinguished lawyer, former Advocate-General Walter Van Gerven, who said that if you want to see what the law is on private claim for damages against private companies, you should look at the law on State liability for breaches of Community law. I am afraid that I disagree with Walter on that subject, for one quite simple reason. State liability depends on the State having committed a 'serious breach of Community law'. If you ask whether all breaches of Article 81 and Article 82 are serious, or if they are not all serious, you ask which ones would be serious, you find that you don't get any intelligible answer from any of the case law or any principle that I have been able to identify. This is not primarily a problem over the unsatisfactory state of interpretation of Article 82; it is I am afraid, simply a result of the fact that State liability for breach of Community law was not based on anything directly relevant to private claims against private companies. So that particular suggestion I am afraid is not going to work and will cause difficulty if anyone tried it.

PROFESSOR DAVID EDWARD

Hew, would you like to comment on those two first.

HEWITT PATE

Sure, briefly. I think on Don's point first, I want to reference what I mentioned as the carefully-worded recommendation on liability. It is not my view that we ought to abolish private liability altogether. Rather the view I stated is the Commission ought to study whether we have the right result now; and again the variables I mentioned were the fact that damages under our system are in all cases paid to the plaintiff, presumably with a handsome percentage to the plaintiff's attorney, the automatic nature of the trebling and then whether three times is the right measure to begin with.

So I think you and I agree that automatic trebling in these cases doesn't make a lot of sense and I am not so absolute in saying there is no place for private enforcement there. Again, even in the case of a follow-on from a successful government section 2 case, and certainly these occur, still these types of cases in my view are getting much less of a clear incentive effect for future conduct because the company who is paying the damages won't know that it was going to be liable based on any transparent or objective measure. It has to await the outcome of the litigation and there is much less likelihood that the result there that occurred to the company that does pay is going to provide much in the way of a clear lesson to other future violators. So in my mind, this is a very different situation than what you have in the cartel enforcement scheme, where these follow-on treble damages really do provide a very important part of the deterrence that we get in the US.

Illinois Brick[16]—not a great deal of difference there. The main point is that it can't make a great deal of sense to have this patchwork case system. If you could find the appropriate way to allocate damages, and a workable way to have those cases adjudicated in court, then of course the proper theory says you want people to be compensated when there has been a violation of the antitrust laws. So it may be that something along the lines of what Professor Hovenkamp has recently been proposing, or something along the lines of what you were arguing for, would work and I completely agree with you that that is a lot more likely to have political attraction than any sort of proposal that would just codify nationally the Supreme Courts rule.

DON BAKER

One just very interesting footnote on *Illinois Brick*:[17] as far as I know, there hasn't been a successful indirect purchaser case tried to judgment; they have been much more of a hold-up settlement. Maybe not hold-up but that kind of thing. Because the causation issue in indirect purchaser is hugely complicated we don't have a situation where there is a state litigation process that is really working other than providing a framework for settling in all cases that are a considerably lower proportion than the risks of federal cases.

PROFESSOR DAVID EDWARD

Good. Right, now what I am proposing to do is to go on to the other half and then open the floor for discussion when we see how much time we have got. First John Temple Lang on State measures restricting competition.

JOHN TEMPLE LANG

The European Commission gave itself the possibility of choosing its priorities for the first time for 40 or 50 years when it persuaded everybody concerned to adopt the Decentralization Regulation [Regulation 1/2003]. The Commission has chosen certain priorities. One of them, as you know, is cartels, and this is obviously right.

What criteria should the Commission be using to chose its priorities?

---

[16] ibid.   [17] ibid.

First, it should look for an area where the law is already in force, so something can be done immediately. Secondly, it should be looking for an area which is important economically, so that the effort will be worthwhile. Thirdly, it should be looking at an area where national competition authorities are not going to be able to do the job and where the Commission itself has to do whatever needs to be done.

That being so, I was disturbed at a conference in St Gallen about ten days ago, that Philip Lowe made his speech announcing the priorities of the Commission, without even mentioning State measures restricting competition. These are clearly important economically, in particular I think in the ten new member countries, but not by any means only there. National competition authorities clearly cannot be expected to do the job completely, although they have got certain possibilities that I will mention in a moment. The rules that the Commission could use if it was brave enough and determined enough are already in force. There are in almost all of our countries a large number of different sorts of State measures which intentionally or otherwise restrict competition. Hew Pate mentioned and Don mentioned real estate legislation; pharmaceutical legislation; physical planning laws prevent hypermarkets being built, except in places where nobody can get at them; licensing of taxis limits the number of taxi-drivers you can have, and therefore limits competition in the taxi business; you have all sorts of over-regulation of different industries and the Commission has been consistently reluctant and slow in dealing with these cases.

Most of the case law that I am going to refer to in general terms has come before the European Court of Justice from national courts. The Court of Justice has frequently said things that make it clear that there is quite a lot of potential in European Community law for the Commission, or indeed anyone else in a position to do so, to challenge quite a lot of government measures, State measures, legislation, statutory instruments and the like. The Commission has been cautious for several reasons. It does no harm to say what they are frankly. First of all challenges of this kind upset governments. Secondly, they are not easy, because although the rules sound clear in principle you have to look in all cases at the justification or the supposed justification for the measure and that involves analyzing the real reasons, analyzing the methods required to achieve the results and deciding the question of proportionality, which always arises.

Some of the measures concern services of general economic interest, and that is a sensitive subject in particular in France, and in particular in the last four or five years. However, it is sometimes said that the legal rules are complex, and I don't think that is true. I am going to tell you what they are in a rather simple way, so that you will see that they are really not so complicated.

First, any national measure that restricts freedom of competition, or freedom of establishment, or freedom of services, must have a legitimate, that is to say a non-protectionist, purpose, and must be no more restrictive than is necessary to achieve that result. That broad principle is true, even if the legislation does not work in such a way as to create a small number of privileged companies. That is a general principle.

The second principle, which is well established by the European courts, is that State measures must not make European competition law ineffective. There are a lot of examples of that principle. It is quite complicated to see all of the implications because, for example, if you could deduct against company tax the fines you have to pay to the European Commission, that would clearly make European Community law ineffective. So there is a rule under Article 10, the cooperation article of the European Community Treaty, that says, among other things, that Community fines can not be deductible for company tax purposes.

Then you have a third rule, that national measures may establish monopolies or give special or exclusive rights to a limited number of the companies only if there is an objective legitimate purpose in the public's interest and if the measure is no more restrictive than is necessary to achieve that purpose. The first principle applies to a situation where the national legislation creates a small group of privileged companies.

Then there is a fourth rule which says that Member States may give an exemption from the rules of the Treaty—a most extraordinary provision in Article 86(2)—but only where it is necessary to do this in order to enable companies that have been given the job of doing something in the general economic interest to carry out the functions that they have been given.

Another rule says that national competition authorities not only may, but must, disregard national legislation if it requires companies to infringe Community law: the *Fiammiferi*[18] judgment of the European Court a couple of years ago.

All of these rules of substantive law are well-established, non-controversial in broad terms. They may be controversial in their application to particular cases, for reasons I have given. There is only one provision of the law which is so controversial that, if I am correct in reading between the lines, the judges in Luxembourg have disagreed over it. That is the question whether a State measure is contrary to Community law only if it leads to a dominant company abusing its dominant position, or whether it can also be contrary to Community law if it establishes a dominant position without

[18] *CFI v Autorita Garante Della Concorrenza E Del Mercato* (Case C-198/01) [2003] 5 CMLR 16.

sufficient justification. I believe that it is the second of those two alternatives, but I have to say that the Court in the *Ambulanz Glockner*[19] case, again a couple of years ago, seems to me to have had considerable trouble over this. The Court finally came down in favour of the rule that there had to be a justification for creating or extending a dominant position, but it didn't actually explain the other case law which says that the measure is illegal only if it leads to an abuse.

So there is a big job that the Commission has not yet apparently decided to tackle, which is much more important than some of the things that the Commission is planning to do. If the Commission doesn't actually take any action, there are several industries throughout Europe in which campaigns to challenge national measures of this kind have already started and a number of other areas are foreseeable.

PROFESSOR DAVID EDWARD

Don. Would you like to comment?

DON BAKER

Hew advocated a serious study of the state action doctrine. That is a really good idea. Based on forty years now, I guess, I have been practising American antitrust law, I think the state action doctrine may be one of the very worst things that we have sort of worked our way into by federalism. Because while the rule doesn't sound too bad there must be clearly articulated state policy to displace competition and there must be active supervision by the state; the courts get awfully sloppy in dealing with this.

One of the worst cases, hence for me one of the most annoying because I brought it when I was an Assistant Attorney General, is a case called *Southern Motor Carriers*[20] in which a group of trucking companies were running cartels on local intrastate carriage and we brought this case. The State Commissions weren't doing anything to supervise them; the companies were running these thinly veneered cartels; and the Supreme Court said that there was adequate articulation in the regulatory statutes which were vague and that the Government didn't contest the active supervision, where as far as I can tell, the Government never found any active supervision.

So the scheme should have gone under. So I think that it would be a fine idea if the Modernization Commission tried to study what's going on in Europe, because it is hard to draw a line between legitimate political deci-

---

[19] *Ambulanz Glockner v Landkreis Sudwestpfalz* (C-475/99) [2001] ECR I-8089.
[20] *Southern Motor Carriers Rate Conference, Inc et al v US* 471 US 48 (1985).

sions to displace competition in favour of some other value. But the politicians really ought to have to take the heat to do that, not write something vague and have it go.

So I think this is a very important recommendation and because it isn't an industry-specific recommendation, you may have a greater chance of getting it through, provided one can come up with some picturesque examples to entertain the public with.

I particularly took your thing about the real estate brokers. I had a great deal of fun and indicted the brokers in Maryland for raising the rates in a very sort of subtle cartel. It was fun and has become one of the landmark cases. So there are so many people who are ready to do it if they are given a little legal cover.

One thing we should mention just for clarity and comparison to Europe. We have something we call the Dormant Commerce Clause Doctrine. The Constitution provides that Congress should regulate interstate commerce. The court has built on top of that a doctrine that says the states can not set up schemes that discriminate against interstate commerce; so a law that says that the shrimps that are harvested in the state have to be processed in the state gets struck down on that kind of thing. So this is a non-antitrust doctrine that is relevant. I guess if I were the Modernization Commission and I was trying to think my way through this, I might try to be more explicit in giving the Government explicit power to enforce the Dormant Commerce Clause issues, rather than leaving it entirely to private parties.

The other thing on the state area I wanted to talk about was Hew's suggestion of pre-empting the state antitrust enforcement. We have had state antitrust laws from before we had the Sherman Act. These antitrust laws now virtually all provide for treble damages. So when you think about these kinds of reforms you have got to think about what goes on at the state level and if for example we knocked out treble damages on non-cartel cases at the federal level one would have to pre-empt the state laws in order not just to have the cases drift into courts where the standards are probably less precise than in the federal courts. Secondly, in terms of the state antitrust enforcers, they have become relatively popular politically at times when the public and the politicians thought that there wasn't enough federal enforcement and I have seen occasionally a very good case. I had one myself where I worked with a state Attorney General when the Clinton Administration decided not to try to block the creation of a newspaper monopoly in Honolulu, the capital of Hawaii. We went out there with a citizen's group and the state Attorney General and blocked it. If one were going to pre-empt, you have to pre-empt in some degree state law as well as state enforcement of federal law. At the moment, the state Attorneys General mostly are, a great bulk of their cases brought under federal law, and so we get cases like *Hartford Fire*,[21] one of the leading international law cases being brought by the state Attorney General.

Last point, Hew, if you send them in a supplemental memo, I would put into it an arbitration of antitrust claims, which is turning in to be a very complicated thing internationally because arbitrations of antitrust work quite well with their disputes between joint venture partners, between licensors and licensees, but when you get these price-fixing cases, in which someone has an arbitration obligation with one defendant and then you have all these other defendants who are jointly and severally liable, that is a subject that is worth serious attention by the Modernization Commission and they are more likely to give it if you push them.

PROFESSOR DAVID EDWARD

Thank you very much indeed, Don.

Hew, would you like to comment at this stage?

HEWITT PATE

It is hard to find any disagreement on this state action. But seriously, if you look even at *Parker*[22] itself, what you have there was a cartel of the raisin producers in California and a cartel that was going to make most of its money from raisin purchasers outside of California. So even at the start, you could really question what was going on with this doctrine. I do agree that maybe this was the place where having the Commission take a look could be of more likely benefit. After all, it is the courts who are going to change this more than the legislators, and so if we can provide some thoughtful leadership there and have the Commission really make some recommendations judges may start to do some things to dial back on the foreseeability rule from the *Southern Motor Carriers*[23] case, for example, that Don was mentioning, where the court instead of forcing the politicians to come straight up to the voters and say: 'We are going to do away with competition', courts have been too willing to accept the idea that if the elimination of competition was just a foreseeable outcome from the passage of the legislation, well then that ought to be enough to create antitrust immunity. For those of you who are interested in this, Michael Greenwood at the American Enterprise Institute is doing a lot of writing on these sorts of

---

[21] 509 US 764, 113 Sup Ct 2891 (1993).
[22] *Parker v Brown*, 317 US 341 (1943).
[23] *Southern Motor Carriers* (n 20).

issues: the political bodies in one state seeking to get benefits from anti-competitive actions that are imposed on citizens outside that state, which in his view ought to be the paradigm case where federal antitrust oversight is needed. But he has got some interesting work in the federalism project at AEI that you might want to take a look at.

On the pre-emption of state enforcement, state activity can be popular. There are areas where state Attorneys General can step in and collect damages for state citizens in context which have proven popular. Some have proven more effective than others. The place where I would really focus on questioning whether there is added value in state enforcement though really is the merger area. At this point, the idea that we have a pendulum swinging back and forth and that there is some sort of gap in federal merger enforcement, I think that was something of a myth. When it was first trotted out in the 1980s, what I think you really had going on was the injection of some economic rigour into antitrust. But at this point, I think the record is pretty clear that you have a relatively stable merger control policy that doesn't have any partisan political content in the United States to speak of. So if there was ever any credibility to this idea that we needed fifty-odd potential state reviewers of mergers to avoid a federal gap, I think the time has passed. So for transactions that involve three, five or more states, certainly for national or global transactions, I think it is a question that really does deserve some study.

DON BAKER

I agree with you on that. I think your reference to one-stop shopping was an interesting one too, where you could have situations where I suppose the feds just chose to stand down. Where, as you know, we get these merger investigations where the parties are responding to the Justice Department or the Federal Trade Commission in five states, or 15 states, which is not a very sensible use of either the state's resources, or the private parties' resources.

ALDEN ABBOTT

Just a couple of quick comments on state action: I agree with what everyone had to say. One interesting thing is the number of commentators that suggested that one should hone in on whether regulatory boards are made up of self-interested members of the profession. If they are, some scholars have argued *ipso facto* they should not be considered, even if they are 'state officials that are engaging in active supervision of the industry with which they deal'. For example, in South Carolina: the South Carolina Dental

Board, a state board, which was made up of dentists tried to exclude dental hygienists in providing services. There are some other examples as well.

Second, I don't think you have the problem in Europe that we do, which is really rooted in the Constitution, though it really goes beyond the First Amendment. What the First Amendment necessitates, the so-called petitioning doctrine; and what if you get an anti-competitive regulation adopted because interests of parties have in effect lied to the regulatory body. How do you handle that? I would presume it would be less of a problem handling that in Europe, than in the United States.

Finally, one more complication and I think one area where Europe seems to be doing quite well is state aids. In the US the Negative Commerce Clause jurisprudence has had mixed results. As Assistant Attorney General Pate mentioned, some might have argued that *Parker*[24] itself involved imposing the sorts of costs on out-of-state residents that you should be concerned about. But more broadly, subsidies to domestic industries, if they are done in the right way, the Supreme Court has found not to violate the Dominant Commerce Clause, where as the same effects were achieved without the subsidy, they might. So that is one complicating aspect of our jurisprudence that perhaps Europe in bringing state aids cases doesn't have to concern itself with.

VAL KORAH

Thank you very much Chairman. I was very interested in John's talk. We had so many countries that believe in a lot of government regulation and government champions and I am worried that the Court seems to be rather loathe to deal with these cases and instead of using Article 86 where the Member State would have to justify its rule, and it would have to be proportionate, they just say it is not an undertaking. Since it is not an undertaking, 82 and 81 don't apply and they are out of everything, and it could be very broad. We started off well with the *Hoffner*[25] case, with a good opinion by Advocate General Jacobs, where he said it all depended on whether it was an economic activity and the German office that dealt with unemployment was held to be an undertaking because it was carrying on an economic activity, although it wasn't charging.

Since then, the Court has not been very consistent. We have had some cases following that, but an awful lot where the Court has just said that it is not an economic activity in cases like the *German Sickness Funds* case. Then of course, it doesn't have to be proportionate. The rules just don't apply.

---

[24] *Parker* (n 22).
[25] *Höfner v Macroton* (Case C-41/90) [1991] ECR I-1979, [1993] 4 CMLR 306.

I don't know how we can persuade the Court to be more competitively orientated and whether the ten new judges will have an effect on these cases.

JUDGE DIANE WOOD

Yes, it seems to me that the lesson on both sides of the Atlantic is one of clarity. Let me explain.

The problem if you go back to the 1943 decision in *Parker v Brown*,[26] is the Supreme Court looked at the Sherman Act and they said the Congress that passed the Sherman Act in 1890 had no concept of interstate commerce, such as the concept that had come into being by the 1940s (it actually came into being really in the 1930s). They said, therefore, because of the federalism concerns we are going to interpret the statute as covering these internal state regulations and in that sense they took a static view of the commerce clause for state action purposes, whereas they had taken an active view of the commerce clause for virtually every other purpose. Whereas, in Europe, you have the benefit of a newer set of governing laws; you have a much clearer sense as I see it in the Treaty of the places where Member State law has to give way to Community regulation, particularly in the competition field. The cases John Temple Lang was talking about reflect the need for the Member States not to throw obstacles in the way of the policies that exist at a Community level. So I actually would disagree with you. Maybe I am a little sensitive about constant accusations of activist judges, but I am really not sure that it is possible for judges to rewrite the Sherman Act, given the way the Supreme Court construed it in 1943, at least any judges other than the Supreme Court itself, because it was really at root a statutory interpretation case. Certainly the article that Hew is alluding to, is one written by my colleague, Frank Easterbrook, called 'Antitrust in the Economics of Federalism', where he says a sensible state action approach might look at, number one, restrictions that inflict costs only on the people within that state and that is in another sense just a tax. Fine, if the people in Arizona want to tax themselves for having expensive lawyers, let them go ahead and do it. Versus something like *Parker*, where 90 per cent of the raisins manufactured in California were sold not only to other states in the US, but internationally, and that was an extra-territorial effect. You could work out a system that looks like that. It just doesn't happen to be the one that we have.

---

[26] *Parker* (n 22).

TIM COWEN

I am picking up on a number of points and the point that was raised by Hew under the Sherman Act section 2, where he makes the point that the company may not realize that it has violated section 2 until well after the fact. There was then a discussion about costs and I think that is a very instructive discussion for the application of Article 82 here in Europe through a decentralized system and perhaps the consequences of that are things that people needed to think about more.

Hew points to the fact that under the Sherman Act section 2 the cases are highly dependant on specific facts and economic analysis and the debate over here in Europe is about making sure that we focus more fully on specific facts and economic analysis. Then I think naturally we will end up logically in the same position of not knowing where people are before the law. That is obviously an issue for us to consider in the future debates on Article 82 which are going on at the moment.

PROFESSOR DAVID EDWARD

I would just say in reply to Val that the judgments of courts are only as good as the submissions that are made to them and one of the difficulties is the wavering of the Commission in its position on this kind of issue.

Panel 4—Economics in Court

PHILIP MARSDEN

I am very pleased to welcome you to our final panel of the day and I am indeed extremely pleased that we have this judges' panel to close the proceedings today. It is called, as you can see, 'Economics in Court'. This is far from a dry topic.

When we ran our judicial training workshop for national judges in Brussels last month the use of economic evidence was on the agenda. One of the striking points that was raised related to the use of 'hot tubs' in the courtroom to address the problem of dirty economists. I am sure we will be raising that exhilarating issue at some point in the discussion today.

To lead this discussion is Frédéric Jenny. He is a great friend of the Institute I am very pleased to say. When he was at the Conseil de la Concurrance, I was very honoured that he was able to find time last year, in particular, to give the keynote dinner address, particularly considering his workload, his teaching schedule and many of the meetings that he was chairing, both at the OECD and in past years at the World Trade Organisation.

Now we also have the honour of congratulating Professor Jenny as I think he is the first economist to be appointed to the Bench at the Cour de Cassation in Paris.

So I very much look forward to the discussion and over to you Frédéric.

JUDGE FRÉDÉRIC JENNY

Thank you very much Philip for your kind words and for your introduction to this panel. Ladies and gentlemen, I will begin to talk on 'Economics in Court'. I thought just to introduce the panel that I would start with a quote. The quote is the following: 'In this Age of Science we must build legal foundations that are sound in science as well as in law'. The quotation is from Justice Breyer in the introduction of the Federal Judicial Centre Reference Manual on Scientific Evidence. I think that it is exactly right for the topic we are going to deal with this afternoon.

Of course the question of building legal foundations that are sound in science, which is generally true, is particularly true in the antitrust area. Indeed over the last fifteen years, there has been a growing consensus that antitrust law, or competition law, should be grounded in sound economic analysis. There is the issue of whether or not a legal decision or judgment makes good or bad economic sense; this has become important to much of the debates in forums like this one and we have heard some of this already this morning. The issue of how to get it right—how to get decisions that make economic sense—has been much debated between competition authorities, in particular at the OECD Competition Committee, but also elsewhere, and of course it has been, as you all know, the object of tense debate over particular decisions which I am not going to refer to directly now.

The areas where the tensions have arisen are mostly abuse of dominance, mergers and verticals, but now I would say over the last two or three years, the debate has shifted a little bit from a debate between non-competition authorities to a debate between economists and the courts and judges and the reason for this is that in many countries where there were relatively new competition agencies, they tried to get it right, they tried to get as much economic reasoning as they could into their decisions and then those decisions found their way to the higher courts and now the issue of course is the extent to which the judicial proceedings can integrate economic analysis. This has increased of course the level of interaction between judges I would say and economists, at least in the area of antitrust. The expectations are raised on both sides, I would say. The economist expects the judge to have the right prior knowledge to understand economic evidence such as is presented in the courtroom and to minimize the cost of errors and to therefore write the decisions in such a way that if they are wrong, they won't create too much damage. On the other side, the judges have high expectations and sometimes they are disappointed by economists, but they expect the economists to provide testable, necessary and sufficient conditions that establish when practices are anti-competitive or when transactions are anti-competitive, and that is where often they are a bit disappointed. Also, they expect the economist to be able to introduce economic evidence in a way which is understandable for non-specialists and again they are sometimes disappointed.

Now, what is underlying those issues, of course, is what kind of education can be given in the area of economics to judges; how much the judge should know; what type of evidence is useful in court; how can you make sure that in the judicial process this evidence is going to be presented?

This topic is a very interesting topic for a conference like this which is based on the Trans-Atlantic dialogue because of course there is a difference at least in culture, I think, between the US and Europe, all Europe, from that point of view, with much more integration of economic analysis in judicial proceedings in the US than there is in Europe, and we will hear about some of the rules or some of the ways in which in the US this issue of interface between economics and law is looked at.

If I categorize what we are going to talk about, I think there are four main issues that we are going to deal with. One on the use and the usefulness of scientific evidence in courts; the second one will be how much economics do judges really need, or should have, and how are they going to get this level of understanding of economics; third, what can the economists bring to the judicial proceedings and how should they deliver it; fourth, how best to organize the interface between the legal professions in general and the economic profession.

Now to address those topics, we have as Philip said earlier a very distinguished panel. I will ask Mr Justice Lightman from the Royal Courts of Justice to start first and he is going to talk to us about scientific evidence in courts. Then we will turn the floor over to Diane Wood, who is as you all know on the 7th Circuit Court of Appeals in the US and she will talk to us about the North American view of this issue and also tell us how this issue has been handled and what lessons we can learn from the US. The last speaker will be President Vesterdorf, who will talk to us about the importance of economics, but also what he expects from economists. Then after those three points of view, we will open the discussion.

So, Justice Lightman.

Mr Justice Gavin Lightman

Thank you very much for your kind introduction. I have particular pleasure attending this Trans-Atlantic dialogue, because in 1961–2 I studied Articles 85 and 86 at the University of Michigan. That, I discovered when I returned to England, was a non-subject here. So I promptly forgot everything I ever knew about it.

By reason of the involvement of issues of expert evidence, competition law cases raise special difficulties for all concerned, and that includes the parties, their advocates and the judge. To the high cost and uncertainty of outcome inherent in all litigation there is added the considerable added cost and uncertainty of adducing, testing and evaluating that expert evidence and the potential for inequality of arms between the parties. In my short contribution, I want to say a word about the problem and the steps available and taken to resolve it. I ask you to appreciate the daunting task of the judge in deciding issues of expert evidence. He, by definition, is a non-expert and yet he has been required to decide a dispute between experts. He may receive a little coaching on the way in the form of expert reports and counsel speeches, but he remains a non-expert. Yet, he has to evaluate and choose between the theses of two experts. It is like a first-year student at university marking the papers of his professors. Concern for the wellbeing of the judge and concern to save costs must underlie the approach of the court and the parties to expert evidence.

I start on the need for expert evidence. There is an overriding public policy why the court should not allow the admission of expert evidence unless it is really necessary and why, if expert evidence is to be allowed, it should be limited to what is absolutely necessary. The reason is the saving of costs, as well as court time. The importance of saving costs is the greater, with the progressive disappearance of public funding and its replacement by conditional fees in this country (and I imagine in some other countries as well). Litigants can be deterred from protecting their rights in court by the cost of doing so and in particular the cost of instructing experts, and there is a reasonable reluctance of lawyers to undertake cases on conditional fees where the outcome depends on expert evidence. The courts should promote access to the court by the financially disadvantaged by removing obstacles to it.

The need for expert evidence may depend on the experience and character of the tribunal before whom the case is to be heard and the experience and identity of the judge or judges manning it, which may well not be certain before the trial. The need is analogous to the need for an advocate to cite authorities in support of propositions of law relied on. A citation may be essential for one judge but may be viewed by another as an insult to his intelligence. An example of the difference in experience lies in the existence of two different tribunals before whom competition cases can arise in this country, namely the Competition Appeal Tribunal and the Chancery Division of the High Court. The Competition Tribunal, in short, hears primarily appeals from decisions of regulators. The Chancery Division hears disputes between private parties. The Competition Appeal Tribunal is a specialist competition tribunal manned by specialists. Accountancy and economic theory principles and language are their daily bread and butter, if not gruel. On the other hand, competition issues arising in the course of private litigation, tried in the Chancery Division, are for many, if not most, judges, a novel and not always appealing experience. Judges of the Chancery Division have in the ordinary course little (if any) such experience or familiarity with economics or accountancy. The sight of a judge trying a case where he lacks the wherewithal to understand and feel at home with the jargon and the exercise he is supposed to be undertaking is not a happy one for the parties, nor is it comfortable for the judge. The explanations by counsel in the course of their addresses can be no substitute for expertise. Differences in the expertise of the judge that may hear the case is likewise crucial to the level at which any expert evidence, the skeleton argument, the examination and cross-examination of witnesses is pitched. But how can you measure the expertise of the judge before whom you will appear before you know who it will be? Broadly you could expect more of a judge in the

Competition Appeal Tribunal than a judge in the Chancery Division. But in case you derive too much comfort from that, you should know that any hearing before the Competition Appeal Tribunal may be chaired by a Chancery judge, for we are all deemed qualified to sit as Chairman of that tribunal. If a judge of a Chancery Division is invited to sit in the Competition Appeal Tribunal, it is an invitation which he cannot refuse.

All these circumstances render it desirable so far as practical that a uniform high level of expertise in accountancy and economics is established and maintained amongst judges trying competition cases whatever the forum. And unless and until this is achieved, the recommendation, in case of any doubt, must be the provision by the parties of an expert report for reference as the judge requires it. The report should be expressed in language readily understood by the intelligent layman and provide the judge with and explain the basic economic and accountancy tools for the task before him. The experienced judge who has no need for it can be invited to leave the report unread and unconsidered.

It is necessary to have in mind that depending on his experience a judge may require a greater or lesser time for pre-reading and please bear in mind the difference between reading time and comprehension time in providing time estimates. I have regularly been given time estimates for reading which give no time for absorbing, let alone thinking. Presumably you want the judge to absorb and think, certainly if you think your case has a chance of winning.

Can I turn to the independence of experts. On matters of expert evidence the judge is very much in the hands of experts. The dependence of the court on the expert has led the Civil Procedure Rules of the United Kingdom court to attach to experts the status of witnesses, whoever calls them, not of the parties that call them, but of the court. Their duty and responsibility for the content of their evidence is to the court, not to the party that calls and pays them. Whilst a party which has seen a draft of his expert's report may ordinarily decide not to call that expert or put that report into evidence, a party may not seek to influence the expert as to its contents or tenor. There is one qualification to this rule: if the expert fails for any reason to deal with a particular issue, the party that calls him may point that out to the expert and invite the expert to fill the lacuna. But he may not indicate how he wishes the expert to fill the lacuna, or invite adoption of any particular approach.

This rule of court has elevated the status of the experts and reduced (but not entirely eliminated) the occasion so often met in the past of experts adopting the role of advocates for the party calling them. Lack of detachment devalues the expert's evidence and reputation. But there is a critical divide in opinion whether the required independence of experts requires not merely independence and detachment of view but also that the expert is neither employed by, nor commercially connected with, the party calling him and so in an economic sense is not dependent on him. There is a divergence of view on this question between the High Court and the Competition Appeal Tribunal. There is a first instance decision of the High Court that a person otherwise qualified to give expert evidence is disqualified from doing so if he is an employee of the party wanting to call him, because of the lack of the necessary independence. The Competition Appeal Tribunal applies no such rigid rule. It is an everyday experience that Government accountants and economists give expert evidence before it for the Government. Any perceived lack of independence in such a case can only go (if to anything), not to the qualification of the expert as an expert, but for the weight of his evidence. A difference in approach between the court and the Tribunal is illogical and undesirable, and the commonsense flexible approach adopted by the Competition Appeal Tribunal is clearly preferable.

I want to say finally something about court and single experts. The system of each party being able to call their own expert evidence has long been the subject of sustained criticism, as calculated to increase costs and weight the balance of the case in favour of the wealthy who can afford the best. I recall the experience when at the Bar I was instructed on behalf of a very substantial company which was the defendant in a worldwide test case on the safety of a drug. Funds without limit were made available, first of all to provide fulltime education in all the relevant disciplines for all of our legal team; secondly, to commission research into the underlying data on which the published research papers relied on by the other side were based and to undermine their case; and, thirdly, to instruct and obtain reports from world experts in each of the disciplines. The other side which was publicly funded could afford none of these. The net result was that the claimants were overwhelmed and abandoned their action. There was no equality of arms. That was an extreme case, but a similar scenario is to be seen today in cases before the court. The question raised is what can be done to ensure equality of arms and to limit the possible exposure of the financially weaker party to a potentially fatal liability in costs if he fails in the litigation.

An available alternative to each party calling its own experts is the appointment by the court of a single expert or a single expert in each discipline. This is satisfactory if the parties agree that the view of that expert is to be accepted without challenge. An alternative is for the parties themselves to agree that they should appoint a single expert. This is perfectly acceptable in some cases and in particular where the sum at issue is small, but it is a gamble which parties (most particularly in substantial cases) are not prepared to take. It involves too much of a risk. It could make the result of the case turn on the identity of the expert. The parties may reasonably require that they should be able to make representations to the expert before he gives his report and (depending on the report of the expert) they may reasonably wish to cross-examine him or present expert rebutting evidence. If any of these options is to be available, the parties will ordinarily be required to retain experts beforehand, to furnish them (prior to the report) with the required representations and (after the report) arm them with the requisite questions and rebutting evidence. At the end of the day, the adoption of this course is likely to require greater costs to be incurred than the conventional course of each side calling one expert. For there will be three, instead of the usual two, sets of costs of instructing experts.

In my experience the closest approximation to justice is achieved where (1) there is a rigorous examination made by the judge whether expert evidence is essential on the issues on which it is directed; (2) there is a limitation of a number of experts to one a side; and (3) at the insistence of the court after the experts have exchanged reports, they actually meet and in their joint report faithfully discharge their duty to agree all they can and to spell out clearly their areas of difference and in detail their grounds of difference. If this exercise is properly carried out, the court and the parties at the trial can concentrate on this third joint report alone. It may also be just to limit cross-examination to a limited time period. This approach however does not obviate the lack of balance resulting from the free availability of funds to one party but not to the other. The party with funds can better train his team, attract the world expert and can better retain the stars of the Bar and solicitors' profession. In my experience, quality does tell. Under the adversarial system the judge is limited in what he can do to maintain a balance, but this approach is calculated to achieve as close an approximation to justice as is possible under our present system.

The Competition Appeal Tribunal, as compared to the High Court, is innovative and informal. This is particularly to be noted in a matter of expert evidence, where for example, it is moving to the adoption of the 'hot tub', the informal discussion of matters of expert evidence between the tribunal and experts. This is to be applauded. It is the occasion for a divergence of practice from the High Court, but a commendable divergence. Past experience does suggest that where the Competition Appeal Tribunal goes today, the High Court belatedly is likely to follow tomorrow.

JUDGE FRÉDÉRIC JENNY

Thank you very much Justice Lightman. We have had an extremely interesting exposé of the UK way of looking at this issue. Diane—the North American Challenge.

JUDGE DIANE WOOD

Let me begin where Justice Lightman left off. I am going to assume for the sake of argument that competition cases, or antitrust cases as we call them in the United States, are cases in which it will almost always be necessary to have an economics expert, or experts as the case may be, at some point along the way. It is a rare case where the relevant market or market power doesn't need to be understood; it is a rare case where the remedies should not be informed by some level of economic expertise.

So let me begin by asking the question: how much economics does the judge really need to know in the end? I think, as Justice Lightman was implying, one might need to draw a distinction between systems in which the judges tend to be generalists, such as the system in the United States and the system here in the UK, putting the Competition Appeals Tribunal to one side, and systems in which the judge is a specialist. In some sense, in the latter sort of systems, there is an expectation that the judge, him or herself, will have attained a certain expertise in the relevant field, which for competition law is economics. Another distinction which I think is important is that between a system that is fundamentally an adversarial system, such as we have in the US and you have in the UK, and one which is fundamentally an inquisitorial system. I don't mean, of course, the Spanish Inquisition; I mean a system in which the judge is primarily responsible for developing the facts of the record and for making sure that the first instance case is presented properly. So with those two distinctions in mind, we might think about what it is we want the judges to be doing. What is the purpose of judicial involvement? For one thing, it may be to guide the original fact-finding. That might suggest that you want the judges to know something about economics. Secondly, it might be to supervise the procedural regularity of the case. In the US that might even mean controlling a jury, but anywhere it means making sure that proper notice has been given, that rights of the defence are observed and other kinds of procedural concerns are satisfactorily addressed. You don't really have to know anything about economics to do that. You have to follow the procedural rules. If that's really all the judges are doing, then maybe we don't need to worry so much. If what the judge is doing, instead of supervising original fact-finding, is reviewing the action of an expert agency, whether it be a US court of appeals looking at the action of the Federal Trade Commission, or whether it be the EC Court of First Instance reviewing a decision of the European Commission, once again, that suggests a slightly different role. The judge needs to evaluate the agency's action intelligently, hopefully with some economic awareness, but it may not be necessary for the judge to have full expertise over the field for which the agency is responsible. Finally, the judge needs to have some way of supervising the experts. Whether it is putting them into the so-called 'hot tub'—which is a phrase that began in Australia by the way, for those of you who don't know—or it is something else, the duty to supervise experts is crucial. Incidentally, the Australians love the hot tub. I think they mean the economics hot tub; they will tell you that it is an excellent system.

In sum, those are a variety of things one might ask the judge to do. What are the procedural tools that we in the United States have given judges to perform the functions that we ask of them? Easily the most important tool today is Federal Rule of Evidence 702. I am just going to read it because it is very short. It says:

'If scientific, technical or other specialized knowledge will assist the trier of fact to understand the evidence, or to determine a fact in issue, a witness qualified as an expert by knowledge, skill, experience, training or education may testify thereto in the form of an opinion or otherwise, if [and this is the crucial part] (1) the testimony is based upon sufficient facts or data; (2) the testimony is the product of reliable principles and methods and (3) the witness has applied the principles and methods reliably to the facts of the case.'

The advisory committee that drafted this particular rule explained that the rule was derived from a very well-known decision of our Supreme Court, *Daubert v Merrell Dan Pharmaceuticals*,[1] a 1993 decision, which then was elaborated in several subsequent cases before the rule was enacted. *Daubert* itself sets forth a non-exhaustive checklist for trial courts who are faced with trying to decide whether a particular expert, whether an economics expert, or some other kind of expert, should be entitled to present testimony. On that checklist we have five things, which the courts stressed were non-exclusive factors.

First is whether the expert's technique or theory can be or has been tested. That refers to the question whether it is challengeable in some objective sense, or whether it is simply a subjective conclusory approach that cannot reasonably be assessed for reliability. Number two is whether the technique or theory has been subject to peer review and publication. The third question asks about the known or potential rate of error of the technique or theory when applied. Fourth, the court looks at the existence and maintenance of standards and controls. And fifth, is whether the technique or theory has generally been accepted in the scientific community. Now, this was a checklist that had scientific evidence very much in mind. On our court, we began to summarize it in a commonsense way, asking whether this was the kind of study and presentation that a person would make if he or she was not in the courtroom. Is this something that one would actually

---

[1] *Daubert v Merrell Dow Pharmaceuticals Inc* 509 US 579 (1993).

do for real business purposes, or is this something that has been concocted just to sound good in court?

Other guidance has come along the way. Along the lines of what I was just saying, it includes whether the experts were proposing to testify about matters growing out of their non-court research and whether the expert has unjustifiably extrapolated from an accepted premise to an unfounded conclusion. In other words, how great is the gap really? Other relevant questions include whether the expert has adequately accounted for obvious alternative explanations, whether the expert is being as careful as he would have been in his regular professional work, and whether the field of expertise claimed by the expert is known to produce reliable results for the type of opinion the expert is being asked to give. One of the examples of fields that do not qualify are theories grounded in astrology. So, don't bring your astrologer to court if you are trying to give your economic evidence.

After *Daubert*, the trial courts were given the job of being the gatekeeper. They were given the job of assessing economics experts, or any other experts, according to these criteria, and they have taken their responsibility very seriously. This set of rules has had the effect of making it more difficult to get an expert qualified to present testimony in the US courts. I give you from the antitrust field the example of a 1999 case from the 7th Circuit in which the authoring judge—no slouch in economics—was Richard Posner. This was one of the brand-name prescription drug cases. The District Court had decided to exclude certain economic expert testimony that had been presented by one Robert Lucas, who had recently won the Nobel Prize for Economics and happens to be at the University of Chicago. Judge Posner, reviewing the case, had this to say in the opinion of the court of appeals:

> The plaintiff's principal economic evidence was that brand-name prescription drugs are indeed priced discriminatorily to the detriment of the pharmacies [who had been the plaintiffs]. The discrimination requires, and thus demonstrates the existence of market power and the charge-back system facilitates discrimination. The defendant spent days cross-examining the plaintiff's principal economic witness, Professor Robert Lucas, and ultimately persuaded the District Court to exclude most of his testimony under the rule of *Daubert*. But what was objectionable about his evidence actually had nothing to do with *Daubert*. It was that the evidence mainly concerned a matter, not at issue, that the manufacturers of brand-name prescription drugs engage in price discrimination, showing that they have market power. Everyone knows this [he wrote]. The question is, whether that market power owes anything to collusion. On that, Lucas had virtually nothing to say. His opinion that

there is price discrimination in the prescription drug industry is one on which an economist of Lucas's distinction should have been able to reach in even less time than the 40 hours he spent working on the case.

Judge Posner told me later that Lucas had accused him of ruining his consulting career, which perhaps he did; I don't know. But in any event, it doesn't matter if you are a Nobel Prize-winning economist. If you aren't going through the hoops, if you aren't meeting the standards of Rule 702, your testimony will not be admitted in a Federal District Court in these days. This illustrates that one of the ways in which the judges are trying to make sure that not only they themselves are educated properly, but that the case is based on some decent foundation, is by being rigorous with respect to what evidence comes in.

Many other devices are also used. One of them is pre-disclosure of expert opinions and usually pre-disclosure of expert reports, so that each side can evaluate the report that the others' expert has prepared. This would be for the experts that a party plans on calling as testifying experts; we have different rules for the people whom the lawyer consults and then thinks something like: 'Oh my gosh, if I put you on the stand my case is lost'. This is obviously not quite the 'hot tub', but it is a way of seeing what the expert testimony is and seeing what kinds of criticisms one's own expert would like to raise against the work of the other side's expert.

It is possible, although still quite rare, for Federal District Courts to appoint the Court's own expert. Judge Kimba Wood (on the US District Court for the Southern District of New York) did so in a case not too long ago. On the other hand, as you may recall, when the District Court in the District of Columbia wanted to appoint its own expert—not in economics—in one phase of the *Microsoft*[2] litigation, it was soundly slapped down by the US Court of Appeals for the District of Columbia Circuit. So that power is something that needs to be exercised sparingly. As Justice Lightman said, it is a move that could have the effect of simply adding costs to the case, and so it is not necessarily going to be useful. But I do think that it reflects a certain scepticism that American judges have about party experts, which is that economists aren't quite like all other experts. I say that with due respect to every economist in the room! I would like to think, for example, that if you were to call a neurologist to testify about a disease of the nervous system, then it wouldn't really matter which medical school the neurologist was associated with. The nervous system just has certain characteristics and the neurologist could describe how the electrical impulses move and what's

---

[2] *United States v Microsoft Corp* 147 F.3d 935 (DC Cir 1998); *United States v Microsoft Corp* 87 F Supp 2d 30 (DDC2000), 253 F.3d 34 (CA DC 2001) (No 03-5030).

wrong with what particular nerve, and so on, and any competent expert would give the same answer. As you know, economics isn't quite one of the hard sciences, and so whether the economist comes from MIT or Berkeley, or the University of Chicago, or the American Enterprise Institute or Brookings, or what have you, may make a difference in how that economist looks at the case. Different schools of thought operate, to a certain degree, under different sets of assumptions. Consequently, one of the reasons that we in the US like having an adversary presentation of economic testimony is because economics is still enough on the social sciences side of the line that we learn more about the underlying assumptions that the particular economist may employ.

Another thing courts can do, aside from being aware of what the economist has brought to the table is, in a cost-saving measure, to sequence the issues in a way that might avoid extensive work, say on damages. A judge might say that the parties should focus only on one issue of market power, and if everyone can conclude that the defendant had no market power, we have saved ourselves all the rest of the work in the case. There is tremendous discretion in the District Courts—the Courts of First Instance in the US— to do that. It is also possible, sometimes, to agree on some neutral sources of expertise, perhaps government studies, perhaps earlier cases.

The final thing I would like to just throw out for you is that there is a distinction that comes up sometimes between facts that really ought to be subject to re-examination in every case and facts that are more legislative in nature, as we would say. I can illustrate that difference from a very different area. We still, from time to time in our court, get black-lung cases (referring to the disease more formally called pneumoconiosis), because there used to be, ages ago, coal mines in Southern Illinois that have long since closed. There are still pension and worker's compensation-type claims that come up from that now-defunct industry. One of the questions has been whether pneumoconiosis, which is caused by exposure to coal dust, is the kind of disease that progresses like asbestosis, so a person might have an x-ray in Year 1 that shows no sign of it, and then no more exposure, but an x-ray in Year 5 that does show signs of it. The federal agency in charge of the miners' compensation scheme decided that pneumoconiosis is a progressive disease. They came to this decision only after a great deal of study: they held all sorts of hearings; they collected vast amounts of medical testimony; they studied actual experience from all over the world. The decision that the disease could be progressive had huge effects on the potential liability of the coal companies, because it meant that anyone who ever worked in the mines some day might come along ten years later and say, 'Now I have pneumoconiosis, please pay me my compensation benefits'. The mining companies keep trying to make the progressivity issue an adjudicative fact.

They want us to re-open the question every time a case is filed, but we have said no. Once this has been decided one can go back to the agency and try to persuade them that they were wrong, but a party is not going to get anywhere with the court. There aren't quite as many legislative facts in economics, but I suppose if somebody wanted to come in and say that the demand curves don't really slope downward, or that some basic economic assumptions should be re-opened, that person would get a much chillier welcome from the courts than the person coming in with particular evidence about a particular industry and, for example, how substitution worked for that product. The distinction between legislative and adjudicative facts, in short, can matter.

I will just quickly wrap up and say economics certainly makes a difference with substantive rules. When should the law reflect a presumption about certain behaviour? Presumptions help judges, to the extent that they exist, because they reduce the amount of evidence that must be taken in each case. In addition, the judge will be educated somehow, by the parties and adversarial system as well as by various entities such as universities and government agencies. In the US we have the Federal Judicial Centre that has programmes; much more controversially there are private groups who have taken it upon themselves to educate judges. Some of the public in the US think that these are brain-washing groups, and they don't want judges to go to these private seminars. Others think that if society is going to trust judges with as much power as it does trust us with, maybe it should trust judges to go to a seminar also. But the jury is out on that. There is legislation introduced from time to time in Congress that would tell judges that they cannot go to seminars that are privately funded any more, but it has never gone too far.

I will leave you with that.

JUDGE FRÉDÉRIC JENNY

Thank you very much, Diane. So it is quite obvious that there are differences of approach between the UK, but I would say more generally Europe, and the US. One of them is that clearly what Diane was telling us is in the context of a general and systematic approach to scientific evidence in courts and there is no real equivalent that I know of at least in Europe. Then Diane went on to question the economist as being hardly a scientist, if I understood well, or at least a sub-scientist.

President Bo Vesterdorf is now going to tell us what he expects from economists.

JUDGE BO VESTERDORF

Thank you. Ladies and gentlemen, the last time I had the honour of participating at a conference organized by the British Institute of International
and Comparative Law, just before Christmas last year, I was invited to
speak about the standard of proof in merger cases. A very interesting and
topical subject in the wake of the famous *Tetra Laval*[3] judgment. Today, I
have been invited to treat a different, albeit in my view closely related,
subject, 'Economics in Court'.

Evidential issues and in particular, the use of economic evidence are, or at
least should be, at the forefront of competition law enforcement, both by
competition agencies and by courts, including of course the courts in
Luxembourg.

Everybody these days on both sides of the Atlantic seems to agree that for
an efficient antitrust regime which promotes economic welfare, economics
and the law must go hand in hand. It is beyond any doubt that economics
has an extremely important role to play at various levels of our competition
law regime, from more generally designing and drafting the basic provisions
of the law and sharing policy by the competition authorities, to more specifically helping lawyers and judges create appropriate legal sub-tests to apply
in particular situations and applying those tests on the basis of economic
evidence in particular cases at hand.

This is of course much easier said than done. As a judge at the Court of First
Instance in Luxembourg for more than 16 years now, I have come to experience first hand the role that economic theory and economic evidence can
effectively play in the adjudication of specific cases before my Court. What
I would like to do today is to not only discuss the reasons why I think
economics has an important role to play in shaping policy, theory and legal
tests, but also try to give you a flavour of the issues a judge has to deal with
when faced with complex economic theories and evidence. Our time is
limited, so I will focus on a few issues that I consider more important or
useful for today's purposes.

To start on a light note, which will immediately give you a flavour of the
difficulties surrounding the use of economic evidence in court, allow me to
begin with a typical economist joke. Frédéric Jenny please excuse me! A
mathematician, an accountant, and an economist apply for the same job.
The interviewer calls the mathematician in and asks 'What does 2 plus 2
equal?' The mathematician replies '4'. The interviewer asks '4 exactly? and

---

[3] *Tetra Laval v Commission* (Case C-12/03 P) not yet reported in the ECR, judgment of 15
Feb 2005.

the answer from the mathematician is clearly 'Yes, 4 exactly'. Then the interviewer calls in the accountant and asks the same question: 'What does 2 plus 2 equal?' The accountant says 'On average 4, give or take 10 per cent, but on average 4'. Then the interviewer calls in the economist and poses the same question. The economist gets up, locks the door, closes the shade, sits down next to the interviewer and says 'What do you want it to equal?'

Being a joke that example is clearly, of course, exaggerated, but it does however pose some relevant questions. Is economics reliable enough to be used for the creation of legal tests? When should judges embrace a particular economic theory in order to create legal sub-tests? What types of economic evidence can be relied upon to help the judge reach conclusions in a particular case? And what should judges do when faced with inconclusive or contradictory economic evidence in any particular case?

But before turning to the more practical evidentiary questions, I would like to spend a few minutes on a more abstract, but equally important, question of what role, or general role, economics play in competition law. As I said earlier, everybody these days seems to agree that antitrust law and economics go hand in hand and the fact that there is a sort of consensus on this point is indeed a remarkable achievement. The United States, a jurisdiction that has embraced this notion perhaps more than any other, has had a tumultuous history of judicial and antitrust enforcement and radical changes in judicial review on the economics of antitrust. Vertical agreements for instance have gone from being per se illegal, to almost being presumed per se legal, or at least being subject to a full rule of reason analysis.

However, the fact that economics should be so influential in this field of the law is hardly surprising: competition law is economic law and its very purpose is to enable the free functioning of the markets in order to increase economic welfare. In addition, most competition laws around the world are couched in very general terms, which allow the judiciary significant leeway in interpreting the law. We are not in the realm of precisely worded statutes that must be merely applied by judges. Article 81, Article 82, and Article 86 and the Merger Regulation are indeed open-ended provisions and without repeating the specific wording with which you are of course all familiar, they basically boil down to one simple question: is the agreement, the conduct or the merger in question, significantly anticompetitive? What is meant by anticompetitive? The myriad permutations and specific situations the judge or authority has to face in reaching a correct answer to this seemingly simple question is precisely where economics can and should play a prominent role.

How? There are, in my view, four different levels where economics can be used to enable correct, or at least as correct as possible, outcomes in competition enforcement. First, in shaping the actual test enacted in the law; second, by helping judges and in particular authorities focus on the broad objectives that the law aims to achieve; third, by helping authorities and judges to create appropriate legal sub-tests that they can apply in a particular situation; finally, by enabling authorities and judges to decide specific cases on the basis of economic theory and evidence.

Let me go briefly through those four elements in turn. First, it is important not to forget that economic theory plays an important role at the very first step, mainly the adoption of the competition laws. It is on the basis of economic theory that most countries adopt their competition laws in order to achieve economic objectives. Article 81, for example, was enacted because established economic theory tells us that cartels invariably lead to a loss of consumer welfare. Many commentators have debated whether Article 82 of the Treaty reflects a certain ordoliberal philosophy of competition and certainly its wording makes sense when one sees it as aiming to protect a free competitive process. The recent debates surrounding the change in the substantive test of the Merger Regulation, or the similar debate which took place in the UK before the adoption of the Enterprise Act, show the legislators are well aware of the relevant issues and legislate in order to pursue a specific economic objective: free competition, and increased economic welfare. Our laws therefore already reflect a particular economic approach, that we as judges, are bound to follow.

Secondly, economics is important in establishing broad-based views on the interpretation of the enacted laws. I have in mind here broad tests or goals that the competition authorities or judges believe the law is aiming to achieve. For example, Article 82 of the EC Treaty prohibits abusive behaviour by dominant companies and gives a non-exhaustive list of types of such abusive behaviour. Whether efficiencies or objective justifications can come into the equation, whether exclusionary abuses must not only harm competitors but ultimately also consumers, or even whether consumer welfare is the ultimate goal, are important questions that the legal provisions have largely left unanswered. These issues may appear too broad and academic in the context of a particular case but it is the duty of the judiciary to interpret the law correctly in the light of the objectives that the legislator intends to achieve. The answers can have a radical impact on how the law is then applied to individual cases.

Thirdly, economics can help authorities and judges to establish more precise legal sub-tests that can be applied in particular everyday situations. The broad text of the competition law allows flexibility as to the application.

One way of applying the law is to employ precise 'effects-based' analysis in every individual case. This approach can of course be good in reaching correct results, or outcomes, in economic terms. However, a precise case-by-case, full-blown, effects-based economic analysis does not always go well hand in hand with legal certainty, or with effective competition law enforcement. Legal certainty is an important objective and it is particularly important for business. Companies need to have certainty and predictability and the judges need to apply the law in a consistent and predictable way. At the same time, competition authorities too need to have predictability and to be able to apply the law in an effective manner. If every single case merited a fullblown costly economic analysis, effective enforcement might indeed suffer. This is precisely where legal sub-tests can become useful. Traditionally, judges have interpreted the broadly drafted competition laws and have created such legal tests that can be pragmatically applied in particular situations. The main advantage of legal tests is that they make the law easier to understand and apply. The main disadvantage is that they remain crude proxies of a precise economic analysis and can thus be either over-inclusive or under-inclusive. An over-inclusive test will catch innocent situations which should not fall within the scope of the antitrust laws. On the contrary, an under-inclusive test will lead to the opposite result, that is, cases that should be caught will escape the competition laws. As an example, an over-inclusive test could be a merger test prohibiting all merger transactions where the parties have more than 40 per cent market share. An under-inclusive merger test could be a test authorizing all conglomerate mergers. It is in order to avoid such crudeness that legal sub-tests have been carefully crafted by the judges faced with specific cases. Conditions, caveats, reversible presumptions and so forth have been added to simple tests, in order to make them more precise and better attuned to economic reality.

You are all familiar with some of those legal tests such as the conditions for collective dominance established in the *Airtours*[4] case, the test for predatory pricing in the *AKZO*[5] and *Tetra Pak II*[6] cases, the refusal to supply tests in *Bronner*[7] and *IMS*[8] or the rebate tests in *Michelin*[9] and *British Airways*.[10] Are these tests good tests in economic terms, and how can economics and economists help judges create better tests? Some of these tests, like the

---

[4] *Airtours plc v Commission* (Case T342/99) [2002] ECR II2585.
[5] *AKZO Chemie BV v Commission* (Case C62/86) [1991] ECR I3359.
[6] *TetraPak v Commission* (Case T-83/91) [1994] ECR II-755.
[7] *Oscar Bronner v Mediaprint* (Case C7/97) [1998] ECR I7791.
[8] *IMS Health v NDC Health* (Case C418/01) [2004] ECR I-5039, [2004] 4 CMLR 28, [2004] ECDR 23.
[9] *Michelin v Commission* (Case T203/01) [2003] ECR II4071.
[10] *British Airways v Commission* (Case T219/99) 4 CMLR 19.

collective dominance *Airtours* conditions, are rather uncontroversial and seem to be fairly well accepted by economists, lawyers and competition authorities. Others, such as the predatory pricing test, are accepted in principle even though refinements are proposed. Others, such as the refusal to supply tests, or the rebate test, remain subject to greater controversy and criticism by lawyers and economists. The debate surrounding the *Michelin* and the *British Airways* cases, in particular, has been rather heated, and my own Court, the CFI, has been criticized for being overly formalistic in refusing to perform a more effects-based analysis of the consequences that fidelity rebates might have in the market in question.

I do not, however, want to spend too much time today on whether those tests are rightly criticized or not. I would nonetheless like to stress that, in my view, extremely rigid per se rules should be very rare in competition law. In most situations, all one can say is that a particular conduct is, *in principle*, presumed to be legal, or illegal. But, in my view, such legality or illegality should almost always be rebuttable if more precise economic or other evidence can establish that in the case at hand the principle simply does not stand. Economic theory and economic evidence can assist judges in being much more aware of the broader debate surrounding a particular conduct and of the economic consequences of a particular legal test that they create. They can thus assist judges in creating more sophisticated legal tests, using more appropriate conditions that are more likely to yield better results.

This brings me to the final part of my talk today: economic input in specific cases before the court. Judges and economists rarely have direct contact (except of course in conferences like the one today), in the way that a competition authority for example does. Even though there are some notable exceptions, in particular in the United States, the judiciary is normally composed of only legal experts with little, if any, direct knowledge of economics. This is not necessarily a handicap, even though, in my view, a specialized judiciary would certainly find it easier to grapple with complex economic theory and evidence.

Over the years, the Community judges at the CFI and the ECJ have been faced with complex economic evidence and have had to make decisions on the basis of contradictory, inconsistent or inconclusive evidence. This is the reality of everyday life and it is almost inconceivable that a case would yield such perfect economic data were there to be no disagreement between the two sides. If it did, the case would most probably not reach the judiciary anyway.

In our current system non-specialist judges come into contact with economics through the evidence presented in court in the particular cases. Our judicial system being a judicial review system where the legality of Commission decisions is examined, makes EC trials very different from US trials. Evidence is more succinct and the parties make less use of direct expert evidence, in particular oral evidence. The first pieces of economic evidence that we are presented with are contained in the party's written pleadings and in the attacked Commission decision. The decision and the pleadings contain evidence in the form of analysis of market definition, theories of harm which fit the particular case, data on market shares, data on the functioning of the market and the interaction between the various players in that particular market. And in the more sophisticated cases, specific use of economic models which use the relevant data to predict or prove a particular outcome. Apart from direct use of such evidence, economic evidence, in the main body of the decision and written pleadings, parties are of course allowed to produce, and do produce, voluminous annexes, containing more specific analyses of particular points, complete with economics graphs that most judges, and at least myself, find difficult from time to time to comprehend. On some occasions, parties make references to economic literature; finally the parties are allowed to present oral evidence and use economic experts at the oral hearing at the court.

I need to stress here that our rules of procedure, in the two courts in Luxembourg, are fairly flexible when it comes to the type of evidence that can be presented during the written and the oral phase of the procedure. This is in contrast to many other jurisdictions such as, for example, the United States where more formal and detailed rules of evidence are applicable. In our proceedings, as long as the adversarial principle is respected, that is that all parties have the opportunity to comment on the evidence submitted before the judge, the judge is indeed entitled to consider any type of evidence he or she finds useful for the purposes of the particular case. The rules of procedure also enable the judge hearing the case to adopt various measures of organization or enquiry, including the appointment of independent court experts.

I would like to make a few points on the type of evidence presented by the parties which, in my view, most judges, at least in my experience from the Community courts, find useful in the competition cases and also on how we, as judges, assess that type of evidence.

First, I cannot stress enough that the most basic, but equally the most important, rule that parties and the economic experts should observe, is to present things clearly. Judges at the Community courts are not expert economists, and presentations making excessive use of jargon and specialist tools such as complicated graphs without any clear explanation will probably not go down very well in the court room. On the other hand, effective presentations in both written and oral pleadings would, in my view, involve a short, concise and easy to understand presentation of the economic theory in question and then a clear application of that theory on the basis of the facts of the case. Evidence of the functioning of the market and practical examples of what is going on in the market, with factual data that can be easily checked and verified, are the type of evidence that most judges find convincing and useful. Any source of data that is found to be reliable can help to prove a contention: internal documents of the parties; market investigations; independent reports; reports made for the purposes of the litigation, or procedure by experts; econometric models, and so on; counter-factual scenarios when presented clearly can also be very useful. For example, what would happen in the marketplace if a dominant undertaking behaved in one particular way? Practical examples with explanations on how the various competitors would likely respond to this conduct and what the concrete effects would be of that conduct should be the type of evidence offered to the judge.

Let me now come to a final point. How do judges assess this economic evidence and what do we do when faced with conflicting, confusing or contradictory evidence? There is no hard and fast rule here. It is up to the court to assess all the evidence produced, interpret the law, decide on what the appropriate legal conditions that should be met are and then assess whether, on the basis of the factual evidence presented, those conditions are met in the case at hand to the requisite legal standard. The requisite legal standard is important. Given that our function is that of judicially reviewing the Commission's decision, which is a task very different from actually re-examining the case on the merits, the review of economic evidence is by implication limited. I am referring here to the economic appreciation of facts and not the actual determination of primary facts as correct or incorrect. That the courts should defer to the Commission's economic expertise in situations of complex economic appreciation is trite in EC competition law and it has a sound basis. The Community judges are not economic experts and it is not their primary task to analyse economic evidence in order to reach conclusions as to economic developments in a particular market. It is the Commission that is entrusted with this task at first instance. The burden is therefore on the applicant challenging a Commission decision to show that the theories advanced by the Commission, or the application of those theories, are tainted by manifest errors of appreciation. Having said that, I should stress that the courts will not of course shy away from checking rather rigorously the economic evidence produced by the applicant and the Commission in order to decide whether the elements produced are correct, but also that all the pertinent elements have been furnished in order to support one or another economic theory in the case at hand.

Allow me to conclude on this point, with a final thought. A lot has been said lately on the role of the courts in competition law enforcement, the relevant standard of review, standard of proof required in competition cases and the role of economics and economic evidence in the adjudication of competition cases. This debate in academic journals and conferences like the one today is more than welcome; it is indeed very necessary. It ensures that decision-makers at all levels of competition law enforcement are much more aware of the issues involved and of the implications of using economic theories and evidence. As far as judges are concerned, it makes us more aware of the need to make clearer distinctions when deciding cases as to facts, legal questions and economic appreciation in order to apply the appropriate standards in the determination of the issue and to handle economic evidence with the appropriate care that it deserves.

The days when economics barely registered on the judicial radars in Luxembourg are long gone, but the difficult task of evaluating complex economic issues and reaching appropriate conclusions in the cases before us remains in front of us. Better and clearer economic evidence can go a long way to enabling the Community judiciary to shift through the issues and decide cases in a more sophisticated way that is in sync with the established economic theories.

Thank you very much for your attention.

JUDGE FRÉDÉRIC JENNY

Thank you very much. Before I open the floor for discussion, I would like to ask Justice Lightman and Diane Wood whether you have comments on what the other speakers have said.

MR JUSTICE GAVIN LIGHTMAN

First of all, there has been a long debate on how far judges in competition cases should be specialists in competition law. Similar issues have arisen in relation to tax and intellectual property cases. The way it is normally put is that, if you are going to attract foreigners (and in particular Americans) to come and conduct litigation in this country, they must be satisfied that judges understand what they are doing. They can be disturbed if they see the judges trying cases in areas of law with which they are not familiar. The general approach adopted in this country is that the judges should be sufficiently equipped to deal with any cases that are called on before them, and that through experience judges can acquire any required expertise. There are exceptions (eg in patent cases) where there is insistence on specialist judges. Competition issues can arise in civil litigation of all sorts, for example, on an assessment of damages and on other issues in private litigation. It is not possible to avoid recourse to non-specialist judges. In the circumstances it is necessary to equip judges generally to try competition issues by the promotion of education of judges and lawyers in competition law, economics and accountancy and by insisting that lawyers put material before the court in readily comprehensible form.

The other matter which I find very interesting is the way that in the European Court there appears to be no barrier to anybody being an expert. In the American courts, the barrier is very high: you have got to show that you are quite extraordinary. In England we have a low threshold, but the judges are flexible and capable of holding that a witness's limited expertise, whilst sufficient to qualify his evidence as expert evidence, is insufficient to attract any substantial weight.

JUDGE DIANE WOOD

I just wanted to pick up for one moment on what Judge Vesterdorf was saying about the creation of rules and presumptions that help judges to manage this kind of testimony. That process, of course, describes the history of the US antitrust laws. They begin with very broad statutory language which, as we were discussing earlier, has something like a common law tone, and then, moving from this very broad language, one first saw distinctions between per se rules and rules of reason and then one began to get hierarchies of what it really meant to talk about the rule of reason. Those kinds of rules certainly can help judges decide what is relevant, what is not relevant and how to approach a case.

We also, of course, have the slightly different model; if you look at mergers, which may be the easiest example, where the agencies have come up with merger guidelines, the courts are quick to tell you these merger guidelines are not binding on them. On the other hand, the guidelines are extremely useful, and courts will look at the methodology that the agency has come up with to try to structure the decision-making. I think that this kind of structured decision-making is another way that we can make the system work with generalist judges. I am not sure that I agree that we need specialized judges in competition cases, but I probably wouldn't say that we need them in intellectual property or anywhere else either.

BO VESTERDORF

I would like to briefly touch upon four different issues that were just raised by my two colleagues: specialized judges; experts in European court proceedings; legal sub-tests; and guidelines.

Specialized judges: when my Court was set up in 1989, it was intended to be a specialist court dealing with competition cases and, as a small side matter, staff cases, with the aim of alleviating the Court of Justice from dealing with such cases. So we were set up as a specialist court primarily intended to deal intensively with fact-finding and verification of facts in competition cases. You should bear in mind, however, that the judges appointed to the CFI, at that point in time, were certainly not, from any perspective, specialist judges. They became specialized gradually because they have had to deal with competition cases, but they were not appointed on the basis that they had a certain expertise in competition law. The broader subject regarding specialist judges for competition cases is an interesting one. I think at least on the European level, ie the Community court level, where judges at the CFI are supposed to verify and check on the Commission's actions in the field of competition law and review very complex files in this field, the time has come, in my view, to create or ensure that we have a specialized competition court. There is a simple, practical reason for this: with the number of judges that sit on the Court today, at 25 (following the recent enlargement), there are simply too many judges for too few opportunities to treat large competition cases as judge 'rapporteur' in order to acquire the necessary familiarity with this field of the law. It is simply a daunting task for a judge who, once in a while, every third or fourth year, is presented with the *Michelin* case, or the *Microsoft* case, as a judge rapporteur; it is indeed somewhat of a challenge. If the Court is, therefore, supposed to deal effectively with such cases, it needs to have people who, on a very regular basis, deal with that type of case. Otherwise it is simply a waste of time and energy and we can certainly not deal with such cases in a sufficiently efficient way. Therefore, I think on this specific topic that there are indeed good reasons to set up a specialist competition court. I have, by the way, as some of you may know, advocated this on many occasions over the last couple of years but with no great success!

It was said that anybody can be an expert in proceedings before the Community courts in Luxembourg. Well, anybody can claim that they are an expert and any party may in fact present a document or report drawn up by somebody called an expert. They will normally have very nice titles, Dr This or That, a number of indications afterwards. We take that evidence as long as it is presented according to the rules of procedure and, in accordance with the rules of procedure, we take it and examine it and we pay attention to it if it merits to be taken into account. This means that, if we feel convinced about the contents of such a document, that it is logical, it is coherent and it is well-documented, then the Court is entitled to give it the weight it considers appropriate. Another perhaps remark on experts in Community courts. It is very rare indeed for the Community courts to appoint their own court experts. We can do it. It has only been done on a very few cases, in a very small number of cases and, in my time in the Court of First Instance, we have not really done it. We have relied upon the evidence presented by the two parties, the Commission and the complainant or the applicant, and taken the evidence for the value that it may have.

Legal sub-tests: we are often in the position that we, the 'lower court', find that we have tried to indicate in our judgments why we reach a specific result, often indicating the motivation behind the result that we get to. In this respect, the judgments often contain an indication of a certain number of conditions that must be met in the particular case at hand. An example is the *Airtours* case where we set out the conditions for collective dominance.

Guidelines: The practice of the Commission to issue guidelines on a large number of issues that DG Comp deals with is indeed a practice that necessitates, on our part, a decision on the value of those guidelines; to what degree should we also as judges feel bound by those guidelines; and to what extent are they sufficiently well established or well drawn-up for the parties to rely upon them; and do they in fact apply or condition the application of competition law by the Commission in a proper way? Therefore, we are more or less led into appreciating a number of sub-conditions on a more informal character.

JUDGE FRÉDÉRIC JENNY

Thank you very much. Somehow the discussion has shifted a little bit. The economists looked terrible at the very beginning of this discussion but they look a tiny bit better now, particularly after President Vesterdorf made a strong case for economic analysis in antitrust cases. I would like to see whether there is any reaction on comments on what has been said before we come to a provisional conclusion of this debate.

SIR JOHN VICKERS

My background is as an economist. So, on the 2 plus 2 principle I will make whatever comment you like. I wanted to make a comment and perhaps ask a question on how these economic factors relate to legal certainty which is often discussed. My view is that there are grounds for optimism in the following sense in Europe. It seems to me we have quite a lot of scope for more of both legal certainty and clearer, firmer, more visible, economic grounding for areas of law that, unlike cartel behaviour, should not be per se. Indeed some of the form-based approaches, far from being good for legal certainty, can be a recipe for legal turmoil, especially when scope for private actions is opening up and I think of the US experience in the late 1960s and early 1970s.

The comments made recently among the judges seem to me to indicate what could be quite a promising way forward. Whether it is a legal sub-test or another jargon-structured rule of reason, where presumptions and burdens might shift as one walks through the analysis, or even simply courts requiring in a judicial review sense that certain key facts are part of the case. If it is an exclusion case, if certain practices are allegedly foreclosing the market, then the question 'how much of the market does that practice apply to?' seems a fairly basic question that should be part of the evidence, otherwise the case would seem to have quite a big hole in it. So some of this perhaps is much more simple than some people fear.

Now how that is to happen is one challenge. Another is how to achieve consistency across the treatment of different kinds of conduct. I think there is a danger if this task is approached, if you like, category of abuse by category of abuse, in the Article 82 sense, then without some clear underlying principles whether they relate to some kind of efficiency standard or consumer welfare standard. There is that danger. So there might be value in a consistent thread in terms of some underlying principles of that kind. But the primary challenge here seems to be on the authorities and, above all, DG Competition through its casework and through guidelines very much welcome the approving remarks made there. Of course for a competition agency guidelines you are making a rod for your own back, but I still think it is one that one ought to make and we hope very much DG Comp will make in this area. The question will then be: how welcome is this to the courts?

JUDGE BO VESTERDORF

I hope I have understood your comments correctly. The answer is a slightly difficult one because on the one hand we as judges have an obligation to make sure, to the extent possible, that there is a coherent and predictable application of competition law in the cases before the court, that we don't shift from one position to another position simply without any economic or any factual difference between the cases. That is obviously an aim in itself and this is why I talked about the necessity of having as large a degree of legal certainty as possible. Therefore, if we can set out in our case law a number of indications formulated in relatively broad terms— that if this or that scenario is the case in the following cases we would normally apply the law in this or that way—like we did in the *Airtours*[11] case, I think is a positive approach.

---

[11] *Airtours* (n 4).

But as I stressed, it is with its limits, because as always, in the individual cases that arise later, the parties will try to explain to us why the facts of that case do indeed differ on significant points from the former cases and therefore you cannot simply apply the fourth prong test of the *Airtours* or the *IMS*[12] case. You can not just simply apply it like that.

Therefore, eventually, at the end of the day as judges we wind up with one case in which we have a certain number of facts before us which are proven to the requisite degree and we have to apply the law to those facts, including of course applying the law to all the economics on the basis of all the economic evidence presented to us. So we are faced with a very difficult task of ensuring legal certainty and at the same time applying the law correctly to the particular set of facts of economic circumstances of the case, which is why I said that per se rules, or rules of that type, must always be treated with some scepticism because they should be rebuttable on the basis of sound economic analysis or any other evidence presented to the judge in any particular future case.

Okeoghene Odudu

I have a question, or maybe a comment, about the role of the economist and economic experts and how it changes the interest with which the judge is concerned or clarifies that competition is concerned with economics. In particular, if you receive lots of economic evidence, does that mean it really is just concerned with economics and, if that's the case, how, particularly in Community law, do you balance this with maybe an Article 6 concern that you should also consider something like the environmental impact with every question with which you're concerned.

Mr Justice Gavin Lightman

I should just say that in the interest of judicial consistency of view, I leave it to Judge Bo to give the answer!

Bo Vesterdorf

Let me try and boil the discussion slightly down to see it from a practical point of view. When we, as judges in the Community courts in Luxembourg, receive any competition case, we always have the great advantage or disadvantage of having a Commission decision before us that is being attacked. That is the framework of all the work in that particular

---

[12] *IMS* (n 8).

case. It is that decision that we have to verify, if it is applying correct legal tests, to correct facts, to correct economic evidence, and we cannot go beyond the framework of that particular decision. So it is both an advantage and to a certain degree a disadvantage. What we will do in practical terms when we receive the case as a judge is of course we start up reading the Commission's decision because that is what is being attacked. Then we will read the application and will find the points in the application where they contest the various parts of the Commission's decision—either facts, economic evidence, other evidence and the application of the legal tests to that set of facts. That is what we are there to do. It is in that context that we, very often, put questions, very precise questions, on facts, not only pure facts, primary facts, but also regarding the economic evidence, in order to get more information, be convinced about the arguments of either of the two parties, but we do not go beyond the case at hand. We cannot do that.

What we try to do, on the other hand, when we set out the motivation for a result, is to think carefully about what this case might mean in other cases in the future. In order to not make too many constraints either on the Commission; too much on the other hand makes sure that there is a sufficient degree of legal control and effective legal control.

JUDGE DIANE WOOD

I just wanted to add a slight comparative note to that. Some years ago, there was a debate in the United States about what did the rule of reason really mean. If you were looking at a case that was not strict hard-core price-fixing, there was a serious question whether there was a need to take other social values into account, whether it was protection of small businesses or local industrial development. There was an analogous discussion here in Europe, looking at what is now Article 81.3. Certainly from the United States' point of view, I think that the resolution of that debate was that if one was talking about the antitrust laws, it was correct to say that they are concerned about a particular thing, namely competition in the market. They are economic legislation. In that sense, it is entirely appropriate to have economics guide decision-making, although economics itself isn't going to tell anyone whether *impermissibly* high market power starts at 80 per cent of the market, or 50 per cent of the market or some other percentage. You have to have a more sophisticated concept of economics, which is certainly not to say that you don't think environmental protection or small business or industrial development or anything else is important. But we have other laws that address those subjects, and it is more efficient to take care of environmental protection under those laws. We reserve competition law, or antitrust law, for a particular set of economic problems; we do not try to pile every concern into the rule of reason, which would break under the strain. Equally undesirably, such a move would destroy any kind of predictability in the competition law for businesses that are in good faith trying to comply with it.

FRÉDÉRIC JENNY

Let me react to some of the things that were said, because there were high points and very low points in this discussion and I am completely schizophrenic about it because I was an economist and am now a judge. What was really depressing was to hear President Vesterdorf say it would be nice if economists could avoid jargon, or complicated graphs that didn't add much to the discussion, or to hear the example in the US where a Nobel Prize of Economics apparently addressed the wrong question and therefore had its evidence eliminated. So there you ask yourself: what are those economists doing? They can't even express themselves. When they express themselves, they don't even address the issue which is at hand, and you get the impression that they are really useless.

On the other side, we have heard in the discussion from President Vesterdorf, and also from Diane Wood, and also finally from Justice Lightman, that the input of economic analysis was extremely important in, and there was no question about this, in competition proceedings, both to establish what the goals of competition law were, to decide the test, and to help the judge actually implement the test.

I think it is generally agreed that economists have a highly logical mind, they work with logical models, they use quite sophisticated econometric methods and somehow they are considered to be unreliable and soft, to take the words of Diane Wood, when one comes to specific cases. So there is really a question there. How can we have on one side those terribly sophisticated people with very solid models and yet be faced with their complete inability or large inability to apply those models to a particular practice, or to devise a practical test to decide whether practice is, or is not, anticompetitive. I think that part of it is due to the fact that economists are not . . . at least micro-economists familiar with IP-related issues. It is a new thing for them to have to apply their models to a particular situation. They are still, to a certain extent, thinking in macro terms, explaining the general relationship between concentration and competition and those kind of things, or the theoretical possibilities provided by the oligopoly model, but have a great deal of difficulty focusing on a natural practice, because they were not so interested, or they were not so interested in their research in doing so.

So what I am really wondering is whether the rules, the very exacting rules, which have been described by Diane and mentioned by Justice Lightman, in the US, are not useful in two ways. First, in simplifying in a sense the work of the courts by eliminating things which are clearly not meeting the standards of proper research, but also in providing guidance to the economist as to what they should do when they try to go from the height of the theoretical models to try to apply those models and say something about a particular case.

I am wondering personally whether in Europe it would be useful to have a set of guidelines of what is admissible evidence from economists and whether it would not in the end make the economists look more reliable than they seem to be considered at this point. I think the sad question of concentration of quotes that Justice Lightman said, quite rightly, that we have to think about how to make economists understandable by regular courts because in any case there are many competition issues which are going to come in front of regular courts, even if we have sometimes courts where the competition issues are concentrated.

But I think that somewhere in those formidable thresholds that had been described, which may be a little less formidable than what has been said, whether there would be something there, that would benefit both the courts and the economist. I really believe this. This topic, by the way, will be taken up in a conference in the fall on the other side of the Atlantic, so we will have time to think again about it.

Antitrust Modernization: Who Needs It? Who Wants It?

Diane P Wood*

I. INTRODUCTION

This afternoon, we heard a very interesting discussion about 'antitrust modernization'. Indeed, it has become quite fashionable of late to undertake ambitious projects to 'modernize' competition laws. Almost exactly a year ago, a comprehensive new set of rules for the competition provisions of the EC Treaty went into effect, which in the aggregate are easily the most important changes in this regime since its infancy. It has not been so long since the UK itself enacted a thorough-going overhaul of its competition laws, bringing them into line with the European model and implementing other desirable reforms at the same time. Not to be left behind, as you already know, the United States has its own Antitrust Modernization Commission, which is charged with studying the US antitrust laws and coming up with recommendations for modernizing them.

'Modernization' sounds like such a great thing, doesn't it? Who wants to be an old fuddy-duddy, clinging to outmoded ways of thinking, quill-pen and horse-and-buggy technologies, and economic assumptions founded on small, isolated, largely agrarian economies? It's more exciting to be 'modern': think of the beginning of Cole Porter's famous song, 'Anything Goes'—'In olden days a glimpse of stocking was looked on as something shocking, but now, God knows, Anything Goes!' But if we look at any 'modernization' movement a little more closely, it turns out that even to use the term 'modernization' is to state a conclusion. The conclusion is that there was something wrong with what went before; that it needs changing; and that the changes will be good. Those who reject that underlying premise and think that the 'old' is well worth preserving, say things like 'if it ain't broke, don't fix it'. More elegantly, they are the ones in the vanguard of the historic preservation movements around the world, of which you have countless examples here in the UK and in Europe more broadly.

The worst of all possible worlds comes when the instincts represented by these two approaches—modernization versus historic preservation—are never reconciled with one another. Almost every day I see an architectural example of this type of failure, and perhaps this unfortunate story has its

---

* Circuit Judge, US Court of Appeals for the 7th Circuit.

UK version as well. About five or six years ago, the Chicago Bears (the perennially unsuccessful NFL pro-football franchise in the Windy City) decided that they needed a better stadium. Throughout the 20th century, they had played at a place called Soldier Field, which is located right on Lake Michigan, and which was built entirely inside a neoclassical outer structure, complete with Doric columns, bas relief decorations, and so on. Soldier Field had earned the distinction of being placed on the US National Register of Historical Landmarks, which meant among other things that it could not be modified without meeting strict criteria of many types. Somehow (and I am mystified about how), the Bears persuaded the Powers That Be to approve placing a new, modern stadium inside and draping over the shell of the old neoclassical building, which is what they did. Many people in Chicago think that the resulting structure looks as if a flying saucer landed on top of Soldier Field and broke at both ends; others less flatteringly refer to the oval-shaped inverted cone that sits on top of the old building as the Toilet Seat. It is actually a very nice stadium once one steps inside and can no longer see the old, forlorn, ridiculously short outer walls and columns. Nevertheless, what makes it nice has nothing to do with historic preservation. Recently the czars of the National Register decided to de-list Soldier Field, and so it will now be possible (should they ever want to spend their money this way) to create a single, architecturally unified, stadium. (Maybe they will even put a roof over it, considering that late November and early December games al fresco in Chicago can be almost painfully cold, and the January Super Bowl is out of the question at present.)

The moral of this story, for antitrust law as well as for anything else, is to begin by deciding whether the 'old' law, or building, or car, is worth preserving or not, by whatever metric makes sense—functionality, artistic quality, cost of maintenance, changed external circumstances, or whatever. Only if it is not worth preserving (or to the extent that it is not) should one then go out and create or purchase the best possible good or service to meet current needs. If the law, or the building, is still fundamentally sound, then wholesale 'modernization' is a bad idea. At most, one needs a surgically focused effort to bring essential systems up-to-date (such as electrical wiring, heating systems, lifts), while at the same time disturbing the old as little as possible and avoiding the Soldier Field-type unintended consequences.

II. ANTITRUST MODERNIZATION IN THE UNITED STATES

Coming back to antitrust law, then, I would like to discuss for a few minutes what, if anything, needs modernizing in the US antitrust system.

You have already heard about the issues that the Modernization Commission—meeting literally right now, as we are enjoying this dinner—has chosen to study. It has identified nine areas for further work, which are as follows:

- Enforcement Institutions
- Exclusionary Conduct
- Immunities and Exemptions
- International Issues
- Merger Enforcement
- 'New Economy' Issues
- Regulated Industries
- Remedies
- Robinson–Patman Act

Rather than adding to this discussion, I would like to shuffle the topics around a bit for the purposes of tonight's talk. I am doing so both in order to make this talk more relevant to an international audience (frankly speaking, what do you care whether the United States insists on keeping the Robinson–Patman Act or not) and in order to keep in mind the question of how desirable modernization is for different aspects of this field. Unlike the Commission, which actually has a serious job to do, I am merely an after-dinner speaker, and so I am going to take full advantage of the fact that (unlike this afternoon's panel) I do not need to worry about the prospects for anything I suggest being enacted into law. This is, as we like to say in the academic world, a 'think piece', and I hope that you don't mind taking it as such.

For convenience, I have divided the issues into the familiar categories of 'procedural' and 'substantive', and I shall take them in that order. Under the 'procedural' heading, it seems useful to consider all types of governmental enforcement authorities separately from private party measures. This is so not only because many countries in the world rely far less on private enforcement than does the United States, but also because the problems one encounters in each are different. Thirdly, before leaving the topic of procedures, I'll look briefly at one issue that is common to all who are entitled to take action under the US antitrust laws, namely, the international reach of those laws (or, what used to be called, invariably in disapproving tones, extraterritoriality). Turning to substance, one can visualize a hierarchy of actions, going from a simple tidying-up of the laws in a way expressly designed *not* to affect substance, all the way up to a total overhaul. I'll explore what might be done to the US laws at each step along the way. Finally, we can consider what sort of 'King's X' we need to put into the laws: what safety valves, exemptions, and exceptions are either necessary or desirable (if any).

III. REFORM OF ANTITRUST PROCEDURES

You may not appreciate, from this side of the Pond, the degree of despair some experienced antitrust practitioners feel about the state of the current system. One long-time observer, who served in the Antitrust Division of the US Department of Justice for a time, practised for many years with a private firm, and chaired the ABA's Section of Antitrust Law, is Ky P Ewing, Jr. He published an article entitled 'Will the New Antitrust Modernization Commission Have the Courage to Tackle Real Issues' in the LexisNexis Antitrust Report in the Summer of 2003. To give you a sense of that despair, I can do no better than to quote Ky's description of 'the challenge' that the Commission faces:

> Our competition policy regime in the United States—viewed from abroad—presents a bewildering hodge-podge of federal and state laws, many of them contradictory to one another in substance, enforced by two federal agencies, fifty-four sets of 'State' attorneys general, and private persons as well. Twelve different federal appellate courts can interpret the federal laws, and fifty-four different 'state' appellate systems can also interact with competition policy. On top of this, the United States has granted at both the federal and state levels an equally bewildering set of exemptions and immunities to antitrust laws. Nor have we even completed the task of deregulating all our industries to the point of having the truly free markets we so often preach to others. A former Assistant Attorney General in charge of the Antitrust Division really was heard to say that 'No one in his right mind would create the mess of antitrust laws we have today.'[1]

That is quite a *cri de coeur*; you can almost see him wringing his hands.

A. Government enforcement

One of the important points Ky mentions, and that everyone acknowledges needs reconsideration, is the one relating to multiplicity of governmental authorities. There are two dimensions here that antitrust experts will find quite familiar: the horizontal one and the vertical one. The horizontal one looks to the number of agencies at a particular level of government, primarily the national level; the vertical dimension relates to what *we* would call the federalism problem—how do the federal authorities relate to the antitrust authorities in the 50 states, the District of Columbia, and the other areas for which the US has responsibility?

---

[1] [Pages 9–10; footnotes omitted.]

The United States is not the only country to have more than one authority at the national level, of course. The UK, France, and Germany, just to name a few, also have more than one national agency. But the US is unique in the degree to which its two national enforcement authorities, the Federal Trade Commission and the Department of Justice, have overlapping mandates. The overlap covers virtually all of antitrust except that the Department has exclusive responsibility for criminal enforcement; for its part, the FTC has sole authority over the consumer protection mission at the federal level. And, like every other country I know, the sectoral regulatory agencies like the Federal Communications Commission, the Securities and Exchange Commission, the Department of Agriculture, and so on, all have some power and responsibility to take competition policy into account.

This state of affairs is not inevitable, from the point of view of the US Constitution. Congress obviously could, if it wished, consolidate antitrust enforcement powers in one single agency, whether it chose to use an independent agency like the FTC or an Executive Branch Department like the Department of Justice. A number of distinguished groups have studied this question over the years. At one point, sentiment was high to abolish the FTC altogether and to give both its antitrust and its consumer protection responsibilities to the DOJ. For a variety of reasons, some having to do with the allocation of oversight authority in the Congress, some with other political support for the FTC, that has obviously never happened, and no one speaks too seriously about it any more. In fact, one can argue (along lines similar to those that Karl Meesen advanced about 15 years ago about the virtues of competition between competition laws) that the United States has benefited from the competition between antitrust authorities. Pragmatically, of course, the agencies make it work, but one could easily imagine legislation (for example) giving sole authority for consumer protection and mergers to the FTC, and conferring the rest of the authority to enforce the antitrust laws on the DOJ.

The problem of the relation between the federal competition authority (or authorities, as the case may be) and the sectoral agencies, is one shared by everyone. Which law, and which agency, should have primacy when competition policy itself is threatened by something another regulator wants to do? Perhaps all of us in this room would say that is an easy question to answer: give the competition authority the final word, if one is serious about implementing competition policy in the nation as a whole. But we must admit, in the next breath, that democratic societies are entitled to choose a more complex mix of policies. Some in the US are now arguing that the market imperfections in our healthcare industry are so profound that we should throw in the towel and abandon any effort to apply antitrust laws there. They raise a serious point, even if that solution may be too extreme. Those who wish to assure universal postal service, or telephone service, or internet access, must similarly compromise the unfettered free market model, which predictably would cut out customers who it is not economical to serve. So, when it comes to other regulated industries, the best one can do is probably to insist on two things: first, a formal role for the competition authority to make its views known, and second, absolute transparency of decision-making by the sectoral agency, including an obligation to explain why it has rejected the competitive model in a particular instance.

Matters are even more complex when we turn to federal/state relations. This is something that has within the last year emerged as a potential issue here in Europe, now that the national authorities and the national courts are not only enforcing their domestic competition laws, but are also fully vested with authority to enforce the EC laws. As I understand it, Europe so far is not saddled with an equivalent of the US *Parker v Brown* doctrine, which more or less allows the states to take actions inconsistent with the federal antitrust laws so long as they are clearly displacing competition with regulation and they are actively supervising their own system. But we do have *Parker*, and more fundamentally a system in which the states retain a degree of sovereignty that might surprise anyone who does not follow the subject closely. The important point to remember is that *Parker* itself is a decision in which the Supreme Court interprets the language of the Sherman Act. Without getting too technical, it rests on the fact that the Commerce Clause of the Constitution was interpreted much more narrowly in 1890 than it was by the 1940s, and the Court assumes that Congress just didn't mean to interfere too deeply with state economic regulations. Congress could change that tomorrow, in my opinion, by exercising its power to pre-empt state legislation that is contrary to the federal antitrust laws. It just has not done so. This bit of procedural antitrust 'modernization' would be, in my opinion, a positive development, although in all candour I would be astounded to see it happen.

The third major topic that is largely procedural relates to the fact that there is a criminal element to the US antitrust laws. Indeed, if you were just to read the Sherman Act, you would see that both section 1 and section 2 begin still today with words indicating that they are describing a felony. Over the years, two very important things have happened: first, the Department of Justice has used its powers to prosecute antitrust crimes sparingly, going after only those who are committing hard-core cartel offences; second, the Department for many, many years has refrained altogether from using the criminal authority conferred by section 2. Sceptics can be forgiven for saying that this 'trust us, we'll be responsible' approach is ultimately unsatisfying. It does not seem too much to ask, if we are about the task of antitrust modernization, to amend the laws so that the criminal offences are defined with the precision that the law generally requires, with careful attention paid to which conduct gives rise to criminal liability, which mens rea level is required, and what defences (if any) will be permitted. This is particularly true given the fact that prison sentences for individual offenders are about to take another leap upward, and the corporate fines are equally impressive.

B. *Private enforcement*

Moving on to private enforcement, I will be somewhat more brief, recognizing that this is still far more important in the United States than it is in the UK or elsewhere. Four issues come to my mind that are candidates for any antitrust modernization effort here: first, what kind of link (if any) should exist between public enforcement proceedings and private actions; secondly, what sort of remedies should be available to private parties, either as damages (trebled or otherwise) or as injunctive relief or divestiture when their suit follows a government action; thirdly, what should the role of alternative dispute resolution be for antitrust matters; and finally, have we reached the right system to handle antitrust violations that affect a large number of consumers, given the current rules barring indirect purchaser suits on the one hand, and the rules allowing class actions on the other.

Taking those points in order, it is easy to review what the present law allows. With respect to the linkage between public and private suits, the answer is that there is some relation, but it is loose. There is no requirement that a private party so much as consult with the FTC, or the DOJ, or any state AG, prior to bringing an action, nor frankly would I want to see one. Often, however, private parties come to the agencies and seek their help. They will plead with the agency to take the case on, which from the private party's standpoint means that the problem may be redressed without vast expenditures of private resources. At the appellate level, private parties urge the agencies to file briefs *amicus curiae*, and the agencies sometimes do so, if the Solicitor General of the United States gives his permission. Finally, if the case is a so-called follow-on case, meaning that it is brought after the Government has obtained an adjudication of an antitrust violation, the Clayton Act makes the result in the government action prima facie evidence of the violation in the private case.

I am not aware of significant criticism of anything I've mentioned so far. The point that raises the most concern is the fact that state attorneys general or private parties (who rely on the same statutory authorization to sue in this respect) are entitled to request and obtain certain forms of injunctive relief and even divestiture from a court even after either the FTC or the DOJ has addressed the case and chosen not to take that step. Especially with mergers, this is genuinely troublesome and in need of reform. (I don't see anything either modern or old-fashioned about this problem, by the way; it's just a problem.) The treble damage issue has been discussed so thoroughly that I really have nothing to add.

The most important new development for private actions is the advent of arbitration and other forms of alternative dispute resolution. For many years people thought that antitrust was not a subject matter suitable for arbitration, because of its public law character. But it is a mixture of public and private law in the United States, and the private side prevailed in 1987 in the Supreme Court's decision in *Mitsubishi Motors v Soler Chrysler-Plymouth,* the first case that recognized that at least an international antitrust claim could be arbitrated. Since then, the courts have allowed antitrust claims of all kinds to go to arbitration. So, for example, the Second Circuit last fall enforced an arbitration agreement in a case called *JLM Industries, Inc v Stolt-Nielsen SA,*[2] which involved allegations that the owners of the world's largest ocean carriers of liquid chemical had conspired to fix worldwide freight rates. Just two months ago, the District Court in New York enforced some arbitration agreements in antitrust litigation against a group of major banks, claiming that they had conspired to set the fees for foreign currency conversions.[3] Banks that inserted an arbitration clause into their cardholder agreement *before* the litigation was brought were entitled to a stay for arbitration; those who tried to change to an arbitral system *after* the litigation was brought were unsuccessful. To the extent that ADR is seen as the 'modern' way to go, it might be useful to acknowledge both its role and its limits in legislation dealing with private litigation.

Class actions continue to be an important part of the private enforcement scene in the United States, despite the fact that their numbers decreased radically after *Illinois Brick* spelled the end to indirect purchaser suits under federal law. The *Currency Conversion* case I just mentioned is a class action, and it is easy to find others. As we can see from Congress's recent passage of legislation that will put most multi-state tort class actions in the federal courts, there are certain efficiencies to grouping together the claims of similarly situated people. There are also risks that largely centre around the lawyers' incentives to negotiate huge fees and the problems of ensuring that the rights of all unnamed class members are respected. There is no reason to expect an antitrust-specific 'fix' rules for class actions, even though we have seen specialized legislation of this kind in the securities area.

---

[2] 387 F.3d 163, 2d Cir 2004.
[3] *In re Currency Conversion Fee Antitrust Litigation,* 361 F.Supp.2d 237 (SDNY 2005).

C. *International reach of the laws*

Things are fairly quiet on the international front. Since the Supreme Court decided the *Empagran* case last June, quite a few courts have dismissed antitrust cases that involved parties harmed in other countries on the ground that they could not show that the injuries the plaintiffs suffered were linked to the effects on US commerce that justified coverage of US law in the first place. I see no real need, aside from an aesthetic one, to tinker with the Foreign Trade Antitrust Improvements Act at this point. What would be helpful, however, would be something that increased the flexibility of the International Antitrust Enforcement Assistance Act of 1994, so that the US authorities could enter into case-by-case executive agreements for cooperation with their foreign counterparts, rather than being forced to solve all problems for all time in a framework agreement first, as the law now requires. Other useful measures go far beyond the field of antitrust, and take us into the area of international judicial assistance. To the extent that courts can work efficiently with one another, whether it is for purposes of serving process, collecting evidence, gathering assets, or enforcing judgments, the possibility of international wrongdoers slipping through the cracks will be diminished.

IV. REFORM OF ANTITRUST SUBSTANCE

Let us turn now to the substance of antitrust law. As I mentioned earlier, someone tasked with 'reform' of the law could do anything from cleaning it up to overhauling it to repealing it outright. I shall assume that the group of people who advocate out-and-out repeal is so small that we can disregard them. But there is work that can usefully be done to improve the laws, and it can be done at several levels. First, there is certainly some house-cleaning to be done with regard to the US laws. Secondly, one could imagine undertaking what I shall call linguistic modernization—redrafting laws in a way that preserves their real substance even though it is changing the words. Thirdly, and more controversially, there is the question whether these laws ought to be modified significantly or ditched for particular 'new' areas, such as information technology industries or claims involving intellectual property rights. Finally, accepting the fact that there will be some safety valves and exemptions, we need to look at the question whether we have the right ones.

A. *House-cleaning*

Most of us discover, to our chagrin, that there is always a bit of cleaning up that we can do, whether it is with our competition laws or with something much more mundane. In Europe, after a few years of operating under your new regime, I predict that more people will be asking what the point is of separating out Article 81(1) from Article 81(3), since it is likely that a unified analysis will emerge (even more so than it has done already). For us, it has been unclear for years what real function is performed by section 3 of the Clayton Act, which prohibits various forms of tying and exclusive dealing, or primary-line price discrimination cases under the Robinson-Patman Act. Maybe this is the time to fold them back into the Sherman Act and spare courts the occasional task of trying to figure out if they have any independent force.

B. Linguistic modernization

At a more ambitious level, one might want to bring the language of our principal antitrust statutes into line with the understanding of what those statutes really address. The name 'antitrust' itself is a relic of the past, and the language of the Sherman Act cannot be understood literally by any American lawyer who is not a legal history buff. What are 'contracts, combinations, and conspiracies in restraint of trade' anyway? Why is the word 'competition' missing from the statute altogether (it does not make its entrance until the Clayton Act, 24 years later). Why does section 2 of the Sherman Act also cover 'conspiracies' to monopolize, and why aren't agreements like that already banned by section 1? These questions may make nice law school examination problems, but it would be preferable to eliminate them if the opportunity to do so is really at hand.

The real trick is to draft the language that would capture what we are doing in a way that did not inadvertently change something that we want to preserve. Section 1 would have to indicate that there is a criminal and a civil component; that a prerequisite to liability is an agreement, which can be explicit or implicit, but which must go beyond conscious parallelism; and, most problematically, it must indicate which agreements are illegal. This would be an opportunity to set forth what the per se rule covers, and what it means to be under that regime: for example, a plaintiff can win without proving market power, and the defendant is precluded from raising certain kinds of justifications in defence. Our fearless drafter could also spell out how the rule of reason works for the cases that do not qualify for per se treatment. In the section 2 area, it would raise the challenge of describing somehow which actions undertaken by a firm with some designated degree of market power should be branded 'exclusionary,' and which ones are good old-fashioned competition. In the merger area, it would be a chance to say something explicit about the distinction we routinely draw among horizontal mergers, vertical mergers, and conglomerate mergers, and it would be a chance to give somewhat greater legal force to the Merger Guidelines that the agencies issue from time to time.

Doing all of this in a way that simply reflects current law and does not change it would be difficult, but maybe it is not impossible. The benefits going forward would not only be greater clarity for anyone subject to the laws; they would also pave the way to more seamless cooperation and coordination with countries around the world who have newer laws that reflect most of these concepts more directly.

C. New technology areas

What about more fundamental change in the law for industries that arguably are *different* from the ones that existed when the antitrust laws were first written? I am not one who believes that the antitrust laws need to make special provision for firms operating in some of today's fast-moving industries, such as information technology. Nor do I think that intellectual property rights are somehow sacrosanct and should be treated more deferentially than ordinary property rights. I feel a bit like the late actor John Houseman (known to generations of American law students as the person who played the dreaded law professor Kingsfield in first the movie and then the TV series *The Paper Chase*) in his ads touting the former brokerage house Smith Barney. He would look earnestly into the camera and say: 'Smith Barney. They make their money the old-fashioned way. They *earn* it.' The antitrust laws have also proven themselves over time, and they have earned their place in the statute books. Even though the answers one gets about market power, likelihood of future exclusion, consumer harm, and the like will certainly be affected by the special characteristics of the IT market, or of IPRs, the *questions* and the analytical structure are still sound.

We may be hearing from the Supreme Court on this subject, if it decides to grant *certiorari* to the Federal Circuit in the case of *Independent Ink, Inc v Illinois Tool Works, Inc.*[4] In that case, the Federal Circuit held that no affirmative showing of market power is required to establish a prima facie Sherman Act tying claim based on a patent; the necessary market power is rebuttably presumed where the tying product is patented. One never knows, of course, but even if the Court decides to let this one pass, the Federal Circuit's decision is a reminder that the idea that IPRs are *sui generis* is still alive and well.

---

[4] 396 F.3d 1342 (Fed Cir 2005).

D. *Safety valves and exemptions*

Last, we can touch very briefly on safety valves and exemptions. I will not discuss the implicit exemptions from other regulatory regimes, because we have already touched on that, nor will I say anything else about de facto exemptions granted by state law because of *Parker v Brown*. That leaves only a few others: the exemption for joint activities to petition government, which is protected by our *Noerr–Pennington* doctrine; the exemption for actions whose effects are felt entirely outside the territory of the United States, also known as the export cartel exemption; and various industry-specific exemptions such as the ones for the insurance industry (which we regulate principally at the state level), agricultural cooperatives, soft-drink bottlers and, most recently, medical residents who have graduated from medical school but who are still receiving mandatory training. The petitioning exemption has strong First Amendment overtones for us, and thus is probably untouchable, despite the fact that the most durable restrictions on competition tend to come from governments. The solution to that problem is not to put a gag order on petitioners; it is to make sure that effective competition advocacy takes place both in legislatures and before regulatory agencies. The export cartel exemption ought to go, even though I believe that its harms are more symbolic than real. Finally, there is little positive that one can say about the industry-specific exemptions except that they are undoubtedly not the only legislation that would not pass a strict test of economic efficiency.

V. CONCLUSION

Like this afternoon's speakers, I too see plenty of work one could usefully do to improve the US antitrust laws. Some of it is true modernization, bringing the vocabulary up to date and making clear that the laws indeed do apply to the newer industries. Some of it is house-cleaning, getting rid of statutory provisions that have out-lived their usefulness. Procedural reform that would make the application of the laws more predictable, transparent, and fair is worth undertaking. But most of the task is in the nature of 'historic preservation'. The antitrust laws in the United States have served us well. The fact that more than 100 countries around the world have also chosen to have competition laws is telling. Imitation is the most sincere form of flattery, and there are many who have thought this model worth emulating. I hope, therefore, that our version of antitrust modernization will both do something useful, but at the same time will not leave us with a monstrosity like Soldier Field, neither fish nor fowl, neither modern nor classical, but a hodge-podge of everything. Like most of us here, I shall watch from the sidelines with interest.

Panel 5—Monopolization/Abuse: Towards Effects-Based Tests

PHILIP MARSDEN

I am very pleased to be launching the second day of our conference with a topic which I personally view as extremely important. To those of you with a North American accent, you may be saying 'Well, why are we saying *towards* effects-based tests?' But of course we are going through a review and a reconsideration of Article 82 here in Europe and it is a reasonably controversial subject. I am very pleased that one of the members of our organizing committee, Dr Helen Jenkins from Oxera, is chairing this panel today on this subject and she is also presenting a paper with us to the Bundeskartellamt in Bonn next week where we will be talking with them about the links between dominance and effects and questioning whether certain assumptions should be made and whether we can move towards some form of more structured consideration of effects-based tests, but not something that is as categorical or as per se as seems to be in the current case law. So it is obviously a very topical issue and I am very pleased that we have got such an interesting comparative panel here; so Helen, thank you very much for chairing this panel and over to you.

HELEN JENKINS

With this morning's first session we focus on what I think is a clear opportunity to exploit the main theme of the conference. That is the Trans-Atlantic Antitrust Dialogue. Here we are going to be looking at abuse of dominance and as Philip has just said obviously here in Europe we are particularly interested in this in the context of the reform of Article 82 being high on the European competition policy agenda. We are very fortunate to have a panel that brings with us some very interesting perspectives with two senior economists from the other side of the Atlantic, with lots of experience of applying dominance jurisprudence and law in a different context with a more effects-based focus and also a lawyer trained in the US, but having practised in Europe for 20 years, to bring a comparative approach across the two in terms of specific cases.

The key area for discussion is to examine the links between the holding of dominance and the effects, anticompetitive or otherwise, of the actions that a firm will take in that marketplace in which they are allegedly dominant. This translates into a question for practitioners of the balance between form-based, or per se, rules and more effects-based tests. Where dominance is used as a shortcut to infer anticompetitive effects, which is really an economic interpretation, we have drawn the analogy with a view of a dominant firm as a bull in a china shop. So a dominant firm must be very careful not to damage its already fragile surroundings and in that view of the way markets work you have a law that looks to enforce the fragile competition that is currently there. This view of market power and the effects of the practice gauged by those who hold it may need revisiting. It is that that the debate we are currently having here in Europe seeks to pursue. Economic theory and practical experience have shown that competitive dynamics can exist even in the presence of large firms and that certain behaviour may be welfare-enhancing, even if it is practised by a dominant firm. So while as we have heard throughout the last day of this conference there is an attraction to, and a need for, certainty in the legal framework, and there must be a reliance on agreed approaches and precedent, this must be balanced against considering what the purpose of this law is, and balanced against the possibility of undertaking more of a detailed assessment of the effects of the different practices.

So we continue this debate here in Europe with the aim of moving towards guidelines that we may hope to achieve, as was suggested through the panel of judges yesterday, with perhaps economists being able to give some indication of necessary and or sufficient tests to look at abuse of dominance. As part of that process, I would now like to ask Greg Werden, Senior Economic Counsel at the DOJ, to open the debate here this morning. Greg has spent many years improving the way economics is used in antitrust investigations and we welcome his perspective this morning from US cases and from economic theory on how actually to move towards a sort of 'test approach' to assessing the anticompetitive effects of dominant firms' activities.

GREG WERDEN

I begin with a few basic precepts of US competition policy on single-firm conduct. You will recognize that not all of these are widely accepted on this side of the Atlantic. But while there is meaningful divergence on some of these points, there is significant convergence on most of them.

First, the goal is to protect the competitive process. Our courts say this quite a bit, although it is often unclear whether they have a firm grasp on what this means. But as expressed by our Supreme Court, the purpose of antitrust law is 'not to protect businesses from the working of the market; it is to protect the public from the failure of the market. The law directs itself not against conduct which is competitive, even severely so, but against conduct which unfairly tends to destroy competition itself.'[1] Distinguishing between these two can be difficult, but the idea is reasonably straightforward. The goal is to protect the process, not the individual competitor, and we allow aggressive competition because that is what the process is all about. Indeed, competition that harms less efficient competitors 'is precisely the sort of competition that promotes the consumer interests that the Sherman Act aims to foster'.[2]

Secondly, when enforcing the law against single-firm conduct, we must take pains to avoid attaching liability to aggressive competitive conduct that harms competitors but is consistent with the goal of maintaining vigorous competition. As the Supreme Court reasoned in its most recent decision under section 2 of the Sherman Act:

> Against the . . . benefits of the antitrust intervention . . . , we must weigh a realistic assessment of its costs. . . . Mistaken inferences and resulting false condemnations are especially costly, because they chill the very conduct that the antitrust laws are designed to protect. . . . The cost of false positives counsels against an undue expansion of liability' for single-firm conduct.[3]

This was not just an idle remark, but rather an important motivating force in the decision. The court found no liability for conduct that may very well have had a significant adverse affect on a competitor, because the Court found that this was not the kind of conduct condemned by the Sherman Act.

Third, quite unlike the present state of the law in the European Union, in the United States no special responsibility is imposed upon a monopolist. As Judge Posner wrote: 'A monopolist, no less than any other competitor, is permitted and indeed encouraged to compete aggressively on the merits.'[4] And as one of our great judges wrote more than half a century ago: 'The successful competitor, having been urged to compete, must not be turned upon when he wins.'[5] The idea is important and fundamental: We want competitors to have the incentive to take risks and to make innovations. To have that incentive, they have to be able to reap the rewards. And if they are going to be hamstrung as soon as they are successful, they will not have the proper incentives.

---

[1] *Spectrum Sports, Inc v McQuillan*, 506 US 447, 458 (1993).

[2] *Copperweld Corp v Independence Tube Corp* 467 US 752, 775 (1984).

[3] *Verizon Communications Inc v Law Offices of Curtis V Trinko*, 540 US 398, 414 (2004).

[4] *Olympia Equipment Leasing Co v Western Union Telegraph Co* 797 F.2d 370, 375 (7th Cir 1986).

[5] *United States v Aluminum Co of America*, 148 F.2d 416, 430 (2d Cir 1945).

To distinguish unlawful exclusionary conduct from lawful aggressive competition on the merits, the US Department of Justice has advocated the 'no economic sense' test. This test was urged on the Supreme Court in our brief on the merits in *Trinko*,[6] which was signed by the two US enforcement agencies and filed by the Solicitor General who represents the United States before the Supreme Court. The test holds that conduct is not exclusionary unless it would make no economic sense to the defendant but for the tendency to eliminate or lessen competition. In *Trinko* the test was only advocated for the one class of conduct in front of the Court at that time, but the Department of Justice has advocated the exact same test in all of its section 2 cases over the past decade.

In *Microsoft*,[7] with which you are all familiar, the Department contended that conduct protecting the defendant's operating system monopoly was exclusionary because it would not make economic sense unless it eliminated competition. This is basically the standard that Judge Jackson applied in the district court in finding Microsoft liable under section 2 of the Sherman Act. In *American Airlines*,[8] we contended unsuccessfully that the defendant drove out rivals by adding money-losing capacity and that distinguishing legitimate competition from unlawful predation requires a common sense business inquiry: whether the conduct will be profitable apart from any exclusionary effects. While rejecting our claim, the Court of Appeals did not reject our test; rather, it found that our evidence did not show that the conduct was exclusionary under our own test.

Most recently in *Dentsply*,[9] the Department argued that the defendant's policies of not using dealers that distributed products of rivals made no economic sense but for the tendency to harm rivals, because the policies cost the defendant something but produced no possible benefit other than reducing competition. The defendant argued that the conduct had efficiency benefits. The District Court, however, rejected those arguments, finding that the policies neither achieved efficiencies nor was intended to do so. After making that finding, the District Court oddly rejected our claim. The Court of Appeals has now reversed that, finding that the conduct did have exclusionary effects.

I turn now to the application of the 'no economic sense' test, and I first want to stress that the test may not be controlling for a number of reasons. Some conduct, for example, aggressive above-cost pricing and new product

---

[6] *Verizon Communications Inc v Law Offices of Curtis V Trinko, LLP*, 540 US 398 (2004).
[7] *United States v Microsoft Corp* 253 F.3d 34 (DC Cir 2001).
[8] *United States v AMR Corp* 335 F.3d 1109 (10th Cir 2003).
[9] *United States v Dentsply International, Inc* 399 F.3d 181 (3d Cir 2005).

introductions, is deemed lawful competition on the merits under US law without any enquiry into its actual effects. Such conduct falls into categories of per se legality, which I call 'prudential safe harbours'. The courts have recognized such conduct is 'almost always' good for consumers, and they do not enquire further on a case-by-case basis to see whether a particular product introduction might be bad, but rather decline to condemn any of them. It is also possible that some other test might be preferred in a particular case because the 'no economic sense' test may turn out to be difficult to apply.

The 'no economic sense' test is applied as of the time the challenged conduct was undertaken, although in some cases there may be more than one such time. And what matters are objective economic considerations at that time. Businessmen make mistakes, and they should not be penalized for those mistakes a second time through the antitrust laws. What they happen to be thinking also is not important under US antitrust law; it is what they do that matters, and that normally can be assessed through a factual enquiry and some economic analysis.

It has often been argued that the 'no economic sense' test cannot possibly work for conduct that costs little to undertake, but this is a misconception of what the test is about. US courts have on occasion referred to 'profit sacrifice' as a test for exclusionary conduct. The 'no economic sense' test is similar to a sacrifice test, but it is not the same, and it does not require anything recognizable as a sacrifice. If there could be such a thing as cost-less exclusion, even that could be dealt with satisfactorily by the 'no economic sense' test, because conduct is exclusionary under the 'no economic sense' test if it can confer no economic benefit other than by eliminating competition.

Short-run sacrifice of profits is also insufficient to make conduct exclusionary under the 'no economic sense' test. Pro-competitive, efficient conduct often entails a short-run sacrifice. Whenever a firm makes an investment, it is giving up profit today in order to get more profit later, and that obviously is not enough to make the conduct exclusionary. Short-term profit sacrifice is insufficient for conduct exclusionary under the 'no economic sense' test, which also asks why it is rational to make the sacrifice. If it is rational for the normal sort of investment reasons, the conduct is not exclusionary, but if it is rational because the conduct excludes competition, the conduct is exclusionary.

Short-run sacrifice also is unnecessary for conduct to be exclusionary under the 'no economic sense' test. When a firm already is dominant and engages in conduct designed to protect its dominant position, it is possible that that conduct achieves its exclusionary effect immediately and therefore does not sacrifice current profit for greater future profit. But short-term profit sacrifice is unnecessary for conduct to be exclusionary under the 'no economic sense' test, which instead asks why the challenged conduct is profitable. If it is profitable only because it maintains the dominant position by hampering the ability of competitors to grow, it is exclusionary. Of course, conduct that protects a dominant position may not achieve its exclusionary effect immediately. Microsoft determined that it was important to do something about emerging competitive threats before they became serious, so the effects of its exclusionary conduct were neither immediate nor definite. It is impossible to have known, and we did not know, what competition eventually would have emerged if Microsoft had not engaged in the exclusionary conduct. But the Court was able to find that the conduct made sense to Microsoft only because it would forestall these nascent competitive threats that might eventually erode Microsoft's dominant position.

We at the Department of Justice find the 'no economic sense' test extremely useful for identifying exclusionary conduct. Used judiciously, it can be the principal tool, if not the exclusive tool, for that purpose. We have used the test primarily to explain why conduct we were attacking was exclusionary. As formulated, however, the test is a necessary condition, which can be used by a defendant to explain why challenged conduct is not exclusionary. That, of course, is a major application of the test, as in *Trinko*, the case in which the Solicitor General advocated the test.

Helen Jenkins

Thanks very much Greg. Now I would like to invite Adriaan Ten Kate who is a European economist who is now a Mexican citizen and has been active in the Federal Competition Commission in Mexico for many years. He is going to bring a particular perspective that comes from a jurisdiction that has been balancing these issues for many years since the early 1990s and to look at the experience they have had and the sorts of tests they use to help inform how perhaps here in Europe we might think about reforming our approach.

Adriaan Ten Kate

Thank you very much. I am going to give you some perspective from Mexico on the Trans-Atlantic Antitrust Dialogue and I want to organize my presentation as follows. First I would like to say something about the Federal Law on Economic Competition in Mexico. Then I want to treat a specific monopolization case. Thirdly, I want make some reflections about form versus effects-based approaches and finally offer you some conclusions.

The Federal Law on Economic Competition in Mexico was enacted in December 1992. The Federal Competition Commission in charge of enforcing the law was created in June 1993 and the objective of the law is to protect competition by the prevention and elimination of monopolies, monopolistic practices, and other restrictions to an efficient functioning of markets. That is, this law distinguishes between two kinds of monopolistic practices: the absolute and the relative ones. *Absolute practices* are hardcore cartel behaviour, bid-rigging, and they are prohibited per se. *Relative monopolistic practices* cover both vertical agreements and unilateral conduct and are assessed under a rule of reason. So by way of comparison with the US, the Sherman Act distinguishes between agreements between two or more economic agents in section 1 and unilateral conduct in section 2. Under the development of US case law, some agreements, the horizontal ones, are prohibited per se, and the other ones, vertical agreements, under the rule of reason, much like the way in which monopolization cases under section 2 are assessed. In Mexico's competition law, we did not follow the distinction between section 1 and section 2 of the Sherman Act, but rather the US case law established division between per se and rule of reason; the absolute practices are per se prohibited and the relative ones are treated under a rule of reason.

Unilateral conduct, which is the subject matter of this panel, under Mexican law only two of them are mentioned explicitly, which is bundling (or tying) and refusals to deal; but apart from that there is a catch-all provision which defines any act that unduly harms competition and these are usually interpreted so as to mean predatory pricing, price discrimination, cross-subsidization and raising rivals' costs and indeed in the Code of Regulation that was issued 1998 this catch-all provision was spelt out further, so as to mean these four types of conducts. The rule of reason under Mexican law comprises two things. One is a market power test. The economic agent that engages in some conduct under the law must have market power for the conduct to be illegal. In the second place there is a test for undue displacement or exclusion of competitors from the market. Particularly the word 'undue' recognizes that displacement on certain occasions may be justified and opens the door for considering pro-competitive effects and indeed those who designed the law in the early 1990s had clearly in mind that much of the relative monopolistic practices, in spite of their apparently anticompetitive nature, may have important pro-competitive effects that should be taken into account in their assessment. So, altogether, one might say that Mexican competition policy started off with a clearly effects-based approach.

I would like to confine myself to a predatory pricing case in the chewing-gum market. The complainant was a fully-owned Mexican company,

Canels, and the defendant was Adams, a subsidiary of Warner Lambert Company. It was about predatory pricing in the chewing-gum market; but the chewing-gum market in Mexico can be split up in two parts: a formal part which stands for sales in supermarkets and similar stores and an informal part of the market which is basically sales by street vendors and very small shops. Adams, the multinational company, happened to be dominant in the formal segment of the market, but Canels, the Mexican company, was rather dominant in the informal segment and Canels was the one that was complaining about the fact that Adams had launched a fighting brand in the informal segment of the market. The Competition Commission held that the relevant market was that for chewing-gum and they did not make the divide between the formal and the informal segments even though the prices in the formal segment almost tripled those of the informal segment. Adams was found to have a market share close to 70 per cent, but that was basically a consequence of the fact that the share was measured in value terms, not in volume terms. Because Adams was present in the higher priced part of the market, evidently that contributed to this 70 per cent. If they would have measured shares in volume it would have rather have been 50/50 more or less. Now, on the basis of the 70 per cent Adams was found to have market power. As far as the conduct is concerned, the Commission handled a price below total cost test, which seems to be very strict and nothing like the Areeda-Turner variable cost test.

So the Commission came to a positive finding; but strangely enough it did not find any evidence for displacement of Canels from the market. So in an original decision the Commission absolved Adams from predatory pricing but it issued a warning against the company that if it should keep behaving the way it did until now the Commission might at any time open an ex officio investigation to follow up the case. Adams didn't like the outcome because they wondered, if they didn't do anything wrong, why were they being warned; but anyway they came away with it, so that was it for the time being. But a couple of months later that warning became true and the Commission opened an ex officio investigation in April 1996 which was practically a replica of the original investigation and, with a finding of market power, the relevant market was exactly defined in the same way as before. The only thing that changed was that the investigation period was moved up for a couple of years and that was sufficient to find that Canels was to a certain extent displaced from the market. That was the missing link in the former part of the investigation. So Warner Lambert Company was found guilty in November 1997 and they were fined accordingly.

Obviously they protested. There was general indignation on several points. First of all, the definition of the relevant market was criticized and it should be broader than just chewing-gum. There were also arguments that the informal and the formal parts should be separated and the market power finding was also criticized because Canels was the one that was stronger in the informal part of the market; obviously they didn't like the total cost test, and argued that it should be average variable cost. Finally, the Commission did not apply any recoupment test. The fact that the Commission did not consider recoupment in this investigation was criticized very heavily by the OECD and on various occasions the OECD has recommended the Mexican Competition Commission to introduce such a test in their assessment of predatory pricing. Still the decision was upheld in May 1998.

But already from the beginning of the ex officio investigation—that was in June 1996—Warner Lambert Company filed a constitutional appeal, not so much against the case but against the competition law, arguing that concepts like relevant market, market power and the catch-all provision of Article 10 were too vague to provide any legal certainty to the economic agents and the outcomes of the investigations would be very unpredictable and the discretion of the competition authority too large. Now this constitutional appeal went up all the way from the lower courts to the Supreme Court and only a year ago in March 2004 the Supreme Court decided that there was no problem with relevant market definition in the law, there was no problem with substantial market power concept, but that the catch-all provision of Article 10 was indeed too vague and it was declared unconstitutional. The Commission is now left without any powers to do something about predatory pricing and discriminatory conduct. One might wonder how that is possible because if you compare it with US competition law and European competition law the catch-all provision of Article 10 is not much vaguer than let's say section 1 of the Sherman Act or Article 81 of the EC Treaty. But you should bear in mind that in Mexico we have a civil law system in which things are expected to be spelt out much further than under a common law system.

Finally, some reflections about form versus effects-based systems. It is often argued that in the EU competition law enforcement is form-based while in the US it is effects-based, which roughly coincides with the distinction between per se and the rule of reason. I believe it is not so simple and much depends on how precisely you fill in form-based and how you fill in effects-based. How do you measure effects? What thresholds are used? So maybe even form-based and the effects-based systems may be very close to each other. The distinction is not so fundamental. Anyway, that was also mentioned yesterday. Form-based approaches usually give more legal certainty, are easier to administer and tend to be more interventionist, at least to the extent that a form-based approach ignores pro-competitive effects of behaviour that in an effects-based approach would otherwise be taken into account. On the other hand, effects-based approaches have also their disadvantages. One of them is that it is very difficult to measure the effects. To measure anticompetitive effects is not even that difficult, but pro-competitive effects are much more difficult and that is seldom commented on, but to estimate pro-competitive effects one should know what would happen without the conduct. If you want to measure the effects of the conduct, then you should know the counterfactuals and that is not at all easy. Usually you can make assumptions about it, but playing around with the counterfactuals may make practically everything possible. Not only changes in magnitude of the effects but even the sign may depend on it.

So what we see in Mexico is basically that it is not exactly a form-based approach. It is rather what I would like to call a form-plus approach, which is essentially form-based, but complemented with a market power test. The market power serves as a proxy for the anticompetitive effects. If there is no market power then these anticompetitive effects are supposed to be small. But as such it misses the pro-competitive effects of behaviour and tends to become interventionist. Now Mexico's competition enforcement, even though in the beginning it started off as an effects-based approach, has become with time rather form-plus with little attention for efficiencies and rather interventionist. Now some people consider this a deplorable state of affairs and others even consider it a betrayal of the cause of those who designed the competition law in the early 1990s. But from my point of view, it is quite understandable and this is for several reasons.

One is that in recently installed competition agencies in developing countries there is usually a great pressure upon those agencies to intervene. There are lots of perceived violations of the competition law. Monopolies: these are very bad people. The big is bad paradigm is still very strong. So people simply expect competition agencies to do something about it. Then coming up with all sorts of arguments that are of an economic nature and are not always understood well by the public at large is sometimes seen as a weakness of a competition authority.

So I would like to conclude this presentation with the observation that our Competition Commission does what can be done, not what should be done but is impossible to do. I am afraid that many competition authorities in developing countries and transition economies will follow more or less the same way.

HELEN JENKINS

Thank you very much Adriaan. So we have had two thought-provoking presentations so far, the first illustrating the different approach that is used in the US and the second showing the difficulties in tensions that exist when trying to use an effects-based test, which was very informative. So I would finally like to ask David Hull from Covington and Burling to strike a comparative note, and a practitioner's note, with twenty years of experience of working in the European jurisdiction. He will be reflecting on how the assessment of tying practices may differ across different jurisdictions.

DAVID HULL

Thank you, Helen. I must admit that I am particularly delighted to be speaking here in the Law Society because, though you may not be able to tell it from my posh accent, I am actually a proud member of the Law Society. Several years ago, I sat for the Bar, and now I'm a solicitor. For those in the audience who often confuse solicitors and barristers, let me just clear up a misconception that many of my friends seem to have: it is barristers who wear wigs, so, though some contend that I could use one, I did not become a solicitor so that I could wear a wig.

As the only lawyer, I find myself out-numbered on this panel. I was in the same position last night at dinner. At my table, there were two economists and myself. I don't know how I allowed it to happen, but the conversation went straight down the very dangerous path of comparing how lawyers and economists think. The word that was used, I think, by one of my dinner companions to describe a lawyer's way of thinking was something like 'mush' because we lack the sharp analytical tools that are available to economists. In an attempt to get some measure of credibility, I said that, before I received my law degree, I read for a degree in economics as an undergraduate. Then one of them proceeded to tell me that there was a study done about people like me who had undergraduate degrees in economics and that, one year out from school, you still could think like an economist, but that, unless you worked as an economist, the study showed that you were back thinking like a normal person (ie someone who is not an economist) again by the time you had been out of school five years. I could only confirm that that is probably true because, when I started practising EU competition law in Brussels about twenty years ago, I actually knew something about economics, but unfortunately economics wasn't in vogue at the time. By the 1990s, when economics came into vogue in EU competition analysis, I had forgotten everything. They then explained to me why it is that the lawyer's way of looking at things is not particularly useful because all we do is compare and distinguish cases. At that point, my heart really sank because that is what I intend to do this morning; so I am afraid the economists in the group may not find my presentation very interesting.

In this context of discussing forms versus effects-based tests, what I want to do is to focus on one practice under Article 82: tying. It is a bit daunting to be talking about tying because there has been so much written about tying in recent years, particularly in the context of the *Microsoft* case,[10] which is a case I would like to use to illustrate my point. I don't want to get into the merits of the case, but simply want to use it for the purpose of comparing the approaches to tying in the US and the EU. The *Microsoft* case is a good case for such a comparison because the fact pattern was very similar in the US case and in the EU case. For those of you who have been on sabbatical for the last few years, let me just remind you that, in the US case, the tying product was the Windows Operating System and the tied product was Internet Explorer, whereas, in the EU case, the tying product was again the Windows Operating System and the tied product was Windows Media Player. Immediately after it issued the *Microsoft* decision, the Commission issued a set of questions and answers about its decision and it went out of its way to say that it had followed the rule-of-reason approach, the same test that the US Court of Appeals had used in the US *Microsoft* case.[11] I want to examine this statement and see if, in fact, it is true or not.

Let me first apologise for having four bullet points on this slide. A friend of mine from the McKinsey consulting firm—who are generally the smartest people in the room, maybe even smarter than the economists—told me that the cardinal rule for all McKinsey consultants is that you never put more than three bullet points on a slide because a normal person—that is, someone who is not a McKinsey consultant or an economist—can only remember three bullet points at a time. Thus, I will leave this slide up here a little longer for the lawyers in the audience.

The US per se test has four criteria:

(1) *The tying and tied products must be two separate products.* To determine whether this test is met, you must determine whether there is a consumer demand for the tied product separately. Do consumers purchase web browsers separately from the operating system? If the answer to that is 'yes', you have two separate products.

(2) *The seller must have market power in the market for the tying product.* Microsoft had market power in operating systems.

(3) *The seller gives consumers no choice but to take the tied product from it.* You can go into a lot of detail about whether a product is tied or not, but the basic idea is, if Internet Explorer is offered free with the Windows Operating System, no one is going to go out and purchase a separate web browser.

(4) *The tying arrangement forecloses competition in the tied product market.*

---

[10] Commission decision of 24 Mar 2004, COMP/37.792. *Microsoft Corp v Commission* (Case T-201/04 R) [2005] 4 CMLR 18 (CFI).   [11] *Microsoft* (n 7).

If you can show that all four of these criteria are met, you have an abuse. As most of you know, in the US version of the Microsoft case, the US Court of Appeals said, 'Well wait a minute. We don't think the per se test works for platform software because we don't have enough experience with the kinds of efficiencies generated by platform software'. The Court of Appeals was particularly concerned about whether the separate products test worked in the context of this case. That test works as a proxy for measuring efficiencies—it is a shorthand way to measure efficiencies. The obvious problem with tying is that it prevents the consumer from choosing to buy a product other than the tied product. As a practical matter, he is compelled to buy the two products together. But, in many instances, if there are no separate products, there is no demand for the products separately, which is another way of saying that the consumer finds the efficiencies generated by the tying outweigh the loss of choice.

The efficiencies you generally hear about are lower transaction costs—that is, the consumer doesn't have to go out and purchase two separate products. If you ask the man on the street why he likes Windows, he will say 'Because everything is all in one package and you don't have to go and buy different functionalities'. That is the transaction cost. Another efficiency consists of the lower distribution costs of not having to maintain two different distribution channels. The Court of Appeals said: 'In this case, there are some other efficiencies, and we are not sure that the separate products test takes these into account. We don't know if the customers really take this into account'. There is something called 'economies of scope' which means you can use the same line of software code in the programme for different functions and don't have to keep on repeating it. Tying is more efficient for software developers who can count on the fact that the web browser functionality is already in the operating system, which means that they don't have to spend time writing the code for that functionality when they are writing their own applications. They can just focus on the applications they are best at writing.

The Court of Appeals concluded that it didn't know enough about platform software to determine if the per se test, and particularly the separate products prong of that test, captures the efficiencies generated by tying, so it chose to use a rule of reason test. The rule of reason test basically says that the plaintiff must first show that the conduct had an anticompetitive effect. If the plaintiff succeeds, the burden shifts over to the defendant to show the pro-competitive effects. If the defendant is successful in doing so, the burden shifts back to the plaintiff who must either rebut the pro-competitive justification or show that the anticompetitive effects outweigh the pro-competitive benefits.

The European Commission has stated that it used this same rule of reason test in the *Microsoft* decision. Let's see if that's true.

At the outset, I would emphasize that the test used in the *Microsoft* case is one developed by the Commission. The European Courts in Luxembourg really never set out a clear test in tying cases. There is very little case law in the EU on tying. In the main tying cases—*Hilti*[12] and *TetraPak*[13]—the ECJ focused on the issues presented and didn't set out a well-rounded test.

As you can see, the Commission's test is virtually identical to the US per se test. The only real difference is that the Commission's test has a fifth criterion: no objective justification. When it set out the test for tying in the *Microsoft* decision, the Commission didn't include this fifth criterion of objective justification, although *Microsoft* pleaded the objective justifications and the Commission's decision discussed these justifications, but it wasn't really part of the Commission's formal statement of its test. If the Commission is saying that it follows the same rule of reason test as the US, if you actually take the Commission's formal statement of its test, it doesn't include this fifth element. It is only via this fifth element that you could have a rule of reason test because, without it, it is just like the per se test.

As most of you know, possible objective justifications are generally considered in Article 82 cases. Thus, whether or not the Commission includes objective justifications in its formal statement of its test, this is part of the test that is applied in practice.

So the question remains of whether the inclusion of an analysis of objective justifications makes the EU test the same as the US rule of reason test? In the case law, when the Commission and the European Courts discuss objective justifications in Article 82 cases, they typically give them fairly short shrift. What you find is that there is a very heavy burden on the dominant firm. First, the dominant firm has to show that tying is indispensable for the realization of the pro-competitive effects and, second, it has to show that the benefits outweigh any harm to competition. Which leads me to conclude that, yes, the EU courts and the Commission do take into account efficiencies in the sense that they look at efficiencies in the context of objective justification, but the burden is much higher on the defendant in the EU system than it is under the US rule of reason test. Thus, as a practical matter, it seems that currently the EU test as it is used in practice resembles the US per se test more than the rule of reason test. The lesson I draw from this in the context of the Commission's plan to issue guidelines on Article

---

[12] *Hilti v Commission* (Case T-30/89) [1991] ECR II-1439, [1992] 4 CMLR 16.
[13] *TetraPak International SA v Commission* (Case C333/94 P) [1996] ECR I5951.

82, and an area where it has really got to focus its efforts, is on fleshing out this aspect of objective justifications. It must think through where the burden of proof should be and also outline in some detail what is meant by 'objective justifications'.

HELEN JENKINS

Thanks very much David. I think now what we might do is take three or four comments or questions from the audience and then ask the panel to comment on those issues that are raised.

VAL KORAH

I have great difficulty in understanding the idea of tying in *Microsoft*. We start with the traditional objection that you are extending your market power from the tying product to the tied product. But the Commission was much more worried about extending the market power in the tying product, in the Operating System for Windows. So it didn't seem to me like a classical case of tying. I realize that there are a lot of answers to the traditional view but calling it tying gave the Commission the advantage that they could use *Hilti* and *Tetra Pack* too to make it easier for them to prove an abuse. They might also have thought of using the *Telemarketing* case,[14] but they didn't. It didn't seem to me that this was at all like tying. It was a question of the indirect network effect, which goes the other way. Just to call it tying so you can take advantage of some precedents seems to me deceptive.

JOHN VICKERS

A question to Greg, seeking clarification on the following point: in your presentation you spoke about the no economic sense test as a principal tool, or the principal tool, and some of your remarks made me think that in some circumstances the test could, in one bound, properly applied, yield the answer of whether a certain conduct was on the right or the wrong side of the line? But in your paper, especially around page 13, it seems to be part two of a two-part test where the first part has to do with whether the behaviour has a tendency to eliminate competition.

So the first part of my question is, is it indeed the second part of a two-part test, or does it get you there in one go sometimes? If it is the second part of a two-part test, what is the standard that tells us whether the first part of the test is met? Is there an independent standard of what is anticompetitive?

---

[14] *CBEM v CLT and IPB* (Case 311/84) [1985] ECR 3261, [1986] 2 CMLR 558.

Is it sort of obvious sometimes, as when 100 per cent market share is created, let's say? Clarification of that would be great.

My second point, if I may, is that some have criticized the test because of the word 'no'. What about situations where some conduct might make a little bit of economic sense? It appears overwhelmingly to be anticompetitive in some other wider, perhaps intent-related, sense.

GREG WERDEN

My formulation of the test used the word 'unless' because the test was designed for application to conduct that did have a tendency to lessen competition. In *Trinko* and many other cases, that was not at issue, but it can be, as it was in *Dentsply*.[15] So, technically the test as I articulated it is really a second part of a two-part test.

What is the first part? One way to think about this first part is that it asks whether the conduct has real marketplace impact. This enquiry distinguishes between effects on competition and effects on competitors; an effect on a competitor plainly is not enough to establish an anticompetitive effect. In addition, the marketplace impact has to be of the sort that could make a significant contribution to creating or maintaining monopoly power. That may be a low threshold, and the hard thinking is not usually associated with the first part of the test, which is usually quite transparent, although it can be tricky.

Your final question asks about the case in which a practice might make a little economic sense, and my answer is that that is enough to conclude that the practice is not exclusionary. 'No economic sense' is exactly the test that we mean to have. If conduct only makes a little economic sense, one might then ask whether the real reason for it was to exclude competition. That is exactly the sort of exercise the 'no economic sense' test is intended to avoid. If the legitimate benefits from the conduct might have been the reason for undertaking the conduct, that is enough.

I also have a comment about the US *Microsoft* case. We, in effect, had two tying theories. The principal theory, which related to practices we called 'tying' as well as to practices we did not call 'tying', is that those practices helped maintain Microsoft's operating system monopoly. This was not a traditional tying theory, and the District Court was confused by it. The District Court took the only tying theory to be the one relating to the impact of the conduct in the browser market. We did not do as well in establishing an anticompetitive effect in that market, but that ultimately did

[15] *Dentsply* (n 9).

not matter. In the Court of Appeals we concentrated on effects in the operating system market, and we did not address those effects under the label of 'tying'. The principal tying theory in our *Microsoft* case was unorthodox, with no precedent in our case law, so the tying case law was not a useful guide to thinking about the conduct. Rather, the exclusionary conduct case law was relevant to the effects of the conduct in the operating system market.

DAVID HULL

I tend to agree and I think the problem in the EU is that the precedents *Hilti*[16] and *Tetra Pak*[17] deal with a completely different situation of consumables and I think that the difficulty that the Commission struggled with, and the Court will be struggling with, is to get away from that precedent and deal with this case by bringing a new theory into this case because existing precedents are not a lot of help; so it would be interesting to see how the Court does that.

BILL BISHOP

I was fascinated by Greg's rely to John Vickers's question when he said 'Well a little is enough and that's what we want'. I guess this is a supplementary question really. Is that because you think that is right in principle? Or is it an instance of something we commonly observe that in American law, that there are quite a lot of per se rules which are favourable to the defendant, presumably designed in order to save big companies from unfair jury verdicts which are believed to favour the little guys, something we don't need to contend with here. I am just wondering whether that is the reason, or whether there is some other reason or principle that would be there, even if all trials were bench trials.

GREG WERDEN

There are two rationales for the approach I advocate. One is that it is right in principle: This branch of competition policy should not be about figuring out the real reason somebody did something or about trying to balance offsetting effects, because that is not workable. In addition, any alternative test runs too great a risk of false positives, particularly in our jury system. The application of a subjective or balancing test cannot be resolved as a matter of law, but rather requires complicated, expensive and error-prone proceedings of some sort, even if not jury trials. So we want a simpler,

---

[16] *Hilti* (n 12).   [17] *TetraPak* (n 13).

clearer test that in some cases can be applied as a matter of law, and that otherwise provides a useful guide for court review.

VANESSA TAMMS

I am just wondering if I could ask Greg Werden in particular to say a little bit about how long it actually takes the investigative phase to actually do these type of tests. As a firm [Virgin Atlantic Airways] that has been on the receiving end of this type of behaviour we tend to be a little concerned about a test that it would take even longer to investigate in practice, just putting aside the merits of doing that in the first place, for a second. In the travel agents case, for example, we are now in Year 12 of this case going on. Admittedly we had an initial decision from the European Commission in 1999, but that was still some six years after we lodged the complaint. So I was just wondering if I could ask you to say a little bit about how long these things actually take in practice.

GREG WERDEN

In the cases I worked on—*Microsoft*, *Dentsply*, and *American Airlines*— our initial investigation phase, pre-complaint, was several years, because it takes that long to fully understand the conduct. That is not the time that potential defendants are most concerned about, however. They are most concerned about the post-complaint time.

The *Microsoft* case was resolved quite rapidly for such a large complicated case. The *American Airlines* case was resolved even faster, because we never got to trial. The district judge said that there was no evidence to support our claim. We took it up to the Court of Appeals, which basically held that a lot of what the District Court has said was wrong, but enough of it was right. In *Dentsply* we had a full trial and an appeal. The defendant has now petitioned for re-hearing en banc in the Court of Appeals and undoubtedly will petition for certiorari in the Supreme Court. The decision from the Court of Appeals came about six years after the complaint was filed, so the case was not as fast as one might hope.

The *Trinko* case took nearly four years. That case never got to discovery, although it took three courts to decide that it did not. The Supreme Court eventually decided that the complaint did not state a claim for relief under section 2 of the Sherman Act, so the plaintiff in that case was not entitled to take discovery. The costs imposed on the defendant were not enormous, even though the case took nearly four years.

HELEN JENKINS

Thank you everybody. I thank the panel and the audience. I think there are still a lot of open questions which remain to be discussed about the role of welfare and the balance between competition and competitors and how principles then get turned into action, which we touched on today by looking at the examples we have heard about. We briefly mentioned the question of whether intent is important or not, which is something that is obviously of major interest to you in Europe. We have also heard about the need for diversity of thought. We have brought some of that diversity today through this panel, and even though I am an economist, I do occasionally use more than three bullet points on a slide even for audiences that aren't economists and I do value that which lawyers bring to the table as well.

The 'No Economic Sense' Test for Exclusionary Conduct

Gregory J Werden[*]

Section 2 of the Sherman Act prohibits the acquisition or maintenance of monopoly power through the use of 'predatory' or 'exclusionary' conduct.[1] In *Trinko*[2] the Solicitor General argued that, when 'the plaintiff asserts that the defendant was under a duty *to assist a rival*, . . . conduct is not exclusionary or predatory unless it would make no economic sense for the defendant but for the tendency to eliminate or lessen competition'.[3] Although the Solicitor General only advocated this 'no economic sense' test for a narrow class of conduct, the Department of Justice has consistently advocated this test in all its cases under section 2 of the Sherman Act.[4] This essay briefly discusses *Trinko* and explains how the 'no economic sense' test is motivated by policies the Supreme Court articulated in *Trinko* and prior cases. This essay also explains the role the test can usefully play in Section 2 cases and why it does not have the flaws of the 'sacrifice' test with which the 'no economic sense' test has been confused.

[*] Senior Economic Counsel, Antitrust Division, US Department of Justice. The views expressed herein are not purported to represent those of the US Department of Justice. Adam Hirsh and David Seidman provided helpful comments.

[1] See *Aspen Skiing Co v Aspen Highlands Skiing Corp*, 472 US 585, 602 (1985).

[2] *Verizon Communications Inc v Law Offices of Curtis V Trinko, LLP*, 540 US 398 (2004).

[3] Brief for the United States and the Federal Trade Commission as Amici Curiae Supporting Petitioner at 15 (emphasis in original), *Verizon Communications Inc v Law Offices of Curtis V Trinko, LLP*, 540 US 398 (2004) (No 02-682), available at <http://www.usdoj.gov/osg/briefs/2002/3mer/1ami/2002-0682.mer.ami.pdf>.

[4] In *Microsoft*, the Department argued that a course of conduct that served to protect the defendant's operating system monopoly was exclusionary because it 'would not make economic sense unless it eliminated or softened competition'. Brief of the Appellees United States and the States Plaintiffs at 48, *United States v Microsoft Corp*, 253 F.3d 34 (DC Cir 2001) (No 03-5030), available at <http://www.usdoj.gov/atr/cases/f7200/7230.htm>. In *American Airlines*, the Department charged the defendant with 'adding money-losing capacity' to drive out rivals by attracting away their passengers and contended that 'distinguishing legitimate competition from unlawful predation requires a common-sense business inquiry: whether the conduct would be profitable, apart from any exclusionary effects'. Brief for Appellant United States of America at 2, 30 (public redacted version), *United States v AMR Corp*, 335 F.3d 1109 (10th Cir 2003) (No 01-3202), available at <http://www.usdoj.gov/atr/cases/f9800/9814.htm>. Most recently, in *Dentsply*, the Department argued that the defendant's policies of not using dealers that distributed products of rivals 'made no economic sense but for their tendency to harm rivals,' because the policies cost the defendant something yet produced no possible benefit other than reducing competition. Brief for the United States at 26 (public redacted version), *United States v Dentsply Int'l Inc*, 399 F.3d 181 (3d Cir 2005) (No 03-4097), available at <http://www.usdoj.gov/atr/cases/f202100/202141.htm>.

I. THE *TRINKO* CASE

Mr. Trinko's law firm selected AT&T to provide its local telephone service. The incumbent local exchange carrier (ILEC) in New York City, a successor of the Bell companies, owned facilities necessary to provide the service, and it was required by the Telecommunication Act of 1996[5] to 'share its network with competitors'.[6] The ILEC, which later became part of Verizon, entered into interconnection agreements with AT&T and others, and it made available its 'operations support system', through which customer orders were placed. Complaints that the ILEC nevertheless failed to fill orders were addressed by a consent decree the ILEC entered into with the FCC. One day after entry of the decree, Trinko filed suit under section 2 of the Sherman Act, alleging that the ILEC failed to provide AT&T with access to its facilities equivalent in quality to the ILEC's own access to them.[7] The district court twice dismissed the complaint for failure to state a claim, and the Second Circuit reversed, holding that the complaint 'may state a claim under the "essential facilities" doctrine' and that Trinko also 'may have a monopoly leveraging claim'.[8]

In its consideration of the case, the Supreme Court initially observed that 'a detailed regulatory scheme such as that created by the 1996 Act ordinarily raises the question whether the regulated entities are not shielded from antitrust scrutiny altogether'.[9] But the Court found that such shielding had been precluded by language in the 1996 Act providing that 'nothing in this Act . . . shall be construed to modify, impair, or supercede the applicability of . . . the antitrust laws'.[10]

The Court then explained why the Sherman Act should not be understood to impose a general 'duty to aid competitors':

> Compelling . . . firms to share the source of their advantage is in some tension with the underlying purpose of antitrust law, since it may lessen the incentive for the monopolist, the rival, or both to invest in those economically beneficial facilities. Enforced sharing also requires antitrust courts to act as central planners, identifying the proper price, quantity, and other terms of dealing—a role for which they are ill-suited. Moreover, compelling negotiation between competitors may facilitate the supreme evil of antitrust: collusion.[11]

---

[5] Pub L No 104–104, 110 Stat 56, codified at 47 USC 251 et seq.
[6] *Trinko*, 540 US at 402 (citing 47 USC 251(c)).   [7] ibid at 404–5.
[8] *Law Offices of Curtis V Trinko, LLP v Bell Atlantic Corp*, 305 F.3d 89, 108 (2d Cir 2002).
[9] *Trinko*, 540 US at 406.
[10] ibid (quoting § 601(b)(1) of the 1996 Act, codified at 47 USC 152 n)
[11] ibid at 407–8.

The Court held that 'as a general matter, the Sherman Act "does not restrict the long recognized right of [a] trader or manufacturer engaged in an entirely private business, freely to exercise his own independent discretion as to the parties with whom he will deal".'[12]

Acknowledging there were 'exceptions' to this general rule,[13] the Court reviewed a particularly notable example—its *Aspen* decision,[14] making clear that the facts of *Aspen* were 'at or near the outer boundary' of circumstances in which 'a refusal to cooperate with rivals can constitute' a violation of Section 2.[15] In explaining why it made sense to impose antitrust liability in *Aspen*, even if not in most other cases, the Court stressed that the defendant had refused even to sell lift tickets to the plaintiff on the terms the lift tickets were sold at retail to skiers.[16] Hence, the Court concluded that the facts of *Aspen* 'suggested a willingness to forsake short-term profits to achieve an anticompetitive end'.[17] The Court thereby hinted at something akin to the 'no economic sense' test.[18]

The Court stressed that the 'cost of false positives counsels against an undue expansion of § 2 liability',[19] and it found that the institutional setting of the case weighed against 'adding . . . to the few existing exceptions from the proposition that there is no duty to aid competitors'.[20] But the Court neither enumerated circumstances in which there is a 'duty to aid competitors' nor articulated a standard for identifying such cases. The Court found no need to 'recognize' or 'repudiate' the essential facilities doctrine invoked by the Second Circuit, because the court concluded that imposing a duty to deal 'serves no purpose' when 'access exists' under a regulatory scheme such as that of the 1996 Act.[21] And the Court rejected the Second Circuit's reliance on 'monopoly leveraging' because 'leveraging presupposes anticompetitive conduct, which . . . could only be the refusal-to-deal claim' the Court was rejecting.[22]

---

[12] ibid at 408 (quoting *United States v Colgate & Co*, 250 US 300, 307 (1919)).
[13] ibid.
[14] *Aspen Skiing Co v Aspen Highlands Skiing Corp*, 472 US 585 (1985).
[15] *Trinko*, 540 US at 409.
[16] ibid.   [17] ibid.
[18] In the wake of *Trinko*, two courts of appeals have suggested that a short-run profitsacrifice is required to make out a s 2 violation, although neither asserted that *Trinko* so held. *Covad Communications Co v Bell Atlantic Corp*, 398 F.3d 666, 675–6 (DC Cir 2005) ('in the vernacular if antitrust law, a "predatory" practice is one in which a firm sacrifices shortterm profits in order to drive out of the market otherwise discipline a competitor'; *MetroNet Services Corp v Qwest Corp*, 383 F.3d 1124, 1134 (9th Cir 2004) (holding alleged conduct did 'not fall within the *Aspen Skiing* exception to the general "no duty to deal" rule' because it did 'not entail a sacrifice of short-term profits for long-term gain from the exclusion of competition').
[19] ibid at 414.   [20] ibid at 411.
[21] ibid.   [22] ibid at 415 n 4.

II. POLICIES UNDERLYING THE 'NO ECONOMIC SENSE' TEST

Although *Trinko* does not adopt the 'no economic sense' test, both it and other Supreme Court decisions from the past twenty years articulate policies motivating that test. First and foremost, the Court has made clear that section 2 of the Sherman Act, which applies to single-firm conduct, sweeps far less broadly than Section 1,[23] which prohibits all concerted conduct that 'imposes an unreasonable restraint on competition'.[24] The Court has described the Sherman Act as a 'consumer welfare prescription',[25] but only Section 1 makes consumer welfare the touchstone for legality.[26]

> It is not enough that a single firm appears to 'restrain trade' unreasonably, for even a vigorous competitor may leave that impression. For instance, an efficient competitor may capture unsatisfied customers from an inefficient rival, whose own ability to compete may suffer as a result. This is the rule of the marketplace and is precisely the sort of competition that promotes the consumer interests that the Sherman Act aims to foster.[27]

'Judging unilateral conduct' less strictly than concerted conduct, the Court reasoned, 'reduces the risk that the antitrust laws will dampen the competitive zeal of a single aggressive entrepreneur.'[28] Put another way: 'Subjecting a single firm's every action to judicial scrutiny for reasonableness would threaten to discourage the competitive enthusiasm that the antitrust laws seek to promote.'[29]

---

[23] See *Copperweld Corp v Independence Tube Corp*, 467 US 752, 767 (1984) ('The Sherman Act contains a "basic distinction between concerted and independent action".') (quoting *Monsanto Co v Spray-Rite Serv Corp*, 465 US 752, 761 (1984)); ibid at 768 ('Concerted activity subject to § 1 is judged more sternly than unilateral activity under § 2.'); ibid at 775 ('the Act's plain language leaves no doubt that Congress made a purposeful choice to accord different treatment to unilateral and concerted conduct'); see also *Spectrum Sports, Inc v McQuillan*, 506 US 447, 459 (1993) ('single-firm activity is unlike concerted activity covered by § 1, which "inherently is fraught with anticompetitive risk") (quoting *Copperweld*, 467 US at 768–9).

[24] *State Oil Co v Khan*, 522 US 3, 10 (1997).

[25] *NCAA v Bd of Regents of Univ of Okla*, 468 US 85, 107 (1984); *Reiter v Sonotone Corp*, 442 US 330, 343 (1979).

[26] Some case law suggests a limited role for a consumer welfare standard under s 2. *Microsoft* raises the possibility that exclusionary conduct may be found to be lawful because the defendant shows it has a legitimate business justification and the plaintiff is unable to demonstrate that the 'anticompetitive harm of the conduct outweighs the pro-competitive benefit'. *United States v Microsoft Corp*, 253 F.3d 34, 59 (DC Cir 2001). The court, however, did not engage is such a weighing, and the relevant conduct already had been found by the district court to be exclusionary under what is essentially the 'no economic sense' test. *United States v Microsoft Corp*, 87 F.Supp.2d 30, 38 (DDC 2000).

[27] *Copperweld*, 467 US at 767.

[28] ibid.   [29] ibid. at 775.

A significant part of the Court's rationale for treating single-firm conduct less strictly than concerted conduct is that single-firm conduct presents a greater danger that procompetitive conduct will be erroneously condemned. That danger is especially severe with exclusionary practices that attract customers away from rivals by offering a better bargain. Offering customers a better bargain is characteristic of the conduct deemed 'competition on the merits',[30] yet it is also precisely how certain conduct, eg, predatory pricing, may exclude competition.[31] Consequently, '[i]t is sometimes difficult to distinguish robust competition from conduct with long-run anticompetitive effects.'[32]

The potential to erroneously condemn procompetitive conduct is obvious with allegedly predatory pricing, and the Court's *Matsushita* and *Brooke Group* decisions emphasized that 'mistaken inferences' of predatory pricing 'are especially costly, because they chill the very conduct the antitrust laws are designed to protect'.[33] But *Trinko* made abundantly clear that this critical tenet of Section 2 law has broader application. *Trinko* explained that 'applying the requirements of § 2 "can be difficult" because "the means of illicit exclusion, like the means of legitimate competition, are myriad",[34] and, quoting *Matsushita*, declared quite generally: 'Mistaken inferences and the resulting false condemnations "are especially costly, because they chill the very conduct the antitrust laws are designed to protect".'[35]

---

[30] The Supreme Court has often referred to, but never defined, the concept of 'competition on the merits'. The Court first invoked the concept in *N Pac Ry Co v United States*, 356 US 1, 6 (1958).

[31] See *Brooke Group Ltd v Brown & Williamson Tobacco Corp*, 509 US 209, 226 (1993) (the 'mechanism by which a firm engages in predatory pricing—lowering prices—is the same mechanism by which a firm stimulates competition; because "cutting prices in order to increase business often is the very essence of competition"') (quoting *Cargill, Inc v Monfort of Colo, Inc*, 479 US 104, 122 n 17 (1986) (quoting *Matsushita Elec Indus Co v Zenith Radio Corp*, 475 US 574, 594 (1986))).

[32] *Spectrum Sports*, 506 US at 458–9 (citing *Copperweld*, 467 US at 767–9).

[33] *Brooke Group*, 509 US at 226; *Matsushita*, 475 US at 594; see also Cargill, 479 US at 122 n 17. The Court's rationale in these cases was in part its judgment that 'predatory pricing schemes are rarely tried, and even more rarely successful'. *Brooke Group*, 509 US at 226 (quoting *Matsushita*, 475 US at 589). As the Third Circuit put it, '*Matsushita* . . . in effect created a *legal* presumption, based on *economic logic*, that predatory pricing is unlikely to threaten competition.' *Advo, Inc v Philadelphia Newspapers, Inc*, 51 F.3d 1191, 1196 (3d Cir 1995) (emphasis in original). After reconsidering that logic, the Tenth Circuit concluded that allegations of predation should not be approached 'with the incredulity that once prevailed' but nevertheless found it appropriate to implement the 'balance the Supreme Court has struck in *Brooke Group*'. *United States v AMR Corp*, 335 F.3d 1109, 1114–15, 1121 (10th Cir 2003).

[34] *Trinko*, 540 US at 414 (quoting *United States v Microsoft Corp*, 253 F.3d 34, 58 (DC Cir 2001) (*en banc*) (*per curiam*)).

[35] ibid (quoting *Matsushita*, 475 US at 594) (citation omitted).

Animating the *Trinko* decision was the notion that striving for monopoly 'is an important element of the free-market system' because 'it induces risk taking that produces innovation and economic growth'.[36] This idea can be traced to Learned Hand's admonition: 'The successful competitor, having been urged to compete, must not be turned upon when he wins.'[37]

Finally, a consistent theme of the Supreme Court's jurisprudence has been that the purpose of Section 2

> is not to protect businesses from the working of the market; it is to protect the public from the failure of the market. The law directs itself not against conduct which is competitive, even severely so, but against conduct which unfairly tends to destroy competition itself. It does so not out of solicitude for private concerns but out of concern for the public interest.[38]

Hence, the mere fact that one competitor's conduct injures another is far from a sufficient basis for presuming that the conduct is improper.[39]

Because distinguishing exclusionary from procompetitive conduct is difficult and error prone, it would chill conduct from which consumers benefit greatly to impose on defendants a burden to defend most aggressive marketplace conduct and refusals to assist rivals.[40] Rather, a significant burden must be placed on plaintiffs to establish that single-firm conduct is, in fact, exclusionary. The 'no economic sense' test properly imposes such a burden by requiring the demonstration that the challenged conduct would not be rational for the defendant absent a tendency to eliminate competition.

Professor Gavil objects 'on procedural grounds' to placing this burden on plaintiffs, arguing that 'consistent with Rule 11 obligations' plaintiffs would find it difficult to make the allegations required '[w]ithout any

---

[36] *Trinko*, 540 US at 407.

[37] *United States v Aluminum Co of Am*, 148 F.2d 416, 430 (2d Cir 1945).

[38] *Spectrum Sports*, 506 US at 458.

[39] As Judge Easterbrook commented: 'Competition is a ruthless process. A firm that reduces cost and expands sales injures rivals—sometimes fatally. . . . These injuries to rivals are byproducts of vigorous competition, and the antitrust laws are not balm for rivals' wounds. The antitrust laws are for the benefit of competition, not competitors.' *Ball Mem'l Hosp, Inc v Mutual Hosp Ins, Inc*, 784 F.2d 1325, 1338 (7th Cir 1986).

[40] See *Olympia Equip Leasing Co v Western Union Tel Co*, 797 F.2d 370, 375 (7th Cir 1986) (Posner, J) ('[T]he lawful monopolist should be free to compete like everyone else; otherwise the antitrust laws would be holding an umbrella over inefficient competitors. A monopolist, no less than any other competitor, is permitted and indeed encouraged to compete aggressively on the merits.') (internal quotation omitted).

opportunity for discovery.'[41] However, a complaint requires only 'short and plain statement of the claim'[42] without significant elaboration of either legal theories or their basis in fact.[43] Despite the suggestion in *Trinko* that conduct is exclusionary only if it involves a sacrifice of short-term profits, courts have refused to dismiss complaints lacking specific factual allegations of sacrifice.[44]

III. THE 'NO ECONOMIC SENSE' IS NOT A TEST FOR SHORT-RUN PROFIT SACRIFICE

There is a widespread misconception that the test advocated by the Solicitor-General in *Trinko* makes a 'short-term profit sacrifice' the touchstone for illegality.[45] This misconception results from the failure to distinguish the 'no economic sense' test from similar tests formulated in terms of profit sacrifice or departure from profit maximization.[46]

Exclusionary conduct was associated with profit sacrifice in several antitrust treatises published in late 1970s. Most often cited is Professor Bork's formulation:

---

[41] See Andrew I Gavil 'Exclusionary Distribution Strategies by Dominant Firms: Striking a Better Balance', 72 Antitrust LJ 3, 55 (2004).

[42] See, eg, *Swierkiewicz v Sorema NA*, 534 US 506, 512 (2002).

[43] See, eg, *South Austin Coalition Cmty Council v SBC Communications Inc*, 274 F.3d 1168, 1171 (7th Cir 2001) (Easterbrook, J) ('It is not necessary that facts or the theory of relief be elaborated.'); *Kirksey v RJ Reynolds Tobacco Co*, 168 F.3d 1039, 1041 (7th Cir 1999) (Posner, CJ) ('The courts keep reminding plaintiffs that they don't to have to file long complaints, don't have to plead facts, don't have to plead legal theories').

[44] See *Covad Communications Co v Bell Atlantic Corp*, 398 F.3d 666, 675–6 (DC Cir 2005) (alleging the defendant's 'refusal to deal was "predatory" . . . suffices to withstand a motion to dismiss because, in the vernacular if antitrust law, a "predatory" practice is one in which a firm sacrifices short-term profits in order to drive out of the market otherwise discipline a competitor'; *AIB Express, Inc v FedEx Corp*, 2004-2 Trade Cas (CCH) ¶74,621, at 100,734 (SDNY 2004) (allegations of significant foregone revenues are sufficient without any indication of avoided costs); *Creative Copier Servs v Xerox Corp*, 344 F.Supp.2d 858, 865–6 (D Conn 2004) (*Trinko* did not alter pleading requirements).

[45] See, eg, Einer Elhauge 'Defining Better Monopolization Standards', 56 *Stan L Rev* 253, 270–1 (2003); Mark R Patterson 'The Sacrifice of Profits in Non-Price Predation', Antitrust, Fall 2003, at 37, 37.

[46] Some prior tests articulated by courts of appeals were quite close to the 'no economic sense' test and did not refer to sacrifice or departure from profit maximization. See *Stearns Airport Equip Co v FMC Corp*, 170 F.3d 518, 524 (5th Cir 1999) ('[A] finding of exclusionary conduct requires some sign that the monopolist engaged in behavior that—examined without reference to its effects on competitors—is economically irrational.'); *Trace X Chem, Inc v Canadian Indus, Ltd*, 738 F.2d 261, 266 (8th Cir 1984) ('To be labeled anti-competitive, the conduct involved must be such that its "anticipated benefits were dependent upon its tendency to discipline or eliminate competition and thereby enhance the firm's long term ability to reap the benefits of monopoly power".') (quoting *William Inglis & Sons Baking Co v ITT Cont'l Baking Co, Inc*, 668 F.2d 1014, 1030 (9th Cir 1981)).

Predation may be defined, provisionally, as a firm's deliberate aggression against one or more rivals through the employment of business practices that would not be considered profit maximizing except for the expectation either that (1) rivals will be driven from the market, leaving the predator with a market share sufficient to command monopoly profits, or (2) rivals will be chastened sufficiently to abandon competitive behavior the predator finds inconvenient or threatening.[47]

Similarly, Professor Posner maintained: 'An exclusionary practice is generally a method by which a firm (or firms) having or wanting a monopoly position trades a part of its monopoly profits, at least temporarily, for a larger market share, by making it unprofitable for the other sellers to compete with it.'[48] And Professor Sullivan suggested: 'Perhaps the characteristic feature of such a predatory thrust is that the predator is acting in a way which will not maximize present or foreseeable future profits unless it drives or keeps others out or forces them to tread softly.'[49]

A highly influential formulation also was offered by economics professors Ordover and Willig: '[P]redatory behavior is a response to a rival that sacrifices part of the profit that could be earned under competitive circumstances, were the rival to remain viable, in order to induce exit and gain consequent monopoly profit.'[50] Although the Supreme Court's *Aspen* decision did not adopt such a definition of exclusionary conduct, it summed up what made the conduct at issue exclusionary by noting that the defendant 'was willing to sacrifice short-run benefits and goodwill in exchange for a perceived long-run impact on its smaller rival'.[51]

---

[47] Robert H Bork *The Antitrust Paradox* 144 (1978). See also *Neumann v Reinforced Earth Co*, 786 F.2d 424, 427 (DC Cir 1986) (Bork, J) ('predation involves aggression against business rivals through the use of business practices that would not be considered profit maximizing except for the expectation that (1) actual rivals will be driven from the market, or the entry of potential rivals blocked or delayed, so that the predator will gain or retain a market share sufficient to command monopoly profits, or (2) rivals will be chastened sufficiently to abandon competitive behavior the predator finds threatening to its realization of monopoly profits').

[48] Richard A Posner *Antitrust Law: An Economic Perspective* 28 (1976).

[49] Lawrence Anthony Sullivan *Antitrust* 113 (1977).

[50] Janusz A Ordover and Robert D Willig 'An Economic Definition of Predation: Pricing and Product Innovation' (1981) 91 Yale LJ 8, 9–10 (footnotes omitted). This test was reformulated and dubbed the '"but for" test' by Steven C Salop and R Craig Romaine, 'Preserving Monopoly: Economic Analysis, Legal Standards, and Microsoft' (1999) 7 *Geo Mason L Rev* 617, 650, 657–8 ('A defendant's exclusionary conduct can be said to have the purpose of monopolizing only if the conduct would have been unprofitable (and thus likely not undertaken) in the absence of increased barriers to competition.').

[51] *Aspen Skiing Co v Aspen Highlands Skiing Corp*, 472 US 585, 610–11 (1985). See also *Advanced Health-Care Servs v Radford Cmty Hosp*, 910 F.2d 139, 148 (4th Cir 1990) ('if a plaintiff shows that a defendant has harmed consumers and competition by making a short-term sacrifice in order to further its exclusive, anti-competitive objectives, it has shown predation by that defendant').

Recent commentators have correctly noted that a short-term profit sacrifice is neither necessary nor sufficient for conduct to be exclusionary.[52] But they have failed to recognize that the 'no economic sense' does not imply that a short-term profit sacrifice is either necessary or sufficient for conduct be exclusionary.

It is obvious that a short-term profit sacrifice is insufficient to make conduct exclusionary, because much pro-competitive conduct entails the sacrifice of current profit in the pursuit of greater profit over the longer term. Investing in R&D or capital equipment sacrifices current profit in order to obtain what is expected to be a significantly greater future profit.[53] It is just as obvious that a short-term profit sacrifice is insufficient to make conduct exclusionary under the 'no economic sense' test. Ordinary investments in opportunities for future profit normally are not exclusionary conduct under that test both because they make economic sense apart from any tendency to eliminate competition and because they have no such tendency. If the defendant's conduct entails a short-run profit sacrifice, the 'no economic sense' test further asks why it is rational to make that sacrifice.

A short-run profit sacrifice also is not necessary for conduct to be deemed exclusionary by the 'no economic sense' test, because the anticompetitive gains from exclusionary conduct sometime can be reaped immediately.[54] Exclusionary conduct can extend the period during which monopoly profits can be reaped. In some cases, the exclusionary impact of such conduct also is immediate, so the conduct increases the monopolist's profit (by preventing a decrease) at the same time the conduct is undertaken. Hence, it is possible, at every point in time, that the exclusionary conduct generates rewards in excess of its costs, so there is no sense in which a short-run sacrifice is made to generate future monopoly profits.[55] Critically, the 'no

---

[52] See Elhauge, above n 45, at 271, 274–94; Steven C Salop, 'Section 2 Paradigms and the Flawed Profit-Sacrifice Standard', Antitrust LJ (forthcoming 2005); John Vickers, Abuse of Market Power (speech to the 31st conference of the European Association for Research in Industrial Economics, Berlin, 4 Sept 2004), available at <http://www.oft.gov.uk/NR/rdonlyres/948B9FAF-B83C-49F5-B0FA-B25214DE6199/0/spe0304.pdf>.

[53] Elhauge, above n 45, at 274–9, makes this point in vastly greater detail. See also Aaron S Edlin and Joseph Farrell 'The American Airlines Case: A Chance to Clarify Predation Policy', in *The Antitrust Revolution* 502, 509, 523 (John E Kwoka, Jr and Lawrence J White eds (4th ed 2004).

[54] The notion that certain kinds of exclusionary conduct require no short-run sacrifice may have first been noted by Thomas Krattenmaker and Steven C Salop 'Anticompetitive Exclusion: Raising Rivals Cots to Achieve Power over Price' (1986) 96 Yale LJ 209, 224. Plaintiff argued that there was 'simultaneous recoupment' of the costs of predation in *Liggett Group, Inc v Brown & Williamson Tobacco Corp*, 748 F.Supp.344, 354 (MDNC 1990).

[55] The three cases discussed in n 4, above, in which the Department of Justice advocated the 'no economic sense' test, all involved conduct alleged to extend the period during which monopoly profits could be reaped. Nevertheless, in both *American Airlines* and *Microsoft*, there was a short-term profit sacrifice.

economic sense' test asks not just whether challenged conduct is profitable, but also why it is profitable.

Because the 'no economic sense' test has been wrongly viewed as a sacrifice test, it has often been erroneously said to be inapplicable when excluding competition costs very little, so there is no meaningful 'sacrifice'.[56] Illustrations from Section 2 cases of exclusionary conduct argued to cost little are attempts to enforce a fraudulently obtained patent,[57] sham litigation or bad-faith administrative filings,[58] and abuse of a private standard-setting process.[59] In each of these illustrations, however, it is impossible to exclude competition without incurring some cost, and applying the 'no economic sense' test means asking whether the cost—no matter how slight—would sensibly have been incurred absent the tendency of the conduct to eliminate competition. In each of these illustrations, the conduct offers no prospect of a positive payoff apart from the tendency of the conduct to eliminate competition, so the conduct is exclusionary under the 'no economic sense' test.[60]

It also has been argued that the 'no economic sense' test certainly cannot be applicable to 'costless exclusion'.[61] A realistic scenario of costless exclusion is quite difficult to imagine, but all costs associated with exclusion easily can be assumed away. Consider, for example, a competitor that sets a match to the factory of a rival, and assume that matches are free, arson is not a crime, and there is no opportunity cost associated with the time it takes to commit the arson. Even in this hypothetical world, the arson is exclusionary under the 'no economic sense' test, because that conduct is entirely pointless as an economic matter apart from its tendency to eliminate competition. To be exclusionary under the 'no economic sense' test, it is sufficient that the conduct confer an economic benefit only if it eliminates competition.

---

[56] See, eg, Elhauge, above n 45, at 281–2; Gavil, above n 41, at 56–7; Reply Brief of Counsel Supporting the Complaint, Rambus Inc. at 10–11 (FTC Docket No. 9302), available at <http://www.ftc.gov/os/adjpro/d9302/040707ccreplybrief.pdf>.

[57] See *Walker Process Equip, Inc v Food Mach & Chem Corp*, 382 US 172 (1965).

[58] See *Cal Motor Transp Co v Trucking Unlimited*, 404 US 508 (1972).

[59] See *Allied Tube & Conduit Corp v Indian Head, Inc*, 486 US 492 (1988).

[60] Commentators have cited *Conwood Co v US Tobacco Co*, 290 F.3d 768 (6th Cir 2002), *cert denied*, 537 US 1148 (2003), as another example of a scenario in which there is no sacrifice. See Gavil above n 41, at 55; Robert A Skitol 'Correct Answers to Large Questions about *Verizon v Trinko*', Antitrust Source, May 2004, at 3, available at <http://www.abanet.org/antitrust/source/may04/skitol.pdf>. In that case, the defendant's sales people removed from retailers the racks on which the plaintiff's products were displayed. That obviously cost the defendant something, and it most likely produced a benefit only by hampering rival's sales. Hence, the conduct likely was exclusionary under the 'no economic sense' test.

[61] See Salop, above n 52.

IV. A ROLE FOR THE 'NO ECONOMIC SENSE' TEST

The phrasing of the 'no economic sense' test suggests that it may be a one-way test. To say that 'conduct is not exclusionary or predatory unless it would make no economic sense for the defendant but for the tendency to eliminate or lessen competition', suggests this test can be used only to exculpate conduct for which this condition is not met. But the reason for the 'unless' formulation is that the 'no economic sense' test provides only a partial definition of exclusionary conduct: The test can be usefully applied only once it has been demonstrated that the challenged conduct actually has a tendency to eliminate or lessen competition.[62] In many cases, injury to a rival may be both clear and all that is required, although a rival's lack of marketplace success cannot automatically be attributed to a defendant's conduct.[63]

The 'no economic sense' test is likely to be most useful when it can play what is essentially the role of a sufficient condition: If challenged conduct with a tendency to eliminate competition would make 'no economic sense' but for that tendency, the conduct is exclusionary. Whenever a plaintiff is prepared to demonstrate that the foregoing two-part condition is satisfied, the 'no economic sense' test provides a logical fulcrum that allows the conduct to be labeled exclusionary.

The utility of the 'no economic sense' test is apt to vary,[64] however, depending on how feasible it is to determine whether the challenged conduct would make 'no economic sense' but for its tendency to eliminate competition. It is doubtful that the 'no economic sense' test would have been well suited to the bundled rebates at issue in *LePage's*.[65] Such rebates implement a form of price discrimination, which can make them profitable even apart from any tendency to eliminate competition, and it may be infeasible to separate the profits from discrimination from the profits from eliminating competition.

---

[62] Although a defendant may rationally expect its conduct to exclude, and may undertake the conduct for no reason but to exclude, the conduct may utterly fail to exclude. Although it was reversed on appeal, this is precisely what the district court found in *United States v Dentsply Int'l, Inc*, 277 F.Supp.2d 387, 419–21, 440–8, 449–53 (D Del 2003), *rev'd*, 399 F.3d 181, 191–4 (3d Cir 2005).

[63] To be considered exclusionary, conduct 'reasonably must appear capable of making a significant contribution to creating or maintaining monopoly power'. 3 Philip E Areeda and Herbert Hovenkamp *Antitrust Law* ¶ 651f, at 83–84 (2d edn 2002). See also *United States v Microsoft Corp*, 253 F.3d 34, 79 (DC Cir 2001) (*en banc*) (*per curiam*).

[64] In the *Trinko* case, an amicus brief filed on behalf of economists William J Baumol, Janusz A Ordover, Frederick R Warren-Boulton and Robert D Willig argued that the 'no economic sense' test generally is appropriate, with the primary exception being some regulated industries. See Brief of *Amici Curiae* Economics Professors in Support of Respondents, *Verizon Communications Inc v Law Offices of Curtis V Trinko, LLP*, 540 US 398 (2004) (No 02-682).

[65] *LePage's Inc v 3M*, 324 F.3d 141 (3d Cir 2003) (*en banc*), *cert denied* 541 US (2004) [124 S Ct 2932].

Even if the 'no economic sense' test determines that challenged conduct is exclusionary, it need not follow that the conduct violates Section 2. A variety of immunities and exemptions limit the application of the Sherman Act.[66] In addition, the case law may effectively place certain types of potentially exclusionary conduct, eg, pricing above cost,[67] in a prudential safe harbor. Although the case law has not explicitly placed much conduct in such a safe harbour,[68] it is impossible to believe that a court would entertain the notion, for example, that merely introducing a new product could be anything but lawful competition on the merits.[69]

In addition, the 'no economic sense' test can be applied only when there is a single, well-defined 'but for' scenario. That often presents no problem because the proper 'but for' scenario is precisely what actually occurred with the exception of the challenged incremental conduct. If so, the issue is whether it made 'no economic sense' for the defendant to undertake the challenged conduct instead of continuing on its prior course. In some cases, however, changed market conditions may make clear that continuing the prior course of conduct would have made 'no economic sense'. In such cases, the 'no economic sense' test may not be useful unless the defendant's choices can be narrowed down to a few, only one of which includes the challenged conduct. The test may be applied to the decision to slash prices 25 per cent in response to entry, but not to the marginal decision to select a cut of 25 per cent rather than 24 per cent. The test does not identify as exclusionary every departure from short-run profit maximization.[70]

---

[66] See generally 1 Philip E Areeda and Herbert Hovenkamp *Antitrust Law* ¶¶ 200–39, at 139–551 (2nd edn 2000); 1A Philip E Areeda and Herbert Hovenkamp *Antitrust Law* ¶¶ 240–62, at 3–285 (2nd edn 2000).

[67] To establish predatory pricing, a plaintiff must show 'that the prices complained of are below an appropriate measure of its rival's costs'. *Brooke Group Ltd v Brown & Williamson Tobacco Corp*, 509 US 209, 222 (1993). The Court held that above-cost prices could be exclusionary but it was unwise to permit liability: 'As a general rule, the exclusionary effect of prices above a relevant measure of cost either reflects the lower cost structure of the alleged predator, and so represents competition on the merits, or is beyond the practical ability of a judicial tribunal to control without courting intolerable risks of chilling legitimate price cutting' ibid, at 223.

[68] An example may be that the use of litigation to assert intellectual property rights cannot violate Section 2 unless it is 'objectively baseless'. See *Prof'l Real Estate Investors, Inc v Columbia Pictures, Inc*, 508 US 49, 60 (1993).

[69] Introducing a new product in place of an existing product raises more difficult issues, and a court might entertain the notion that such conduct might be exclusionary. While considerable skepticism is appropriate in a challenge to a product design decision, design changes may constitute unlawful exclusionary conduct. See *United States v Microsoft Corp*, 253 F.3d 34, 64–7 (DC Cir 2001) (*en banc*) (*per curiam*).

[70] In the *American Airlines* case, the court of appeals rejected one of several price-cost comparisons proposed by the government on the grounds that it asked only whether the defendant 'failed to maximize short-run profits'. *United States v AMR Corp*, 335 F.3d 1109, 1119 (10th Cir 2003). The court, however, mischaracterized the proposed comparison. See Gregory J Werden 'The American Airlines Decision: Not with a Bang but a Whimper', Antitrust, Fall 2003, at 32, 34 and n 35.

Finally, the 'no economic sense' test is not designed to identify all single-firm conduct that harms consumers by excluding competition.[71] A critical premise for the 'no economic sense' test is that some potentially harmful conduct must be tolerated to avoid even greater harms from chilling risk taking and aggressively competitive conduct. A policy of prohibiting all single-firm conduct injuring consumers also would be unworkable: In most cases, there is no satisfactory way to trade off shortrun benefits from injecting competition into one market against long-run costs from the reduced innovation and economic growth that may flow from reduced risk taking throughout the economy.

V. APPLYING THE 'NO ECONOMIC SENSE' TEST

The application of the 'no economic sense' test is at least conceptually straightforward. If challenged conduct allegedly threatened to create a monopoly because of a tendency to exclude existing competitors, the test is whether the conduct likely would have been profitable under the assumption that a monopoly was not created because the existing competitors were not excluded. If the challenged conduct allegedly maintained a monopoly because of its tendency to exclude nascent competition, the test is whether the conduct likely would have been profitable under the assumption that the monopoly was not maintained because the nascent competition flourished.

Applying the 'no economic sense' test in these ways may avoid the need to determine directly whether profit gains from challenged conduct should be attributed to legitimate competition on the merits or illegitimate elimination of competition. This is a cardinal virtue of the test, because antitrust law has never defined 'competition on the merits'.[72] This does not mean, however, that applying the 'no economic sense' test is without difficulties. Particularly problematic would be a case in which the inevitable outcome of the competitive process would be a single surviving competitor.[73]

Under the 'no economic sense' test, conduct can be exclusionary even if it produces some efficiency gain or consumer benefit.[74] That conduct

---

[71] See Salop and Romaine, above n 50, at 658 ('Exclusionary conduct that escapes condemnation under this test can nevertheless lead to anticompetitive effects on consumer and aggregate economic welfare').

[72] For an attempt to do so, see Elhauge, above n 45.

[73] This can be the case in the presence of powerful network effects, which make competition 'for the market' rather than 'in the market'. See generally Gregory J Werden 'Network Effects and Conditions of Entry: Lessons from the Microsoft Case' (2001) 69 Antitrust LJ 87, 89–91.

[74] Professor Gavil, above n 41, at 53, wrongly criticizes the 'no economic sense' test for finding conduct not to be exclusionary if it produces 'any efficiency gain'.

produces some gross benefit plainly is an insufficient basis for concluding that it makes economic sense, because there has been no consideration of cost. The 'no economic sense' test may deem conduct to be exclusionary unless it has a positive expected payoff, net of costs and not including any payoff from eliminating competition.

The 'no economic sense' test does not enquire into the actual impact of the challenged conduct, but rather into the reasonably anticipated impact of the conduct. The 'no economic sense' test is applied as of the time the challenged conduct was undertaken on the basis of reasonable expectations at that time.[75] Actual effects can provide powerful evidence of the reasonably anticipated effects, but actual effects also can be entirely irrelevant.[76] Many business decisions ultimately prove unprofitable because of misfortune or ineptitude, and the antitrust laws do not add insult to injury by deeming as exclusionary all unprofitable conduct.[77] Marketplace conduct also may prove highly profitable for reasons that could not have been anticipated when it was undertaken, and such unanticipated profits should not preclude a finding that the conduct was exclusionary. Finally, some conduct may have exclusionary effects that were unforeseeable when that conduct was undertaken, and such effects should not be a basis for condemning the conduct long after the fact.

The foregoing does not imply that the 'no economic sense' test is based on intent.[78] In applying the test, what matters are the objective economic considerations for a reasonable person, and not the state of mind of any particular decision maker.[79] Conduct should not be condemned because the

---

[75] There may no single time at which particular conduct was undertaken. A defendant pursuing a course of conduct for a considerable time may periodically reevaluate the wisdom of the conduct both in the light of new information on projected costs and benefits, and in response to changes in the economic environment. In such a case, the 'no economic sense' test is applicable at several different times, with potentially different results.

[76] The best evidence may be detailed business plans made by the defendant, which estimate the costs and benefits of alternative courses of conduct.

[77] Accord William J Baumol 'Principles Relevant to Predatory Pricing', in *The Pros and Cons of Low Prices* 15, 23–5 (Swedish Competition Authority 2003), available at <http://www.kkv.se/bestall/pdf/rap_pros_and_cons_low_prices.pdf>.

[78] It is at least misleading for Professor Gavil to argue that the 'no economic sense' test 'could be interpreted as little more than a test of "intent".' Gavil, above n 41, at 52.

[79] Modern Section 2 jurisprudence generally rejects an intent-based approach. See *United States v Microsoft Corp*, 253 F.3d 34, 79 (DC Cir 2001) (*en banc*) (*per curiam*) ('in considering whether . . . conduct . . . is . . . exclusionary for purposes of § 2, our focus is upon the effect of that conduct, not upon the intent behind it'); *Ball Mem'l Hosp, Inc v Mutual Hosp Ins, Inc*, 784 F.2d 1325, 1339 (7th Cir 1986) (Easterbrook, J) ('Vigorous competitors intend to harm rivals, to do all the business if they can. To penalize this intent is to penalize competition'); *Barry Wright Corp v ITT Grinnell Corp*, 724 F.2d 227, 232 (1st Cir 1983) (Breyer, J) ('"intent to harm" without more offers too vague a standard'); Areeda and Hovenkamp, above n 63, ¶ 651b, at 72–6 (2nd edn 2002) ('Despite loose language, . . . the courts . . . have focused on conduct while talking about intent.').

decision maker did not clearly focus on, or even was unaware of, sound economic reasons for the conduct. And exclusionary conduct should be condemned even if the decision maker's rationale for undertaking the conduct was not profit maximization:[80] Burning down a rival's factory is exclusionary conduct even if the defendant is a pyromaniac and never considered the economic benefits of the conduct.[81]

VI. CONCLUSIONS

By placing on plaintiffs a significant burden to demonstrate that challenged conduct truly is exclusionary, the 'no economic sense' test implements important policies the Supreme Court has articulated in recent decades. Principal among them is that the application of Section 2 must guard against the risk of 'false positive' determinations that challenged conduct is exclusionary. To maximize the consumer benefits from competition, it is essential to allow some conduct to go unremedied even though it harms consumers. Doing otherwise would chill risk taking and aggressively competitive conduct from which consumers benefit greatly.

The 'no economic sense' test may not be useful in every Section 2 case, but it is very useful in most such cases, including cases of 'low-cost exclusion,' which critics consistently cite as examples of cases in which the test cannot be applied. The 'no economic sense' test does not requires a profit sacrifice, especially in monopoly maintenance cases. Nor does the 'no economic

---

In *Trinko* the Supreme Court employed language suggesting an intent-based test by indicating that forsaking short-term profits in *Aspen* 'revealed a distinctively anticompetitive bent', and in contrasting *Aspen* with *Trinko* as to whether the defendant's prior conduct shed light 'upon the motivation of the refusal to deal' and whether it was prompted 'by anticompetitive malice'. *Verizon Communications Inc v Law Offices of Curtis V Trinko, LLP*, 540 US 398, 409 (2004). It is unlikely, however, that the Court intended any significant role for subjective motivation. Had the *Trinko* Court wanted to craft an intent-based test, it would have included the initial clause of the famous *Colgate* dictum: 'In the absence of any purpose to create or maintain a monopoly.' *United States v Colgate & Co*, 250 US 300, 307 (1919). By omitting this clause when it quoted the dictum (540 US at 408 (quoted in text accompanying note 12 above)), the Court sent the clear signal that subjective motivation is not what matters.

[80] Many s 2 cases mention the possibility of rejecting a business justification as 'pretextual' (eg, *Eastman Kodak Co v Image Tech Servs, Inc*, 504 US 451, 461, 484 (1992)), but few have explicitly focused on the state of mind of decision makers. A notorious case that did is *Image Tech Servs, Inc v Eastman Kodak Co*, 125 F.3d 1195, 1219 (9th Cir 1997) ('Evidence regarding the state of mind of Kodak employees may show pretext, when such evidence suggests that the proffered business justification played no part in the decision to act').

[81] If s 2 made liability turn on a decision maker's state of mind, it would have to admit an insanity defence of sorts, but no such defence appears ever to have been suggested for civil antitrust cases. Of course, there must be some room for an insanity defence in a criminal antitrust case, since like other violations of criminal law, a criminal antitrust violation requires a guilty state of mind. See *United States v US Gypsum Co*, 438 US 422, 435–43 (1978).

sense' test make the mistake of deeming exclusionary any current sacrifice of profit in the hope of greater future profit. Plaintiffs and defendants alike should find the 'no economic sense' test, when properly understood, to be of great value in assessing possibly exclusionary conduct, as should the courts.

Unilateral Conduct under Mexican Competition Law: Form-Based versus Effects-Based Approaches

Adriaan Ten Kate*

I. INTRODUCTION

It is often argued that European competition law enforcement is form-based, ie focused on the form of conduct, whereas in the US it is more effects-based, ie it is rather the economic effects of the conduct that matter. Without a doubt, this is an oversimplification of a more complex reality. How an effects-based approach works out in practice depends on many factors, eg on how effects are estimated and what kind of thresholds are used. Likewise, form-based approaches can take many different shapes. Thus, the real differences between the two systems may rather depend on the way in which the details are specified. Still, I believe there is some truth in the distinction and it seems that recent modifications in EU policies towards mergers and Article 81 cases were inspired by the desire to introduce more economic analysis (effects) in their assessment. Whether the treatment of abuse of dominance under Article 82 will undergo similar changes is an open question and currently under debate.

The purpose of the present paper is to shed some light on this debate from the perspective of a development country that enacted its competition statute in the early nineties. It is particularly interesting to examine the difficulties the Mexican competition authority has encountered to implement the outspoken effects-based approach the designers of the law had in mind while drafting the statute. Today Mexican competition law enforcement seems to be better described by, what I would call, a *form-plus* approach, that is, an essentially form-based system but complemented with a market-power test.[1] In such an approach competition law enforcement runs the risk of becoming overly interventionist because it tends to ignore the pro-competitive effects of conduct and agreements.

* Head of the Economics Department of the Federal Competition Commission, México. The opinions expressed in this paper are of the author and need not coincide with those of the Competition Commission.
[1] In such an approach market power is used as a proxy for the anticompetitive effects of conduct or agreements—ie in its absence the latter are unlikely to be significant. Thus, the test introduces an element of effect in the otherwise form-based approach. However, market power has little to do with the potentially important procompetitive effects of conduct so that the latter tend to be ignored in a form-plus approach.

In this paper I first discuss the basic features of the Mexican competition law, the distinction it makes between absolute and relative monopolistic practices, how they are treated (per se or rule of reason) and where unilateral conduct (abuse of dominance/monopolization) fits into the picture. Then, I describe two outstanding unilateral-conduct cases: one of predatory pricing in the chewing-gum market and the other about refusals to deal and price discrimination in the wholesale market for pay-TV signals. Both cases are illustrative of the way the competition authority usually handles such conduct, and merit some afterthought. After this follows a discussion comparing form- and effects-based systems from an implementation point of view. In the conclusions I address the question why it is that Mexico's competition law enforcement has ended up largely as form-plus system.

II. THE MEXICAN COMPETITION LAW

Mexico's Federal Law on Economic Competition (FLEC) makes a distinction between absolute and relative monopolistic practices. Absolute practices are horizontal agreements, such as hard-core cartel behavior and bid-rigging, and are prohibited per se. Relative practices cover both vertical restraints and unilateral conduct and are assessed under a rule of reason.

By way of comparison, the Sherman Act divides trade-restrictive conduct in (i) agreements between two or more economic agents (section I); and (ii) unilateral conduct, called monopolization (section II). In US case law agreements are further split up in horizontal and vertical agreements. The former are prohibited per se; the latter are assessed under a rule of reason together with monopolization cases. The distinction between absolute and relative monopolistic practices of the Mexican law ignores the distinction between agreements and unilateral conduct of the Sherman Act but follows the divide between per se and rule of reason developed under US case law. See the diagram.

Comparison US–Mexico

	Horizontal Agreements	Vertical Agreements	Unilateral Conduct
US–Sherman Act	section 1		section II
Assessment	per se	rule of reason	
Mexico–FLEC	absolute	relative	

The Mexican rule of reason implies that, for relative monopolistic conduct to be illegal, the responsible economic agent must have substantial market power and there must be an *undue* displacement or exclusion of competitors from the market, either in effect or intentionally. The latter requirement introduces the possibility to take account of the pro-competitive effects of the practice under investigation. Particularly the word 'undue' recognizes the fact that it is the very purpose of sound competition to displace competitors from the market and that it cannot be the intention of the law to discourage competition on the merits, not even in cases where the firm in question has market power. Such an effects-based approach has clearly been on the minds of those who designed Mexico's competition law in the early 1990s. In an accompanying paper they underscored the potentially pro-competitive nature of apparently anticompetitive behaviour, giving a variety of specific examples.[2] They also stressed the importance of a balancing of pro- and anticompetitive effects on a case-by-case basis.

A list of relative monopolistic practices is provided in Article 10 of the FLEC. Among the vertical agreements considered there, exclusive dealing, exclusive territories and resale-price maintenance are mentioned explicitly, whereas unilateral conduct only comprises tying and bundling, and refusals to deal. There is however a separate catch-all provision for 'any conduct that unduly harms competition'. The latter provision has commonly been interpreted as to cover practices such as predatory pricing, cross subsidization, price discrimination—which often goes hand in hand with refusals to deal—and raising rival's costs. In fact, in the regulations to the FLEC which were issued early in 1998, the catch-all provision was spelled out further so as to include precisely the four above-mentioned types of behaviour.

A striking feature of the FLEC is that it does not prohibit exploitative abuses of dominance. Having market power and its exploitation are perfectly legal; only exclusionary abuse is prohibited. This is the more surprising because the Mexican Competition Law came to replace another law which granted extensive powers to the Executive to control the prices of a vast basket of products.[3] In fact, in the mid-1980s more than half of Mexico's aggregate value of production of goods had been under some form of price control by the Ministry of Trade and Industrial Promotion (MTIP), a proportion which was reduced significantly during the late 1980s with the structural adjustment programmes adopted during that period.

---

[2] See Gabriel Castañeda, Santiago Levy, Gabriel Martínez, and Gustavo Merino *Antecedentes Económicos para una Ley Federal de Competencia Económica* (Dec 1992).

[3] Ley sobre Atribuciones del Ejecutivo Federal en Materia Económica, Diario Oficial de la Federación, 30 Dec 1950 and its reforms.

The decision to abstain from prohibiting exploitative abuses of dominant positions seems to have been taken deliberately, in recognition of the fact that market power does not only reflect a lack of competition today but can have been obtained as a result of fierce competition on the merits in the past.[4] Apart from that, it was considered that competition authorities should not be turned into price regulators. Such an approach was entirely in accordance with the criteria for the assessment of monopolization cases developed under US case law.

Altogether, the Mexican competition law enacted in 1992 is quite a modern competition statute designed with the help of experienced competition agencies and the OECD. It draws extensively from the US antitrust experience, particularly from the distinction between per se and rule-of-reason assessment of anticompetitive behaviour. It might even be argued that the Mexican law is more modern than US or EU laws, in particular in its treatment of vertical agreements and unilateral conduct under one and the same rule-of-reason test and in the fact that it does not outlaw resale-price maintenance per se.

Thus, Mexican competition law enforcement started off with a typically effects-based approach. This does not mean that there is a mandate to strictly quantify the pro- and anticompetitive effects of the investigated practices according to some welfare standard, which I believe everybody would agree is virtually impossible, but it implies a recognition of the fact that vertical restraints and unilateral conduct may have significant beneficial effects which must be taken into account on a case-by-case basis.

III. MONOPOLIZATION CASES

Making an assessment of how these criteria have been brought to practice in monopolization/abuse-of-dominance cases resolved by the Federal Competition Commission (FCC) during the first decade of Mexico's competition regime, goes beyond the scope of this paper. I confine myself to a brief description of two noteworthy cases. The first concerns a predatory pricing complaint by the chewing-gum manufacturer *Canel's* against *Adams*, a subsidiary of *Warner Lambert Cy*; the second refers to *PCTV*, a joint venture of regional cable distributors for the acquisition and resale of TV programmes, which discriminated against or refused to deal with outsiders.

---

[4] See Castañeda et al (n 1).

A. Canel's v Adams/ Warner Lambert[5]

In June 1994, exactly one year after the creation of the Federal Competition Commission (FCC), Canel's filed a complaint against Adams for predatory pricing in the chewing-gum market. Canel's is a fully Mexican-owned firm whose main product is chewing-gum; Adams was a subsidiary of the multi-national drugs and confectionery manufacturer Warner Lambert Cy, producing chewing-gum as part of a wider basket of candies and confec-tionery. Canel's main product (Canels 4's) had traditionally been sold through informal channels, like street vendors and small shops, but was gradually penetrating the formal part of the market (supermarkets) where the presence of Adams' star performer, Chiclets 4's, was much stronger in spite of its higher prices.

As early as 1985 Adams had launched a fighting brand named Clarks, almost indistinguishable from Canels 4's and selling at a price significantly lower than that of its branded product Chiclets 4's. After a dispute about industrial property rights, Adams changed the presentation of Clarks slightly but continued selling at the low price. At that time there was no competition law but price interventions were pervasive so that Canel's asked the MTIP for mediation. Several settlements were reached through commitments by Adams to charge certain minimum prices but all these settlements were breached after some time through aggressive marketing strategies with deep discounts and similar incentives.

Shortly after the enactment of the competition law Canel's turned to the FCC accusing Adams of predatory pricing by selling Clarks systematically below costs in order to drive Canel's from the market or at least to prevent it from penetrating the formal segment of the market further. For the FCC it was the first case of this type and in the absence of precedents it estab-lished a number of criteria to assess such cases. Some of them had to do with the cost concept and with the way in which indirect costs should be allocated among products in the case of multiproduct firms, others with the likelihood of success of exclusion. Apart from that, the mandatory market power test was applied.

The relevant market was defined as that of chewing-gum. Candies and other confectioneries were not considered close enough substitutes to exer-cise any pricing discipline over chewing-gum. Somewhat more surprisingly, the formal and the informal distribution channels were taken to belong to the same relevant market, in spite of the fact that prices in the formal

---

[5] Comisión Federal de Competencia, *Informe Annual 1997*, 73 and Gaceta de Competencia Económica, *Chicles Canel's / Chicle Adams / Grupo Warner Lambert México*, No 14 (Sept–Dec 2002) 289–398.

segment more than doubled prices in the informal segment. This decision was justified with arguments of supply substitution, ie as Chiclets 4's was virtually the same product as Clarks, the production capacity of the former could readily be switched to produce the latter. The market was considered to have national coverage mainly because at that time import tariffs from the US were still considerable (in 1994 18 per cent *ad valorem*).

A finding of market power for Adams was established considering (i) its superior market share (above 60 per cent); (ii) the fact that it was able to unilaterally raise its prices above competitive levels without its competitors being able to counteract this behaviour, as evidenced by the fact that it could maintain the price of Chiclets 4's significantly above that of Clarks and Canels 4's without losing market share; and (iii) strong entry barriers mainly consisting of the strength of Adams' brand and sunk investment costs.

Regarding costs, the FCC established that for there to be a conduct in violation of the FLEC, price must be below average *total* cost for an extended period of time. Below-cost pricing for introductory purposes or temporary promotion campaigns would not fall in this category. With respect to product-wise cost accounting it was held that indirect costs should preferably— ie unless there are specific reasons not so do so—be distributed according to sales costs, not to sales values, as Adams had done in its own accounting exercise, the latter because taking sales value as a basis for cost division would allocate a much higher proportion of indirect costs to the more expensive product Chiclets and so disguise eventual losses incurred with Clarks. Regarding the likelihood of successful exclusion the FCC held that predatory conduct must induce losses to the victim; otherwise the exclusionary intent would not be credible. In other words, if Canel's would turn out to have made positive profits, it was considered competition would not be threatened.

Applying these criteria the FCC resolved the case in February 1996 by declaring no violation of the law, mainly because Canel's had not been able to demonstrate that it had suffered losses during the period Adams had been selling below cost. It warned Adams, however, that if the presumption of predatory pricing would continue it might initiate an ex-officio investigation any time in the future. In spite of this favourable resolution Adams filed an appeal before the FCC protesting against the warning (why are you warning me if I did nothing wrong?) and against some aspects of the criteria for cost accounting. In the final resolution the FCC maintained its position with some minor adjustments in the phrasing of its warning and of the criteria for cost accounting.

Canel's was unpleasantly surprised with this outcome. Particularly the fact that it should have demonstrated losses was difficult to understand where it was precisely the below-cost pricing by Adams it had targeted as a violation of the law. Moreover, Canel's itself had also a considerable market share. In the informal segment of the market where the predatory pricing actually occurred it was in fact the largest player of the two. Perhaps the resolution would have raised less confusion if the FCC would have linked the likelihood of success of the exclusionary conduct more directly with an analysis of the evolution of market shares, which could have been performed in a straight-forward way without the need of cost-accounting exercises.

However, a few months later (April 1996) the FCC started an ex-officio investigation due to the persistence of aggressive pricing strategies by Adams which at that time had become part of Grupo Warner Lambert México (GWLM). The results of the new investigation were quite similar to those of the previous one but by moving the period of investigation a couple of years ahead Canel's could demonstrate to have suffered losses systematically. It was until November 1997 that the FCC resolved by declaring the existence of price predation in violation of the FLEC, ordering GWLM to abstain from such conduct in the future and imposing a fine. Once more, GWLM appealed before the FCC but the arguments were rejected and in May 1998 the Commission confirmed its previous resolution without any modifications.

The way in which the FCC handled this case was heavily criticized both inside and outside Mexico. Within Mexico there was the usual skrimmage about whether the relevant market was defined properly and whether GWLM had any market power. However, the defendant's arguments that the market should be wider were weakened by the fact that it had hardly protested against the market delineation of the original investigation. Regarding market power, GWLM's market share in the chewing gum market was held to be approximately 70 per cent, which was not accepted by the defendant. Anyway, the shares were measured in terms of sales values, not volumes. Without a doubt GWLM's market share would have been significantly lower, probably slightly above 50 per cent, when measured in terms of volumes, because in the formal segment of the market where GWLM was the dominant player, prices almost tripled those of the informal segment.[6] In this respect, a market share of just above 50 per cent would probably be considered low in monopolization cases in the US but sufficient in abuse-of-dominance cases in the EU. Canel's cause was further

---

[6] It should be admitted that measuring market shares in terms of sales values is inconsistent with the argument about supply-side substation used earlier to justify joining formal and informal sales in a single relevant market. Indeed, if the production capacity of Chiclets 4's can readily be switched to the production of Clarks it is volumes that matter not values.

weakened by a badly timed interview with the plaintiff's CEO in a business magazine in which he bragged about the success and expansionary ambitions of the company.[7]

From outside Mexico the decision was criticized for three reasons. In the first place, it was considered that the total cost criterion adopted by the FCC was too severe and not in accordance with international practice which relies more on variable cost. In the second place, the Commission was accused of protecting national companies against foreign competition in spite of the almost universal consensus that competition law enforcement should be neutral in this respect. This accusation seems somewhat opportunistic because in none of the resolutions is there any discriminatory language, or a preference for national companies, if present, would have become clear from many other cases. The third objection had to do with the absence of a recoupment test. For predatory pricing to be successful it is not only necessary that competitors be effectively driven out of the market (or disciplined); there must also be recoupment of predatory losses. If recoupment is not possible, there is no harm to competition even if competitors are expelled from the market. Since *Brooke Group*[8] the recoupment test has become widely accepted as a criterion for the assessment of predatory pricing cases in the US and some other countries, though not in the EU.[9] Since then the OECD has recommended Mexican competition law enforcers on several occasions to introduce such a test.[10]

Already in the course of the ex-officio investigation GWLM filed a constitutional appeal (amparo) before the Judicial System, seeking protection against the vagueness of the phrasing of Article 10's catch-all provision and similar concepts of the law, such as 'relevant market' and 'substantial market power'. According to GWLM this would leave defendants in a position of great legal uncertainty, particularly in view of the allegedly arbitrary way in which the FCC had established its own criteria to define these concepts in the case at issue. After the final resolution of the ex-officio investigation, issued in May 1998, GWLM filed another amparo alleging that the FCC had transgressed principles of due process, among others. Followed a skrimmage among all participants in the procedure—defendant, plaintiff and the FCC—and the judicial system, in which both amparos went all the way up to the Supreme Court and the FCC had to reinstate the investigation procedure in 2002 arriving at essentially the same outcome as

---

[7] José Ramón Huerta *Canel's: Pegó Su* Chicle, Expansión, No 718 (18 June 1997) 58.

[8] *Brooke Group Ltd v Brown & Williamson Tobacco Corp*, 509 US at 209 (1993).

[9] See Gunnar Niels and Adriaan Ten Kate 'Predatory Pricing Standards: Is There a Growing International Consensus?' (2000) 45 Antitrust Bulletin 787.

[10] See, eg, OECD, *Mexico: The Role of Competition Policy in Regulatory Reform* (1999) 27.

in 1998. However, at the end of the day (in March 2004) the Supreme Court held that the concepts of relevant market and market power were sufficiently specified in the FLEC so as not to give rise to legal uncertainty, as claimed by *GWLM*, but it protected *GWLM* against the vagueness of the catch-all provision, so annulling the FCC's finding of an anticompetitive practice.

This Supreme Court decision has effectively declared the catch-all provision of Article 10 unconstitutional and has left the FCC unarmed in its struggle against predatory and discriminatory conduct by dominant firms. Currently, proposals are under way to amend the competition law in such a way as to incorporate the descriptions of predatory and discriminatory pricing, cross-subsidization and raising rivals' costs, which are now in the Regulations of the FLEC, into the text of the competition law itself, which would solve the constitutional controversy. The fate of these proposals remains uncertain, however.

B. *Telecable de Oriente v PCTV*[11]

In August 1999 *Telecable de Oriente* and some other regional cable TV operators filed a compaint against *Productora y Comercializadora de Televisión (PCTV)* for relative monopolistic practices in violation of the FLEC. The alleged offenses were refusals to deal, price discrimination and exclusivity in the sales of bundled TV programmes. The FCC admitted the complaint and started an investigation.

PCTV is a joint venture of regional cable operators founded before the enactment of the competition law with the aim of enhancing their bargaining power vis-à-vis programme producers in order to obtain TV programmes and channels at conditions more favourable than would be possible through individual negotiations. PCTV also bundles those channels, and adds some value by incorporating mostly local advertising before reselling them to its members and other interested parties.

PCTV's members are regional cable operators who are not competing amongst each other because at the time PCTV was founded there was only one concession per region. The picture changed with the issuing of a new Code of Regulations for Telecommunications which allowed for so-called 'second concessions'.[12] The plaintiffs were holders of such second concessions. They had a double second-mover disadvantage: one due to the economies of scale involved in building the cable network infrastructure

---

[11] Comisión Federal de Competencia, Gaceta de Competencia Económica, No 15 (Jan–Apr 2003) 462–502.
[12] See Art 23 of the Reglamento de Telecomunicaciones, issued in Oct 1990.

and the other at the side of programme acquisition where they lacked the critical mass necessary to obtain favorable conditions. No wonder they tried to acquire content from PCTV at the same terms as granted to their members. Less wonder PCTVs shareholders did not want to share for free the benefits of their past efforts with what they saw as unwelcome competitors. After the adoption of the Code of Regulations PCTV changed its statute and rules of operations so as to exclude second concessionaries from membership and charge them prices for content higher than to its members.

In the course of the investigation horizontal market segmentation was added to the list of alleged monopolistic practices. Some of the plaintiffs had argued that the members of the Board of Directors of PCTV, who themselves were holders of concessions in different regions, had implicitly agreed not to invade each others territories and to defend their territories against entrance of newcomers with the afore-mentioned change of the statute. Horizontal market segmentation is an absolute monopolistic practice defined in Article 9 of the FLEC, which is forbidden per se.

In the first round of the investigation the relevant market was defined as that of distribution and commercialization of content for cable TV at the national level and PCTV was held to have market power because its members served more than 80 per cent of all cable TV subscribers in Mexico. Moreover, it was considered there was sufficient evidence to conclude that PCTV and its Board members had committed the alleged practices. Thus, the FCC accused PCTV by October 2002 of all the monopolistic practices that figured in the complaints, ie clauses for exclusive distribution in Mexico with content producers, refusals to deal with, and discrimination against, non-members as well as market segmentation. The latter accusation was not against PCTV but against its Board members.

In its defense PCTV argued that the relevant market definition adopted by the FCC was incorrect; in the first place because *PCTV* does not participate in the distribution of TV signals but only in their commercialization; in the second because it is not only cable operators to which it resells content but also to distributors using other technologies such as microwaves (MMDS) and satellite (DTH) to broadcast their signals, and third because it should also include the open channels which are available to everybody by antenna but which must be included in any package because consumers find it important to have access to them through their subscriptions.

Regarding market power PCTV argued (i) that the number of subscribers of its members was an inadequate base for measuring market shares; (ii) that there were other firms commercializing content for pay-TV, offering channels not necessarily the same as PCTV but of the same kind as PCTV's channels and thus competing with PCTV's supply; (iii) that individual cable operators could also acquire content directly with programme producers because *PCTV* had no exclusivity but only what was called 'first choice' with some programme producers (ie programme producers reserved the right to sell directly to operators not served by PCTV); and (iv) that there was sufficient room in the market for non-members of PCTV to form their own joint venture for acquiring content.

As regards the relative monopolistic practices (price discrimination and refusals to deal) the defendant asked the FCC to consider the fact that, when second concessionaries were given access on equal terms to programmes and channels offered by PCTV, they would actually be free-riding on the achievements of a joint-venture they didn't help to establish in the first place. Moreover, regarding exclusivity PCTV disclosed its contracts with programme producers to the FCC, from which it became clear that it was indeed 'first choice' that prevailed. Exclusivity was only present with some channels with relatively low ratings.

With respect to the absolute monopolistic practice of market segmentation the arguments of the defendants were rather formalistic. In the first place, it was claimed that it was not the members of the Board of Directors but the assembly of shareholders that had the power to change the statute of the association. In the second, it was argued that neither the members of the Board nor the shareholders were competing amongst each other because they were holding concessions in different regions so that the fundamental condition for absolute monopolistic practices—that there be an agreement between competitors—was not satisfied.

In its final resolution the FCC admitted that the relevant market should be defined as that of commercialization (not distribution) of content to pay-TV operators irrespective of the technology used to transmit the signals to the final consumers. Only the defendant's argument about open channels was not accepted because the FCC considered those channels just a supplement to the restricted channels even though they played an important role in consumer choice. Moreover, the FCC presented the results of an extensive analysis of substitute channels offered by other firms commercializing TV content from which it appeared that the choice of cable operators that were no members of PCTV was not so limited as claimed by the plaintiffs. All these elements annulled its previous finding of market power and the FCC absolved PCTV from the commission of the alleged relative monopolistic practices.

In contrast, the FCC held up its charge for absolute monopolistic practices by market segmentation. It argued that, whatever the precise role of the members of the Board or the shareholders, the change of the statute of *PCTV* had been a vehicle to withhold its members from entering other regions with second concessions for which they would be perfect candidates. The fact that they were no actual competitors did not imply that they were no potential competitors and, in fact, with any geographical market segmentation potential competitors are no longer actual competitors precisely due to such an agreement.

PCTV appealed this resolution before the FCC and proposed a settlement consisting in a modification of its statute so as to admit new shareholders, subject to an evaluation of its market power in 2005. *PCTV* argued that the market was changing rapidly and that by that time there would be more competition by second concessions and from MMDS and DTH technologies. This proposal was accepted by the FCC by which the conflict was settled for the time being.

III. IN HINDSIGHT

Some outside observers consider the final resolutions in the chewing gum war as the worst antitrust essays written by the FCC since its creation. Whether they are right or wrong is not up to me to judge but there is little doubt that the backlash of the case, ie the recent declaration of unconstitutionality of the catch-all provision of Article 10 due to its vagueness, is an important setback for competition policy in Mexico. Ironically, the phrasing of the catch-all provision of Article 10 ('any act that unduly harms or impedes competition') is hardly vaguer than that of Section I of the Sherman Act ('every contract [. . .] in restraint of trade') or of Article 81 of the EC Treaty ('agreements [. . .] which have as their object of effect the prevention, restriction or distortion of competition'). This can only be understood in light of the fact that Mexico has a system of civil, not common law.

In contrast, the final resolution in the case of the cable TV operators would perhaps qualify as one of the best antitrust essays in the history of the FCC. Indeed, the resolution gives testimony of a careful listening to the arguments of the defendants and of a thorough analysis of all the issues brought up by both plaintiffs and defendants during the procedure.

It should be noticed, however, that in both cases most of the arguments have focused on three elements. First, on whether the investigated conduct matched the description of relative monopolistic practices as provided in Article 10 of the FLEC; secondly, on the definition of the relevant market; and thirdly, on whether the defendants had substantial power in that market. Little attention has been paid to displacement and exclusion of competitors from the market and even less to whether such displacement was 'undue'. In the chewing gum case the likelihood of displacement of the plaintiff was addressed by considering its current losses but no attention was given to recoupment. In the PCTV case the impediments to entry to related markets were mentioned in relation to absolute monopolistic practices where they should not play a role but in none of these cases was the undueness of eventual foreclosure mentioned.

One may wonder, for example, what would have happened if the FCC would have been able to hold up a positive finding of market power for PCTV. Everything seems to indicate that such a finding would have resulted in an establishment of an infringement of the FLEC. Questions on whether the shareholders were entitled to appropriate the benefits of their past investments by not sharing them with newcomers and on whether vertical risk sharing implicit in non-linear pricing schemes between PCTV and its clients were sufficient to justify its discriminatory conduct remained largely unanswered. Likewise, in the chewing gum case the battle was about the definition of the relevant market and market power, and only a bit about the successfulness of displacement, but recoupment, which immediately addresses consumer harm, remained unattended.

Altogether, although Mexican competition law was designed in the spirit of an effects-based antitrust regime, at least with respect to the assessment of relative monopolistic practices, the cases presented in this paper clearly suggest that its application has mainly focused on the form of the conduct and a market-power test with little attention for the possible economic justifications for the conduct under investigation. As I argue below, this is not so surprising in view of the enormous difficulties involved in an evaluation of economic effects in general and of the even greater difficulties to defend such evaluations in Court.

IV. FORM-BASED VERSUS EFFECTS-BASED SYSTEMS

In a form-based approach a conduct is illegal for what is done, irrespective of its effects. In an effects-based approach it is rather the effects of the conduct which determine whether it is legal or not. If the effects are beneficial, or at least not harmful, there is no offense even if the conduct is anti-competitive in its form. In competition law the distinction between form- and effects-based approaches roughly coincides with that between per se and rule of reason. Under per se an agreement is illegal for what is agreed; under a rule of reason it is only illegal when its net effects on welfare are negative in the case at issue.

As a general rule form-based regimes are easier to implement than systems based on effects. This is due to the difficulty to measure effects. To estimate the effects of conduct on welfare one must make assumptions about what would have happened without the conduct, ie about the counterfactuals. All too often, the magnitude of effects, and sometimes even their sign, hangs critically on these assumptions so that 'dancing with the counterfactuals' makes practically everything possible.[13]

A direct consequence of the fact that economic effects are difficult to determine is that an effects-based system provides less legal certainty than a form-based system. In a form-based system it is easier to know whether what one is doing is right or wrong. In an effects-based system what one does may be wrong only for the outcome of some complicated economic model or reasoning that for many people are far-fetched or at least debatable.

Finally, it is commonly held that form-based regimes are less permissive than their effects-based counterparts and to the extent that the latter provide efficiency justifications for conduct that would otherwise be prohibited this is indeed the case. Still, the degree of intervention also depends on what exactly is permitted in a form-based system and on the way in which the effects are measured and on what welfare standard is adopted in an effects-based system. For example, with a consumer welfare standard the system will be less permissive than with a total surplus standard.

V. THE FORM-PLUS APPROACH

Most systems are somewhere in between purely form-based and purely effects-based. Effects are usually not measured quantitatively (assuming that that would be possible at all) but are rather approximated with form-based rules. The most common mixture of a form-based and an effects-based system is what I called above the form-plus approach, which stands for an essentially form-based system complemented with a market-power test.

In such a system market power is used as a proxy for the anticompetitive effects of the conduct at issue. Pro-competitive effects, on the other hand,

---

[13] For example, it is often argued that exclusive dealing imposed by car manufacturers upon their dealers is to avoid free-riding by competitors and so encourage the transfer of the know-how required for after-sale services, among others. One may wonder, however, what would happen without exclusive dealing. Would dealers give up loyalty and trade other marks? And would the manufacturer indeed stop transferring know-how? If so, would he compensate his dealers with lower wholesale prices? And what would the dealers do? Would they buy the required know-how with their own money? And so on. Without an answer to these questions it is impossible to estimate the effects of exclusive dealing. Put another way, the free-riders argument is qualitatively correct but to estimate the effects quantitatively one must know the counterfactuals to begin with. Thus, an economic effects analysis of conduct is equally as speculative as guessing what would happen without that conduct.

are usually unrelated to market power and can well be substantial for dominant firms. Thus, a market power test alone fails to consider the pro-competitive effects of conduct. As a consequence, form-plus approaches are usually overly interventionist and may unduly punish pro-competitive behaviour.

In light of the foregoing, classifying European competition law enforcement as form-based and US antitrust as effects-based seems somewhat simplistic. Yet, there is little doubt that European competition law is more formalistic, legalistic and interventionist than US antitrust. Perhaps the European system is closer to the form-plus approach described above.

VI. CONCLUSIONS

It is sometimes argued that the enforcement of the Mexican competition regime has gradually drifted away from an effects-based approach and has become more interventionist than originally envisaged by the designers of the law. In fact, Mexican competition enforcement has come closer to the form-plus approach which seems to prevail in Europe. This is not only the case for unilateral conduct but also for vertical restraints for which a simple finding of market power is often considered sufficient to declare the conduct illegal. Moreover, there are strong voices advocating to reform the FLEC in such a way as to prohibit exploitative abuses of market power and to introduce the concept of collective dominance, not only in the ambit of merger control but also for the assessment of relative monopolistic conduct. A proposal to amend the law accordingly is currently under discussion.

Some scholars, and of course many defendants, consider these developments as deplorable. According to them Mexican competition law enforcement has gone the wrong way. Even if they were right, one should recognize that in most developing countries—and Mexico is no exception—there are a number of forces at work pushing competition policy in that direction. What is more, some of these forces are equally present in the more advanced countries, which would provide some food for thought for competition officials in traditional jurisdictions who consider the introduction of more economic elements in the assessment of their cases.

In the first place, newly installed competition agencies in developing countries are usually under great pressure to 'perform'. All too often, to get the legislation through greater than realistic expectations had to be raised about the benefits competition policies can bring to the society. In the popular view the big-is-bad paradigm is still strong and price increases are perceived as devilish. So the public at large expects the competition authority to remedy such evils. How is it possible then that our competition agency sits back in its chair, with its arms crossed, seeing how gas prices go up or how Walmart eats up pop 'n mom stores one after another without doing anything about it? In such circumstances temptations to intervene are strong and it is not at all easy for a competition authority to 'keep its head cool' and justify non-intervention on the basis of economic concepts that are often complicated, counter-intuitive and not always well understood by the public.

In the second, recently installed agencies in developing countries are not only under great pressure to perform; they are also anxious to perform mostly out of a professional vocation to promote competition in an environment where it is most needed. As a general rule competition officials in such countries are little aware of all the pitfalls antitrust enforcement has gone through in traditional jurisdictions and prefer to leapfrog the lessons from the Chicago school rather than to learn them.

In the third, it is easy to say that an effects-based system is superior to a form-based or a form-plus approach but one should recognize that the enormous difficulties involved in estimating the welfare effects of conduct with any degree of reliability, particularly the pro-competitive ones, make an effects-based approach definitely less administrable. Even in the more experienced jurisdictions pro-competitive effects are seldom determined in a quantitative way. It is more a matter of knowing that they exist and adjust the assessment criteria accordingly. That is not easy to explain to plaintiffs or defendants and less so to judges.

Altogether, it is unsurprising that Mexico's FCC has opted for an essentially form-plus approach and has gradually become more interventionist, much like European competition enforcement. This in spite of the original intentions to implement a fully effects-based system. It is also likely that many other competition agencies in developing countries and transition economies will follow suit.

Reform of Article 82: Where the Link Between Dominance and Effects Breaks Down

Gunnar Niels

The reform of Article 82 is high on the EU competition policy agenda. Many commentators are of the view that abuse of dominance cases should move away from the current form-based approach to an effects-based approach. This article explores one of the fundamental shortcomings of the current approach—the use of dominance determinations as a shortcut to infer inter-competitive effects.

The European Commission's review of its policy on abuse of dominance is one of the main policy issues in EU competition law in 2005. This review follows the substantial changes made in recent years to the other two pillars of competition law: merger control, and restrictive agreements under Article 81 of the EC Treaty. One outcome of these previous reforms is that EC policy on mergers and agreements has been brought more into line with current economic thinking.

The general expectation is that the abuse of dominance provisions in Article 82 will follow a similar path. EU case law on abuse has for years been criticised as legalistic and interventionist, and the current review is seen by many as an opportunity for change. Various commentators have stressed the desirability of moving towards an approach that emphasises the actual or expected economic effects of allegedly abusive behaviour by dominant firms, rather than its form.[1]

Perhaps less attention has been paid thus far to where it is exactly that the current approach fails. Many have argued that Article 82 protects competitors rather than competition—but how does this come about? This article explains that one of the fundamental shortcomings in the current case law is the virtual per se prohibition of certain practices once a firm is deemed to be dominant—in other words, dominance is used as a shortcut to infer anti-competitive effects. This can be misleading, as the implied link between dominance and effects does not always hold.

---

[1] See J Vickers (2004) 'Abuse of Market Power', speech to the conference of the European Association for Research in Industrial Economics, Berlin 3 Sept; and Competition Law Forum Article 82 Review Group (2005) 'The Reform of Article 83: Recommendations on Key Policy Objectives', European Competition Review 1, 179–83.

I. BULLS IN A CHINA SHOP

Article 82 policy has traditionally been influenced by the 'ordo-liberal school'. In essence, this school of thought emphasises individual freedom as the primary objective for competition policy, and considers that the presence of dominant firms weakens the competitive process and reduces the economic freedom of other market participants.

The notion that the mere existence of dominant firms is dangerous for competition is still deeply embedded in EU law. A dominant firm is in effect regarded as the proverbial bull in a china shop—it must be restrained to prevent it from inflicting further damage to its already fragile surroundings. As formally established in *Michelin* (1983), a dominant firm has a 'special responsibility not to allow its conduct to impair genuine undistorted competition on the common market'.[2]

This view on how competition works appears somewhat outdated. Economic theory and practical experience over the past 30–40 years have shown that competitive dynamics can function well even if a market has some very large players. (Indeed, large players and/or temporary positions of market power can improve competitive dynamics.) The theory has also established that certain behaviour can have positive efficiency effects, even if practised by dominant firms. In other words, using the bull analogy to describe dominant firms does not fit well with current thinking on how markets work.

The shortcomings of the current approach to Article 82 arise from a combination of the following three policy aspects:

- EU case law has only one threshold for dominance, regardless of the type of practice at hand;
- this threshold is set relatively low; and
- the threshold constitutes the basis for a form-based per se prohibition of certain behaviour.

With regard to the first of these, it is important to bear in mind that market power is a matter of degree—Microsoft has market power, but so has a small corner shop (provided there are few other shops nearby). Dominance can be interpreted as a very high degree of market power—one that enables a firm of sustain prices above the competitive level without inducing customer switching or competitor entry.

The assessment of dominance can be a useful intermediary step in the analysis of an alleged abuse of dominance. In particular, many types of

---

[2] Case 322/81, *Michelin* [1983] ECR 3461.

behaviour are likely to be of little competitive concern if the accused firm is not dominant—in other words, dominance is a necessary condition, and can be used to filter out cases *below* the threshold. However, in EU law, dominance is also used the other way around—ie, to apply virtual per se prohibitions to firms above the threshold.

This policy approach can be problematic. From an economics perspective, the competitive effects of any business practice will depend on, first, the type of practice in question, and second, the degree of market power of the firm in question. The current 'one-size-fits-all' dominance threshold—the traditional market share rule of thumb of 40–50 per cent (combined with some indications of entry barriers) still seems to be the norm[3]—is arguably set too low to allow for any strong inferences of anti-competitive effects, as discussed in this article.

This is not to say that a per se prohibition above a certain dominance threshold can never be the correct policy approach. Such a prohibition might be justified if the threshold were set sufficiently high—some types of behaviour (such as refusal to deal or margin squeeze) are often invariably anti-competitive if engaged in by a firm with a near-monopoly. In this respect it is worth noting that some recent EU cases have referred to the concept of 'super-dominance', which might be a reasonable threshold above which the behaviour under investigation can be presumed to have anti-competitive effects.[4]

However, if the current, lower threshold for dominance is maintained, this can only be used as an intermediate step in the analysis of actual or likely anti-competitive effects—ie, as a necessary but not sufficient condition. A further assessment of those effects is required.

II. PREDATION AND TARGETED DISCOUNTING

Predatory pricing and targeted discounting are practices where the link between dominance and effects may not hold. US antitrust law has established the 'recoupment test' for predation cases, which places strong emphasis on whether market structure is such that predation is feasible (and

---

[3] This rule of thumb for the dominance threshold appears to have been confirmed in the recent Coca-Cola undertakings (Case COMP/39.116/B-2, announced on 19 Oct 2004) with respect to exclusivity, rebates and tying, which apply to those countries where Coca-Cola's soft drinks represent more than 40 per cent of national sales (and more than double the share of the nearest competitor).

[4] Super-dominance was first defined as a 'position of overwhelming dominance verging on monopoly', in Opinion of Advocate General Fennelly of 19 Oct 1998 on *Compagnie Maritime Belge* and *Dafra-Lines*, Joined Cases C-395/96 P and C-396/98 P, para 137.

hence the initial losses from predation can be recouped through subsequent monopoly profits).[5]

While sometimes criticised as overly harsh on complainants, the recoupment test has consumer welfare at its heart, as it essentially allows any aggressive price cut as long as there is no prospect for successful monopolisation of the market.

In contrast, EU law has explicitly rejected the recoupment test—it considers pricing below the acceptable level (see below) by dominant firms as abusive in itself if there is a risk that competitors are eliminated, and therefore sees no need to establish the feasibility of predation.[6] Another (more economic) justification for rejecting the recoupment test might be that the possession of dominance in itself means that feasibility of predation is likely. However, the conditions for recoupment are typically more stringent than those for dominance, as defined in EU law. (For example, a very high market share is needed from the start, and greater emphasis is placed on the possibility of successfully maintaining monopoly prices in future.)[7]

Instead, predatory pricing cases in the EU focus primarily on the relationship between prices and costs. In the AKZO judgment (1993), the European Court of Justice determined that predation can be presumed if a dominant firm sets prices below average variable costs (AVC).[8] As such, this test is reasonably in line with economic theory, which also identifies marginal cost (or some variant) as a relevant price floor for predation cases. Yet the risk is the pricing below AVC by dominant firms is outlawed per se, without any consideration of whether such pricing:

- actually has negative effects on competition, which is not always the case—for example, below-AVC pricing during one month only (the basis for the UK Office of Fair Trading's finding of predation in *Aberdeen Journals*[9]) is arguably not sufficient to infer an anti-competitive effect;
- may be justified on efficiency grounds—for example, if there are strong network effects, below-AVC pricing may be required to gain critical mass, even in the absence of any competitors.[10]

---

[5] *Brooke Group Ltd v Brown & Williamson Tobacco Corp* 509 US 209 (1993).

[6] Case C-333/94P, *Tetra Pak v Commission* [1996], ECR I-5951.

[7] See G Niels and A Ten Kate (2000) 'Predatory Pricing Standards: Is there a Growing International Consensus', Antitrust Bulletin, 45, 787–809.

[8] Case C62/86, *Chemie v Commission* [1991], ECR I-3359 [1993] 5 CMLR 215. Prices in the range between AVC and average total cost are deemed predatory if the purpose of the conduct was to eliminate a competitor.

[9] Case No CA98/5/2001.\

[10] See A Ten Kate, and G Niels, (2003), 'Below-cost Pricing in the Presence of Network Externalities', in Swedish Competition Authority in *The Pros and Cons of Low Pricing* (Stockholm 2003).

The link between dominance and effects on competition may also not hold in targeted discounting and 'fighting brands' cases. Targeted discounting arises where a dominant firm sets low prices only for those customers who are using, or likely to switch to, a competitor, but keeps other prices unchanged (the *AKZO* case is an example), Fighting brands—or fighting ships in *Compagnie Maritime Belge* and fighting titles in *Aberdeen Journals* (both cases referred to above)—are also specifically targeted at competitors. They are priced low, while the price of the main brand remains unaffected.

In 'standard' predation cases, economic theory establishes a link between market share and the likelihood of success of predation—the higher a predator's market share, the quicker it can depress market price, and hence the greater the chance that rivals will leave the market soon.[11] With targeted discounting and fighting brands, however, this link does not hold because the predator is not reducing the prices on all its products in the market. Take the example in Figure 1. A dominant firm with 90 per cent of the market pitches a fighting brand (representing 10 per cent) against the competitor with 10 per cent market share. The firm therefore only sets below-AVC prices for the fighting brand, keeping the price of its main brand unaffected. In other words, the predator is not using the full weight of its dominance (ie its 90 per cent share), and hence the possession of such dominance is not directly informative on the actual or likely effects on competition.

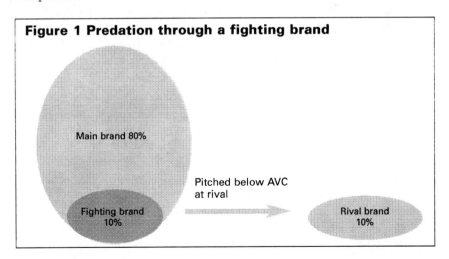

Figure 1 Predation through a fighting brand

Main brand 80%

Pitched below AVC at rival

Fighting brand 10%

Rival brand 10%

[11] To give an example, if market demand is inelastic (elasticity = –0.5), and 'quick and dirty' predation requires the market price to be cut by 40 per cent, a predator with a 10 per cent market share would have to triple its output; a predator with 40 per cent still must increase output by half; while a predator with 90 per cent heads to increase output by only 20 per cent.

This is not to say that complains about these forms of predation should be rejected outright. The point is that the actual or likely effects of targeted discounting or fighting brands need to be assessed more carefully, and cannot be inferred from the position of dominance in the broader market as such.

III. VERTICAL FORECLOSURE

Form-based rules have also been applied to practices that may result in vertical foreclosure by dominant firms, such as exclusivity requirements and loyalty incentives on distributors. Under EU law, dominant firms are virtually prevented from engaging in any such practice. Again, such a per se approach may be overly intrusive and unrelated to the actual or likely effects on competition. The existence of dominance is a necessary but not sufficient condition for this to apply. Whether a significant part of the distribution channel is indeed foreclosed must also be assessed. For example, if a dominant firm with 60 per cent of the market imposes exclusivity requirements on 10 per cent of all distributors, the foreclosure effect is probably limited. In this case, a prohibition seems less appropriate than if, say, 60 per cent of the distribution channel were foreclosed, particularly if such exclusivity generates certain efficiency benefits (which would also need to be assessed as part of the effects-based test).

The treatment of loyalty rebates illustrates the shortcomings of the form-based approach in EU law. In two judgments in 2003—*Michelin II* and *British Airways*—the Court of First Instance confirmed the long-established EU policy that dominant firms are only allowed to offer discounts that relate to cost savings, but not to encourage loyalty.[12] Any considerations of the actual or likely effects of such discounts on competition are deemed irrelevant.

For example, in *British Airways*, the concern was the the loyalty incentives offered by the airline to travel agents were retrospective—ie, paid on all ticket sales above the performance target, and not just on the incremental sales above that target—and could thus induce agents who are close to their sales target to promote British Airways rather than rival airlines. The form of this incentive scheme was considered an abuse, without much consideration of the effects. One such effect could have been the foreclosure of sales channels to Virgin Atlantic, a new competitor and complainant in this case. However, Virgin had continued to gain market share throughout the affected period, which indicates that the competitive effect of the loyalty

---

[12] Case T-203/01, *Michelin v Commission*, Judgment of 30 Sept 2003; and Case T-219/99, *British Airways v Commission*, Judgment of 17 Dec 2003.

schemes was probably limited. For the US court that reviewed the same facts, this was one reason (among others) to reject the complaint that Virgin had filed in that jurisdiction.[13] In contrast, the European Commission simply made the point that Virgin would have had even more success in the absence of the loyalty schemes.

IV. ABUSE IN A RELATED MARKET

A final illustration of where the link between dominance and effects may not hold refers to the principle that dominance in one market can also be abused in a related market.[14] This principle means that, in practice, dominant firms can be subject to the same per se prohibitions in those related markets. In terms of the analogy used earlier in this article, the bull is feared not only inside the china shop, but is also considered capable of inflicting damage as soon as it sets foot outside. Such concerns may overstate the power of dominant firms.

For a more accurate assessment of the competitive effects of an alleged abuse in a related market, it is necessary to establish the precise link between the two markets and to identify the mechanism through which such abuse would work. In some cases there may well be links that enable this type of abuse—for example, where markets are vertically related and one provides an important input to the other, or where the two products are complements. Such links may facilitate leveraging practices such as refusal to supply, tying and discrimination. Making the existence of such links between the two markets explicit is an important part of any effects-based test, but this is not always done in practice—it is often simply taken for granted that a dominant firm can do harm in neighbouring markets.[15]

Furthermore, an assessment of this type of practice would need to consider the actual or likely effects on competition in the related market—is the practice in question likely to result in monopolisation of the related market, or does it merely give the dominant firm some competitive edge in that market? If the latter holds, there is arguably little cause for concern. The likely effects will depend on the relative strength of the dominant firm and other competitors in the related market. Dominance in the first market in itself is no guarantee of success in the second market. Even a company like Microsoft might find it hard to monopolize every market it ventures into.

---

[13] *Virgin Atlantic Airways Ltd v British Airways Plc*, 257 F.3d 256 (2d Cir 2001).

[14] Case C-333/94 *Tetra Pak v Commission* [1996] ECR I-5951.

[15] See, eg, G Niels, and H Jenkins (2000) 'Predation or Innovation? How Competition Authorities Deter Dominant Firms from Entering New Markets' European Competition Law Review 21:6, June, 287–90.

V. CONCLUDING REMARKS

The Commission's review of its policy on Article 82 will lead to a greater consideration of the current economic thinking on abuse of dominance, and there will be much debate on how far this should go. Admittedly, there has as yet been relatively little analysis of the potential negative effects on consumers of the current form-based approach—most of the criticisms that have been made are based on anecdotal evidence, or simply on ideological grounds. This article has set out one of the main shortcomings of the current approach, namely its reliance on the dominance determination as a shortcut to inferring anti-competitive effects. This can lead to incorrect, and probably too much, intervention against many types of business practices by firms that are considered dominant.

A move to some form of effects-based test has been advocated. From an economics perspective, this would be a more appropriate approach to Article 82 as it would allow greater emphasis on efficiency and consumer welfare. Such an effects-based test does not necessarily mean—as some may fear—fully quantifying and weighting all the costs and benefits of the alleged abusive behaviour. Often, it may simply involve the consideration of a range of economic indicators of actual and likely competitive effects that go beyond the assessment of dominance, such as the likelihood of success in excluding competitors and possible efficiency benefits. Dominance would then merely be one of the indicators of relevance to the assessment of allegedly abusive practices.

Panel 6—Unilateral Effects Analysis (Oracle PeopleSoft)

MARK WILLIAMS

Today's session is about unilateral effects in merger control. What are unilateral effects? In practice, unilateral effects have come, rightly or wrongly, to be almost synonymous with what economists might call static oligopoly theory, those mathematical models of competition in markets, in part derived from the pioneering work of Cournot and Bertrand in the last century, and increasingly embodied these days in merger simulation models of ever increasing complexity. But given our transatlantic theme, I think it also seems appropriate to focus our discussion today on unilateral effects and related issues in the recent Oracle PeopleSoft merger, because that was examined both in the US and the EU. We will find out later that partly the EU analysis was not actually under the new SLC test.

Also, given our theme, I think we are particularly lucky in our panel today in that we have three distinguished speakers, all of whom were in one way or another involved in the *Oracle PeopleSoft*[1] debate. My first speaker on my left will be Thomas Vinje, Partner of Clifford Chance, based in their Brussels office. He is particularly known for his expertise at the interface of antitrust and IP law and for its application in the context of technology markets. He is also well known for his work for the interoperability alliance in *Microsoft*[2] and I think for Oracle in the PeopleSoft merger as well. Our second speaker needs no introduction, Greg Werden, because you have already seen him this morning, but I cannot introduce him for this session at least without emphasizing the pioneering work he has undertaken on merger simulation. Merger control, as we know, is some form of looking into the future and more than most, I think, he has done a lot to build and to recognize the limitations of merger simulation models. Equally relevant for today's purposes, he was significantly involved in the DOJ's work on the US arm of *Oracle PeopleSoft*. Our final speaker is Dr Bill Bishop, founder and Chairman of Lexecon Limited, the antitrust economics consultancy. For the last 15 years, as all of you here will know, Bill has been involved in many of the most prominent European antitrust matters, most recently for Sun Microsystems in the EC case against Microsoft and for Oracle in the EU proceedings.

---

[1] *United States v Oracle, Inc* 331 F.Supp.2d 1098 (ND Cal 2004).
[2] Commission decision of 24 Mar 2004, COMP/37.792. *Microsoft Corp v Commission* (Case T-201/04 R) [2005] 4 CMLR 18 (CFI).

THOMAS VINJE

Thank you very much. This indeed does appear to be the way of the future, a second panel with one lawyer and three economists. It won't be that long until the economists are hiring the lawyers for these cases!

A very brief introduction to the case. There was one overlap area between the two parties, Oracle and PeopleSoft: enterprise application software, which is the back office sort of stuff that automates processes in organizations. The overlap area was particularly related to human resources, software and financial management solutions. The merging parties, Oracle and PeopleSoft, were numbers 2 and 3 in enterprise application solutions globally; SAP is number 1. The overall enterprise applications market is highly fragmented and, allegedly, more concentrated in the high end. There was no consideration of a single dominance theory in this case. It was indeed a gap case with respect to the old Merger Regulation. There was no basis for any single dominance theory. For quite some time, as we will see in just a moment, the Commission focused upon a coordinated effects theory and then turned to a non-coordinated, or otherwise called, unilateral effects theory.

Mark has introduced the unilateral effects theory but just in case there may be some in the room who are not particularly familiar with it the concern in a unilateral effects case is that the reduction in competition will occur without coordination. In other words, the merged entity will find it rational to raise prices without expecting a similar reaction from non-merging rivals. This is typically an issue with differentiated product markets where the merging parties are close substitutes and non-merging rivals are less close.

I am going to give you a brief run through the case just to give you a feel for what kind of process it was. It really was quite a saga; it was the longest-running merger case ever. It began on 6 June 2003 with the announcement of the deal. Between mid-June and mid-October we had informal discussions with the case team. There were two substantial information requests and finally in October we filed the form CO. On 17 November we received an Article 6.1 (c) decision that was focused on coordinated effects. There was some brief mention of vertical issues but no mention of unilateral effects. Between mid-November 2003 and mid-March 2004 we continued to have informal discussions with the case team and with the DG Comp hierarchy; all of those discussions were focused on coordinated effects. On 19 December we received what became called by my team 'The Christmas Gift', a very substantial information request, and there appeared to be concern on the part of the Commission that there was a possibility of things becoming disconnected, one might say, between the United States and the

European situation and the clock was stopped for failure to comply with the Christmas Gift information request. It continued to be stopped until after the DOJ filed its challenge in the District Court in San Francisco on 26 February. Soon thereafter followed the Statement of Objections (on 12 March 2004) which focused mainly on non-coordinated or unilateral effects. So we found out, actually only about four or five days before the Statement of Objections, that we were now facing a unilateral effects case and not a coordinated effects case.

So we immediately had access to file. We could say quite a lot about the access to file in this context because for those of you who have not faced an access to file in the context of a hostile merger notification it is quite an experience. An entirely different session could be devoted to that with I think some usefulness. In any event we had a rather rapid access to file. We raced to prepare a response to the Statement of Objections, now on the basis of a unilateral effects theory, and on 31 March began a two-day hearing. I think it was one of those few cases where the hearing actually made a difference. I say that with all due respect to Serge but I think in many cases the writings are more important. But in some few cases the hearing really makes quite a substantial difference. I think this was one case where it really did hit home.

Then over the next few days, after the hearing, we had some rather intense discussions with the DG Comp hierarchy and on 14 April, after the fourth information request was sent, the clock was stopped again. So then we entered into quite a lengthy period of time between mid-April and early October where we responded to that information request. That one came to be known by my team as the 'Information Request from Hell' and indeed it was very demanding; I am not saying inappropriately demanding but extremely demanding in terms of the bid data that it requested. The US trial occurred during this period between June and July. That decision came on 9 September. During this period we had communications with the Commission regarding all of the data submissions that we were required to make and finally on 26 October the clearance decision arrived. I am not going to say much more about the interaction between the two sides of the Atlantic, but I think you can see from this time-line that there were some very substantial ways in which things had to be coordinated on the two sides of the Atlantic.

Now I shall say a few words about the decision and then I will turn to some observations and some unanswered questions about unilateral effects.

The relevant product market: this was one of the more controversial aspects of the case. The Commission, like the DOJ in the United States, defined the product market as consisting of human resources and financial management solutions for high functionality, high-function solutions for HR and FMS, and high-function solutions, typically purchased by LCEs, which stands for large complex enterprises. The proxy used for large complex enterprises was large organizations of 10,000 employees or more than 1 billion euros in revenue with so-called complex functional needs. Now, you might ask what is high-function software? This was also a very controversial issue with respect to which we had many discussions. In any event, as found in the decision, high-function software has certain undefined characteristics regarding scalability, configurability, sophistication, pricing, reliability, quality and brand recognition. The Commission basically found that it was difficult to get one's head around what high-function software really meant, so it adopted a proxy, being the net licence value for any particular deal of over 1 million euros. Basically, if the deal was worth over 1 million euros then it had to be high-function software according to this process. Now this market definition was rejected by the United States Court but it was maintained in the Commission's decision. This product market definition is a critical element of the decision.

With respect to geographical market, the Commission concluded that the market was global and it used econometric evidence—a discount analysis—to show that the average discount did not vary depending upon the location of the bid and on that basis the Commission concluded that the geographic market was global. That was contrary to the DOJ's limitation to the US market and we feel at least that the reason the DOJ limited the geographic market to the US was that that thereby limited the significance of SAP. In that context I might note that the news came out just yesterday that, not in this particular high-function software market, but more generally in the EIS market, SAP has just surpassed Oracle in the EIS market in the United States for the last year. So the Commission used a global geographic market; the DOJ used a US market; but the US Court agreed with the Commission on this so it adopted a global market.

Then we come to the really critical decision which was the fundamental lynch-pin for the Commission's decision. The Statement of Objections said that there are only three players in this high-function software market: Oracle, PeopleSoft and SAP, and that was the fundamental basis for the concerns raised in the Statement of Objections; basically, that this was a three-to-two merger. But after receiving all of the data, the bid data that was submitted through the 'Information Request from Hell', the fourth one, and data obtained from the United State's trial, the Commission concluded in its decision that it had to include in that relevant product market not only Oracle PeopleSoft and SAP, but also Lawson, Entencher, IFS, QAD and *Microsoft*. So the new data showed that those players had won some bids for high-function, FMS, HR software, that they had been runners-up in a larger number, and they participated in bids over 1 million euros. So that analysis of the bid data was critical in determining that there were more than three players in the relevant market. But again, in the difference between Europe and the United States, contrary to the US District Court, the Commission excluded outsourcers and 'best of breed' point solution vendors from the product market. Again, one cannot underestimate the importance of the bid data analysis in this case, in particular with respect to determining who the market participants were. The Commission conducted its own analysis on the bidding data, and Lexecon conducted analyses as well, and it concluded that there was no significant distinction between the behaviour of Oracle when competing against SAP and PeopleSoft and when competing against other bidders and thus that the bidding data could not be relied upon to justify a finding of a narrow market for large enterprises comprising only Oracle, PeopleSoft and SAP. So this was really the fundamental basis for the decision.

The Commission then went on to consider the analysis of the competitive effects after having determined what the relevant product market and the relevant geographic market were and who the players were in the relevant market. But, and very interestingly, the Commission did not employ a traditional market structure analysis. Indeed, the decision does not even provide market shares. So what did the Commission do? Again it went back really to the decisive effect of the Commission's conclusion on who participated in the market. The Statement of Objections, based upon its conclusion that post-merger there would be a market containing only two players, Oracle and PeopleSoft, in other words that this was a three-to-two merger, the Statement of Objections found that there would be a significant group of customers for whom there would only be one supplier left after the merger. The basis upon which the Commission concluded there would be only one supplier left for certain customers was quite different from the basis employed by the DOJ, but nonetheless it was concluded that there was this group of some customers who would really only have one choice. This, in itself, in the Statement of Objections appeared to be decisive; if you read the Statement of Objections it appeared that that was enough for the Commission essentially to determine that the merger could not go forward. So, you can see how the change in the conclusion on market participation led the Commission to abandon its conclusion that there was this group of customers who would be left without choice and that appears to have been decisive in the decision allowing the Commission to let the merger go forward.

The Commission did also engage in certain econometric analysis. In the Statement of Objections the Commission referred to a merger simulation.

The Statement of Objections was indeed partly based upon that merger simulation which showed harmful effects. The decision abandoned any reliance upon the merger simulation on the basis that the merger simulation relied upon in the Statement of Objections was based upon a market of only three players and since the Commission concluded that the market had more players than three, the merger simulation obviously was no longer valid. But something which was not really explained in the decision is why the Commission didn't then undertake a merger simulation based upon that broader market participation. I will come back to merger simulation in just a moment. The Commission did however rely upon a bidding data analysis and particularly upon discount analysis. The Statement of Objections relied upon what the Commission admittedly called a crude and simplified discount analysis provided by PeopleSoft and the Statement of Objections did rely in part upon that for the concerns expressed therein. Based upon the much greater quantity of data available after the information request had been complied with and data had come from the US trial, Lexecon undertook a very extensive discount analysis. The Commission, the Chief Economist's office, undertook its own discount analysis and the regressions undertaken did not show that Oracle discounts were affected by either the number of bidders or the identity of the bidders in the final round.

So, just to put the grounds for the decision in a nutshell, I think you could put them into three categories. The first one was by far the most important, namely the conclusion that it wasn't a three-to-two merger. There was no group of customers confronted with an absence of choice post-merger. Secondly, the econometric analysis didn't provide any evidence of harmful effects. Again, the merger simulation was abandoned; the discount analysis did not indicate any harmful effects. In the light of time I will leave you to read these factors but it is very interesting that the Commission's decision said that there were additional factors supporting the conclusion that Oracle would not be able profitably to increase prices. I think that these factors would undermine the DOJ's theory of the case, but I will leave that to Greg to address.

Now very briefly some observations. First, and again this could be a topic for quite another discussion for another day, but hostility matters. This would have been an entirely different case had it not been a hostile take-over bid. Indeed I wouldn't even have been so surprised for it to have been a first phase case. We were really ambushed by the way the case went in the beginning after it became apparent that PeopleSoft was playing the antitrust card as its main defence against the take-over. But hostility mattered in all sorts of ways. Secondly, evidence matters. It matters a lot, especially in unilateral effects cases. Also, it was clear from this case that the CFI cases on the standard of proof, *Airtours*[3] of course in particular, seem to have had an impact on the Commission. I think the Legal Service clearly is particularly, not surprisingly, chastened, one might say, by the CFI cases and does not wish to march off to Luxembourg to defend a case absent a solid evidentiary basis. Third, another reason why one can conclude from this case that evidence matters is that the additional bid data that was obtained after the hearing made a difference. That is what caused the Commission to change its conclusion from prohibition to clearance. In this regard I think it is interesting to note that the Commission collected more and different bid data than the DOJ.

So one note I would say for you lawyers, the few remaining ones, in unilateral effects cases in particular or where it appears that unilateral effects might be an issue, and it is hard to tell when it might be an issue, gather your data early. In that regard, I would say though, and this was a difficult lesson to learn I must say, learned with some pain, there is, I fear, often going to be a gap between the Commission's expectations as to what parties can produce in terms of data and the party's actual ability to produce the data and I think that gap reflects another gap, which is the gap between the way antitrust enforcers view the world and the way business people actually view the world in which they compete, and I fear that lawyers are often stuck in the middle between those two views. But Oracle was simply not able to provide lots of the data in the form the Commission wished it to do in terms of filling in the spreadsheet, because those factors weren't relevant to the way it did its business, and so it simply was not something that was available.

Do economics matter? Yes, certainly. Much more than before in light of the court cases and in light of the change to the substantive test. Clearly they matter much more. I'm not sure the *Oracle PeopleSoft* decision tells us much in this regard, except for the fact that the discount analysis clearly contributed to the clearance in that case. A practical pointer for the few remaining lawyers again, especially in cases where unilateral effects might be an issue, employ your economists early and try to gather the data from the client early and undertake as best you can a variety of analyses early: diversion analysis; discount analysis; merger simulations.

One more point with respect to economics: the Chief Economist's role clearly matters. I think one can reach a significant conclusion about a case depending upon whether a member of the Chief Economist's team is added to the case team for your merger case. If a member of the Chief Economist's team is added get ready for quite a ride.

---

[3] *Airtours plc v Commission* (Case T342/99) [2002] ECR II2585.

Finally, with respect to observations on three-to-two mergers, one can conclude, if there is any point one can reach from *Oracle PeopleSoft*, that three-to-two mergers are going to be problematic. Whether one can conclude vice versa, that no unilateral effects prohibitions will occur unless it's three-to-two, I am not so sure about, but if it is three-to-two get ready for a ride.

Trans-Atlantic convergence. Well, clearly there was coordination amongst the authorities, but I would actually suggest that there was more lack of convergence than convergence in this case. The US Court and the Commission disagreed on the product market definition, for example.

I shall very soon end but I just want to leave you with the unanswered questions, which I fear are more important than the answered ones in this case.

First, when is the Commission going to employ a traditional market structure analysis and when is it going to use econometrics or what one might call direct measurement of the effects of a merger? It is simply not clear from *Oracle PeopleSoft*. I don't think it is clear from the Commission's practice more generally; so I don't think we have an answer to that question.

Secondly, if a unilateral effects theory is pursued in a case, which one? And what is it going to look like? I think probably on both sides of the Atlantic, but perhaps more on this side than the other, unilateral effects is a new-born baby in a way and it is a moving and evolving target. So again, get ready for a ride if you are involved in a unilateral effects case.

What is the real meaning of the 25 per cent market share threshold in the guidelines?—the sort of safe harbour principle in the guidelines? Especially if the Commission doesn't provide any market shares, if it doesn't calculate any market shares, and there is a direct measurement of effects. Does the 25 per cent threshold mean anything? And what econometric analysis is the Commission going to employ? I can't really answer that question. What is a sufficient price increase to justify a prohibition in a unilateral effects case? I don't know that. In what percentage of deals must the price rise, whatever it must be, occur? We don't have an answer to that question. Is the prohibition threshold close competitor or closest competitor? We don't have an answer to that. Quite a number of other questions are answered neither by *Oracle PeopleSoft*, nor by the horizontal merger guidelines, nor by anything else, I fear.

I shall try to answer the question Mark asked me to seek to address. What is going to satisfy the courts? One thing I can say in that regard is that there are more economists on this panel than lawyers. There may even be more economists in the room than lawyers, but those guys down in Luxembourg are lawyers. So we, handling these cases, are going to have to present economic evidence to them in a way that we as lawyers and they as judges being lawyers can understand. So that is going to be a challenge both for the lawyers and the economists.

What about merger simulation? That is the question Mark was particularly interested in. It is pretty clear from *Oracle PeopleSoft* that the Commission is going to use merger simulations. It is a much bigger question whether the court will credit them, whether it will give them any credence. Indeed, there are some statements in the *Oracle PeopleSoft* decision which undermine the credibility of merger simulations and emphasize that the simulations are only as good as the assumptions upon which they are based because that is the nature of mergers. I am not an expert on merger simulations but as best I do understand them they are based upon a number of assumptions regarding elasticities of demand and the like. So I think the bottom line, not surprisingly, is that the extent to which the courts will credit merger simulations will depend upon the solidity of the evidence that underpins the assumptions which underline the simulation and I think one should keep in particular *Airtours* in mind there. The assumptions underlying the simulations are going to have to be based on reasonably solid evidence or I don't think you are going to see much heed paid to them in Luxembourg.

MARK WILLIAMS

Thank you very much. Our next speaker is Greg Werden. As I mentioned earlier, he has played a pioneering role in development of merger simulation as well as involvement in *Oracle PeopleSoft*. So now over to the economists.

GREG WERDEN

I will open with a comment on Trans-Atlantic convergence: The fact the two agencies came to different conclusions in the *Oracle* case does not mean they took divergent approaches. Any two decision-makers looking at identical facts—and they were not identical facts—will on occasion come to different conclusions. We lose some cases in court because judges come to different conclusions when they look at the same facts. There were differences between the analysis of the European Commission and that of the US Department of Justice, but I do not think they were important. Although the European Commission approached the case somewhat differently than we did and came to some different conclusions, this case is evidence of convergence, rather than divergence.

Turning to unilateral effects, I begin with some history. Competition policy towards mergers evolved long before industrial organization economists came to embrace game theory. In the United States a fairly modern merger policy began to emerge as early as the late 1940s, and it was firmly in place by the early 1960s. When game theory came to dominate economists' thinking about competition, new light was cast on existing models giving rise to unilateral effects. These models had been around for a long time: The Cournot model dates to 1838; the Bertrand model dates to 1883. Until the game theory revolution, economists tended to think these models did not make a lot of sense. But in the 1970s and 1980s economists concluded that prior generations had it all wrong. By the early 1990s unilateral effects analysis was important at the two federal enforcement agencies in the United States, and it was officially incorporated into policy through the 1992 Horizontal Merger Guidelines, which introduced the term 'unilateral effects'. Since the early 1990s, many of the merger challenges by the two federal enforcement agencies in the United States have been based on unilateral effects theories.

The idea of unilateral effects is very simple: By internalising the competition between the merging firms, a merger alters their incentives, causing them to change their 'actions', to use a technical game theory term. If their actions were setting prices, a unilateral anticompetitive effect would cause them to raise prices. Models giving rise to unilateral effects differ with respect to how competitors interact. Competitors may set prices; they may set quantities; they may bid; and if they bid they may bid in various formats. So there are many distinct unilateral effects models. Depending on the facts of any particular case, one of these models might be useful in understanding the likely unilateral effects of a merger and possibly even in quantifying those effects through a merger simulation analysis. I say 'may be useful' because it isn't necessarily true that any of these models fits the industry well enough to be especially useful, although the insights from these models are quite general and economists would always draw on them.

It brings me to the *Oracle* case. As was already mentioned, Oracle and PeopleSoft competed in a sale of enterprise resource planning software, which automates central operating functions of large organizations. This case focused on two different types of software. We use slightly different acronyms in the United States than are apparently used in Europe for these products, but I think they are the same products. Human relations management software (HRM) deals with pay, benefit and other employee matters; financial management systems (FMS) deal with receipts, accounts receivable and the like. All of this is fairly standard accounting software used by all kinds of organizations. The US Government's theory in the case was that some organizations demand high-function software for various complex accounting purposes and that these particular customers spend a lot of money and go through a complicated process of up to three years' duration to procure and implement this software. Critically, the US Government's theory was that this process entails an entirely separate competition for each of these organizations. We also thought that these competitions were best modelled as an oral auction. One difference with the European Commission is that they thought a sealed bid auction better described competition.

Oracle's acquisition of PeopleSoft would increase the winning bids to a significant number of organizations according to the US Government's theory of the case, because the merging firms offered the two best choices for certain organizations. Because each organization represented a separate competition, nothing mattered in that competition other than how competing vendors stacked up for that customer. So if Oracle and PeopleSoft were the two best choices, their merger would change the outcome of that competition and cause the winning bid to be higher.

To explain how competition works in oral auction, I have constructed an example based on a real auction. Let us suppose that there is a live auction, with four bidders interested in a Wedgwood jug. One is willing to pay £100, one £110, one £120 and one is willing to pay £200 for this jug. So how does each one bid? Game theory has this all worked out, but it is also very intuitive. Each bidder keeps bidding until the level of the bid reaches what that bidder is willing to pay, and the winner slightly outbids the person willing to pay the second most. Here, the bidder willing to pay the second most is willing to pay £120, so if the bid proceeds in increments of £1, the winning bid is £121. Even though the winning bidder is willing to pay £200, he doesn't have to pay that much because nobody else is willing to bid more than £121.

If the bidder willing to pay £120 and the bidder willing to pay £200 team up somehow—for example they get married—that changes the outcome of the auction because they bid as a team and only have to outbid the person willing to pay £110. So they win the auction at a bid of £111 instead of £121. There is an anticompetitive effect only if the two bidders willing to pay the most team up. If any other pair of bidders does so, neither the winning bid nor the winning bidder changes. The allegation in the *Oracle* case was that for some customers, we did not say all or most, but for an important number of customers, Oracle and PeopleSoft were the two best options.

Before I go on, I want to comment about two points in Thomas's presentation. First, we found that the market was limited to the United States, while the Commission found a worldwide market. The software was easily transported throughout the world. It cost next to nothing to ship, and although

I do not think this is actually done, it could even be emailed. Nevertheless, vendors visited the customers in order to try to win the competition, and after winning, they spent a lot of time with the customers. So an in-country presence was important, and SAP did not serve US customers out of its European offices. But the more important point is that there was an entirely separate competition for each customer, which meant that the European customers and the Asian customers were irrelevant to the effect of the merger in the United States. Our main rationale for saying the market was limited to the United States was that the rest of the world had nothing to do with the effect of the merger in the United States. That the average level of discounts did not vary much from one country to the next was a coincidence, since the competition was separate for every customer. Discounts within the United States varied widely.

Secondly, Thomas commented on the merger simulation done by economists in the European Commission. The European Commission used a sealed-bid auction model, while we used an oral auction model. Oral auction analysis is much simpler; indeed, with a few simplifying assumptions, it becomes a back of the envelope exercise. R Preston McAfee, who is an expert in auction theory and was one of our witnesses, conducted simulations that predicted average price increases of 5–11 per cent for high-function FMS software and 13–30 per cent for high-function HRM software. Key inputs to these simulations were what you might refer to as the market shares of Oracle, PeopleSoft and SAP. Technically, that characterization is not right because each auction is best thought of as a separate market, and the shares reflect rates of success over many different auctions. But things like market shares were central inputs into this process. Oracle objected to modelling competition in this industry as an oral auction, or any other kind of auction. Most of the objections were trivial in my view, and the Court repeated them in its decision without comment. The Court rejected the simulations only because it found that the shares on which the simulations were based were the wrong shares. The Court found that many more than just three firms were competing.

I have one further comment on a difference in analysis between the US and the European Commission, which arguably amounts to an error on the part of the Commission. As we thought about high-function software, there were no bright lines that divided customers that bought it from customers that didn't and probably no bright lines dividing what was, and what was not, high-function software. That made it a messy case that was hard to win in court. Nevertheless, we decided that it did not make sense to draw bright lines based on the size of the organization (or based on anything else), but that is something the Commission apparently did. Doing that introduces an error into the data analysis because some software is mischaracterized as high-function. Our view was that not all large organizations bought high-function software and that only Oracle, PeopleSoft, and SAP had ever won a bid for high-function software. Others had won bids to supply large organizations, but those large organizations were not buying high-function software.

Many organizations used software with lower functionality, and lots of other vendors produced such software. No set of organization characteristics neatly separated those using high-function software from those not using it. No particular aspect of high functionality explained why it was required by those organizations using it. A number of these organizations were witnesses at the trial, and the particular functionality they demanded was different from one to the next, based on the particularities of their businesses. One other complication stressed a lot by Oracle was that the software was purchased in a package with other software, not just the two kinds we were talking about, but rather a suite of business applications, and other vendors provided other software in that suite.

In his decision in the case, Judge Walker did not even acknowledge the possibility of a separate competition for each customer. Either we did not make ourselves clear, which I think is a real possibility, or he chose to ignore what we were saying. Some people think it was the latter—that he did not want to explain why our theory did not make sense, so he instead said we had a different theory. He applied the analytic framework commonly used for differentiated consumer products. In this framework all customers face the same set of prices, and all of his analysis in this case was based on the assumption that all business organizations face the same set of prices on what is essentially an off-the-shelf software product. Our view is that he evaluated the evidence through the wrong lens, and that is why he came to a different conclusion that we did.

For example, Judge Walker held that 'diversion ratios' are the key determinant of the magnitude of the unilateral competitive effects, and he criticized us for not presenting any diversion ratios. Diversion ratios are critical when all customers face the same prices. When merging firms raise price in order to exploit the market power they gain over some customers, they lose the business of other customers who are not willing to pay the higher prices. Thus they trade-off the business they lose against the higher revenues they earn on the business that they keep. With this trade-off, diversion ratios are absolutely critical in determining unilateral effects. But in *Oracle* diversion ratios were totally meaningless; they don't exist in an oral auction case. Because the prices are different for each bidding situation, there is no trade-off. If Oracle and PeopleSoft could size up customers accurately, there would be no customers lost as a result of raising the bids, because they would not raise bids to any customers they would lose. Of course, there is a factual issue in the case of whether they could effectively do that, and Oracle maintained that they could not. Judge Walker did not agree or disagree with Oracle on that, but rather did not comment on the issue.

Interestingly, Judge Walker decided to write a treatise on unilateral effects. I imagine he thought there was not an extensive analysis of unilateral effects in the case law, so he should do everybody a favour and provide one. His treatise is essentially dicta because he decided the case primarily on the basis of a traditional structural analysis. The most notable thing about his treatise is that it omitted important unilateral effects theories, including the Government's theory in this case. He never mentioned auctions or anything resembling auctions as a possible unilateral effects theory. Nor did he mention bargaining theory, which the Government has relied on in hospital merger cases. Economic theory provides many distinct unilateral effects analyses, all of them potentially relevant in merger cases, but Judge Walker did not acknowledge that.

Also interesting is that while we were writing the post-trial brief, Judge Walker issued an order stating what literature he had read and asking whether there was anything else he should be aware of. Our post-trial brief directed him to several relevant articles, but his opinion does not cite a single authority not listed in his order. We cited literature on unilateral effects with auctions because that was our theory, but his opinion did not cite any of that literature. I am gratified that he cited my work, but it seems clear that large parts of the decision were written before the post-trial briefs were filed.

Judge Walker not only identified the wrong model as the relevant one, but also identified the wrong economic literature as providing the economic underpinnings of the model he did apply. And he seems to have misunderstood the fundamental role of consumer preferences. He wrote that 'the issue is not what solutions the customers would *like* or *prefer* for their data processing needs; the issue is what they *could* do in the event of an anti-competitive price increase by a post-merger Oracle.'[4] But this simply is not right. The issue is precisely what customers prefer to do, because customers actually do what they prefer to do. They do not do what they could do but prefer not to do.

I also think it is unmistakable that Judge Walker set the bar way too high for unilateral effects. He maintained that a unilateral effects theory cannot be sustained without a demonstration that the merged firm would have essentially a monopoly position. This means that he would have ruled

---

[4] *United States v Oracle, Inc*, 331 F.Supp.2d 1098, 1131 (ND Cal 2004).

against us even if he has agreed that there were only three competitors. He framed the issue in *Oracle* as whether 'PeopleSoft and Oracle are engaged in localized competition to which SAP is not a party',[5] which is most unfortunate, and I fear that other judges are going to get the wrong message. It is very clear in economics that significant unilateral effects can occur despite the presence of several rivals, and even if the merging products are not especially close substitutes.

There is some good news, however. Judge Walker discussed at length the difficulties in defining the relevant market in differentiated products unilateral effects cases, and he was right about that. Economists have long argued that it is not helpful to draw bright lines when the lines in reality are not bright, and Judge Walker recognised that. He also correctly explained that market shares may be poor predictors of unilateral effects from mergers involving differentiated consumer products. Economists have long pointed that out as well. And, as he suggested, diversion ratios are much more important than market shares for mergers involving differentiated consumer products. So he followed the economic literature on all these points.

One last note is that he made very positive comments on the use of merger simulation. He did not rely on it, but after pointing out the problems of using market definition and market shares to analyze unilateral effects, he commented that:

> modern econometric methods hold promise in analyzing differentiated products unilateral effects cases. Merger simulation models may allow more precise estimations of likely competitive effects and eliminate the need to, or lessen the impact of, the arbitrary factors inherent in defining the relevant market. For example, some merger simulation methods compensate for potential errors in market definition.[6]

This is correct, and it is very positive that he would say something like this. It will take some time, but I think that our courts will come around in unilateral effects cases to the view that market definition and market shares cannot play the central role and that other modes of analysis can be more helpful. In many non-merger cases in the United States, courts have acknowledged that there may be better ways to demonstrate anticompetitive effects than defining the market, assigning market shares, determining whether the defendant has market power and therefore drawing certain inferences. Many cases under section 1 of the Sherman Act have endorsed going more directly to competitive effects analysis, but until *Oracle* no

[5] ibid at 1168.   [6] ibid at 1122.

merger case had done so. This quote from Judge Walker is a first step down the path I think the courts will be taking in the United States.

MARK WILLIAMS

Thank you very much Greg for that lively perspective from the United States' view. Our next speaker is Bill Bishop of Lexecon who is going to give a more European perspective on this.

BILL BISHOP

I have titled this talk 'Unilateral Effects: History, *Oracle* and Simulation' and that is because I have divided it into three unequal parts. I am going to start with just a little bit of history about how we got here because no-one had heard of unilateral effects until 13 years ago. The term was only christened then. It is quite an interesting intellectual history; so here is my bit of history, very simplified.

I am going to start with the structure of economics and the structure of merger control law. This, by the way, is based on some work I did with an academic friend and colleague of mine, Bill Kovacic, who was previously General Counsel of the United States Federal Trade Commission and has now gone back to the academic world. If you look at the structure of the law today you will find it has got three parts. Merger to monopoly, that is the American term—we would call it single firm dominance on this side of the Atlantic. Secondly, unilateral effects. I think our technical term is non-coordinated effects. Third is tacit collusion or collective dominance here in Europe. That actually corresponds to three parts of economics fairly closely. The first is the economics of monopoly versus competitive markets which goes back famously to a famous book published in 1776, Adam Smith's *Wealth of Nations*. The second part is—Mark already really referred to it under these terms—static duopoly theory. That was worked out by two Frenchmen, Auguste Dan Cournot and Josef Bertrand, in the middle of the 19th century. That corresponds quite well to unilateral effects-type analyses. Of course, there have been many successive things but that is the foundation. Thirdly, the law of tacit collusion or collective dominance is represented today in economics by what is known as dynamic oligopoly theory. A process by which firms learn that they are competing with one another and learn to trust, punish and that sort of thing and achieve an outcome better than they otherwise might, and better than the merger control authorities think they really ought to.

This correspondence is pretty obvious once it is set down and yet no-one saw it that way as little as 13 years ago. If you look at that economic logic and that legal history then you will find that logically number 2 comes before number 3. After all, you are going to get more excited and worried about two people being able to coordinate without achieving a better outcome, without any signalling or anything like cooperation between them, before you get interested in a lot of people. Historically in economics, number 2 comes before number 3; it is 19th-century theory, not 20th. But in legal history actually the order is different. In legal history number 1 comes first; that is, the concern about monopoly comes first. Then number 3 and only at the end, number 2. The road by which it evolved is peculiar and identical in fact on both sides of the Atlantic, but with different time lines.

In the United States the merger control began with the Sherman Act and was really about merger to monopoly only for the first 60 years of its existence. It wasn't until the Celler-Kefauer Act in 1950 that control of mergers, where there was merger into an oligopoly that simply reduced competition in some way, became possible; it wasn't really until the late 1950s that the Celler-Kefauer Act was put out. I put that date as 1950, but it could have been 1957 just as well, or 1958. Then a peculiar thing happened. The United States Government issued merger guidelines, very clear economics based ones, in 1981 or 1982, and judges began to read them and they said, 'Wait a minute. You guys are bringing this merger case saying it is all about coordination and we don't believe that; this is not the kind of market in which people can coordinate'. The United States Government suffered six defeats in about 1989, 1990. Greg was there through all of this and he can comment if I fall into error. Bill Kovacic's favourite is the *Baker Hughes* case,[7] because two of the judges that decided that are now on the United States Supreme Court. After these defeats, the economists and lawyers inside the enforcement authorities went back to school as it were and said, 'Wait a minute. Something is going wrong here. We firmly believe we were right to oppose these'. And they said, 'Yeah, actually the reason is our true theory was not about coordination; it was really about unilateral effects' and they christened this theory 'unilateral effects' and that is how it spread around the world, in the manner that's normal; most innovation of this business does happen in the United States and that's still true and is likely to be true for some time to come.

On the right-hand column there I have given the same, exactly identical, evolution in Europe. We begin with merger to monopoly. Many Member States believed that the Merger Control Regulation could only be applied to single firm dominance. The Commission always rejected this, and asserted

---

[7] *United States v Baker Hughes, Inc* 908 F 2d 981 (DC Circuit 1990).

its jurisdiction in the spring of 1992 in the *Nestlé/Perrier* case.[8] But it remained controversial and it really wasn't until the *Gencor* case,[9] in my opinion, that it was clear that the Commission had jurisdiction over collective dominance. So instead of 1992 you could put 1997 as the critical date. At this point we had number 1 and number 3. We had monopoly and we had collective dominance. Then the crisis came, and just as in the United States it was defeat in court that did it. Again, the judges looked at what the Commission had said about what its theory was and it said: 'We just don't believe that it works in this case'. That is what the *Airtours* case[10] is all about.

Lack of correspondence between the Commission's theory and the facts of the case. The Commission itself by now decided perhaps it had better learn a little bit about unilateral effects, which it had been ignoring for nine or ten years, because it realized it had the same problem that the Americans had identified they had. There was a gap. So in November, I think it was, of 2002, just six months after the defeat in court, Commissioner Monti announced that the test would be changed so as to accommodate the gap, if there was a gap, and that would clearly permit unilateral effects-type analysis. Of course, it didn't come into force until 2004 and we had hangover cases such as *Oracle* which had to be decided under the old law and that played an important part in the way the *Oracle* case was analysed.

That basically is the story of how we got here from there. There have been a number of comments about the economists sort of appearing to take over this business; actually it is illusion. If you look at the path by which this arrived in our law, it appears to be all driven by economics. But ask yourself was it economists using empirical methods and theories inspired by scientific methods? Was that what revealed that there was a gap here? No it wasn't actually. It was the dialectical processes of the law that revealed it. I did a little search for articles by economists and lawyer-economists on mergers before 1990. That is not easy to do, but I couldn't find a single incidence of anyone identifying what we now call the gap or unilateral effects-type needs. It simply wasn't perceived by anyone until the judge said: 'Just a minute. Here are the words, the guidelines and what people say about them and it does not correspond to the facts of this case. Yet there does seem to be another type of problem'. So this is about as clear-cut an example as you could get of the way in which law and economics are inevitably intertwined in antitrust law.

---

[8] Case IV/M190 [1992] OJ L356/1; [1993] 4 CMLR M17.
[9] Case T-102/96 [1999] ER II-753, [1999] 4 CMLR 971.
[10] *Airtours* (n 3).

That's my little history lesson. Again, Greg is here to correct me, if I have fallen into error. I am now going to turn to my second part, which is the *Oracle* case. We have heard a lot about this and I am perhaps going to go through this a little more quickly than I had originally intended because you might get a little exasperated with endless accounts of the studies done.

Main economic issues. Was there a high end market for this? Who competes in it? I will skip the bit about the geographic market. Unilateral or non-coordinated effects analysis of course turned out to be central, but there was a long period of coordinated effects— for the first eight of the 16 months the European Commission was concentrating on that, probably because they were worried that they didn't have jurisdiction over unilateral effects under the law that has now passed away.

On product market definition. Well, the first pass was high-function HR and FMS purchased by large customers with complex functional needs. That was defined by proxies, corporate customers with larger than 10,000 employees or a billion euros in revenue, and deals—that is, purchases of complex software—worth more than a billion euros in net license value to Oracle or one of its competitors. The other points I think have been covered. It is very difficult to find clear conceptual criteria or practical proxies of this and, as Greg has outlined, the United States Government said that there is not much point in even trying, but there was still a unilateral effect anyway. It has to be said that a key development in the EC case was the conclusion of who is in the market. The decision, unlike the original Statement of Objections, accepted a significant fact, therefore, that this was not a simple three-to-two merger.

Now to unilateral effects specifically. Of concern of course, as always, is reduction in competition without coordination in the sense in which you are only raising your price because you know, or at least believe, that the other chap will also raise his, cooperating with you. This is typically an issue in differentiated product markets when merging parties are relatively close substitutes to each other and the non-merging rivals are less close. Other things, as Greg has said, can be unilateral effects, but this is where the analysis begins and where as a practical matter is usually the case in which the authorities are concerned. So, the real question then becomes how closely do the parties compete? How closely do other rivals constrain them? Hence, looking at bidding data becomes a natural way to look at it. The Statement of Objections reached adverse conclusions, but without very much data. This was a contested take-over first as Thomas has mentioned, and PeopleSoft submitted a very simple analysis, claiming the discounts were higher when the number of bidders was higher. Oracle later collected detailed information in response to this on 600+ bids and quite a lot of econometric analysis. I will come to that in a minute.

Key questions: Do the number of rival bidders affect Oracle's discounts and does the identity of rival bidders, especially PeopleSoft, matter? Is it true that prices are higher when they know it is PeopleSoft that is the best substitute? That was the enforcement theory on both sides of the Atlantic in one form or another. Eventually there was no systematic evidence of this found, and the Commission finally agreed with this, possibly reluctantly. The response to the Statement of Objections: here this is a very partial analysis that had been submitted by the bidder, but relied on by the Commission in its Statement of Objections and the result depended entirely on eight anomalous observations where the discount was positive—with a list price of £100 and the price was £130, lets say, and no theory of how this came about. In fact, it also had a low, what is called an 'R squared' in this business, a very low percentage of the variation explained, only eight per cent of the variation in prices explained. If these eight anonymous observations were excluded it was pretty clear that the result fell away. Well, I said that more data was collected and there was quite a lot of extensive analysis of bidding situations. I think that has really been covered so I will skip to the next slide.

This is a general point. The aim is to identify who are the credible bidders for a particular type of contract and assess whether the merging parties are particularly important constraints. Of course, the Commission claimed that PeopleSoft was the most important constraint. Market definitions are typically difficult in bidding markets; again Greg has said quite a lot about this. I entirely agree with those general points. In fact, it is pretty useless. Nevertheless, it is a brave man who goes before a competition authority or in front of a courtroom, which has got all these precedents about market definition and says, 'Market definition is for the birds'. It is not actually what either officials want to do or lawyers going before officials want to do.

The last point that is perhaps worth saying is that who competes for different types of contract can be informative, but a very important limitation to any bidding analysis is that customers may not invite, typically will not invite, all potential suppliers to bid. It actually costs resources to bid and people will bid more vigorously if they know they have a decent chance of getting the job. I have to say as an occasional bidder myself that if someone rings me up and says, 'Well, we have invited eleven people to bid for this'. I usually say 'Thank you very much' and put down the phone. If, on the other hand, a sensible person rings up and says, 'Well, actually this is going to be an important case and we want you to take this seriously and we are only considering one other firm', then I will consider it very seriously. The world is just like that. So the number of people bidding and the identity of customers is less informative than our simple bidding models sometimes assume.

To estimate the effects of a merger using the variation of the number and the identity of the bidders is assumed to be a natural experiment. You look at the number of bidders; you look at the particular competitor and whether his presence makes any difference. So, in the additional analysis after the Statement of Objections in *Oracle*, carried on of course during the eight month stopping of the clock—as somebody once commented, it was not so much a stopping of the clock, as a stopping of the calendar and of course, entirely by coincidence, the Commission started the clock again after Judge Walker had given his opinion in the United States and entirely by coincidence, made the same decision—the data looked at the effect of the number of bidders on Oracle's discounts, the identity of bidders and controlled for various characteristics; especially the size of the sales opportunity was extremely important. All kinds of things become possible if you adopt lots of data controlling for different factors with the black arts of econometrics. I should say this is not something that any economist carries out unless he is a true specialist in econometrics. This is highly specialized stuff and I, myself, wouldn't dream of doing it. I have a department of colleagues who are econometricians The results show that suppliers other than Oracle and PeopleSoft competed to supply the large enterprises, but only on a limited number of occasions. There was no consistent evidence that a larger number of bidders led to higher discounts or that the discounts were higher with three, rather than two. There was no consistent evidence that PeopleSoft made any difference to the level of discounts. The Commission took these results and redid it and came to the same conclusions, to the same results.

Now, I have already said that there are some problems with bidding analysis. Technically this is known as omitted variable bias. It is a common problem in cross-sectional data. If an omitted variable is correlated with the explanatory variables in any way you just get wrong results or unreliable results. Quite a good example here was that the PeopleSoft data had not controlled for the size of the deal, the size of the business opportunity. In fact, it turned out that when we sold the bigger data set and had the data on the number of the size of the deal as well, it turned out that we had a very simple explanation that really was omitted variable bias, but what was happening here was that big deals attracted more bidders. Surprise, surprise! Big deals attract more bidders! Also maybe the employing corporation spending more money is perhaps more concerned to get people in to offer bids. So in fact the number of bidders was proxying for the size of the deal. Once you control the size of the deal, the number of bidders made no difference. As I said, customers may not negotiate with all credible suppliers. So that argues for a bit of humility, I think, among analysts doing these sorts of things. My experience, in 15 years now of doing empirical work in merger analysis, is that it is never a magic bullet. It is frequently, usually, informative. It is better than the untutored prejudices of either the parties or the officials or the complainants. But it is, in the end, a tool of analysis that informs an intelligent decision, but it isn't a piece of magic.

So that's *Oracle PeopleSoft*. The third part on simulation; I can be brief here. We have heard something about simulations already. Thomas made some observations on them and Greg as well. I am simply going to ask one question: when are they robust and reliable? Some people want to say they never are and others want to say, 'Gosh, this is the way for the future and this is what's going to give us the right answer'. I am going to advance a market criterion. As economists we are famous for thinking markets are a good thing and market tests are a good way of discriminating between things, so I have a simple market criterion for reliability: that the simulation is reliable when it is actually used by businessmen in making decisions. Let me explain what I mean here. Business frequently has to predict the outcome of some strategic choice. That is a common feature of business decision-making. That is what simulations yield. They yield what are known in our trade as comparative statics results for big changes in the commercial environment, in the competitive environment. So they could be used in merger planning. Question: Does business actually use them? After all, if the simulation gives better results than the untutored intuitions of people involved, then the businessmen using them will make money at the expense of those who don't use them. So are they used? Well actually sometimes they are. One of my most instructive experiences I had in this business, was a little-known merger called Sydkraft and Groenige, a Swedish merger about three years ago, and I went into Rue Joseph II with the client to talk about some aspects of the merger early in Phase 1 and I met on the opposite side of the table the very economist who later was seconded from the Chief Economist team to work on *Oracle PeopleSoft*, Klaus Benson. I just about collapsed when he announced that he had done a simulation of this merger. Who had ever heard of such a thing? A simulation for merger in Phase 1, two weeks after the case began? It turned out that it was a serendipitous simulation in that he had found a Danish electricity transmission company, which had built a model of the Nordic Scandinavian Pool, which was what the case was all about and—he was an enterprising chap, Danish himself—he said to them, 'Oh, by the way, if I were to give you some other numbers could you plug it into your model and tell me the results?', to which the transmission company said, 'Yeah, sure. Of course'. And so Mr Benson got a merger simulation. Fortunately for my clients it showed that there would be no effect of the merger, but this is not accidental that it should be electricity. Of course it is used. There are big models used all the time because it is quite a ripe field for this type of analysis. It is not easy to say reposition a brand as you could with an advertising campaign in fast-moving consumer goods. You are talking about giant facilities costing hundreds of millions which churn out electricity and which is a commodity product, at least within any one 'time slice'. So, I conclude that this is actually a reasonable test for when simulation is likely to be reliable if it is actually used.

I want to give one final caution here. Transitions matter. New theories take a while to be accepted. You can look somewhere in the back page of the *Financial Times*, it is hard to get through it without some reference to the way in which the Black Scholes models and its variants dominate financial markets today. That is true. It has been true since about 1981 or so . . . 1981/1982. But the Black Scholes theorem was proved in the Spring of 1973, so if you had applied my little market test in say 1976 you would have concluded that it is not used, so therefore, it is not reliable. Well, you'd be wrong because it takes time for new techniques to be used. My guess is that the McKinseys and Bains and Boston Consulting Groups of this world are trying to indeed use simulation in cases where it is likely to be reliable. But if a lot of time goes by and we don't see more of it then it will not be good news for simulation in my view.

MARK WILLIAMS

Now, unlike *Oracle PeopleSoft*, I don't have the ability to stop the clock, but we have got a few minutes for questions. Do we have any questions?

ALDEN ABBOTT

Alden Abbott. Could it be that the market for simulations is affected by the existence of antitrust law? That is, firms and business planning don't engage in simulations precisely because they are afraid that they will be used in the event there is any litigation.

BILL BISHOP

That is very interesting actually. I thought when you began the sentence you were going to say the opposite, that they use simulations because they think they might be used by the authorities and therefore the actual use of them was uninformative. But you are suggesting they might use them but for worries about having to be revealed. That is an interesting question and part of the complication of all this. My sense is that simulation is quite appropriate in certain kinds of heavy industries and actually isn't all that revealing in industries where you can change the parameters more quickly. I may be wrong about that. Greg may have another perspective?

GREG WERDEN

I think merger simulation is both most useful and most often used with differentiated consumer products. In this context nearly all economists agree about the theory applied and about how to apply it. At issue mainly are the details of the econometrics. There may be cases in which this analysis is not very helpful because it is easy to reposition products, but those cases are quite rare in my experience.

If there are no more questions, I will make Bill happy by commenting on his history lesson. First, it should be noted that the US has had a merger law since 1914. Section 7 of the Clayton Act was amended in 1950 by the Celler-Kefauver Act to eliminate an important loophole. Only stock acquisitions could be challenged from 1914 to 1950, but there was merger enforcement before 1950, and modern structural merger analysis began to emerge in the *Columbia Steel*[11] case of 1948. Second, the losses in court Bill mentioned had little to do with the introduction of unilateral effects. All of those cases turned on the definition of the market or entry, and none specifically rejected a coordination theory. Addressing entry was one of the principal reasons for revising the Guidelines in 1992. Not all of the new material on entry added by the 1992 Guidelines has been influential, but entry did cease to be the key issue it once was. New material on competitive effects was added in 1992 to incorporate the current thinking on the subject, which had changed since 1982.

MARK WILLIAMS

Good. Well thank you very much for that. I think I had probably better wind proceedings up now. To summarize there are some thoughts going through my mind. Are we beginning to see the slow move towards the end of market definition? The second conclusion that is coming out in my mind here, but I would say this, is quite clearly the importance of not theoretical economics, but the importance of empirical economic analysis. We can theorize, we can speculate, but ultimately it is 'what does the data say?' And finally, the most important conclusion: hire your economists early.

---

[11] *United States v Columbia Steel Co*, 334 US 495 (1948).

Unilateral Effects from Mergers: *The* Oracle *Case*

Gregory J Werden*

At the end of 2004, Oracle Corp. announced the completion of an acquisition begun over 18 months earlier with its tender offer for the shares of PeopleSoft, Inc. The acquisition had been challenged by the US government and several states on the primary grounds that it would have significant unilateral (non-coordinated) anticompetitive effects.[1] On 9 September, following a 19-day trial and extensive briefing, Judge Vaughn Walker held that the government failed to establish that the acquisition would violate US antitrust law, and on 1 October the government announced that it would not appeal his decision.

The *Oracle* decision was the first to provide an extensive discussion of unilateral effects, and it is highly significant that Judge Walker was receptive to unilateral effects theories and to the use of economic theory in analyzing and quantifying unilateral effects. But these positive aspects of his decision could be overshadowed by shortcomings in its articulation of the relevant economic analysis. Judge Walker inaccurately stated the conditions under which a differentiated products merger gives rise to significant unilateral effects, and he took an overly narrow view of the range of valid unilateral effects theories.

The discussion below first briefly summarizes the US government's view of competition between Oracle and PeopleSoft and its unilateral effects theory. That summary serves as a foundation for an assessment of Judge Walker's treatment of unilateral effects, which curiously never addressed the specific theory the government actually presented. Concluding comments highlight his important insights on the advantages of greater reliance on economic models in the assessment of unilateral effects from differentiated products mergers.

* Senior Economic Counsel, Antitrust Division, US Department of Justice. The views expressed herein are not purported to represent those of the US Department of Justice. Tom Barnett and Craig Conrath provided helpful comments.
[1] The 26 Feb 2004 complaint is available at <http://www.usdoj.gov/atr/cases/f202500/202587.pdf>.

I. THE US GOVERNMENT'S THEORY OF THE *ORACLE* CASE[2]

Oracle and PeopleSoft competed in the sale of Enterprise Resource Planning (ERP) software, which provides tools for efficiently automating essential operating functions within large organizations. The US government's complaint focused specifically on Human Relations Management (HRM) software, which deals with pay, benefit and other employee matters, and Financial Management Systems (FMS), which deal with receipts, accounts receivable and the like.

HRM and FMS software products have widely varying degrees of functionality in terms of the number of transactions and users supported, and in terms of the ability to accommodate various complexities and adapt to a user's particular and changing needs. Some organizations require, and acquire, products with much greater functionality than others. The procurement of the HRM and FMS software products with the greatest functionality entails a six to eighteen month process in which customers work with (generally two) vendors to determine what HRM or FMS software to use and negotiate a price for it. A period similar in length is then required for the customer and vendor to implement the software.

The complaint focused on the particular HRM and FMS software products it labeled 'high-function',[3] and it alleged there were just three vendors of high-function HRM and FMS software—Oracle, PeopleSoft, and the German company SAP AG. The US government argued that Oracle's acquisition of PeopleSoft would result in substantial increases in the amount paid to license HRM or FMS software by many customers for which the high-function HRM or FMS software of Oracle and PeopleSoft were the two most attractive options.

---

[2] The facts of the case are presented here in a highly simplified form and largely from the US government's point of view. The concise views of the litigants on the facts and the law can be found in their post-trial briefs. Plaintiffs' Post-Trial Brief (Redacted Public Version), available at <http://www.usdoj.gov/atr/cases/f204500/204591.pdf>; Oracle Corporation's Corrected Post-Trial Brief (Public Version), available at <http://www.oracle.com/peoplesoft/OraclePostTrialBrief.pdf>. Judge Walker's lengthy decision provides far greater detail on the facts, and readers also may consult the US government's even longer Proposed Findings of Fact (Public Version), available at <http://www.usdoj.gov/atr/cases/f204500/204565.pdf>.

[3] The government's post-trial brief explained that high-function software 'tracks thousands of transactions and supports thousands of concurrent users', allows a user to 'mold the software to meet its business needs without expensive and inefficient software customization', can 'perform multiple related transactions seamlessly . . . and with a high degree of ease and sophistication', is capable 'of handing international aspects of a business, such as multiple currencies, multiple languages, and multiple legal regimes', can 'accommodate rapid growth, acquisitions, and reorganizations', and is able 'to reflect actual units of business, rather than a pre-set business organization, and usefully link the data from those units'.

A fundamental aspect of the US government's unilateral effects theory was that each procurement through which high-function HRM and FMS software was acquired represented an entirely separate competition and the price charged by a vendor in any one of these competitions was set independently of its prices in other competitions. High-function HRM and FMS software products are customized; their use entails an ongoing relationship with the vendor; and they are licensed on terms that preclude sublicensing. Consequently these products cannot be arbitraged, so economic forces do not operate to eliminate or limit prevent price differences across customers. There was also considerable evidence that vendors offered different customers significantly different discounts off list prices.

The US government's theory analogized the procurement process to an auction and maintained that the acquisition would eliminate PeopleSoft as a bidder. In many auctions the absence of PeopleSoft would allow Oracle to win with a higher bid than it or PeopleSoft otherwise would have made. The government identified customers that recently had procured high-function HRM or FMS software for which the absence of PeopleSoft would have been highly significant. However customers differed in complicated ways, and the government could not point to particular characteristics of organizations that universally caused them to require high-function HRM or FMS software or necessarily caused them to find the products of Oracle and PeopleSoft more attractive than those of SAP.

II. JUDGE WALKER'S TREATISE ON UNILATERAL MERGER EFFECTS IN
     DIFFERENTIATED PRODUCTS INDUSTRIES

Oracle was not the first US merger case litigated on a unilateral effects theory. In *Staples* (1997) and *Swedish Match* (2000) proposed mergers were enjoined on the basis of such theories. In *Gillette* (1993), *Kraft* (1995) and *Long Island Jewish Medical Center* (1997) courts found there was insufficient evidence to sustain challenges to mergers based on such theories. But none of these decisions discussed unilateral effects theories at length or articulated particular elements of proof. Judge Walker sought guidance from economic and legal literature rather than precedent, and he provided other judges with a treatise on unilateral effects. To borrow from Dr Johnson, a judge writing about economics 'is like a dog's walking on its hinder legs. It is not done well; but you are surprised to find it done at all'.

Judge Walker's treatise focused on the theory he deemed relevant in *Oracle*, in which the merging firms sell competing differentiated products that are the first and second choices for a significant number of customers. His presentation of that theory began badly by citing the wrong economic model as its basis. Economists rely extensively on the Bertrand model in analyzing the unilateral effects of mergers involving differentiated consumer products. Theoretical analyses include Shapiro (1996), Werden (1996), and Werden and Froeb (1994), and analyses of particular mergers include Hausman, Leonard and Zona (1994), Hausman and Leonard (1997), Nevo (2000), and Werden (2000). Judge Walker (p. 1113) cited instead the model of 'monopolistic competition'.

The Bertrand model was introduced by Louis François Bertrand (1883). From the game theory perspective through which economists now view competitive interaction, it is a model of a 'simultaneous-move' 'one-shot' game, which means competitors interact just once and all decide at the same time what actions to take. To determine which actions competitors take, economists apply the concept of 'Nash non-cooperative equilibrium', developed by John F Nash, Jr (1951), which defines an equilibrium as a set of actions by competitors such that none has an incentive to alter its action in light of the actions being taken by its rivals. The Bertrand model posits that the actions of competitors are the prices they charge, so the Bertrand–Nash equilibrium is a set of prices such that each competitor is happy with its price, given its rivals' prices.

In the Bertrand model a merger combining two differentiated products, and not reducing costs, necessarily leads to price increases (Deneckere and Davidson, 1985), even if only very small price increases. The merged firm finds it in its unilateral self-interest to raise the prices of both products because raising the price of either causes an increase in sales and profits for the other. Shapiro (1996) usefully presents this intuition and discusses factors affecting the magnitudes of the price increases. Werden and Froeb (2005) survey literature on the analysis of differentiated products mergers using the Bertrand model.

The model of monopolist competition was introduced by Edward Chamberlin (1933, ch 4) and Joan Robinson (1933), who pioneered the analysis of differentiated products, but their model always has been used to address different questions than the Bertrand model. The model of monopolistic competition assumes that entry into an industry is entirely free and is used to examine how the entry that occurs compares with the social optimum (Archibald 1987).

Far more important than Judge Walker's citation to the wrong economic model was his misleading characterization of the conditions necessary for significant unilateral effects from mergers involving differentiated products. He appears to have imposed conditions more stringent than economic theory supports and more stringent than the US enforcement agencies had applied.

The Horizontal Merger Guidelines (HMGs) promulgated by the US Department of Justice and Federal Trade Commission (1992, § 2.21) state that:

> Substantial unilateral price elevation in a market for differentiated products requires that there be a significant share of sales in the market accounted for by consumers who regard the products of the merging firms as their first and second choices. . . . The price rise will be greater the closer substitutes are the products of the merging firms, i.e., the more the buyers of one product consider the other product to be their next choice.[4]

Judge Walker (p. 1117) insisted that 'the factors described' by the HMGs 'are not sufficient' because the HMGs' discussion 'emphasizes only the relative closeness of a buyer's first and second choices' while 'the relative closeness of the buyer's other choices must also be considered in analyzing the potential for price increases'.[5] To make out a unilateral effects case Judge Walker (p. 1117) opined that 'a plaintiff must prove not only that the merging firms produce close substitutes but also that other options available to the buyer are so different that the merging firms likely will not be constrained from acting anticompetitively'.[6]

Unilateral merger effects are significant only if customers would not readily substitute away from the merging products in the event their prices rose slightly, but non-merging products need not be substantially different from the merging products. Differentiated products arise primarily in consumer goods industries in which brands are important, and what determines the unilateral effects of the merger of sellers of differentiated consumer products are consumer preferences among brands. Consumers may have strong preferences, and products strongly preferred by many consumers have considerable market power. When two strong brands merge the prices of both may increase significantly. The most important factor in determining

[4] Similarly, the guidelines issued by the European Commission (2004, ¶ 28) state: The higher the degree of substitutability between the merging firms' products, the more likely it is that the merging firms will raise prices significantly. For example, a merger between two producers offering products which a substantial number of customers regard as their first and second choices could generate a significant price increase. Thus, the fact that rivalry between the parties has been an important source of competition on the market may be a central factor in the analysis.

[5] Judge Walker (1117) asserted that the HMGs 'later acknowledge as much in section 2.212'. But that section addresses only the scenario in which buyers 'limit the total number of sellers they consider' and 'either of the merging firms would be replaced in such buyer's consideration by an equally competitive seller not formerly considered'.

[6] As explained below Judge Walker would have been correct if he had been discussing the US government's unilateral effects theory based on an English auction model, but he was not discussing such a model.

the magnitude of the unilateral price increases following the merger is the proportion of the sales lost by each merging product that is recaptured by the other when the price of the first product is increased slightly. Shapiro (1996) dubbed these proportions 'diversion ratios'.

Judge Walker may have misunderstood the central role played by consumer preferences and diversion ratios. He (1167–8) made much of the fact that many customers prefer FMS and HRM software from SAP over that from Oracle or PeopleSoft. But consumer preferences obviously differed, and what mattered was not how often SAP's FMS and HRM software were the first choice of customers, but whether SAP's products were a close substitute for the products of Oracle and PeopleSoft when SAP was not a customer's first choice.

Judge Walker (1131) asserted that 'the issue is not what solutions the customers would *like* or *prefer* for their data processing needs; the issue is what they *could* do in the event of an anticompetitive price increase by a post-merger Oracle.' The most natural reading of this dictum is totally at variance with the economic theory. Consumers 'could' do anything, but what matters is what they would do, which is what they 'prefer'.[7] It should not be assumed that products are close substitutes just because they appear similar to an outside observer.

Most importantly Judge Walker appears to have adopted the mistaken view that a differentiated products merger can produce significant anticompetitive effects only if the merged firm would occupy a near-monopoly position. In explaining the basic theory he (1170–1) adopted the terminology of one of the defense experts, who used the word 'node' to describe a narrow region of a 'product space' that 'is defined by characteristics of the product'. Judge Walker (1170) explained: 'The unilateral effects theory is concerned about there being only one vendor operating inside the node, thereby being able to increase price unilaterally'. Thus he (1118) held that when 'a plaintiff is attempting to prove that the merging parties could unilaterally increase prices', the 'plaintiff must demonstrate that the merging parties would enjoy a post-merger monopoly or dominant position, at least in a "localized competition" space'.

Judge Walker (1123) indicated that his notion of dominance was 'essentially a monopoly . . . position'. He (1123) held that the 'presumption of anticompetitive effects' in the HMGs (§ 2.211) was 'unwarranted'. That presumption arises under certain circumstances if the merging firms'

---

[7] Judge Walker may have understood this but chose his words unwisely in attempting to say that a slight preference for a product would not prevent switching to alternatives in the event of small price increase.

combined market share is at least 35 per cent. In assessing the evidence presented at trial Judge Walker (1168) also framed the central question as whether 'PeopleSoft and Oracle are engaged in localized competition to which SAP is not a party', and he (1166–9, 1172) rejected the challenge to the proposed acquisition because the evidence failed to demonstrate that was so.[8]

Judge Walker's unilateral effects treatise is mistaken if read to say that a differentiated products merger can produce significant unilateral anticompetitive effects only if the merged firm would be 'dominant'. This can be seen by considering a special case in which the price effects of a differentiated products merger are given by Shapiro's (1996) simple formula. If the merging firms are identical and consumer demand is linear, the proportionate increase in price from a merger is given by $md/2(1-d)$, in which m is the pre-merger price–cost margin for both merging products (price minus marginal cost, all divided by price) and d is the diversion ratio from either merging product to the other.

Suppose the diversion ratios between two merging products are both one-third, so when the price of either is increased slightly the substitution to the other amounts to one-third of the decrease in sales of the first merging product. Suppose also that both merging products have pre-merger price–cost margins of 40 per cent, which is in the range commonly observed. Simple arithmetic reveals that the merger increases the prices of both merging brands by 10 per cent. This is a significant unilateral effect, yet non-merging products account for two-thirds of the diversion away from either merging product as its price is increased.

---

[8] It is possible to understand Judge Walker to have held only that the US government did not prove what it set out to prove. This interpretation is suggested by the way in which he (1166) began his discussion of the government's evidence: 'Plaintiffs rest their theory of anti-competitive effects on an attempt to prove that Oracle and PeopleSoft are in a 'localized' competition sphere (a 'node') within the high function FMS and HRM market. This sphere does not include SAP or any other vendors, and a merger of Oracle and PeopleSoft would, therefore, adversely affect competition in this localized market.'

It is also possible to understand Judge Walker to have found facts sufficient to decide the case against the government under a correct view of unilateral effects. This interpretation is suggested by the way in which he (1172) began his findings of fact on unilateral effects: 'The court finds that the plaintiffs have wholly failed to prove the fundamental aspect of a unilateral effects case—they have failed to show a 'node' or an area of localized competition between Oracle and PeopleSoft. In other words, plaintiffs have failed to prove that there are a significant number of customers (the "node") who regard Oracle and PeopleSoft as their first and second choices.'

This passage refers to a 'node' in a space of consumer preferences, although Judge Walker defined a 'node' as a region in a space of product characteristics. The passage also indicates not just that SAP competed with Oracle and PeopleSoft but also that very few customers found the products of Oracle and PeopleSoft to be their first and second choices.

Another useful demonstration can be made with the 'logit' model of consumer demand, variations on which are commonly used by economists in the analysis of differentiated products (Werden and Froeb 2002b, Werden, Froeb and Tardiff 1996). In this model each consumer makes a choice from a set of alternatives. The utility associated with an alternative is modeled as the sum of two components—one common to all consumers and one that is customer-specific. The latter component is treated as random because it cannot be observed, and a convenient assumption as to its statistical distribution leads to the logit model.

Consumer preferences in the logit model have a property simplifying the assessment of the unilateral merger effects: When the price of one alternative is increased slightly, the substitution away from it is distributed over the others in proportion to their shares as first choices. The simplest version of the logit model specifies the common component of demand as $\alpha - \beta p$, in which p is the price of a choice, α is a constant that indicates that choice's average preference and β is a constant that determines the degree of substitutability among alternatives.

Consider the merger of any two brands in a six-brand market with logit demand, and assume that all brands have the same sales, so the merging brands are neither dominant nor isolated from other brands. The 40 per cent margins in the prior example can be replicated by assuming all brands are priced before the merger at €1, the pre-merger demand elasticity at the market level is 0.5 and β is 2.9. These assumptions produce diversion ratios almost exactly half as large as before (0.16). There is no simple formula for the price increases resulting from a merger, but they work out to be 5.7 per cent for the two merging brands,[9] and competition authorities are likely to view such price increases as significant.

Contrary to what readers are apt to take away from Judge Walker's decision, the Bertrand model is generally used to analyse differentiated products mergers, and it indicates that mergers can cause significant price increases even if the merging firms face substantial competition. For a merger to produce significant price increases, the merging brands must be next-closest substitutes from the perspective of a significant number of individual customers. But when viewed from the overall perspective of all customers collectively, the merging brands need not be especially close substitutes.[10]

---

[9] The only additional assumption necessary for these calculations is that the marginal cost of each of the brands does not vary with the quantity produced.

[10] The logit model makes this clear because all brands are, by definition, equally close. The substitution pattern described above causes the cross elasticity of demand for each brand to be the same with respect to the price of any given brand, which makes brands equally close substitutes by one reasonable measure.

III. JUDGE WALKER'S TREATISE ON UNILATERAL EFFECTS OMITTED IMPORTANT
THEORIES, INCLUDING THE US GOVERNMENT'S THEORY

Judge Walker (1113) began his treatise on unilateral effects by asserting that
they come in just two strains—the one considered in the previous section
and one in which the merged firm is dominant because of a cost advantage
over smaller rivals.[11] This taxonomy appears to exclude several unilateral
effects theories well accepted by economists, notably those based on
auction models.[12] This is curious because Judge Walker (1169–70)
described the use of an auction model by one of the expert witnesses to
predict the effects of Oracle's proposed acquisition.[13] Either Judge Walker
did not appreciate that the unilateral effects of mergers in an auction model
may differ from those in the Bertrand model, or he ignored the differences.
In any event a striking fact about his decision is that Judge Walker never
acknowledged that the government was arguing that the acquisition would
have significantly differing effects on different customers, which is characteristic of an auction model but not a Bertrand model.

There are many types of auctions associated with many economic models
(Klemperer 2004, ch 1)). The most familiar type of auction, and the type in
which it is simplest to analyze a merger's unilateral effects, is the English
auction. When the auctioneer sells items to bidders in an English auction,
the level of bids ascends and bidding is open: Bidders shout out their bids
or communicate them in any number of other ways. The auction continues
as long as the bidding is advanced, and the selling price is the final bid.
English auctions are commonly used to sell art, antiques and collectibles.

Consider an auction in which the four bidders value a Victorian Wedgwood
jardiniere at £100, £110, £120, and £200. As the bidding progresses the
first bidder drops out at £100, the second at £110, and the auction ends
when the third bidder drops out at £120. The winning bidder pays £120 or
a small increment more, which in this example is far less than he is willing
to pay. If the two bidders willing to pay the most were to merge (perhaps

[11] The HMGs (§ 2.2) identified two classes of unilateral effects, and in one the product is
homogeneous and firms are distinguished primarily by their production capacities. The EC's
guidelines (¶¶ 32–5) also mention that scenario. The court's dominance theory falls within this
class, as does a theory based on the Cournot model.

[12] Within the class of unilateral effects involving differentiated products, the HMGs (§ 2.21
n 21) specifically mention an auction model, and the EC's guidelines (¶ 29) refer to 'bidding
markets'. Dalkir, Logan and Masson (2000), Froeb and Tschantz (2002), Tschantz, Crooke
and Froeb (2000), and Waerher and Perry (2003) analyze mergers in the context of auction
models. Werden and Froeb (2005) present insights from this literature.

[13] Acting for the US government, R Preston McAfee modelled competition as an English
procurement auction (the meaning of which is explained presently). His model predicted price
increases of 5–11 per cent for high-function FMS software and 13–30 per cent for high function HRM software.

by getting married), the winning bid would fall to the third-highest value, £110.

If the auctioneer procures an item from the bidders rather than sells to them, the level of bids descends. The winner is the bidder able to provide the good or service at the lowest cost, and the winning bid is the second-lowest cost of any bidder.

In an English auction the winning bid is affected by a merger only if the merging bidders have the two highest values (when they buy) or two lowest costs (when they sell). Consequently a merger may affect the winning bid in relatively few individual auctions. Even if infrequent these effects can be substantial if the third-highest value or third-lowest cost differs significantly from the secondhighest value or second-lowest cost.

In the Bertrand model generally applied to differentiated products, the merging firms cannot raise prices just to customers for which their products are the first and second choices. Price increases are moderated, often greatly, by the fact that a price increase for one of the merging products would cause some customers to switch products of non-merging firms. The extent of this moderating effect is determined mainly by diversion ratios, which are often low, causing the unilateral effect of mergers to be insignificant. In an English auction there is no switching to products of non-merging firms because bidding to one customer is independent of bidding to another.

Judge Walker (1172) explained that Oracle contended that an auction model was 'wholly inappropriate' because the customers were 'extremely powerful at bargaining' and software vendors did 'not simply "bid" for business' but rather engaged in 'extensive and prolonged' negotiations 'with the purchaser having complete control over information disclosure'. But this sort of power and control by customers characterizes a procurement auction, and the negotiations that follow the bids may only turn what is essentially a sealed-bid auction into what is essentially an English auction.[14]

Judge Walker did not endorse any of Oracle's objections. He (1158–61, 1170) rejected the specific application of an auction model by the expert on the sole grounds that the assumed winning bid shares in his model were 'unreliable data' because a far greater range of products should have been included. Judge Walker never attempted to explain why an auction-like

---

[14] Analysis at the European Commission used a model of a sealed-bid auction largely on theory that vendors would not believe what Oracle told them about competing offers (Bengtsson 2005). Oracle argued somewhat differently that the procurement process would not reveal enough to vendors to cause them to bid differently to different customers.

analysis, with a separate competition for each customer, was not the right analysis in the case.[15]

Judge Walker (1167) found the US government's evidence unpersuasive in part because '[d]rawing generalized conclusions about an extremely hetero-geneous customer market based upon testimony from a small sample is not only unreliable, it is nearly impossible.' But he failed to notice, or preferred to ignore, that no generalization was required given the government's contention that Oracle would raise price to just selected customers. Judge Walker (1172) also found the government's evidence wanting because it lacked econometric estimates of diversion ratios. But he failed to realize, or declined to acknowledge, that diversion ratios are irrelevant in the English auction model the government used to analyze the merger. Diversion ratios are critical in the Bertrand model, because manufacturers cannot raise prices to just selected customers, and the effects of mergers depend critically on the proportion of the sales lost by raising prices to all customers that is recaptured when some switch to products combined by the merger. But there are no lost sales in an English auction model.

The US government's theory of the *Oracle* case relied heavily on the notion that high-function HRM and FMS software was sold through a procure-ment process resembling an English auction and having a separate compe-tition, with separate prices, for each customer.[16] Judge Walker neither acknowledged that this was the government's theory nor recognized that auction models provided an important class of unilateral effects theories distinct from those based on the Bertrand model.

IV. CONCLUSIONS

Judge Walker followed the traditional structural approach to merger analy-sis, and as a practical matter his (1132, 1158–61) important holdings were that the relevant markets were not limited to high-function HRM and FMS software and that the competitors in the relevant markets were not limited to Oracle, PeopleSoft and SAP.[17] But the most interesting aspect of his deci-

---

[15] Near the end of his decision Judge Walker (1172–73) indirectly addressed the evidence on whether prices differed significantly across customers. He rejected an analysis of Oracle's pricing to 222 customers because it was not a 'formal stud[y] of price discrimination' and did not consider the pricing of PeopleSoft or SAP. But Judge Walker was addressing not the merits of the government's unilateral effects theory in general, but rather only one expert's justifica-tion for not having presented econometric evidence.

[16] Having a separate competition for each customer means nothing ties the effects of the merger on US customers to the effects of the merger on non-US customers. That, in turn, explains the government's argument that geographic scope of the markets was just the US.

[17] The US government relied heavily on the testimony of customer witnesses (1125–30), but Judge Walker (1130–1) questioned the 'grounds on which these witnesses offered their opin-

sion may be its stress on the limitations of the structural approach and its suggestion of an alternative that economists have advocated.

Judge Walker (1120–23) iscussed at some length the 'difficulties in defining the relevant market in differentiated product unilateral effects cases', which long have been noted by economists (Werden and Rozanski 1994). He (1121–22) also explained that market shares may not be good predictors of unilateral competitive effects with differentiated products. Werden and Froeb (1996, 73–8) demonstrate this systematically by evaluating mergers in randomly generated industries. Most interestingly, Judge Walker (1122) declared:

> Despite the problems with qualitative analyses, modern econometric methods hold promise in analyzing differentiated products unilateral effects cases. Merger simulation models may allow more precise estimations of likely competitive effects and eliminate the need to, or lessen the impact of, the arbitrariness inherent in defining the relevant market. For example, some merger simulation methods compensate for potential errors in market definition.

Merger simulation generates quantitative predictions of unilateral merger effects using oligopoly models such as the Bertrand model or an auction model, after first calibrating the models to match critical features of the industries. Economists have advocated and employed merger simulation in cases involving differentiated consumer products, eg Hausman and Leonard (1997), Werden and Froeb (2002a, 70–8), Werden (1997). It may be hoped that the lasting impact of Judge Walker's decision will come not from the shortcomings of his unilateral effects analysis, but rather from his positive comments on the use of modern economic analysis.

Despite the fact that the European Commission came to some different conclusions, the case exposed no apparent methodological or policy differences. Rather the European Commission benefitted from Judge Walker's decision and took a somewhat different view of complex facts. Hence another positive feature of Oracle may be progress toward convergence between US and European competition policies.

---

ions', faulting their testimony for failing 'to present the cost/benefit analyses that surely they employ' in making procurement decisions. Although he acknowledged the 'preferences of these customer witnesses for the functional features of PeopleSoft or Oracle products', he (1131) found that 'the issue is not what solutions the customers would *like* or *prefer* for their data processing needs; the issue is what they *could* do in the event of an anticompetitive price increase by a post-merger Oracle'. In addition, Judge Walker (1136, 1138–9, 1141) identified what he saw as significant gaps in the knowledge of several of the government's other industry witnesses.

REFERENCES

Archibald, GC (1987), 'Monopolistic competition' in John Eatwell et al (eds) *The New Palgrave: A Dictionary of Economics* vol 3 London: Macmillan 531–5.

Bengtsson, Claes (2005), 'Simulating the effect of Oracle's takeover of PeopleSoft' in Peter van Bergeijk (ed) *Modelling European Mergers: Theory, Competition Policy and Cases* Cheltenham, UK: Edward Elgar.

Bertrand, Joseph LF (1883), 'Review of "Théorie Mathématique de la Richesse Sociale" and "Recherches sur les Principes Mathématiques de la Théorie de Richesse"', Journal des Savants 67 499–508. A modern translation by James Friedman appears in Andrew F Daughety ed *Cournot Oligopoly* Cambridge: Cambridge University Press 73–81, 1988.

Chamberlin, Edward H (1933), *The Theory of Monopolistic Competition* (8th edn 1962) Cambridge Mass.: Harvard University Press.

Dalkir, Serdar, John Logan, and Robert T. Masson (2000), 'Mergers in symmetric and asymmetric noncooperative auction markets: the effects on prices and efficiency' International Journal of Industrial Organization 18(3) 383–413.

Deneckere, Raymond and Carl Davidson (1985), 'Incentives to form coalitions with Bertrand competition' RAND Journal of Economics 16(4) 473–86.

European Commission (2004), 'Guidelines on the assessment of horizontal mergers under the Council Regulation on the control of concentrations between undertakings' OJ C 31/03.

Froeb, Luke and Steven Tschantz (2002), 'Mergers among bidders with correlated values' in Daniel J Slottje (ed) *Measuring Market Power* Amsterdam: Elsevier 31–45.

Hausman, Jerry A and Gregory K Leonard (1997), 'Economic analysis of differentiated products mergers using real world data' George Mason Law Review 5(3) 321–46.

Hausman, Jerry, Gregory Leonard, and J Douglas Zona (1994), 'Competitive analysis with differenciated products' *Annales d'Economie et Statistique* 34 159–80.

Klemperer, Paul (2004), *Auctions: Theory and Practice* Princeton: Princeton University Press.

Nash, John (1951), 'Non-cooperative games' Annals of Mathematics 54(2) 286–95, reprinted in Andrew F Daughety (ed) (1988) *Cournot Oligopoly* Cambridge: Cambridge University Press 82–93.

Nevo, Aviv (2000), 'Mergers with differentiated products: The case of the ready-to-eat cereal industry' RAND Journal of Economics 31(3),395–421.

Robinson, Joan (1933), *The Economics of Imperfect Competition* 2nd edn London: Macmillan 1969.

Shapiro, Carl (1996), 'Mergers with differentiated products' Antitrust 10(2) 23–30.

Tschantz, Steven, Philip Crooke, and Luke Froeb (2000) 'Mergers in sealed versus oral auctions' International Journal of the Economics of Business 7(2) 201–12.

US Department of Justice and Federal Trade Commission (1992), Horizontal Merger Guidelines.

Vickrey, William (1961), 'Counterspeculation, auctions, and competitive sealed tenders' Journal of Finance 16(1) 8–37.

Waehrer, Keith, and Martin K Perry (2003), 'The effects of mergers in open-auction markets' RAND Journal of Economics 38(2) 287–304.

Werden, Gregory J (1996), 'A robust test for consumer welfare enhancing mergers among sellers of differentiated products' Journal of Industrial Economics 44(4) 409–13.

Werden, Gregory J (1997), 'Simulating the effects of differentiated products mergers: a practical alternative to structural merger policy' George Mason Law Review 5(3) 363–86.

Werden, Gregory J. (2000), 'Expert report in *United States v Interstate Bakeries Corp. and Continental Baking Co*' International Journal of the Economics of Business 7(2) 139–48.

Werden, Gregory J and Luke M Froeb (1994), 'The effects of mergers in differentiated products industries: logit demand and merger policy' Journal of Law, Economics, & Organization 10(2) 407–26.

Werden, Gregory J and Luke M Froeb (1996), 'Simulation as an alternative to structural merger policy in differentiated products industries' in Malcolm Coate and Andrew Kleit (eds) *The Economics of the Antitrust Process* Boston: Kluwer Academic Publishers 65–88.

Werden, Gregory J and Luke M Froeb (2002a), 'Calibrated economic models add focus, accuracy, and persuasiveness to merger analysis' in Swedish Competition Authority (ed) *The Pros and Cons of Merger Control* 63–82.

Werden, Gregory J. and Luke M. Froeb (2002b), 'The antitrust logit model for predicting unilateral competitive effects' Antitrust Law Journal 70(1) 257–60.

Werden, Gregory J and Luke M Froeb (2005), 'Unilateral competitive effects of horizontal mergers' in Paolo Buccirossi (ed) *Advances in the Economics of Competition Law* Cambridge, Mass: MIT Press.

Werden, Gregory J, Luke M Froeb, and Timothy J Tardiff (1996), 'The use of the logit model in applied industrial organization' International Journal of the Economics of Business 3(1) 83–105.

Werden, Gregory J and George Rozanski (1994), 'The application of section 7 to differentiated products industries: the market delineation dilemma' Antitrust 8(3) 40–3.

FTC v Swedish Match, 131 F.Supp.2d 151 (DDC 2000).

FTC v Staples, Inc, 970 F.Supp.1066 (DDC 1997).

New York v Kraft General Foods, Inc, 926 F.Supp.321 (SDNY 1995).

United States v Gillette Co, 828 F.Supp. 78 (DDC 1993).

United States v Long Island Jewish Medical Center, 983 F.Supp.121 (EDNY 1997).

United States v Oracle, Inc, 331 F.Supp.2d 1098 (ND Cal 2004).

Panel 7—Keynote Speech by Philip Lowe

MICHAEL HUTCHINGS

We are here to honour a competition conference and it just made me think what does competition mean for most people? For most people competition means sports. One of the main sports that people indulge in in a competitive way is running. Well this is very apt because we have here two Philips. We have the Philip who has organized this conference and we have the Philip who has come to speak to us. So you might call this the race of the Philips. I am told by a little bird that our Philip has recently run in the London Marathon and I think he achieved quite a good time; something a little over three hours. I haven't actually heard the time of our guest speaker, but I suspect that he might be just a little ahead of that, and I think Philip Marsden has got to do some faster running to catch up because Philip Lowe is a very keen and successful runner.

That's his real activity. His part-time activity apart from that is running the Competition Department in Brussels, which he has done as we all know superlatively well. I am not really going to talk about that because we all know about that. I do want to thank him and commend him for his support of this Institute, his support of this event. He has been to a number of events at the Institute including previous conferences and meetings of the Competition Law Forum. I do really, really appreciate this because he told me last year at the dinner something about his travel schedule, which is shuttling between Brussels, Beijing, New York, Sao Paulo and every other quarter of the world and it is really extremely kind of him to take time out to be with us today. Philip Lowe.

PHILIP LOWE

I would like to thank you very much for your kind words of introduction and promise the Commission's continued support to this Institute. This conference is just one example of the high quality of the debate and dialogue which the Institute has been at the centre of. And the dialogue which it has organized brings together not just people in the UK and Europe, but those from across the Atlantic as well.

Chairman, when you referred earlier to sports, I thought we were going to have a whole series of questions on the joint selling of Premier League TV soccer rights, but I understand now that you are really interested in *Microsoft*,[1] so we can go on to that as well if you want.

I remember saying to one of my Commissioners years ago, 'Commissioner, I think you should lift up your eyes to the hills and see this great project which we are involved in'. He wasn't terribly keen on that idea actually; he just wanted to get the next set of decisions out of the door. I have persisted with the same idea with every Commissioner I have had since, but I have always had the same reply.

You know we have a new set of Commissioners. Regime change in Brussels is a regular event, and unlike results of general elections, it does actually result in new faces walking around the corridors in Brussels. And they naturally ask themselves exactly what are they supposed to be doing here as Commissioners and what all the officials are supposed to be doing. Where are we going in competition policy is of course an interesting question.

Neelie Kroes—with all the enthusiasm of a neophyte to competition policy—arrived in Brussels in September of last year. Due to difficulties between the new Commission and the European Parliament, we even had a period of three months where Neelie Kroes and Mario Monti worked in the same building.

You will find that Neelie Kroes comes from a different world to many people in Brussels in the sense that she tells things as they are, she wants to know how things work as they are, and the first thing she said to us was: 'Well, President Barroso wants to have a more competitive Europe. How are we going to help him with our competition policy?'

Of course, at least two thirds of us said, 'Well, it's obvious. Competition policy is good for competitiveness'. People involved in competition policy do say things like that. We take a decision against a company. We say: 'Competition has won'. It is all over once the decision is taken. We rarely look at what happened afterwards. We say: 'We have taken the decision. We have fought against the evils of private monopoly or State aid and we have won in the name of the consumer'. Which is of course, a very interesting statement, but a very declaratory one. The challenge which Neelie Kroes put to us of saying, 'Well what precisely are we going to do to help Europe become more competitive?' made us think a lot more about what precisely we are talking about: whether phrases like 'competition has won', 'competition is bringing results for consumers', really mean something.

So we had to reinvent ourselves, to move away from just being an agency inside the Commission, in order to take part in the political debate that

---

[1] Commission decision of 24 Mar 2004, COMP/37.792.

began at the end of last year as to what kind of challenges Europe has, and in what way a competition policy can contribute to solving these challenges, and to creating a more competitive Europe. And we need to remember here of course, that competition policy is on the whole about facilitating—creating a framework and enforcing rules—and not about paying people money or inflicting regulations on them. Some analysis was produced by our colleagues in the Commission highlighting Europe's poor record in productivity, growth and in innovation in many key sectors; its ageing work force; its inflexible labour markets. What the Commission started out by saying was: 'Well, we really have to show that we are contributing to more jobs and more growth in Europe. We should do that by giving new impetus to what the Heads of State established in 1999 as a new agenda for Europe, the so-called Lisbon Strategy.'

What is the Lisbon Strategy about? It is basically about improving the supply-side factors of performance of European industry and European business in general, and providing the support to that in terms of infrastructure, research and development, innovation, and so on. So in February of this year the Commission put forward a range of proposals which the European Council subsequently accepted. The European Council was concentrating on negotiations with Turkey at the time, so the revamped Lisbon Strategy didn't get much media coverage. But the Council did endorse the Commission's new strategy.

There are some very down-to-earth things in it. One is trying to make sure that European legislation is not actually hindering competitiveness, but is rather facilitating it. Another is making sure that there is a favourable framework for investment and innovation, both by private and public bodies. Removing existing regulatory and other obstacles to competition in the internal market, including distortions arising from private behaviour, was also included in it. The guidelines which the European Council adopted in March explicitly recognized the need for open and competitive markets as a means to improve competitiveness.

Obviously competition cannot produce more competitive business in itself. But competition is a necessary condition for businesses to start to become competitive. It is virtually a truism that unless you have the benchmark of the performance of those competing against you to provide the same services to the same customers, you are never going to be able to assess whether your performance is at an adequate level. So that recognition of the need for open and competitive markets clearly put a focus again on the question which Neelie Kroes put to us, 'What is competition policy going to do for the Lisbon agenda?'

Naturally, we came back with some of the proposals we have always said before. We said, 'We're going to enforce the antitrust rules, enforce the merger rules, and enforce the State aid rules in a way which is going to make sure that businesses are finally competitive!' We also however said, 'Well, we can look beyond just attacking anticompetitive conduct of private firms, and of governments through State aid, and look at the sectors of the economy where quite clearly competition isn't working'. The reasons why competition is not functioning effectively may simply be because of a lack of an enterprise culture in the sector concerned. But it can equally be because the framework of regulation around markets is so heavy that competition can't take off. It could be that national regulation or European regulation is preventing new entrants coming into the market. It could be that despite a lot of single market legislation, which is aimed to create a level playing-field in Europe, no-one is in the end getting on their bike and competing in each other's markets.

Several examples came to mind. If you look at the banking sector there is a lot of consolidation domestically. But it is not so obvious that any of our European banks are making a genuine effort to compete for new markets, new products, or new services elsewhere in Europe. If you take another example—the energy sector—we have got a lot of legislation now consensually agreed mostly with the governments but also with the incumbents in the energy sector. The acceleration directives are gradually introducing more open energy markets for industrial and residential users. In principle, this should allow people to choose the best energy provider around. But if you look more closely at energy markets, you do not see users switching very often between energy providers. In fact, you can even ask if there is any gas-to-gas competition in Europe at all. Why doesn't it exist? For a variety of reasons. A large percentage of supplies are covered by long-term contracts. Long-term contracts certainly help the security of supply. But they are not very helpful if you are trying to create a minimum degree of liquidity in order for people to compete, to offer the best energy prices, the best energy supplies, in order to improve the competitiveness of Europe.

That by the way was one of the reasons why we were extremely worried about the proposed merger between the gas and electricity monopoly in Portugal. The parties quoted Commission documents stating that the energy market in Europe would in principle be completed by the year 2007 and that there would already be an Iberian market before this. Yet when you analysed in practical terms whether those markets will ever be created in a real competition sense, the prospects were much bleaker. The reality is that the European legislation on energy liberalization is a permissive factor; but issues as to how networks work and where there are barriers to entry are so glaringly obvious that there are serious grounds for concern. Of course, you can say, well this isn't just simply a problem of regulation or the competition rules. There is for example insufficient interconnection capacity to allow a real European energy market to get going. Correct. This is why we are looking at the competition problems of the sector in a holistic sense, including the need to develop trans-European infrastructures.

So while competition policy needs to deliver strong law enforcement, it also needs to focus on how markets are working in sectors which are key to European competitiveness. The sector enquiries we have launched will deliver messages both for antitrust enforcement priorities and for regulation. Maybe some legislation is too strong. But some of it may need to be strengthened. If you want to move gas from Zeebrugge to Budapest, you have got to negotiate with five different networks, five different sets of tariffs, and five different sets of balancing conditions to ensure that the gas you put in is sold to your customer at the destination at the right price. This is the nuts and bolts of markets, but some of them are not yet working. So to contribute to European competitiveness, we need active law enforcement and a systematic examination of new and existing legislation for its impact on competition and competitiveness.

You might say, 'Well, every national authority has done this sort of advocacy for years. Why hasn't DG Competition been doing it at the European level?' To a large extent, it has already been doing it. But, as every single national authority also knows, it is difficult to get some messages across when there are powerful forces acting in other directions.

With the backdrop of the political context in which our work is being pursued, it is fairly obvious that the new EU competition regulations in place since 2004 give us a greater margin of manoeuvre to adapt how we enforce the law to wider policy priorities. Regulation 1/2003 helps to promote a competitive Europe based upon a rather predictable level playing-field of parallel application of Articles 81 and 82 by the Commission and national authorities within the new system. We have the potential for more effective competition law enforcement without a notification system. The agencies involved can establish enforcement priorities. Where necessary, after discussion with each other, they can select those cases which it makes sense for them to handle and direct other cases elsewhere. There is no exclusive competence of any agency in any particular area of the economy. This means that each of the agencies in the European Competition Network has to address the question as to which portfolio of cases it makes sense for it to deal with and which of those its sister agencies should be dealing with. The key notion in Regulation 1/2003 is of an authority which is 'best placed' to carry out an investigation, to pursue a case and to impose an effective sanction or remedy.

I should like to highlight here some of the factors which are influencing the way in which we are establishing enforcement priorities in DG Competition. Quite clearly, cases involving an EU-wide or global market definition are likely to come to the Commission and where we probably have the most developed investigative capacity. There are also likely to be cases with links to other areas where an EU-wide approach is relevant, for example in sectors such as telecoms and air transport where European internal market legislation is in place.

On the merger side, the division of powers between national jurisdictions and the European jurisdiction is on a different basis than Regulation 1/2003. The fundamental concept is that above a certain combined turnover of the parties, a merger is more likely to be more of European relevance, whereas those below those thresholds can be left to the laws applied at national level. Yet, here too, we see a very rapid convergence of the way in which we analyse cases from a substantive point of view. The change to a new substantive test in EU merger control ('significant impediment to effective competition') is part of that. At the same time, the new provisions for referral of cases between authorities contain the notion of 'the most appropriate authority' to handle a case. Interestingly, the facility to request referral of a case either to Brussels or to a national capital, has again concentrated attention on the notion of which authority is 'the most appropriate' to deal with the case. This is generally the authority which can deal most effectively with the case, in terms of knowledge of markets, management of the investigation and capacity to impose sanctions. These are essentially the characteristics of the 'best-placed authority' of Regulation 1/2003. So the concepts of most appropriate and best-placed authority in both regulations are very similar in the end. It is interesting to note that something like 10 per cent of our present volume of merger notifications has come from referrals under the new system. So maybe this is a reflection of how the new system corresponds to multiple filings and that is in itself a very good reason for having done it. At the same time, with 25 different national jurisdictions covering a market of over 450 million people, it is very likely in any case that more mergers which affect several markets are going to come to Brussels.

As opposed to fixing antitrust enforcement priorities, where the objective is to focus on areas of greatest competition concern, the enforcement priorities we establish in the merger field do not affect the choice of cases, except in so far as cases can be re-allocated between agencies. The resources we devote to merger work are determined to a significant extent by the judicial review which we are subject to. The amount of evidence we need to provide in order to establish a case, and take a negative or positive view about it, is a crucial issue.

In the last 18 months, we have seen some increase in merger control activity, but certainly not at the levels of 1999 and 2000. We are approximately at about 20 per cent above 2004 and 2004 was about 15 per cent above 2003. But the proportion of complex cases in second-phase investigation is significantly lower. That being said, we always have to bear in mind that we have to meet our merger deadlines and provide the correct analysis and the correct proof for every particular decision we take. With a finite amount of staff resources, our 'absolute' priority to pursue merger investigations places some limits on the scope of antitrust enforcement activity.

But there is still a lot of margin of manoeuvre. When I came back to DG Competition three years ago, we had four categories of cases in antitrust: Priority 1, Priority 2, Priority 3 and Priority 4. As I found out very quickly, cases under the categories Priority 2, 3 and 4 were never dealt with. Cases under Priority 1 were only resourced to about a third of what was required. We also used to set ourselves the objective of taking 50 decisions and issuing 50 Statements of Objection every year. In practice we were never able to get to more than 50 per cent of this target. However, even this performance amounts to quite a lot of cases: 25 decisions on individual antitrust cases; 25 Statements of Objection issued. Yet when you actually analyse *why* we pursued some cases rather than others, it is not clear that they relate directly to issues of, for example, substantial consumer harm (which is our stated policy focus). Nor have they arisen from a more Lisbon agenda-related analysis of where markets are not functioning effectively. In fact our file of around 1,000 outstanding cases (formal and informal) is generated by a whole panoply of complaints and other representations, the majority of which find their origin in allegations of anti-competitive conduct by one competitor against another. Very few are generated by consumer complaints.

How should we react to this? One could say, 'Well, we in the Commission are primarily there to protect the individual firm and individual business against anti-competitive practices and structures on the market'. Fair enough, but of course we can't investigate *all* anti-competitive conducts and structures. We have to select. One can also ask, in an EU with 26 competition agencies acting together, whether there is not a large amount of scope for establishing priorities across and between agencies. To what extent, too (as we will come on to later on), is the absence of any significant framework for private enforcement driving cases to public agencies which, generally speaking, could be dealt with directly by the courts?

Our broad assessment is that we have to plan our use of staff resources in accordance with time-lines and in relation to achievable 'outputs'. Those outputs must ultimately translate into tangible benefits for the competitive process and for consumer welfare. There are some areas of enforcement activity which are traditional for the Commission, but which undeniably remain areas which have to be dealt with at European level. One example is the interaction we have with the sectoral regulators in the telecoms field on control of market power following liberalization. Another is the accompaniment of the process of liberalization in the different transport sectors, as well as in energy and financial services. There is a plethora of regulations in these fields which aim to create a new dynamic of competition in the European Single Market. Despite this, however, there is a large volume of complaints, not just from individual consumers, but also from business consumers, for example about the way financial services are provided. Perhaps as a Commission we have given too much focus in Brussels to creating a level playing-field in terms of shareholder and consumer protection, but we have paid insufficient attention to consumer welfare. Are markets in Europe providing more competitive goods and services at lower costs and greater quality? That is where EU competition policy has a vital complementary role to regulatory action. Its focus must be on the welfare of consumers, as individuals or businesses.

There are of course forms of anti-competitive conduct where the harm to consumers is clear and substantial, such as cartels. It is therefore inevitable that the Commission is going to have to be a major player in this area. Neelie Kroes has made it clear that this has got to be one of our major enforcement priorities. In the last few months we have been able to carry out some further reorganisation in order to concentrate our expertise on anti-cartel work in a single directorate. There are also often sectors of global scope where arguably the Commission has developed some specific expertise. We certainly are becoming experts on Microsoft! I hope we are also becoming experts on the IT sector as a whole. There are other practices which emerge where the conduct of a multi-national corporation has similar effects in many Member States. Here it makes sense for the Commission to undertake an investigation and provide for a solution or a settlement which is in the interests of the European Union's jurisdictions as a whole.

I referred previously to the launching of two sectoral enquiries. I want to outline rapidly what we expect the likely outputs of those enquiries will be. Unlike under UK legislation, Regulation 1/2003 does not allow us to impose remedies or fines on the basis of the results of the sectoral enquiries. But they can be a trigger for new antitrust investigations and they also can inform our merger policy. I might say they can also inform our State aid policy. Look at the influence that the compensation of stranded costs has had on the energy sector. By authorizing State aid to compensate stranded costs at a high level, the Commission has in the end allowed incumbents in the energy sector to raise barriers to entry. Perhaps we should have been paying more attention to this five or six years ago when the European energy directives were being negotiated. At the same time, if governments had not compensated the incumbents for stranded costs, at the level which they wanted, there would arguably have been sustained resistance to energy liberalization in a number of Member States. So maybe there are arguments on both sides. But if we really want the benefits of liberalization to flow through to consumers and society as a whole, then we need to be very strict and rigorous about tackling competition problems in each sector, not just by enforcing the competition rules, but also if necessary by changing legislation which is hindering effective competition.

Sectoral enquiries can of course spiral from one thing to another, just as Article 82 enquiries can. You start off with one problem, you get one complaint, you think that is very interesting, so you set five or six people on it and after about 18 months they receive another complaint which is very nice and then you go on to the next one. Then you have rapidly forgotten what the original problem you were trying to solve is. Our general concern, if we are going to make competition policy effective and relevant, is that when there is a problem on the market, it should be possible for the Commission, or for any other agency, to intervene in a meaningful timeframe, which actually relates to the problem as addressed and promotes a solution. That is very important in areas where markets are moving very fast, in new technology areas. What is the point of investigating a corporation for 10 years and then imposing a remedy on it in relation to a market which has since been completely revolutionized? So speed, as well as rigour, is essential to an effective investigation. That is why, as far as our sectoral enquiries are concerned, we want to limit them in time. The energy enquiry which we are launching will deliver preliminary results which can be fed into the process of legislative review by the end of this year. For both the financial services enquiry and the energy enquiry, we have set the final deadline for results at the end of next year.

The outcomes may involve adapting our antitrust enforcement priorities and/or adapting merger or State aid policy. But these will inevitably be some conclusions on the extent to which European and national legislation is making markets work effectively.

So that is just a taste of how competition policy looks in Brussels under the new Commission. I haven't mentioned a range of initiatives which you have been discussing in this conference over the last two days. The effort to produce Article 82 guidelines is one of them. Certainly we aim to produce a draft guidance document for the end of this year. But we will carefully measure whether they produce real guidance rather than simply consolidate case law. We have also promised a Green Paper on private enforcement, and

I sincerely hope we will reach that objective. We have talked in general terms about the need at a certain stage to complete the guidelines in merger policy to cover both vertical and conglomerate mergers. I don't see that happening in 2005, but I do see us starting serious discussions on this in 2006.

Finally, I know you're not so interested in it, but I have to mention again the State aid reform. We have had such a long period where we have debated for years a more economic approach to antitrust and merger policy. Those of you who have been involved in the State aid control have probably discovered a complex architecture of rules and regulations. You may have asked yourself occasionally what the ultimate objective of State aid control is. Who or what are we protecting? Competitors? The competitive process? The consumer? And are we using economics in the right way to achieve our objective, whatever it is? In broad terms, we are probably protecting the competitive process more than consumers, but in the longer run, consumers should also benefit.

Secondly, economics has to play a bigger role in this policy. We have to make clear what our underlying analytical methodology is, using in particular concepts of market failure and competitive distortion.

Thirdly, it takes us now on average between 25 and 33 months to close a major State aid case. And the vast majority of the Commission's final decisions are positive. So there is a lot of dissatisfaction from both Member States and business that the State aid procedures should be brought up to date. Timely delivery of State aid decisions is as relevant to business timetables as in antitrust and mergers.

MICHAEL HUTCHINGS

Philip has kindly agreed to answer a few questions and we have a few minutes before we are going to take a quick break for coffee.

ALAN RILEY

I was going to ask you about your communication strategy in the light of the success the Commission has had with cartel-busting, particularly with the 2002 Leniency Notice. My argument would be surely DG Competition should be using the success they have had in order to build more understanding of competition law, more political support for what they do, and potentially more support for more power and more resources.

I am worried that perhaps DG Competition isn't doing this. I will tell you why. I drafted a parliamentary question for one of the British MEPs asking how many leniency applications the Commission had actually obtained under the new Notice. The answer is 92 from February 2002 to November 2004, which is fantastic. I am sure the Antitrust Division would have been singing those statistics from the top of the Capitol building in Washington, whereas I had to actually extract them out of DG Competition. It seems to me that the Commission is to some degree missing a trick here. That it could actually first of all politically make itself far more popular with the Member States and with the Parliament and, secondly, actually use it to drive political support for the changes wanted in the policies that you have talked about.

PHILIP LOWE

I agree with you to about 85 per cent. I would just say , however, that if I announced how many leniency applications—and we do regularly announce how many we have in progress in these speeches and elsewhere— I still have one major problem: I have got to them out of the door in terms of decisions.

Last year, compared with 2003 and 2002, we only took I think six decisions against hardcore cartels. There are several reasons for that. One reason is that in 2000 and 2001, the cases concerned were either relatively simple or of international dimension and well investigated by a number of competition authorities. Most of the new cases we have had since then involved an enormous number of parties and systematically require litigation, at least on the level of fines.

But I agree with you that we are not selling our work well enough. Not only do I agree with you, Neelie Kroes also agrees with you because she started her mandate by saying more or less what you have just said. Are we good at advocacy? I think that we have got a long way to go! But the first thing that you have to establish before you advocate how effective you are is to make sure you are effective and credible. Credibility means achieving results. Credibility also means attacking those areas where you are not achieving results as well so that when you say how successful you are in cartels, someone doesn't immediately pipe up and say, 'Yes, but your Article 82 record is a disaster'. But I think we're getting there. I really do. We have had to readjust our merger policy and practice disciplines which are proportionate to the impact of our decisions on the business community. An absolutely healthy message has come out from the *Tetra Laval*[2] decision of the Court of Justice: 'Listen Commission. The more ambitious you are in

---

[2] *Tetra Laval v Commission,*(Case C-12/03 P) not yet reported in the ECR, judgment of 15 Feb 2005.

the theories you have about mergers, the more evidence you must show that you have got'. That seems to be basically common sense. There is plenty more common sense around. For example, if you want to use an economic theory, make sure you use one which you have got data to test it. But don't pretend that you have got a case if you've only got a theory without data which you haven't tested. Because then investigation is just speculation.

We have come a long way in EU merger control, building on the success it had already. In cartels, we have got to get back to the achievements in terms of decision-making we had in 2001 and 2002. We have set the objective of taking 10 decisions this year. It requires redeploying staff from one part of DG Competition to the other. That requires us to go through the exercise, which I have referred to earlier, of establishing enforcement priorities. If we can't do that, we can sing a lot of nice songs and not deliver. I think that if we can sing the song of a successful effective merger regime, a successful anti-cartel regime and a limited number of significant antitrust actions, particularly under Article 82, then we have built up the case for going to, for example, our own budgetary authority in the year 2007 and saying, 'Right, we have cleaned up the stables. Now look at the record. Give us more resources to go on'. I think that will happen, but I don't think that budgetary authorities are particularly impressed if we just only tell part of the story. We have got to tell the whole story and that's what Neelie Kroes and I want to do over the course of the next year.

JOHN WOTTON

Philip, I was wondering how far the Commission's priorities in terms of taking up the cases are, or should be, influenced by what one might call national considerations, for example, the availability of national remedies, the accessibility of the national courts to the complainant, and the willingness or otherwise of the national competition authority or authorities that might otherwise handle the case to take the case up?

PHILIP LOWE

I am not the only one in the room who is qualified to comment on that but I would just say that if there was anyone under the impression in the process of negotiation of modernization that the new regime would allow the Commission to refer cases to national authorities, then this was an illusion. The reality has been quite different. We are moving into a period of more effective enforcement, but it isn't a situation in which the Commission is in a position—nor national authorities by the way—to dictate from one authority to the other which cases they should take up.

As a matter of fact, the majority of cases which have been discussed between us for 81 and 82 have been situations in which some of the smaller agencies have said to us, 'We can't handle this case from a technical point of view, or we are not strong enough to handle this case vis-à-vis our government. Can you do it, even though the problem is national?' I think it is fair to say honestly that our reply to that is, 'Well, I'm sorry, we have to establish priorities for the European jurisdiction as a whole, and if we take this case, or that case, simply on the grounds of incapacity at national level, or lack of independence and power of the competition agency, I think that we would not just weaken the local agency, we would weaken the Commission'. It is important that the Commission displays its priorities clearly out to the Member States and to agencies. It can be influenced obviously, but there must be a genuine argument that there is a European-wide dimension to the cases which we take up.

So yes, it would help too if there was greater accessibility of national courts for complainants to resolve problems. I think we have had a number of discussions about that inside the European Competition Network. It is certainly true that the possibilities for a court action remain hindered, not just in some cases by capacity, but also by genuine differences in procedure and problems of delay. I think it would also be an illusion to think that businesses could find redress through national courts by preliminary rulings in Luxembourg, unless there was the dramatic reform of the timetable on which that is possible.

But in the first instance, a national court influenced, where necessary, by a national competition authority should in our view be one major route to redress. In so far as we can also try to build a better framework for private enforcement, this will help too.

Panel 8—Roundtable with Heads of Agencies

PHILIP MARSDEN

Welcome everybody to the final session of this two-day conference. It gives me great pleasure to be able to introduce this session because it is something that we have shamelessly borrowed in a transatlantic sense from the ABA, and their famous agency heads' coffee clutch, which is designed to make them feel comfortable, but of course, highly caffeinated, and thereby provoke a very interesting discussion.

Our genteel interrogator this year is David Lawsky from Reuters. With all respect to the other commentators in the room, I have to say that I find his articles which come out frequently to be extremely incisive and I think that benefits from the fact that he has his own obviously Trans-Atlantic perspective, having reported on antitrust issues in the States for several years and now being based in Brussels and being able to comment on what some people (he may not say this), but some people might refer to as a more gentlemanly system of competition.

David, thank you very much, and agency heads, thank you very much for joining us.

DAVID LAWSKY

By now I think you probably know at least some of these people. Philip Lowe who just spoke to you, the top ranking civil servant in DG Comp; Tihamér Tóth, who is the Vice-President of the Hungarian Competition Authority; Hew Pate, the Head of Department of Justice Antitrust Division; and Sir John Vickers, of course Head of the Office of Fair Trading here in London.

What we are going to do is, we have got a few topics we are going to try and hear. At the end of each topic, we'll more or less open the floor for a few questions; so be thinking of your questions. We will try to take two or three questions and then let the panel deal with them. We want to have time for ideas that you have, or questions that you have; we'll try to save a little time at the end for topics that you want to raise that we don't raise here.

So I think we will get started. We will start with private law suits. We had a question yesterday that Hew dealt with about, if you recall, that you might wind up with a free-for-all if things were as they are now with a very broad Article 82. So I am going to go on beyond that and key off something that John Temple Lang said yesterday. With the problems of loser pays, the lack of discovery and some other difficulties, it wasn't really clear to me, even with the green paper that you are going to have out later this year, how in the world we were ever going to get started with private lawsuits here. What John suggested, if you recall, was that once auditors realise that there is tax-payers' money that is being lost because there are no follow-on lawsuits, that that would put pressure on municipalities and others to bring lawsuits.

I want to start with Hew, where you do have a very well-adopted private lawsuit system, to bounce that idea off you to see what you think about that.

HEWITT PATE

Well, I think John Temple Lang's idea has a great deal of merit to it. I have cautioned several times that Europe ought to worry a little bit about moving all the way towards the American system, at least in this context, and it is important to keep in mind that the different situations call for different types of remedies. In the cartel situation, I am not as concerned or sceptical. I think it is very clear that private cartel litigation in the United States is a big part of the deterrent against that sort of conduct and I think if the experience here turns out to be anything like ours, public procurement cases are among the very best and among the ones that get the most public support.

I think it is harder than you might believe to study bids or to collect data and thereby determine where there are going to be cartel cases. We have tried that with varying success over the years. This type of study can help you find the right place to look for the cases where you are going to have the biggest benefit and where you are going to not be as hampered by some of those impediments that John described yesterday.

DAVID LAWSKY

Phil, have you had a chance to begin to look at this or think about this for the green paper yet?

PHILIP LOWE

Well, I don't want to repeat any of the discussions you already had yesterday. I think that we certainly will be wanting to position ourselves somewhere away from the extremes on the other side of the Atlantic. We will certainly concentrate on damages, redress for harm. We want to be able to see consumer groups, consumer associations, being able to take representative action in specific cases. I certainly agree with Hew that the cartel area is an easy one for us to go ahead with. However, as to public procurement on this side of the Atlantic, there is another legal framework for complaint, which may not necessarily be directly relevant to the framework which we would create under Regulation 1. Our idea would basically be that this would be private enforcement of 81 and 82. But I agree that any party who has suffered through cartelization of a tendering procedure should get redress.

DAVID LAWSKY

Private enforcement could, of course, encompass a municipality in a sense. But the private enforcement that, I think the follow-on cases with the *Lombard* case[1]—are people here familiar with the *Lombard* case? There was a group of banks in Austria in 2002 that conspired quite openly to have high interest rates for consumers. They were very open about it. You caught them, you fined them and since that time there has been a consumer group, one of whose members is in fact the Austrian Government, that has been trying to do follow-on suits. They have run into all kinds of difficulties. One of them has been discovery. In fact they won a lawsuit against you a week or two ago telling you to go back and look more carefully at 48,000 pages of documents to see whether or not you could give them your own records, which of course, that is all you do. You won't do anything else.

PHILIP LOWE

I think what the Court objected to is that we took a global approach to the issue of discovery and said, 'You can't have any of it!' What we were concerned about was the implication that this evidence could be used against individuals, which the judge in particular was looking for at the time, without there being a due process of equivalent quality and sanctions which is guaranteed under Regulation 1. So I think that we will have to look back at that case and see which parts of the evidence are relevant to the problem which we were worried about. The Court rapped us on the knuckles for having taken a global approach.

DAVID LAWSKY

If you have to do that for every case—why don't we ask a couple of the

---

[1] *Austrian Banks ('Lombard Club')* [2004] OJ L56/1.

national authorities—if you have to start doing that for cases, I don't see how you will be able to do anything else. What do you see might begin to get private lawsuits going?

TIHAMÉR TÓTH

If I may start by saying that private enforcement is a novelty in Hungary, so we are still very far from the American example, which is not necessarily the best thing, I believe.

Nevertheless, the Office is just about to propose an amendment to the Hungarian Completion Act which would enable private parties to bring lawsuits. Plaintiffs will be able to rely not only on European but also the similar Hungarian antitrust provisions before the courts, which is a good thing, I believe, to have the same level playing-field. Nevertheless, I believe that private enforcement will not be a cornerstone of competition policy implementation, in Hungary at least. Still it can have at least two advantages. First, it allows the competition office to concentrate on the most important cases. I know that complainants were not very happy hearing that, but nevertheless we can say that complainants should now turn to courts, not to the Office. The second advantage will be felt especially in the field of cartels. If there are follow-on court cases, then it can be something like an extra deterrent effect for cartel members.

SIR JOHN VICKERS

You ask about where these cases might come from. We have had some in the UK and there may have been some cases not in the public domain that have been settled as well. It is important not to forget those. Now I don't know about those; you don't *see* those of course.

One direction is clearly the follow-on action, for example an action for damages in a cartel case, and it could well be a municipality which has been on the wrong end of that. We have had some construction industry cartel cases where municipalities have been victims of that and it seems fine to my mind for them to follow on and recover damages. In terms of the 'Should we go to the US system?' question, of course as Hew was explaining yesterday, that is a cocktail of things: treble damages, class actions, contingency fees and all the rest, which are not unique to antitrust; they are part of a wider legal system. It is one where, if I heard right, there are not civil fines. So you need to think of a package of incentives in all this and I don't think there is any likelihood of the UK, or indeed anywhere else in Europe, going to a system of treble damages and all the rest and of course we do have a system of administrative fines, subject to appeal. I wouldn't advocate going, as it were, the whole hog to the American system, especially going for some parts of it but not the other parts. That might also have undesirable effects.

The second direction is that there may be competition points taken in cases that are originally about something else. It might be a contract dispute, it might be a patent infringement case, where indeed the defendant against whom that private suit has been brought counter-challenges with some competition points. There are some UK cases where that has been a feature as well, even in the early days that we have had.

Third would be the *de novo* case brought by a private plaintiff where the authorities have not picked up the particular ball. I think that's probably less likely, and going to be less frequent than the other two.

As to whether this is all good or bad, on the whole I think it's a positive thing in so far as these private actions complement what the authorities are doing. It also removes the authority's monopoly over bringing cases which I think has some advantages in addition. But it being a good thing does depend crucially on substantive law being sensible. In jurisdictions where substantive law has gone in odd places, like perhaps the US and vertical agreements in the late 1960s and much of the 1970s, there you could get a lot of private actions that may be very damaging to economic efficiency. But this underlines the point that if you get the substantive law right then these things work together as complements.

TIHAMÉR TÓTH

Should private enforcement become a daily reality in Europe it would be interesting to see that not only the European Commission and national authorities will have a chance to contribute to the formulation of European competition policy, but also that national judges will take an active role. It would be very interesting, I believe.

PHILIP LOWE

I think John makes a good point; there are plenty of situations where competition issues arise in the course of other litigation. The major problem is not linked to private enforcement as such. When there are cases of Articles 81 and 82 in national courts, I am pretty confident that the national competition authorities will educate the courts, where they are not educated already. But I do fear a situation where the courts are bogged down in requests for preliminary rulings from Luxembourg on aspects which we have not covered in our guidance.

DAVID LAWSKY

Is that made worse because you cannot appeal from the national courts into the EU courts on these cases?

PHILIP LOWE

Can you or can't you? I think a system of private enforcement must explicitly foresee preliminary rulings on issues of law and also on some issues of assessment of the facts.

DAVID LAWSKY

There are instances, I think we have seen it with the beer case here, where sometimes people think that judges should seek a preliminary ruling and ask for guidance from Luxembourg and they don't. They just presume to know the law. Does that pose any kind of a problem?

PHILIP LOWE

It causes us an existential problem in the long term. In the case you are referring to and others, it is natural that judges may decide to take a view which is, in the Commission's view, not consistent from time to time with previous case law and ongoing Commission policy. It is up to us to intervene in those situations, whether indirectly through the national competition authority or directly through *amicus curiae* briefs, or through opinions which we give on request, or even when we are not requested. Having done that, then it is for the legal system to resolve it. Even if national courts keep the cases to themselves, they will probably raise it to the national Supreme Court, and the Supreme Court will have to decide whether it needs a preliminary ruling in Luxembourg.

SIR JOHN VICKERS

It is not always a bad thing if the national courts have the courage to take these decisions. We had in our consumer law work a case of *First National Bank*[2] that went to the House of Lords and it was a point about the Unfair Contract Terms Directive. There, the House of Lords made a judgement. We actually lost that particular case, but in terms it was very helpful to us on a wider front. Had it gone to Luxembourg for two or three years, who knows what would have happened. In many ways it was better to get reso-

---

[2] *Director General of Fair Trading v First National Bank Plc* [2001] UKHL 52.

lution in a shorter time. So I make that point, just in case people think it is necessarily bad if national judges fail to send truck-loads of questions to Luxembourg.

DAVID LAWSKY

Hew, how do you decide when to file an *amicus* brief or get involved in a private case?

HEWITT PATE

Well, for us, with *amicus* briefs, if the Supreme Court is hearing a competition-related case, we almost certainly are going to look hard at filing a brief. Lower court cases are difficult; we very rarely file *amicus* briefs in District Court proceedings and in the Court of Appeals somewhere in the middle. But we don't necessarily have an agenda as to what area of competition we would focus on. It depends a little bit on what private litigation is coming up. So, for example, a couple of years back in *Trinko*,[3] we did something very unusual and filed a brief urging the Supreme Court to take a case because we thought it was important, but the much more common situation is for our Supreme Court to request the views of the United States.

So it is often governed by what rolls up on the beach.

DAVID LAWSKY

Before I do everything else, before we turn to the audience, do we have any questions?

HAROLD CAPLAN

I hope I am not going to make an impertinent suggestion to Mr Philip Lowe, but could I suggest when he is talking or thinking about private enforcement he might have a word with his friends in another directorate called, or which used to be called, Home and Legal Affairs, who have established a rather under-developed network of structures throughout Europe for the resolution of disputes by non-judicial means. It hasn't got very far yet, and maybe if he's serious about it, he could help them to get on with it.

---

[3] *Verizon Communications Inc v Law Offices of Curtis V Trinko, LLP*, 540 US 398 (2004).

BERT FOER

Two questions weren't addressed on the private enforcement side. One is the aggregation of small claims in class actions or something of that nature and the other is contingent fees. If you are going to have antitrust cases brought by private plaintiffs you have got to have some motivation for attorneys who are not otherwise willing to participate and in the absence of treble damages, and perhaps in the absence of class actions, I am wondering what your thoughts are on how to motivate the activity that would be necessary to provide additional enforcement.

STEVEN ANDERMAN

The cocktail of measures that John Vickers referred to gave examples, but there is one further element of the cocktail that isn't always publicised very much and that is the way the American courts, at least some of them, treat the issue of proof of causation and how there is a certain tone of generosity in the treatment of burden of proof of damages. There is no hint of anything like that at the legislative level in any of the European proposals, but it is something that really has to be thought about because if there is a serious policy of encouraging private enforcement then something needs to be done about the aid to the plaintiff in getting past the usual European, certainly the UK, burden of proof. It is almost impossible to meet, except in the most egregious of cases.

I have been told that at least one European country, I think it is Sweden, has come up with some way of easing the burden of proof, so that if you can actually show an infringement you get help with the proof of damages. I don't know, since I haven't looked at the detail of the Swedish legislation, I don't know whether that is punitive in the sense that it is almost like an exemplary damages kind of idea, or whether it is simply part of the Swedish culture or judicial cultural notion, if something is wrong, there should be a way to compensate the person that suffered the wrong. But the point is that part of the cocktail that would be needed would be a conscious effort to deal with this problem of proof of damages in a competition case since the obvious difficulty is you are having to prove what would have happened if something else hadn't happened.

DAVID LAWSKY

Why don't we start with the third one first, the burden of proof, which I think was also something that was dealt with in St Gallen by Professor Clifford Jones. I wasn't there for that, but I read his paper. It was the same point and I think it is a very interesting point. Hew, why don't we start with you since you're familiar with the way it's done in the States.

HEWITT PATE

Start with me, but go backwards. Yes, I think it is well-known in private antitrust litigation in the States that if you can make your showing of liability then you face a relaxed burden in terms of what sort of expert projections might be admissible to try to prove damages. So undoubtedly, it makes a big difference.

The problem is that this is just one more part of this terrifically powerful cocktail that we have—to use the idea that is attributed to John. So we have methods of aggregation, as Bert is talking about, we have contingent fees, and so we motivated the plaintiff's trial bar right the way into private jet aircraft in the United States and it has been a very powerful motivation. So I think this idea of what is a workable mix, is a good way to think about it. You wouldn't want to have every part of the system stacked in favour of private actions, but there may be a mix that does give you that additional deterrence. Again, the type of case matters. In a cartel case you are going to have a cartel period to compare to another period whereas in a section 2 or Article 82 sort of situation, you are imagining a hypothetical but-for world and you may have very questionable incentive and deterrent effects for future parties because of the indeterminacy of the liability. So, different types of cases may need a different cocktail to get the best result.

DAVID LAWSKY

The specific example that was given in the paper I read was actually *Crehan*[4] and that there was a very high level of proof. I wonder if you can comment on that John.

SIR JOHN VICKERS

I am not close to that case, but Steve, I believe, was suggesting on this side of the Atlantic that this is yet another hurdle to cross and of course it is part of the *Crehan*[5] litigation and the Lords may say something very interesting on this. I am not sure that it is quite as difficult as maybe Steve was suggesting, but that would be less clear to me.

---

[4] *Courage v Crehan* (Case C-453/99) [2001] ECR I-6297, [2001] All ER (EC) 886.
[5] ibid.

On the point about contingency fees, which is one of the things that Bert raised, this is part of a much wider public policy issue and it is not just competition law. Again we have got to think that there are lots of other bits involved. I have personally no difficulties with that. That seems fine. My favourite example was a Judge Kaplan, who I believe in the *Auction Houses* case[6] in the US auctioned the right to represent the class—it was a sealed bid auction—and said if they get a certain amount of money damages the law firm will get 25 per cent of the excess above whatever number they bid. So different lawyers made different bids, and I believe David Boies's firm got that. So that was a very nice example of using the competitive process through the auction to determine the identity of the lawyer and the level of the fee.

HEWITT PATE

Part of that auction is going to be who can really get compensation to the people who are hurt. Our Federal Trade Commission has been active in scrutinising some of these situations where attorneys are making very handsome fee awards but consumers are left with coupons that don't really accomplish very much. Bert Foer's question looks at the right thing, which is how do you really get the consumers compensated? It should not be about the lawyers.

PHILIP LOWE

I am first of all going to say one thing about process. And that is, if I knew exactly what was going to be in our Green Paper on private enforcement, I would tell you. But it is going to be pretty comprehensive in its coverage and hopefully it will raise a number of, or all, the issues you have just raised about the cocktail of incentives and obligations which need to be provided, and it should raise the issue of balance between them.

DAVID LAWSKY

Do you want to talk about the Home and Legal Affairs suggestion?

PHILIP LOWE

There are a number of things which have gone on in the Commission over the past few years. Some of them are have proved to be very effective, others not. There is a whole raft of legislation, apart from competition legis-

---

[6] *In re Auction Houses Antitrust Litigation*, 197 FRD 71 (SDNY 2000).

lation, which foresees the possibility of redress where there are alleged infringements which cause damage to parties. When complaints about those infringements have been dealt with in Brussels, the approach has been relatively legalistic. The infringement is normally an infringement against the application of a law in a Member State. The Commission issues warning letters and then opens cases in the courts in Luxembourg. The whole process goes on and on, by which time all the people concerned have grown old and the original problem isn't so much relevant any more. What has been useful, and I think Mr Kaplan was referring to it, is that there are plenty of complaints which can be dealt with by administrative means; when, for example, the person or the business concerned doesn't know which part of the administration they should need to engage with to solve their problem. So in the last three years our colleagues in the internal market area set up something called 'Solve It'. This is the kind of name, by the way, which we need for our competition policy! Solve It is a network of officials in the national administrations and in the Commission who take on the mission of trying to solve people's problems in relation to application of EU law. And they have had some very good successes in getting basic redress or just simply a change in policy, a change in treatment of individual cases, and that is all very good.

But I think we have to go on from there and look at the issue of the legal consequences. There are plenty of people and organizations which do not simply get persuaded to behave correctly by being named and shamed. They need to have the serious threat of litigation and that is what we will be concentrating on in the private enforcement Green Paper. And as John and Hew said, strengthening the private enforcement system, which must by necessity have its focus in national courts, is going to make it much clearer what the deterrents are and what the sanctions are to infringing competition law.

DAVID LAWSKY

I would like to talk a little bit, or ask a little bit, about confidentiality, what is called 'redaction' in the United States. When I reported in the United States, there generally were two forms of briefs and decisions that would come out; one which was for the parties, which included commercial secrets or other kinds of things that could be damaging to the companies; and the public version. As I recall there was maybe a few days' lapse, but here in Europe in a number of countries it seems to be a major issue. You've been taken to court before you can release decisions over what should be redacted. I don't understand why it is so simple in the States and why it is so difficult here. I wanted to ask, would everyone here, maybe get this reconciled.

HEWITT PATE

I don't know if it's simple. We have put a good deal of effort into releasing redacted versions of briefs and other things. I think if you step back, the reason that we do it so quickly is because of the underlying expectation. We find that it varies from judge to judge but it is very likely when we are on a case, we are going to be confronted with a judge who has very little patience for the idea of confidential corporate information, very little patience for the idea of sealing parts of what is a public proceeding. Judge Walker, in the *Oracle* case,[7] for example, took a very hard line against what he viewed as unnecessary sealing. So any time we have a filing coming up, we are going to have a team of attorneys who are ready to try to produce a redacted accessible version just as quickly as possible; hopefully, as you say, within a few days. That doesn't mean that it is always easy to do, but that is just the underlying expectation that we need to make it available whenever we can, as quickly as we can. That is in the civil context. On the other hand, grand jury testimony, for example, in the United States is treated with a very high degree of confidentiality. So there are some places where we place a lot of emphasis on keeping things confidential, but in the type of case you mentioned, we are just used to that as the expectation.

SIR JOHN VICKERS

First of all we must make sure we are comparing like with like. When the DOJ is taking an action you are there in court. In the course of administrative proceedings, that is clearly a different context. We may well end up in court or before the tribunal and that has its own transparency provisions. Within the administrative proceedings, I would say there is quite a contrast between merger and non-merger. With mergers, where until even five years ago the OFT was publishing nothing, now we publish something on every case and redacted versions typically come out in a matter of days on the sort of timescale that you mentioned. We are just doing Phase 1, of course, and matters do or don't go to the Competition Commission for Phase 2. In non-merger work, it is different and there are a number of questions and we may be seeking wider views on this, on how we should walk the line between preservation of commercially confidential information before any decision has been taken, and on the other hand, a natural desire to be open.

We have had a few issues go to the tribunal on this sort of point. The tribunal has said what it has said and it is very early days here and quite often I think our instincts would be towards more openness than what we have always done. So that is an evolving story.

---

[7] *United States v Oracle, Inc* 331 F.Supp.2d 1098 (ND Cal 2004).

I think the main point in doing Trans-Atlantic comparison, as is the theme of the conference, is to not forget that one is administrative pre-appeal and the other's in court.

DAVID LAWSKY

Predictably, what you do is release to the public your final decisions; you also have to give within your administrative proceedings, for example, a Statement of Objections, one to third parties and that's not such a difficult piece of work I guess. But it is very difficult when it comes to your final report about anything, I have noticed. Why is this?

PHILIP LOWE

The whole point of this administrative proceeding is to provide a solution and not be part of the problem. Therefore, the protection of commercially sensitive information before the decision has been reviewed right the way down the track is, in the European system, essential. We have a number of points where our due process depends on our being transparent with a particular intermediate decision, or with the final decision, which means, of course, that we come across the well-known problem in this room that the parties concerned may or may not want to cooperate fully with us in providing a non-confidential version within a reasonable period of time. Or alternatively, provide a non-confidential version which is really limited to protecting commercial secrets and not to protecting issues of strategic value, but not of commercial sensitivity as such. This means from time to time we have to take a formal decision to produce the non-confidential version, which can be challenged in the court, if the parties themselves don't agree.

I can understand fully that this is a comparison which is negative from the European point of view. That being said, there are some advantages to this system. I read the FTC's explanation of the cruise ship merger with interest and the FTC and DOJ now frequently do produce an explanation of decisions. It is a discipline which is placed on us, first phase and second phase, because we have got both, which I personally believe is quite healthy. The parties themselves, if they are going to expedite, if they are going to go to Luxembourg and get, in their view, redress for any decision which we have produced, have also an interest in providing a version which doesn't damage their interest and then it doesn't damage other people's interests either. Don't forget, all our cartel activity decisions are reviewed in the courts. All of them.

So I think there is no reason to be particularly pessimistic about this area. I think it is a sign that this is a system which is subject to a due process, but where there are clearly interests to be played against, if you are the public authority, against what the private party might say.

HEWITT PATE

I don't know why the comparison is one you would necessarily take to be negative. One of the big complaints we get from private parties is that they don't have available the equivalent of a Statement of Objections and that some of our staff are much more transparent than others in revealing to parties what the potential competitive problem is that the parties need to address if the authority is not going to take action. In terms of transparency at the back end, the US Federal Trade Commission and, as you said, the DOJ, have really for the first time recently put in place procedures to explain the reasons for non-action. That is something we haven't done at all until recently and something we are getting started with because we think the model over here is in some ways more respectful of the idea of rule of law—explaining the basis for your decisions.

That doesn't mean that I think we ought to go all the way down the road of allowing a party to challenge a non-action. But again, if you go back to the cocktail, you have to remember in the US system if a party doesn't like the fact that there has been non-action, they can go take a crack at it themselves under our system.

So there are just two different systems. Likewise in the merger context, before we reach a decision we keep information confidential. In a case of non-action we may release very little. So you just need to understand the differences. It is a bit of an apples and oranges thing.

DAVID LAWSKY

It is a bit of an apples and oranges issue, but as you say there are lessons to be learned in both directions. There are some ways in which there is more transparency here than in the United States and vice versa. This is more a question of timing. The reasoned non-intervention that you're talking about . . . that you learned from the model over here . . . John, you had some thoughts on that too, I know.

SIR JOHN VICKERS

Well, it follows directly from what Hew was just saying. Put in very simple terms, people want to know, businesses want to know, practitioners want to know, where in the authorities' view the line is between the merger that's ok and the merger that isn't and where the line is between lawful and unlawful behaviour under 81 and 82 and domestic equivalents.

Now if the only things that go public are infringement decisions, then that gives some clues as to where the line is in the view of the authorities. I stress that because it is all subject to review and correction by the courts. But surely one can do better than that and guidelines are one way to try and give a fuller picture, but the reasoned non-intervention is another way, not just in the merger area where we have been publishing and where we have to publish—used to publish some, now we publish all clearance decisions, as well as reference decisions to the CC suitably redacted—but also in Competition Act cases, we have been in some cases explaining why we did not intervene.

These are sometimes long documents. The *Sky*[8] case comes to mind there. Sometimes they are very short. Things like *Edinburgh Buses*,[9] there was the *BA/ABTA*[10] question, there was the refusal to supply questions involving *DuPont*.[11] We think that puts out there quite a bit of our thinking and our philosophy on where the line is.

Hew said if people don't like a non-action, they can have a go at it themselves. Of course, in our context, they can have a go by taking us to the Competition Appeal Tribunal for our non-actions and indeed quite a lot of our time and I think maybe all the time of the regulators with concurrent powers before the tribunal has been about non-actions. Indeed our success rate on our actions is very high compared to that of our non-actions.

So it is not just either/or; there is that other way of having a shot at it here.

DAVID LAWSKY

Tihamér, how do you handle it in Hungary in terms of explaining non-actions?

TIHAMÉR TÓTH

Under Hungarian administrative law we are obliged to give our reasons even for cases which involve non-actions. This is reasonable because all our decisions can be reviewed before courts; also directly affected complainants or competitors can turn to the courts and challenge a non-intervention decision there, which happens frequently. It is an open question, but a great

[8] Office of Fair Trading Decision of 8 May 2001.
[9] Office of Fair Trading Decision of 29 Apr 2004.
[10] Office of Fair Trading Decision of 11 Dec 2002.
[11] Office of Fair Trading Decision of 2 May 2002.

number of decisions, around 40 per cent, involve non-intervention decisions, which is a fairly big number compared to the European average.

PHILIP LOWE

The number of clearance decisions which are questioned in Luxembourg is also significant.

DAVID LAWSKY

Next topic. You all participate in a number of international agencies. I think of the International Competition Network, which is coming up in June; the OECD which meets I am not sure how many times a year; the WTO also has something for antitrust; the European Competition Network for the agencies here; you have, Tihamér, I think, something like 115 people in your agency. Do you do anything besides go to international conferences?

TIHAMÉR TÓTH

That is the question really! First of all, you can't implement competition policy without having regard to international developments. It is very important for us to go to conferences like this, to participate at different levels of international cooperation. You haven't mentioned that we also have a regional type of cooperation for Central and Eastern European countries called CECI, Central European Competition Initiative, where we discuss actual issues like public procurement cartels or sale below cost-type issues. Another example is that this year a regional centre of the OECD in Budapest has been established. Based on this institution we are meant to teach, to throw the seeds of competition policy to the Balkan States and to the post-Soviet countries. It is very demanding. It is rather a rhetorical question, but where should it end? Should there not be something like a share of work between these international organisations?

PHILIP LOWE

This is a common concern because we have got core business to do. But we have also a lot of issues of convergence and coherence to discuss. I would distinguish the European Competition Network nevertheless from the other international fora which we are in, in so far as cooperation within the ECN is based on parallel application of the same law, with a specific role for the Commission to ensure coherent application of the law. Do we spend too much time coordinating within the ECN? Well, John, I and the other Directors General of national authorities meet at most twice a year in that context. But our colleagues who are dealing with individual sectors or individual types of problems may meet in sub-groups of the ECN. It is inevitable that those agencies which are most interested in the problem concerned turn up to be represented in these sub-groups. Are they also generally speaking the agencies which have the most resources? Probably yes. On the other hand, the work done for example by the ECN financial services or energy sub-groups or on cartels is ultimately to the benefit of the rest of the agencies who cannot participate. So I think that on the whole it is progressing quite well.

I think a similar degree of discipline is necessary in OECD and in the ICN. In the ICN, we have spent quite a lot of time trying to work out where the focus of discussion should be, so it could bring in most of the members on issues which are directly relevant to their activities. I think certainly in the merger area, there has been major progress; whether or not all ICN members turn up at all the meetings, they have all benefited from the work done.

Cartel work is a similar area where we can reap low-hanging fruit. I think there are more general issues where, with or without a very large audience in front of us, we are going to discuss issues of ideology and philosophy. A good example is the relationship between competition law and IPR—which is never about ideology in the end, but about cases!

Another horizontal issue of importance is information exchange.

I think both these issues are very, very important. Both need to be discussed regularly. But they are not going to have the same operationality for us in terms of what we are achieving in the merger and cartel area and what we are doing inside the ECN in terms of hard results.

DAVID LAWSKY

In terms of resources for smaller agencies like an agency that has fewer people on its entire agency than there are PhD economists in the US DOJ and FTC combined. How should they use their resources, given all these various international groups that we are supposed to have? Do we have too many international groups? Is that too much of a hot potato to throw out here?

PHILIP LOWE

Just to add a word on the European Competition Network, we don't just have exchange of information about cases. Everyone's now got access to each others' case law and economic research. So none of us are landing hard on a new sector or a case without the cushion of knowledge and experience in the ECN as a whole. I would like to think that that would apply more widely as we go into second-generation agreements with other jurisdictions outside the EU.

SIR JOHN VICKERS

I would apply principles of competition and choice to your question. One fact about these meetings is that you don't have to go. With all the conferences as well; I mean two great conferences are Fordham and the ABA. I have once been to Fordham in five years and never been to the ABA. You don't have to go.

In terms of competition, there have been in a sense two new entrants about four or five years ago. One was the ICN which you have mentioned, which I think has done a lot of good in its own right and in a very efficient way. It has no premises, no fixed secretariat, mainly virtual working routes, and so on. It really is quite inclusive across all the new agencies and although the membership is entirely agencies, the private sector involvement with the work has been very open and I think it has been admirable how much various private sector participants have done, often at the cost of their individual time. I think the ICN has actually been a positive competitive stimulus for the OECD meetings because it has done some things differently and better. Then it just moves ahead. This is why we think competition is good in markets, so why not here as well? The other new entrant was the ECA which is the network of European authorities and there again we had a meeting. John Fingleton organised one in Dublin where he deliberately chose a room that could fit at most 25 people, compared with these enormous ballroom-type things where you get hundreds round. It was an incredibly good meeting. I think that was a bit of competitive stimulus for the Director Generals' meetings in Brussels. We had a phase where we had two meetings under each banner, which is too many, so we now have one of each a year and, in the old days, it used to be two DGs' meetings as well, so there can be some trimming down as well.

PHILIP LOWE

A national authority chairs the ECA meeting and the Commission chairs the ECN meeting.

SIR JOHN VICKERS

Yes. And we are operating in working groups and all the rest, partly to learn and you do learn a lot from the experience of others, but also there have been a number of very big European questions. The merger review, the Article 82 review, and so on, the technology transfer block exemption. These are all debates we want to be part of. Not just to get the wisdom of Brussels, but also to have a say in the evolution of that wisdom.

David Lawsky

This is where you are all going to make suggestions to Philip to take back. There have been questions about what Neelie Kroes should focus on. There are three focuses in discussions with some people; you talked a little bit about the focus in your speech, but one would be on a governmental focus, so that the revised Lisbon Agenda, reducing and targeting State aid, which you didn't mention, but it is something which you have talked about before. A second would be a sort of non-governmental focus; the revision of Article 82 which you are working on, coordination of the immunity applications, cartel control where you are establishing a special unit. The third would be a mixture of the two. Sector queries, which would require some enforcement against companies to point the way towards reforms, and possibly involve some State aid. So you can do everything, but you can't do everything all the time. What do you think would have the most lasting effects? How would you counsel Philip to make suggestions to Ms Kroes? What would be most helpful to your agency of these?

Tihamér Tóth

What I would like to point out is that it is clear that there is a relationship between the priorities set at European level and between the priorities along which national authorities work. If you set your priorities at European level, that more or less determines the priorities which a national authority has to follow. It happens spontaneously as well. For example you have mentioned the importance of sector enquiries. By chance we are just about to finish two sector enquiries in Hungary: one in the electricity sector and the second in a certain part of the financial sector.

Sir John Vickers

I have a lot of sympathy with what Philip said in his remarks, particularly starting with the basics, for any authority; having a reasonable flow of good, well-explained decisions is in a way the basis for everything because if you don't do that, then other things are on a much weaker foundation. So I think that is an extremely important thing. In all authorities that I know well a lot of investment has been going on into improving processes, priority-setting and all the rest. So Philip said a few things about that which struck a lot of chords with me.

On the policy front, to do with the development of and explanation of policy, it seems to me that huge advances have been made by DG Competition in the area of Article 81. The reform to the Verticals Block Exemption in the late 1990s was an extremely important step. The focus in recent years—and we were very much behind and were pushing with others the leniency notice that was discussed earlier—the drive against horizontal cartels has been incredibly successful. The merger reforms—partly stimulated by the courts in Luxembourg—have been extremely positive. We have got the Horizontal Guidelines which is the most important chunk of the sort of triptych of guidelines, as Philip mentioned, the Verticals and Conglomerate are to follow. The two areas where policy is less clear are Article 82, again much discussed at this event, and State aids as well where national authorities don't have enforcement responsibilities, but it is an area of huge interest and importance.

Now going beyond that, and I don't know how the dynamics of the new Commission will work, but I think it has struck many people for a long time that sometimes there is very little trace of competition thinking, or sometimes even market thinking in quite closely adjacent areas of Community policy. The influence of DG Comp in screening legislation is one of the things that Philip put up. It is not just the new legislation; it is also going back over the accumulated stock of legislation. If DG Comp could have the authority and credibility to exert a positive influence in those areas, that could be hugely beneficial for the European economy and consumers.

HEWITT PATE

So, as the American on the panel, anything I say is by definition the most presumptuous advice. I guess Mario is a little bit of a hard act to follow. Mario Monti came in and did some very fundamental things to reform competition law. The question is, what do you do to follow that? I think that having heard and read things Commissioner Kroes has said so far, she is on the right track.

Number one, there has been an emphasis on cartels. I think that is the fundamental place to be in terms of enforcement against private anticompetitive acts. The second thing is to look at ways to address State impediments to competition. So State aids is an important part of that—that isn't a part of my portfolio in our jobs, so I have nothing to compare it with really. But some of the things that the Commission has been doing in terms of enquiries into professions—ways in which governmental action can actually hinder competition—is important. If you stay focused on those two, I think you are going to find a sound way forward.

ORIT DAYGI-EPSTEIN

It seems to me that there is kind of a shift between concentration on the demand side and consumers and now moving towards competitiveness and towards looking at competitors. I think that it was important to concentrate on consumers and consumer interests and important things have been done in order to empower consumers and I wanted to know what the Commission and national competition authorities intend to do further, whether they would like to kind of say enough has been done and we will leave things as they are? I think private enforcement and the green paper seems very good. But I think, in practice, I am not very optimistic whether it will work and, perhaps other things, for example, a more active role of competition authorities, may be the solution in a way. That is the first question. The second one is regarding priorities of competition authorities. I was wondering how do you set your priorities and how do you know whether you address the real issues; the fact whether the people in a way, the citizens are really satisfied with the way you operate?

DAVID LAWSKY

Why don't we start with the problem of how you stay in touch with the public and what kind of feedback you get. I mean I have always noticed that in writing about this it is a pretty abstract subject, even in highly publicised cases and how much the public actually wants to know about what you're doing is sometimes unclear beyond the specialised audiences that we write for.

PHILIP LOWE

Just because this Commission is talking about a more competitive Europe, it doesn't mean to say we have just abandoned our consumer orientation. We certainly confirm that consumer orientation and it is a dynamic one. We look both in the short term and in the long term. So that is the starting point. The question then is what are the areas of the economy which through the action of competition policy, could be encouraged not just to be more competitive, but also to deliver more competitive services and goods to consumers, whether they are European or others. Our job is naturally concentrated on Europe.

It is often very difficult to gauge the right feedback from various elements of society on what is best for consumer welfare. Certainly, economic studies tell you how price is behaving, how concentration is developing and how choice may be affected. Mario Monti, and we under him, put a great deal of emphasis on trying to develop more relationships with consumer organizations, whose input into many of our cases was very patchy. They played a big role in the debate on the revision of the Car Block Exemption Regulation. But frequently, when we have asked them to take part in a view about a merger, they gave us no views on it, either because they had no resources, or because they had no views. On the other hand, you have got to look at the balance of evidence in an investigation. It may sound heretical, but in some situations competitors can tell you very accurately what consumers want. It is the balance between what the parties say, what the competitors say, and what consumers say, which hopefully gets you near to what the truth is.

Now going on from that sort of abstract language, the next question which will almost certainly be, 'Well, is this Commission going to start taking decisions in the interests of efficiency of business and trample over the interests of consumers because it wants to create national or European champions?' That debate has been certainly taken place externally, on the front page of Financial Times, and on the back page and front page of Handelsblatt. As far as our only policy and practice is concerned, we have got to get the market definition right, and we have got to get the competition assessment right in our investigations. But at the end of the day, we have got to ask ourselves, what is the best result for consumers? We don't have a competition law which allows us to say that in any market without any potential competition you can ignore the consumer in one country, because there are efficiencies to be gained in another country. This would be perfectly acceptable within the EU if there was a European-wide market. But we are not in a position to trade off the interests of consumers in different, nationally defined, markets. We search for remedies to deal with consumer harm where markets are defined more narrowly than Europe or the world. So a more competitive Europe, yes, but consumer welfare needs to be maintained and improved. Why did we choose sector enquiries in financial services and in energy? Well, for one major reason, we heard from every single industrial and individual energy consumer that liberalization wasn't delivering the results which were expected. In the area of retail banking, the other day one of our colleagues in the European Competition Network said, 'Actually, our agency hasn't received any complaints in the retail banking area'. But he was referring to competitors' complaints. He wasn't referring to *consumer* complaints. That shows, I think, that we have already a dynamic consumer orientation which we are going to maintain.

HEWITT PATE

Just to sound a sceptical note on the idea of direct consumer involvement: I don't think there is a great deal of popular appetite for discussion of the ins and outs of competition law. We need to do things on behalf of consumers and to seek the best result for them, but the notion that we are really communicating very frequently to a consumer audience, I think is a false one. In fact, there is a danger to the extent that antitrust becomes a subject of popular discussion. Expectations can be created that don't really have much to do with sound law or economics. Bert Foer plays a valuable role in developing antitrust policy because he represents a certain point of view, for lack of a better word, sort of the American antitrust left. It is not because he is somehow channelling consumers. Not that we disagree all the time, but in instances where Bert and I disagree, the value is that if I am taking a less interventionist position, he forces me to justify it. But the idea that we are going to somehow do an American idol-type phone-in or Eurovision Song-type phone-in to figure out much how to do antitrust, is just not realistic.

DAVID LAWSKY

I am sure some of you in the room have had the experiences that I've had, where you've been in a social gathering and somebody finds out that you are associated with antitrust and competition policy, and he says, 'Oh that sounds of interest. I read something in the paper about *Microsoft*.[12] Tell me about it'. And after about 45 seconds, their eyes glaze over. In my experiences, they don't really want to know in any detail about how antitrust works.

SIR JOHN VICKERS

It partly depends which cases come along. If you are doing a lysine cartel then that is quite hard to explain why that matters to consumers. If you're doing Sotheby's and Christies, you can explain why that matters to some consumers but maybe not the population in general. It just so happens that two of our most important cases, the *Replica Football Kit*[13] and the *Toys Price Fixing*[14] cases, happen to be in the sectors which were immediately

---

[12] EU: Commission decision of 24 Mar 2004, COMP/37.792. *Microsoft Corp v Commission* (Case T-201/04 R) [2005] 4 CMLR 18 (CFI). US: *United States v Microsoft Corp*, 147 F.3d 935 (DC Cir 1998); *United States v Microsoft Corp* 87 F.Supp.2d 30 (DDC 2000), 253 F.3d 34 (CA DC 2001) (No 03-5030).

[13] *Umbro Holdings Ltd v Office of Fair Trading*. The various rulings in this case are available from: [2003] CAT 25, 26, 29, 30; [2004] CAT 3; and [2005] CAT 22.

[14] *Argos Ltd and Littlewoods Ltd v Office of Fair Trading*. The various rulings in this case are available from: [2003] CAT 10, 16, 24; [2004] CAT 5, 24; and [2005] CAT 13; 15, 16.

consumer-facing and there was quite a bit of coverage of them; not going into the intricacies of the law and its enforcement, but I think that as a sort of incidental by-product it helped get the message through.

I think, uniquely on the panel, I am from an authority that has consumer responsibilities, as well as competition law responsibilities and the way to make a lot of consumer law work as best we can, is not just to enforce it, but is also to communicate loud and clear about some issues out there in the marketplace, including raising consumer awareness. So we do quite a lot of communication on that front, for example in areas of scams or things currently riding on the internet or hazards of some kinds of doorstep selling and things of that sort. I know that the FTC in the US—we at the OFT have smaller feet—has a similar footprint in that regard given the relative size of the countries. On this, are we looking at consumers or producers? I think if you are properly market-oriented, you are looking at both at the same time. You don't change the direction of view and look at one side or the other, although productivity and competitiveness are words with a 'producerist' tone to them. The only productivity worth its name is productivity to deliver what people want and indeed you find something very much to that effect in Adam Smith.

As to the particular rights of consumer organixations and consumers, we touched on that in the context of private actions before. We, of course, for several years now, and indeed now enshrined in statute, though it existed previously, have the super complaint process, where designated consumer bodies can bring to our attention a matter which they think we should look at and we are committed to giving some kind of public response within the period of 90 days. The response might be, 'No, we don't think there is anything there'. But that is an attempt to rebalance a bit in a world which would otherwise just have a lot of very well-resourced complainants pursuing their commercial interests. Quite a few of our market studies and indeed one or two references of markets to the Competition Commission have originated that way, which again shows the value of not leaving us with a monopoly of wisdom, which we certainly don't have.

DAVID LAWSKY

Tihamér, you have said that you have had a lot of consumer groups in other forms, but have you done anything that has touched a nerve, that has got a sort of overwhelming response?

TIHAMÉR TÓTH

I fully agree with the previous speakers, but nevertheless I have thought that especially from the point of view of a smaller or less-known competition authority, although we have 15 years of experience, nevertheless I believe it is very important for us to adopt, from time to time, so-called consumable, easily understandable, decisions which are of direct concern to the consumers, like a restaurant cartel or a taxi cartel. So you need to have cases like this in order to establish or to strengthen your credibility. We also have lots of consumer deception cases, which contribute to our fame, I hope. Thirdly, I would like to mention the importance of competition advocacy as well which can be well publicised. For example, we had some success in at least postponing a municipality decree in Budapest which would regulate the taxi market, which was likely to have caused a 50 per cent raise in price, which is not good for consumers. It is easy to explain actions like this and we need to have actions like this.

PHILIP LOWE

Some of the most attractive cases for consumers are some of the most difficult cases to deal with because they are about excessive pricing. Judging by the amount of fan mail or anti-fan mail we receive, our major enforcement priority should be to cut cross-channel ferry fares, slash mobile roaming charges, have a harmonized pricing system for medical products throughout Europe and make sure you can buy a car anywhere in Europe at the cheapest price. The first two cases run against the issue of legally proving excessive pricing. The last two run against general frustration of citizens as consumers that there isn't competition across Europe to the benefit of them. But as citizens, they might take a different view as to whether health systems or taxation systems should be harmonized across Europe.

BERT FOER

Hew mentioned the AAI; I don't see us as representing the left, I see us as representing the centre. Our group is market-oriented and we see market failures perhaps more often than you do and think the Government can intervene successfully more often than you may, but we are basically in the middle together, Chicago and post-Chicago. What I wanted to say to John is we are actually making a film right now about the lysine cartel[15] for a television audience—it will also probably be about the *Microsoft* case—and

[15] Between 1993 and 1996, the world's five leading producers of Lysine, an animal feed additive, colluded to fix both prices and sales quotas. The discovery of the cartel led to the prosecution of the cartelists and the levying of fines of more than $100 million in the US and Canada and more than 105 million euros in the EU. (Source: <http://www.achive.official-documents.co.uk>).

what we want to do is attempt, for the first time that I am aware of in the US, to tell a story for a mass audience as to why antitrust is good for consumers and for businesses. We have a real problem that people don't understand why there is antitrust, or why it is useful, and therefore they don't support it particularly politically. I think that's what we need to build.

MICHAEL HUTCHINGS

Just to throw a bit of a spanner in the works: the consumer interest. I think there is a perception amongst some consumers that there is a problem with competition regulation that has perverse results. I think people get very frustrated that they hear of people who are able to fly halfway round the world for £10 or 1p or something and yet when they book their flight they have to pay three hundred and something pounds. Or they get very frustrated that competition has resulted in total confusion in the mobile and telephone market generally. A lot of the perceived benefits of competition have actually resulted in confusion or frustration amongst consumers. I am not suggesting this is a real problem. I think it comes back to something that I think Philip mentioned in his presentation which is the importance of advocacy and actually explaining constantly to the world what it is you are trying to achieve.

PHILIP LOWE

This gives me an opportunity to talk about *Microsoft*, which is a corporation we greatly respect!

But first I want to talk about air transport, which is a good example where, generally speaking, deregulation has produced an enormous amount of competition, particularly for point-to-point travel. It stimulated all sorts of new offers, new offers nevertheless which need to be explained. Inevitably if someone is running a business, they need to have some predictability about how many people get on their plane. Otherwise they are going to go bust and most of them are going bust, except for some very good low-cost operators. These low-cost operators have calculated quite carefully how they price for a £1 or a £120 ticket. Gradually, consumers are realising where they can get the best value and how you should avoid getting the worst offers. Basically, in the air transport industry, buy your ticket early and don't change it and the airlines will take you there for nothing. But if you arrive the day before, it will cost you a lot of money. That is a business model which seems to be still robust and which consumers can gradually understand.

In the area of IT inter-operability, it is vital to keep avenues for innovation and market development open. It is frequently all too tempting for IT companies to keep those doors and windows closed in their own strategic interest. Innovative companies obviously need to be remunerated adequately for the innovation which they themselves have actually created. But in exceptional cases there are some limits which need to be respected.

In our case with Microsoft on server-to-server interoperability, we already have the background of concern throughout the world that servers should be able to operate with client PCs, whoever the server manufacturer is. But many people ask us what we mean by server-to-server inter-operability. The answer is that if you use a PC and it is in a group of PCs, then there are functions such as filing, printing and mail, which are managed by servers together in a group. They need to communicate with each other. Our problem in this area has been it wasn't possible to talk to a Windows server unless you are in another Windows server. So you could do everything in a group of servers as long as they were all Windows servers. The people who complained to us about Microsoft said: 'this is a situation in which we are not asking a company to reveal patented information which they will not be remunerated for. We are not even asking them to reveal any code which they regard as secret. We are asking them to give information which tells you how to talk to another member of a server family'.

This is a point which I think can influence the views of consumers and citizens. If you translate the whole issue of inter-operability to things which people use every day, whether it is mobile phones or smart phones, or the relationship between your PC and your mobile, the message is understandable. People want to see competition on the merits between operators who can actually offer something which is getting better and better for the consumer. Our case is more technical because it is related mainly to corporate users, or to institutional users, who are buying Oracle as opposed to Windows, and they don't want the constraint of having to say that forests of servers have to be all Windows and there is no possibility of combining the two. Of course there may be efficiencies from having all one brand, or all one product, when you buy your computers or buy your servers. Some airlines choose only to fly Boeing, or only to fly Airbus for that reason. But many want the choice, and it seems to us that in the area of inter-operability there is something which is common to both the US case and ourselves, that this is a key issue of leaving doors open, allowing new products to develop in a way which, while not harming the remuneration to innovation, nevertheless allows markets to expand and prosper and bring benefits to consumers.

SIR JOHN VICKERS

Michael's two examples of aviation and mobile phones show he needn't worry. I can understand a world of acutely jealous people would not like any departure from uniform pricing or wouldn't want any product differentiation, but surely in those areas competition and choice have driven enormous consumer benefits, among which are inspiring the long-standing incumbents to better performance than would otherwise have been the case. My worry might be that, in terms of perverse effects, utterly well-intentioned so-called consumer protection measures—I don't know whether the Passenger Compensation Regulation is of this category—could have the perverse effect of making life much worse for consumers, despite their intention.

HEWITT PATE

I think Philip has unwittingly shown the degree to which the general public may not have an appetite for the stuff, but my eyes didn't glaze over. I am glad he went to the part of the *Microsoft* case where we have more often agreed that with respect to bundling. Obviously we have a concern about where the Commission ought to take this in terms of long-term competition involvement of bureaucrats in designing products but, on the inter-operability side, our remedy has largely been along the same lines as what the Commission is pursuing. There is a difference in that the Commission found liability for a refusal to license, whereas for us it was part of a remedy after a violation was proven. But we continue to work together well. I am very heartened by what Philip has said. I think you are seeing in the newspapers a lot of articles placed there perhaps by folks who have a commercial interest in urging the Commission to require Microsoft to do open-source licensing, to not be able to protect its source code, to have to meet some undefined innovation index in order to get remuneration for licences. All of those things—which might well be way beyond the Commission's order or the Court of First Instance's initial look—would be quite problematic. But that is not what I'm hearing from Philip and I think therefore we have a lot of complementarity there. There is less excitement than you might have liked maybe on the *Microsoft* one.

DAVID LAWSKY

Before Stephen Walzer closes the conference I would ask you to join me in thanking our panel.

STEPHEN WALZER

Ladies and gentlemen, it falls to me to say just a few words to conclude the conference. I have served as the Acting Director of the Institute now for some five months. My first impressions when I joined back in January were of an excellent bunch of guys, really hardworking, who wanted to do well and provide an excellent service for their members. I have now got closer to them, so my first impressions have been reinforced. The sessions of yesterday and today have offered a standard of excellence which frankly I have now come to expect. Thanks very much for the hard work of Philip Marsden and to the excellent support of Michael Hutchings.

We have seen gathered in this room, the movers and the shakers, if I may say so, of competition law and policy, from practice, from industry and especially from the regulators. In the UK from John Vickers, Paul Geroski and their teams and particularly from further afield. I would like to express our gratitude to Hew Pate and his colleagues who have crossed the Atlantic to share their views with us, and to Philip, who has come from Brussels, sparing important time from a very busy schedule, and to Mr Tóth also, from the Hungarian Competition Office, who I know has also got a very busy schedule. We are equally grateful to you, our participants, for adding your time and your value particularly to the excellence of the conference, making the session such a success.